AUSTRIA IN COLOR

KURT PETER KARFELD

AUSTRIA
IN COLOR

TEXT BY
GORDON SHEPHERD

PRINTED AND PUBLISHED BY
ÖSTERREICHISCHE STAATSDRUCKEREI, VIENNA

THE PATTERN OF AUSTRIA

The country which this book brings to life has sat for one thousand years on the busiest crossroads of Europe. Armies, both Christian and heathen, have rolled across it in battle. Great migrations of peoples have spilled over its frontiers. The trade routes and the cultures of a continent have met here, clashed here, and finally joined hands. There has often been equilibrium, but there has never been rest.

This is the key to all things Austrian. To understand the land and its people, the visitor must seek and find this shifting quicksilver balance in the Austrians' art, their architecture, their politics, and even in their food, their dress, and their language.

Each people has at least one characteristic mark which stamps their approach to life, a mark which has been moulded by their particular history as a nation. It is reserve which dominates the British character, and it is Britain's life as an island race which has produced this mood of detachment. It is the desire for novelty and new horizons which stamps the American approach, and the fairly recent pioneer origin of the American people is the mainspring of this urge. With the Austrians, the central theme is compromise, a theme dictated for them by their geographical exposure which, for centuries, has compelled them to absorb the unfamiliar and to come to terms with the intruder. The Austrian may not have been born with this gift. But he was forced to develop it. His character is, in the truest sense, the reflection of his past and the image of his present.

Austrian baroque architecture—that happy fusion of northern solidity and southern fantasy—is often quoted as the classic expression of this Austrian compromise in practice. But it is only one example typical of many. The palaces, castles, monasteries, and churches shown in the following pictures all have a main theme which holds good for the Austrian nation as a whole—to create and to survive by adaptation.

The combination of old and new which results is, of course, in no way an Austrian prerogative. All ancient countries are forced to dress up their present alongside their past. Indeed, Rome and Athens, whose classical ruins slumber alongside the luxury hotels, are better examples of such contrasts than Vienna, where modern architecture has so far done little to transform the traditional face of the town.

But the unique Austrian achievement has been to preserve the old character amid the new setting. The Romans and Greeks of today are no longer the peoples whom Augustus and Pericles ruled. But the Viennese, one feels, have remained essentially the same folk with that same gentle and insidious philosophy which sweetened life for Caesar's garrison legions in Vindobona, the Vienna of nearly 2,000 years ago. The result of this happy gift is that even those things which the Austrians have copied from their neighbours take on a specifically Austrian character. Thus even Austrian baroque architecture itself, though based on foreign inspiration, could only exist in the form which the Austrians gave it amidst their own countryside. The Austrian pattern is not just the passive mixture of alien colours. It is the blending of the rose-grower who, from the shoots of two or three blossoms will bring to life a new flower, with a vitality and a character all of its own.

The pictures which follow were certainly not selected deliberately to show that Austrian universality which has also come from her "crossroads history". But even without intention, many examples appear in these pages—Belvedere Palace in Vienna, the home of a European as well as an

5

Austrian soldier; Dürnstein Castle in the Wachau, where an English king captured on his return from the Crusades was held for one of the fattest ransoms of the Middle Ages; Bernstein in the Burgenland, the best preserved of a long chain of fortresses which once formed the frontline of the Christian world against the heathen east; the fairy tale castle of Hochosterwitz in Carinthia, whose very spelling shows the trace of a long-vanished Celtic occupation; Beethoven's house among the vineyards of Vienna, and Haydn's church on the edge of the Hungarian plain, monuments to two of the giants of world music who lived and worked in Austria; and finally Salzburg where, once a year, the world still comes to hear their compositions amid the works of Mozart, Austria's special son.

The Austrian countryside as depicted here typifies as much as the buildings the lesson of her history—dividing and at the same time blending the different streams of European culture and commerce. Two great themes run through these landscape pictures. They are the Danube and the Alps: Europe's longest river and Europe's greatest mountain range. It is along this river since time immemorial that the merchandise of East and West have been exchanged and the inland fleets of peace and war have sailed. And it is through the lovely valleys which vertically pierce the Austrian Alps that the caravans of the north have moved down to the Mediterranean shores since the earliest trading times. Better than any words or dates, the banks of this river and the passes of these mountains illustrate the destiny which the Austrian people have been called on to fulfil.

But these landscape pictures can tell us even more. The Austrian provinces are not only one of the vital connecting links of Europe's commerce and communications. They are also, geologically and botanically, a transition ground from west to east, and from north to south. This is true of Austria's mountains, her plains, and her lakes. The

Tyrolean Alps, majestic though they are, are set in a minor key to the even mightier peaks of Switzerland, and it is in Austria that this great range tails off eastwards in countless minor chains until it finally dies away in the soft hills of the woods which overlook the capital. Vienna's famous Kahlenberg is not just a picturesque look-out point. It is also the last spur of that great Alpine massif which rises 500 miles to the west. Similarly, the rich cornfields of Lower Austria and the Burgenland are not merely the bread-basket of Vienna. They are the beginnings of that great Central European plain into which, on Austrian soil, the Alps subside. It is in the Austrian Burgenland, among the squat brown houses of the villages and on the reedy shores of Lake Neusiedl that one can sniff the first melancholy-sweet breath of the "puszta". Even the Austrian lakes form a half-way stage in colour and in temperature between the icy and ice-blue lakes of the north and the warm sapphire waters of Como or Lugano.

If these ageless influences of nature have left their mark on Austria's buildings and her culture, and even on the plants and trees of her countryside, it is obvious that they have also indelibly stamped the character of her people. As a nation, the Austrians are unprejudiced, unenvious, and politically unambitious. The first quality springs from their unbroken contacts over the centuries both with neighbours and with distant intruders belonging to different races and religions.

The other two qualities have sprung, partly from this, but partly also from the violent ups and downs of their own history. The Austrians have held and lost great influence in the councils of the world. They began in the first Millennium as the inhabitants of a small feudal mark, set up by the lords of Bavaria to guard the eastern approaches of Christian Europe—a sort of suicidal outer drawbridge which had to be defended because it could never be raised. It was not until 1156—when the outlines of an integrated nation state had already appeared in France and England—that the Austrians became even a separate dukedom, with some legal independence of their own. Through the acquisition of Styria, Carinthia, Krain, and the Tyrol this inner Austrian dukedom grew gradually into one of the most powerful territorial units of Central Europe. Finally, in the 16th century, and under the leadership of those same Habsburgs who had expanded Austria's basic provinces, the dukedom grew by dynastic marriage and war into one of the greatest European land powers of all time, extending to Burgundy, Spain, Hungary and Bohemia, and crowned with the dignity of the Holy Roman Empire.

This unwieldy complex was divided soon after its formation into a western and an eastern half, ruled respectively from Madrid and Vienna. The eastern part, inadequately called Austro-Hungary, survived intact until the 20th century as the massive guardian of conservatism and stability in Central and Eastern Europe. Then, in 1918, the dynasty, the far-flung provinces, the dignity, the prosperity, and the power disappeared almost overnight. Though weakened by internal tensions, the Empire was destroyed only by war. By November of that year, the Austrian people found themselves territorially back at the same starting point which their ambitious rulers had won for them 500 years before. But now, it was not a strong and rising dukedom which straddled the Enns and the Danube, but a dazed and enfeebled republic, facing a ring of hostile neighbours.

From this painful cycle in their own fortunes the Austrians have learned instinctively to rate the human and the spiritual values of life higher than the political. They have learned indeed what an ungrateful, exhausting and dangerous imposture the search for power can be. It is an attitude which could be of service to a world seeking an alternative to the rule of force.

These same qualities and this same history have made the Austrians—and particularly the Viennese—one of the most receptive of peoples. Theirs is not the mondaine cosmopolitanism which eagerly grasps at any new experience for its own sake and seeks to be Europe's arbiter and pioneer of taste and intellect. Indeed, perhaps because he has absorbed so much in the past, the Austrian of today will hesitate before modifying his own way of life with still more foreign notions. But even those ideas which he is reluctant to copy he is willing to respect. He is glad to have almost anyone enter his country and, once there, prepared to let him argue his case and live his life in peace.

Even as an occupied state in the ten years after the Second World War, Austria's laws of political asylum were exemplary. And despite the tensions of the Cold War in those difficult years and despite the physical pressure of foreign garrisons which stood on opposite sides in that Cold War, the Austrian government managed to have these rights of asylum carried out in practice on its soil. This constant stream of destitute refugees threw a heavy strain on an already stricken Austrian economy. Austria's hospitality was sometimes deliberately misinterpreted and sometimes genuinely misunderstood. Yet the country continued then with its task, and will continue as a free country now, so long as there are refugees who clamour for asylum along its borders. This attitude is remarkable yet understandable. To the Austrians, the political refugees of the twentieth century are just another phase in that constant shifting of peoples which they have had to live with in the Danube Basin for nearly two thousand years. This is the deeper cosmopolitanism. It consists not of imitation but of tolerance.

To some extent, of course, the Austrian's natural sympathy for foreigners is explained by the simple fact that the blood of nearly all the nations of the continent flows in his veins. Almost any European foreigner and certainly any Central European neighbour is the Austrian's "alter ego". The mere list of races who peopled the Austrian lands at the dawn of civilization illustrates this mixture—

7

Illyrians, Celts, Romans, Teutons, Avars, Slavs, and Magyars, to name only a few. But a big role was also played by political chance, by the fact that for nearly six hundred years, from the late 13th to the early 20th century, the destiny of the Austrian people themselves became entangled and identified with the destiny of that great supra-national empire mentioned above.

The historical accident that, in 1273, the Swabian Count Rudolf assumed the leadership of the then German-speaking world and founded in Vienna the dynasty of the Habsburgs completed the cosmopolitan education of the Austrians. Till then, theirs had been the instinctive universality possessed by all races with mixed blood. But, as the Middle Ages moved into modern times, and that same dynasty still sat and ruled from Vienna, the Austrians learned their universality all over again—from their imperial office desks.

At its zenith, this empire "on which the sun never set" stretched to the borders of the then civilized world: at one end was the warm breath of Madrid and at the other the rough wind of the Asiatic steppes. And, for centuries, the Austrian was the "primus inter pares" of this company, the first member among all this motley family of nations, the people of the same blood and language as the Emperor himself, and therefore his natural choice as servants and administrators. One can compare that old Austria, which many of these photographs depict, to a vast landed estate, run too long on feudal lines, but managed on the whole with benevolence and justice. On this estate, the Austrians became the liveried stewards and game-keepers, stationed in all remote corners of the great property, as well as in Vienna itself, and preoccupied not with any national issues of their own, but rather with the problems of the fifteen different races whom they had to administer.

The fact that they were concerned more with the day-to-day business of empire than with their own fate brings us to another salient feature of the Austrians of today—their late development as a nation-state. It is no coincidence that the pictures in this book contain no national monuments comparable with George Washington's statue or Nelson's Column in London. For the Austrians reached this 20th century without a specifically national history of their own. Nationalism was the force which, throughout the 19th century, threatened the federal structure on which the Empire was built; and the Austrians, as the first servants of the dynasty, could only indulge in it at the cost of disloyalty to their masters. Thus when, in 1918, the great empire of which they had been the ruling instrument collapsed around them, they had to seek for a patriotism of their own on which to start life again as a small republic.

In the relatively short space of time that has passed since, the Austrians have managed, despite a total of seventeen years of foreign occupation, to find this national identity which the Empire unwittingly withheld from them. This has meant shaking off all the nostalgia of imperialism on the one hand, and on the other, the even more difficult task of reducing to proper perspective their relationship with their German cousins in the north. But at last this Austrian people, so old in tradition, have found the one thing which even their long history denied to them—a political personality of their own.

The traditional tolerance of the Austrians as well as their newly developed national identity are two characteristics over which there is little room for dispute or misunderstanding. But many other popular beliefs about them are based on illusions whose persistence is as strange as their origin.

There is, for example, the notion that the Austrians are a lighthearted, feckless people with little or no thought for what tomorrow may bring. In actual fact, their cheerfulness is balanced by an almost equal dose of wistful melancholy, and these two strains are perfectly represented in their music. Austrian music can rightly be taken as the expression of the nation's way of life. But it must be studied in its entirety, and not in those sections which the outside world will persist in substituting for the whole.

The charm and the immortality of Johann Strauss are beyond argument. It is however high time to dispose of the sickly legend that his waltzes form a sort of magic and universal key to both Austria's culture and her character. In some ways, indeed, the Viennese waltz is exceptional rather than typical, and so was the atmosphere in which it was born and in which it flourished.

The Vienna of Johann Strauss's days was a doomed capital living through a sort of false springtime. This was the socalled "Gründerzeit", when a sudden economic boom, based on the first delayed effects of industrialization and a modern credit system, happened to coincide with a lull in those domestic and international conflicts which were soon to tear the empire savagely apart. Strauss was the symbol of this new middle class wealth; the symbol also of this Fata Morgana of Austro-Hungary's political stability, a deceptive vision which was destroyed for all time by the cannons of the First World War. There is nothing novel in this paradox. Other civilizations and other empires have lived through this same sudden blaze of sunshine which comes immediately before the long night.

But the picture of the Austrians which spread to the furthest corners of the earth with Strauss's melodies in the 1870's was particulary misleading. For, as a people, they never have had and they never will have that bursting energy and youthful confidence which vibrates through most (though not all) of these famous tunes. A truer keynote to their character could be heard, even then, in the older musical background of the age — the sad, but good-tempered resignation of Schubert. And, as events were to prove, this also turned out to be a better sign-post of the tragedy lying ahead for Austro-Hungary than the brightly-painted park bandstands of Johann Strauss.

It should be noted, incidentally, that a strong, bitter-sweet undertone also lies beneath the music of Vienna's winegardens, the equally famous "Heurigen Lieder", which have helped to perpetuate the Strauss legend. Taken as a whole, this popular music is far less gay and uninhibited than French or even English drinking songs. Death stalks through the choruses of the Heurigen Lieder as well as life, and as many of their themes are devoted to nostalgia over the past as to contentment over the present. Not that this makes them any the less attractive. They are possibly the best drinking songs in the world, and the Vienna winegarden is certainly the best setting in the world for such music. But this is precisely because both of them cater in equal measure for the twin effects of alcohol— exuberance and melancholy. To dwell only on the gaiety is, in other words, to underestimate Vienna's contribution to the cult of the grape.

So much for the Strauss myth of light-headed gaiety. The illusion about the fecklessness of the Austrians is just as far off the mark. It is true that, politically, Austria's history has left her with a certain fatalism which even her new national spirit has not shaken off. But in their private lives, few people make such earnest and conscientious endeavours to ensure themselves against the hazards of the future as do the Austrians. If they have a mania, it is for security, not for extravagance.

To have a pension to look forward to is the very summit of the Austrian's material desires in life. Out of a total working population of over two million it is estimated that at least three quarters are in pensionable jobs of one sort or another. And no fewer than 760,000 are actually retired and drawing pensions. Not long ago, at an Austrian school in Styria, the teachers conducted an inquiry as to what their pupils wished to do for a living. Among the junior grades, who were unversed in the hard economic facts of life, the most popular career chosen was that of "pensioner". That could only happen in Austria.

This demand for security stretches far outside the ranks of bureaucrats and the like who, in any country, prefer a fixed certainty to a variable uncertainty. In Austria, it pervades also the artistic and commercial world. The typical actor or musician in this country is either state-paid or state-subsidized. Most of the colourful artists and singers of the Vienna Opera are in fact established civil servants with solid pensions to look forward to when their charms begin to fade and their voices no longer reach up to the third gallery.

The same urge for security before adventure stamps the Austrian businessman. Perhaps this comes from his inborn inclination to deadsafe markets such as those his ancestors enjoyed for generations in the old empire. Perhaps it is due to his late contact with the industrial revolution, or to Austria's lack throughout her history of overseas possessions. But whatever the reason, it is the spirit of caution, not the spirit of the gambler which possesses him. He is very often a successful industrialist, as the splendid steel mills, power plants, and textile factories of the country show. But he is rarely a successful salesman. Characteristically enough, his many inventions have, as often as not, been developed by other nations. Risk—that factor on which business in the capitalist world is normally built up — is anathema to the Austrian. And even those who do gamble and win are usually content with the initial prosperity which results. The millionaire bent on doubling his fortune every decade of his life is an unthinkable figure for Austrians. They have no business tycoons; not only because their economy is relatively small but also because their mentality is totally unsuitable. Their aim is an ample sufficiency and not a riotous surplus.

This attitude brings with it a certain lack of enterprise which sometimes handicaps the Austrian on the world stage. But he cherishes a sneaking feeling that his approach is the right one; and the more "manager disease" spreads among the more bustling nations, the more this view is shared elsewhere in the world. For what the Austrian's life loses in excitement and the chance of great wealth, it gains in relaxation and the prospect of solid comfort.

This, more than anything else, is the keynote to the "Gemütlichkeit", that easy-going and good-natured approach to life, for which the Austrian and above all the Viennese is famous. Here is no myth that needs exploding, and no legend that needs correcting. In this respect at least, there is no contrast and no interruption between Austria's imperial past and her republican present. Austrian Gemütlichkeit runs like a bright ribbon even through the tragedies of the nation's life. The ribbon is light in texture but tough, and indestructible because it is so intangible.

Obviously, this Gemütlichkeit must have certain material preconditions. It would be almost unattainable, for example, in a country which did not grow its own wine. Any nation lucky enough to live under the shadow of the grape-vine has a natural warmth which comes harder to those peoples who have to import their sunshine by the bottle from abroad. But even among the quality wine-growing countries of Europe, Austria holds a unique position. She is the only land where, year after year, the people account for virtually the entire crop themselves. The wine output of Austria in 1953, for example, reached the respectable total of 18,174,046 gallons. The Austrians drank the lot—apart from 345,290 gallons, or barely 2%, which went for export.

To transfer this crop from the vineyard to the palate, an impressive retail organization is maintained. Vienna alone has roughly 7,500 establishments at which a glass of wine can be had at any hour of the day, not counting the hundreds of wine-gardens scattered on the wooded outskirts of the city. There are, in fact, few streets anywhere in the capital where it is necessary to walk more than 250 yards with a thirst. And though not as cheap as the fresh air of the Vienna Woods, the open wine of Austria is within the reach of most (as the disposal of the annual crop would indicate). An "Achtel", or a full wine-glass measure, can be had in the modest inns for a few pence. This is an enjoyment whose broad popular base enhances it for all.

Another material factor in this happy philosophy of life is, of course, the physical beauty of the countryside and the ready-made facilities for enjoyment which it offers. Austria is one of those fortunate lands whose attractions are spread liberally over the four seasons: the winter snow of the mountains gives as much joy and sport to native and foreigner alike as the summer sunshine of the lakes and forests. And the result is about the nearest thing to mass but unorganized recreation which any modern society can boast. These relaxations can be indulged in by all classes with all incomes. Here again, we come up against that essential undertone of Austrian life—the happy undertone of pleasures shared and multiplied by the very process of division.

In Vienna too, the traditional Austrian Gemütlichkeit is helped by nature. No capital of the world has a green belt of such depth and unspoilt beauty so close to its concrete heart as Vienna possesses in its famous woods. They encircle the whole north-western approaches to the capital and can be reached, even on the tortoise backs of the city's trams, in less than half an hour's journey from Vienna's centre.

But, in the capital, Nature has also been partly helped by man in building the cradle for a pleasant life. True, Vienna is not lovely in the exotic or romantic style of many another European beauty-spot. Though commonly thought of as the greatest Danubian city and though geographically the centre of the whole Danube basin, it is not even built on the river along which its destiny flows. The Danube near Vienna is, for the most part, a muddy, grey-green waterway, disciplined like a canal with unin-spiring artificial banks, and forced to run outside the city proper, through the flood-control area of the eastern plains. Vienna's only "river", the so-called "Wienfluss", is, in fact, a docile trickle of water as shallow as a children's paddling pool, which wanders down one of the city's parks in a special concrete bed ten times as big as itself. All this is aesthetically a loss, as the contrasting arrangement of Prague, Budapest, Florence, Paris and London —to name only a few of Europe's "river-cities"—will show.

Yet, even in this aesthetic loss, there is a specifically Viennese gain. For the very fact that the planners of the city did not allow it to be cut into two by their river meant that the centre of the capital gained in compactness and character. Vienna's "Innere Stadt", that bustling octagon of narrow streets enclosed by the broad Ringstrasse, is one of the most concentrated and self-contained centres to be found in any major city. There is much that is beautiful outside this centre. But the passing stranger who, with only three hours in Vienna to spare, walks carefully through this Inner City will take away with him the unforgettable essence of the capital, even should he never return. Palaces, and at the head of them the old Imperial Hofburg; churches, and above all the Cathedral of St. Stephen's; the cultural shrines of Austria, notably the Burgtheater and the rebuilt Opera itself; museums and monuments from an earlier age and luxury shops and hotels of today: Vienna's past and her present are lovingly pressed together in his tiny space less than two miles across. What other capitals have sprawled, Vienna has thrown into one, behind what were formerly the fortress walls of the medieval town.

The result of this compactness is an intimacy which no other city of such size can boast. The visitor who is receptive to this appeal becomes, in 24 hours, an honorary resident. This is "Gemütlichkeit" in operation and again, it springs from a pleasure shared. Vienna is one of the few sight-seeing capitals of Europe which has no "tourist centre" and no tourist complex.

Its native citizens and its most casual visitors merge naturally into one.

But neither the vineyards of the Kahlenberg and Nussdorf nor the wine gardens all around them; neither the broad spread of the Vienna Woods nor the friendly turmoil of the Inner City could, by themselves, have created the Austrian's philosophy of life. "Gemütlichkeit" is a personal characteristic. The face which it shows to the world may be an anonymous image of a whole capital, a whole people and a whole country. But it is born in the individual. And if it ever perishes, it is in the individual that it must first of all die.

Applied to the tormented world of today, this Austrian way of life becomes an appeal to reason. What it stands for in the political sphere is not the concern of this book. Nor indeed is its political content unique, whatever special qualifications and opportunities Austria may possess. All small nations, pressed between the great power blocks of the world, aim naturally at peaceful reconciliation. But what the Austrian philosophy aims at in the sphere of ordinary social relations is almost unique, at least among the modern industrialized peoples of the world. For, alone among these nations, Austria preaches and practises the philosophy of leisure. Austrian "Gemütlichkeit" is an isolated protest against the paradox of our Machine Age in which man constantly has more time placed at his disposal and yet steadily has less time to spare.

More perhaps than any European people since the Ancients, the Austrian still tries to build his real life around his leisure hours. Here he will show reserves of energy which are astounding. The young Viennese clerk or worker will cheerfully do overtime on a Friday in order to spend Saturday and Sunday on a ski-ing trip to the mountains—standing overnight in a crowded train; and fully prepared on arrival to march up to his chosen peak with a 30 lb. rucksack on his back. The Austrian is not, by disposition, "queue-minded". But he will stand in line with the patience of Job and the tenacity of a mule in the hope of securing a last-minute ticket for a sold-out performance at one of his concert-halls or opera houses.

This love of leisure is not simple hedonism, and it is certainly not pure laziness—the Austrian works steadily enough for his free time, as his remarkably low post-war record for industrial strikes shows. It is rather based upon the instinctive feeling that there is more to life than the amassing of money or the quest for power. "Gemütlichkeit" is an appeal for perspective, relaxation and tolerance in this frantic and vicious age. There could be no greater mistake than to think of its message purely in terms of the wine-garden's conviviality. The Austrian would never think of his own philosophy of life as a crusade. Yet a crusade without banners is, in fact, what it is.

No introduction to Austria and its people, however superficial, would be complete without some account of the provincial basis of the nation's life. Indeed, without this, no introduction would even be intelligible. For Austria is not simply divided into nine parts, as Caesar's Gaul was into three. It is rather the nine separate parts which go to make up Austria.

Despite all the centralization which the machinery of a modern Federal Republic has brought, the ancient provinces remain the real units of Austrian life. They were there, not only before the Republic, but even before the Habsburg dynasty which preceded it. And 20th century parliamentary techniques are as powerless to centralize them out of existence as was the bureaucracy of the Empress Maria Theresia two centuries before. Nor, today, would the attempt be made. Here again, the Austrian has struck his famous balance. Vienna and the provincial capitals have reached a division of labours which works, considering the difficulties, with remarkable harmony, and serves to strengthen the political structure of the Republic as a whole. For the activity and the influence of the provinces, with their contrasting background and character, not only help to preserve what is best in the nation's old traditions. They help also to guarantee what is best in the Republic's new democracy.

The provinces act as an automatic check on the aspirations of each other; and together they act as a counterweight to the supremacy, however loyally acknowledged, of the federal capital. Control is the essence of free government. To some extent, the provinces in their capacity as provinces fulfil this function in Austria more effectively than the National Parliament in Vienna. In a very real sense, therefore, they are the guardians of Austria's future as well as of her past.

For this reason, it is with historical, as well as pictorial justice to Austria that the photographs on these pages should depict each separate component of the Austrian state: Vienna, Lower Austria, Upper Austria, Styria, Carinthia, Salzburg, Tyrol, Vorarlberg and the Burgenland. Their varied character which the pictures show is not only a matter of landscape and geographical position. It is also implicit in the very different circumstances in which they were joined together as the successive pieces of an Alpine jig-saw puzzle; and, not the least, in the span of nearly ten centuries which were needed to achieve this union.

The historical and strategic heart of the whole complex is the area of Lower Austria which surrounds the capital. This was the original "Ostmark" of 976, as established by the Holy Roman Empire and allotted to the Babenbergs to secure the Empire's unsettled flank. It originally stretched only from the River Enns to the upward curve of the Danube near Spitz in the Wachau Valley, but seventy years later the same energetic Babenbergs had already extended their fiefdom eastwards of Vienna to the banks of the River Leitha.

Vienna itself, though first mentioned in documents as early as 881, only assumed its permanent importance for Austria in the early 11th century as the seat of the Babenberg rulers. For nearly 900 years this city remained the centre of the Austrian lands, and for over two-thirds of this enormous span it was also the capital of the Austrian Empire, and the seat of the Habsburg dynasty which succeeded the Babenbergs. Yet here is straight away a typical paradox. Though it is the oldest and most venerable of Austrian possessions, Vienna is juridically the youngest of Austrian provinces: it did not achieve that constitutional status until 1922, perhaps because the earlier centuries had always taken its significance for granted.

One by one, the other provinces of present-day Austria were added to the "heart-lands" of the Habsburg realm: parts of Upper Austria in 1156: Styria in 1192; Carinthia in 1335; Tyrol in 1365; Vorarlberg in 1375; and finally, the spiritual principality of Salzburg in 1805, as compensation for the loss of Tuscany. All these regions were the acquisitions of the dynasty—some by inheritance, some by grant, some by marriage, and some by purchase. Only one was added territorially by the Austrian Republic—the area of Western Hungary which was taken over by Austria in 1921 as the province of the Burgenland.

This long dynastic struggle by which the Austrian people built up their present home explains much in the position of the provinces today. These provinces are nearly as old as the counties of Britain, and have seen even more vicissitudes. Yet they have preserved over the centuries a great deal of the independence which the English counties have long ago lost. This is largely because, until 1918, they were still among the principal administrative units of the Empire, each reflecting in its own government that balance between dynasty on the one hand, and local landowners, industrialists, clergy, craftsmen, and ordinary citizen-voters on the other, which became typical of domestic political life in Austria towards the end of the Habsburg era.

13

Between 1919 and 1929, the Federal Republic made heavier inroads than the Empire into the authority of the provinces. Apart from the traditional prerogatives such as defence and foreign policy, the capital secured powers of exclusive jurisdiction and internal security, and even the complete control of higher education throughout the country. Yet, despite this, Federal Austria and its different provinces are today still juridically separate bodies and, internally, each province has retained the sole right to administer its sub-districts, as well as keeping certain privileges of local government vis-à-vis the Republic as a whole. In this way, the needs of sovereignty in a modern state have been balanced against the local traditions of the Middle Ages.

The siting of the various provincial capitals reflects their historic role in strategy and commerce. Bregenz, for example, is the gate to the Swiss Alps; Innsbruck to the Italian Alps; Klagenfurt to the Adriatic; and Graz to the great south-eastern hinterland of Yugoslavia and Hungary. Others, like Linz, are among the main road, rail and river junctions of Central Europe; and, in the case of this flourishing Upper Austrian capital, a major industrial city in its own right. It is their independent role as communication centres which give these provincial capitals an importance and a separate vitality which nothing can efface.

Our superficial introduction to the Austrian state and its people can fittingly close with this survey of the provinces. For the rich and varied spectrum of provincial life reflects again the essential pattern of Austria. This country "which God loved" remains the connecting link of a whole continent; and today, the connecting link is made doubly strong because an alloy of old and new has been poured into the metal.

There is the poetry of great events as well as the poetry of beauty in this view of Vienna from the Belvedere Palace. It was down the slopes of the Vienna Woods shown in the distance that, on 12th September 1683, the relief army descended to do battle with the Turks in their great siege of the Austrian capitel. This was in fact a siege of Christendom, and the victory which Austrian and Polish arms gained on that day was a victory for Christendom. It was, incidentally, in this same historic battle that Prince Eugene of Savoy, who later built the Belvedere Palace, began his long career as a European soldier and statesman. He had entered the service of the Austrian army in the year of the Turkish invasion after his services had been refused by Louis XIV of France due to his slight build.

And it was in the same gardens of this Belvedere Park that the Austrian people celebrated their most joyous event as a modern republic. On 15th May 1955 the paths and lawns shown here were covered with tens of thousands of Viennese who had gathered to watch the signature, in the Marble Chamber of the Palace, of the State Treaty which restored to Austria her freedom and identity after seventeen years of foreign occupation.

There is thus a gap of two and a half centuries separating the days, in very different settings, when Eugene of Savoy and the Foreign Ministers of the four great 20th century powers looked from the windows of Belvedere at this view. But the spire of St. Stephen's Cathedral in the foreground and the Vienna Woods on the horizon were there on both occasions.

15

The whole complex of the Belvedere Palace was built between 1714 and 1722 by Lukas von Hildebrandt as a summer residence for the great European soldier, statesman and man of letters Eugene of Savoy. The site chosen was a long sloping meadow just outside the fortifications of the old town. Though the Upper Palace, a glimpse of which is shown here, is normally thought of as Prince Eugene's home, this building was almost entirely used during his lifetime for audiences and banquets. The Prince himself lived in the long, one-storey "Lower Belvedere", a master-piece of intimate baroque architecture which Hildebrandt constructed to the Prince's orders at the foot of the sloping site.

Prince Eugene's Palace stood under no happy star. His heirs ransacked it after his death for everything they could sell, and most of the beautiful furnishings and pictures which the Prince had collected during his lifetime, as well as his irreplaceable private archive, were dispersed. Fortunately, the Palace itself was shortly afterwards acquired by the ruling house of Habsburg.

In the hands of this unhappy dynasty, it lived through some typically tragic moments. Though no one realized it at the time, the most poignant of these was the famous Court Ball and Gala held in the Belvedere in April 1770 to bid farewell to the Austrian Archduchess Maria Antonia two days before her marriage with Louis XVI of France. As Queen Marie Antoinette, she was to die on the scaffold with him 23 years later.

It was not until 1910 that the Belvedere Palace received a permanent royal resident worthy of its style. And even then there was a tragic destiny in the choice. This last inhabitant of the Palace was none other than the Archduke Franz Ferdinand, Heir-Presumptive to the Austrian throne, who was murdered at Sarajewo in June 1914.

This house, the so-called "Beethoven House", at Heiligenstadt on the slopes of the Vienna Woods, was lived in by the great composer in 1817. It was one of the many quarters Beethoven took up in the restless years between 1792 and his death in 1827 which he spent in the Austrian capital. No major works were composed in this building, but it was at a house in the Probusgasse a few yards away that the Second Symphony was written in the summer and autumn of 1802.

The name Probusgasse recalls, incidentally, the role which the ancient Romans played in establishing Vienna for all time as a winegrowing centre. It was the Roman Emperor Probus who, in the latter part of the Third Century A. D., authorized his garrison in the province of Noricum, as Roman Austria was then called, to help in constructing the vineyards on the slopes of the Danube.

The wine which Beethoven tasted was the ultimate descendant of these vines, and wine from the same stock can be drunk in this same house today. In summer and in winter, the Beethoven House at Heiligenstadt is now one of the most popular "Heuriger" of Vienna.

The roof of Vienna's famous St. Stephen's Cathedral is itself a symbol of the fusion of new and old which makes up the Austria of today. The coat-of-arms traced out in coloured tiles on the side of the roof shown here are those of the Habsburg dynasty with whom, for more than 600 years, Austria's triumph and tragedy as an empire were shared. But on the other side are shown the arms of the young Austrian Republic together with those of the City of Vienna.

Twice in its long history the great cathedral has been gutted. The original 12th century edifice was almost completely burnt down in 1258. The construction of the main features of the present Gothic building stretched from 1304 until 1450. A large part of this, one of the most beautiful cathedrals of the Middle Ages, was destroyed in April 1945 when, during the last days of fighting in the capital, sparks from blazing houses nearby set fire to scaffolding around the cathedral's tower and roof.

The whole of Austria contributed to the rebuilding of the capital's main landmark. The province of Lower Austria provided the new flooring; Upper Austria the new great bell; Styria the great gate; Carinthia the chandeliers; Tyrol the glass windows; Vorarlberg the pews; Burgenland the marble communion bench; Salzburg the tabernacle; and Vienna the roof. It was a day of national rejoicing when, in April 1952, the cathedral, rebuilt for the second time in its history, was complete again.

This panorama of Vienna is taken from the tower of St. Stephen's Cathedral. It is a vantage point 450 feet above the ground which has been put to many uses since the original tower was completed in 1433. For centuries, it was the main military look-out of the capital. It was from here that emergency light signals were flashed when the Turks closed in on the capital in the 17th century, and it was from here that the advance of the first relief columns was observed.
When the days of land sieges passed away, St. Stephen's spire became the highest observation point of Vienna's fire service. The fireguard post, which was sited just over halfway up the spire, was only dissolved in 1955.
The view shown here also spans the centuries. In the left foreground is St. Peter's Church, built by the great baroque architect Fischer von Erlach on the site of an earlier church dating from the 8th century. In the background are the twin towers of the Votiv Church, erected in the 19th century in memory of the Emperor Franz Joseph's escape from an attempted assassination in 1853. And on the extreme right of the picture is one of the largest modern buildings of post-war Vienna, the so-called "Ring Tower" which was finished in 1954.

For all its richness, this ornamental bowl from the Art Museum of
Vienna is a modest example of the capital's treasures. Quite apart
from the world-famous picture galleries, Vienna has the largest collection
of drawings in the world (the Albertina with over 1,000,000 items);
one of the most important Egyptian collections in existence; as well as
many specialized treasures such as collections of old ceramics; arms
and armour; musical instruments; coins; historical carriages; and wall
tapestries.

Nor is science neglected. Vienna also houses one of the greatest collections
of plants and minerals in Central Europe, and the Technical Museum
counts among its exhibits the first petrol-driven car of the world, constructed in Vienna in 1875.

Above all, it possesses in the collection of crown and state treasures
(the so-called Schatzkammer) something unique not only in its beauty
and variety. There is no more complete assembly of crown jewels in
existence, and none which symbolizes so faithfully the whole history
of a people for over a thousand years.

This little country-house on the edge of the Vienna Woods has been chosen as typifying the so-called "Biedermeier Age" in which it was built—that period of peace and false security which stretched between the end of the Napoleonic wars and the national uprisings of 1848.

The comfort and extravagance which were among its main characteristics are both reflected in this extraordinary house—built in 1810 in a carefree mixture of Gothic and oriental styles by an Austrian banker named Geymüller who had made his fortune in the Napoleonic era. A fitting tenant was soon found to match its oriental exterior. During the Congress of Vienna in 1815 the envoy of Turkey was lodged here, and it was in this year that the house acquired its private mosque.

The fortunes of Baron Geymüller did not even last as long as the brief Biedermeier age itself. His heir and nephew got through the money in record time and became the inspiration of Raimund's wellknown comedy "The Spendthrift".

The rich and unspoilt Burgenland, of which a typical harvest scene is shown here, is the most easterly of Austria's provinces and the most recently acquired. Parts of it belonged to the Habsburg empire for two hundred years between the 15th and 17th centuries, but it was not until 1921 that the young Austrian Republic won the province as it now exists from neighbouring Hungary. Border skirmishes as well as a three-year diplomatic tussle were needed to end the dispute. Even then, all four "Burgen", or fortresses, from which the area originally got its name (Pressburg, Ödenburg, Wieselburg, Eisenburg) remained in Czech or Hungarian hands.

But though the Burgenland is young as an Austrian province, it is the most ancient of all Austro-Germanic colonizing areas. It was here that over eleven hundred years ago Charlemagne established Franconian settlers in a feudal mark set for defence purposes on the borderline of the Teuton and Slav worlds. And ever since, these cornfields have been the highway for invading armies from the East.

This glimpse of a vineyard in Lower Austria symbolizes one of the province's many sources of wealth and principal claims to fame. Lower Austria is the geographical and historical heart of the country, since it was around this fertile area north and south of the Danube that the Austrian state had its origin in the feudal mark of the Babenbergers, a thousand years ago.

The region has always been famous for the quality and variety of its wines. One of the principal wine-growing areas lies north of the river and has been popularly known for centuries as the "Wine Quarter".

But though the vineyards are the most picturesque among the natural riches of Lower Austria, they cannot compare in economic importance with the great oilfields in the plains of Marchfeld east of Vienna. With their annual output of over 3,5 million tons, they have turned Austria into Europe's second oil producing country, surpassed only by Rumania in quantity. It was on the plains where the oil derricks now rise that the founder of Imperial Austria's greatness, Rudolf of Habsburg, laid down the political and military basis for his dynasty with his defeat of the Bohemian King Ottokar in 1278. It was on the same plains that, over 500 years later, Austrian armies successfully challenged the might of Napoleon.

Culturally as well as geographically, the Burgenland is a transition ground between the Alps of Central Europe and the great plains of the East. This Burgenland village scene, with its low-slung houses and its goose-pond, already brings the atmosphere of the Hungarian "puszta".

But the most remarkable natural phenomenon of the province is undoubtedly Lake Neusiedl, which, over twenty miles long and some five miles wide, straddles the Austro-Hungarian border. Though it is the largest of Austria's lakes, it is nowhere much more than three feet deep and can be waded through in calm weather with comfort. The birdlife of the lake is as unique as its other properties, and species are found on its shores which are unknown anywhere else in Europe.

The province is also of considerable sociological interest. Its mixed population typifies the tolerant fusion of races and creeds which characterizes Austria as a whole. Of its 300,000 inhabitants, roughly 40,000 are Croats and over 10,000 Magyars, and there is a strong Protestant element among the predominantly Catholic population. But, in less than two generations, these different strands have been woven into the single thread of a harmonious Austrian province.

This tiny town on the shores of Lake Neusiedl, with little more than 1,500 inhabitants, has become famous for two things—its wine and its storks. The quality of the neighbouring vineyards was established in the Middle Ages, and in 1364 the people of Rust were given the right to seal wine barrels with the municipal coat-of-arms.

The stork-life of the town is one of the most famous natural curiosities of Austria. There is scarcely a roof-top in the town without the strange silhouette of a stork's nest.

The so-called "Humpback World" (Bucklige Welt), a stretch of which is shown here, belongs to the most peaceful and unspoilt of Austria's many undiscovered regions. Geologically, this area 50 miles south of Vienna is one of the last connecting links joining the Central Alpine Massif to its final spurs in the Rosalien and Leitha mountains which overlook the Hungarian plain. Though the Humpback World can boast some respectable peaks over 5,500 feet high, its main characteristic is this open and softly rounded hill country which is found relatively seldom in the Austrian landscape. Its quiet beauty has inspired many writers, including Austria's national poet Anton Wildgans.

A feature of this countryside is that, despite its proximity to the capital, it has the sparse population and untouched natural calm of the most remote alpine region. The small towns and villages hidden in the folds of these hills are favourite inexpensive holiday centres for the Viennese in both summer and winter. The area also contains pilgrimage centres, such as St. Corona, which are of more than local renown.

Bernstein Castle in the southern Burgenland. However idyllic it appears on this picture, this 13th century fortress has had anything but an idyllic past. Since the early Middle Ages it formed one of the principal strongpoints in the long chain of forts built to guard the Austrian land from invasions across the eastern plains. Bernstein itself, though besieged by Mongols, Magyars and Turks, and involved in countless minor actions, never surrendered. Its banners are still preserved in the armoury of the castle, which is now adapted for use as a country-house hotel.

This curiously built baroque church in Eisenstadt, provincial capital of the Burgenland, has held the tomb of the great Austrian composer Joseph Haydn since 1820, and is popularly known as "the Haydn Church". Though Haydn was born on the border of the adjoining province of Lower Austria, his name is most closely associated with Eisenstadt since it was at the Palace of the Esterhazys, only a few hundred yards away from this church, that he worked between 1761 and 1790 as house conductor and composer to the Prince. It was here that many of his most famous works were written, and the operas and concerts of the Palace helped to create the reputation of Eisenstadt as "the Versailles of the East".

In June 1954, Eisenstadt was the scene of a Haydn occasion that was both gruesome and touching. The skull of the composer, which had been removed from the grave soon after his burial by misguided admirers, was finally reunited, after nearly 150 years of separation, with the composer's other remains. A long motorcar cavalcade, mainly in mourning but partly in celebration, crawled at a funereal pace from Vienna to Eisenstadt for the ceremony.

The old town of Eisenstadt overlooks the unbroken stretch of the Hungarian plain and, since prehistoric times, fortifications have been built on the site. The town was made the capital of the Burgenland after the loss of Oedenburg (Sopron) to Hungary in 1921.

The Rax and Schneeberg mountains (each well over 6000 feet high) shown on this panorama belong to the chain of Vienna's "backgarden peaks" which rises less than 60 miles south-east of the capital. Though they are equipped with everything the foreign tourist needs, from Alpine rest huts to large luxury hotels, it is primarily as the weekend and holiday playground of the Viennese that these mountains are known. They provide the capital not only with its nearest high mountain air but also with Vienna's water supply, renowned for its quality. The springs which feed the water pipes down to the capital rise in the area shown on this picture.

Nearby is the Semmering pass (3000 feet high), the natural watershed between the Vienna Basin and the neighbouring province of Styria, and, for centuries, a vital link in the trade route connecting the Austrian capital with the Adriatic sea.

It was here that, in 1728, a new pass road was built in the record time of 48 days, to facilitate the journey made in June of that year to Fiume by the Emperor Charles VI. Seventy years earlier, when his predecessor had travelled across the mountain to take the homage of the Styrian nobility, 3000 oxen were needed to pull the carriages over the primitive road. The new pass could be negotiated "with comfort in a twohorse carriage".

The Semmering is also the site of Europe's first mountain railway. It was completed in 1854 under the direction of the Austrian engineer Karl von Ghega, who pushed through his plan despite the ridicule of most railway experts of the day, including the famous Stevenson in England. For six years, 4000 workers laboured through four million working days to build the three miles of tunnels and viaducts needed to scale the height. At its inauguration, the Semmering railway was one of the most progressive engineering feats of its day, and it will always remain one of the most difficult and daring.

This traditional national costume from Lower Austria is that of a winegrower in the Wachau Valley. It is only one of sixty or seventy distinctive national costume forms which still exist in Austria; and to these basic types must be added countless variations, with subtle changes not only from valley to valley, but from village to village.

Nearly all of these genuine costumes are accurate reproductions of the peasant festival dress of former centuries. The further west one goes in Austria, the older these costumes seem to be in origin. Most of those from the Danube Valley, for example, (like this one with its characteristic golden head-dress) date from the early 19th century. In Tyrol and parts of the Salzburg province, costumes from the 18th century are not uncommon. In the great Bregenz forest of Austria's westernmost province of Vorarlberg, costumes even survive in their original 16th century form.

It should be noted that many items of Austrian national dress commonly thought to be traditional are, in fact, relatively recent innovations, largely influenced by the modern world of fashion. To these belong, in its current form, the so-called "dirndl" of the Salzburg province.

Much that is typically Austrian finds expression in these costumes, whether old or new—the warmth of the land, the astounding variety and tenacity of its local traditions, the pride of the people in them, and the legendary charm of Austria's womenfolk.

The majestic Abbey of Melk, whose towers rise over 350 feet above the Danube, is not only one of the largest and loveliest of all baroque buildings in Central Europe. Its own history symbolizes the triumphs and tragedies of the Austrian people over the last 1,000 years. The original edifice is thought to have been built as a castle for the Babenberg dynasty as long ago as the last quarter of the 10th century. About one hundred years later, it was handed over by the same ruling house to the Benedictine monks from St. Lamprecht, and its long history as an Abbey began.

But this transfer from temporal to spiritual hands did not spare the building from the military perils of the Middle Ages. Already in the 14th century it had been reconstructed as a powerful fortress, and few armies who moved up the central Danube valley passed it by. In 1683 it was besieged by the same Turkish army which tried in vain to take Vienna. It was a fire which finally destroyed the original structure, however, and the building as we see it now was constructed on the same site by the famous architect Jakob Prandtauer between the years 1701 and 1738. The two western towers which overlook the river were added last of all by a pupil of Prandtauer's.

Even in its new ecclesiastical form, the Abbey of Melk was destined to play its part in most of the great campaigns of imperial Austria. It was here, for example, in 1805 and again in 1809 that Napoleon resided during both of his advances on the Austrian capital.

The Kuenringer "Danube pirates", who ruled Duernstein from the 12th century, would have remained an obscure feudal family had not one of their chiefs, Hadmar II, gone down in history as goaler to the captive Richard Lionheart of England. It was here that the English king, captured near Vienna on his return from the Crusades, was imprisoned in 1192 while the English collected the ransom demanded by Leopold of Austria for his freedom.

Duernstein is another of the many Danube edifices to bear the full brunt of the campaigns which swept over Austria. In March 1645, during the 30-Years-War, the original building was reduced to a ruin by Swedish troops, and has never been rebuilt since. All that remains today of King Richard's prison are the outer ramparts and a jagged remnant of the keep, silhouetted against the horizon. But the town itself was destined to see further battles. It was near Duernstein that, in November 1805, the allied armies of imperial Austria and Russia scored one of their triumphs against Napoleon's troops.

The Wachau valley, of which Duernstein is one of the venerable jewels, is unquestionably the most beautiful stretch of the Austrian Danube. Its vineyards which stretch through almost every village from Krems to Melk, are among the most renowned in the country. The valley is at its loveliest when a carpet of apricot blossom stretches down, every spring, from the hills to the banks of the river. So many thousands of Viennese and foreign visitors now make their spring-time pilgrimage to the Wachau to see this sight that the narrow twisting road of the valley became incapable of taking the traffic. A new and modern highway—called the "Wine Road"—is now being built, which will run also through Duernstein.

The village of St. Wolfgang on the Upper Austrian lake of the same name was a goal of pilgrims long before it became a goal for tourists. According to local legend, it was the holy Wolfgang, Bishop of Regensburg, who built the original church here with his own hands, and released a healing spring from the ground underneath it.

The present parish church of St. Wolfgang contains one of the finest pieces of Gothic carving in existence—the famous altar screen created by Michael Pacher in the late 15th century. This little church also boasts other notable altar pieces from the 17th and early 18th centuries.

Medieval documents show that pilgrimages to St. Wolfgang were already flourishing in the 14th century. Its fame as a holiday centre, on the other hand, dates from the last 50 years. The symbol of its touristic importance is the "White Horse Inn" on the shores of the lake, whose name has been carried by operettas to all corners of the earth.

St. Wolfgang is in the centre of the Salzkammergut group of lakes. The Schafberg peak, shown rising above it on this picture, is well over 5,300 feet high but can be comfortably reached by Austria's oldest cog-wheel railway. The panorama from the top takes in not only the whole Salzkammergut region but also the mountains of Styria to the south, the plains of Bavaria to the west, and the Czech mountains of the Böhmerwald to the north.

The Mondsee, 15 miles east of Salzburg, is one of the warmest and the quietest of the famous chain of lakes which run through the Salzkammergut.

Since prehistoric times, men have sought rest and shelter under the gigantic "Dragon's Wall" shown on this picture—a face of rock which rises sheer from the blue waters. Traces still survive of lake-dwellings built on stilts on these shores some two thousand five hundred years before Christ. Even the lake's name is surrounded with legend. According to one version, it was called "Moon Lake" because, in the 8th century, the local ruler Duke Odilo II lost himself while hunting at night behind the rock-face and was only saved from plunging to his death in the lake by the moon suddenly breaking through the clouds. A more prosaic explanation is that both lake and village got their name through being used as a post station (Mansio) in Roman times.

There is, however, nothing legendary about ecclesiastical importance of Mondsee. Its famous abbey was a centre of learning and religion for a thousand years after its foundation in 748 by monks from Monte Cassino in Central Italy. Mondsee's attractions for the modern tourist in search of simplicity and peace are equally well-founded.

The history of the Abbey of Krems-
muenster stretches back beyond the
six centuries of Habsburg rule and
beyond even the dynasty of the
Babenbergs which preceded them. The
original abbey was founded in the
eighth century by Tassilo Duke of
Bavaria and shows traces of the
colonization of Austria by missionary
monks from Ireland in the early
Dark Ages.

It was built in its present form in
the late 17th and early 18th century
by Jakob Prandtauer, the architect
of Melk. Like Melk, it did long service
as a fortress as well as an abbey before
assuming its peaceful baroque identity.
Though the abbey is ancient, its
abbots have kept up with the times.
The present building possesses an
observatory and is the seat of a
wellknown ecclesiastical college.

Few Austrian towns present such a happy combination of the beautiful and the useful as this Upper Austrian city on the river Enns. Its old buildings are a pleasing mixture of late Gothic, Renaissance, and baroque styles. But though the unspoilt atmosphere of the city is almost medieval, its function as the seat of Austria's greatest car industry is highly utilitarian. This industrial tradition stretches back unbroken to the earliest Christian times. Iron was worked here even in the days of the Roman occupation. In the 13th century, an Imperial Privilege gave Steyr the right to have all the iron ore and timber from the nearby iron mountain offered first for public sale on its market square for the space of three days. The locksmiths, armourers, and cutlers of the city exploited this privilege to build up an industry which flourished unchallenged throughout the Middle Ages.

Steyr was threatened in the 16th century by Turkish invaders, and barely was that threat repulsed when the town was ravaged by the wars of religion. The 30-Years-War and the Napoleonic campaigns also took their toll of the city, and it was in the house of the "Lion Apothecary" that the armistice of Christmas Day 1800 was signed between Austria and France.

Yet throughout this troubled history the ancient iron industry of the town kept functioning—now wilting, now flourishing. Finally, in 1869, the "Austrian Manufacturing Company" was founded, to complete the town's transition into the modern industrial age. The present Steyr-Daimler-Puch company, through it has abandoned armaments production for that of motor vehicles, still continues in the 20th century the thousand-year-old iron working tradition of the town.

Graz, the beautifully situated capital of Styria, is a good example of a major Austrian town which has preserved something of the charm and intimacy of more leisured days despite its position as one of the political, strategic, and economic centres of the country.

This peaceful view, for example, is taken from one of the main squares in a bustling city of over 226,000 inhabitants. The clock tower, which crowns the Schlossberg-hill in the background, has dominated the panorama of the city ever since its construction in 1561. The great bell alongside it has been tolling for the people of Graz on days of festival or in times of danger ever since it was cast in 1587.

In modern times, Graz has not contented itself with keeping up with events but has marched ahead of them, especially in the fields of commerce and learning. Its university boasts four Nobel Prize winners. Its Technical College has produced two scientists of European renown. Its spring and autumn trade fairs are Austrian's main link with the traditional markets of South East Europe.

Eggenberg Castle near Graz owes its creation in the seventeenth century to a phenomenon which was rare for those times. It was built by Johann Ulrich von Eggenberg who, despite his bourgeois ancestry from a merchant's family at Radkersburg, achieved the highest noble rank of Prince of the Empire in 1623 for services to the Habsburg dynasty. Two years later, he built this castle as his seat.

Though he could not quite keep up with the current mode of kings and have a room for every day of the year, he did his best to build on the grand scale by having exactly 365 windows put into the castle. But the family of Eggenberg was not destined to survive long after reaching the apex of its remarkable career. In 1755, the male line died out, and the castle passed into other hands.

Styria is above all the province of the hunter. It is therefore fitting that this, the most important castle of the provincial capital, should even today be a museum of the shoot and the chase.

The weirdly beautiful "Ore Mountain" of Styria is the biggest mineral treasure of Austria after the oilfields of the eastern plains. But unlike the oilfields, whose discovery and exploitation was left till the 20th century, the industrial history of the Ore Mountain dates from the beginning of Christian times.

The profile of the mountain is a strange combination of prehistoric nature and centuries of man's activity. Originally, 60 great steps, each nearly 40 feet high, were cut into its side. Today, these have been reduced to the 30 giant shelves shown on the picture, each over 70 feet high, and more than 700 yards long.

The flourishing and progressive iron industry which now works the mountain's treasures has been nationalized since the end of the Second World War. It operates without the fear that its precious source will run out in the near future. The reserves of the Ore Mountain are still estimated at about 330 million tons. At the current excavation rate of some 2,5 million tons a year, this is enough to keep the blast furnaces of Austria fully working for well over another 100 years.

This mountain typifies a phenomenon rare in the Machine Age. Like the great factories which encircle it, it blends happily into the landscape, with an artificial grandeur of its own. Austria is lucky enough to have a heavy industry in her economy without a Black Country on her landscape.

The Styrian paper-making town of Frohnleiten, on the banks of the swiftly running river Mur between Bruck and Graz, is yet another of those examples of Austrian provincial industrial centres which have preserved both their historic character and their beautiful natural setting.

The migration of cattle up to the "Almen", or mountain pastures, in spring, and their return to the valleys in autumn are among the most picturesque sights which Austrian country life has to offer. Both are great days in the annual calendar of the villagers, and both are celebrated with a strong dash of ancient superstition as well as traditional custom.

The "Auftrieb", or procession up to the pastures, is normally held towards the end of March on the lower slopes, from where, about the middle of June, the cattle are taken to the highest pastures. Certain days, such as a Friday or Sunday, are considered incorrect or unlucky. Before the cattle leave their sheds in the village, the old Christian ceremony of protecting them from mishap on their journey is still widely observed. They are given a last meal of sanctified Christmas bread, and touched with holy willows. Even the loud cracking of whips which accompanies the beasts on their climb is not designed to drive them forward by force, but is rather a ceremonial affair dating from heathen recipees for scaring away evil spirits.

The "Abfahrt", or procession down from the alpine pastures, can take place any time up to the end of September. This is an occasion for general rejoicing. The last week before the descent, the so-called "Schoppwoche", is traditionally devoted in all the alpine huts to singing, dancing and drinking. The last night on the mountains before the move (in Tyrol called the "Grünnacht", or green night) forms the climax at which the celebrations last from dusk till early dawn, when the cattle are set moving.

Though the picture opposite is a modest example, such processions can often be very elaborate. The men and women who have attended the herds throughout the summer months put on their finery. The leading cow wears an enormous bell around its neck and often carries on its horns a head-dress of golden tinsel and glass pearls. The other cattle are given little wreaths of alpine flowers.

Once the procession gets safely down to its home village, it is greeted with music and the characteristic blank rounds of mortar fire which accompany most alpine celebrations. This, however, can only take place if no mishap has overtaken the herd during its pasturing time. If one of the animals should have died, or a disease have broken out, the celebrations are cancelled, and special mourning wreaths of deep violet and black are hung on the returning cattle.

Behind all this maze of tradition and superstition there are the practical outlines of a highly important agricultural activity. Austria's milk cows alone number well over a million head, and their milk production in 1955 was over 2,5 million tons.

This Christmas fir tree, whose lights shine in a snow-covered Salzburg landscape, expresses what is a relatively modern tradition. Illuminated Christmas trees are first mentioned around the year 1600 in Central Europe, but the customs from which they derive go back much further. The ceremony is allegedly a survival of the heathen belief that the new life energy developed after midwinter by all trees and bushes should be carried into people's homes to radiate its power among all who dwell there.

Relics of this older belief are still to be observed in many a peasant house of the Austrian countryside, where sprigs of fir or pine trees are nailed over the door or hung over portraits of the Holy Family in the living room.

It was at Oberndorf, an old settlement of boatmen on the river Salzach, not far from these mountains, that the world's most famous Christmas song was composed. On Christmas Eve of the year 1818, the village organist Franz Gruber and his friend the priest Josef Mohr respectively composed the music and words of "Silent Night, Holy Night". The little church of St. Nikolaus where the song was first played, no longer stands. But the song will last as long as Christmas itself.

The origins of the famous Salzburg spa of Bad Gastein are another charming mixture of legend and fact. The local folklore has it that the warm healing springs of the town were discovered in 1680 by hunters pursuing a wounded stag. The documentary history of the springs dates from the 14th century, and among the first of the spa's many prominent guests was the later German Emperor Frederick III, who visited the springs in 1436 shortly before his ascent to the throne. Gastein, as the world knows it today, was built up largely in the 19th century when its waters —a combination of temperature and radio-activity unique in the world—attracted the sick and the prominent from all continents.

In recent years, the spa has also developed into a winter sports centre of the first rank. A cable railway and many ski-lifts have been built on the surrounding mountains, and it has become the venue of international championships.

The so-called "Perchten", shown climbing through the snow in the foreground of this picture, give a typically Austrian contrast of old with new. With their weird head-dresses, bells and chains, they symbolize, among other things, the coming forces of spring, and their noisy race down the hills every January 6th is one of the most picturesque sights of the Salzburg province.

This view of Salzburg shows the fortress, the old landmark of the town and surrounding countryside, towering over the festival theatre, the 20th century centre of the city's musical life.

The music festivals themselves are, however, older than is generally supposed. They date from 1842, when the Salzburg memorial for Mozart was unveiled. The International Mozart Foundation was constituted already in 1870, and the construction of the Mozarteum Music Conservatory was begun in 1910. But it was only in the 1920s, under the inspiration of men like Max Reinhardt and Hugo von Hofmannsthal, that the festivals developed into red-letter days in the world's calendar of culture.

Though Mozart was born in a house a few hundred yards from the scene of this picture, he spent only part of his working life in the service of the Prince-Archbishops who ruled Salzburg in his day. In 1777, at the age of 21, he left their employment temporarily, and, four years later, severed all permanent connections.

The flourishing city of Salzburg is the capital of the Austrian province of the same name. Today, its principal source of income is the tourist trade, which reaches a hectic peak with the five weeks of the festival season.

52

AUSTRIA, BY AUSTRIA'S GREATEST POET

(Franz Grillparzer, 1791—1872)

". . . It is a goodly land
Well worth a kingly venture.
Where did you ever see its match?
Look round about: wher'ere the eye may rest
It laughs as the bride does to her lover;
With luscious green and meadows flow'r-beset,
Embroidered blue and yellow with flax and saffron fields,
Its mellow air perfumed with herbs—
A nosegay, wreathed by the Danube's silver.
Gaily the valleys broad stretch up
To hillocks, where the generous sun
Casts golden burnish on the juicy grape.
The hunter's realm, dark forests, crowns the whole;
And God's mild breath that hovers over it
Warms and ripens and makes the pulses throb
As in the frozen steppes they never will.
Thus is the Austrian gay and frank:
Owns willingly his faults, and never hides his joy;
Envies not, lets others envy him . . .
Oh goodly land! Oh fatherland!
Twixt Italy the child and manly Germany
Thou liest—a red-cheeked stripling.
May God preserve thy youthful heart,
May he redress what other hands have spoiled".

(English translation by J. H. Blumenthal, 1931)

If Salzburg's music festivals have a drawback, it is that they sometimes tend to obscure the city's claim to fame in its ow
right. For even had W. A. Mozart never been born in the narrow Getreidegasse, Salzburg would surely have won inte
national renown as one of the world's loveliest cities.

A good idea of its concentrated beauty is given in these two views of the Cathedral square. In one, the misty silhouet
of the 900-year-old fortress is shown against a foreground of colonnades. The other shows a close-up of the "Immaculat:
statue, a symposium of lead-moulded figures erected in 1771.

Many of the town's most beautiful buildings arose in the first half of the 17th century, and it is from this period that t
famous Cathedral also dates. It was constructed between 1614 and 1628 by Santino Solari on the site of an 8th centu
basilica.

It is in this square that the open-air performances of the morality play "Everyman" are held during the festival seaso
The anonymous play, whose English text dates from the first half of the 16th century, was first performed in this natur
setting in 1920, and has ever since remained a standard feature of the festival programme. The dramatic highpoint of th
particular production of the work are the invisible admonishers whose voices sound out from the facade of the Cathedr
and even from the parapets of the fortress high above.

Austria's southern most province of Carinthia is not only a borderland between two states. In culture, climate, landscape, and population it is a transition ground between Central Europe and the Italian and South Slav worlds.

This view of the Drau river valley, which runs west to east across the province not far from the Italian and Jugoslav frontiers, typifies this characteristic. There is still a strong reminder of the Alpine theme which dominates the Austrian countryside. But the open and friendly fields in the foreground give a strong hint of the sun-drenched Italian South which lies only a few miles off.

Carinthia's role as a crucible of nature makes it one of the richest and most versatile of the Austrian provinces. Apart from timber, there are large deposits of coal, magnesite, lead and zinc ore, and its rivers and mountains supply an important and steadily expanding hydro-electric industry. The landscape—and particularly the many lakes—guarantee a constant stream of tourists and holiday-makers, while Carinthia's position on the age-old trade route between Vienna and Venice gives it permanent importance as a communications link.

Carinthia gets its name from the Celtic race of the Carnians who were absorbed in the Roman Empire at the beginning of the Christian era. The region flourished under Roman rule as one of the chief centres of the iron industry of Noricum, as Roman Austria was called.

Remarkable fresh evidence of this Roman civilization has been brought to light since the Second World War by the important excavations carried out by the Provincial Government on the Magdalensberg, a rise near the old Carinthian town of St. Veit. The work so far carried out is enough to show that this was a Roman settlement of considerable importance, which served less as a military fortress than as a peaceful provincial centre. Public interest in these discoveries has been so great that a new motor road has been built to link this and other inaccessible sights of Carinthia to the main north-south route.

Hochosterwitz Castle in Carinthia is, in its romantic style, one of the loveliest in Austria. It is one of the few still to remain in possession of the original owners—the Khevenhüller family who built it in the second half of the 16th century. It is also unusual in that it was never submitted to a major siege though, in the times of the second Turkish invasion, it gave asylum to many of the local people. This relatively untroubled history is partly due to its construction which would daunt the heart of the fiercest invader—14 successive castle gates and many bastions guarding the steep ascent to the summit of the limestone peak on which it was built. But, as its relatively recent origin shows, the castle itself dates from the era when these massive stone dwellings were already losing their importance as fortresses and becoming instead ornate places of residence.

This picture of sunset over Lake Wörther, with its almost tropical blaze of colours, shows how strongly the influence of the South pervades the Carinthian atmosphere.

The Wörthersee is the largest and most frequented of the 200 odd lakes which are dotted all over the province. Its busiest tourist centres are Pörtschach and Velden, and the whole of the socalled "Austrian Riviera" which stretches between. Here, all the sophisticated apparatus of an international holiday region has been created—flower carnivals, "concours d'élegance" for fashions and automobiles, roulette casinos, major tennis tournaments, and numberless congresses. This northern coast of the lake is doubly busy since, in addition to its tourist attractions, it lies on the main road and rail route between Vienna and Northern Italy.

The southern shores of the lake, though they boast one of the best golf courses in Austria, are on the whole less sophisticated and more idyllic. The picturesque peninsula of Maria Wörth juts out halfway along this southern side—an ancient pilgrimage centre with two old churches, one of which dates from the 10th century.

In temperature as well as in setting, the Wörthersee has a breath of the warm South. Bathing can often go on comfortably until well into the autumn, at a time when the lakes of northern Austria are only for the hardiest fanatic.

Heiligenblut in Western Carinthia is the picturesque gateway to the great Gross-
glockner road, one of the most modern alpine pass routes in Central Europe.
The sharp snow-covered peak of the Grossglockner towers up in the background.
   Nearly 12,500 feet high, it is the highest of all Austria's countless mountains.
It was first scaled in the year 1800 by a village priest from the East Tyrol.
Today, the whole region around the peak and the huge six-mile-long Pasterze
   glacier below it form a special reservation area for winter sports enthusiasts.
The great motor road over the Glockner is some thirty miles long and was
built between 1930 and 1935, despite the serious economic troubles which the
First Austrian Republic was then facing. Its highest point, the so-called Hochtor, or
High Gate, was already used by the Romans as a crossing point of the
   Tauern Range to which the mountain belongs.
Despite its inevitable associations with the Grossglockner road, Heiligenblut is
an Austrian beauty spot in its own right. Its name comes from a local legend
   that some of the holy blood of Christ was brought here for preservation.

Lake Millstatt, in the centre of the province, is one of the most peaceful of the larger Carinthian lakes, despite its accessibility on the main east-west route from Lienz to Klagenfurt, the provincial capital. Long stretches of its shores are unspoilt and unbuilt-upon, like the section shown in this view. Yet the increasing flow of tourists and holiday-makers is forcing Millstatt to adopt more and more of the up-to-date methods used by its sophisticated sisters like Lake Wörther. And nearby, at Radenthein, lies an ever-expanding centre of Austria's magnesite production.

The lake itself is the bed of an Ice-Age glacier stream which ran here between two wooded peaks on the southern edge of the Tauern Range. Though more than 1800 feet high, the climate of the lake is remarkably mild.

Among the main sites of the town of Millstatt is a former Benedictine monastery with an 11th century church and a lime-tree one thousand years old in its ground.

The ancient lime-tree typifies the age-old history of the Millstatt area as a cultural settlement. Celtic and other remains which have been dug up from the banks of the lake show that pre-Christian peoples sougth shelter on these shores. Roman graves have also been found here to testify to the part Millstatt already played at a time when most of present-day Austria was one of the northern bastions of the Roman Empire.

The connected and documented history of the villages on the lake is as old as the town of Millstatt itself, and suggests that by the early Middle Ages a flourishing community existed all around these shores.

The Dolomite mountains of Lienz, shown here in midwinter, are one of the many grandiose chains which dominate the landscape of the East Tyrol region. These peaks, known in local dialect as "The Monsters", are the most easterly spurs of the Italian Dolomite range.

Until 1918, the present areas of North, East, and South Tyrol were one united Austrian province. The transfer of the South Tyrol to Italy after the First World War severed all common boundaries between the other two parts.

The East Tyrol is today one of the most peaceful as well as most beautiful of all Austria's mountain regions, having remained outside the main stream of tourist traffik.

Few things express more strikingly the deep religious sense which characterizes the people of Tyrol than these socalled "Marterle", which can be found dotted on pathways and peaks all over the mountains of the province.

Strictly speaking, they are burial or memorial signs for ordinary persons who died or were killed by accident on the spot marked. In this form, they usually countain a picture of the deceased, with the details of his death and the request that passers-by should pray for his soul.

In a broader sense, these "Marterle" are simply wooden or stone posts carrying a holy picture, or else crucifixes or small religious statues which still fall short of a mountain chapel proper.

The word almost certainly derives in some form from "martyr" or "martyria".

The Virgen Valley, which lies well over 3,000 feet high in the East Tyrol, is typical of scores in the province—a gently sloping basin of meadows and woods, divided by a mountain stream and leading up on either side to the snow-clad peaks of the Alps. Characteristic of most of these valleys are the isolated and beautifully tended farmhouses of the local peasants, whose very solitude adds to the tranquillity of the scene. Yet even the remotest of these valleys are often directly linked with the world of great events which seems to have passed them by. Near the village of Hinterbichl, for example, which lies at the end of this particular valley, is situated the summer school of the world-famous Vienna Choir Boys.

The picturesque dress which these villagers from Praegarten in the East Tyrol are wearing is as much of a uniform as an ancient peasant costume: it is the garb of the Tyrolean Riflemen, a self-defence organization formed by the free men of the province in the late Middle Ages. Among the many actions which the ancestors of these villagers fought in these same costumes was the famous rebellion of the Tyrolean peasants against Napoleon under Andreas Hofer in 1809. The proud martial tradition which these costumes express is also a proud democratic one. From the early 15th century, the free citizens and peasants of Tyrol were represented in their provincial diets on an equal footing with the local nobility and clergy.

This palette of contrasting moods and colours shows the range of the Carinthian landscape. In the background, a mountain peak typical of any alpine chain in early spring; in the foreground, a rich mixture of meadow, pine and birch.

The wealth of Carinthia is also shown in this view. Over 40% of the province is forest, and timber is one of its principal products. Here, we are on the lower slopes of the wooded belt, which ends in this part of the Eastern Alps at about 5,500 feet. But there is already enough space for the birch, with its characteristic longing for light and air, to get its head clear.

This panoramic view of Innsbruck, the ancient and lovely capital of the Tyrol, shows many of the historic and natural landmarks of the city. The twin-towered church in the foreground, the socalled Hofkirche, contains what is perhaps the most important German sculpture of the Renaissance period. This is the monument worked in metal for the marble sarcophagus of the great Habsburg Emperor Maximilian I. The church itself was built in 1553-63 to take his tomb, though in fact the ruler was buried in Wiener Neustadt, Lower Austria.

Behind the church is the palace built by Maximilian as his town residence. The documented history of Innsbruck goes back far beyond the Habsburg dynasty. It was first named in records in the early 11th century and was established as a fortified town as early as 1180.

In the background towers the peak of the Patscherkofel mountain, whose rounded cone-shape is one of the rarest sights in an Alpine range. It is a wellknown centre for holidaymakers and tourists in summer and winter alike.

The valley of the Inn, shown here from the village of Mösern, is the largest of all the valleys of Tyrol and, at the same time, the most important communications and industrial artery of the province. In this lovely broad valley are situated not only Innsbruck, the provincial capital, but all the larger Tyrolean towns and the local industries associated with them such as Jenbach (machinery); Wörgl (wood fibre products); Kufstein (metal and timber); Wattens (glass); and Imst, to name only one of the textile centres.

It is from the Inn valley that the narrower side valleys of the Tyrol branch off—like the Oetz, the Ziller, the Stubai and Paznaun valleys, each one a holiday centre in its own right. Parallel to the river run the main road and rails links which connect the Alps to Eastern Europe, and at right angles across the valley run some of the main north-south routes of the Continent. To combine all this activity and all this importance, and yet remain as peaceful and unspoilt as this view suggests, is an Austrian speciality.

Though the province of Tyrol is always thought of as a mountain region, it also contains some of Austria's loveliest and most unspoilt lakes. This is one of them—the Achen Lake which lies a few miles north of the main Innsbruck—Wörgl road, to which it is linked by the excellent motor route shown. The lake is some 3,000 feet high and is noted locally for the unusual deep blue of its water.

Nearby are one of Tyrol's oldest castles and one of her newest power plants. Tratzberg Castle already appears in the chronicles of the 13th century and, some 300 years later, it belonged for a time to the Fuggers, the famous German merchant and banking family. The power plant, which is named after the lake, is a major link in Austria's great hydro-electric chain. Thus even near the shores of this idyllic mountain lake, the new and the old of Austria are found close together in a characteristic blend.

The Grossvenediger Mountain (just over 12,000 feet) shown on this picture is the second highest peak of Austria, being surpassed only by the Grossglockner, a glimpse of which was given in an earlier scene.

The "Venediger" is one of the finest skiing and climbing mountains in Austria. The ascent can be made via a chain of rest-huts which, outside the great wintersports centres, still form the backbone of the Alpine tourist industry. For the skier, the enormous untracked slopes which lie beneath the peak of the Venediger provide perfect natural deep-snow runs.

The glaciers and streams of this mountain region also form an inexhaustible reservoir for Austria's hydro-electric power plants which are among the greatest in Europe.

The mountains of the Ziller Valley, not far from Innsbruck in the Tyrol, crown one of the loveliest and most popular Alpine regions of Austria. The peaks shown are typical of the savage beauty of this range, which contains no fewer than 132 glaciers. They afford many difficult climbs for the enthusiast, and it is on mountains such as these that the climbers of many nations have trained for their conquest of the great peaks of the Himalayas or the Andes.

In autumn, this region is famed for its chamois shooting, and some of the record trophies of the world have been shot in this area of the Alps.

The Ziller Valley itself forms a complete contrast to the lonely severity of these peaks. It is dotted with picturesque villages, whose "Kirchtage", or open-air church festivals, are among the most colourful in the country.

The winter sports centre of Seefeld lies on Austria's most beautiful railway—the Kar-
wendelbahn—which climbs up from Innsbruck, boring through the legendary Martin's
Wall on its way. The resort lies some 3900 feet high and, as the picture shows, is perched on
a huge plateau between the encircling mountains. Despite the ever increasing number of
modern hotels, it is still the 15th century parish church which dominates its attractive
silhouette.

The attraction of Kitzbühel, the most famous winter resort of the Austrian Tyrol, is not to be explained simply by its
unique "ski-circus" nor by the variety of its lodgings, which range from the simplest pension to the most luxurious international hotel. The secret of its appeal is that, despite the chromium-plated efficiency of modern tourism, it has clung
on miraculously to the atmosphere and appearance of a medieval town. This, more than the cable railways and chair lifts,
draws year after year its record stream of tourists who outnumber many times over the 7,000 odd residents of the town.
Kitzbuehel's happy combination of old and new is well illustrated in this scene. In the upper foreground is the line of the old
defence wall, drawn in front of the 500-year-old pencil-spired church. The slit in the mountain wood in the background
marks the path of the modern cable railway which leads up to the Hahnenkamm peak.

74

This view of the Silvretta mountains of the Vorarlberg, with the giant wall of a power dam driven into their side, typifies the union of science and nature, and of old and new, which makes up Austria's westernmost province.

The Silvretta group of the Rhaetian Alps stretches from Switzerland across the Vorarlberg and into the neighbouring province of Tyrol. The chain is studded with peaks over 10,000 feet high and is scored with countless glaciers. Such Alpine regions are the reservoirs of Austria's so-called "white gold" or hydro-electric power.

The construction shown here is part of the Illwerk Power Plant with an annual capacity of some 1,000 million kilowatt hours a year, which is being constantly expanded. In addition to feeding Austria's home needs and enabling projects such as the electrification of the federal railways to be carried out, the hydro-electric industry makes an important contribution to the country's trade balance. The Illwerk, for example, sends over one third of its output to Western Germany.

This plant is one of a gigantic chain constructed or developed throughout the Austrian Alps since the Second World War. The biggest of these projects is that at Kaprun in the Salzburg province. Another important one has been built on the Danube at Ybbs Persenbeug, 60 miles west of Vienna.

In addition to the deliveries to Germany, Austria exports her electric power to most of her other neighbours. Yet all the stations completed and planned do not account for half of the country's hydro-electric potential, which is estimated at the astronomic figure of 40,000 million kilowatt hours a year.

It is difficult to guess from this picture of the beautiful Vorarlberg town of Rankweil that an important regional centre of Austria's textile industry is tucked away between the slopes of the mountains. Yet for all its natural beauty, the province of Vorarlberg, which borders on Switzerland, is relatively the most industrialized in Austria. It is textile plants which form the backbone of this provincial industry, and this fact finds its annual expression in the Trade Fair of Dornbirn, a few miles north-east of Rankweil, which has become one of the leading textile exhibitions of Europe.

In appearance and character, Rankweil is anything but a miniature industrial centre. The 600-year-old Liebfrauen Church dominates the skyline just as serenely as it did in the days when Rankweil was more known for its pilgrimages than for its cloth.

This view of the evening waters of Lake Constance brings us to the westernmost boundary of Austria, and at the same time completes the gamut of variations in the Austrian landscape. For here, though the nearest ocean lies over two hundred miles away, the mood of the open sea is somehow recaptured in the midst of the Alps. The lake's mild climate and the plentiful crops of fruit and wine which grow on its shores help the Mediterranean illusion for the visitor.

Bregenz, on the Austrian shore of the lake, is now noted above all for its summer festivals. Started after the Second World War, these have succeeded in giving a new and picturesque setting to the classical operettas of Vienna. Every year, as the main attraction of the festival, one of these works is performed on a giant floating stage as the so-called "Play on the Lake". Thus, even at the westernmost tip of Austria, the spirit of Vienna is preserved through adaptation.

TECHNICAL DATA

All pictures taken in Agfacolor by Kurt Peter Karfeld and Dr. Irmtraud Karfeld

Page						Page					
15	View of Vienna	F: 9	$1/60$ sec.	2 p. m.		40	St. Wolfgang	F: 6,3	$1/100$ sec.	1 p. m.
20	Cathedral Roof	F: 4,5	$1/200$ sec.	12 noon		50	Christmas Tree	F: 2,3	$1/1$ sec.	5 p. m.
21	View from Cathedral	F: 6,3	$1/50$ sec.	5 p. m.		51	Gastein	F: 12,5	$1/100$ sec.	11 a. m.
17	Belvedere Gate	F: 11	$1/75$ sec.	11 a. m.		52	Festival House	F: 4,5	$1/25$ sec.	6 p. m.
18	Beethoven House	F: 4,5	$1/60$ sec.	4 p. m.		54	Cathedral Square	F: 3,5	$1/30$ sec.	8 a. m.
22	Ornamental Bowl	F: 3,5	$1/15$ sec.			55	Madonna	F: 12,3	$1/25$ sec.	5 p. m.
23	Biedermeier House	F: 9	$1/60$ sec.	10 a. m.		56	Drau Valley	F: 12,5	$1/60$ sec.	10 a. m.
24	Harvest Scene	F: 12,5	$1/100$ sec.	2 p. m.		59	Lake Woerther	F: 3,5	$1/20$ sec.	7 p. m.
26	Farm House	F: 9	$1/60$ sec.	3 p. m.		58	Hochosterwitz	F: 6,3	$1/100$ sec.	12 noon
27	Rust	F: 9	$1/60$ sec.	11 a. m.		61	Heiligenblut	F: 9	$1/60$ sec.	11 a. m.
31	Haydn Church	F: 6,3	$1/60$ sec.	10 a. m.		62	Lake Millstatt	F: 5,6	$1/60$ sec.	4 p. m.
32	Rax Mountain	F: 12,5	$1/50$ sec.	12 noon		68	Mountain Birch	F: 6,3	$1/60$ sec.	5 p. m.
28	"Humpback World"	F: 6,3	$1/50$ sec.	5 p. m.		64	Alpine Crosses	F: 4,5	$1/25$ sec.	7 a. m.
29	Bernstein Castle	F: 9	$1/100$ sec.	11 a. m.		65	Lienz Dolomites	F: 5,6	$1/25$ sec.	10 a. m.
25	Chapel	F: 12,5	$1/60$ sec.	10 a. m.		66	Tyrol Costumes	F: 6,3	$1/100$ sec.	3 p. m.
35	National Costume	F: 5,6	$1/60$ sec.	6 p. m.		67	Virgen Valley	F: 9	$1/60$ sec.	2 p. m.
37	Melk Abbey	F: 9	$1/50$ sec.	5 p. m.		69	Innsbruck	F: 4,5	$1/25$ sec.	6 p. m.
38	Duernstein	F: 9	$1/100$ sec.	11 a. m.		72	Grossvenediger	F: 12,5	$1/100$ sec.	11 a. m.
42	Kremsmuenster	F: 12,5	$1/100$ sec.	1 p. m.		73	Zillertal Alps	F: 9	$1/100$ sec.	3 p. m.
43	Steyr	F: 6,3	$1/60$ sec.	9 a. m.		70	Inn Valley	F: 6,3	$1/100$ sec.	11 a. m.
41	Salzkammergut	F: 12,5	$1/50$ sec.	8 a. m.		71	Lake Achen	F: 6,3	$1/200$ sec.	1 p. m.
44	Graz	F: 6,3	$1/100$ sec.	5 p. m.		74	Seefeld	F: 9	$1/100$ sec.	3 p. m.
45	Eggenberg Castle	F: 9	$1/100$ sec.	11 a. m.		75	Kitzbuehel	F: 12,5	$1/60$ sec.	10 a. m.
47	Erzberg	F: 6,3	$1/60$ sec.	9 a. m.		76	Ill Power Plant	F: 6,3	$1/60$ sec.	3 p. m.
48	Mountain Cattle	F: 9	$1/75$ sec.	12 noon		78	Rankweil	F: 9	$1/60$ sec.	11 a. m.
46	Frohnleiten	F: 9	$1/60$ sec.	11 a. m.		79	Lake Constance	F: 4,5	$1/60$ sec.	5 p. m.

A·N·N·U·A·L E·D·I·T·I·O·N·S

Multicultural Education

00/01

Seventh Edition

EDITOR

Fred Schultz
University of Akron

Fred Schultz, professor of education at the University of Akron, attended Indiana
University to earn a B.S. in social science education in 1962, an M.S. in the
history and philosophy of education in 1966, and a Ph.D. in the history and
philosophy of education and American studies in 1969. His B.A. in Spanish
was conferred by the University of Akron in May 1985. He is actively involved
in researching the development and history of American education with a primary focus on the history of ideas and social philosophy of education. He also
likes to study languages.

Dushkin/McGraw-Hill
Sluice Dock, Guilford, Connecticut 06437

Iona College
Libraries

Visit us on the Internet
http://www.dushkin.com/annualeditions/

Credits

1. The Social Contexts of Multicultural Education
Unit photo—United Nations photo by Y. Nagata.
2. Teacher Education in Multicultural Perspective
Unit photo—© 2000 by PhotoDisc, Inc.
3. Multicultural Education As an Academic Discipline
Unit photo—© 2000 by Cleo Freelance Photography.
4. Identity and Personal Development: A Multicultural Focus
Unit photo—Ed Keating/New York Times.
5. Curriculum and Instruction in Multicultural Perspective
Unit photo—Courtesy of Dushkin/McGraw-Hill.
6. Special Topics in Multicultural Education
Unit photo—Sara Krulwich/New York Times.
7. For Vision and Voice: A Call to Conscience
Unit photo—Courtesy of Digital Stock.

Copyright

Cataloging in Publication Data
Main entry under title: Annual Editions: Multicultural Education. 2000/2001.
    1. Intercultural education—Periodicals. I. Schultz, Fred, *comp.* II. Title: Multicultural education.
ISBN 0–07–236566–8   370.19'341'05   ISSN 1092–924X

© 2000 by Dushkin/McGraw-Hill, Guilford, CT 06437, A Division of The McGraw-Hill Companies.

Seventh Edition

Cover image © 2000 PhotoDisc, Inc.

Printed in the United States of America   1234567890BAHBAH543210   Printed on Recycled Paper

Staff

iii

In publishing ANNUAL EDITIONS we recognize the enormous role played by the magazines, newspapers, and journals of the public press in providing current, first-rate educational information in a broad spectrum of interest areas. Many of these articles are appropriate for students, researchers, and professionals seeking accurate, current material to help bridge the gap between principles and theories and the real world. These articles, however, become more useful for study when those of lasting value are carefully collected, organized, indexed, and reproduced in a low-cost format, which provides easy and permanent access when the material is needed. That is the role played by ANNUAL EDITIONS.

New to ANNUAL EDITIONS is the inclusion of related World Wide Web sites. These sites have been selected by our editorial staff to represent some of the best resources found on the World Wide Web today. Through our carefully developed topic guide, we have linked these Web resources to the articles covered in this ANNUAL EDITIONS reader. We think that you will find this volume useful, and we hope that you will take a moment to visit us on the Web at **http://www.dushkin.com** to tell us what you think.

As we begin this new century, the debate over multiculturalism and schools is continuing. We can hope that this new century will be a gentler and more humane century than the past one. We have much in common as human beings and as the heirs of great civilizations; yet we must also cherish and value those cultural values and heritages that make us unique and diverse. An education for transformative intellectual and social development should focus on those things that emancipate and liberate us from cultural stereotypes. All voices should be included in the dialogue regarding how to achieve such educational goals. How we best help our students to develop their voices and to be heard is a major question for all concerned teachers.

The concept of multicultural education evolved and took shape in the United States out of the social travail that wrenched the nation in the late 1960s, through the 1970s and 1980s, and into the present decade. The linkages between diverse and coexisting ethnic, racial, and socioeconomic heritages have been explored. There has been enthusiastic support for the idea of a volume in this series exclusively devoted to multicultural education. Having been teaching and studying multicultural education for 29 years, it is a pleasure to serve as editor of *Annual Editions: Multicultural Education 00/01.*

The critical literature on gender, race, and culture in educational studies increases our knowledge base regarding the multicultural mosaic that so richly adorns North American cultures. When the first courses in multicultural education were developed in the 1960s, the United States was in the midst of urban and other social crises, and there were no textbooks available. Educators who taught in this area had to draw heavily from academic literatures in anthropology, sociology, social psychology, social history, sociolinguistics, and psychiatry. Today, there are textbooks available in the area, but there is also a need for a regularly, annually published volume that offers samples from the recent journal literature in which the knowledge bases for multicultural education are developed. This volume is intended to address that need.

The National Council for the Accreditation of Teacher Education (NCATE) in the United States has in place national standards requiring that accredited teacher education programs offer course content in multicultural education. A global conception of the subject is usually recommended, in which prospective teachers are encouraged to develop empathetic cultural sensitivity to the demographic changes and cultural diversity that continues to develop in the public schools as a result of dramatic demographic shifts in the population.

In this volume we first explore the social contexts for the development of multicultural education. Its role in teacher education is then briefly defined in the essays in unit 2. In unit 3 the nature of multicultural education as an academic discipline is discussed, and several issues related to this topic are explored. The readings in unit 4 look at multicultural education from the perspective of people in the process of developing their own unique personal identities, in the context of their interactions with their own as well as others' cultural heritages and personal life experiences. The readings in unit 5 focus on curriculum and instruction in multicultural perspective. Unit 6 addresses special topics relevant to development of multicultural insight, and the essays in unit 7 explore alternative visions for multicultural education and the need for a critically conscious quest for emancipatory educational futures for all people of all cultural heritages.

Once again we are including important World Wide Web sites that can be used to further explore article topics. These sites are cross-referenced by number in the topic guide.

This year I would like to acknowledge the very helpful contributions of the advisory board members. Their assistance in finding useful sources is appreciated. I would also like to acknowledge Dr. Stephen H. Aby, research librarian at the University of Akron, whose assistance is greatly valued.

This volume will be useful in courses in multicultural education at the undergraduate and graduate levels. It will add considerable substance to the sociocultural foundations of education, educational policy studies and leadership, as well as to coursework in other areas of preservice and inservice teacher education programs. We hope you enjoy this volume, and we would like you to help us improve future editions. Please complete and return the form at the back of the book. We look forward to hearing from you.

Fred Schultz

Fred Schultz
Editor

Contents

UNIT 1

The Social Contexts of Multicultural Education

Five articles discuss the importance of a multicultural curriculum in sensitizing students to an integrated world society.

The concepts in bold italics are developed in the article. For further expansion please refer to the Topic Guide and the Index.

The concepts in bold italics are developed in the article. For further expansion please refer to the Topic Guide and the Index.

UNIT 4

Identity and Personal Development: A Multicultural Focus

Six articles consider the interconnections between gender, social class, racial and ethnic heritage, and primary cultural values.

UNIT 5

Curriculum and Instruction in Multicultural Perspective

Seven articles review how curriculum and instruction must be formulated to sensitize young people to the multicultural reality of a national civilization.

The concepts in bold italics are developed in the article. For further expansion please refer to the Topic Guide and the Index.

UNIT 6

Special Topics in Multicultural Education

Ten articles explore some of the
dynamics of implementing
multilingual programs.

The concepts in bold italics are developed in the article. For further expansion please refer to the Topic Guide and the Index.

The concepts in bold italics are developed in the article. For further expansion please refer to the Topic Guide and the Index.

UNIT 7

For Vision and Voice: A Call to Conscience

Four selections address the concerns that must be kept in mind for the future improvement of our educational system.

The concepts in bold italics are developed in the article. For further expansion please refer to the Topic Guide and the Index.

This topic guide suggests how the selections and World Wide Web sites found in the next section of this book relate to topics of traditional concern to students and professional educators involved with the study of multicultural education. It is useful for locating interrelated articles and Web sites for reading and research. The guide is arranged alphabetically according to topic.

The relevant Web sites, which are numbered and annotated on pages 4 and 5, are easily identified by the Web icon (◎) under the topic articles. By linking the articles and the Web sites by topic, this ANNUAL EDITIONS reader becomes a powerful learning and research tool.

TOPIC AREA	TREATED IN	TOPIC AREA	TREATED IN
African Americans	16. Parental Influences on Career Development 34. Dissin' "the Standard": Ebonics As Guerrilla Warfare 36. Looking at the Schools ◎ **18, 24, 29**		24. Making the Most of the Classroom Mosaic 25. Noteworthy Books about Latinos for Children and Adolescents 26. Class Web Sites Can Offer Enhanced Access ◎ **20, 22, 24, 25, 26, 30, 31**
Aims of Multicultural Education	1. Americanization and the Schools 2. "Celebrating Diversity vs. Preparing for the Mainstream"? Should We Consider Another Choice? 3. Celebrating Diversity vs. Preparing for the Mainstream: A Pseudo-Controversy? 4. Violence That Creates School Dropouts 5. Paying Attention to Our Children 10. Different Mirror 11. Idolatry of Multicultural Education 12. Why Standardized Tests Threaten Multiculturism 13. Failing to Marvel 38. Outsider's View Inside 39. Call for a Multicultural Revolution 40. Who Shall Have the Moral Courage to Heal Racism in America? ◎ **4, 5, 6, 8, 9, 12, 14, 30**	**Empowerment of Students**	12. Why Standardized Tests Threaten Multiculturalism 39. Call for a Multicultural Revolution ◎ **24, 29**
		Field Experiences in Multicultural Perspective	6. Prospective Teachers' Attitudes toward Urban Schools 7. Predictors of Success in Urban Teaching ◎ **10, 11, 12, 13, 15**
		Hispanics	15. Culturally Authentic Bias 16. Parental Influences on Career Development 20. Respect in the Classroom 25. Noteworthy Books about Latinos for Children and Adolescents 32. Testimonies of Latin American Women ◎ **4, 17, 18, 19, 22, 23, 24, 29**
Anthropology of Education	18. Therapeutic Moment? ◎ **18, 22**	**Historical**	5. Paying Attention to Our Children 27. Children and Play in the Holocaust
Bilingual Education	21. Changing Face of Bilingual Education ◎ **20, 22**	**Holocaust**	27. Children and Play in the Holocaust
Celebrating Diversity vs. Preparing for the Mainstream: The Debate	1. Americanization and the Schools 2. "Celebrating Diversity vs. Preparing for the Mainstream"? Should We Consider Another Choice? 3. Celebrating Diversity vs. Preparing for the Mainstream: A Pseudo-Controversy? 10. Different Mirror ◎ **14, 15, 18, 22**	**Identity Development**	14. Reducing the Effects of Racism in Schools 15. Culturally Authentic Bias 16. Parental Influences on Career Development 17. From La Belle Sauvage to the Noble Savage 18. Therapeutic Moment? 19. On the Teaching and Personal Construction of Educational Equity 20. Respect in the Classroom ◎ **10, 11, 12, 16, 17, 18, 19, 28**
Core Curriculum: The Debate	1. Americanization and the Schools 10. Different Mirror ◎ **4, 5, 6, 7, 8, 9**	**International Perspectives**	29. Expanding Roles of Teachers for the 21st Century 38. Outsider's View Inside ◎ **22, 29, 32**
Critical Theory and Multicultural Education	12. Why Standardized Tests Threaten Multiculturalism 39. Call for a Multicultural Revolution ◎ **13, 14, 15, 18, 22**	**Language**	21. Changing Face of Bilingual Education 23. Using Stories to Introduce and Teach Multicultural Literature 33. Issue of "Authenticity" in California Language Restoration 34. Dissin' "the Standard": Ebonics As Guerrilla Warfare ◎ **20, 21, 22**
Culture and Cognitive Styles	22. Relationship between Culture and Cognitive Style 33. Issue of "Authenticity" in Californian Language Restoration ◎ **23, 24, 29, 30**		
Curriculum and Instruction	20. Respect in the Classsroom 21. Changing Face of Bilingual Education 22. Relationship between Culture and Cognitive Style 23. Using Stories to Introduce and Teach Multicultural Literature	**Language Restoration**	33. Issue of "Authenticity" in California Language Restoration 34. Dissin' "the Standard": Ebonics As Guerrilla Warfare ◎ **20, 21, 22**

● AE: Multicultural Education

The following World Wide Web sites have been carefully researched and selected to support the articles found in this reader. If you are interested in learning more about specific topics found in this book, these Web sites are a good place to start. The sites are cross-referenced by number and appear in the topic guide on the previous two pages. Also, you can link to these Web sites through our DUSHKIN ONLINE support site at *http://www.dushkin.com/online/*.

The following sites were available at the time of publication. Visit our Web site—we update DUSHKIN ONLINE regularly to reflect any changes.

General Sources

1. Educational Resources Information Center
http://www.accesseric.org:81
This invaluable site provides links to all ERIC sites: clearinghouses, support components, and publishers of ERIC materials. You can search the ERIC database, find out what is new, and ask questions about ERIC.

2. Education Week on the Web
http://www.edweek.org
At this *Education Week* home page, you will be able to open archives, read special reports, keep up on current events, look at job opportunities, and access a variety of articles of relevance in multicultural education.

3. Global SchoolNet Foundation
http://www.gsn.org
Access this site for multicultural education information. The site includes news for teachers, students, and parents, as well as chat rooms, links to educational resources, programs, and contests and competitions.

4. Multicultural Publishing and Education Council
http://www.mpec.org
This is the home page of the MPEC, a networking and support organization for independent publishers, authors, educators, and librarians fostering authentic multicultural books and materials. It has excellent links to a vast array of resources related to multicultural education.

5. National Education Association
http://www.nea.org
Something about virtually every education-related topic can be accessed at or through this site of the 2.3-million-strong National Education Association.

6. Phi Delta Kappa
http://www.pdkintl.org/home.shtml
This important organization publishes articles about all facets of education. By clicking on the links at this site, for example, you can check out the journal's online archive.

The Social Contexts of Multicultural Education

7. American Psychological Association
http://www.apa.org/psychnet/
By exploring the APA's "Resources for the Public," you will be able to find links to an abundance of articles and other resources that are useful in understanding the factors that are involved in the development of prejudice.

8. Association for Moral Education
http://www.wittenberg.edu/ame/
AME is dedicated to fostering communication, cooperation, training, curriculum development, and research that links moral theory with educational practices. From here it is possible to connect to several sites on ethics, character building, and moral development.

9. Center for Innovation in Education
http://www.educenter.org
This is the home page of the Center for Innovation in Education, self-described as a "not-for-profit, non-partisan research organization" focusing on K–12 education reform strategies. Click on its links for information about and varying perspectives on various reform initiatives.

Teacher Education in Multicultural Perspective

10. Awesome Library for Teachers
http://www.awesomelibrary.org/teacher.html
Open this page for links and access to teacher information on many topics of concern to multicultural educators.

11. Education World
http://www.education-world.com
Education World provides a database of literally thousands of sites that can be searched by grade level, plus education news, lesson plans, and professional-development resources.

12. Teacher Talk Forum
http://education.indiana.edu/cas/tt/tthmpg.html
Visit this site for access to a variety of articles discussing life in the classroom. Clicking on the various links will lead you to electronic lesson plans, covering a variety of topic areas from Indiana University's Center for Adolescent Studies.

Multicultural Education As an Academic Discipline

13. Canada's Schoolnet Staff Room
http://www.schoolnet.ca/home/e/
Here is a resource and link site for anyone involved in education, including bilingual education teachers, parents, volunteers, and administrators.

14. Goals 2000: A Progress Report
http://www.ed.gov/pubs/goals/progrpt/index.html
Open this site to survey a progress report by the U.S. Department of Education on the Goals 2000 reform initiative. It provides a sense of what goals that educators are reaching for as they look toward the future.

15. Teachers Helping Teachers
http://www.pacificnet.net/~mandel/
This site provides basic teaching tips, new teaching methodology ideas, and forums for teachers to share their experiences. Download software and participate in chat sessions. It features educational resources on the Web, with new ones added each week.

Identity and Personal Development: A Multicultural Focus

16. Ethics Updates/Lawrence Hinman
http://ethics.acusd.edu

This site provides both simple concept definition and complex analysis of ethics, original treatises, and sophisticated search engine capability. Subject matter covers the gamut from ethical theory to applied ethical venues. There are many opportunities for user input.

17. Kathy Schrock's Guide for Educators
http://www.capecod.net/schrockguide/
This classified list of Web sites is useful for enhancing curriculum and teacher professional growth.

18. Let 100 Flowers Bloom/Kristen Nicholson-Nelson
http://teacher.scholastic.com/professional/ assessment/100flowers.htm
Open this page for Kristen Nicholson-Nelson's discussion of ways in which teachers can help to develop children's multiple intelligences. She provides a useful bibliography and resources.

19. The National Academy for Child Development
http://www.nacd.org
This international organization is dedicated to helping children and adults reach their full potential. This page presents links to various programs, research, and resources.

Curriculum and Instruction in Multicultural Perspective

20. American Indian Science and Engineering Society
http://spot.colorado.edu/~aises/aises.html
This is the AISES "Multicultural Educational Reform Programs" site. It provides a framework for learning about science, mathematics, and technology by which minority students and their teachers can make meaningful cultural connections to teaching and learning; it also provides Web links.

21. Child Welfare League of America
http://www.cwla.org
The CWLA is the United States' oldest and largest organization devoted entirely to the well-being of vulnerable children and their families. This site provides links to information about issues related to the process of becoming multicultural.

22. STANDARDS: An International Journal of Multicultural Studies
http://www.colorado.edu/journals/standards/
This fascinating site provides access to a seemingly infinite number of international archives.

Special Topics in Multicultural Education

23. American Scientist
http://www.amsci.org/amsci/amsci.html
Investigate this site to access a variety of articles and to explore issues and concepts related to race and gender.

24. American Studies Web
http://www.georgetown.edu/crossroads/asw/
This eclectic site provides links to a wealth of resources on the Internet related to American studies, from gender studies to race and ethnicity. It is of great help when doing research in demography and population studies.

25. Early Intervention Solutions
http://www.earlyintervention.com

EIS presents this site to address concerns about child stress and reinforcement and suggests ways to deal with the negative behaviors that may result.

26. National Institute on the Education of At-Risk Students
http://www.ed.gov/offices/OERI/At-Risk/
The At-Risk Institute supports research and development activities designed to improve the education of students at risk of educational failure due to limited English proficiency, race, geographic location, or economic disadvantage.

27. National Network for Family Resiliency
http://www.nnfr.org
This organization's home page will lead you to a number of resource areas of interest in learning about resiliency: General Family Resiliency, Violence Prevention, and Family Economics.

28. National Parent Information Network/ERIC
http://npin.org
This is a clearinghouse of information on education for parents and for people who work with parents.

29. Patterns of Variability: The Concept of Race
http://www.as.ua.edu/ant/bindon/ant101/ syllabus/race/race1.htm
This site provides a handy, at-a-glance reference to the prevailing concepts of race and the causes of human variability. It can serve as a valuable starting point for research into and understanding of the concept of race.

30. U.S. Department of Education
http://www.ed.gov/pubs/TeachersGuide/
Explore this government site for examination of institutional aspects of multicultural education. National goals, projects, grants, and other educational programs are listed here as well as many links to teacher services and resources.

For Vision and Voice: A Call to Conscience

31. Classroom Connect
http://www.classroom.net
This is a major Web site for K–12 teachers and students, with links to schools, teachers, and resources online. It includes discussion of the use of technology in the classroom.

32. EdWeb/Andy Carvin
http://edweb.cnidr.org
The purpose of EdWeb is to explore educational reform and information technology. Access educational resources worldwide, learn about trends in education policy, and examine success stories of computers in the classroom.

33. Online Internet Institute
http://www.oii.org
A collaborative project among Internet-using educators, proponents of systemic reform, content-area experts, and teachers who desire professional growth, this site provides help for integrating the Web with individual teaching styles.

We highly recommend that you review our Web site for expanded information and our other product lines. We are continually updating and adding links to our Web site in order to offer you the most usable and useful information that will support and expand the value of your Annual Editions. You can reach us at:
http://www.dushkin.com/annualeditions/.

www.dushkin.com/online/

5

Unit Selections

1. **Americanization and the Schools,** E. D. Hirsch Jr.
2. **"Celebrating Diversity vs. Preparing for the Mainstream"? Should We Consider Another Choice?** Gary K. Clabaugh
3. **Celebrating Diversity vs. Preparing for the Mainstream: A Pseudo-Controversy?** Edward G. Rozycki
4. **The Violence That Creates School Dropouts,** Christine Clark
5. **Paying Attention to Our Children: Educational Dilemmas for Americans,** Patricia Albjerg Graham

Key Points to Consider

❖ What should every student learn about cultural diversity and his or her own cultural heritage?

❖ What facets of the history of the human struggle for civil rights should be taught to students?

❖ What should students learn about other nations and other democratic traditions?

❖ How can the mass media more effectively inform the public on issues related to cultural diversity?

❖ What can educators do to help students better understand the social contexts in which they live?

❖ What should every student know about cultural diversity and equality of opportunity?

❖ What should everyone know about our common humanity?

 **Links** **www.dushkin.com/online/**

7. **American Psychological Association**
   http://www.apa.org/psychnet/
8. **Association for Moral Education**
   http://www.wittenberg.edu/ame/
9. **Center for Innovation in Education**
   http://www.educenter.org

These sites are annotated on pages 4 and 5.

We begin this new century with spirited dialogue regarding multiculturalism and schooling in this demographically changing and ever more culturally pluralistic region of the world. The struggle for open-mindedness and justice with regard to matters of race, culture, and gender continues. The role of teachers in teaching students acceptance of human diversity and difference is being intensely discussed.

The power of culture cannot be ignored in shaping peoples' conceptions of social reality. Every person needs to develop his or her own social vision of life as it relates to actual cultural realities in society.

The United States is becoming an ever more multiculturally unique nation. Canada is also experiencing major changes in its cultural composition due to its very generous immigration policies. Both nations face multicultural futures. Some demographic projections indicate that within 5 years a majority of the total American elementary and secondary school student body will be composed of youth who are "persons of color," the children of the rainbow coalition—Native American, African American, Asian American, and Hispanic.

Multicultural national communities face special challenges in daily life. Such societies also have unique opportunities to develop truly great culturally pluralistic national civilizations in which the aesthetic, artistic, literary, and moral standards of each cultural group can contribute to the creation of new standards. Groups can learn from one another, they can benefit from their respective strengths and achievements, and they can help one another to transcend problems and injustices of the past. We ought, therefore, to see the multicultural national fabric that is our social reality as a circumstance of promise, hope, and pride.

In examining the social context of multicultural education, we need to help teachers and education students to sense the promise, the great social opportunity, that our multicultural social reality presents. We have the task of empowering students with a constructive sense of social consciousness and a will to transcend the social barriers to safety, success, and personal happiness that confront, in one form or another, almost one-third of them. It is essential that we invest in all the children and young adults of multicultural nations, in order that great social promise and hope may be brought to fulfillment in the future.

We can ask ourselves certain very important questions as we work with children and young adults in our schools. Are they safe? Are they hungry? Are they afraid? Are they angry? Do they have a sense of angst; are they filled with self-doubt and uncertainty as to their prospects in life? For far too many children and adolescents from all socioeconomic groups, social classes, and cultural groups the answers to these questions are "yes." Far greater numbers of children from low-income minority cultural groups answer "yes" to at least

some of these questions than do children from higher socioeconomic families.

Having done this, educators and civic leaders should consider a few questions. What are the purposes of schooling? Are schools limited to their acknowledged mission of intellectual development? Or, are schools also capable of advancing, as did classical Greek and Roman educators, education in honor, character, courage, resourcefulness, civic responsibility, and social service? This latter concept of the mission of schooling is still the brightest hope for the full achievement of our great promise as a multicultural society in an interdependent world community of nations.

What are the obstacles to achieving this end? Each child must be able to advance intellectually in school as far as may be possible. We need to help children develop a sense of honor, self-respect, and pride in their own cultural heritage, which will lead them in their adult years to want to serve, help, and heal the suffering of others. We need intellectually curious and competent graduates who are knowledgeable about their own ethnic heritages and committed to social justice for all persons, in their own nation as well as in the community of nations.

The problems we face in achieving such an intellectual and social end are significant. Developing multicultural curriculum materials for schools and integrating them into the course content and activities can help to sensitize all students to the inherent worth of all persons. All youth deserve the opportunity to learn about their own cultural heritages.

North American nations have qualitative issues to face in the area of intercultural relations. Our problems differ because of very different national experiences and very different school systems. Around the world other nations have to wrestle with providing adequate opportunity for minority populations while maintaining high intellectual standards. The articles in this unit attempt to discuss all of these concerns, and they attempt to address the thoughtful concerns of those who have studied the rhetoric of debate over multiculturalism in school curricula.

There have been dramatic demographic changes in the characteristics of the world's population and in the interdependence of the world's nations in a global economy. We must reconsider how we develop human talent in our schools, for young people are the ones who will be the most basic resource in the future. Some unit essays give important background on the history of the civil rights movement in the United States as well as on the origins of many racial and cultural stereotypes that have inhibited the efforts of educators to help young people become more accepting of cultural diversity.

The unit essays are relevant to courses in cultural foundations of education, educational policy studies, multicultural education, social studies education, and curriculum theory and construction.

The Social Contexts of Multicultural Education

Americanization and the Schools

E. D. HIRSCH, JR.

When the Marxist government of the state of Bengal announced, in the early eighties, that the supposedly elitist, colonialist teaching of English would be discontinued in government-run primary schools, many on the left denounced the decision itself as elitist, because it would deprive the masses of the many economic and social advantages of speaking the world's language, and only the affluent private-school elite would henceforth have that privilege.

So wrote Salmon Rushdie in an essay on recent cultural life in India.[1] During the same period of the 1980s in the United States, the American academic Left exhibited little consciousness of such practical complexities. It adopted the kind of view enunciated by the state government of Bengal, that to impose elitist Anglo culture on Hispanic kids or inner-city blacks was disrespectful to their culture and a denial of their dignity and rights. American culture, they said, needed to be replaced by something more representative of the diverse ethnic origins of the nation's inhabitants. But, among the romantic particularists who mounted this argument, there was little agreement about which multicultural elements needed to be introduced into schooling and thus into the common public sphere, or even if there should exist a common public sphere.

I do not see any difference between the duty of the public schools to Americanize the children of immigrants and the duty of those schools to Americanize all schoolchildren. That duty becomes ever more pressing as the American social fabric becomes more fragile, a condition that has been brought about in part because the public schools have lost their way over the past five decades. It is not certain in any case that ethnic identity has to be sacrificed in the course of Americanization. But one thing is certain. A failure to master the nuanced use of English in speech and writing places a severe limit in the United States on one's opportunity, and freedom, and the amount of money in one's purse.

In this brief essay, I shall treat bilingualism and multiculturalism together as a common subject. Bilingualism might qualify as a separate topic in some rare instances in kindergarten or first grade when effective teaching of the way letters translate into sounds will require bilingual expertise by reading teachers. I don't intend to enter into the complex details of those instances. Such expertise in the teaching of reading is all too rare and it is not what is normally meant by *bilingualism*. The dominant meaning of the term is the right of children not to lose or neglect their parents' native language and culture when acquiring mainstream American culture.

That public schools should help preserve and enhance ethnic identities other than, or in addition to, Anglo-American literate culture has appeared as one of the many new rights announced in the 1980s, though it is a sentiment that goes back to early romanticism and the writings of Fichte at the start of the nineteenth century. When this romantic, ethnic particularism is expressed as a right, it unifies the two movements of bilingualism and multiculturalism. The sentiment of particularism pairs the question of how to school immigrants with the question of how to school African Americans, who are understood to have a right to preserve their ethnic identity just as immigrants do. This linking has made the bilingual movement and the multicultural movement in education sisters under the skin. They are both versions of romantic particularism.

E. D. Hirsch, Jr., is the University Professor of English and the Humanities at the University of Virginia and author of Cultural Literacy: What Every American Needs to Know *(1987). A slightly edited version of this article appeared as "English, Si" in the fall 1997 issue of* Freedom Review.

Their mortal enemy is Enlightenment cosmopolitanism—the universalist civic and political ideal under which America was founded, and which has proved to be the most durable and humane political principle yet devised.

* * *

Too often, debates about schooling make children pawns (as in Bengal) in a struggle between elite groups of grownups who ignore the rather obvious practicalities of economic and political life. These practicalities will require from children, after they become adults, an ability to communicate effectively with others in a nation's policy and economy. Those Americans who lack effective mastery of English, including mastery of the shared background knowledge that enables its nuanced use, are destined to stay poor and alienated from mainstream social and political life. Hence, the practical result of an "anti-elite" multicultural and bilingual orientation in elementary schooling has been to deepen the disadvantage of the children of the unassimilated and to enhance the advantage of the already-assimilated English-speaking elite (whatever their original ethnic identities), and thus to exacerbate class differences. Multiculturalism and bilingualism have been cultural policies that have preserved the economic status quo and even widened the gap between rich and poor.

In 1988, I was chatting at a university cocktail party with a young member of the academic Left (a category I had hitherto used for myself) who upbraided me for wanting to perpetuate the language and culture of the elite in America's public schools, instead of working to change American culture. I replied that during the long period it would take before professors managed to change the linguistic competence required to get a job at IBM or to understand a serious newspaper, the withholding of "elite" culture from disadvantaged students would simply prevent them from earning a good living or participating in political life. With eyes set unflinchingly on a brave new future, my interlocutor, who was a child of privilege, uttered words I will not forget: "That's a sacrifice I'm willing to make." The remark left me speechless, but I treasure the epitomizing moment.

Although a more inclusive curriculum is desirable and inevitable in America, the militant bilingualism and multiculturalism of the 1980s made American schools even more confused and rudderless places than they had already been. For five decades, American schools had accepted the primacy of process over content, arguing that specific knowledge is almost irrelevant, whereas thinking skills are of paramount importance. But under the pressure of the multicultural movement the one exception to the anti-content idea became multicultural content. Not surprisingly, a generation emerged that knew Rosa Parks but not Eleanor Roosevelt—which would have been acceptable if the choice had been made as the result of open discussion and decision making instead of pure drift.

Right-wing critics of the schools are mistaken in thinking that such anomalies have been the result of a left-wing plot. On the contrary, those who are familiar with the schools and their history know that there was not a plot, only curricular drift, punctuated sporadically by multicultural pressures.

The main victims of this curricular incoherence have been the children on whose behalf romantic particularism claimed to speak, just as the main victims of ineffective bilingual programs have been the immigrant children whom the programs were supposed to benefit. Ineffective bilingualism, like incoherent multiculturalism, breeds communicative incompetence. And communicative incompetence—the inability to read, write, speak, and listen to nuanced English—condemns Americans to lives of poverty and alienation. The main beneficiaries of these programs have been adults who derive jobs or status or power as advocates of bilingualism or multiculturalism.

The sacrifice of children to these adults is one of the themes of Jim Sleeper's eloquent new book *Liberal Racism:*

> The air inside the edifice of liberal racism is growing stale, and it is scented with death. The inhabitants of that edifice are discovering that racial narratives do not cultivate democratic predispositions, that Ebonics and much of what passes for bilingualism do not enrich civic dialogue, and that racial multiculturalism offers nothing to mixed-race children and others who want to escape their immigrant or racial corrals. Racial narrators who deny that reading dead white males such as Thoreau and Whitman can stimulate young blacks now as it did Richard Wright and Ralph Ellison, are really denying that black kids can be taught to read the American literature that is their precious heritage too. Some multiculturalist pedagogues want not the "inclusion" they claim to seek but a ritual certification of exclusion that garners them paychecks, moral cachet, and sometimes opportunities to exploit others of the same color in the name of race loyalty.[2]

The imposition by American public schools of mainstream Anglo culture on black and Hispanic children has been denounced as cultural and linguistic imperialism. But the use of the bludgeon-word *imperialism* masks a nontrivial distinction. The word usually means an external imposition by a conqueror on a colonized or conquered land. Americanization, on the contrary, is the internal imposition of a school-based culture and language within the public schools of a nation. Such *internal* imperialism is practiced by all modern countries, and, for that matter, all smaller-scale ethnic, tribal, or family units. A common language in any group is usually a consequence of cultural imperialism. Since the practice is universal, it may be supposed to be a social necessity. Those who reproach American schools for their cultural imperialism would think it odd to say that Anglo-American children who attend school in Mexico are being culturally subjugated when they have to learn Mexican history and Spanish through total immersion. To attach a powerful pejorative term to a benign and even necessary school practice is not only rhetorical overkill; it masks an impracticality that perpetuates injustice as well as disharmony and lack of community.

New citizens and citizens-to-be deserve the same Americanization as other American children. All American children need to be Americanized in a deeper sense than merely learning common American attitudes and lingo from TV and the streets. To decide what immigrants need to know to be Americans, it's necessary to decide what the children of longtime citizens need to know to be Americans. This system of common knowledge and root attitudes needs to be imparted in school not just to achieve a citizenry competent to role itself, but also to achieve community, social peace, and, not least, economic justice.

These were precisely the ends that Horace Mann enumerated in his great 1848 paean to the common school, in his *Twelfth Annual Report* as secretary to the Massachusetts State Board of Education. To Mann, the common school implies a common curriculum, which will not only create thoughtful, voting citizens but also accomplish two main social ends: It will eliminate "the fatal extremes of overgrown wealth and desperate poverty," and

> . . . by enlarging the cultivated class or caste will open a wider area over which the social feelings will expand; and if this education should be universal and complete, it would do more than all things else to obliterate factitious distinctions in society.

This expansion of the social feelings has as its shared object love of country. The nation is the matrix of this social sentiment—matrix from *mater*, like its analogue, patriotism from pater. In his brilliant book on nationalism, *Imagined Communities,* Benedict Anderson distinguishes between nationalist sentiment and patriotism. The first is an aggrandizing sentiment that defines one's group in terms of its distinction from alien groups that are potential enemies to be overcome or excluded. Thus, nationalism implies self-definition at the expense of the other. It is allied to ethnic particularism, which is the root of the extreme versions of bilingualism and multiculturalism.

Patriotism, by contrast, implies love of country without necessarily implying hostility to the other. Where the nationalist is an aggressive defier, the patriot is a reluctant martyr. American patriotism is built of shared knowledge, attitudes, loyalties, and values—including the values of non-exclusion and toleration. Americans have proved that it is possible to feel patriotism for a cosmopolitan, diverse country, which is loved more for its vital diversity than for its racial or ethnic purity. Such was Walt Whitman's patriotism, and Melville's. For most of its history, the United States has imagined itself as a patriotic rather than a nationalist state. George Washington thought of himself and was celebrated as Cincinnatus—the warrior hero who wishes only to return to his hearth and farm once the necessary sacrifice and service to the *patria* is finished.

From an early day, Americanization was imagined to consist not in narrow, nationalist indoctrination but in a special universalist sentiment appropriate to a nation of nations. For Mann, this was to be the sentiment inculcated by the common school. This was also the America celebrated by Whitman, who embraced multitudes, and by Herman Melville. Literary critics have seen Melville's *Pequod*—the ship in which Ahab pursues Moby Dick—as a symbol of America, its crew being made up of all the races and nations. Melville had made that theme explicit in his earlier novel, *Redburn* (1849).[3]

> There is something in the contemplation of the mode in which America has been settled that, in a noble breast, should forever extinguish the prejudices of national dislikes. Settled by the people of all nations, all nations may claim her for their own. You can not spill a drop of American blood without spilling the blood of the whole world. . . . We are not a narrow tribe of men—No: our blood is as the flood of the Amazon, made up of a thousand noble currents all pouring into one.

With depth and passion, Melville followed this idea of a non-ethnic, non-nationalistic, cosmopolitan America into political and psychological subtleties that have never been equaled. It is worth quoting the rest of the short chapter from *Redburn*.

> For who were our father and mother? Or can we point to any Romulus and Remus for our founders? [Thus denying we are a blood tribe.] Our ancestry is lost in the universal paternity, and Caesar and Alfred, St. Paul and Luther, Homer and Shakespeare are as much ours as Washington, who is as much the world's as our own. We are the heirs of all time, and with all nations we divide our inheritance. On this Western Hemisphere all tribes and people are forming into one federated whole; and there is a future which shall see the estranged children of Adam restored as to the old hearthstone in Eden.

The New World will redeem the Old by rejecting "national dislikes" and forming a "federated whole." Here, on this new continent, humankind has a new chance to free itself from the curse of ethnic hostility. Our new "Eden" yields a promise of a more-than-political redemption. Then, suddenly, in the words that follow, these quasi-religious allusions will lead Melville to full-scale religious/political sentiment in one of the most remarkable passages in American literature:

> The other world beyond this, which was longed for by the devout before Columbus' time, was found in the New, and the deep-sea-lead that first struck these soundings, brought up the soil of Earth's Paradise. Not a Paradise then or now; but to be made so, at God's good pleasure, and in the fullness and mellowness of time. The seed is sown, and the harvest must come; and our children's children, on the world's jubilee morning, shall all go with their sickles to the reaping. Then shall the curse of Babel be revoked, a new Pentecost come, and the language they shall speak shall be the language of Britain. Frenchmen, and Danes, and Scots; and the dwellers on the shores of the Mediterranean, and in the regions round about; Italians and Indians, and Moors; there shall appear unto them cloven tongues as of fire.

It is a stroke of prophetic genius that Melville should have foreseen that the need for a common language is the key to a trans-ethnic future. One may be what one may be in blood or race or ethnicity, but the political jubilee morning can arrive only when all shall speak a common language, and "the curse of Babel be revoked." To stress the importance of this secular redemption, Melville wittily (and humorously) inverts the biblical story of the Pentecost. In the Bible, it will be remembered, the apostles suddenly began to speak different languages to carry the Gospel to all nations (Acts, 2):

> Suddenly there came a sound from heaven as of a rushing mighty wind, and it filled all the house where they were sitting. And there appeared unto them cloven tongues like as of fire, and it sat upon each of them. And they were all filled with the Holy Ghost, and began to speak with other tongues.

In Melville's reverse pentecost, "there shall appear cloven tongues as of fire," and all those who now speak different tongues shall, in the "new Pentecost," speak the language of Britain. This mythos of Americanization has not lost its pungency and capacity to inspire.

By contrast, the romantic defense of particularism is a false profundity, and ultimately a muddle. Many of those who advocate bilingualism and a particularistic version of multiculturalism are very quick in the next breath to defend their positions with universalistic references to equal rights and other democratic principles whose foundations lie entirely in Enlightenment universalism—that all humans are fundamentally the same, that all have equal rights, that the harmony of the polis is more fundamental than religion, or race, or home culture. Particularists have no hesitation in momentarily abandoning their theories to take advantage of these universalistic principles.

This political and philosophical contradiction at the heart of American particularism is so gaping that the view cannot plausibly sustain itself. To be coherent, American particularism must either give up its claim of the ethnic and cultural essence of human nature, or else its claim to democracy and universal civic rights.

NOTES

1. S. Rushdie. 1997. Damme, this is the oriental scene for you! *The New Yorker*, 23 and 30 June: 54.
2. J. Sleeper. 1997. *Liberal racism*. New York: Penguin Books, 176.
3. All quotations from Melville's *Redburn* are from Chapter 33.

"Celebrating Diversity vs. Preparing for the Mainstream"?

Should We Consider Another Choice?

"Celebrating" diversity is another matter. The most obvious difficulty is that the beliefs and practices of various cultures are, in many instances, incompatible with one another.

by Gary K. Clabaugh

GARY K. CLABAUGH is a professor of education at La Salle University in Philadelphia, Pennsylvania. He directs La Salle's Graduate Program in Education and coordinates arts and sciences graduate programs.

Educators certainly must understand cultural differences. Otherwise, they are incompetent. "Celebrating" diversity is another matter. The most obvious difficulty is that the beliefs and practices of various cultures are, in many instances, incompatible with one another. And in spite of the urgings of pedagogical Pollyannas, educators often have to choose among them.

Such conflicts are easily evident. Suppose, for example, I teach a class that has some youngsters whose culture of origin does not value timeliness. (There are many such cultures. When I resided in Jamaica, for example, I quickly discovered that

events scheduled for, say, 2:00 might not start until 3:00 or even 3:30.) And let's further suppose that the rest of the children in my class share cultural backgrounds that place a high value on showing up at the scheduled time. If I, as teacher, am committed to the "celebration" of difference, what shall I do about the "soon come" kids' different time sense? It seems clear the rest of us should not wait patiently until these particular kids trickle in to class and then give them a round of applause for manifesting difference. And if I just ignore their tardiness, that might start something no one could live with. Besides, there are school policies to consider. In the final analysis, then, I must insist on timeliness—though I could do it in an understanding way. I might even ask these kids to tell the others about their culture's sense of time. But even if I am understanding, I just can't have it both ways.

And what about youngsters who don't agree with their parents' continued commitment to the values and practices of their culture of origin? When that is the case, on whose side should an educator who "celebrates" difference be? I recall a news story, for example, concerning a young lady of eighteen. She and her family were originally from India. True to their cultural tradition, her parents arranged a marriage for her to a much older man. But she was in love with an American her own age and she refused to cooperate. Her parents were about to ship her back to India against her will when she ran away. Her mother and father reported her missing, and the story made the news when local authorities refused to look for her once they discovered the circumstances. By the time the young lady finally surfaced, she was married to her American boyfriend. Now let's suppose that while this scenario is hatching she is in my class and seeks my advice. Should I "celebrate" her family's cultural values by encouraging her to obey her parents and return to India to marry? And if she understands herself to be an American rather than an Indian-American, should I emphasize her Indian origins anyway?

Similarly, suppose I have a young lady from Saudi Arabia in my class. Her parents, traditional Muslims, absolutely refuse to let her read literature by and about women because, from a Saudi point of view, such reading encourages "immodesty" and "impiousness." If I am her English teacher, and also committed to the celebration of diversity, should I side with her parents and refuse to help her learn anything that might undermine her culture of origin? If I discover that she is still secretly reading the likes of Kate Chopin or Harriet Arnow, should I tell her parents? On a broader scale, it is undeniable that many of the world's cultures reject equal rights for women. When they do, should a celebrationist educator encourage kids to commemorate *that* difference?

Many other cultural practices raise similar problems. We're told, for instance, that corruption in Congo (formerly Zaire) has reached such extraordinary levels that the society is best described as a "kleptocracy." So let's imagine that I get a youngster from Congo in my class who is fresh off the plane. And let's further suppose that his parents offer to grease my palm if I give their kid an "A". Should I take the money and celebrate this particular cultural difference with a night on the town? I think not. Nor should I use the money to throw a pizza party for the class, explaining to the kids how the parents of a classmate made it possible. In the final analysis I just have to say no, and consider reporting the offer.

Then there are cultures that define themselves by their hatred for others. The identity of many Bosnians, for instance, appears to be entangled with their hatred of Serbs, and vice versa. So let's suppose I

And if we are to prepare kids for specific social roles, we should concentrate on parent and citizen, not corporate minion.

have kids from both cultures in my classroom. Should I celebrate their diversity by honoring their mutual loathing? "Look kids, do you see how Myraslav is refusing to sit with Muhammed? Well, he is fulfilling a cultural tradition that is hundreds of years old. Isn't that wonderful!"

For any reflective educator, the "celebration" of difference is clearly problematic. It can even be a massive foolishness when, taken to its logical end, it promotes a radical tolerance that makes moral judgment impossible. But is it the only alternative to prepare kids for the "mainstream"? Let's hope not.

Consider the misbegotten, but currently popular, notion that educators should devote their energies to preparing graduates that meet the "needs" of business and industry—turning out more compliant Dilberts! Now that is a truly loathsome mission. Imagine getting youngsters

ready to serve corporate executives who get paid huge bonuses for mercilessly laying off thousands of employees, who reduce cubical sizes to 4' x 4' to fit in more staff members, who "empower" more of the staff but only on things that have no real importance, who encourage quality circles but are deaf to suggestions, who permit employees to recommend their replacements after they've been fired, or who "improve employee morale and productivity" with "fresh, gender-sensitive" carpet and paint colors. No, thank you! (By the way, these are not imaginary examples. They are actual practices selected from just one day's entries in the on-line Dilbert Zone's contest, "Top 50 Stupidest Company Initiatives Planned for 1998.")

Fashioning students to suit the appetites of business executives may "prepare them for the mainstream," but it certainly does not help them cope with, or resist, the instability of modern life. Nor does it sharpen their perception of the dangerous problems that confront humanity or help them search for personal meaning. Yet they will need to do such things, and do them well. Ironically, it does not even insulate them from the bitter winds that sweep today's workplace. That's because no matter what kind of compliant corporate lackeys educators produce, they will still be laid off the moment it increases the chief executive's income or serves the corporate bottom line.

As educators we should not be celebrating diversity *or* preparing kids for the mainstream. We should be helping youngsters develop more fully as individuals. To do that we need to help them learn how to learn and how to reason more critically. And if we are to prepare kids for specific social roles, we should concentrate on parent and citizen, not corporate minion.

Celebrating Diversity vs. Preparing for the Mainstream: a Pseudo-Controversy?

by Edward G. Rozycki

Should schools celebrate diversity? Never mind what this question boils down to in practical terms: we need entertainment.

Jack Sprat could eat no fat; his wife could eat no lean. And so betwixt the two of them they licked the platter clean.

—Mother Goose,
Nursery Rhyme

Education, particularly public education, is such an exhausting undertaking that not infrequently we find educators distracting themselves from substantial problems, such as funding programs, maintaining buildings, or replacing classroom equipment, by an obsessive focus on a vaguely formulated question. Should schools celebrate diversity? Never mind what this question boils down to in practical terms: we

EDWARD G. ROZYCKI is a twenty-five-year veteran of the school district of Philadelphia. He is an assistant professor of education at Widener University, Chester, Pennsylvania.

need entertainment. Should schools prepare children for the mainstream? Again, don't bother us with critical analyses—we need simplicity. Formulated as a controversy, the question makes the distraction from bottom-line hard issues even more recreational: should the schools celebrate diversity or prepare students for the mainstream? Instead of evaluating costs and benefits, assessing risks and dealing with a reality of shades of gray in which today's allies may be tomorrow's adversaries, we want black-and-white—or at least starkly multicolored—choices.

If we look at the apparent debate on whether schools should celebrate diversity or prepare students for the mainstream, we find that it is problematic in two different dimensions. In the first, there is a multitude of probably factually false or questionable assumptions that underlie the debate and enable its formulation. In

the second dimension, in which we assume that some consistent sense can be made of the proposals to "celebrate diversity" and to "prepare students for the mainstream," several difficult questions arise about exactly how such proposals should be implemented. Lets look more closely at these two dimensions.

"Celebrating Diversity"

What does "celebrating diversity" assume? How is one to understand this phrase? Can we expect there will be a common understanding of it? It is not unusual to find that "diversity" as defined by school policies, legal precedents, and government regulations is not what real students, parents, educators, and other members of the community perceive as diversity. There is substantial controversy as to whether such categories as *black, white, Asian, Hispanic, middle-*

 From *Educational Horizons*, Spring 1998, pp. 113-115. © 1998 by Edward G. Rozycki. Reprinted by permission.

class, underclass, *homosexual, straight, special,* or *regular* demarcate real or generally important distinctions in the world. Many of these distinctions have been argued to be little more than mythological constructs that serve political agendas. Educators, under pressure to avoid controversy, tend to treat these distinctions as given, as though they were rocks that could be arranged into a garden—read "program"—with minimal problems; only technical skill is needed. That is a delusion.

How does one prepare for something—especially when it is not clear what one is preparing for? Our society changes quickly.

In actuality, educational benefits— e.g., admissions, diplomas, scholarships, etc.—are distributed in our population based on several distinctions among personal attributes: sex, race, height, ability, effort, choice, need, wealth, handicap, potential, and achievement. The use of these distinctions represents a consensus, often unstable, about their "reality" and importance. They threaten, at any moment, to break out into conflicts that too frequently impinge on the day-to-day activities of the schools. Little wonder, then, that

educators are disposed to discuss them infrequently, and out of earshot of the public.

Do school activities of "celebration" necessarily have a positive effect on students? Does any experienced teacher believe that students can't tell what is merely lip service and what is substantial commitment? And don't they nonetheless often confuse the two? As they pass through adolescence students tend to be "unrealistically" idealistic: they assume adults are hypocrites. Do educators believe that school activities of "celebration" can offset this?

Plato believed that evil was the result of *nothing more* than ignorance. This prejudice infects the thinking of many educators today. So it is that we find programs proposed on the grounds that knowledge of difference—or what passes for knowledge—increases tolerance of difference. A cautious respect for fact requires us, however, to allow that whether Plato was right, and to what extent, are matters to be determined by careful research. What we have engaged in, instead, is experimentation with children whom the law has entrapped for us as subjects.

"Preparing for the Mainstream"

What is the mainstream? Is it the same at different times and places? One need only travel from town to town across these United States and discover how different "the mainstream" can be.

On the other hand, is "the mainstream" merely a slogan for pushing "English Only" programs, or for cutting back on music and the arts in public schools, or—as I observed at one school board meeting—for getting rid of Macintosh computers and replacing them with IBM clones? Don't these possibilities make it reasonable to rein in our enthusiasm about how readily the schools respond to their role as "preparer"?

How does one prepare for something— especially when it is not

clear what one is preparing for? Our society changes quickly. But for their perennial underfunding, public schools could all too easily be overresponsive to calls to prepare students for some external condition or another.

I interviewed for a position some years ago with a major educational research corporation. I was to develop a description of a vocational-education project so that it could be replicated across the country. The project had a 100 percent job placement rate for its graduates. It was working then on pilot funds received from the federal government. The corporation hoped that with an adequate description, a substantially larger grant could be obtained.

I asked how it was possible to get 100 percent placement. My interviewer told me that this was done by offering prospective employers a stipend to offset future wages to be paid. No student was accepted into the program unless an employer had been found who had accepted the agreement. When I asked how such arrangements could be replicated across the country, given that we did not control our economy the way the Soviets did, I received the reply, "Ed, that is the one question around here that we never ask."

I did not accept the job. Someone else did. The description was written up. The government grant was secured. This was in 1975. That project has left no traces. Its perpetrators have advanced in reputation and position.

Suppose There Were a Consensus on "Celebrating Diversity"

Many assumptions underlie the debate over whether the schools should celebrate diversity or prepare for the mainstream. No less problematic is the situation in which we postulate that those assumptions are founded on reality and then proceed to try to implement either alternative.

What exactly are we going to celebrate? Cultural differences? As defined by whom? Everyone? Or just those claimed by a vehement constituency? What about ethnic differences? Or gender differences, or religious differences, or differences in sexual preference? Count up all your categories and divide them into 180 (on the average) school days. Apportion them among different classes. What could this mean in terms of curricular effects? Something more than nonsense or sentimentalities?

What would count as celebration? Banners, special assemblies, speeches from notables? Will anyone do research to see if there is a negative effect on SAT scores? Will anyone do any research to check if the students are positively affected by this focus on what makes them, as individuals, different from others? Whose welfare is being considered here?

How different should students be allowed to be, and who will and should have the authority to deny permission? Difference often generates conflict; and conflict is a common means of maintaining difference. Dare we as educators push this very far? Doesn't the family, the church, or the community have any responsibility here? Do the schools have the resources to succeed here where they fail?

Suppose There Were a Consensus on "Preparing for the Mainstream"

Given that there were a consensus, what problems would still exist with "preparing for the mainstream"? The problem of "which mainstream?" would still exist. Should we focus on the culture and economy of New York, Chicago, or Los Angeles to make the choice? Who is this "we"? There are more than 15,000 school boards in this country. What are their ideas of what the mainstream is, or should be?

There are less comfortable questions. Should the people whose preferences and practices define the mainstream be permitted (by whom?) to do so? Do the major TV networks define it? How about the religious right, or academic left? Do they define the mainstream to some extent? How can this be changed, if it should?

How about a boring question: do schools have the resources to effectively define, or redefine, much less implement preparation for, the mainstream? What about time lag? Kids spend twelve spotty years in basic education—less than they do in front of the TV. How fast does the mainstream change? Specialists find it hard to keep up personally with developments in their own fields. How can schools keep up across the spectrum of the curriculum, if this curriculum is supposed to respond to changes in the "mainstream"?

Licking the Platter Clean

If educators do not attempt to get answers to the questions raised by the assumptions underlying either "celebrating diversity" or "preparing for the mainstream," nor for the real problems of implementation to be answered (even assuming consensus on those ideas), they might better spend their time on pursuits unrelated to education. How about a P.D. James mystery? Even simple physical activity clears the mind far better than expatiation on vague concepts.

Think of the millions of hours of educators' time spent each year on contemplating and arguing about concepts that are as vague as their professional discussion is haphazard. As diverting as such controversy may be, it consumes resources that might be put to better use.

The Violence that Creates School Dropouts

By Christine Clark

"To know others, one needs to know self; multiculturalism teaches the history of self and others."

—*study participant, 1993*

Violence invades, violates, and destroys multicultural communities in increasing proportions in the 1990s. While educators, among others, try to contend with the reality of violence in the classroom and in the community at large, their strategies for so doing converge around collectively distancing themselves and their work from violence and its manifestations, in essence suppressing it.

In the Eurocentric educational setting, the primary tactic employed to deal with violence or violent behavior is to move the violent or behavior-problem student out of the regular classroom into some type of special education. At best, special education is characterized by a behavior-problem student being moved into a special education classroom with other behavior-problem students, for some or all of the school day (Massachusetts State Department of Education, 1991).

Occasionally, a behavior-problem student is able to turn her or himself around in the special education classroom, which focuses on teaching the student to control, not understand and resolve, behavior problems and return to the regular classroom. More often, however, the placement of a behavior-problem student into a special education classroom becomes but the first step down a long and twisted staircase that this student will take en route to developing a disdain for all schools, and formal

Christine Clark is an assistant professor of Curriculum & Instruction and Multicultural Education in the College of Education at New Mexico State University, Las Cruces, New Mexico.

education in general, and a propensity, if not a predilection, for a long rap sheet.

As a result, educators must come to recognize that they are treating violence as an abstraction as they try to get on with the "business" of instruction. How can we expect to be effective in any community (but especially multicultural communities) if we see one of the most influential forces in these communities as an abstraction; in essence, not really seeing it at all?

Certainly, multicultural education has been more successful than Eurocentric education in attempting to comprehensively explore with each and every student the impact of various forms of violence and its manifestations on their identity development and, subsequently, their ability to be successful in school (Walsh, 1991). However, as long as we continue to lose even one student to the streets it has not been successful enough.

My research interest in violence began with my own first conscious personal experience with violence, around age four. How that experience and subsequent experiences impacted on my identity development and, in turn, on my ability or lack thereof to be successful in school emerged as a persistent question in my mind for the next twenty-five years of my life. Coupled with this personal experience, ten years of professional experience working with violent adolescent and adult offenders in educational contexts has further nurtured my desire to look critically at the relationship between violence, identity development, and academic success.

In considering the research on the impact of race on both individual and group identity development by Bailey Jackson (1976) and Rita Hardiman (1979), I began to surmise that my experiences of violence, as an individual (as Christine) and as a group member (as a woman), which had impacted upon my identity development

and subsequent success or failure in school, might be shared by others with similar experiences. In wanting to test this hypothesis qualitatively, I thought initially about interviewing gang members, since they were very likely to leave school and their experiences were among the most plagued with violence as we generally conceive of it. But after reflecting on my work experiences in the mental health field, I realized that usually those in the most extreme circumstances of any kind are the ones least likely to call attention to themselves. Given this, I decided to broaden the criteria upon which I would identify interviewees for a study on this subject to include any young person who had left school under any circumstances before finishing high school and who had not yet completed a General Equivalency Diploma (GED).

This article is based on my study entitled, *Multicultural Education as a Tool for Disarming Violence: A Study Through In-Depth Participatory Action Research* (1993). The study investigated the perceptions of young people who had left school before completing high school or a GED about the general factors leading up to their leaving school. Additionally, it looked at what, if anything, could have been done to prevent them from leaving or could be done to get them to go back. In particular, the study focused on finding out what role various forms of violence and its manifestations, as both the research participants and I defined them, played a part in their leaving school or might play a part in their return.

I defined violence in the study as either "initial" or "reactive" as it was initiated by members of social groups with access to power at the institutional level of society and directed towards members of social groups who lacked access to power at the institutional level of society. Initial violence was said to be manifest in four ways: (1) physically (e.g., police brutality), (2) economically (e.g., the ability of only some to access adequate healthcare), (3) politically (e.g., the "hidden curriculum" of public education as Eurocentric), and (4) psychologically (e.g., homosexuality defined as "deviant"). Reactive violence was said to be manifest in only one way, physically (e.g., the Los Angeles riots).

Participants in the study consciously defined violence as only physical, without distinguishing between the initial and reactive contexts of it. However, they described, in a very critically conscious fashion, both initial and reactive violence and its manifestations when discussing their relationship with peers, family, teachers, and school structure.

Elaine, a 37-year-old African-American study participant, details her experiences with peers, the effect of many manifestations of violence, especially economic violence, in these experiences, and the ensuing impact on her academic success:

I was doing good in junior high until I got with a crowd of friends. Because we lived in a project, and when you live in a project and being on welfare everybody tries to be like everybody else. You want to fit in. So you act like everybody else around.

My grades were good in school until my friends were around, then I had to be like the class clown. I had to do things to get attention; I always wanted attention. Because of this, I stayed back in seventh grade. Then the next semester, I got on trial, and they put me to the ninth grade because they said I could do the work. I just had to stay away from the people, the crowd that I was hanging with. Then I did good.

I passed eleventh grade to the 12th grade. Then I met my kids' father. He wasn't in school; he had just come from Florida. When school get out, a lot of older guys that are popular in the neighborhood will come up there to see the girls who's coming out. That was the thing back then. They come up there to see what they can see. I happened to be coming down the stairs one day, and he seen me and I seen him and it was love at first sight; we just connected. He was a handsome guy and quite popular. And a lot of women would have been glad to be with him, and I just felt so important because I was the chosen one.

When I met him, the thing was hanging out. They had a bar up here on the square. That was the place that all the younger teenagers go to drink, smoke marijuana. You're welcome in there; they serve you. They didn't care. And I wanted to be a part

of that and hang with my boyfriend and that was his scene, and so I thought that's what fun was about.

I lost my focus on school when I started hanging with this crowd and the drugs and drinking. I was no longer doing homework or anything, and if it was something I didn't understand I'd just say, "Well I don't understand it anyway so why do it? I don't have to do it. Teacher ain't gonna take time to show me. Forget it, just go ahead and medicate [use drugs and drink]."

All my peers, they wasn't doing anything in school. Half of 'em had already dropped out. But they'd sneak into the school, and I'd meet 'em in the bathroom or I'd see 'em in the hallway, they'd get my attention so I'd get out of the classroom. Or they'd just come up when school would get out, and we'd hang out. I had like four months left of school before graduation, but I hooked up with this crowd and I dropped out, I quit.

Here, peer group identity is integrally tied to class identity. The lack of a school culture to affirm the socioeconomic experience of Elaine and her friends led them to accept the master narrative which dictated that "hanging out," not school, will prepare them for their financial futures.

Carlos, a 16-year-old Puerto Rican study participant, describes family physical violence and its impact on his school success:

My stepfather basically grew me up. But the way he used to handle things when you doing something wrong, he never used to talk, he used to yell "scram." When I was younger, I would listen, because he is a man and I was just a child. But as I grew up I said, "this can't happen like this," and I started standing up to him.

We used to fight, physically. He used to hit me. I used to fight him back, and that used to make him even madder. But, I was the type [to say], "I'm not gonna take that, 'cause you're not my father." So I guess he was kind of feeling some kind of insult or something. But, since he did hit me and because he's not my father, I never used to like him; I used to look at him like he was nobody.

Parents shouldn't do that anyway, 'cause if you have a child you really want them to do okay in school and to be able. You can't go up to them with anger and everything, 'cause all they'll do is get scared. What's gonna be good if your son or your kid is fighting everything?

At one point it came down to, he was on the school phone and the teacher was there. She said, "your father wants to talk to you," and I was talking to him. And he was arguing with me about something, and he said that he was gonna hit me and this and that. And I told him "If you hit me you better kill me 'cause if you don't I'm coming for you."

That got him real pissed off. He came to school, I was real young, and he came with a blackjack [a type of billy club] to hit me. I carried a .22 caliber [gun], which he knew about, and I ran out the school. I caught him in the woods. I wouldn't have the guts to shoot him because he'd do me up [beat me] and I don't know how my mother would feel, so I scared him and he left. Later we ended up talking, and everything was fine for awhile. But then he was handling the same thing the same way, more with anger and fierce instead of sitting down [talking].

When school could no longer even provide temporary reprieve from his stepfather's abuse, it lost what little purpose it once served for Carlos. By fourth grade Carlos left school for good to join a gang whose pledge to protect him from his stepfather held more promise. Here, the gang is more in touch with Carlos' home culture than is the school and, therefore, better able to equip him with the skills he needs to survive.

John, a 17-year-old European-American study participant, explains his only experience of violence, both physical and political, with teachers and its resulting impact on his academic interest:

I got along with teachers except one, an English teacher. In his class, maybe ten students and most of them would be all my friends, we'd just mess around, talking, and then he'd kick me out of the class. He threw a couple of other people out too. And at the end of the class he ended up having no kids in his class. And then there was one time when I asked to get out of class, 'cause he told me to do my work and I forgot my book. And I had my fingers on the desk, and he slammed another book down on my desk and hit my fingers. He definitely did it on purpose 'cause he had a fistfight with a student once that came to this school. They fought right in the hallways. So he had kind of a bad reputation with students. I just walked out of his class after this incident, and everything just went downhill after that, I started skipping school.

And, nothing ever happened to the teacher for doing that to me.

John learns from life, in contrast to what he may have been told in the classroom, that schools are not necessarily democratic institutions. The rules for those with and without access to political power differ; if you have it you can use it to hurt those without it and go unpunished.

Vanessa, a 23-year-old African-American study participant, relates her experiences of especially psychological violence as it pertained to school structure in general:

I remember we sat in rows of desks, three desks behind you and seven people to a class. And in the slow class—you know, learning disability—the teachers stand by you, but they don't really help. I had problems reading, and I couldn't really spell words or nothing. Like on the paper I could see it, I could write it down, but I couldn't write it down the way I saw it.

From first through sixth I used to do good, got As and Ss [satisfactory grades]. But it was like every time I do something they give me the same. Every time I went to a different grade, I do the same work over and over. It was like I had the same class for three years; I did the same work over and over. That's a lot of why I didn't do my work. I knew it, and I was getting bored. And then in seventh grade, it all started to go down from there, like I said. It just seemed like they didn't care in school, so I didn't care either. They knew what was going on at home but, you know, they didn't care. At one point, the school did call DSS, and a social worker came to the house and was gonna take us kids away. But my mother talked to them, and we got to stay. That was the wrong thing for them to do. That made things worse; 'cause I never wanted to tell anybody anything that was wrong after that, 'cause I was scared they was gonna take us away.

After ninth grade, I just asked my mother, "Could I quit school?" She said she don't want me to, but it's up to me; it's my decision, I'm going to regret it the rest of my life if I do. And so I decided to do it, and she signed me out. I didn't have to talk to a guidance counselor or nothing. We just went up there, and she signed me out. And that was it.

Vanessa highlights how being labeled "slow" not only led teachers to expect less of her but to encourage her to expect less of herself. The sheer boredom which en-

sued caused her to leave school, psychologically the healthiest choice.

Study participants further detailed how violence affected their identity development and, in turn, their ability to be successful in school in two major ways. First, it created in them a sense of themselves as either invisible, without representation, or bad, with only negative representation. Second, it discouraged them from attempting to communicate their basic emotional and academic needs to their peers, parents, or teachers and simultaneously . . . discouraged their peers, parents, and/or teachers from reaching out to communicate with them.

Thomas, a 19-year-old Native-American and European-American study participant, described how he became increasingly disillusioned by school in direct proportion to his inability to escape this teachers' negative characterizations of him. In tenth grade he became uncontrollably bored with school, having come to the realization that teachers were passing him on to the next grade when they had not taught him anything. This, he said, was evidenced by the fact that today he still has trouble reading and writing at even a basic level. Prior to this realization, Thomas had been under the impression that he was learning in special education classes the same skills as those in mainstream classes, only that he was learning those skills differently.

Thomas believed that part of the impetus for his teachers' passing him was to "get rid of" him because, he admits, beginning around seventh grade, he would verbally intimidate (but never hit) them when they got him mad. Teachers got Thomas mad by giving him the same worksheets to do over and over again, by looking over his shoulder while he did them instead of giving him the space to try and do the work on his own, and by chastising him publicly for having casual conversations with other students in the course of doing his work; in general, by being too strict, too formal, too controlled.

These practices alone made Thomas wonder if his teachers were discriminating against him, but when they began calling him a "juvenile delinquent" to his face he was pretty certain they were. All of Thomas's teachers were white, mostly female, but he did not believe that more racial or gender diversity among them would have made much of a difference. As he said, "It's not who they are, it's how they are." Thomas was unable to find a positive image of himself anywhere in the school environment. Inevitably then, Thomas left school to pursue such a picture of himself elsewhere.

Stacy, a 16-year-old Jamaican and African-American study participant, explains his attempts to engage in reciprocal and

meaningful dialogue with respect to the learning environment and his academic future with various school personnel:

After public school, I got placed in this program. The teachers I got now are all white; so are most of the other students. When I hear we are getting a new intern to work here, or a new kid in the program I ask, "Is he African American?" I always ask that. And sometimes they'll say yes, and sometimes they'll say no. I don't get depressed. It don't bother me but if they say yes I get happy. That's cool, that's good, more mixture here. Because right now it's like to me the mixture here is like a box of Cap'n Crunch cereal, the milk and me. But if we get some more African Americans, I think it'll be a mixture of Cocoa Puffs, and it'll be better for me.

I'm learning a lot in this program and I'm trying to let 'em know that my attitude is changing. When I first came here I would fight, and one of the teachers here was gonna restrain me and I didn't know him so I pulled a razor blade on him.

I regret it now. I've grown attached to a lot of people here. But I feel like I'm gonna make it back to public school no matter what they tell me. I'm a make it and become a doctor. And some of the teachers here tell me, "Well, don't you think that's a kind of big goal for you?" and I say, "No, that's a little one." The teacher's here hear you say this and tell you it's an unrealistic goal and ask, "Do you think you can make it?" I say, "I don't think, I know," I really feel it.

But the teachers in public schools told me, "You ain't gonna make it. Look at, you know, you being bad, you ain't gonna make it. You ain't gonna make what you want. You'll become somebody that's living off of track [gambling] and drinking Night Train [a cheap, strong wine] or whatever." That hurt but I told 'em, "I'm a prove you wrong. When you come into my hospital asking me to make some surgery on you or do an autopsy on your body or whatever, I'm a prove you wrong." That's it.

Discouraged from sharing his dreams with peers or teachers, Stacy stops trying. He concluded, somewhat in contrast to Thomas, that it is both how and who "they" are that allows communication to occur.

Discussion with the participants in the study converged around the need they expressed for multicultural education to disarm the violence that characterized their Eurocentric educational experiences. In general, study participants believed that conflict between students of different racial, ethnic, linguistic, and other social groups erupt outside of school because of a lack of knowledge about each other's cultures. Animosity is then made worse by the lack of an in-school environment and curricula that encourage multicultural awareness, knowledge, and understanding among students of various social groups.

Elaborating on this theme, Vanessa recounted a comment made by one of her friends to a newspaper reporter who was interviewing high-school students about violence in schools, "If you clean the school system to where it is more of a multicultural diversity in areas of learning, then the streets will start to clean up." Waverly, a 24-year-old African-American study participant, stated his belief that more multicultural education is an imperative. In particular he would have wanted to learn more about Black history because, he said, "To know others, one needs to know self; multicultural education teaches the history of self and others."

Stacy had this to say:

I feel that, in public school systems, they should get a lot more of African-American history and others. 'Cause when you talk about race I get mixed up. Back then what was the Spanish [Latina/o]? They were a different color from black and different color from white. They had a race somewhere. Were they recognized as blacks or whites? I ask this question, and people can't answer it. But this is a question I always got on my mind and whenever I hear about race I'm always gonna ask it. And if you can't answer it, then that means either you need to get some more teaching or you need to have some other people come help teach. Sometimes I get bored here 'cause I don't got nobody else my color or no learning about it.

And Carlos, expanding upon what Waverly and Stacy said, explained:

I think mainly why kids just drop out is just problems they have that they don't have to talk with somebody, and just ain't into the work. [They] just don't make it interesting. Everyday they opening a book, the same book, onto the same pages. That isn't interesting. Like if you want to teach a kid about history I would go about it this way. I want to teach a kid the history of this city, sightseeing and everything. I would take a car, and I would take 'em and give 'em a pad and a book and tell 'em to take notes. Because they sightseeing they getting active, they getting into it. They not just sitting in a class doing the same thing with the same book.

And if you want to teach a person math and counting I would get real money, get real items with tags on them and candy and other things they like. And spread out the money, and they go up to you and want the candy bar. And you say, "How much is this candy bar?" And they say, "forty cents" and give you fifty cents and then you ask how much change they are going to get back.

Make it active, make it active, make it active and interesting. Move around more and talk more. Make it easier for them to understand. If you can get them to get into it a certain way then keep using that method. That's work. That way worked for me so a little while after I learned. I also learned in the program I'm in now that if I talk more to the teachers and let 'em know I got problems with this and that, if they would listen, then things got easier.

I think that we should also learn about all different people's cultures in school, and it should be blended in all year round in one whole book not just once a month. Because you know as you can see Black people from where they came from are making a whole lot of progress. 'Cause a lot of people say it's the minorities that do all the crime, which is wrong, completely wrong. 'Cause it's not the minorities.

'Cause look at Black people. Before, they weren't even on television. Now they on television. We had a Black person running for president. They have culture and history themselves; a human is a human. I would like to learn about everyone's history including my own. I've never really learned anything about my own, only how to cook Puerto-Rican food and what the first Puerto Ricans [Tainos] ate and how they lived, but not no main history like the first Puerto Rican to do this or that. Nothing like that. That would be real interesting.

The desire for multicultural education is quite coherently articulated here. The study participants make impassioned requests for multicultural curriculum content, multicultural pedagogies, multicultural membership and interaction among students, teachers, and parents, and multicultural school structure. Ultimately, all the study participants argue that student resistance to school as well as violence in schools and communities is all due in large measure to the schools' and society's resistance to dealing with issues of diversity and to developing and implementing multicultural education, and the impact of the physical, economic, political, and psychological violence inherent in this resistance.

Overall, the study pointed toward making changes in Eurocentric education that multicultural education and its proponents have championed for a long time. The problem here is not primarily that multicultural education is not known, but rather that it is not being implemented, either at all or comprehensively enough to effect the targeted changes. In the context of a conservative political climate in which "the fiscal bottom line" is the clarion call to solidarity, it is ironic that even the frugal fiscal effectiveness of various multicultural educational programs (for example, the marked decrease in prison recidivism eventuated when inmates leave incarceration with marketable skills) can be ignored.

The implications of this study have relevance for all schools, educators, and parents. It is important for all persons involved in young people's lives to become aware of, knowledgeable about, and understanding of the real conditions of existence of young people, which today necessarily include some form of violence, and to reflect this in the organizational structure, curricula, and interpersonal interactions of which young people are a part.

References

Clark, Christine Elise. (1993). Multicultural Education as a Tool for Disarming Violence: A Study Through In-Depth Participatory Action Research. University of Massachusetts, Amherst, MA: Unpublished dissertation.

Hardiman, Rita (1979). *White Identity Development.* Amherst, MA: New Perspectives, Inc.

Jackson, Bailey (1976). *Black Identity Development.* Amherst, MA: New Perspectives, Inc.

Massachusetts State Department of Education Regulations (1991). Chapter 766, Program Prototypes 502.0–502.12.

Walsh, Catherine E. (1991). *Pedagogy and the Struggle for Voice: Issues of Language, Power and Schooling for Puerto Ricans.* New York: Bergin & Garvey.

PAYING ATTENTION TO OUR CHILDREN

EDUCATIONAL DILEMMAS FOR AMERICANS

PATRICIA ALBJERG GRAHAM

Periodically, Americans pay attention to our children's educations. Whenever we do so, inevitably we find ourselves deeply mired in contradictory accounts of their experiences. Newspapers abound with graphs revealing how poorly or how well US children take academic tests compared to each other and compared to others around the world. People seeking a simple indicator of a complex situation find a test score, and its relative standing among others tested, a handy guide of whether children are doing well or badly. Others, who are convinced that the public schools need fixing, seek a single solution— vouchers, perhaps, or charter schools—as the remedy. Still others observe that in some states there is five times as much spending on students in some school districts as in others ($15,744 versus $2,932 during 1994–95 in Illinois, for example) and argue that equalization of expenditure is the cure-all.

Education is an important issue for nearly all Americans, but for almost none is it the most central issue in our lives. As an important but rarely preeminent question, we often discuss it superficially and seek one comprehensive solution. Our disappointment increases when no panacea materializes; but by that time, our sons and daughters are already grown and our interest in education has receded, since only a few of us worry about the educations of other people's children.

Ms. Graham is a professor at the Harvard Graduate School of Education.

Why, then, does education present itself as such a persistent dilemma in the United States? I believe that there are three fundamental explanations: We change our minds about what the central tasks of schools should be; we want teenagers to get high school diplomas, but we are deeply ambivalent about what the content of their adolescent experience should be; and we are unsure how important school itself is in children's education.

First, we change our minds about what the central task of schools should be, and we expect schools to accommodate immediately to these shifting priorities. To a remarkable degree American schools historically have faithfully delivered what American society sought from them. When changes in society's expectations for these schools occurred, as has happened during the last dozen years, the schools have had difficulty making a complete and rapid adjustment to the new expectations. While American schools have always had a core commitment to academic achievement for some apparently gifted children, including children of the poor, the emphasis for the vast majority of the other students has changed significantly.

Schools do deliver what society wants, but slowly and incompletely. During this century society has set four principal but different goals for our schools:

1900–25: *Assimilation.* Schools were the principal institution in which the many European immigrants and their children encountered an emerging and distinctive American

Reprinted from *Current*, May 1998, pp. 3-7. Originally appeared in *Daedalus*, Vol. 127, No. 1, "Science in Culture," Winter 1998, pp. 225-236. © 1998 by the American Academy of Arts and Sciences. Reprinted by permission.

culture. The schools understood that their primary mission was to "Americanize" the children into loyal and acculturated American citizens.

1925–54: *Adjustment.* The new and dominant progressive education movement, committed to the "whole child" (with special attention to the child's mental and social health), became codified after World War II as the Life Adjustment Movement in which 20 percent of students were to be educated for college, 20 percent for vocational training, and the remaining 60 percent with "general life skills," or how to adjust to life.

1954–83: *Access.* Again, after the 1954 desegregation decision in Brown v. Board of Education, schools were used as institutions to serve the broad goals of the society by providing access to those previously denied it. This emphasis continued with special attention to children of poor families in the Elementary and Secondary Education Act of 1965 and the Education for All Handicapped Act (PL 94–142) in 1975.

1983–present: *Achievement.* The current effort to universalize academic achievement as a goal of the many and not just of the few is the most radical goal of all. The enunciation of this sentiment came most poignantly to the American people in the 1983 report of a Reagan-appointed commission on American education, entitled *A Nation at Risk.* Yet even in this last decade the increases in school budgets have been concentrated in special education, not regular academic education.

Richard Rothstein and Karen Hawley Miles recently examined expenditures for nine school districts between 1967 and 1991, which revealed that real school spending increased by 61 percent in that period. They found that the share of expenditures going to regular education dropped from 80 percent to 59 percent, while the share going to special education climbed from 4 percent to 17 percent. Of the net new funds spent on education in 1991, only 26 percent went to improve regular education, while about 38 percent went to special education for severely handicapped and learning-disabled children. Per-pupil spending on teacher compensation also grew as a result of more intensive staffing—in particular, the hiring of more resource- and subject-specialist teachers.

SPECIAL EDUCATION In their study of the spending in New York state school districts, Hamilton Lankford and James Wykoff found that the $5 billion increase in expenditures (a 46 percent increase in real per-pupil spending) over the 1980–1992 period was primarily spent on teachers and on disabled students. These researchers suggest that the implementation of PL 94–142 and associated state requirements led school districts to "substantially increase their spending on special education students" at the expense of nondisabled students.

Certainly the needs of special education students are great. The emphasis, however, has been on academic achievement for all. We have been much longer on rhetoric, usually referred to as "standards," than on imaginative and effective interventions to assist teachers in helping ordinary children learn more. New funds go to special education; new demands for academic achievement encompass all students.

These rapid changes in priorities for schools have left teachers and administrators gasping. They have occurred at a time when school personnel, especially teachers, are much older and more experienced than was the case earlier in this century. For example, at the turn of the century the median age of American teachers was twenty-six; hence at least half the teachers were being prepared for teaching and entering the field at a time when assimilation was the reigning emphasis for schooling. Today the median age for public-school teachers is forty-two, and fully 30 percent have more than twenty years of experience. Many of them were thus prepared for teaching in the waning days of adjustment and the rising period of access; neither period demanded the kinds of skills and attitudes for teachers that achievement does today. Therefore, one of the greatest challenges for those involved with schools today is to assist teachers who were trained for one set of school emphases in becoming effective with an altogether different set. For example, I entered teaching the year the Progressive Education Association disbanded (1955), and no one expected me then to teach American history according to today's national standards. How does one mobilize a tenured teaching force prepared to do one kind of teaching to become capable of and willing to do something quite different? That is the mystery of professional development.

In "A Revolution in One Classroom: The Case of Mrs. Oublier," David K. Cohen shows the contrast between one teacher's (Mrs. O's) perception of how a mathematics workshop focused on the understanding of mathematical ideas has changed her teaching and that teacher's actual practice. Cohen's observations of Mrs. O's classroom reveal that while the social organization of her class, the teaching materials she uses, and the lessons are all new, Mrs. O's pedagogy has essentially remained unchanged. Schools abound with Mrs. Os, teachers who seek to incorporate new and presumably more effective teaching techniques but who for a variety of reasons fail to do so.

SECONDARY EDUCATION

Second, we want our teenagers to get high-school diplomas, but we are deeply ambivalent about what the content of their high-school experience should be. America has led the world in the twentieth century by providing broad and nearly universal secondary education, and for most of the century our means of achieving such widespread access has been to modify the curriculum of the high school, reserving rigorous academic courses for a relatively small minority of our youngsters. The percentage of teenagers who graduated from high school (or in more recent years gained high-school equivalency through a GED) increased dramatically from less than 10 percent in the early years of this century to approximately 50 percent in the middle years of the century; today, 85 percent of American teenagers receive a high-school diploma or its equivalent.

The first federal aid to schools was the Smith-Hughes Act of 1917, which provided funds for vocational education in the high school as a supplement or an alternative to the traditional classical or college-prepatory curriculum. As the fraction of students continuing in high school increased through the middle years of the century, more and more efforts were launched to alter the high-school curriculum to make it more appealing to students who were neither academically inclined nor intending to attend college. The Life Adjustment curriculum at the end of the progressive education movement captured the emphasis on staying in school but not necessarily learning much. In short, the twentieth-century American strategy has been to keep children in school by changing the curriculum while holding the pegagogy constant. A more effective approach undoubtedly would have been to modify the pedagogy, so that it attracted learners, while holding constant the curriculum that society believed all children should learn. But the intent was to prevent dropouts, not to create learners. Furthermore, the effort was successful.

Diplomas were a goal, and thus antidropout programs were important; however, in anti-intellectual America, achievement itself has not been broadly sought for most children until recently. If the approaches to learning academic material were not modified to appeal to a broad variety of students, then inevitably many high-school students, beset with the hormonal and cultural consequences of adolescence, would find high school itself boring. In the absence of a compelling need to be interested in schoolwork, they sought other alternatives. For many—especially for white, middle-class youngsters—the preferred alternative was paid employment.

PART-TIME EMPLOYMENT

Working during the school year provides many advantages; mostly, it brings in money, which occasionally is saved but more commonly is used to buy the desirable but nonessential goods that many teenagers crave. Money from working brings these goods without delay. This immediacy appeals to many teenagers whose capacity for delayed gratification—advocated by teachers as a benefit of education—is limited. "Greed, not need" explains the high rate of American youth employment during the school year, according to Ellen Greenberger and Lawrence Steinberg, who argue:

> It is difficult to say whether the increased consumer spending of young people preceded or followed their increased participation in the part-time labor force, but the two forces obviously fed one another. As more teenagers developed expensive tastes and a hunger for luxury goods, they found it necessary to go to work; and as more youngsters entered the labor force and began earning money that they could spend as they wished, more money was spent on developing and expanding the youth market.

Many parents also support their adolescents' employment during the school year. Exhausted parents often take comfort in the security of knowing that their sixteen-year-old is under supervision while flipping hamburgers—and is happy with the money. They take further consolation in the hope that he or she is developing a good work ethic, and some are relieved that they do not have to supervise their child at home, insisting that the homework get done. All, undoubtedly, are thankful that their children are not driving around looking for opportunities to use drugs or alcohol.

Estimates vary, but approximately half of high-school students work during the school year with estimates for white students being significantly higher than for blacks and somewhat higher than for Hispanics. A 1990 New Hampshire survey found that 70 percent of all teenagers held jobs and that more than 84 percent in grades 10 through 12 worked; 45 percent worked more than twenty hours per week during the school year.

These figures are in sharp contrast to the national rate of black teenage unemployment—32 percent of those who are seeking jobs. As Richard Freeman and Harry J. Holzer have observed, "Young blacks have made advances in both occupation and education. Yet their employment problem has worsened, reaching levels that can only be described as catastrophic. . . . In many respects, the urban unemployment characteristic of Third World countries appears to have taken root among black youths in the United States."

Nearly everyone would agree that working a little (less than ten hours per week during the school year) is not harmful, and possibly beneficial. Similar concurrence exists at the other end of the spectrum—working more than twenty hours per week during the school year is detrimental. For those students, grades suffer, less rigorous curricula are pursued, and often health is impaired because of insufficient sleep or inadequate exercise. Less easy to measure is the impact of a short-term job with its immediate rewards compared to the patience required to take demanding courses and work hard enough to do well in them. Although immediate transition to the work force may be easier for someone who has worked extensively during high school, upward mobility is more likely for someone with a strong high-school and college record; calculus is more valuable in terms of discipline than a perfect attendance record at McDonald's.

A recent comparison of youth in Minneapolis and Sendai, Japan, reveals considerable differences in use of time and money. Nearly three-quarters of the Americans work, while only one-fifth of the Japanese do. Average weekly income (from both job and parents) was $205 for the American youths and $86 for the Japanese; nearly all of the Japanese youths' income came from parents, while only half of American youths' income came from their parents. Other findings included that Japanese watch more weekly television (16.7 hours) than Americans (12 hours) and that fewer Japanese reported experiencing stress each week (43.4 percent) than Americans (71.2 percent).

The United States is atypical in its pattern of youth employment while enrolled in school. Beatrice Reubens, John Harrison, and Kalman Rupp reported in 1981 that almost 70 percent of all sixteen- and seventeen-year-old students were in the labor force during the 1978–79 school year in the United States, compared to 37 percent in Canada, 20 percent in Sweden, and less than 2 percent in Japan. We tend to prolong adolescence while providing the conveniences (but not responsibilities) of adulthood. By encouraging part-time work during the school year, both in high school and for many college students, we delay the time that young people need to assume full obligations of adult life.

Young people often have money for luxuries because they continue to live at home and enjoy a parental standard of living that would not be available to them if they were dependent upon themselves for support. Researchers who examined young-adult living patterns found that between 1977 and 1986 increasing proportions of high-school seniors reported that "living in luxury" was important to them, and that parents tolerate coresidence with their adult children if they did not seek daily funds from their parents. In short, a young person can continue the pattern of high-school employment and using income for frills while parents supply the necessities—as long as the child does not seek direct support [from] parents for day-to-day expenses. College, too, becomes a much longer process, with many adult students working part time and studying part time, further blurring the boundary between adolescence and full-fledged adulthood. Over half the undergraduates today are over twenty-one years of age—formerly the typical age of graduation from college.

The ambivalence we exhibit about the content of our adolescents' educational experiences is also illustrated by our commitment to high-school athletics. H. G. Bissinger captures the intensity of community enthusiasm for winning high-school football teams in *Friday Night Lights*, revealing adults much more concerned about the teams' prowess than about children's learning. In the face of these pressures brought by students, their parents, and the local community, schools traditionally have relaxed academic demands in

ATHLETICS

order to accommodate student employment and facilitate athletic eligibility. No wonder we are ambivalent about our adolescents' educational experiences.

Finally, how important is school itself in children's education? Scholars ranging from the late James S. Coleman and Lawrence A. Cremin to Christopher Jencks have quite properly reminded us of the limited role that schools play in children's education. Analytically there is no doubt that these writers are correct in identifying families, communities, religious institutions, television, and (now) electronic devices as cumulatively much more important than school alone in the education of the young.

One profound irony of those of us who understand this analytic contribution, and who have the wealth necessary, is that we make enormous efforts to get our children into the best possible schools. As parents, we often select our place of residence based in large part on its proximity to good schools for our children. Although we know that we will supplement our children's education in many important ways beyond what the school provides for them, we still believe that the school itself is a crucial educational intervention for our children. We want schools with good teachers, often defined as ones who have had sound undergraduate academic instruction and who are effective in reaching their students. We want principals with good judgment and effective administrative skills. We want facilities, buildings, libraries, athletic equipment, and computers that will attract and challenge our children. Most of all, we want other students whose families share our educational values. In short, those of us who best understand the limited role schools play in education want the very best schools for our children, and generally we get them.

QUALITY OF SCHOOLS The irony rests on the fact that while most families want the best for their children, many are not aware of the quality of their schools. As Richard Murnane and Frank Levy point out in *Teaching the New Basic Skills*, the families of the Zavala School in Austin, Texas, also recognized that their children needed good schools. The average annual family income at Zavala is $12,000, and since many families speak only Spanish, the school was the way for their children to learn English. These families saw that success in school was their children's best hope to avoid the poverty of their parents. Imagine the shock of the families when they learned that their children, who had been receiving mostly As and Bs on their report cards, scored in the bottom quartile on the Texas achievement tests. Here was a school that was fooling its clients by pretending that they were doing well, when in fact the teachers were not demanding rigorous work from them. Murnane and Levy recount the pain of the parents when they realized that their children were being cheated by the very institution they believed was their children's best hope for having a better future; they also report how the parents, the new principal of the school, and newly committed teachers, plus some outside advocates, gradually and with difficulty turned the school around and truly improved the achievement of the children.

In short, schools are more important for the children of the poor than they are for the children of the affluent. While prosperous families arrange for a variety of beneficial educational activities for their offspring, school is often the only constructive educational experience that children living in poverty may have. It is thus an extraordinary tragedy that the worst schools—whether in terms of faculty and administrative skills or per-pupil expenditures—serve the children who most need excellent schools, the children of the poor, while the best ones serve the children who have the most educational alternatives, the children of well-educated and prosperous families.

These three dilemmas—the changing central purpose of schooling in America, the ambivalence Americans exhibit about their adolescents' educational experiences, and the contradictory commitments we hold about the relative importance of schooling to education—tax our imaginations to understand and our will to resolve. What is most impressive, however, is the historic capacity of Americans to adapt their educational institutions, albeit slowly, to meet and fulfill the shifting expectations placed upon them. Again, we have the opportunity to demonstrate this ability.

Unit 2

Key Points to Consider

❖ Why is multicultural education so frequently seen as an isolated, segregated part of teacher education programs?

❖ What are the reasons for so much resistance to coursework in the area of multicultural education in teacher education programs?

❖ What can we learn about teaching styles and methods from case studies of teachers from cultures other than our own?

❖ Why can it be said that our understanding of the relevance of multicultural perspectives on teacher education emerged from the struggle for human rights in general?

❖ What seem to be the major points of disagreement about the role of multicultural education in teacher education programs?

❖ What attitudes need to change regarding multicultural education?

 **Links** | **www.dushkin.com/online/**

These sites are annotated on pages 4 and 5.

At a time when the minority student body at the elementary and secondary school levels is beginning to approach 50 percent of the school population, fewer students from cultural minorities are choosing teaching as a career. This social reality within teacher education programs in the United States only underscores the need for multicultural education, as well as for coursework in specific cultural studies areas in the education of American teachers.

Multicultural educational programming of some sort is now an established part of teacher education programs, but debate continues as to how it can be integrated effectively into these programs. The National Council for the Accreditation of Teacher Education (NCATE) has established a multicultural standard for the accreditation of programs for teacher education in the United States. Many educators involved in teaching courses in multicultural education have wondered why such coursework is so often a segregated area of teacher education curricula. And many who are involved in multicultural teacher education believe that all teacher educators should become knowledgeable in this area. Teaching preservice teachers to respect cultural diversity can enhance their ability to respect individual students' diversity in learning styles and beliefs. Prospective teachers need to be sensitized to the reality of cultural diversity and to the need to learn about the values and beliefs of their students.

There is still much misunderstanding within the teacher education establishment as to what multicultural education is. This will continue as long as many of its opponents consider it a political rather than an intellectual or educational concept. If all children and young adults are to receive their educational experiences in schools that nourish and respect their respective heritages as people, all teachers must learn those intellectual and affective skills that can empower them to study and to learn about diverse cultures throughout their careers. Multicultural education course content in teacher education programs is about both cultural diversity and individual students from differing cultural heritages.

Teachers will have to consider how each student's development is shaped by the powerful force of those values prevailing in his or her home and neighborhood. In a civilization rapidly becoming more culturally pluralistic, resistance to overwhelmingly Eurocentric domination of social studies and language arts curricula in the schools will continue. About 5 billion of the approximately 6 billion people on Earth are people with a non-Eurocentric conception of the world. Scholars in the social sciences, humanities, and teacher education in North America, who study minority-majority relations in the schools, now realize that the very terms "minority" and "majority" are changing when we speak of the demographic realities of the cultural configurations existent in most major urban and suburban educational systems. This is also true when we consider minority-majority relations in vast isolated rural or wilderness areas where those of western or northern European descent can be found to

be "minorities" in the midst of concentrations of indigenous peoples. Many teachers will teach students whose values and views of the world are very different from their own, hence the relevance of teachers learning how to learn about human cultures and belief systems in order that they can study the lives and heritages of their students in the schools.

Many teachers of European ethnic heritage are having difficulty understanding the importance of the fact that North American society is becoming more culturally pluralistic. From a multicultural perspective, one of the many things course content seeks to achieve is to help all prospective teachers realize the importance of becoming lifelong learners. The knowledge base of multicultural education is further informed by the history of the struggle for civil rights in North American societies. Multicultural educational programming in teacher education programs seeks to alter how prospective teachers perceive society as a whole, not just its current minority members. We must take a broad view of multicultural education. Culturally pluralistic themes need to be apparent throughout teacher education programs and integrated into the knowledge bases of teacher education. Broadly conceived, multicultural education seeks to help members of all ethnic, cultural backgrounds to appreciate one another's shared human concerns and interrelationships; it should not be conceived as simply the study of minority cultural groups. Teachers need to be prepared in such a manner that they learn genuine respect for cultural as well as personal diversity.

Teachers should be prepared to take a global perspective of the world and to think critically about the issues confronting them, their students, and society as a whole (seen as part of an interdependent community of nations). Multicultural education should not be politicized. It should be a way of seeing the world as enriched by cultural and personal diversity. Preservice teachers should learn from case studies that exemplify and report on the differing cultural traditions in child rearing, entry into adulthood (rites of passage), and varying cultural styles of child-adult interaction in school settings.

The essays in this unit explore why it is important not to see multicultural education as just a political concept, but rather as an area of critical inquiry from which we can all learn alternative diverse styles of teaching appropriate to the learning styles and cultural backgrounds of students. The articles stress the importance of teachers being able to learn differing ways, share in social interaction in classroom settings, and to see the impact of race, gender, and social class on their ideas about themselves as teachers, how they perceive other teachers, and how they perceive their students.

This unit's articles are relevant to courses that focus on introduction to the cultural foundations of education, educational policy studies, history and philosophy of education, and curriculum theory and construction, as well as methods courses in all areas of teacher education programs.

Teacher Education in Multicultural Perspective

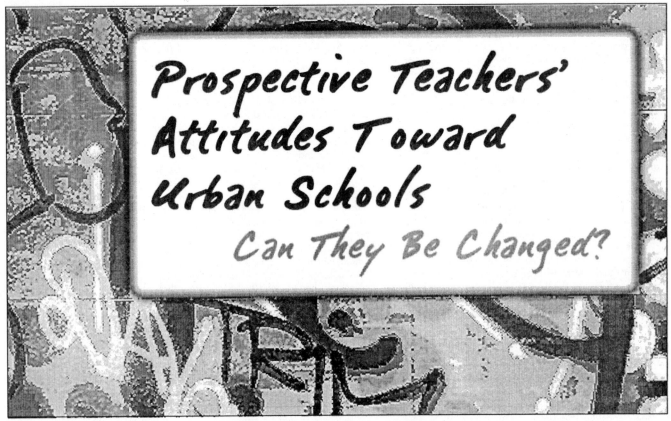

Prospective Teachers' Attitudes Toward Urban Schools
Can They Be Changed?

By Terrence C. Mason

Much of the research on preservice teachers' attitudes and beliefs about teaching suggests that altering those beliefs constitutes a difficult, if not impossible, task (Richardson, 1996). On the other hand, we know that beliefs influence teacher behavior and expectations (Cooper, Baron, & Lowe, 1975), and that an important goal of teacher education is to lead prospective teachers toward developing beliefs about teaching that will maximize learning for all students. Current demographic changes are producing a student population that is increasingly diverse; even the meaning of the term minority must now be reconsidered. Meanwhile, the ethnic and cultural composition of the teaching force remains relatively unchanged.

Under these circumstances, educators must continue to ask whether those entering teaching hold attitudes about cultural and socioeconomic diversity that will enable them to meet the needs of the students they will encounter in the classrooms of

Terrence C. Mason is an assistant professor in the Department of Curriculum and Instruction at the School of Education, Indiana University, Bloomington, Indiana.

the 21st century. Some who have studied this issue conclude that they do not (Garcia, 1994; Gomez & Tabachnick, 1992; Haberman & Post, 1992), and that being white and middle class presents a serious obstacle to becoming a successful teacher of minority children.

A key question one might ask here is, "Why be concerned about urban schools?" This question can be answered by citing the demographic shifts referred to above and the impending high demand for teachers in urban areas populated largely by non-white, low-SES students. But such pragmatic justifications fall short of identifying the real reason why educators should care about the educational futures of inner-city children.

In a recent doctoral seminar discussion, I was reminded by one of my students that sometimes educational practices need not be supported by elaborately constructed logic or reasoning. To advocate for quality schooling for urban students, or any students for that matter, is, as she put it, "just the right thing to do." A similar view was advanced by John Goodlad in his 1990 book, *Teachers for Our Nation's Schools*. One of 19 postulates for reforming teacher edu-

cation articulated by Goodlad recommends that teacher education programs be infused with the understanding of and commitment to the moral obligation of teachers to ensure equitable access to and engagement in the best possible K-12 education for all children and youths" (p. 292).

In keeping with this principle, the American Educational Research Association's Division on Teaching and Teacher Education (Division K) has recently adopted an equity policy urging teacher educators to respond to the disproportionate representation of poor, non-white students among low achievers, non-academic tracks, and drop outs. According to this policy, "Failure to do so threatens the stability of democratic societies and mocks the principles of equity and social justice upon which these societies are founded" (American Educational Research Association, 1998). Thus, if we are to take at all seriously the responsibility of educating children in a democratic society, we cannot pursue policies that ignore the needs of all its children.

In 1979 Vivian Paley published *White Teacher*, an account of her career as a school teacher and the development of her understanding of how her own cultural biases affected her teaching. Paley candidly relates how her unconscious stereotyping of African-American students interfered with her ability to treat them as individuals and meet their needs. Through a critical examination of her own teaching practice, however, she gained valuable insights into the meaning of diversity and offered an example of how, at least for one teacher, differences in culture need not impose a barrier to becoming a successful teacher of "other peoples' children" (Delpit, 1988).

If not all teachers possess Paley's extraordinary reflective capacity, how can we bring about fundamental changes in teachers' beliefs and attitudes? Is it possible to create learning experiences for prospective teachers to encourage more productive and democratic attitudes toward teaching? Can teacher educators influence the early socialization of preservice teachers to enhance their understanding and appreciation of cultural diversity?

While one method of improving future teachers' attitudes toward such students has been direct exposure and interaction through field experiences, interpretations of recent studies of the impact of these programs have lead some educators to question the value of this approach (Haberman & Post, 1992). Indeed, some believe that this exposure increases rather than diminishes preservice teachers' negative attitudes and confirms their reluctance to seek positions in inner-city schools.

In this article I will review two recent studies that challenge this view and offer some suggestions about how teacher educators might work with preservice teachers to overcome stereotypical views of students from diverse backgrounds.

The Urban Field Experience Debate

A common suggestion for improving the preparation of teachers for inner-city schools has been the inclusion of an urban field experience prior to student teaching (Haberman, 1987). This experience would enable preservice teachers to understand the unique conditions and demands of socially, culturally, and economically diverse groups of students by working with these students under the direction of successful urban educators. In a study conducted with Post (1992), however, Haberman found that students' initial attitudes toward low-income, minority students, whether positive or negative, were maintained in spite of completing an field experience with low income, urban students. According to these authors, "people perceive what they believe" (Haberman, 1993, p. 86).

Haberman hypothesizes that college students' beliefs about the educability of urban pupils stem from attitudes that are deeply enculturated and highly resistant to change. He concludes that the inner-city

field experience represented a "fruitless path" lacking potential for changing prospective teachers' beliefs or behavior (1993, p. 85).

Other critics of current field experience practices argue that field experiences may encourage utilitarian teaching perspectives (Tabachnick & Zeichner, 1984) "that tend to encourage acquiescence and conformity to the existing, conservative routines found in the schools" (Goodman, 1986, p. 111). According to this view, we cannot expect incoming teachers to develop more positive attitudes toward culturally or socio-economically diverse students (i.e., those that affirm diversity, foster equitable teaching practices and social justice, and diminish stereotyping) simply by placing them in classrooms with practicing teachers who

employ ineffective teaching practices. On the contrary, the opposite is likely to happen.

In contrast to Haberman's results, others have found that field experiences have altered students' perceptions in significant ways. Based on a meta-analysis of the effects of early field experiences, Malone (1985) concluded that the impact on preservice teachers' attitudes and on their teaching performance may be the most profound among those students placed in low SES schools. Malone further concluded that, when exposed to teachers working in such schools, many prospective teachers feel that they possess the energy and resources to educate students more effectively than the teachers they observe in those settings, a finding echoed by other investigators (Hoy & Woolfolk, 1990; Weinstein, 1988).

Similarly, in spite of the lack of attitude change, Haberman and Post (1992) did find that teacher candidates' sense of personal efficacy and motivation to pursue urban teaching was enhanced by the inner-city field experience. Others have suggested that, when properly supervised, early field experiences can lead prospective teachers toward richer understandings of the needs of today's students and provide opportunities for important attitudinal change particularly regarding issues of student diversity (Gomez & Tabachnick, 1991; Ladson-Billings, 1991). The key here is "when properly supervised." Recently developed teacher preparation curricula have attempted to control the structure and content of preservice teachers' field experiences and have found that this approach improves their ability to teach in culturally and socially diverse schools (Burstein &

Cabello, 1989; Gipe, Duffy, & Richards, 1989).

Overall, the available research indicates that the impact of preservice field experiences, particularly in urban settings, remains under question. With that in mind, let us consider the following two studies that support the value of field experiences in the formation of positive attitudes toward teaching in urban, low SES settings.

Urban Schools and Suburban Schools

In a recent publication (Mason, 1997), I reported the results of a two-year study designed to gauge the impact of urban-based field experiences on the attitudes of preservice teachers which addressed the following research questions:

To advocate for quality schooling for urban students, or any students for that matter, is... "just the right thing to do."

1. Do preservice teachers become more positively disposed toward teaching in an urban setting as a result of an urban field experience?
2. Do preservice teachers' attitudes toward inner-city, low-income, and minority students improve as a result of completing an inner-city field experience?
3. How do attitudes toward low-income, minority students of preservice teachers who complete an inner-city field experience compare with those who complete one in a suburban school attended predominantly by European-American, middle-class students?

Over a period of four semesters, data were collected on junior and senior level undergraduates (N=176) enrolled in an undergraduate elementary certification program at a metropolitan, public university in New England. As a requirement of the program, these students completed an eight-week, field-based practicum in conjunction with instructional methods courses in mathematics, language arts, social studies, science, and health. They spent two full days a week working with elementary students in a self-contained classroom under the supervision of the classroom teacher and a faculty member from the university's department of teacher education. During the practicum they observed and assisted the classroom teacher and planned and carried out instruction including a "miniunit" based on social studies and language arts content.

Some of these preservice teachers (n=75) were placed in "inner-city" schools in which a large proportion of the students were African American and Latino and from low-income families. These schools were located in, or directly adjacent to, a large metropolitan area. Another group of students (n=101)were placed in suburban, middle-class schools for their practicum attended by few minority or low-SES pupils (less than 2 percent of the total school population).

All undergraduates participating in the study were administered a questionnaire prior to the beginning of the field experience to assess various attitudes related to inner-city teaching. They rated the extent to which they were interested in pursuing teaching in the inner city (5=very interested; to 1=not at all interested). In addition, based on some of the issues raised by

Vivian Paley . . . was able to self-reflect and alter her own beliefs and practices, but even she relied on reactions from fellow teachers and her student teachers. . . . [I]n the absence of such guidance and reflection [cultural] conflicts could ultimately lead to frustration and failure.

Haberman (1987) and others, a set of potential problems associated with urban schools commonly cited by teachers was developed. Using a scale from 1 to 10: 1 indicating that it would not represent a problem, and 10 indicating that it would represent a serious problem, they rated the extent to which they believed a series of educational issues posed difficulties for teachers in inner-city schools.

They also rated the extent to which these same issues presented problems for teachers in suburban schools. These issues were student(1) ability, (2)language proficiency, (3) motivation, and (4) cooperation with peers, (5) parental support, (6) general teacher morale, (7) school discipline, and (8) administrative support. In order to compare overall attitudes toward teaching in these two settings, ratings of these potential problems were combined to form an overall "inner-city" and "suburban" attitude rating.

At the completion of the eight-week field experience, these preservice teachers were administered the same questionnaire.

Participants also responded to rating-scale type questions focusing on the impact of their methods courses and the field experience on their knowledge about cultural diversity and their preparation to teach in urban schools. At the end of the field experience they rated their perception of the overall quality of teaching displayed by the cooperating teacher in their field placement classroom, and provided written narrative comments on the impact of the field experience on their preparation for teaching.

Based on the location of the schools where these prospective teachers completed their practicum, a "natural field experiment" was made possible for comparing the impact of the two types of field experience settings on attitudes toward inner-city students. Detailed results of this study have been reported elsewhere (Mason, 1997), but the major findings can be summarized as follows:

- The effect of the field experience on interest in urban teaching was positive overall for all participants regardless of field placement, however,

- Following the field experience, 55 percent of the urban group indicated that they were more inclined to pursue inner-city teaching versus 20 percent of the suburban group. (Statistically significant differences were maintained from pre-to post- between the urban and suburban groups.)

- All participants perceived urban schools as generally more "problematic" than suburban schools both prior to and following the field experience but,

- Experience in inner-city classrooms did not diminish prospective teachers' attitudes toward urban schools and improved perceptions in certain key areas (student motivation and language proficiency, discipline, and parental support.)

- Participants in the urban field experience group reported gaining more knowledge than did those in the suburban group about students from different cultural backgrounds from their methods courses.

Three elements differentiated this intervention from those reported in other studies where beliefs and attitudes were found to be more intractable. The first of these concerns the *supervision* of participants in the field experience. The second involves the overall *structure and content* of the field experience and its relation to other elements of the teacher preparation curriculum, and the third relates to the *duration of teaching responsibility* in the field experience. Let us consider the impact of these three elements on the results of this study.

Structure

The urban field experience was integrated with a teaching methods course focusing primarily on Social Studies and Language Arts, and the activities that the field experience participants engaged in were connected to the curriculum of the field experience classroom. For example, the theme or topic for the "mini-unit" was generated in conjunction with the cooperating teacher and was aligned with subject matter being covered in the classroom. The field experience students were encouraged, however, to employ alternative teaching strategies presented in their methods classes such as inquiry-based instruction, learning centers, and cooperative learning. In this manner, the content of the field experience was derived jointly from ideas about curriculum from university coursework and the specific context of the field placement classroom.

The field experience also followed several courses in which issues related to student diversity were addressed. It is, therefore, not surprising that the urban field experience enhanced the acquisition of knowledge of cultural diversity. As a result of their experiences in the field setting, those in the urban group were able to develop a"schema" for multicultural concepts. Learning about the theory and practice of multicultural education in the university classroom combined with the urban field experience made the information about culture and ethnicity and its implications for teaching more meaningful for the urban group.

Duration of Teaching Responsibility

Preservice teachers completing the field experience in this study were required to spend a minimum of 96 hours, two full days a week, over an eight-week period in their field placement, a large part of which was spent actively engaged in teaching. As a result, they learned enough about their students to discover effective ways of carrying out instruction, and had the opportunity to overcome the initial frustrations and unsuccessful efforts that many preservice teachers encounter.

By contrast, in the study reported by Haberman and Post (1992) of a relatively small group of college sophomores (n = 23), the field experience group only participated for a period of six weeks in a summer school program during which they had limited responsibility for actual classroom teaching. The sustained teaching experience afforded to those in the present study very likely contributed to their more positive attitudes toward the students and schools they encountered during the field experience.

Supervision

The role of the university supervisor with undergraduates who have limited experience in culturally diverse settings is also relevant. All field experience participants in this study, regularly met individually and in groups with their field experience supervisor. In most cases the supervisor was one of the social studies or language arts methods course instructors who was able to link methods course content with the field experience activities. All field experience students were observed teaching in their field experience placement classroom by the supervisor on two or more occasions.

Individual conferences accompanied each observation where concerns about teaching and learning, the content and structure of the lesson and unit, the individual and group needs of the pupils, and any other issues that arose could be discussed. Through continuous contact between the field experience student and the supervisor, support for innovative teaching practices that were consistent with student needs could be maintained, and the tendency to adopt the "conservative routines" referred to by Goodman (1985) and others (Tabachnick & Zeichner, 1984) could be avoided.

Different Methodolgy; Similar Findings

In a study employing a qualitative rather than quantitative approach, Olmedo (1997) also found that under the right conditions the attitudes toward children of color in urban school settings held by predominantly white, middle-class undergraduates could be improved. Similar to the study described above these undergraduates were enrolled in teacher preparation program leading toward elementary certification and participated in a one-semester field experience in an urban school. Data for this study conducted in a large Midwestern university were drawn from the journal entries of sixteen white undergraduates in which they reflected on their field experience in relation to readings and discussions from a course that accompanied the field experience.

Analysis of the journal entries produced a number of important themes reflecting changes in beliefs and attitudes on the part of these students over the course of the study. Initially, the participants believed that they must "discipline the unmotivated," "pity the victim," "be colorblind," and that, "the system was the problem" (Olmedo, 1997, p. 250). As a result of the field experience combined with the discussions and readings, however, these attitudes eventually were replaced by a new set of assumptions about the schools and students they were teaching. For example, participants came to realize that, "children

want to learn," and "good teaching can take place even in inner city schools." Furthermore, they acknowledged "diversity within diversity;" that is, they recognized that considerable variability existed among students within ethnic and racial groups. Finally, they concluded that "being color blind was not good pedagogy (Olmedo, 1997, p. 251). To be fair and equitable they needed to incorporate cultural differences into the ways that they planned and carried out their teaching.

Olmedo attributes the success of this intervention to the use of small group rather than large, whole-class discussions, readings focused on accounts of teachers' experiences working in urban schools (e.g., Paley, 1979; Kohl, 1991), and the reflective, autobiographical narratives produced by the preservice teachers. By employing these methods she was able to observe important changes in the assumptions that her white, middle-class students made about teaching in an urban, multicultural setting. Olmedo concludes that,

> As a result of their interaction with students of color and diverse language backgrounds in the classroom, these prospective teachers became aware of the fact that issues related to multicultural education were not just "politically correct" doctrines to be discussed in the university, but were real concerns to be addressed by teachers in the schools, including decisions about the curriculum, the selection of materials, and classroom language. Moreover, their experiences in the fieldwork presented challenges to the deficit views of inner city schools which they had previously accepted as social reality. (Olmedo 1997, p. 256)

Implications and Future Directions

A colleague of mine recently described an incident involving a white, female undergraduate who was student teaching in an urban elementary school attended by predominantly African-American, low-income children. As is common practice, the student teacher devoted a part of the school day to reading aloud to her pupils. During this daily reading time, several of the girls in the class sat together and combed and braided each others' hair. The student teacher found this behavior to be inappropriate and unacceptable and asked them to stop. This led to ongoing conflict and considerable tension between the student teacher and the girls.

When she told the story to my colleague, who was serving as her student teaching supervisor, the student teacher expressed her displeasure with the girls' lack

of respect for her authority and felt justified in breaking up the coiffure session. In response to this, my colleague pointed out that hair grooming was an important aspect of the girls' culture, and that perhaps in denying the girls the opportunity to do this, the student teacher was being insensitive to a cultural norm that differed from her own values. Besides, would hair braiding really interfere with the girls' ability to understand and appreciate the story being read? The student teacher reflected on this, reconsidered her position, and allowed the girls to resume their hairstyling sessions during story time.

In relating this anecdote, my colleague lamented how ill-prepared our students are to successfully teach in situations where they do not share the same cultural background as their students or are not knowledgeable enough about their students' culture. I, however, interpret this scenario somewhat differently; I see it as important and powerful learning. It is very possible that an incident such as this would lead this student to acknowledge her own cultural "baggage" and adopt a more generalized reflective posture towards what she assumes about her students and their behavior. It might also lead her to value the importance of cultural differences and to seek out information about the history, customs, values, and cultural practices of her students. Because this student teacher was skillfully guided by her supervisor to reconsider her actions in light of her own biases she was able to take a step toward becoming an effective teacher for those students.

Paley, as an experienced teacher, was able to self-reflect and alter her own beliefs and practices, but even she relied on reactions from fellow teachers and her student teachers. Of course, in the absence of such guidance and reflection this incident, combined with other similar conflicts, could ultimately lead to frustration and failure. The role of close field supervision reported in my study (Mason, 1997) or the guided reflection described by Olmedo (1997) cannot be underestimated here as we look for the keys to success in preparing teachers for urban schools.

While the field experiences examined in the two studies reviewed here yielded positive results, still more can be done to improve school-based experiences in urban settings. Teacher preparation programs should include specific, structured activities aimed at increasing awareness and understanding of cultural diversity within the context of the communities where students carry out their field work "to sensitize teachers to values, lifestyles, and cultures different from their own and generate a respect for human diversity" (Zeichner, 1990; p. 118).

It is also crucial that effective cooperating teachers in urban schools be identified to work with prospective teachers. Although a university supervisor can sometimes attenuate the impact of a weak cooperating teacher, the influence of an exemplary model classroom teacher is invaluable. Finally, teacher educators themselves must become actively involved in the day-to-day operation of urban schools to become credible mentors for prospective urban teachers.

Future Research

The findings of the two studies reviewed here support the possibility that preservice teachers' attitudes can be influenced and altered by well conceived and structured field experiences. Such attitude change is crucial if we are going to prepare the kind of teachers who will meet the diverse and complex needs of students in the 21st century. The debate surrounding the worth of field experiences in teacher preparation will no doubt continue, but rather than dismissing their impact on the formation of positive attitudes toward urban schools and students, it would seem more worthwhile for future research to continue to examine the nature of those experiences and their contribution to attitude change.

This view coincides with that of Wideen, Mayer-Smith, and Moon (1998) regarding how we should approach future inquiry into the role of preservice teachers' beliefs as they enter teaching. Based on an exhaustive analysis of recent research on the process of learning to teach, these authors conclude "that the fixed nature of prospective teachers' beliefs should remain an open question rather than an accepted assumption until the impact of the more robust programs of teacher education has been fully analyzed" (p. 144). Teacher educators, therefore, must continue to implement such programs and systematically study their structure and effects.

Results of the two studies reviewed here focus on preservice teachers; but we know that the more important questions regarding attitudes and beliefs concern practicing teachers. While, as Olmedo (1997) points out, we should not minimize the significance of affecting change in preservice teachers, we need to continue examining what occurs when teachers assume responsibility for their own classrooms. Do the positive dispositions toward urban classrooms and culturally diverse students reported here persist?

We also must reconsider how we define urban or inner-city schools in relation to other types of school settings. In his analysis of demographic changes occurring in many parts of North America, particularly in the West, Kaplan (1998) notes that the distinction between urban and suburban is becoming blurred as students from a wide range of cultural, socioeconomic, and ethnic backgrounds populate schools in all types of communities, and as suggested at the beginning of this article, the majority is no longer the majority in many places.

Future studies may need to find other ways to characterize the sociocultural composition of schools to accurately portray the backgrounds of the students who attend them. With these considerations in mind, research should be designed to gain insight into ways to better prepare teachers to understand and value the varied cultural backgrounds of the students they will increasingly find in classrooms everywhere.

References

American Educational Research Association. (1998, Fall). *Division K Newsletter.*

Burstein, N.D., & Cabello, B. (1989). Preparing teachers to work with culturally diverse students: A teacher education model. *Journal of Teacher Education,* 40, 9–16.

Cooper, H.M., Baron, R.M., & Lowe C.A. (1975). The importance of race and social class information in the formation of expectancies about academic performance. *Journal of Educational Psychology,* 67, 312–319.

Delpit, L. (1988). The silenced dialogue: Power and pedagogy in educating other people's children. *Harvard Educational Review,* 58, 280–298.

Garcia, E.E. (1994). *Understanding and Meeting the Challenge of Student Cultural Diversity.* Boston: Houghton Mifflin.

Gomez, M. & Tabachnick, B.R. (1991). Preparing preservice teachers to teach diverse learners. Paper presented at the annual meeting of the American Educational Research Association, Chicago.

Gomez, M., &Tabachnick, B.R. (1992). Telling teaching stories. *Teaching Education,* 4(2),129–138.

Goodlad, J.I. (1990). *Teachers for Our Nation's Schools.* San Francisco, CA: Jossey-Bass.

Gipe, J. P., Duffy, C.A. & Richards, J.C. (1989). A comparison of two types of early field experiences. *Reading Improvement,* 26(3), 254–265.

Goodman, J. (1986). Making early field experience meaningful: A critical approach. *Journal of Education for Teaching,* 12(2), 109–125.

Haberman, M. J. (1993). Diverse contexts for teaching: Implications and Reflections. In O'Hair, M. J. & Odell, S.J. (eds.), *Diversity and Teaching.* Fort Worth, TX: Harcourt, Brace, Jovanovich.

Haberman, M. J. (1987). *Recruiting and Selecting Teachers for the Urban School.* ERIC Clearinghouse on Urban Education, New York, NY.

Haberman, M.J., & Post L. (1992). Does direct experience change education students' perceptions of low-income minority students. *Midwestern Educational Researcher,* 5(2), 29–31.

Hoy, W.K, & Woolfolk, A-E. (1990). Socialization of student teachers. *American Educational Research Journal* 27, 279–300.

Kaplan, R. (1998). Travels into America's future: Southern California and the Pacific Northwest, *The Atlantic Monthly,* 282(2), 337–61.

Kohl, H. (1991). *I won't learn from you: The role of assent in education.* New Jersey: Milkweed.

Ladson-Billings, G. (1991). When difference means disaster: Reflections on a teacher education strategy for countering student resistance to diversity. Paper presented at the annual meeting of the American Educational Research Association, Chicago.

Malone, M.R. (1985). Preservice field experience in teacher education: A quantitative synthesis. Paper presented at the annual meeting of the American Educational Research Association, Chicago, Illinois.

Mason,T. C. (1997). Urban field experiences and prospective teachers' attitudes toward inner-city schools, *Teacher Education Quarterly,* 29–40.

Olmedo, I.M. (1997). Challenging old assumptions: Preparing teachers for inner-city schools. *Teaching and Teacher Education,* 13(3), 245–258.

Paley, V.G. (1979). *White Teacher.* Cambridge, MA: Harvard University Press.

Richardson, V. (1996). The role of attitudes and beliefs in learning to teach. In J. Sikula (Ed.) *The Handbook of Research on Teacher Education,* 102–119. New York: Macmillan.

Tabachnick, I.R. & Zeichner, K (1984). The impact of the student teaching experience on the development of teacher perspectives. *Journal of Teacher Education,* 35(6), 28–36.

Weinstein, R. (1988). Preservice teachers' expectations about the first year of teaching. *Teaching and Teacher Education,* 4(1), 31–40.

Wideen, M., Mayer-Smith, J., & Moon, B. (1998). A critical analysis of the research on learning to teach: Making the case for an ecological perspective on inquiry. *Review of Educational Research,* 68, (2), 130–178.

Zeichner, K. M. (1990). Changing directions in the practicum: looking ahead to the 1990s. *Journal of Education for Teaching,* 16(2),105–132.

Predictors of Success in Urban Teaching:

Analyzing Two Paradoxical Cases

❀ ❀ ❀ ❀ ❀ ❀ ❀ ❀ ❀ ❀ ❀ ❀ ❀ ❀ ❀ ❀ ❀

By Terrence C. Mason

Preparing teachers for the rigors of teaching in today's schools represents a formidable challenge for educators. Given the sometimes difficult conditions in our inner-cities, that challenge is in many ways compounded. Identifying the conditions that can foster effective teaching and learning in the urban school and with traditionally underrepresented student populations has emerged as an important issue for educators. In conjunction with this debate and as moves toward learner-centered or "constructivist" approaches to teaching have gained momentum in many schools, some have begun to question whether the teaching methods such as those associated with "whole language" and "process writing" are the most suitable or effective methods of teaching low-income, minority students (Delpit, 1988; Reyes, 1991).

Terrence C. Mason is an assistant professor in the Department of Curriculum and Instruction at the School of Education at Indiana University, Bloomington, Indiana. He thanks the two undergraduate teacher education students referred to in this article ficticiously as Sam and Jennifer who allowed him to use their stories to form the basis of this case study.

Using case study methods (Yin, 1984), the research reported here compares two undergraduate teacher education students' performance in an urban field experience. Through an analysis of what the students did in those field experiences, the impact of their efforts on student learning, and the conditions they were working under, I will attempt to identify some of the factors that contributed to one student's successful teaching and another's frustration.

Data Sources and Methods

Data for this study consist of a variety of materials documenting an urban field experience completed by two undergraduate elementary education students attending a public, metropolitan university in New England. Background information gathered on the students, notes from observations and conferences, students' written work, evaluation materials from the course and field experience, and follow-up interviews constitute the data from which the case studies were developed.

The field experience was connected to a senior-level general teaching methods course and took place in a K-6 elementary school where these two teacher education students were placed in self-contained third-grade classrooms under my supervision as the instructor for the methods course. During the six-week field experience, three mornings a week the students observed, worked with third-grade students, assisted the cooperating teacher, and planned and taught lessons from a thematic unit they had developed. As their methods course instructor, I observed and conferenced with the students regularly, conducted seminars with the field experience students placed in the same school, evaluated their written work, and interacted with them frequently regarding their field placement work.

The Setting: Henry Barnard School

Housed in a physical plant that bore the ill effects of decreasing budgets caused by the economic decline of the late 1980s, Henry Barnard School served several hundred low SES students, most of whom were African American, and some from families that had come from the Caribbean. It was a "neighborhood school" where most students lived in single or multifamily homes, or in a large government subsidized housing project. Most of the staff, which was racially mixed, about half white and half African

From *Multicultural Education*, Spring 1999, pp. 26-32. © 1999 by Caddo Gap Press, Inc. Reprinted by permission of *Multicultural Education*, the magazine of the National Association for Multicultural Education.

American, had been at the school for many years and were nearing retirement.

Instruction was generally traditional, with students in seated in rows, working under the direction of the teacher or individually for long periods of time each day. Maintaining order and achieving student compliance were major concerns for teachers in this overcrowded school. It was not uncommon to hear teachers yelling desperately at their students in an effort to restore order in the classroom.

Teachers were often frustrated in their efforts to teach, and as a result, in some classrooms, particularly in the upper grades, students appeared restless and bored. The primary grades evidenced less apparent antagonism between students and teachers.

In many respects, Henry Barnard was a typical urban school of the 1990s, facing the challenge of educating students from poor and, in some cases, troubled home backgrounds and social circumstances. Completing the field experience at Henry Barnard provided prospective teachers with a glimpse of "the real world" that many educators face.

The Undergraduate Students

The students selected for the case studies here were not chosen at random. One of these students embodied many of the characteristics that would seem to distinguish an individual who would achieve success in an inner-city classroom (maturity, confidence, persistence, a strong sense of purpose, and commitment to teaching) while the other student did not necessarily appear to possess these characteristics.[1]

As a result, one would have been expected to do well in the urban classroom while the other would have very likely encountered difficulties. Their actual effectiveness as teachers in their field experience classrooms, however, did not conform to such a prediction. The following are descriptions of the two undergraduate, elementary education students whose teaching performance in an inner-city field practicum is the basis of this study.

Jennifer, a white female in her early twenties, came from a middle-class background typical of the predominantly suburban-based, first-generation college students who attended the state university. Initially, she planned to complete her field experience in one of the suburban elementary schools that were available for the field practicum. Following my plea to students that teachers needed to be committed to educating all children regardless of their social backgrounds, ethnicity, or family circumstances, she somewhat reluctantly volunteered to take an assignment in an inner-city school.

Among the students enrolled in the course, Jennifer seemed to be one of the least self-assured. She spoke infrequently in class, doing so in a voice that was enthusiastic but somewhat nervous. Her appearance characterized her as [a] young woman from a fairly traditional background, not unlike many who enter the field of elementary education at this particular institution. She was similar to many other teacher education undergraduates, generally devoted to children, but largely unprepared for the exigencies and rigors of the urban school. Based on her background and the challenges she would face in an urban elementary school, located in a neighborhood ravaged by poverty, drugs, and gang activity, one could not be optimistic about her chances of success. Her request, however, was honored and she was placed in a third grade classroom at Henry Barnard for the field experience.

According to his responses to a questionnaire that students completed at the beginning of the term, Sam, the second subject of this study, had spent some time in the business world and had come back to school to enter teaching because he had found the world of insurance sales personally and professionally unfulfilling. Several months as a substitute teacher with what he indicated were some "pretty tough kids" led him to select the inner-city option for his field experience.

Sam was a white male in his mid-20s who seemed bright and a bit more worldly than some of his peers; he was relaxed in class, possessed a clever wit, and was comfortable speaking his mind about any topic that came up in class. On several occasions, as we discussed social issues in class, he expressed his view that the history we learned in school was dominated by the ideas and values of the white, middle class and that his eyes had been opened to other interpretations of history in classes that he had taken in the last couple of years.

His opinions clearly suggested that he was interested in social change and he believed that teachers had a role in bringing it about. This disposition, coupled with his strength of purpose, relaxed, confident manner, and apparent genuine concern about improving the lives of all children, suggested that he would have a strong likelihood of success teaching students in an urban classroom. He was, therefore, placed in a third grade classroom at Henry Barnard.

In the Classroom

During the first week of the field practicum, Jennifer appeared in my office somewhat disturbed about the fact that her cooperating teacher had not given her any leads on a topic for her unit. She was told by her cooperating teacher that she could choose whatever she wanted, but felt unsure about this since she did not know the curriculum or the students well at this point and she was concerned because an initial outline for their unit projects was due the next week. I assured her that she could take some extra time and that I was sure that she would come up with a topic soon.

I began to wonder whether Jennifer's primary concern was to meet course requirements and to do well on her assignments, and that the real task, namely meeting the needs of her 20-some third graders, had not yet sunk in. Within a week or so, this problem was resolved as she chose to do a unit on weather and "the water cycle." As I began my rounds in the school over the next few weeks observing other students, I didn't see or hear from Jennifer and assumed that she was getting along alright.

During the first seminar session that I conducted with the field practicum students at Henry Barnard, Sam shared with the group his growing concern about the classroom he had been placed in and his role within it. He characterized the class as completely out of control and described himself as a kind of referee responsible solely for trying to maintain order, break up fights, and keep the children from physically harming each other. Since I had placed other students with this teacher in previous years, I knew that her classrooms were not always the most orderly or well managed, but I did not realize the severity of Sam's predicament. I thought that the students were just testing Sam's resolve, that he would assert himself in time. Unfortunately, I did not get involved with the situation.

Several weeks into the field practicum, I heard about another incident that caused me further concern about Sam's effectiveness in his field experience classroom. An instructor for a math methods course had observed Sam presenting a lesson to the class which had not gone well; the students were inattentive and disruptive and Sam had resorted to harsh reprimands and threats in order to try to restore order. He had trouble sticking with his lesson plan because of the behavior problems and, according to my colleague, was not able to teach the lesson successfully. When I spoke to Sam about it later he did not have any real explanation for what happened; he felt he just got overwhelmed and panicked. We decided that better planning both in terms of the content and procedures he used in the lesson and how he would deal with student misbehavior could help him do better and we both were satisfied that when I came to observe he would be able to avoid repeating the same scenario. In retrospect, I can see Sam's problem was considerably more serious than I thought and that a stronger intervention on my part would have been warranted.

Observation Day

The irony of these two paradoxical cases is heightened by the following observations that I conducted on the same morning in their respective third-grade classrooms at Henry Barnard School. The following is a brief summary of those two observations based upon the notes I took and the evaluation summary I completed:

Background to the lesson. Sam had grappled with his topic of "community" for some time. He wanted to relate aspects of the community where the children lived to their daily lives, but had difficulty determining the appropriate level of difficulty for the material he wanted to present. He expressed his belief that the students in the class would not be interested in mundane, abstract ideas about how communities work and he wanted to find a way to engage them in the lessons and activities that he would include in the unit. We had met in my office on campus to discuss the unit, and I thought he had some pretty good leads on ideas to pursue. The lesson I was to observe involved the students' exploring the newspaper and finding familiar items, pictures, advertisements for products, etc.

Observation summary. As I entered the classroom I was warned to watch my step because one of the children had vomited on the floor just moments before my arrival, creating a stir in the classroom. I tried to reassure Sam by not appearing disturbed or surprised by this and positioned myself in an out-of-the-way spot in the back of the room. Normally a detailed, written lesson plan is given to me when I arrive for an observation; Sam provided me with a very brief, hastily written plan that did not include much detail. For some reason, the teacher had reacted to the vomiting incident by squeezing all the students into half the classroom away from the front door creating very tight quarters, adding to the complexity of the teaching situation for Sam.

He commenced the lesson, giving directions to the students about what they were to do with the newspaper that each had at his or her desk. He spoke very loudly and rapidly and began almost immediately to interject desists and threats in a fairly harsh and exasperated manner ["Listen to me, I want you and Greg to. . . if you don't I will take it away" (the newspaper)]. He had promised a reward (pencils) to the students who cooperated and did as they were instructed.

It was clear that he was not at ease and seemed to be anticipating that the students would not cooperate with him. The students were actively paging throughout the newspapers but without any apparent pur-

pose. Sam continued to explain to the students, over the commotion of rustling newspaper and the undertone of chatter and giggling, that they were to locate and write down the page numbers of items listed on sheet of paper (weather report, local and national news stories, ads for familiar neighborhood businesses, etc.). It was not clear whether the students understood these directions as they continued leafing through the paper focusing mainly on the pictures of various kinds of merchandise and clothing depicted in the advertisements. Sam began to circulate among the students attempting to get them to focus on the task of searching for the items on the list. He became progressively more exasperated, resorting to a variety of threats and repeating " 'Scuse me!" numerous times in a loud voice in an attempt to gain the class's attention. These efforts met with little success as most of the students continued to be disruptive and pay little attention to the task at hand.

Finally, after 15 or 20 minutes, Sam positioned himself at the front of the class, hands thrust into his pockets, seeming to be disgusted and defeated by the situation, calling for the students' attention in order to hold a discussion about what they had found in the newspaper. He was unable to quiet them down enough to have this discussion, so he closed the lesson by telling the class that they had done "better than on Monday, most had done well, but others, and you know who you are, acted like this was a joke." He ended the lesson by declaring "time's up" and asking them to clean up the newspapers. Sam hastily removed himself from the front of the class and left the room. The cooperating teacher took over the class and I headed into the corridor to find Sam to debrief and discuss the lesson.

When I got to Sam he was visibly upset, angry, and frustrated. He was clearly not pleased with what had happened. He immediately began to vent his hostilities toward the students, the cooperating teacher, and to some extent himself for failing so miserably at maintaining control of the class. For a few minutes we tried to examine what might have caused this to occur, but he was so upset that I decided to end the discussion and schedule a time to meet later on campus after he had calmed down and we could analyze the lesson more clearly. Besides, I had another observation in a few minutes and would not be able to get to the heart of the matter with Sam in so little time.

After observing Sam, I was apprehensive about what I would encounter in Jennifer's classroom. Given her quiet, reserved manner I was wondering how she would cope with students who were disruptive or hostile. After all, this was the same grade level (3rd grade) in the same school, so why

would I expect the students to be more receptive or cooperative that those in Sam's class?

Observation summary. I arrived in the classroom before the students returned from recess. Jennifer had a lesson plan waiting for me that clearly outlined the sequence of activities she planned to engage in with her students. Several sets of demonstration materials had been set up around the front of the room—a hot plate with water to be boiled, and a wind machine were ready to be used in showing the students how evaporation occurs and air moves to create the "water cycle."

When the students entered the classroom, Jennifer immediately got the students' attention by writing the term "water cycle" on the board and asking the students if they knew what a "cycle" was. She explained that it was something that goes around and gave an example of a number pattern "1-2-3" that repeated itself over and over creating a cycle. She then asked one of the students to come to the chalk board and spread water on a part of it with a wet sponge. Jennifer asked the students to be watching what would happen to the water over the next few minutes as she continued with her lesson. The students began to voice their interpretations of what was happening. "The water is going through the board." "The water is going up." They anxiously responded to this and expressed their ideas, their theories of what was happening without becoming boisterous or out of control.

Jennifer then introduced the term "evaporation" and demonstrated how water becomes steam and evaporates rapidly when boiled. She wanted the students to be able to see the process of evaporation take place, so she asked them to leave their desks and come forward to the front of the class. Since she was worried about the danger of boiling water and a crowd of third graders pushing close to see, she had put a "boundary line" with tape on the floor in a semi-circle a few feet from the table where the water was boiling. She explained that they would have to stay behind that line if they were going to watch. For several minutes the students huddled around the water boiling and Jennifer talked about how the steam was similar to fog and clouds and that this was a part of the water cycle. At one point, two students began to push and shove each other and one of them became very upset with the other and began to cry. Rather than stopping the lesson and diverting the other students' attention to the outburst, Jennifer continued to explain and discuss as she moved in and separated the two children so that they could cool down. She diffused a potentially disruptive situation and was able to continue teaching.

The lesson continued with actual demonstrations of the processes of condensation and precipitation in which the students were actively involved in observing, manipulating objects, predicting, and reflecting on what they saw. The concepts, related to the "water cycle" were made tangible to the students through demonstration. Their natural curiosity and interest were aroused as phenomena that they had experienced (steam from hot water, condensation on the bathroom mirror) were connected with new concepts related to the causes of various types of weather. The students in this class remained focused on the teacher and the lesson content that she was addressing. They participated actively without becoming disruptive and continued to be interested and engaged for the remainder of the lesson, approximately 40 minutes.

Other Performance Indicators

The end of semester evaluations completed by Sam and Jennifer's cooperating teachers reflected the notable differences in teaching success evidenced by the descriptions above. The cooperating teachers rated the students on a one to five scale (one being low; five being high) on professionalism, knowledge of content, and lesson implementation. Sam got straight 3's (an unusually low rating for students in this field experience), while Jennifer received straight 5's. Comments the teachers made also reflected the two students' overall performance. "Jennifer has done a fantastic job knowing the strengths and weaknesses of the children in a very short time. She pulls from their strengths so all will meet success with this wonderful weather unit." vs. "Sam enjoys the youngsters. He tries very hard to work with them on a one to one basis. He needs to work on group classroom control. He needs to spend some time preparing for needs of all levels of children."

Results from other work completed for the course related to the field experience provides further support for the differences in Jennifer's and Sam's ability to provide effective teaching. The major written assignment for the course was an instructional unit write-up, much like a portfolio, documenting and reflecting on the student's field experience. Sam turned in a largely incomplete write-up that did not reflect the criteria for the unit assignment; many elements were missing and incomplete. A learning center related to the thematic unit topic was never implemented in the classroom as required.

Jennifer, on the other hand, submitted a complete unit write-up that reflected the quality of effort of her successful teaching performance. Not surprisingly, Jennifer completed the course with an "A" while Sam managed to get a "C+" based in part

on some high quality work and test results early in the semester.

Follow-Up Interviews

To gain Sam and Jennifer's perspective on their teaching experience at Henry Barnard School, I conducted a follow-up interview with each of them approximately two years after the field experience semester. The interviews were tape recorded with notes later transcribed from the tapes. The questions focused on their recollections of the field experience, what they learned from it, the factors that contributed to their performance, and what had been different about subsequent teaching experiences. The following is a summary of Sam and Jennifer's responses to these questions.

Jennifer expressed that she learned that "kids were kids" and that they needed to have learning experiences that were fun and meaningful. She described how she approached the weather unit by having the students actually place thermometers in cold water to gain an understanding of the meaning of temperature. She said that this may not have been necessary with other students, for example those with whom she worked later during student teaching in a more suburban setting, but the inner-city kids needed more direct experience with these concepts and materials since they had not experienced them before. She adapted her teaching in this way and created connections between these activities and more abstract concepts like changes in weather, cloud formations, and how the weather affects other people. She gained confidence from the inner-city experience because she was quickly able to become integrated into the activities of the classroom, and developed a positive rapport with the students early on.

Jennifer attributed her success in the experience to the support she received from the cooperating teacher who gave her the freedom to make some decisions (selecting unit topics) but then supported her with constructive criticism and positive comments. She also cited her own motivation to succeed and her understanding that she was "there for the kids" and her belief that even though she was only there for a short time, it could make an important and significant difference in the lives of the children in the class. She said that she came into the situation ready to work and to set goals.

Later in student teaching she taught in a school that was, as she put it, "not very diverse." It was located in a predominantly middle-class community with relatively little ethnic diversity. However, she pointed out that the classroom she taught in was an "inclusion" classroom with a variety of special-needs students and support staff to work with them. She said that this experi-

ence taught her the importance of meeting the needs of all kids. Thus, a different form of diversity in this setting enabled her to learn to make appropriate adaptations for the students she encountered, a skill she had already demonstrated in another way at Henry Barnard School.

Sam described his field experience in very different terms. Although he believed that it was, in retrospect, valuable as a learning experience, he too attributed the outcome of his field experience to the cooperating teacher. According to Sam, "she had no control from day one; the kids owned her." By this, he meant that she was not able to establish an orderly, respectful, and, therefore, productive environment in the classroom, and as a result, neither was he. He observed, furthermore, that there was an atmosphere of negativity throughout the classroom. He noted that there were no "routines, discipline, or morals" established in the classroom by the teacher.

Sam said that initially he was unwilling to ascribe responsibility for his difficulties to the teacher, but as he continued there, he became convinced that this was not a "normal" class, an observation that was confirmed when he had the chance to observe other classes in the same school where the conditions were substantially more positive.[2] He affirmed his conviction that it was the teacher that made a difference, its "how you handle it." His subsequent teaching experience had taught him that how he approached his teaching would determine how things went; that "kids are kids." Days that he was lethargic, Sam stated, were days when the students would be lethargic too.

Following the negative experience at Henry Barnard, he was somewhat reluctant and anxious about student teaching the next semester; but somehow he did not feel that this classroom had been representative so he was optimistic that he would succeed. He also acknowledged that he did not have a firm understanding during the field experience of what his students could do or the kind of instruction they needed. He also realized that he had not put enough time into planning for instruction and that more attention to this had made a remarkable difference in his later teaching. Sam also expressed a belief that the role that he had been assigned in the field experience classroom of "referee," breaking up fights and helping to maintain order, made it difficult for him to assume the role of teacher and gain the respect of the students that one needed to teach.

Analysis and Conclusions

The case studies of these two undergraduates' field experience describe how

Jennifer was able to successfully plan and teach lessons, while Sam was systematically unable to do so. Jennifer provided instruction that was intellectually stimulating and motivating for her students. She was able to gain and maintain her students' attention and intervene in appropriate ways when disruptions occurred. She was also successful in establishing a warm and nurturing learning climate. Sam, however, encountered consistent failure in his efforts to create positive learning experiences for his students. He did not establish his authority with his students and was, therefore, unable to teach effectively. He frequently lost his patience with students, becoming harsh with them, and on at least one occasion abandoned a lesson midstream. There was little evidence from the backgrounds of these two students to predict this kind of outcome, so why did it occur?

Obviously, the point here is not merely to compare the performance of two students in their field experience practicum. What meaning can we make from their stories to help us better understand the characteristics of effective teaching in urban classrooms and ways to provide better teacher preparation for urban schools? Is there a useful explanatory framework for interpreting these cases?

A model for teaching and learning articulated by Roland G. Tharp and Richard Gallimore (1988) based, in part, on Lev S. Vygotsky's (1978) principle of "assisted performance" offers a lens through which we can interpret the events described in these cases. According to this perspective, individuals, particularly novices, acquire new knowledge, abilities, and skills through explicit forms of interaction with more competent others or experts. We can identify two sets of "novices" in these case studies, the children in the classrooms who are in the process of acquiring basic knowledge and literacy, and the two field experience college students who are learning to teach. For both groups the presence or absence of crucial forms of assistance may have accounted for the outcomes observed here.

Assisting Elementary Students

Tharp and Gallimore (1988) identify five main categories of methods for assisting performance: *modeling, contingency management, feeding-back, instructing,* and *questioning.* These can be used individually or in combination to render new and unfamiliar concepts comprehensible to those at the initial stages of a learning process. The third graders in this study were making their first steps toward grasping basic concepts, literacy skills, and the conventions associated with learning in a school setting. For this reason, it is essential that learning be supported directly by one or

more of the kinds of assistance suggested by Tharp and Gallimore. How and why did Jennifer accomplish this while Sam did not?

In the account of Jennifer's lesson observation we can identify several elements of assisted performance. To begin with, she *modeled* and directly *instructed* the key concepts that she was focusing on in her lesson. She recognized that the students needed clear, unambiguous examples and demonstrations of the phenomena related to the "water cycle," so she provided them. She also asked direct questions that connected familiar experiences to more abstract ones (e.g., the concept of "cycle" being related to a pattern of numbers that repeats itself).

In contrast, Sam's direct interaction with the class during the observed lesson did not focus on the concepts or skills that the students needed to complete the newspaper task. He assumed that the hands-on, discovery-oriented nature of the task would be sufficiently motivating and clear for the students to work independently. Sam acknowledged later that one of his problems in the field experience was not knowing what to assume about what these children knew or could be expected to do. His assumption that his students could construct meaning out of the newspaper task on their own is typical of what Lisa Delpit (1991) refers to as teachers "keeping secrets," requiring students to discover concepts and not explicitly teaching what they know and want their students to know. While Sam was probably not consciously attempting to withhold knowledge from his students, his assumption, based on a pedagogy drawn from white, middle-class culture, was inadequate for his students who did not share that same cultural experience. Sam would contend, and perhaps rightly so, that his unsuccessful teaching was due to the absence of assistance from another source, those who were in the position of teaching him how to teach.

Assisting Prospective Teachers

In the follow-up interview, when asked what accounted for her ability to successfully teach her students during the field practicum, Jennifer cited her cooperating teacher as a major source of support and guidance. Specifically, it was the *feedback* ("constructive criticism") and praise (*contingency management*) given to her that enabled her to gain confidence and develop an effective repertoire of teaching strategies.

Sam received little of such support. His cooperating teacher did not offer suggestions or critiques of his teaching or guidance in overcoming the problems he was having planning appropriate activities or managing the behavior of the students. In addition, the cooperating

teacher was unable to provide a *model* for Sam to imitate or learn from as he struggled with the class. From my perspective, as the university supervisor, my mistaken perception that Sam possessed the skills necessary to overcome the challenges he was facing combined with my misreading of the severity the problems in the classroom kept me from becoming sufficiently involved soon enough to avert the difficulties he experienced.

So why was assistance present in some of the situations described here and absent in others? Again, drawing from the work of Vygotsky and his current interpreters, we can consider the concept of the *zone of proximal development* (ZPD) as an important construct in explaining what occurred here. The ZPD represents "the distance between the child's individual capacity and the capacity to perform with assistance" (Tharp & Gallimore, 1988, p. 30), and thus represents the "space" where the learner can benefit from guidance, support and direct teaching from others. If a teacher assumes that learners are beyond the ZPD, and thus capable of functioning independently with respect to a particular skill or domain of knowledge, then assistance may not be provided. Such was the case when Sam assumed that his students could carry out the newspaper activity on their own, and when Sam's cooperating teacher and supervisor believed that he could pull himself up by the bootstraps in his field experience classroom.

Jennifer, on the other hand, viewed her students as capable learners but in need of directed and explicit forms of teaching in order to succeed. By acknowledging this and adopting the teaching strategies outlined above she was teaching in the zone of proximal development of her students. Her cooperating teacher, by providing the necessary support and guidance to Jennifer, also seemed to be responding to Jennifer's ZPD and providing the kind of coaching that Jennifer needed to succeed.

One Size *Doesn't* Fit All

Students who receive much of their instruction directly from the teacher generally do better than those who are expected to learn on their own or from one another. To learn independently, students must be able to read, understand, and follow directions. They must be able to identify key concepts and to correct their own errors. Furthermore, they must be willing and able to sustain sufficient levels of concentration and effort. (Brophy, 1982)

This statement is consistent with what some critics of the ways that whole language, process writing, and other learner-centered approaches to teaching are being applied to urban, low SES, non-white classrooms. Although it was written as a summary of the process-product research carried out over twenty years ago, its message is echoed currently by Delpit (1988), Maria de la Luz Reyes (1992), and others who maintain that students who have been excluded from the sources of power provided by the ability to use language in conventional ways ("edited English," Delpit, 1991) need explicit forms of instruction aimed at developing fundamental competence.

As we have seen, Jennifer organized her teaching to render the subject matter "meaningful and fun" for her students. However, she made sure that she provided the appropriate direction and experience for the students to grasp key concepts, including some activities (actual measurement of temperature) that were needed for the particular group she was teaching. Important ideas were identified in advance (evaporation, condensation, precipitation) and conveyed *directly* through instruction and hands-on experience.

Sam, on the other hand, wanted his students to "experience" the newspaper directly, but provided little foundation for what the students were actually to learn from the activity. Without a clear focus, the door was left open for the students to define for themselves what they would do. For many of them it was to disrupt others and to use the newspapers in ways that were not connected with any learning purpose. An approach that might have worked in a classroom with extremely compliant students was inappropriate and unproductive for students in this urban setting.

Thus, a "one size fits all" (Reyes, 1992) approach to teaching that does not consider the cultural, economic, and social characteristics of the learners, will not result in success. While both Sam and Jennifer expressed the belief that "kids are kids" in their follow-up interviews, the actions they took toward their students varied considerably. Although Sam was contending with multiple difficulties in his classroom, he nonetheless did not adapt his instruction to the needs of the students, while Jennifer did so in a variety of ways.

Case studies such as these are useful as research insofar as they are generalizable and address important phenomena for understanding teaching and learning. The implications of the somewhat surprising findings obtained here lead us to consider what the critical elements that determine

success in urban teaching really are. Is it appropriate motivation, attitude, and predisposition, or is it what happens to prospective teachers once they actually begin to work with students in classrooms? It is, no doubt, some of both.

We can conclude, however, from the evidence provided by Sam and Jennifer's cases that the assumptions that we make about our students and the actions we take based on those assumptions can have a powerful influence on learners' success. To teach well, then, we must know our students well. Only when that is the case can we expect to identify and implement teaching strategies that will work.

Post Script

Seldom do teacher educators have the opportunity to systematically follow their students after the completion of their teacher preparation programs. Since Sam and Jennifer represented unique and somewhat anomalous cases, I decided to keep track of their professional paths beyond the course they took from me and after their graduation. I was interested in seeing if the pattern established in the field experience/methods course would continue. Both Sam and Jennifer went on to successfully complete student teaching the next semester in schools located in the same greater metropolitan area as Henry Barnard School but in adjacent school districts outside the inner city. The schools were somewhat culturally and economically diverse but they were not located in neighborhoods where the degree of poverty and the challenges for teachers were as acute as at Henry Barnard.

Evidence from his student teaching evaluations and letters of recommendation from the cooperating teacher and student teaching supervisor suggest that Sam became a highly successful and effective elementary teacher. Jennifer's classroom teaching performance continued to be outstanding. They both met all graduation requirements successfully, received initial teaching certificates, and began to apply for teaching jobs. Sam obtained a full-time teaching position in a third grade classroom in the district where he student taught. Jennifer is also currently teaching.

In a way, we are lucky here. Both individuals in this study were able to realize their potential and ultimately achieve teaching success. But we cannot leave these matters up to the vagaries of luck. Teacher educators need to consider new paradigms

and methods in teacher preparation (see Manning & Payne, 1993) to provide the kind of supported learning experiences that constitute powerful teaching.

Notes

1. Martin Haberman (1992) and his associates have developed a questionnaire to identify potentially successful candidates for urban teaching. In a 35-minute interview candidates are evaluated on factors such as persistence, response to bureaucracy, and fallibility. The students in this study *did not* undergo such an interview but, as suggested by their descriptions here, in many ways they reflected the characteristics described by Haberman.
2. Following this field experience, I arranged for Sam to observe in another teacher's classroom to see how that teacher was able to provide a dynamic, active learning environment where students were able to express themselves, but where mutual respect between the teacher and the students was maintained.

References

Brophy, J. (1982). Successful teaching strategies for the inner-city child. *Phi Delta Kappan*, April, 527–530.

Delpit, L. (1988). The silenced dialogue: Power and pedagogy in educating other people's children. *Harvard Educational Review*, 58, 280–298.

Delpit, L. (1992). A conversation with Lisa Delpit. *Language Arts*, 68, 541–547.

Feiman-Nemser, S. & Remillard, J. (1996). Perspectives on learning to teach. In F. Murray, ed. *The Teacher Educator's Handbook: Building a Knowledge Base for the Preparation of Teachers*. San Francisco, CA: Jossey Bass, 63–91.

Haberman, M. (1992). Predicting the success of urban teachers (The Milwaukee Trials), *Action in Teacher Education*, 15, 1–5.

Manning, B.H. & Payne, B.D. (1993). A Vygotskian-based theory of teacher cognition: Toward the acquisition of mental reflection and self-regulation. *Teaching and Teacher Education*, 9, 4, 361–371.

Reyes, M. de la Luz. (1992). Challenging venerable assumptions: Literacy instruction for linguistically different students. *Harvard Educational Review*, 62, 427–446.

Tharp, R.G. & Gallimore, R. (1988). *Rousing minds to life: Teaching, learning, and schooling in social context*. New York: Cambridge University Press.

Vygotsky, L.S. (1978). *Mind in society: The development of higher psychological processes*. (M. Cole, V. John-Steiner, S. Scribner, E. Souberman, Eds. & Trans.), Cambridge, MA: Harvard University Press.

Yin, R.K. (1984). *Case study research: design and methods*. Beverly Hills, CA: Sage.

Service Learning Helps Future Teachers Strengthen Caring Perspectives

KEVIN J. SWICK

The need for caring teachers has always received considerable attention in teacher education. As Noddings (1992) noted, "Coming to recognize the transforming ecology that is possible through the caring ethic means engaging teacher education students in experiences with teachers and others who embrace this ethic in their lives" (4). One means of strengthening the caring skills of future teachers is through meaningful service learning (DeVitis, Johns, and Simpson 1998), a form of learning by which teacher education students contribute to the lives of their students and strengthen their own efficacy. In this article, I explain the importance of caring in teaching and present ways that service learning can be used to strengthen the caring skills of future teachers.

Caring Experiences Strengthen Students and Teachers

The caring process confirms our prosocial competence and enriches everyone's "voice," which is the core of the self (Gilligan 1993). Strengthening our voices is key to our continuing growth and helps us realize that experiences are meaningful and worthy of further attention. As teachers, for example, recognize that their nurturance is making a difference, they realize a new sense of power in themselves (Kohl 1998). Children gain a more in-depth understanding of themselves as they learn how to care for others, and they achieve new competence in their play and work (Coles 1997).

Two important elements of dialogue between teachers and students are also strengthened through caring: the reflective aspect of thinking and the attention one gives to

Kevin J. Swick is a professor of instruction and teacher education in the College of Education at the University of South Carolina, Columbia.

the views and feelings of others (Ruddick 1995). As teachers care for children and young people, they are likely to inquire about their own strengths and needs and thus reflect on means for improving their caring skills. Caring is an *intentional* process that requires us to plan and think about our actions (Noddings 1992). It enables us to learn from our experiences, to use our personal and collaborative resources to enrich itself, and to trust in the voice that tells us we are caring and worthy people (Ruddick 1995).

Serving Promotes Our Caring Perspectives and Skills

From the time we are very young, we learn that sharing increases our access to others and thus broadens our sources for learning. Prosocial behaviors, such as aiding a person who is injured or helping to build houses for those who are homeless, enable us to realize caring as a part of our growth and that of others (Goldstein 1997; Noddings 1992; Wuthnow 1995).

Serving others provides three elements that are essential to caring (Wuthnow 1995): (1) opportunities to respond to the needs of others; (2) possibilities for learning more about being a caring person; and (3) situations for reflection that strengthen our skills to be lifelong learners. Each of these elements needs to be integrated into development and learning, particularly that of teacher education students.

Opportunities to serve. The opportunity to serve others meets the need for security, thus empowering each person to gain the resources and validation that are essential for a healthy identity (Erikson 1982). In a very real sense becoming a teacher has more to do with helping people (including the teacher) become lifelong learners than it does with "teaching" others (Cohen 1995). From helping

From *The Clearing House*, September/October 1999, pp. 29-32. Reprinted with permission of the Helen Dwight Reid Educational Foundation. Pulished by Heldref Publications, 1319 Eighteenth St., NW, Washington, DC 20036-1802. © 1999.

others, we gain the power to see ourselves and others in positive and growing ways (Chaskin and Rauner 1995).

Learning about caring. Learning what it takes to become a caring person is best realized through service (Wuthnow 1995). In service we gain numerous important attributes and competencies (Pipher 1996; Wuthnow 1995), such as the following:

- Knowledge of the area in which one is serving
- Knowledge and understanding of the needs of others
- Insight into one's skills as they emerge and develop in various helping roles
- Insight into the empathic nature of common human needs such as safety, security, love, and belonging
- Perspectives about how caring is an empowering process that all of us use to increase our integrity
- Perspectives about the importance of caring in our development as growing persons
- Ideas about how to strengthen our caring skills

Reflection: Being responsive learners. Service offers many opportunities for reflection: feedback about one's goodness, learning to improve one's helping skills, ways of seeing others as helpers, and experiences for renewing our sense of identity (Noddings 1992). We validate our significance in the community (Kinsley 1997) and come to realize that with our support other people can become skilled helpers in the community (Wuthnow 1995).

Service Learning in Teacher Education: Nurturing Caring Teachers

Involvement in service can foster insights that strengthen the caring skills and perceptions of teachers (Erickson and Anderson 1997). As one student teacher engaged in helping at an after-school program noted (Swick et al. 1998),

I never thought of myself as doing so much helping, especially with middle school students. But these students want a caring adult around them like a security blanket. I am seeing my role as a teacher in a much larger sense—that of guiding and nurturing young people. (148)

Service learning can engage teacher education students in activities that promote caring inquiries similar to those they will experience in teaching. The following are two case examples of such efforts as students have reflected on their service learning.

Assisting at the Nurturing Center

My experience at the Nurturing Center (a program that facilitates the rehabilitation of abusing families) initially evolved from my selecting it as the place to do my service learning for my Family Life in Early Childhood Education course. I went through the training and was assigned to help out in the classrooms with three and four year olds. During my third day at the center I was assigned to read to a little girl named Brenda. This was the beginning of

what has become a truly close friendship. She was in need of a great deal of attention and stuck with me like glue from our first contact. She had been sexually abused and her mother had been beaten often by the father. Brenda's mother left her abusing husband and found shelter at Sister Care, which referred them to the Nurturing Center. . . .

As Brenda came to trust me, she began to join in with the other children and to take an interest in other things in her environment. Brenda's mother also became more confident in her skills and began to reach out to others for support and strength. She joined in with the Center's parent support group, enrolled at the university for several courses, and began to establish the basis for a new life. Her husband is a wealthy lawyer in the community. One day during lunch at the Nurturing Center I got to know Brenda's mother and we hit it off right away. I offered to stay with Brenda as she needed and we have developed a really nice friendship. We even had a picnic at the zoo and have been on walks and shared books we both enjoy.

Little did I know that my service-learning experience would blossom into a close friendship too! I can say for sure that I will be a different teacher as a result of this experience. Now I can see that there are other Brendas in the world and most likely they will be in my classroom. Not all will have been abused but many will have special needs and those needs must be attended to if we expect children to learn in positive ways. Caring is more than just helping someone feel good, it is helping them grow too! In the process you grow and become a better human being.

Helping in the Real World of Kindergarten

I have always wanted to be a kindergarten teacher. I love young children but really only had contact with children whose values were like mine. Then our professor in Family Life in Early Childhood Education said we were to do thirty hours of service in a setting with children and families as a part of the course. I selected the inner-city school near campus and asked to be placed in a kindergarten.

From the start I realized the children were in search of love. They were all after me to be with them: "Play with me!" "Read to me!" "Eat with me!" The teacher (Mrs. Jackson) explained that many of the children did not have many adults who spend time with them. She also explained that for many children this was their first experience in a group setting. The children and the parents loved the teacher; some parents and grandparents volunteered regularly in the classroom. What impressed me was the respect this teacher showed for all of the children and their parents.

Two of the most powerful experiences I had were going on a home visit and being a helper on the annual field trip to the ocean. In the home visit I saw a world I had never experienced before. Here are some of my notes on the home visit: "We visited Josh's grandmother. Josh and his grandmother live in a public housing apartment. It is in need of repair. Miss Albert (Josh's grandmother) welcomed us and apologized for 'the mess.' She thanked us for all that we were doing for Josh. 'Is he behaving better?' We assured her that he was and that he was doing some good work too! Josh was pleased at our comments and smiled and continued to play nearby. We shared some drawings Josh had made and some of his other work too. Miss Albert said that Josh was better at home, too—'he is really learning a lot at school,' she said. She was concerned, though, about letting him play outside. 'The gangs hang out and it is a bad influence,' she said. 'I keep him in here but I don't know what I can do as he gets older—and really right now he needs kids to play with.' We offered to see if we could get him in the after-school program activities at school.

"She also had many concerns about paying the heating bill. We told her who to call at the Salvation Army—in our community they have a heating aid support program that helps pay high utility bills for people in need. Mrs. Jackson also said she would have the school social worker visit and see what she could to do help with some of the needed repairs. As we ended the visit, Miss Albert was gracious and said she would continue reading to Josh nightly."

The field trip was equally enlightening. TO THE OCEAN read the sign on our bus. Twenty-six children, two teachers, five parents, and I made the trip to Myrtle Beach, South Carolina, to spend the day learning all about the ocean. But I really spent the day serving and learning. I was responsible for guiding three children, organizing all of us for our picnic lunch, doing the "bus checks," and preparing a report on what I gained from the experience (which I later presented at a school faculty meeting.) Excerpts from my report tell the real story of what I learned: "You really have to be prepared on a trip like this and be ready for anything. One child had an accident and we were ready with back-up clothes. Children know so much more than what we see in the classroom. One of my children (Janelle) was drawing stories in the sand about how fish swim. I had no idea she had so many serious thoughts about living things—Wow! . . . The children learn to care for each other and learn how they can contribute to the group by helping with lunch, watching out for each other, and taking turns in using the materials. . . . I noticed how much my three children watched me and copied what I did! If I shared things, they were soon sharing with each other too."

These case examples highlight three important benefits of service learning in teacher education. Service learning

1. expands student understanding of what caring means when it is contextualized in real settings;
2. engages students in situations with positive mentors who model competence and caring in their interactions with children and adults; and
3. requires students to reflect on and to articulate what specific service experiences mean to them in relation to both their career and personal growth.

Service Learning as a Transforming Process

We know that there are "points of transformation" at which teachers develop new images of themselves and their modes of functioning (Ayers 1995; Coles 1993; Noddings 1992). For both teacher education students and experienced teachers, service learning provides a structure for nurturing three important realizations:

• One can be a caring person—that is, one can contribute, learn, and be responsive to others in meaningful and reciprocal ways (Noddings 1992).

• Caring and community improvement are interactive processes that depend on the empowerment of every person (Wuthnow 1995).
• Service to others requires paying attention to ourselves as growing persons (Coles 1993).
• Professional growth is also supported by service learning. Through it, teacher education students
• gain a more comprehensive understanding of the "persona" of being a teacher, including the significant influence of teachers in the lives of children and families (Erickson and Anderson 1997);
• experience the rudiments of the caring inquiry style (Myers and Pickeral 1997);
• interact with professional role models, such as community leaders and teacher leaders (Waterman 1997);
• are challenged to contextualize "caring" within settings that require specific skills and service activities (Root 1997);
• experience the complexities of being a caring teacher and thus have experiential knowledge to consider as they construct their understanding of teaching as a career (Kinsley 1997);
• study and experience ways in which service learning can be used as an instructional methodology (Root 1997);
• engage in roles that encourage them to re-think how they respond to the totality of the lives of children and families (Alt 1997): and
• reflect on the importance of serving all children (Erickson and Anderson 1997).

Student teachers learn meaningful approaches through the experiential and reflective service learning activities in which they participate. Tutoring, mentoring, creative uses of technology, inquiry strategies, teacher-coaching, and cooperative learning are some instructional modes that students indicate they either acquire or refine through service learning (Swick et al. 1998). When service learning is combined with on-site reflective activities, students also participate in discussions that extend their understanding of these varied methods of instruction (Root 1997). Of particular value is the opportunity to ask questions about why certain approaches are used, why teachers relate to children in different ways, and what has occurred when an activity or approach is ineffective (Swick et al. 1998).

Service learning is a potentially transforming process for teachers and the children and families they serve. Children and families gain new sources of support, thus strengthening their skills to be proactive in school and the community. Teacher education students are empowered to be more responsive and caring. As a teacher educator has noted (Swick et al. 1998),

Service learning helps our teacher education students transform their understanding of their roles as a teacher. They come to realize that teaching is more than giving children knowledge; it is about caring for and with children as learners and persons who have great potential to care for self and others! I am encouraged about the experiences our students are having. They are talking and writing about caring insights I have not seen before in the usual practica assignments. (142)

REFERENCES

Alt, M. 1997. How effective an educational tool is student community service? *NASSP Bulletin* 81 (591): 8–16.

Ayers, W., ed. 1995. *To become a teacher: Making a difference in children's lives.* New York: Teachers College Press.

Chaskin, R., and D. Rauner. 1995. Youth and caring: An introduction. *Phi Delta Kappan* 76 (9): 667–74.

Cohen, M. 1995. Reconstruction alternatives: Opening the curriculum. In *To become a teacher: Making a difference in children's lives,* edited by W. Ayers, 89–98. New York: Teachers College Press.

Coles, R. 1993. *The call of service: A witness to idealism.* Boston: Houghton Mifflin.

———. 1997. *The moral intelligence of children.* New York: Random House.

DeVitis, J., R. Johns, and D. Simpson. 1998. *To serve and learn: The spirit of community in liberal education.* New York: Peter Lang.

Erikson, E. 1982, *The life cycle completed: A review.* New York: W.W. Norton.

Erickson, J., and Anderson, J., eds. 1997. *Learning with the community: Concepts and models for service-learning in teacher education.* Washington, DC: American Association for Higher Education. (Published in cooperation with the American Association of Colleges for Teacher Education.)

Gilligan, C. 1993. *In a different voice: Psychological theory and women's development.* Cambridge, MA: Harvard University Press.

Goldstein, C. 1997. *Teaching with love.* New York: Peter Lang.

Kinsley, C. 1997. Service learning: A process to connect learning and living. *NASSP Bulletin* 81 (591): 1–7.

Kohl, H. 1998. *The discipline of hope: Learning from a lifetime of teaching.* New York: Simon and Schuster.

Lipsitz, J. 1995. Prologue: Why we should care about caring. *Phi Delta Kappan* 76 (9): 665–67.

Myers, C., and T. Pickeral. 1997. Service-learning: An essential process for preparing teachers as transformational leaders in the reform of public education. In *Learning with the community: Concepts and models for service-learning in teacher education,* edited by J. Erickson and J. Anderson, 13–41. Washington, DC: American Association for Higher Education. (Published in cooperation with the American Association of Colleges for Teacher Education.)

Noddings, N. 1992. *The challenge to care in schools.* New York: Teachers College Press.

———. 1995. Teaching themes of care. *Phi Delta Kappan* 76 (9): 675–79.

Pipher, M. 1996. *The shelter of each other: Rebuilding our families.* New York: G.P. Putnam's Sons.

Purple, D. 1998. Service learning: A critique and affirmation. *Encounter: Education for Meaning and Social Justice* 11 (2): 22–27.

Root, S. 1997. School-based service: A review of research for teacher educators. In *Learning with the community: Concepts and models for service-learning in teacher education,* edited by J. Erickson and J. Anderson, 42–71. Washington, DC: American Association for Higher Education. (Published in cooperation with the American Association of Colleges for Teacher Education.)

Ruddick, S. 1995. *Maternal thinking.* Boston: Beacon Press.

Swick, K., L. Winecoff, M. Rowls, R. Kemper, N. Freeman, J. Mason, J. Somerindyke, and T. Williams. 1998. *University of South Carolina service-learning and teacher education: Final report, 1998.* Columbia, SC: Department of Instruction and Teacher Education. (Final SLATE Report submitted to AACTE in conjunction with the USC-AACTE SLATE Project funded by AACTE and the National Corporation for Service Learning-Higher Education.

Waterman, A., ed. 1997. *Service learning: Applications from the research.* Mahwah, NJ: Lawrence Erlbaum.

Wuthnow, R. 1995. *Learning to care: Elementary kindness in an age of indifference.* New York: Oxford University Press.

Why Aren't Teachers Using Effective Multicultural Education Practices?

NANCY P. GALLAVAN

Today's K–12 teachers are given many classroom responsibilities, including the charge of "multicultural education." Much has been written documenting the importance of multicultural education and outlining strategies for integrating effective strategies. Infusing culturally responsive and responsible pedagogy across the curriculum has been shown to ensure greater success for every student (Cole, 1995; Sparks, 1994).

Teachers play a vital role in deciding how to translate educational theories into appropriate practices as they plan curricular content, select materials, facilitate instruction, assess their students, and interact with families, especially when considering effective multicultural education practices. And beyond curriculum, instruction, and assessment, teachers' formal and informal interactions with students communicate strong messages that guide and reinforce their students' attitudes about specific course content and the learning process in general. Teachers easily convey their own attitudes and personal perceptions about the subject matter, their values about learning, their students, the community, and society-at-large as they teach their classes (Nieto, 1996; Sleeter, 1992). Multicultural education permeates all that is taught and how it is taught.

Yet, university graduate students in the field of education often report that effective multicultural education practices are missing in many K–12 classrooms. This study was designed to gain insights from experienced teachers accounting for this frequently heard observation. The findings in this article identify five major categories for why teachers are not using effective multicultural education practices as reported by experienced teachers. The supporting reasons are relevant not only to individuals teaching multicultural education courses as part of a teacher education program, but are essential for understanding the absence of effective multicultural education throughout the entire teaching profession. Becoming aware of these findings will help

teacher educators, school administrators, staff developers, and, most importantly, K–12 teachers address these concerns directly and successfully in their own multicultural education practices while promoting educational reform and systemic change.

DESIGN OF THE STUDY

The average K–12 teacher in the United States fits this description: white, female if they teach elementary school, male if they teach secondary school, have a master's degree (or are working toward earning one), have taught for at least 10 years, are in their early 40s, are married with employed spouses, are middle-class, and participate regularly in community and civic organizations (Edlefelt, 1997).

Practicing teachers from the area schools who enroll as graduate students in my multicultural education courses match this general description. Over a two-year span, students from four of these courses were selected to participate in a study designed to explore why average teachers report that effective multicultural education practices are not being used by experienced teachers. A total of 113 graduate students contributed to the data collection and analyses. The participants included: 95 white students and 18 students of color (specifically African American, Hispanic, Asian American, and Native American Indian); 89 females and 24 males; 9 students with master's degrees or higher, and 104 in the process of earning a master's degree (the major purpose for enrolling in this course); 58 elementary school teachers and 55 secondary school teachers; an average teaching career of only 6 years, an average age of 33; 72 married; and all considered themselves middle-class with 85 reporting that they participate regularly in community and civic organizations. However, the area K–12 school district student population is 54% white and 46% students of color with approximately 20% of these students living in lower income homes.

This study was conducted toward the end of the semester, following a series of learning experiences exploring and describing various effective multicultural education practices for successfully infusing culturally responsible and responsive pedagogy across the curriculum. These students were well-equipped and prepared to analyze teachers and the profession critically.

Students in each of the four courses were asked to brainstorm and list all the possible explanations for why experienced teachers are not using effective multicultural education practices. Students were assured that no right or wrong answers existed; they simply needed to reflect upon their own teaching experiences, observe the teachers around them, and consider the teaching profession in general while creating their lists for the next class session.

During the second class session, students were placed into small discussion groups to share their reasons and compile their lists. Their lengthy conversations validated the need to conduct this examination among experienced teachers and posed an ideal concluding assignment for a graduate class in multicultural education. Each group's list was consolidated into a single list. Then the consolidated lists for each of the four groups were condensed into one large list. Interestingly, similar conversations were held in each of the four groups, and the same items were found on each of their lists.

An exciting and vital series of discussions accompanied this study; the graduate students deliberated at length, attempting to differentiate among effective, ineffective, or absent multicultural education practices. They concluded that all teachers are responsible for infusing culturally responsible pedagogy into their classrooms just as they are responsible for using effective teaching strategies in other subject areas to meet students' individual needs and interests. These powerful conversations helped the students to identify and understand a major concern associated with the field of multicultural education.

THE FIVE MAJOR CATEGORIES

Graduate students participating in this study identified more than 50 reasons why teachers aren't using effective multicultural education practices. As the trends began to emerge, students organized their reasons into five major categories to better manage and understand their data (see Table 1). The five major categories included:

1. Teachers do not know or understand what multicultural education is
2. Teachers do not know how to use effective multicultural education practices
3. Teachers are not motivated to learn effective multicultural education practices

4. Teachers are resistant to learn effective multicultural education practices
5. Teachers do not realize their full responsibilities as educators for using effective multicultural education practices

Reasons from Teachers

Teachers Do Not Know or Understand What Multicultural Education Is.

In all four courses, the principal reason given by every group distinctly stated that *most teachers lack a clear definition or understanding of what multicultural education is.* Because these graduate students were nearing the end of their courses in multicultural education, they fully understood what multicultural education encompasses and could articulate various descriptions and approaches. They were well-versed in the research of Banks (1995), Gay, Gollnick and Chinn, Nieto (1996), Sleeter (1992), Smith (1992), and others. Yet the primary concern the graduate students had encountered in their own teaching experiences (before taking this course in multicultural education) and when talking with other teachers about multicultural education was the ability to establish a clear operational definition. The overriding question repeatedly arose: How can experienced teachers use effective multicultural education practices if they don't know what multicultural education is?

The graduate students offered many reasons to account for this concern. Many experienced teachers, especially older teachers who earned their college degrees more than 10 years ago, were not required to take any courses specifically related to multicultural education. These teachers completed their undergraduate degree programs, and most likely their master's degrees, before state mandates requiring multicultural education courses as part of the licensure or certification process. These teachers have become acquainted with multicultural education concepts and practices through a variety of avenues based on their own interests and levels of motivation or the insights and incentives of their school and district administrators. Cultural diversity was not a clearly defined educational issue when many of them began their teaching careers (McCall, 1995).

For some teachers, however, courses in multicultural education were included either at the undergraduate or graduate course level, but the multicultural education concepts frequently were constructed as additive to education rather than infused into the curriculum and instruction (Banks, 1995). Similarly, a few teachers may have completed a course labeled multicultural education that was actually more of an ethnic studies course—not a course exploring multicultural education inclusive of people, policies, programs, process, and practices. Courses such as these did not elucidate the meaning of multicultural education.

The graduate students also reported that many experienced teachers are working in schools where no or few multicultural education in-services have been offered. When in-services are conducted, often they are extremely short, catered to fit into the school schedule, and held before or after the regular school day. The teachers reflected that this brevity generally makes the in-service superficial in content coverage and, again, communicates an additive approach for using multicultural education practices.

Some graduate students shared that teachers who have been exposed to some multicultural education in-services felt the information had been presented as a personal attack on them as white, middle-class, "prejudiced" teachers, responsible for past social injustices. These teachers reflected on the in-service sessions as generating more negative hostility and defensiveness rather than focusing on student acceptance and academic achievement. This reaction to multicultural education in-services has been shared by other teachers in other studies (Greeman & Kimmel, 1995; Pang, 1994).

One graduate student summarized, "I wish our school would dedicate a full day or more of staff development to learning more about multicultural education, ourselves, and society as we did during this course rather than just trying to fix 'those children' and improve test scores in quick little in-services. It seems like we should do this right."

Teachers Do Not Know How To Use Effective Multicultural Education Practices.

In addition to not knowing what multicultural education is, most teachers are *unsure how to use effective multicultural education practices*, particularly how to integrate and infuse culturally responsive and responsible pedagogy across their curricula. The graduate students reported that some teachers may be acquainted with this terminology; yet few teachers are clear as to the meaning of the terms, especially for infusing cultural diversity and applying effective strategies into subject areas other than social studies or literature. The graduate students reported the trend for teachers to decontextualize curriculum in order to address multicultural education concepts. This observation parallels findings substantiated in research related to integrating multicultural education into university teacher education programs (Ladson-Billings, 1994).

Teachers also lack the skills for incorporating alternative and authentic assessments to match and expand culturally diverse student learning styles. Most teachers are unclear how to design meaningful assessment procedures that genuinely empower students and demonstrate student achievement in various ways.

Discussions related to infusing multicultural education across the curriculum generated the observation that teachers are uncertain how or when to teach prejudice reduction, equality, and tolerance. These skills are missing for most teachers, and the teachers have had no preparation to teach these subjects regardless of their assigned content areas. And not only are teachers unprepared to teach these concepts, teachers reported that their colleagues are uncomfortable teaching about most multicultural educational topics and issues. Compounding their lack of knowing what multicultural education is and how to use effective practices, teachers frequently consider multicultural education as a controversial subject entailing race relations and human equity—discussions they tend to avoid in their classrooms. Often, these topics are viewed as sociology and psychology, not an objective related to math, science, or other curricular content.

A graduate student participating in this study shared that "Most of the teachers at my school claim that they are treating all students fairly; they act like teaching multicultural education is someone else's responsibility and not a part of *all* classrooms and school events. I think many teachers avoid multicultural education because they don't really know what it is or how to bring it into their teaching strategies. They are afraid of controversy or getting off the subject in their classrooms."

Teachers tend to view using effective multicultural education practices as requiring too much time to prepare and infuse adequately. Most teachers seem overwhelmed by the number of responsibilities they have been given and are reluctant to take on any more. They see gaining more information about multicultural education as an infringement on their time. The learning should have been provided by their teacher preparation programs or the school districts for whom they now work—not an additional requirement for working with low-achieving students.

Likewise, it was reported that most teachers would prefer a packaged multicultural education program just as they are supplied for teaching most other subject areas. Teachers might consider teaching multicultural education if a complete program with student textbooks, teacher guides, and prepared materials was provided for them with all the necessary tools for effective multicultural education.

Teachers Are Not Motivated To Learn Effective Multicultural Education Practices.

A third major category that emerged from this study identified this finding for a variety of reasons. Graduate students reported that many teachers *simply are not interested in learning about effective multicultural education practices*; they claim that there is little or no time to learn about such practices. This belief extends to teachers' perceptions that to prepare and infuse effective multicultural education practices into their current teaching styles requires too much time—time that they feel is necessary to attend to other classroom responsibilities.

Teachers stated that time to learn effective multicultural education practices could be provided by school administrators if their administrators valued the notion or if this idea was supported by the school district admini-

Table 1. Why Aren't Teachers Using Effective Multicultural Education Practices?
Five Major Insights from Experienced Teachers

I.   **Teachers Do Not Know or Understand What Multicultural Education Is.** Teachers report that:

1. There is no clear understanding or operating definition of multicultural education or for valuing cultural diversity
2. Multicultural education was not an education issue during their teacher preparation
3. No course was required or available in their undergraduate teacher preparation program
4. No course was required or available in their graduate education degree programs
5. Courses in multicultural education were taught via an additive approach
6. Courses in multicultural education were taught via an ethnic studies approach
7. Few or no building in-services are conducted for teachers in schools
8. Building in-services are too brief due to school schedules
9. Building in-services treat multicultural education in a superficial manner
10 Building in-services become negative leaving many teachers feeling helpless or hostile

II. **Teachers Do Not Know How To Use Effective Multicultural Education Practices.** They report that:

1. They are unsure how to integrate multicultural education into their current curriculum without decontextualizing content
2. They are unsure how to infuse concepts into instructional practices
3. They are unsure how to incorporate alternative & authentic assessments to meet cultural differences
4. They are unsure when to teach about prejudice reduction, stereotyping, tolerance, etc.
5. They are uncomfortable teaching about race relations and human equality
6. They are uncomfortable teaching about feelings at all
7. They are charged with too many responsibilities and cannot add more
8. They have too little teaching time to add more to curriculum
9. They perceive that effective multicultural education requires too much preparation time and energy
10. They want a set program such as a packaged set with prescriptive textbooks and guidebooks.

III. **Teachers Are Not Motivated To Learn Effective Multicultural Education Practices.** They state that:

1. Most classroom teachers simply are not interested in multicultural education
2. Multicultural education practices are not important
3. Multicultural education is not valued in concept by building or district administration
4. Multicultural education is not supported with time, money, or resources by administration
5. Teachers have no personal time to take multicultural education courses
6. Teachers don't need more courses toward maintaining their license or earning their next pay raise (the motivation for taking most courses)

stration. One graduate student added, "Multicultural education issues were a high priority a few years ago, and a flurry of intensive activities happened at that time. Then we zipped on to another new concern; one that seemed to have more money attached to it." Teachers acknowledged that they would be motivated to continue learning effective multicultural education practices if the administration provided the time and resources to attend classes and purchase materials.

Most teachers are not going to pursue these endeavors on their own time and with their own money. Experienced teachers, particularly those who have completed their masters degrees, are less likely to enroll in university courses to earn additional credits toward their salary increase. These teachers can earn credits toward maintaining their teaching licenses through other means and usually do not select courses that address cultural diversity, especially if multicultural education is not a goal or emphasis of the administration.

In one of the more revealing findings of this study, the graduate students reported that most teachers are not motivated to learn effective multicultural education practices

because *they feel there is no need to change their current approaches.* Teachers do not internalize a need to know or infuse the ideals of a culturally responsible and responsive pedagogy. In many situations, their students are achieving well and the community is pleased with the school. Teachers are occupied with addressing other educational needs or interests and receiving support to bring new concepts and practices into their classrooms. Their professional and personal conversations do not focus on the need to learn effective multicultural education practices.

Teachers Are Resistant to Learning Effective Multicultural Education Practices.

The belief that teachers are not motivated to learn effective multicultural education practices is strengthened by their resistance to learn them. Many different reasons were given, rationalizing teacher resistance.

Some teachers feel that they currently are using effective multicultural education practices in their classrooms. Unfortunately, these teachers incorporate global studies or ethnic studies into their course content and consider these to be effective multicultural education practices.

7. Teachers don't feel there is a need in their current classroom
8. Teachers don't feel there is a need in their current school community
9. Teachers don't feel there is a need in their current educational circles
10. Teachers don't feel there is a need for multicultural education within the society-at-large

IV. Teachers Are Resistant to Learn Effective Multicultural Education Practices. They claim that:

1. They are already using effective multicultural education practices
2. They consider their teaching global studies as multicultural education
3. They consider their teaching ethnic studies as multicultural education
4. They have traveled or lived in other countries and consider that to be multicultural education
5. They feel that multicultural education is too concerned with race relations and controversial issues
6. They feel professionally threatened by their lack of multicultural education knowledge and skills
7. They don't need multicultural education since they match the culture of their students and school community
8. They think that multicultural education is only for teachers in "at-risk" schools
9. They teach in an inner-city or "at-risk" school and have learned what multicultural education is from their own professional experiences
10. They are persons of color, minorities, etc., &, therefore, they are knowledgeable from their own lifelong experiences (regardless of the experiences)

V. Teachers Do Not Realize Their Full Responsibilities for Using Effective Multicultural Education Practices. Teachers need to:

1. Learn how to infuse culturally responsible and responsive pedagogy across the curriculum so all learners are provided equitable educational opportunities regardless of the subject area and community environment
2. Teach all children about all children—locally to globally
3. Role-model learning about others to their own students in both formal and informal interactions
4. Role-model learning about others to families and the school community
5. Facilitate communication with families and the community
6. Role-model learning about others to colleagues and all levels of school administration
7. Role-model learning about others to preservice and student teachers
8. Promote more people of color in becoming teachers and school administrators
9. Be a well-educated person and professional in today's society
10. Understand that the United States is changing in a positive direction in the local and global scene, and that multicultural education is a tool that will help us individually and nationally to be more successful; multicultural education is not a threat

Some teachers have traveled extensively or have lived internationally; they label those experiences as multicultural education. These teachers have confused their global travels and personal backgrounds with cross-cultural experiences and are resistant to modifying their practices (McDiarmid, 1992; Renyi & Lubeck, 1994).

Similarly, some teachers are resistant to learning effective multicultural education practices because they feel anything multicultural is overly concerned with race relations and controversial issues. This reinforces the first major finding that teachers do not know or understand what multicultural education is. The graduate students report that teachers just want to teach their assigned subject areas. Experienced teachers also resist learning effective multicultural education practices if they believe that their own professional knowledge, skills, and status are threatened. They do not want to change what they believe works.

This belief is supported when teachers perceive that they culturally match their students and community. Teachers are resistant to learn or use effective multicultural education practices if they feel that their classrooms are not multicultural. Learning multicultural education is viewed by some experienced teachers as necessities required for preservice teachers or professionals teaching in inner city schools to learn about "those types of children" (Tomlinson, Callahan, Tomchin, Eiss, Imbeau, & Landrum, 1997). These teachers do not realize that all children benefit from learning about all kinds of children. Some teachers assigned to inner-city schools or schools labeled as having "at-risk" populations state that they have learned to use effective multicultural education practices by virtue of their daily experiences regardless of what they are actually doing in their classrooms. The graduate students in this study questioned if what they observed in these schools would constitute effective multicultural education practices (Deering & Stanutz, 1995; Shultz, Neyhart, & Reck, 1996).

This study also showed that it is not only white teachers who exhibit a lack of understanding of cultural diversity and resistance to multicultural education. Some teachers of color state that simply by being a person of color they fully understand multicultural education. These individuals claim that their personal lives have provided them with enough empirical evidence to be multiculturally astute and are more attentive to multicultural education concerns than their white counterparts. Obviously, all teachers bring unique experiences to their teaching repertoire; some teachers reap the benefit of a greater diversity of life experiences than other teachers. However, all teachers gain from formal instruction offered in multicultural education as they learn more about others as well as themselves (Goodwin, 1994).

Teachers Do Not Realize Their Full Responsibilities as Educators.

The graduate students in this study concluded that *most teachers do not fully realize or accept their responsibilities as educators.* Because many teachers do not know or understand what multicultural education is, and they do not know how to use effective practices, *teachers are not providing the best education opportunities that they can for their students regardless of the students' backgrounds and learning needs, the curricular content area, and the quality of instruction.* Teachers need to learn how to infuse culturally responsible and responsive pedagogy across the curriculum and throughout the school environment to assure equitable learning opportunities for all students.

All teachers are responsible for teaching students about all kinds of people both during formal instruction and during informal, casual conversations. Experienced teachers do not realize what strong influences and powerful role models they are for young people as they demonstrate the importance of being aware of others, valuing cultural diversity, and behaving respectfully toward others. Frequently, young students never even realize how they were exposed to negative role-modeling by their teachers (Cabello & Burstein, 1995).

Teachers serve as essential role models as they demonstrate the importance of learning about other students, families, and the community. These integrated learning experiences facilitate stronger communication between schools and homes. Often, teachers express frustration that their students' parents do not visit or support their children's schools; using effective multicultural education practices could extend a greater welcome. Likewise, teachers inform and support one another; it is important for teachers to demonstrate and reinforce learning and use effective multicultural education practices within all educational environments.

Experienced teachers also serve as role models not only to their K–12 students but also to preservice teachers completing field placement and student teaching assignments. Universities and school districts rely on these experienced teachers to blend educational theories with useful practices. Yet, as with all areas of curriculum and instruction, some experienced teachers exhibit ineffective or harmful teaching practices, especially regarding multicultural education. If preservice teachers do not observe their field placement teachers modeling effective teaching strategies for infusing multicultural education, the preservice teachers are less likely to integrate strategies across their curriculum and instruction (Deering & Stanutz, 1995).

This concept is particularly noteworthy if schools want to increase the number of teachers of color. The graduate students in this study linked the growing number of children of color, the need for all students to learn about all people, the observation that experienced teachers do not use multicultural education practices effectively, and the few numbers of teachers of color as conditions everyone involved with education must acknowledge and work to change.

Teachers need to understand that as well-educated and successful individuals, they must realize and accept their full responsibilities for using effective multicultural education practices. They must be willing to change as the United States and the world change.

SUGGESTIONS FOR EDUCATIONAL REFORM AND SYSTEMIC CHANGE

This study, which was designed as a concluding exercise in a graduate course to apply theories of multicultural education, revealed clear implications for the experienced teachers enrolled in these classes. The graduate students began the exercise casually, looking at possible connections between the ideals of this course and their own educational environments; the inquiry seemed rather simplistic: "Why aren't experienced teachers using effective multicultural education practices?" At the end of the exercise, the findings strongly implied that many changes need to occur. These findings provide teacher educators, school administrators, staff developers, and, most importantly, experienced K–12 teachers with many reasons for change, organized into the identified five major categories. These categories furnish educators with a quick and useful review of teacher beliefs and behaviors generated by experienced teachers.

Effecting change is challenging. Average experienced teachers, such as the graduate students enrolled in these multicultural education courses, have established themselves comfortably within their schools and communities, and many are resistant to change. They seem sure of who they are. They consider themselves competent and confident in their teaching practices, perceptions that have been reinforced positively and frequently by their students, colleagues, and school administrators. Yet, all too often, these same teachers lack the knowledge, skills, and beliefs about diversity that are necessary to ensure student achievement and success (Ladson-Billings, 1994).

To ensure that culturally responsible and responsive pedagogy is infused into all classrooms, continued efforts must be made to reach out to all teachers, administrators, and staff members while building upon their years of teaching and variety of educational experiences. Opportunities for all school personnel to learn more about multicultural education and for valuing cultural diversity will help to reform education and ensure that all children will be successful in school and in life (Larke, 1992).

Teachers, staff, and administrators must be provided meaningful staff development in-services by qualified and well-prepared facilitators who will help teachers to know and understand what effective multicultural education is to them as human beings and as professionals. All school personnel will benefit from quality staff development in-services that advance their abilities to know themselves, to honor and respect every individual, to communicate more effectively with one another, and to assure consistently equitable educational opportunities for students and their families. These experiences establish a deeper understanding for the values, beliefs, and meaning of multicultural education.

Likewise, all teachers, staff, and administrators need to see and experience effective multicultural education practices that provide safe, healthy, and welcoming educational environments. School personnel need to be shown how to ensure the use of culturally inclusive language and curriculum throughout all of the policies, programs, materials, and resources helping them to know and understand how to use effective multicultural education practices. Demonstrations introducing multicultural literature, authentic use of books and materials, and culturally inclusive displays need to reflect the nation's and world's cultural diversity in realistic and genuine ways. Likewise, school personnel need to be aware that classroom and school-wide events need to honor and respect diverse student and community populations.

Teachers also will benefit from in-services that help them to develop their skills to implement a variety of instruction strategies and ensure increased academic achievement of all students. Many teachers welcome additional instruction demonstrating the use of alternative and authentic forms of assessment that reflect fair and impartial teaching and testing programs, even as a growing emphasis is placed on test scores and academic performance.

Teachers continue to report that administrators play a key role to guarantee equity in all education environments for students, families, and teachers. Teachers and administrators working collaboratively are seen as being instrumental for motivating teachers to learn effective multicultural education practices, reducing teacher resistance, and establishing teachers' responsibility for using effective multicultural education practices. Administrations must provide the financial resources, facilities, time, and staffing for additional staff development opportunities for teachers. Administrators can introduce enriched and comprehensive curriculum and educational programs for students while requiring fair and impartial assessments and testing programs. For these to be successful, administrators need to be well-acquainted in effective multicultural education practices, curricular development, instructional strategies, their teachers, and

their communities through an openness to new and creative approaches that value cultural diversity. Through the educational leadership and staff development opportunities provided by insightful administrators and supported by culturally sensitive teachers, more teachers and school personnel will be using effective multicultural education practices.

REFERENCES

Banks, J. A. (1995). Multicultural education: Historical development, dimensions, and practice. In J. A. Banks, & C. A. M. Banks (Eds.), *Handbook of research on multicultural education* (pp. 3–19). New York: Simon & Schuster Macmillan.

Cabello, B., & Burstein, N. D. (1995). Examining teachers' beliefs about teaching in culturally diverse classrooms. *Journal of Teacher Education* 46(4), 285–295.

Cole, R. W. (Ed.). (1997). *Educating Everybody's Children: Diverse Teaching Strategies for Diverse Learners*. Alexandria, VA: Association for Supervision and Curriculum Development.

Deering, T. E., & Stanutz, A. (1995). Preservice field experience as a multicultural component of a teacher education program. *Journal of Teacher Education* 46(5), 390–395.

Edlefelt, R. A. (1997, September–October). A profile of America's teachers. *ATE Newsletter* 31(1), 5, 7.

Goodwin, A. L. (1994). Making the transition from self to other: What do preservice teachers really think about multicultural education? *Journal of Teacher Education* 45(2), 199–132.

Greenman, N. P., & Kimmel, E. B. (1995). The road to multicultural education: Pothole of resistance. *Journal of Teacher Education* 46(5), 360–369.

Ladson-Billings, G. (1994). What we can learn from multicultural education research. *Educational Leadership* 51(8), 22–27.

Larke, P. J. (1992). Effective multicultural teachers: Meeting the challenges of diverse classrooms. *Equity & Excellence in Education* 25(2–4), 133–139.

McCall, A. L. (1995). Constructing conceptions of multicultural education: Preservice teachers' life experiences and teacher education. *Journal of Teacher Education* 46(5), 340–351.

McDiarmid, G. W. (1992). What to do about the differences? A study of multicultural education for teacher trainees in the Los Angeles Unified School District. *Journal of Teacher Education* 34(2), 83–94.

Nieto, S. (1996). *Affirming diversity: The sociopolitical context of multicultural education* (2d edition). White Plains, NY: Longman.

Pang, V. O. (1994). Why do we need this class? Multicultural education for teachers. In Schultz, F. (Ed.), *Annual editions in multicultural education, 97/98* (pp. 80–83). Guilford, CT: Dushkin/McGraw-Hill.

Renyi, J., & Lubeck, D. R. (1994). A response to the NCSS guidelines on multicultural education. *Social Education* 58(1), 4–7.

Schultz, E. L., Neyhart, T. K., & Reck, U. M. (1996). Swimming against the tide: A study of prospective teachers' attitudes regarding cultural diversity and urban teaching. *The Western Journal of Black Studies* 20(1), 1–9.

Sleeter, C. E. (1992). Restructuring schools for multicultural education. *Journal of Teacher Education* 43(2), 141–149.

Sparks, W. G., III. (1994). Culturally responsive pedagogy: A framework for addressing multicultural issues. *The Journal of Physical Education, Recreation & Dance* 65(9), 33–38.

Tomlinson, C. A., Callahan, C. M., Tomchin, E. M., Eiss, N., Imbeau, M., & Landrum, M. (1997). Becoming architects of communities of learning: Addressing academic diversity in contemporary classrooms. *Exceptional Children* 63(2), 269–283.

Nancy P. Gallavan is Assistant Professor of Elementary School Social Studies and K–12 Multicultural Education at the University of Nevada, Las Vegas.

Unit Selections

Key Points to Consider

❖ What should be some minimal standards of practice in the field of multicultural education?

❖ What should be the qualifications for persons who wish to become specialists in multicultural education?

❖ It has been argued that all American students should learn the multicultural reality of our nation. Why is this true? How can it be accomplished?

❖ What does it mean to speak of multicultural education as an interdiscipline?

❖ What issues are raised by total infusion models of multicultural education in teacher education programs?

❖ What should all American students know about racism and prejudice by the time they graduate from high school?

❖ How do we help people learn to accept cultural diversity? What can teachers do to foster acceptance of cultural differences?

 **Links**   # www.dushkin.com/online/

These sites are annotated on pages 4 and 5.

Multicultural education emerged as an area of scholarship out of the social upheavals of the 1960s and the concern of many in the scholarly community that there was a critical need for research-based knowledge of the cultural contexts of education. Much of our early knowledge base came from critically important research in anthropology and sociology (as well as psychiatric studies of the impact of prejudice and victimization on targeted racial and cultural minorities), from the 1920s to our present time. These studies examined intercultural relations in all sorts of urban, suburban, small town, and rural settings in the United States. They used ethnographic field inquiry methods developed by anthropologists and later used by some sociologists and educators. The earliest of these studies, from the 1920s through the 1950s, focused on such concerns as child-rearing practices, rites of passage into adulthood, perceptions of other cultural groups, and the social stratification systems of communities and neighborhoods. Studies of how victimized and involuntarily segregated racial and cultural groups responded to being "targeted" for discriminatory treatment documented the intercultural state of affairs in American society in the 1930s and 1940s.

As the civil rights movement of the 1950s in the United States continued to grow in momentum throughout the 1960s, continued anthropological and sociological inquiry about the education of minority cultural youth continued to develop. Out of the urban and other social crises of the 1960s emerged a belief among those educators concerned about questions of racial and cultural justice that there was a serious need for an area of educational studies which would specifically focus on the study of intercultural relations in the schools from a "multi-" cultural perspective. It would challenge the by-then-traditional Eurocentric melting pot visions of how one became "American." The problem with the Eurocentric "melting pot" was that it was a very exclusionary pot; not everyone was welcome to jump into it. The philosophy of a culturally pluralist democracy in which all cultural heritages would be treasured and none rejected became attractive to those who witnessed the arbitrary and cruel effects of racial and cultural prejudice in schools, as well as in other areas of life in "mainstream" society.

The belief that all teachers should respect the cultural heritages of their students and that all students have the right to know their cultural heritages and to develop pride in them began to spread among socially concerned educators. The studies that had been conducted on intercultural relations among teachers and students by the early 1970s clearly demonstrated the need for an academic discipline that would focus on building knowledge bases about our multicultural social reality as well as on how to teach about other cultural heritages and to improve the quality of instruction in multicultural school settings. Many of us realize today that all young Americans need to know about the American experience from a multicultural perspective that rejects and transcends the old Anglo- and Eurocentric presuppositions of melting pot theories of assimilation into American social life.

As part of the movement for civil rights, persons from non-English-speaking backgrounds also sought to guarantee that their children would be given the opportunity to grow up both bilingual and bicultural. By the time the U.S. Supreme Court handed down its decision in *Lau v. Nichols* in 1974, there were dozens of cases in the federal court system concerning the causes of bilingual education and English as a second language.

The academic leadership of the nation's cultural minorities and many other concerned scholars have forged a competent community dedicated to the task of setting standards of practice for multicultural education as an academic discipline. There is spirited dialogue going on in the field as to what these standards of practice should be as well as about what academic qualifications people ought to have to conduct multicultural education. James Banks, professor of multicultural education at the University of Washington, and others are concerned about the future survival and development of multicultural education as an academic discipline that must also maintain its focus on classroom practice as well as on defensible theoretical constructs.

Multicultural education must develop an ongoing cadre of competent scholarly leaders to direct the further development of the field as well as to ensure that attempts to merely infuse multicultural content into existing teacher education course content does not dilute the academic quality of multicultural education or the standards of practice in the field. Multicultural education is an interdiscipline that draws its knowledge base from anthropology, sociology, social history, and even psychiatry. Focused, adequately prepared specialists in this new interdiscipline are necessary on school faculties if it is to maintain its academic integrity.

The essays in this unit reflect concerns regarding academic standards and goals for multicultural education as the field continues to develop and to enter a new period in its history. The authors of these essays raise important qualitative issues that must be addressed as the time approaches when a majority of Americans will be from "minority" cultural heritages and when traditional conceptions of minority and majority relations in the United States will have little meaning.

This unit's essays are relevant to courses in curriculum theory and construction, educational policy studies, history and philosophy of education, cultural foundations of education, and multicultural education.

Multicultural Education As an Academic Discipline

A Different Mirror

A Conversation with Ronald Takaki

How can education reflect all voices in our history? Can multiculturalism reunite our fragmented society? Educator and historian Ronald Takaki discusses the power of a curriculum that mirrors many ethnic perspectives.

Joan Montgomery Halford

A pioneer in the field of ethnic studies, Ronald Takaki has written nine books on diversity in American society, including the widely acclaimed A Different Mirror: A History of Multicultural America (1993) and A Larger Memory: A History of Our Diversity, With Voices (1998). Takaki, the grandson of Japanese immigrants in Hawaii, has bridged many cultures as a student, a scholar, and an activist. As a young professor, for example, he taught the first black studies course offered at the University of California, Los Angeles, shortly after the Watts riots. Recently, Takaki spoke with Educational Leadership about diversity and education.

How do you define multicultural education?

The multiculturalism I have been seeking is a serious scholarship that includes all American peoples and challenges the traditional master narrative of American history. The traditional master narrative we've learned in our schools says that this country was founded by Americans of European ancestry and that our ideas are rooted in Western civilization. But when we just look around at ourselves, we realize that not all of us came from Europe. Many of us came from Africa and Latin America, and others were already here in North America. And others, like my grandfather, came from a Pacific shore. It is not only more inclusive, but also more *accurate* to recognize this diversity. The intellectual purpose of multiculturalism is a more accurate understanding of who we are as Americans.

Multicultural education has been misrepresented by the critics of multiculturalism, especially Arthur Schlesinger Jr., who presents multiculturalism as ethnic separatism in his book *The Disuniting of America*. What Schlesinger has done is to equate multiculturalism with Afrocentrism. But Afrocentrism is not multicultural, it's monocultural. And so what Schlesinger has done is to reduce multiculturalism to the shrillness of ethnic separatism manifested in some versions of Afrocentrism.

Does multiculturalism risk being treated as a fad?

I don't think it will be a fad because of the changing face of America. By 2001, whites in California will become a minority group just like African Americans, Asian Americans, Latinos, and Native Americans—and 2001 is only three years away. Within three years in California, we will all be minorities. California is only the thin end of a larger entering wedge. Researchers have projected that by around 2050, all of us in the United States will be minorities. In the coming multicultural millennium, we will be reminded of our diversity every day. It would be a danger for multicultural education to be a fad. It needs to be up front and central.

I often think about the Los Angeles riots of April 29, 1992. That night on our TV screens, we saw the black smoke rising to the skies above Los Angeles, the Korean stores burning out of control, and the frightening violence on the streets. But the most powerful image that was beamed out of L.A. that night was the trembling face of Rodney King. Many of us still hear his words echoing in our minds. He said, "Please, people, we're stuck here for a while. We can get along, we can work it out." The question is, How do we work it out? How do we get along unless we learn more about one another in a systematic and informed way? Multiculturalism can help reunite America.

A few months ago, a white elementary school teacher in Brooklyn chose to teach the book **Nappy Hair,** *which celebrates African American hair, to her predominantly African American class. The teaching of the book provoked parents in the school to make physical threats against the teacher. Incidents such as this have frightened educators. How can educators safely address diversity in the classroom?*

It's very important for educators to explain clearly to parents what they are doing and why they are doing it. Educators must work with parent organizations to explain why, for example, we're teaching a book called *Nappy Hair*. Had that school had open discussions about the texts that teachers would be using in the classroom, parents would know that teachers don't make decisions about what they'll be having their students read in isolation from the community.

But there is a larger problem here. Many parents who complain don't at-

tend the parent-teacher meetings. In many cases, these parents are working long hours, and it's very difficult for them to get to meetings in the evening or the late afternoon. The social and economic contexts make this kind of information sharing very difficult. And that's something that needs to be kept in mind.

Educators such as E. D. Hirsch advocate teaching a curriculum of core knowledge. What is your opinion?

I agree with Hirsch. There's knowledge that I think every American should know. There should be a core. The question, however, is, What should be the content of this core? This is where Hirsch and I differ.

At the back of Hirsch's best-selling book, *Cultural Literacy, What Every American Needs to Know*, a 66-page appendix lists terms that every cultural literate person should know. If you look at this list, you'll find that it's very Eurocentric. For example, the list includes Ellis Island, but it omits Angel Island. How many Americans have heard of Angel Island? People who live in San Francisco can see Angel Island in the middle of San Francisco Bay. We think of Angel Island as a place to bike, hike, and picnic. However, Angel Island was also the site of the immigration station for Chinese and Japanese immigrants; the remains of it are still there. We need to include Angel Island in a list for cultural literacy.

So I agree with Hirsch that we need a core, but the question is, Whose core will this be? I would like this

core to be reflective of a more accurate understanding of who we are as Americans.

Do you think the standards movement is helpful in promoting this core?

The problem is that these standards are often set by bureaucrats. More educators should come together and determine what core knowledge is and engage one another in dialogue and debate. Just the term *standards* is intimidating. It suggests rigidity. Knowledge is something that is more vibrant, more fluid. I would be reluctant to endorse or promote standards. The question is, Where are the standards going to be made? Many people making them in the agencies are not educators.

How do class differences factor into multicultural education? People often

discuss multiculturalism in terms of race and ethnicity, but what about class?

Class is very important. Most of us wouldn't even be here if it were not for the demand for the labor of our ancestors. Jews, for example, were needed as workers in the garment industry. And the Irish were needed to build the railroads and to work in the textile mills. My Japanese grandfather would not be here had it not been for the need for his labor on the sugar plantations of Hawaii.

where multiculturalism can bring us together. When we examine our history, we will all find that we are linked to one another in terms of our class in intricate ways.

Take, for example, slavery. How many Americans really know why slavery was established in what would become the United States? Many people have this notion that slavery just began when the first 20 Africans were landed by a Dutch slave ship in Jamestown, Virginia, in 1619. But actually, those first 20 Africans were not slaves. They became indentured

slavery was such a profitable institution, why didn't these white planters bring in more labor from Africa? Well, they had this vision of Virginia as a reproduction of English society in the New World. Hence, there was resistance to the importation of large numbers of non-English, especially laborers who did not look European.

The Virginia planters did not want to bring in Africans, but they did bring in large numbers of white indentured servants from England and Ireland. But these white indentured servants had the right to bear arms. That was an English right. In 1676, they engaged in Bacon's Rebellion; the rebels burned down Jamestown. And the rebellion was repressed only after British troops came to Virginia.

The intellectual purpose of multiculturalism is a more accurate understanding of who we are as Americans.

Class is a hidden reality of American history. We overlook class, but class is central to the ethnic experience, including the experience of European immigrant groups. This is

servants. There was no law for slavery in the English colonies at that point.

Even in 1675, 55 years later, blacks constituted only 5 percent of the total population in the Virginia colony. If

After Bacon's Rebellion, the planter class realized that it would be dangerous to depend on a white laboring class that had the freedom of assembly and the right to bear arms. At that point, the planter class decided to shift from white indentured servitude to enslaved African labor. African labor was denied the right of assembly and the right to bear arms. The working class could be disarmed because of race. By 1740, the black population in Virginia had risen from 5 to 40 percent. This was when slavery became an institution.

The point I'm making involves the relationship between class and race. Racial diversity was forged in the crucibles of white class conflict. Black workers were used and pitted against white workers. And white workers who were also economically exploited and degraded thought that they belonged to a white aristocracy. During the Civil War, these white workers went to war and were killed to defend an institution that did not benefit them economically or socially.

So when the president is asked to apologize for slavery, the question I have to ask as a historian is, Apologize to whom? It's not just to Africans and their descendants, but also to the white workers who were then pitted against these newly imported workers from Africa. Race is tied intricately to class. When we understand

this intricate tie that binds us, we begin to see that we do share much common ground in class.

Why do you distinguish between race and ethnicity?

In American history, Americans who had distinct physical characteristics because of their skin color or the shape of their eyes represented an ethnic group because they had different religions and different cultures—but they also represented a racial group. And people were stigmatized because of their distinct physical characteristics. And this led to legislation against them, like slavery, the Chinese Exclusion Act, and the internment of Japanese Americans. Neither Italians nor Germans were interned during World War II. You have to make a distinction between ethnic experience and racial experience. To lump together race and ethnicity violates this complex reality.

I am a scholar who strives to make the distinction between race and ethnicity. European immigrant groups were ethnic groups. They represented different religions. And Catholics and Jews suffered the oppression of ethnocentrism inflicted upon them by a Protestant America. But because they were white, they were eligible for naturalized citizenship, and they were able then to exercise political power and advance their economic and social interests.

On the other hand, Asian immigrants were not eligible for naturalized citizenship. The Naturalization Act of 1790 specified explicitly that to be eligible for naturalized citizenship, you first had to be white—and it used the term *white*. You might think, "That was 1790." Well, this law was in effect until 1952. And because of this law, my grandparents never became U.S. citizens. How is that for an example of the difference between race and ethnicity?

What are your thoughts on bilingual education?

Students who go through a good bilingual education program learn English with greater competency and rapidity than students who are just immersed in English-only classrooms. Teaching students in their native languages gives them cultural dignity.

Bilingual education doesn't disunite us. It's not a cultural separatism. Actually, it lets America be America, to use the phrase of Langston Hughes: "Let America be America where equality is in the air we breathe." For us to acknowledge the native languages of others is to embrace equality for them.

Talk with us about your stance on affirmative action.

Most Americans support affirmative action. In January 1997, the *New York Times* reported that only 25 percent of Americans polled actually wanted to abolish affirmative action. Another 25 percent said they want to continue affirmative action as is. And about 40 percent said let's mend it, not eliminate it. Most of us as Americans realize that we belong to a nation that—to use Lincoln's language in his Gettysburg Address—is dedicated to the "proposition" of equality. We believe in equality and fairness, and we realize that the playing field is not a level one. A person's life chances depend largely on where he or she resides or goes to school. And so we need to create a more level playing field.

The government is an important instrument to do this. Now, when we think of affirmative action, we usually think of it in terms of affirmative action for underrepresented racial minorities. But actually the primary beneficiaries of affirmative action have been white women. Affirmative action has opened up opportunities for them to enter professions such as law, medicine, and business in increasing numbers. With Proposition 209 in California, there was a misrepresentation of affirmative action as a racial program.

I have written a draft of a pro-affirmative action initiative, the California Equality Initiative, for the ballot in 2000. The California Equality In-itiative revises the principle and policy of affirmative action. My initiative reads that in order to act affirmatively in the promotion of equality of opportunity, it shall be lawful for the State of California to consider race, gender, or socioeconomic class disadvantage as criteria in the selection of qualified individuals for education, employment, and government contracting. This law does not permit quotas, but it does allow the consideration of the above three categories.

What I've done in my draft is to include socioeconomic class disadvantage. I've been teaching at the University of California, Berkeley, for almost 30 years now. And I don't find white students or even black or Chicano students from the working class and the lower class. The average family income of our students exceeds $100,000 a year; we are an elite university in terms of class. And if we want to practice our commitment to equality of opportunity, then we have to practice it in terms not only of race and gender but also of socioeconomic class disadvantage.

Class is a hidden reality of American history.

And students who come from the lower classes and the working classes are at a disadvantage.

They have lower SAT scores for one thing. They don't have the family resources to take those expensive SAT preparation courses. Further, students who are admitted to Berkeley are given what's called a *bonus point* for advanced placement courses or honors courses. So if you have the privilege of attending an elite suburban high school where you can find an abundance of AP courses, then you are awarded five points; an *A* is regarded as five points for AP courses. And so we have students with 4.0 GPAs who are black and Latino who are competing against white and Asian students with 4.2, 4.3, and 4.4 GPAs. And this is unfair.

In the epilogue of A Larger Memory, *you write movingly about your high school religion teacher, Dr. Shunji Nishi. Could you tell our readers how Dr. Nishi made a difference in your life?*

When I was a teenager, I was not academically inclined. I was growing up in Hawaii, and my parents had a restaurant near the beach. I became a very good surfer. In my Episcopalian high school, I didn't do especially well. I was required to take a course in religion that was taught by a teacher named Dr. Nishi, a Japanese American with a Ph.D. I was curious and impressed. I can remember going home and saying to my mother, who had been born on a plantation and who had only an 8th grade education, "My teacher's name is Dr. Nishi. He's Japanese American and he has a Ph.D. What's a Ph.D.?" And she looked at me and she said, "I don't know, but he must be very smart." A light bulb went on in my head. I thought maybe I too could become a Ph.D., Ronald Takaki Ph.D.

Dr. Nishi became a role model for me. He wrote comments on my papers: "How do you know this is true? Is this point valid?" Often, he wrote, "Interesting." Occasionally, he wrote, "Insightful." A relationship developed between the two of us. During the second semester of my senior year, as I was walking across campus, Dr. Nishi saw me and he said, "Ronald, I think you should go away to college. There's a fine liberal arts college in Ohio called the College of Wooster. Would you like to go to the College of Wooster?" I immediately blurted out, "No, that's too far away." I had never been off the island. I could not imagine going all the way to Ohio to attend college. But Dr. Nishi asked, "Would it be OK if I wrote to the college to tell them about you?" And I said fine.

A month later I received a letter from the dean of the College of Woos-ter and the letter read, "Dear Mr. Takaki, you have been accepted to the College of Wooster, but please fill out the application form." When I look back at this, I realize that this was an early version of affirmative action. This dean was offering me an opportunity to pursue educational equality. He hadn't even received my transcripts to know what my GPA was, and it wasn't that high. This dean had not received my SAT scores, which were not that high, either. I think he decided on the basis of that letter written by Dr. Nishi that I represented quality. How do you measure—how do you quantify— "insightfulness"? It's not something that we can reduce to numbers. We have become prisoners of quantitative instruments and quantitative measurements of merit and quality. I also think this dean thought it would be good for the College of Wooster to have greater ethnic diversity, that it would be good to have Asian Americans.

This experience changed my life. I accepted the invitation to go to the College of Wooster, and that sent me on the path that led me to this conversation we're having. Had it not been for Dr. Nishi, had it not been for this dean taking a risk and admitting me, I would not be a professor at the University of California, Berkeley.

When I got to Wooster, most people did not see me as an American. My fellow white students would ask me questions like, How long have you been in this country? Where did you learn to speak English? I realized that I didn't look American to them. My name didn't sound American, yet my grandfather came here in 1886. As a family, we've been here longer than many European immigrant groups, longer than the Italians, the Irish, and the Polish. And yet no one would ask them, How long have you been in this country?

I could have changed my name to Ron Taylor, but that wouldn't have helped. I began to think about what it means to be an American and how many people did not see Americans except in terms of a European perspective. After I earned my degree at Wooster, I decided to pursue a Ph.D. When I came to Berkeley, I was swept up in the Civil Rights movement. And this is what stirred me to study race in America.

You use the term hidden reality *to characterize the stories left out of American history. How do educators begin to give voice to these hidden realities?*

We need to do our homework. When I went to college, multicultural research was not available to me. And the master narrative of American history wasn't very critical of our past. But now this scholarship is in our schools of education. The new generation of teachers will have a more accurate understanding of American history. And it's important to have this accurate understanding if we're going to get along with one another. We're going to find out about these hidden histories because multicultural scholarship has emerged.

Multiculturalism is an affirming of what this country stands for: opportunity, equality, and the realization of our dream.

Ronald Takaki is Professor of Ethnic Studies in the Department of Ethnic Studies at the University of California at Berkeley, CA 94720. **Joan Montgomery Halford** is Senior Associate Editor of *Educational Leadership* (e-mail: jhalford@ascd.org).

Editor's note: To order the April 1999 *EL on Tape* audiotape featuring this live interview with Ronald Takaki, contact the ASCD Service Center. Price: $9.95 (member); $11.95 (non-member). Stock no. 299043.

THE IDOLATRY OF MULTICULTURAL EDUCATION

A PROPHETIC PRAGMATIC ALTERNATIVE?

BY JEFFREY AYALA MILLIGAN

MULTICULTURAL EDUCATION has significantly influenced schooling in the United States for at least the last two or three decades (Banks, 1992). Its proponents have argued, compellingly, that education that excludes the experience and contributions of women and diverse cultural groups is miseducative of those excluded groups as well as the privileged groups represented in such schooling (AAUW, 1992; Sleeter, 1991).

American education has generally responded to such criticisms by attempting, with varying degrees of success, to be more inclusive in its enrollments, curricula, methods, and aims. But multicultural education has also become one of the most controversial issues in education (Aufderheide, 1992; Barber, 1992). Critics argue that multicultural education erodes the nation's sense of a unifying cultural heritage and substitutes political correctness for enduring academic values as a criterion for

---

Jeffrey Ayala Milligan is an assistant professor in the Center for Curriculum and Instruction, Teachers College, University of Nebraska, Lincoln.

deciding questions about curricula, methods, and aims (Bloom, 1987; D'Souza, 1991).

Thus, the so-called "culture wars" rage on (Gates, 1992). Though there are serious and substantial philosophical differences between multiculturalists and their critics, much of the smoke and confusion of the culture wars stems at least in part from the lack of any substantial agreement about what multicultural education is. This ambiguity allows critics to set up multiculturalist straw men for easy criticism and enables defenders to rally supporters of their views against the "racist" and "patriarchal" status quo.

Much of the real fighting in the culture wars, however, occurs on terrain at the heart of multicultural education: the concepts of inclusion and empowerment. Though there are a variety of different approaches to multicultural education—Sleeter (1991) has identified at least five—each is vitally concerned with these two issues.

Decades ago, John Dewey (1938, p. 5) recognized that such social conflicts usually manifested themselves as educational controversies and challenged educational philosophers to look for an alternative plan

of operations proceeding from a level deeper and more inclusive than those represented by either of the contending parties. I propose, therefore, to accept Dewey's challenge by offering a critique of what I will claim is the idolatry (Barfield, 1965) implicit in the concepts of inclusion and empowerment.

However, as one generally sympathetic to the underlying moral purpose of multicultural education, I will argue further for the relevance of Cornel West's (1989) prophetic pragmatism as an alternative philosophical framework for education that responds to that underlying moral purpose while eschewing the idolatrous tendencies of contemporary multicultural education. Following West's (1993a, p. x) plea to move beyond Eurocentrism and multiculturalism, I will conclude with a call for prophetic pragmatic education as an alternative to multiculturalism.

THE IDOLATRY OF INCLUSION

The concept of inclusion in multicultural education rests upon the categorization of individuals into groups, for to determine

---

who should be included it is necessary to determine who has been excluded. Thus multicultural education tends to focus on the same categories that were previously constructed to exclude certain groups of people from the mainstream of society: race, culture, ethnicity, gender, sexual orientation, etc.

These categories, however, are problematic. For instance, they are incoherent. They include categories defined by skin color (Black, White), by culture (Hispanic, Native American), by geography (Asian-American), and by gender (male, female). Yet multicultural education frequently ignores other social groupings—religious identity, for instance—that are often a more important source of self-identification for many individuals (Nord, 1995; Milligan, 1996a, 1996b, 1998).

All too often multicultural education reifies the categories it uses by treating them as if they were accurate descriptions of an objective social reality rather than contingent social constructions, created by outside observers, which often ignore the identities constructed and claimed by the individuals supposedly included in such categories. They become, in effect, idols: man-made objects whose createdness is forgotten (Barfield,1965). While their creation may well benefit in real ways those categorized, Said (1979) and Foucault (1991) have shown how they clearly benefit the categorizers. The process creates a whole new discipline through which the categorizers create and claim power and often inspire resistance among those categorized.

Even if we accept such categories as useful, if imperfect, markers of groups historically excluded from the mainstream and therefore candidates for inclusion by multicultural education, the idolatry of inclusion still presents problems. There is, for instance, what Jane Roland Martin (1992) has termed "the problem of curricular abundance." There are far more cultures represented in our schools than can be realistically included in the curriculum in any meaningful way. Choices must be made. But how do we choose? On what basis? Does the curriculum have to reflect the diversity present in a particular school, a district, a state, or the nation? Who chooses? Categorization gives us more idols than we have room for in the temple. Therefore, the concept of inclusion does not rescue the multicultural educator from the process of exclusion or its potentially negative consequences.

The idolatrous reification of categories also presents problems regarding the ends of multicultural education. Is its purpose the reinforcement of cultural identity? If so, should such reinforcement affirm cultural values that, say, oppress women (Milligan, 1998)? Or is multicultural education's aim to produce citizens who are multicultural?

What might this mean? Does it mean students identify with more than one culture? Or does it mean that they are familiar with more than one culture? Which ones? How many is enough?

Might this be a form of "multi" cultural imperialism in which we impose through education relativistic cultural values that contradict the values of particular cultures (Gaddy, Hall, & Marzano, 1996)? Does it mean than students are tolerant of other cultures? What about the problem of moral relativism? Are there some cultural values—oppression of gays and lesbians, for instance—that are morally unacceptable? The categorization through which the value of inclusiveness is operationalized creates these problems. It cannot answer them without resorting to its antithesis—exclusion—thereby perpetuating the practices and the resulting tensions that fuel the culture wars.

THE IDOLATRY OF EMPOWERMENT

Most approaches to multicultural education do not focus entirely on categories of race, culture, gender, etc. as potential targets for inclusion. Rather, they attempt to refine those categories by paying attention to the distribution of social power (Sleeter, 1991). Empowerment of the disempowered is thus an important purpose of multicultural education, particularly the more critical approaches. In a society marred through much of its history by racism, sexism, and homophobia, attention to categories of race, culture, gender, and sexual orientation are a convenient, if imperfect, way of identifying the likely victims of disempowering social injustice and their victimizers. Thus there are really only two categories: the disempowered and the powerful.

While this simple dichotomy would seem to solve the problem of curricular abundance discussed above, it in fact constitutes another potentially idolatrous move that conceals the constructedness and fluidity of power. The insights of postmodernists like Foucault (1991) and others define a conception of power as a product of social discourse among various subject positions. Power is claimed or constructed through such discourse. Therefore, a particular subject position may possess power in one context yet be relatively powerless in another: a white woman, for instance, may enjoy a certain degree of social power as a result of her race and at the same time be disempowered in a sexist society. Furthermore, power is fluid; changes in social discourses can change the configurations of social power. Thus determining who are the powerful and who are the powerless becomes complicated indeed.

Other implications of the idea of empowerment seem contradictory. For instance, the notion of empowerment suggests either that the powerful share power with the powerless or that the powerless create power or take it from the powerful. In the first of these options the powerless are passive recipients of a gift from the powerful. As Ruiz (1991) asks, "what kind of power are they willing to give up" (p. 222). And Freire (1990) notes that such potentially "false generosity" preserves the power of the giver over the recipient in the very act of giving.

Does such multicultural education empower the powerless or the multicultural educator? Is this empowerment at all (Ellsworth, 1989)? The second option assumes that the powerless are not, in fact, powerless. If this is indeed the case, then what justification is there for multicultural education as empowerment?

> ...A PROPHETIC PRAGMATIC MULTICULTURAL EDUCATION WOULD HAVE AT ITS HEART A MORAL VISION OF JUSTICE AND LOVE RATHER THAN A BEWILDERING MULTIPLICITY OF REIFIED IDENTITIES.

AN ALTERNATIVE APPROACH TO MULTICULTURAL EDUCATION?

Postmodernism's deconstruction of the multicultural educator's categories has led some theorists to question the very viability of the idea of collective, transformative action implicit in multicultural education. The deconstruction of these categories seems to leave us with an aggregate of individual subject positions defined by the peculiarities of their particular positions rather than collective positions defined by similarities. Thus, individual resistance, rather than collective transformation, is the only possible change (Roman, 1993).

While such a retreat from the complexity and difficulty of multiculturalism's tranformative agenda maybe understandable, it is not justified. For multicultural education recognizes that the existential predicament of individual human beings—"death, despair, disillusionment, disease" and institutionalized forms of oppression (West, 1994, p. 140)—is an objective reality that falls disproportionately on the poor, on women, and on people of color. Multicultural education constitutes, in effect, a response, through education, to respond to a moral imperative to "alleviate the plight of the wretched of the earth" (West 1989, p. 235).

The critical deconstruction of the categories multicultural education has heretofore relied upon is not a call to abandon this moral imperative. It is, rather, a call to liberate that moral imperative from the idolatry of inclusion and empowerment. In the remainder of this essay, I will offer a rough, tentative sketch of a means of doing just that.

PROPHETIC PRAGMATIC EDUCATION

Cornel West's (1989) critical revision of the pragmatic tradition offers a philosophical framework whereby the moral imperative of multicultural education might be rescued from the idolatry of categorization. His *prophetic* pragmatism draws critically on three distinct intellectual traditions: the normative vision of Afro-American protestant Christianity, the critical insights of progressive Marxism, and the historicist sensibilities of American pragmatism (West, 1989, pp. 211–239). It critically revises each of these traditions by highlighting their strengths and combining them to compensate for the shortcomings of the others. Thus the

> . . . distinctive hallmarks of a prophetic pragmatist are a universal consciousness that promotes all-embracing democratic and libertarian moral vision, a historical consciousness that acknowledges human finitude and conditionedness, and a critical consciousness which encourages relentless critique and self-criticism for the aims of social change and personal humility. (West, 1989, p. 232)

Prophetic pragmatism locates itself within the tradition of American pragmatic philosophy running from Emerson through Dewey to contemporary pragmatists like Richard Rorty (West, 1989). Pragmatism's contribution to West's project is a historicist vision that recognizes the socially constructed and contingent nature of knowledge claims and the products of human cultures such claims ground. Thus pragmatism eschews the idolatrous tendencies of a multicultural education founded solely on the concepts of inclusion and empowerment because it foregrounds the contingency of all such social constructs (West, 1989, pp. 98–99).

However, pragmatism is deficient, according to West (1989, pp. 102–111), in its inadequate theorization of political and economic forces and its overly optimistic Emersonian theodicy. The first of these deficiencies is compensated for by deploying the insight of progressive—Gramscian—Marxist critique to understand how political and economic forces affect power relations and the lives of the poor (West,1991a, p. 87). But Marxism's inadequate theorization of culture and tendency toward the idolatry of power and class are balanced by pragmatism's insight into the historical contingency of all such crude categorizations and its democratic rejection of Marxist-inspired totalitarianism (West, 1989, pp. 69–111).

Pragmatism's second deficiency—its blindness to the existential reality of tragedy and evil—is compensated for by the normative vision of an Afro-American protestant Christianity which recognizes the dignity and fallenness of human beings called to struggle toward ethical ideals unattainable within history (West, 1982, pp. 15–20). Thus it provides a moral orientation which simultaneously grounds relentless criticism of injustice, recognizes the inability of fallible human beings to ever fully achieve these ethical ideals, and provides the loving criticism that sustains individuals in their struggle toward them.

While West's prophetic pragmatism is rooted in his Christian faith, he is nevertheless critical of the racism, sexism, and homophobia endemic to many religious communities (West, 1988, p. 210). Furthermore, his philosophy of prophetic pragmatism is not necessarily Christian or even religious. West acknowledges the prophetic energies of secular and other religious traditions (1991b, p. 129). However, unlike the mainstream of multicultural education, he recognizes that

> . . . the culture of the wretched of the earth is deeply religious. Since the Enlightenment most of the progressive energies among the intelligentsia have shunned religious channels. And in this day of global religious revivals progressive forces are reaping the whirlwind. Those of us who remain in these religious channels see clearly how myopic such an antireligious strategy is. The severing of ties to churches, synagogues, temples, and mosques by the left intelligentsia is tantamount to political suicide. (West, 1989, pp. 233–34).

West's project recognizes and harnesses the tremendous potential for ameliorative change present in religious communities and exemplified in the civil rights movement. But it does so without promoting one faith over another or religiosity over secularism and holds those religious communities accountable to critical scrutiny.

West calls for "race-transcending" prophetic leaders "who critique the powers that be and who put forward a vision of moral regeneration and political insurgency for the purpose of fundamental social change for all who suffer from socially induced misery" (West, 1993b, p. 46). Thus his prophetic pragmatism suggests a revision of multicultural education in the iconoclastic spirit of jazz, "an improvisational mode of protean, fluid, and flexible dispositions toward reality suspicious of either/or viewpoints, dogmatic pronouncements, or supremacist ideologies" (West, 1993b, p. 105).

It suggests a vision of multicultural education that would not ignore the reality of gender, religious and cultural identity, sexual orientation, or the unequal distribution of social power. It suggests a vision of multicultural education that would transcend those categories by recognizing their contingency and foregrounding the moral imperative implicit in multicultural education rather than reifying cultures as so many distinct individual identities that can be invited to a party or power as a physical currency that can be redistributed like taxes.

CONCLUSION

What would such a revision of multicultural education look like? It is impossible to do more than offer a rough sketch in the confines of this article. However, it is clear that a prophetic pragmatic multicultural education would have at its heart a moral vision of justice and love rather than a bewildering multiplicity of reified identities.

It would recognize and welcome the fact that this moral vision will be expressed in a variety of religious and not just secular languages. It would deploy and teach careful but relentless critique of all failures to realize that moral vision from within a supportive context governed by an ethic of love. It would eschew the idolatry of inclusion and empowerment without losing sight of the need to "alleviate the plight of the wretched of the earth."

Prophetic pragmatism may not bring peace to the culture wars, but it may well offer a less divisive plan of operations for multicultural education than the competing idolatries of eurocentrism and multiculturalism.

REFERENCES

American Association of University Women. (1992). *How schools shortchange girls.* New York: Marlow & Company.

Aufderheide, P. (1992). *Beyond p.c.: Toward a politics of understanding.* St. Paul, MN: Graywolf Press.

Banks, J. (1992). Multicultural education, history of. In M.L. Alkin (Ed.), *Encyclopedia of educational research,* vol. 3. New York: Macmillan.

Barber, B. (1992). *An aristocracy of everyone: The politics of education and the future of America.* New York: Oxford University Press.

Barfield, O. (1965). *Saving the appearances: A study in idolatry.* New York: Harcourt Brace Jovanovich.

Bloom, A. (1987). *The closing of the American mind.* New York: Simon & Schuster.

Dewey, J. (1938). *Experience and education.* New York: Collier Books.

D'Souza, D. (1991). The visigoths in tweed. In P. Aufderheide (Ed.), *Beyond p.c.: Toward a politics of understanding.* St. Paul, MN: Graywolf Press.

Ellsworth, E. (1989).Why doesn't this feel empowering? Working through the repressive myths of critical pedagogy. *Harvard Educational Review,* 59, (3), 297-324.

Foucault, M. (1990). *The history of sexuality,* vol. 1. New York: Vintage Books.

Freire, P. (1990). *Pedagogy of the oppressed.* New York: Continuum.

Gaddy, B., T. Hall, & R. Marzano. (1996). *School wars: Resolving our conflicts over religion and values.* San Francisco, CA: Jossey-Bass.

Gates, H. (1992). *Loose canons: Notes on the culture wars.* New York: Oxford University Press.

Martin, J. (1992). *The schoolhome: Rethinking schools for changing families.* Cambridge, MA: Harvard University Press.

Milligan, J. (1996a). Multiculturalism and the religious right: Is dialogue possible? *Journal of Thought,* 31 (1), pp. 45–54.

Milligan, J. (1996b). Religion, public education, and Dewey's call for an intelligent theory of education. *Educational Foundations,* 10 (3), pp. 69–84.

Milligan, J. (1998). Gender and the limits of inclusion: Should multiculturalism include fundamentalism? *Religious Education.* In press.

Nord, W. (1995). *Religion and American education: Rethinking a national dilemma.* Chapel Hill, NC: University of North Carolina Press.

Roman, L. (1993). White is a color! White defensiveness, postmodernism, and anti-racist pedagogy. In C. McCarthy & W. Crichlow (Eds.), *Race, identity and representation in education* (pp. 71–88). New York: Routledge.

Ruiz, R. (1991). The empowerment of language-minority students. In C. Sleeter (Ed.), *Empowerment through multicultural education* (pp. 217–229). Albany, NY: State University of New York Press.

Said, E. (1979). *Orientalism.* New York: Vintage.

Sleeter, C. (1991). *Empowerment through multicultural education.* Albany, NY: State University of New York Press.

West, C. (1982). *Prophesy deliverance! An Afro-American revolutionary Christianity.* Philadelphia, PA: Westminster Press.

West, C. (1988). *Prophetic fragments: Illuminations of the crisis in American culture and religion.* Grand Rapids, MI: William B. Eerdmans.

West, C. (1989). *The American evasion of philosophy: A genealogy of pragmatism.* Madison, WI: University of Wisconsin Press.

West, C. (1991a). *The ethical dimensions of Marxist thought.* New York: Monthly Review.

West, C. & bell hooks. (1991b). *Breaking bread: Insurgent black intellectual life.* Boston, MA: South End Press.

West, C. (1993a). *Beyond eurocentrism and multiculturalism, vol. 1: Prophetic thought in postmodern times.* Monroe, LA: Common Courage Press.

West, C. (1993b). *Race matters.* New York: Beacon Press.

West, C. (1994). *Keeping faith: Philosophy and race in America.* New York: Routledge.

Why Standardized Tests Threaten Multiculturalism

Statewide standardized tests force students to sacrifice learning about the cultural complexities that define our society.

Bill Bigelow

Under the banner of "higher standards for all," Oregon has joined the national testing craze. In fall 1998, the Oregon Department of Education field-tested its first-ever statewide social studies assessments. Many teachers were dismayed to discover that the tests were a multiple-choice maze that lurched about helter-skelter, seeking answers on World War I, Constitutional amendments, global climate, rivers in India, hypothetical population projections, Supreme Court decisions, and economic terminology.

Given the broad scope of the standards and the resulting randomness of the test questions they generated, an infinite number of facts could appear on future social studies tests. Teachers worry that to prepare our students for the tests, which students must pass to earn Oregon's 10th grade Certificate of Initial Mastery, we will have to turn our classrooms into vast wading pools of information for students to memorize.

The tests in Oregon are part of a national standards movement that has a democratic veneer. Proponents insist that all students will benefit from "higher expectations" and greater teacher, principal, and school "account-

ability." But as the Oregon example shows, standardization of social studies curriculums and assessments is hostile to good teaching. Social studies standardization threatens a multicultural curriculum—one that attempts to explain the world as it really exists; speaks to the diversity of our society; and aims not only to teach important facts, but also to de-

velop citizens who can make the world safer and more just.

Multiculturalism is a search to discover perspectives that have been silenced in traditional scholastic narratives. Multiculturalism attempts to uncover

At its core, multicultural teaching is an ethical, even political, enterprise. It recognizes our responsibility to fellow human beings and to the earth. It has heart and soul.

"the histories and experiences of people who have been left out of the curriculum," as educator Enid Lee emphasizes (1995, p. 9). Because multiculturalism is an undertaking that requires new scholarship and constant discussion, it is necessarily ongoing. Yet as researcher Harold Berlak points out, "Standardization and centralization of curriculum testing is an

© Hulton Getty Images

The "one best answer" approach on standardized tests vastly oversimplifies complex social processes, such as the unionization of industrial workers.

effort to put an end to a cacophony of voices on what constitutes truth, knowledge and learning and what the young should be taught. It insists upon one set of answers" (Berlak, in press).

A Lack of Critical Sensibility

Creating an official, government-approved social studies curriculum is bound to be controversial. Thus, state education officials "tried to stake a neutral ground" to win approval for the state's version of social reality (Learn, 1998). Not surprisingly, this attempt to be neutral and inoffensive means that the standards the state produced lack a critical sensibility and tend toward a conservative *Father Knows Best* portrait of society. For example, one typical 10th grade benchmark calls for students to "understand how the Constitution can be a vehicle

for change and for resolving issues as well as a device for preserving values and principles of society." Only? Is this how, say, Frederick Douglass or the Seminole leader Osceola would have seen the Constitution? Shouldn't students also understand how the Constitution can be (and has been) a vehicle for preserving class and race stratification—for example, Dred Scott and *Plessy* v. *Ferguson*—and for maintaining the privileges of dominant social groups? Abolitionist William Lloyd Garrison called the Constitution an "agreement with Hell" for its support of slavery.

The school curriculum will inevitably reflect the contradictions between a society's myths and realities. But a critical multicultural approach examines these contradictions, whereas standardization tends to paper over them. For example, another bench-

mark, "Explain how laws are developed and applied to provide order, set limits, protect basic rights, and promote the common good," similarly fails the multicultural test. Whose order, whose basic rights, are protected by laws? Are all social groups included equally in the term *common good*? Between 1862 and 1890, laws in the United States gave an area the size of Texas and Oklahoma to privately owned railroad companies, but gave virtually no land to African Americans freed from slavery. Viewing the Constitution and other U.S. laws through a multicultural lens would add depth to the facile one-sidedness of Oregon's "neutral" standards.

Standards Miss the Multicultural Mark

Indeed the "R" word, *racism*, is not mentioned in the 1998 11th grade field tests or in the social studies standards adopted in March 1998 by the Oregon board of education. Even if the only yardstick were strict historical accuracy, this would be a bizarre omission: The state was launched as a whites-only territory by the Oregon Donation Act and in racist wars of dispossession waged against indigenous peoples; the first constitution outlawed slavery but also forbade blacks from living in the state, a prohibition that remained law until 1927.

Perhaps state education officials are concerned that introducing the concept of racism to students could call into question the essentially harmonious world of "change and continuity over time" that underpins the standards project. Whatever the reason, students cannot make sense of the world today without carrying the idea of racism in their conceptual knapsack. If a key goal of multiculturalism is to account for how the past helped shape the present, and an important part of the present is social inequality, then Oregon's standards and tests earn a failing grade.

Despite the publication of state social studies standards and benchmarks, teachers or parents don't really know what students are expected to learn until they see the tests, which were developed by an out-of-state assessment corporation, MetriTech. As Wade W. Nelson points out in a frank article, "The Naked Truth About School Reform in Minnesota" (that might as well have been written about Oregon) (1998),

> The content of the standards is found only in the tests used to assess them. Access to the tests themselves is carefully controlled, making it difficult to get a handle on what these standards are. It seems ironic to me that basic standards—that which every student is expected to know or be able to do—are revealed only in tests accessible only to test-makers and administrators. This design avoids much of the debate about what these standards ought to be.

When we look directly at the tests, their limitations and negative implications for multiculturalism become most clear. Test questions inevitably focus on discrete facts, but cannot address the deeper, multifaceted meaning of facts. For example, in the field tests that Oregon piloted in fall 1998, one question asked which Constitutional amendment gave women the right to vote. Students could know virtually nothing about the long struggle for women's rights and get this question right. In contrast, they could know lots about the feminist movement and not recall that it was the 19th and not the 16th, 17th, or 18th Amendment (the other test choices) that gave women the vote.

Because there is no way to predict precisely which facts will be sought on the state tests, teachers feel pressured to turn courses into a "memory Olympics"; we simply cannot afford

© Hulton Getty Images

If a key goal of multiculturalism is to account for how the past helped shape the present, and an important part of the present is social inequality, then Oregon's standards and tests earn a failing grade.

to spend the time probing beneath the headlines of history.

Last year, my students at Franklin High School in Portland performed a role-play on the 1848 Seneca Falls, New York, women's rights conference, the first formal U.S. gathering to demand greater equality for women. The original assembly was composed largely of middle- to upper-class white women. I wanted my students not only to appreciate the issues that these women addressed and their courage, but also to consider the limitations imposed by their race, class, and ethnicity. Thus in our simulated 1848 gathering, my students portrayed women who were not at the original

conference—enslaved African Americans, Cherokee women who had been forcibly moved to Oklahoma on the Trail of Tears, Mexican women in the recently conquered territory of New Mexico, poor white New England mill workers—as well as the white middle- and upper-class reformers like Elizabeth Cady Stanton and Lucretia Mott who were in attendance.

In this more socially representative fictional assembly, students learned about the resolutions adopted at the original gathering and the conditions that prompted them, and they also saw firsthand how more privileged white women ignored other important issues, such as treaty rights of Mexican women, sexual abuse of enslaved African Americans, and workplace exploitation of poor white women, that a more diverse convention might have addressed.

The knowledge that my students acquired from this role-play consisted not only of "facts," although they learned plenty of these. They also exercised their multicultural social imaginations, listening for the voices that are often silenced in the traditional U.S. history narrative and becoming more alert to issues of race and class. However, this kind of teaching and learning takes time—time that could be ill-afforded in the fact-packing pedagogy required by multiple-choice tests. And after all their study, would my students have recalled which amendment gave the women the right to vote? If not, they would have appeared ignorant about the struggle for women's rights.

Likewise, my Global Studies students spend the better part of a quarter reading, discussing, role-playing, and writing about the consequences of European colonialism. They read excerpts from Okot p'Bitek's poignant book-length poem, *Song of Lawino,* about the lingering psychological effects of colonialism in Uganda; role-play a trial on the colonial roots of

deportations of foreign-born labor organizers, affect union membership?

And how about the Oregon test's reductive category of "worker"? Shouldn't students be alert to how race, ethnicity, and gender were and are important factors in determining one's workplace experience, including

kinds—racial, gender, class, linguistic, ethnic, national, environmental—to make explanations and propose solutions. It recognizes our responsibility to fellow human beings and to the earth. It has heart and soul.

Compare that with the sterile fact-collecting orientation of Oregon's standards and assessments. For example, a typical 49-question high school field test piloted in 1998 included seven questions on global climate, two on the location of rivers, and one on hypothetical world population projections. But not a single question in the test concerned the lives of people around the world or environmental conditions—nothing about increasing poverty, the global AIDS epidemic, rainforest destruction, unemployment rates, global warming, or efforts to address these crises. The test bounded aimlessly from one disjointed fact to another.

The tests represent the authority of the state, implicitly telling students, "Just memorize the facts, kids."

the Irish potato famine; and examine how Asian economies were distorted to serve the needs of European ruling classes. But when confronted with multiple-choice questions that demand that they recall isolated facts about colonialism in 1914, would my students answer correctly? As these examples illustrate, a multicultural curriculum is not so much about teaching facts as it is about nurturing a fuller understanding of society.

Misrepresenting Social Realities

Not surprisingly, Oregon's "one best answer" approach vastly oversimplifies complex social processes—and entirely erases ethnicity and race as categories of analysis. One question on a recent test reads: "In 1919, over 4.1 million Americans belonged to labor unions. By 1928, that number had dropped to 3.4 million. Which of the following best accounts for that drop?" It seems that the correct answer must be A: "Wages increased dramatically, so workers didn't need unions." All the other answers are clearly wrong, but is this answer "correct"? Do workers automatically leave unions when they win higher wages? Weren't mechanization and scientific management factors in undermining traditional craft unions? Did the post-World War I Red Scare, with systematic attacks on radical unions like the Industrial Workers of the World and

union membership? For example, in 1919, professional strikebreakers, hired by steel corporations, were told to "stir up as much bad feeling as you possibly can between the Serbians and the Italians." And more than 30,000 black workers, excluded from AFL unions, were brought in as strikebreakers (Zinn, 1980, p. 372). A multicultural awareness is vital to arriving at a full answer to this Oregon field-test question. But the state would reward students for choosing a historical sound bit that is as shallow as it is wrong.

What Tests Communicate

Another aspect of these tests is especially offensive to teachers: They don't merely assess, they also instruct. The tests represent the authority of the state, implicitly telling students, "Just memorize the facts, kids. That's what social studies is all about—and if teachers do any more than that, they're wasting your time." Multiple-choice tests undermine teachers' efforts to construct a rigorous multicultural curriculum because they delegitimate that curriculum in students' eyes: If it were important, it would be on the test.

At its core, multicultural teaching is an ethical, even a political, enterprise. Its aim is not just to impart lots of interesting facts—to equip students to be proficient Trivial Pursuit players—but to help make the world a better place. It highlights injustice of all

Indeed, the test's randomness may reveal another of its cultural biases. Oregon's standards and assessments make no distinction between knowledge and information. The state's version of social education would appear to have no purpose beyond the acquisition of large quantities of data. But for many cultures, the aim of knowledge is not bulk, but wisdom—insight into meaningful aspects about the nature of life. Writing in *Rethinking Schools,* Peter Kiang makes a similar point about the Massachusetts Teacher Test that calls into question the validity of enterprises such as these. He writes that

> by constructing a test based on a sequence of isolated, decontextualized questions that have no relationship to each other, the underlying epistemology embedded in the test design has a Western-cultural bias, even if individual questions include or represent "multicultural" content. Articulating and assessing a knowledge base requires examining not only what one knows, but also how one knows. (Kiang, 1998/99, p. 23)

Students "know" in different ways, and these differences are often cultural. Oregon nonetheless subjects all students to an abstract, data-heavy assessment device that does not gauge what or how they have learned. As Kiang points out, test makers address multicultural criticism by including individual questions about multicultural content—for example, by highlighting snippets of information about famous people of color like Martin Luther King Jr., Cesar Chavez, and Harriet Tubman. But these "heroes and holidays" additions cannot mask the fundamental hostility to multicultural education shown by standards and assessments like those initiated by Oregon.

The alternative? I want the state to abandon its effort to turn me into a delivery system of approved social information. I want it to support me and other teachers as we collaborate to create curriculum that deals forth-rightly with social problems, that fights racism and social injustice. I want it to acknowledge the legitimacy of a multicultural curriculum of critical questions, complexity, multiple perspectives, and social imagination. I want it to admit that wisdom is more than information—that the world can't be chopped up into multiple-choice questions and that you can't bubble-in the truth with a number-two pencil.

References

Berlak, H. (in press). Cultural politics, the science of assessment and democratic renewal of public education. In A. Filer (Ed.), *Assessment: Social practice and social product.* London: Falmer Press.

Kiang, P. (1998/99). Trivial pursuit testing. *Rethinking Schools. 12*(2), 23.

Learn, S. (1998, December 22). Oregon looks for middle ground with its draft history standards. *The Oregonian,* p. B2.

Lee, E. (1995). Taking multicultural, anti-racist education seriously. In D. Levine et al. (Eds.), *Rethinking schools: An agenda for change* (p. 9). New York: The New Press.

Nelson, W. W. (1998). The naked truth about school reform in Minnesota. *Phi Delta Kappan 79*(9), 681.

Zinn, H. (1980). *A people's history of the United States.* New York: Harper-Collins.

Bill Bigelow is a social studies teacher at Franklin High School, 5405 S. E. Woodward, Portland, OR 97206 (e–mail:bbpdx@aol.com). He is coeditor of the education reform journal *Rethinking Schools.*

Failing to Marvel:

The Nuances, Complexities, and Challenges of Multicultural Education

By Paulo M. Simões de Carvalho

The only phenomenon with which writing has always been concomitant is in the creation of cities and empires, that is the integration of large numbers of individuals into a political system, and their grading into castes or classes.

—Claude Lévi-Strauss,
Tristes Tropiques, 1955

On 16 November, 1532, in the Inca city of Cajamarca an encounter took place between two cultures that would ultimately decide the fate of one and preeminence of the other. It involved a meeting between Atahualpa, the last great Inca ruler, and the Spanish Dominican Friar, Vincent Valverde. Depending on the sources consulted, the episode unfolded in a variety of ways, but the end result was that the meeting concluded with the death of Atahualpa a few days later and with it the transference of the Inca empire to Spanish control.

At its most base level, Atahualpa's death was the result of a misunderstanding of cultural symbols. According to Francisco de Jeréz, the official Spanish chronicler to Juan Pizarro's expedition of 1532, the tragic encounter occurred during the administer-

Paulo M. Simões de Carvalho is a graduate student in history at the University of California at Berkeley. He thanks Judith Lessow-Hurley of the College of Education at San José State University for assistance in the preparation of this article.

ing of the *Requerimiento*, a royal edict of religious justification required to read before acts of conquest were undertaken.[1] It seems that when Fray Valverde handed Atahualpa a book (his missal), the Inca chief rejected it by tossing it to the ground.

Atahualpa's rejection of the book handed him represented many things at once. For the Spanish it signaled his rejection of their Christian God and more abstractly his rejection of writing and literacy as an expression of Western civilization and of the Spaniard's belief in their cultural superiority. Atahualpa's fatal error was that he did not realize that the revered book embodied the very essence of Western religion and culture at the time. His failure to marvel was enough to warrant the subsequent conquering of his kingdom.[2]

But the Spanish had proven just as ignorant. Only days before during a previous encounter the Spaniards were offered *chicha*, a ceremonial Inca drink. Their response had been similar to Atahualpa's; they rejected the mysterious substance presented to them by throwing it to the ground with the effect of equally insulting their hosts.

Although the events of 1532 might seem historically remote, their lessons bear a significant message into the present. It is a message that educators of multiculturalism would do well to heed. As demonstrated by both the Spanish and Inca alike, the misinterpretation of another culture's symbols can have disastrous effects. The fundamental risk in multicultural educa-

tion is that educators might unknowingly be tempted to interpret other cultures through Western lenses and, in doing so, diminish the very essence of the cultures they are trying to sustain.

The dilemma of the multicultural educator of what to emphasize in choosing the curriculum (what to value or deprecate, to emphasize or de-emphasize) is much the same as the dilemma of the anthropologist or ethnographer of today. This is because the very notion of "culture" is seen as a newly-problematic object of description.

The postmodernist critique underscores the limits on one's ability to understand and authentically define the culture of the anthropological "Other." Indeed, a close look at current trends in historiography and anthropology reveals the postmodernist revolution now taking place in the textual analysis of past histories and ethnographies. In the past polyvocality was restrained and orchestrated in traditional histories and ethnographies by giving to one voice, that of the historian or anthropologist, a pervasive, authorial function.

Today dialogism and polyphony question the textual, nuanced, monophonic authority characteristic of sciences that have claimed in the past to authentically represent other cultures.[3] Both historians and anthropologists have become self-reflexive, recognizing that in our interpretations of other cultures we are subconsciously and inescapably tied to our own cultural bias.

From *Multicultural Education*, Spring 1998, pp. 14–17. © 1998 by Caddo Gap Press, Inc. Reprinted by permission of *Multicultural Education*, the magazine of the National Association for Multicultural Education.

Knowledge is a power construct, and our creation of knowledge is culturally driven. With this in mind we must consider, indeed recognize, that historically our knowledge of, and attitudes toward, other cultures have been shaped by a centuries-old, at times subconscious campaign to elevate—even justify—the superiority of the West at the expense of the rest of the world. Or, as Columbia University literary scholar Edward Said might note, we are actively engaged in contact with other cultures to mystify, exoticize, even trivialize them. It is a process by which we subordinate and conquer other cultures with a virtual bombardment of universal, yet ultimately Western ideas.[4]

Within this critique multiculturalism, both as a theory and self-reflexive mode in attempting to define other cultures, is a Western, liberal construct. It is nothing more than a dialogical link toward an understanding of ourselves. In the words of James Clifford, a leading authority of postmodernist anthropological thought, "*culture* is always relational, an inscription of communicative processes that exist, historically, *between* subjects in relations of power."[5] It is essentially a problem of epistemological and cultural relativism that looms large.[6]

Multiculturalism presumes a naive universalism that all cultures can share the same values. More specifically, there is the operative belief that all cultures can coexist in a type of melting pot. This is most apparent in the Western values that govern our public schools. *De jure* and *de facto* segregation aside, it is perhaps only in the public school system where many cultures combine to form North American society. This is the only institution that begins to approximate the true image of the melting-pot community.

Accompanying the Western, liberal construct of multicultural education are various critiques of the limits of multicultural representation. Can an educator today authentically recognize and appreciate the many cultures in modern classrooms in states with such ethnically diverse populations as California or New York? How does postmodernism apply to the situation? Hans Bertens, a student of the critique, puts it as follows:

Postmodernism interrogates the power that is inherent in the discourses that surround us—and that is continually reproduced by them—and interrogates the institutions that support those discourses and are in turn supported by them. It attempts to expose the politics that are at work in representations and to undo institutionalized hierarchies, and it works against the hegemony of any single discursive system—which would inevitably victimize other discourses—in its advocacy of difference, pluriformity, and multiplicity. Especially important are its interest to those who from the point of view of the liberal humanist subject constitute the "Other"—the collective of those excluded from the privileges

> **The fundamental risk in multicultural education is that educators might unknowingly be tempted to interpret other cultures through Western lenses and, in doing so, diminish the very essence of the cultures they are trying to sustain.**

accorded by that subject to itself and its interest in the role of representations in the constitution of "Otherness."[7]

Multiculturalism, like postmodernism, carries with it many nuances. Its structure is much like the one depicted in Edward Said's *Orientalism* in that it has a tendency to dichotomize the human continuum into we-they contrasts and to essentialize the resultant Other—to speak their mind.[8] It is a one-sided equation in which the culture of the Other is placed within a Western framework, interpreted and qualified by Western values, and ultimately subjugated to Western deconstruction.

In multicultural education, the process of deconstruction takes place mainly through English language literacy. As the British scholar Ali Rattansi notes, in Great Britain the education of minority ethnic groups (primarily West Indian) is antithetical to anti-racism. Citing the 1985 Swann Report, a study that focused on the challenges of ethnic minority education in England, he states that:

The expectation that Asian minorities would simply blend into a ho-mogenous British or even English stew, perhaps adding some harmless spice, was revealed as not only hopelessly unrealistic but symptomatic of a form of racism which regarded "Britishness" and "Westernness" as the only touchstones of cultural value.[9]

For Rattansi, English language literacy becomes an analog for the "enforced cultural assimilation" of immigrant cultures. Writing in a postmodernist vein, he explains that the assimilationist thrust behind multicultural education is at its root essentialist.

Like all essentialism it assumes an obvious, definable, homogenous essence (British or Western culture) into which the hapless migrant might be inducted, given a suitable dose of English and an undiluted diet of the official school curriculum.[10]

As in Great Britain, public schools in the United States are in the business of making good "citizens." It is a term that is defined by the dominant, white, Anglo-American culture. Our educational curriculum is designed to solidify the ideals of our nation-state as exemplified in the U.S. Constitution, a document all educators are sworn to uphold. Conceptually, multicultural education is ideologically encumbered. Implicit in multiculturalism is that there exists a certain universalism in terms of cross-cultural values, mores, etc. But a universalism on whose terms, by whose definition? Moreover, a central goal of educational curriculum in public schools is that all children attain literacy by the time they graduate. But literacy on whose terms, in what language, and confined to whose cultural agenda?

In 1955 the French structural anthropologist Claude Lévi-Strauss wrote in his epochal *Triste Tropiques,* a study of the Nambikwara Indians of Brazil, that the primary function of writing or literacy was "to facilitate slavery."[11] He was not implying that writing as an ingenious method of communication and a means of preserving knowledge was in itself a form of chattel, but rather a means of ordering knowledge, of constructing and confining it.

Lévi-Strauss was touched by a pinch of imperialist nostalgia, a sympathy and admiration for the noble savages of his study. He lamented the inroads of Western civilization into the indigenous cultures of the Brazilian Amazon and correctly postulated that with the introduction of Western writing came a cultural clash. Writing, and the power of knowledge associated with it, placed the Nambikwara—and their lack of it—at the lowest rung of the ladder of Western cultural achievement.

Language has always been the companion of empire because it confines knowledge. In Great Britain as in the United States, English is the dominant language spoken in public schools. Instruction in English is the principal method by which ethnic minority cultures are consumed by the dominant culture. As such, the pedagogy of public education in this country becomes one of an imperialism of speech and ideas.

Cultural attitudes toward literacy vary. As Westerners we apply a certain sanctity to literacy as an expression of cultural achievement. We are surprised when we encounter other cultures that do not share this belief.

The complexities of the argument come into greater focus through comparative study. Again, Great Britain, whose culture is essentially the "mother culture" of the United States, offers a particularly alarming example of a do-good model of multicultural education gone awry.

The publication in Britain of the Pakistani writer Salman Rushdie's *The Satanic Verses* in 1989 provoked riots among Muslims. They viewed the work as heretical and blasphemous of the very foundation of Muslim culture and race. Book-burning demonstrations took place and Muslims appealed to the British government to ban sale of the book. These actions were met by a typically Western, liberal response that justified both the book's printing and condemned its burning.

The British political scholar Talal Asad raises important questions related to the Rushdie event and multiculturalism. One, "When immigrants bring new practices, beliefs, and discourses with them to Britain [or by comparative extension to the United States] do they extend the scope of British [or American] life or are they (conditionally) tolerated by the authentic British [or American] who are also the cultural majority?" And two, can cultural diversity be tolerated if it conflicts with the identity, or essentialism, of the dominant culture?[12]

For the Muslims, the Rushdie affair required they shed an inherent part of their culture—a reverence of the sacredness of print and its uses. It also required that they assimilate to an extent the values of the dominant culture. For Rattansi, the Rushdie affair "exposed the weakness of any benign multiculturalism premised on the assumption of easy harmony and pluralism."[13] But what of Rushdie? It could be argued that his fame came not from his book, but rather from the response it drew from Muslims around the world (including from the Ayatollah of Iran who issued a death sentence to the suddenly rocketed-to-fame writer). Rushdie seems to have correctly called the bluff of the posture of Britain's dominant culture toward multiculturalism and all it entailed. Writing before the fact, Rushdie proclaimed his prognosis

of the assimilationism implicit in Britain's soft handling of multiculturalism. Himself a product of a multicultural world, the region of East Pakistan and India—a world of identities fabricated by the legacy of British colonial rule—Rushdie sees the problem of Britain's confrontation with her multiculturalism as the problem of cultural identity in the post-colonial dialect.

Rather than resist acculturation, Rushdie embraces it, for India is nothing more to him than an imaginary homeland, a power/knowledge construct of Great Britain and of the West. For him culture evolves and assimilation is a process of that evolution. His view holds that although the world's movement toward the English language can be termed a kind of "linguistic neo-colonialism." It could be considered just plain pragmatism on the part of many of the world's governments and educationists, according to your point of view."[14]

Rushdie takes up the issue of the power of language and the meaning and impact of the literacy that accompanies it. He views problematically the genre of "Commonwealth literature," which for him is like the genre of multicultural literature produced in the United States. All, however, is written in English, a fact that sets parameters, confines, and reduces authenticity. For Rushdie, such genres portray voices of fabricated identities—fabricated identities similar to the one Said's *Orientalism* laments so eloquently. He writes:

> What we are facing here is the bogey of Authenticity. "Authenticity" is the respectable child of old-fashioned exoticism. It demands that sources, forms, style, language and symbol all derive from a supposedly homogenous and unbroken tradition. Or else.[15]

On this point, Rushdie suggests that Commonwealth and multicultural literature combine to segregate and form a "ghetto" out of the culture they hope to expose.

> Not only [i]s it a ghetto, but it [i]s actually an exclusive ghetto. And the effect of creating such a ghetto [i]s to change the meaning of the far broader term "English literature"—which I'd always taken to mean simply the literature of the English language—into something far narrower, something topographical, nationalistic, possibly even racially segregationist.[16]

Perhaps it is not surprising that Rushdie defends the assimilation aspects of multiculturalism with respect to its evolution-

ary power both upon the minority and dominant culture. If language is a prominent feature of both culture and colonization, then according to Rushdie:

> Those peoples who were once colonized by the language are now rapidly remaking it, domesticating it, becoming more and more relaxed about the way they use it—assisted by the English language's enormous flexibility and size, they are carving out large territories for themselves within its frontiers.[17]

For Rushdie no culture, minority or dominant, can remain static. And multiculturalism's feigned efforts to preserve the Other's culture through Western lenses is contrary to his and the post-modernist's dialectic. If anything, it is merely part of it.

It is the opinion of this author that multiculturalism (and the educational approach and curriculum associated with it) reveals more an identity crisis within the dominant culture of the United States than of one within the perceived "minorities" that it professes to rescue. It is part and parcel of the politics of blame in a society where the racial minority population is booming. It operates, still however, within the discourse of the West. In the words of Said, "it shuts out even as it includes, compresses, and consolidates."[18]

Teachers take cultural baggage into the classroom of which frequently they are not aware. They instill values that are in many instances uniquely Western and at times uniquely North European. In the experience of this author and educator, many teachers profess a faith in the goals of multicultural education but do not realize that, in accordance with the post modernist critique, in and of itself multicultural education is an impossibility.

In multicultural environments many voices clamor for expression. The challenge of the multicultural educator is to recognize those voices but at the same time recognize his or her own as that of the West and, more specifically, that of the dominant culture. In essence, multicultural educators, like anthropologists, need to become critically self-reflexive. Ali Rattansi puts the dilemma quite succinctly and perhaps, in closing, it is worth citing here.

> The educational prescription is therefore a curricular dose of knowledge about those "other cultures," taught in a variety of sometimes imaginative ways. The problem with this is not merely that there has been very little serious thinking within multiculturalism about how "cultural understanding" ac-

tually occurs, about its forms, mechanisms and limits. What, after all, does it mean to *understand* any culture, including one's own, whatever that might be in ethnic, class, or any other terms? The more subversive possibility is that the discourse of prejudice contains an element that threatens the foundations of multiculturalism from within. That is, there is a contradiction between the *rationalism* of the multiculturalist project, which recommends a reduction of prejudice by teaching a combination of facts and cultural empathy, and the insistence, also within the discourse of prejudice, that prejudice involves a strong element of *irrationalism*.[19]

Notes

1. For an introductory discussion see Charles Gibson, *Spain in America* (New York: Harare and Row, 1996), 38–47.

2. For the most up-to-date treatment of the event see Patricia Seed, "'Failing to Marvel': Atahualpa's Encounter with the Word," *Latin American Research Review* 26:1 (1991): 7–32.

3. James Clifford & George E. Marcus, *Writing Culture: The Poetics and Politics of Ethnography* (Berkeley, CA: University of California Press, 1986), 15.

4. See Edward W. Said, *Culture and Imperialism* (New York: Alfred A. Knopf, 1993).

5. Clifford & Marcus, 15.

6. Ali Rattansi, "Changing the Subject? Racism, Culture and Education," in Ali Rattansi & J. Donald, eds., *'Race', Culture, and Difference* (London, United Kingdom: Sage, 1992), 39.

7. Hans Bertens, *The Idea of the Postmodern: A History* (London, United Kingdom: Routledge, 1995), 8.

8. See Edward W. Said, *Orientalism* (New York: Vintage Books, 1979).

9. Rattansi, 13.

10. *Ibid.*, 15.

11. Claude Lévi-Strauss, *Tristes Tropiques* (New York: Penguin Books, 1992), 296–299.

12. Talal Asad, "Multiculturalism and British Identity in the Wake of the Rushdie Affair." *Politics and Society* 18 (1990): 458–459.

13. Rattansi, 39.

14. Salman Rushdie, *Imaginary Homelands: Essays and Criticism, 1981–1991* (New York: Granta, 1991), 64.

15. *Ibid.*, 67.

16. *Ibid.*, 63.

17. *Ibid.*, 64.

18. Said, *Culture and Imperialism*, 22.

19. Rattansi, 28.

Unit Selections

Key Points to Consider

❖ What are the primary gender issues in multicultural school settings?

❖ What should children learn about the cultural heritages and values of other children in their schools?

❖ How do social class differences relate to misunderstandings among students from different social positions in a community?

❖ What can educators learn from developing close communications linkages with the families of their students?

❖ What challenges do minority students encounter that majority students in a desegregated school do not encounter?

❖ How does community structure affect adolescent identity development?

❖ What can teachers do to foster positive personal identity development in their students?

 **Links** | **www.dushkin.com/online/**

These sites are annotated on pages 4 and 5.

People are impacted by many social forces as they interact with others in the process of forming themselves as individuals. Multicultural education can help students as well as teachers to identify those social forces that affect their personal development.

The development of each person's unique concept of self (the development of one's identity as a person) is the most important developmental learning task that any of us undertake. The preschool, elementary, and secondary school years are ones in which each of us learns critically important cognitive and affective strategies for defining ourselves, others, and the world. Multicultural education seeks to help people develop intellectual and emotional responses to other people that will be accepting and empathic. There has been much psychological and psychiatric research over the past few decades on the differences between prejudiced and tolerant (accepting) personalities. One opportunity educators have as they work with students in school settings is to provide good examples of accepting, tolerant behavior and to help students develop positive, affirmative views of themselves and others. Gordon A. Allport, in his classic book *The Nature of Prejudice,* commented in his chapter on "The Tolerant Personality" that we could be "doubly sure" that early instruction and practice in accepting diversity is important in directing a child toward becoming a tolerant person. Thus, we take up the topic of personal identity development in this unit.

As educators we need to see the interconnections among such factors as gender, social class, position in society, racial or ethnic heritage, and the primary cultural values that inform the way people see the world and themselves. We need to be sensitive to their visions of who they are and of how things are in the world. We need to "see our clients whole." It is important for teachers to set positive examples of acceptance, open-mindedness, empathy, compassion, and concern for the well-being of each student.

We need to help students to understand themselves, to define their strengths and their concerns, and to empower them to encounter their own personal social reality critically. This is a task each person must learn to do in childhood and adolescence in order to empower themselves to interpret and evaluate their own experience. This task can be integrated and effectively achieved within the intellectual mission of the school. One way to do this is to encourage students to critically interpret and evaluate the texts that they read and to discuss issues in class openly and actively. Each student needs to be able to explore the boundaries of his or her intellectual strengths and weaknesses and to explore the social boundaries encountered in school and out of school.

Multicultural education is intended for and needed by all students in order for them to develop a sensitivity to the many varying heritages and backgrounds that make up the United States and Canada and to forge their own conception of who they are as people. Why should only one cultural heritage be thoroughly taught while all others are essentially ignored in elementary and secondary school years in a pluralistic national social environment, the demographics of which are changing so dramatically? Cultural values are of primary importance in the process of a person's conceptualization of him- or herself. This unit's articles explore various models of human interaction and the psychosocial foundations for the formation of knowledge bases of students. How students form social groups in culturally integrated school settings is explored along with the behavioral differences among members of "loose-knit" and "tight-knit" social groups in desegregated school settings. The ways in which students define themselves and their possibilities as they move across or are trapped within their perceived social boundaries in school and community settings are explored. How educators can better utilize the knowledge bases of minority cultural families in assisting minority students to achieve better social integration into mainstream school settings is also examined. The importance of educators trying to establish more effective communications linkages between students' family and cultural environments is further examined. The multiple social roles students frequently have to play, both in and out of school, are another phenomenon in personality development that receives analysis in these essays.

Students live in a hierarchy of social contexts in which their racial, cultural, gender, and social class backgrounds, and the degree of their personal identification with each of these factors, influence their important choices and decisions regarding their own identity. Some of the research on how teachers can achieve more effective intercultural socialization is also considered. One of the questions being studied in desegregated school settings concerns the circumstances in which higher rates of intercultural friendship develop. How do we get all cultural group members to learn each others' cultural heritages? Helping students to learn from the cultural perspectives of other groups so that all students might better comprehend alternative, diverse definitions of their social environments is one of the tasks of multicultural education. Another purpose of multicultural education programming is to teach tolerant, accepting attitudes toward others of differing cultural backgrounds. Allport and several other major psychiatrists and social psychologists of past decades have taught us that prejudice and tolerance (acceptance) are learned behaviors. We can learn to be accepting, caring, compassionate persons. Educators are not powerless in the face of the prejudiced view many students bring to school from their homes.

The essays in this unit are relevant to courses in educational policy studies and leadership, cultural foundations of education, sociology or anthropology of education, history and philosophy of education, and curriculum theory and construction, among others.

Reducing the Effects of Racism in Schools

By modifying curriculum and instruction and by addressing expressions of racism, schools can help students move beyond tolerance to acceptance, understanding, and celebration of racial and cultural differences.

Sandra Parks

At the C. W. Henry School, an urban, multiethnic middle school in Philadelphia, Pennsylvania, Merri Rubin helps her students work with students from an upper-middle-class, white suburban school to compose, produce, and perform a musical on racial tolerance.

> ## We have shifted from concerns about segregation to issues of equity.

Funded by the Southern Poverty Law Center and the American Music Theater Festival, this project not only features the content of interethnic understanding, but also requires students from different racial, cultural, and economic backgrounds to work together.

At Dreher High School in Columbia, South Carolina, Annette Walker serves as faculty advisor for the school's racial task force. Although the school's population is racially balanced, students initiated the task force to move beyond tolerance to acceptance, understanding, and celebration of racial and cultural differences. The task force meets weekly to share information that is sometimes controversial and difficult to talk about. Students build trust and empathy and gain experience in dealing with racial issues.

Like Rubin and Walker, educators are increasingly undertaking a daunting educational reform—reducing the effects of racism in schools. In the last 40 years, as a profession and as individuals, we have shifted from concerns about segregation—removing legal constraints or policy barriers based on race or gender—to issues of equity—ensuring that all students experience challenging instruction that supports their personal, academic, and professional growth. However, research on the resegregation of U.S. schools (Orfield & Eaton, 1996) and the inequalities in school funding (Riddle & White, 1993) indicates that significant issues remain unresolved.

Confronting the Roots of Racism

To make continued progress toward solving problems of access and equity, we must confront the root cause of such practices and policies. To mitigate the fears, misconceptions, and disappointments that racism creates and to develop learning communities where diversity contributes to the richness of learning, we must remedy the insidious and pervasive effects of personal and institutional racism.

First, educators must address a tough issue: humankind's difficulty in acknowledging racism and its consequences. Like other conditions that create dysfunctionality in individuals, relationships, and institutions, racism thrives on denial. Unless one holds extremely bigoted beliefs, most people do not perceive the influences of racism in themselves or in their peers. Fair-minded, service-oriented educators consider racism to be inconsistent with the values that attracted them to teaching and therefore do not recognize that their own attitudes and behavior may be tinged with its effects.

To confront racism in their own attitudes, individual educators must be willing to examine unconscious, often deeply held assumptions; to acknowledge their own privilege or resentments; and to recognize how their own values, priorities, and attitudes, and those of others of different ethnic or cultural groups, are expressed in community life and in school. To heal personal and institutional racism requires preservice and inservice education characterized by insight and sensitivity that is unprecedented in current professional development practices.

Getting Started

Recognizing racism involves acknowledging beliefs, attitudes, and symbols that are legitimized by those with cultural and political power and are so-

From *Educational Leadership,* April 1999, pp. 14-18. © 1999 by the Association for Supervision and Curriculum Development (ASCD). All rights reserved. Reprinted by permission.

cialized in successive generations (Derman-Sparks & Phillips, 1997). Once educators acknowledge the nature of racism, they can explore the relationship between racism and other issues, such as teen violence, safe schools, gang behavior, drop-out and suspension rates, diversity and equity in per-

soning, emotional intelligence instruction, and critical thinking.

Abatement involves reducing the tensions and barriers created by intercultural or interracial discord. Unless strained relations have erupted into incidents that the public cannot ignore, teachers and administrators tend to

- changing dispositions of certainty about other cultures to become curious and receptive of new understandings, and
- understanding others' experiences and transforming one's own assumptions and views before seeking solutions.

Minimizing racism in schools involves a careful examination of the total educational program.

sonnel policies and school administration, poor achievement among students of color, inequity in school funding, and the needs of children living in poverty. Such school problems directly or indirectly reflect past or present racism and may not be meaningfully remedied until racism is addressed.

To approach this initiative, teachers and administrators identify the conditions that reducing racism would ameliorate. Once educators clarify the immediate and long-term benefits of reducing racism, they can decide what combination of interventions for prevention, abatement, and healing will address local needs and goals.

Often, school districts undertake diversity training or a multicultural education program without being clear about what they expect such initiatives to accomplish. For example, if student behavior at a local high school reflects racist attitudes, instituting a multicultural education program aimed at preventing racism is not likely to address immediate conflicts and reduce tensions. Peer mediation, conflict resolution, or antiviolence education may be necessary initially to create a culture of openness before students can realize the benefits of multicultural education.

Prevention involves classroom instruction and professional development that identifies racist influences and prevents them from taking hold in hearts and minds. Such efforts include antiracism curriculums, peace education, global education, moral rea-

minimize or deny divisive influences. Abatement involves techniques to mitigate distress, such as conflict resolution, peer mediation, and diversity training for faculty. It also includes activities to promote communication and interdependence, such as service learning, cooperative learning, and community mentoring.

Healing the effects of racism is the approach with which individuals and communities have had the least experience, although it offers remarkable opportunities for personal and institutional renewal. For people of color, healing entails developing a greater understanding of and security in their own ethnic identity, viewing their own and other ethnic groups more objectively, establishing meaningful relationships and coalitions with whites and other groups, and becoming antiracist in their own spheres of influence. For whites, this process includes developing an understanding of their own racial and cultural identity, engaging in a self-examination of their participation in racism, working effectively in multiracial settings, and becoming actively antiracist (Tatum, 1995).

Sherlock Graham-Haynes (1998), who implemented a racial healing project with youth groups in Massachusetts, describes elements of the process:

- developing experiential and conceptual knowledge of the oneness of the human family,
- respecting the spiritual and material values of cultural groups,
- gaining understanding of one's own and others' experiences and challenges,

Program Changes

Minimizing racism in schools involves a careful examination of the total educational program to ensure that

- curriculum promotes cultural competence and appreciates ethnic diversity;
- instructional methods promote cooperation, interaction, and success for all students, regardless of background, language proficiency, social class, or learning style;
- assessment practices include alternative methods that allow for cultural differences and encourage community review to ensure an equitable appraisal of students' work;
- a school culture of oneness supports growth of all students; and
- public conversation and policy making are sensitive to the perceptions and values of the total community.

Multicultural education is the key curriculum reform in combating racism. Cultural competence is the necessary but not sufficient condition for students and teachers to acknowledge and appreciate the values, experiences, and contributions of all groups within the human family. Meaningful multicultural education allows students to relate the strengths and values that have sustained people from other cultural groups to the students' own challenges, experiences, and struggles.

The public's growing awareness of the value of multicultural education is reflected in a 1998 Ford Foundation poll of 2,011 registered U.S. voters. Ninety-four percent believe that the growing diversity in the United States makes it important to understand people who are different from themselves. Sixty-six percent believe that colleges should explicitly increase diversity in higher education. Seventy-two percent believe that students are more likely to learn workplace skills, such as teamwork, problem solving, and communication, if college courses teach about diversity (Marklein, 1998).

However, the Florida College Student Diversity Study, also funded by the Ford Foundation, surveyed 610 randomly selected students at 11 Florida public and private institutions, including 2 traditionally black colleges. It reported that 58 percent of the students believe that diversity education creates division and conflict. Forty percent characterize diversity education as nothing more than political correctness, with more African American or Hispanic students than white students expressing that view (Van Norstrand, 1998). Such findings remind us that one residual effect of racism in the lives of people of color is an understandable skepticism about positive change in racial attitudes. Because meaningful multicultural education must deal with substantive issues that touch people's lives, perhaps a generation of students and teachers may be uncomfortable and disappointed as the content and the conduct of multicultural education evolve toward greater effectiveness in combating racism.

Banks (1993) describes five components of multicultural education that play a direct role in reducing racism:

■ Content integration: using examples, data, and information from a variety of cultures to illustrate the key concepts, principles, generalizations, and theories in subject areas.

■ Knowledge construction: helping students understand how knowledge is created and influenced by factors of race, ethnicity, gender, and social class.

■ Prejudice reduction: developing strategies to help students acquire positive racial attitudes.

■ An equity pedagogy: using instructional techniques that promote cooperation and include the learning and cultural styles of diverse groups.

■ An empowering school culture: creating a learning environment in which students from diverse racial, ethnic, and social groups believe that they are heard and are valued and experience respect, belonging, and encouragement.

Components of a Multicultural Curriculum

Because of their discomfort with racism and lack of preparedness in dealing with it, teachers seek well-articulated curriculums to help themselves and their students address the issue effectively (see box). Although implementing these programs may not change racial attitudes, each of the following initiatives contributes to students' understanding and openness about issues surrounding race if the topic is addressed directly in classroom discussions and instructional materials.

■ *Character education* helps students understand that the qualities of being a good person are expressed in practices across cultures and are not exclusively demonstrated by individuals in one's own group.

■ *Moral education* clarifies principles of ethical behavior that promote understanding, respect, caring, and fairness toward all people.

■ *Peace education* demonstrates the quality of human interactions when divisive influences have been minimized or eliminated.

■ *Peer mediation and conflict resolution* enact strategies for reducing discord created by overt or covert racism.

■ *Emotional intelligence instruction* helps students manage fears or resentments resulting from misapprehension or from experiences of interracial conflict.

■ *Service learning* builds community and gives students purposeful experiences with people of ethnic groups or social classes with whom they do not commonly interact.

■ *Antiviolence education* teaches students to recognize problematic situations and to take steps to reduce violence that results from racist influences, such as gang behavior.

■ *Critical thinking* instruction teaches strategies for making well-founded judgments, uncovering assumptions, evaluating sources of information, analyzing arguments, fostering fair-mindedness, controlling impulsivity in action or belief, and considering other views.

■ *Global education* addresses racism as a human problem. In addition to the spiritual and interpersonal principles that students learn in confront-

Antiracist Resources

Anti-Bias Curriculum: Tools for Empowering Young Children. Guidelines, activities, and resources. Washington: National Association for the Education of Young Children, 1509 16th St., N.W., Washington, DC 20036.

Teaching Tolerance. Practical materials, resources, and techniques for elementary and secondary classrooms. Used in 55,000 schools, its video-and-text teaching kits *America's Civil Rights Movement, The Shadow of Hate,* and *Starting Small: Teaching Tolerance in Preschool and the Early Grades* are free upon written request. Education Department, Southern Poverty Law Center, P. O. Box 548, Montgomery, AL 36101-0548.

A World of Difference. An antiprejudice and diversity awareness program for educators and families provides an interdisciplinary curriculum, instructional materials, activities, and resource

guides for K–6 classrooms. A World of Difference Institute, Anti-Defamation League of B'nai B'rith, 823 United Nations Plaza, New York, NY 10017.

Facing History and Ourselves. A course for grades 8–12 uncovers the roots of prejudice in students' own lives. It offers case studies of the Holocaust and U.S. history and relates historical and personal examples of racism to students' own actions. Facing History and Ourselves National Foundation, 16 Hurd Rd., Brookline, MA 02445.

Racism and Human Development. A 15-week course for upper division or graduate studies. Activities can serve as a guide for secondary or postsecondary curriculums. Course goals are described in *Teaching/Learning Anti-Racism* by Louise Derman-Sparks and Carol Brunson Phillips (New York: Teachers College Press, 1997).

ing racism, they gain greater understanding of their national history, world history, global conditions, and current events. They can identify racist influences that underlie international conflicts and the challenges needed to overcome them.

A Long-Term Challenge

Healing the effects of racism is a long-term, voluntary process of personal and institutional transformation. Mandated staff development and quick-fix remedies frustrate and disappoint teachers, students, and the community. Educators must take time to define the issues, to examine best practices, and to honor the evolutionary nature of personal and community change. Educators who undertake the goal of reducing racism find several program development factors to be significant:

■ Individuals and institutions must commit themselves to healing the effects of racism. They must become comfortable about their own and other people's discomfort about race. Learning to face racism and to talk about it transformatively with others requires compassion toward oneself and others and sufficient intellectual character to not abandon the effort as it becomes distressing.

■ Individuals who pursue their own inner work regarding racism and who are sufficiently knowledgeable about the transformative process can mediate such conversations.

■ Understanding and confronting racism involve recognizing its expression across all cultural groups.

■ Effective multicultural and antiracism instruction in preservice teacher education is crucial to decreasing racism in the long term.

■ Meaningful change involves confronting racism at both a personal and an institutional level. Teachers, administrators, teacher educators, and community advisors must all have an opportunity for change and self-renewal.

■ School programs must ensure a quality education for children of poverty. Past and present conditions of racism contribute to reduced expectations, opportunities, and resources for students of color who live in poverty. The influence of racism result in policies and conditions that are debilitating for children and young adults, perpetuating rather than reducing the cycle of poverty.

■ White administrators, teachers, and teacher educators must largely undertake leadership responsibility. To identify subtle but insidious racism within past and present policies, community relations, and instructional practices, decision makers must become aware of their own beliefs and dispositions. In most school districts, this introspective task is undertaken by educators of European descent who may not have previously understood the perceptions of people of color or appreciate the personal challenges that individuals of other ethnic groups experience in their own schools or districts. Examining one's own attitudes and experiences of racism is a complex process that requires time, compassion, and commitment (Kivel, 1996).

■ Decision makers who seek to remedy the effects of racism depend on constituents who understand and support such efforts. That constituency becomes frustrated and confounded by public policies and utterances that disclose racist connotations or that support the conditions or attitudes that perpetuate the effects of racism.

The organizational health of schools rests on the values, behaviors, and attitudes of all its members. Although racism may be covert, it nevertheless affects the moral life of schools, the vitality of faculties and students, and the peace and well-being of all participants. To reduce the effects of racism in the lives of students and teachers, schools must move beyond teaching tolerance to become "beloved communities," learning environments free of "the daily dose of tension, suspicion, and distrust that crosses racial lines in both directions and eats away at human potential on every side" (St. Rain, 1998)—a worthy undertaking for a new millennium.

> To reduce the effects of racism in the lives of students and teachers, schools must move beyond teaching tolerance to become "beloved communities."

References

Banks, J. (1993, September). Multicultural education: Development, dimensions, and challenges. *Phi Delta Kappan, 75*(1), 22–28.

Derman-Sparks, L., & Phillips, C. B. (1997). *Teaching/learning anti-racism.* New York: Teachers College Press.

Graham-Haynes, S. (1998, October). Workshop materials. Durham, NC: ReOrganics.

Kivel, P. (1996). *Uprooting racism: How white people can work for racial justice.* Gabriola Island, BC, Canada: New Society Publishers.

Marklein, M. (1998, October 7). Diversity education important to voters. *USA Today*, p. 12A.

Orfield, G., & Eaton, S. (1996). *Dismantling desegregation: The quiet reversal of Brown v. Board of Education.* New York: Norton.

Riddle, W., & White, L. (1993). *Variations in expenditures per pupil among local educational agencies within the states.* Washington, DC: Congressional Research Service.

St. Rain, J. (1998). *Nine reasons to work for race unity: A Baha'i perspective.* Bloomington, IN: Special Ideas.

Tatum, B. (1995, October). *Stages of racial/ethnic identity development in the United States.* Paper presented at the meeting of the National Association for Multicultural Education, Washington DC.

Van Norstrand, D. (1998). *The 1990 Florida college student diversity education study.* Coral Springs, FL: Mar's Surveys.

Sandra Parks is an author of professional and student books on analytical thinking and a staff development consultant on multicultural education at Thinking Works, P.O. Box 468, St. Augustine, FL 32084.

Culturally Authentic Bias

Just because a book is "multicultural" doesn't mean it is free of stereotypes. Many cultures have stories replete with bias.

BY MARTA I. CRUZ-JANZEN

As an elementary school teacher, I constantly searched for exciting literature to share with my students. My motto: A good book a day keeps the blues away. I was particularly eager to find good multicultural books. Often, I rushed to grab everything—anything—I found.

One day, I was brought up short by a comment from one of my fourth grade students. We were reading "The Rainbow Colored Horse," a popular legend from Puerto Rico. There are numerous versions of the story, but in this one, a poor young man wins the "hand" of a beautiful and wealthy Spanish "senorita" even though the two have never met. Her father had offered her in marriage, without her consent, to any man who could perform the required feat.

"That's a stupid way to find a husband," my fourth grader said. "Just because some guy can ride a horse and throw a ball on your lap doesn't mean that you are going to like him. You just don't marry anyone off the street."

I stopped to think. I realized that, despite good intentions, I was perpetuating stereotypes in the name of multiculturalism.

Over the years, I have come to an important understanding. Many cultures have stories that are replete with biases that can hurt children. Just because a book is "multicultural" doesn't mean it is free of bias.

In the Latino culture, which I know best, there are any number of biases. In the children's literature, there is a litany of beautiful Spanish "senoritas" who sit quietly in their balconies or town plazas looking their best and waiting for caballeros to per-

Growing up biracial in Puerto Rico made me aware at a very young age of the racism in Latino culture.

form noble feats and claim them in marriage. The stories are entirely about men, including fathers, brothers, and total strangers, making decisions for women.

Some will say that these are only children's songs, games, and popular folklore. Why worry so much? But these tales can have a cumulative effect on children and promote negative attitudes and perceptions.

MULTICULTURAL RACISM

Growing up biracial in Puerto Rico made me aware at a very young age of the racism in Latino culture. Although family and friends called me triguena (wheat colored), I recall classmates' and even teachers' cruel taunts because I stood out. They told me,

"Eres una mosca en un vaso de leche" (You are a fly in a glass of milk). When I powdered my face, children laughed and called me Cucarachita Martina. I was reminded, "No eres arroz con leche" (You are not rice with milk). When I dressed in my best, I was taunted, "La puerca de Juan Bobo" (Juan Bobo's pig).

Arroz Con Leche (Rice With Milk), Cucarachita Martina (Cockroach Martina), and Juan Bobo (Simple John) are part of the rich Puerto Rican oral tradition. They are culturally authentic folklore. I grew up disliking these stories and characters and shied away from using them in my own classroom. They always brought back painful memories of how I was taunted. I continue to be concerned about the use of such folk tales in today's classrooms by teachers who seem to be unaware of their subtle, damaging messages.

In Arroz Con Leche, children in a circle sing: "Rice and milk wants to wed a little widow from the capital state, who can embroider and knows how to knit, and in the same safe place her needle does keep." A child inside the circle responds: "I am the little widow, a daughter of the king. I want to get married and cannot find with whom." The group sings back: "If you are so beautiful and can't find with whom, here you have plenty, choose at your taste." Children imitate church bells: "Ti-lin, Ti-lan, . . ." The child inside chooses among the players: "With you, yes. With you,

From *Rethinking Schools,* Fall 1998, p. 5. Reprinted by permission. *Rethinking Schools,* an urban educational journal.

no. With you, my dear, I will marry." The chosen child steps inside the circle and the game begins again.

Arroz con leche is a sweet hot cereal for children. It is also a popular expression for a light-skinned and often preferred child—as white as rice and milk and just as desirable or sweet. This is not unique to Latino culture; other cultures have references for very "fair" children. We often hear "milk and honey" for blond children and "peaches and cream" for those with rosy cheeks.

The game Arroz Con Leche reflects Latino gender and racial biases favoring boys and light-skinned people. In the game, a man seeks and chooses a wife and sets his expectations: She must be a good cook, seamstress, and tidy housekeeper. The wife sets no expectations for her husband; she just wants to get married, and it doesn't matter much to whom.

Cucarachita Martina is another popular folk tale. Martina is a beautiful, hard-working cockroach who finds a gold coin while sweeping and immediately spends it on face powder to make herself even more beautiful in order to find a husband. She is dark-skinned. Historically, Spanish women (as do other women around the world) powder their faces to appear lighter. As a child, I often heard Black Latinas mockingly called "cucarachas empolvas" (powdered cockroaches).

Martina cleans house and polishes all day, then sits on her balcony with her powdered face, displaying her worthiness of marriage. Martina marries Perez Mouse because he has the sweetest voice. We never find out what skills Perez possesses besides singing "Chui, chui, chui" and being a charmer. Martina takes care of him until he succumbs to his curiosity and greed and falls into the hot stew she is preparing.

JUAN BOBO THE 'NOODLEHEAD'

Juan Bobo (Simple John) depicts a silly "noodlehead." He is Puerto Rico's favorite fool and simpleton and has been the mainstay of jokes and laughter for generations.

Juan Bobo does nothing right. His mother is presented as a single woman who overdresses in bright provocative clothing and excessive jewelry, even when going to church. In one of the stories, Juan Bobo dresses the family pig as his mother. Even today, people who dress excessively are labeled "La Puerca de Juan Bobo" (Simple John's pig).

Supposedly, Juan Bobo embodies the essence of Puerto Rico—the jibaro; the humble, earth-loving, country and mountain folk. The jibaro is the true Puerto Rican and a product of three cultures: Taino Indian, African, and Spaniard. Juan Bobo is frequently portrayed as either a dark Black person or a light-skinned person with broad nose, thick lips, and curly hair.

Juan Bobo purportedly stands for the honest, simple, and uncorrupted life of country folks against the pompous arrogance, excess, and falsehood of those in the city (i.e., the aristocratic Spaniards and those imitating them). But too often Juan Bobo is instead a mockery of the jibaro. Among Puerto Ricans, it is highly insulting to be called either jibaro or Juan Bobo.

Persons of African and Indian ancestry are the majority in most Latino countries. Yet the folklore and literature—adult's and children's alike—predominantly present characters of Spanish ancestry. Country folks and Latinos of color tend to disappear or are presented as ignorant and superstitious, as criminals, servants, and buffoons. Those in power are white Latinos.

Arroz Con Leche, Cucarachita Martina, Juan Bobo and other culturally authentic stories have been translated into English and other languages in recent years. They can now take their messages across cultures. As teachers search out multicultural literature, it's important to remember that the biases and myths that hurt us can sometimes be multicultural!

Marta I. Cruz-Janzen, a former bilingual teacher in the New York City and Denver public schools, currently is Assistant Professor of Education at the Metropolitan State College of Denver.

Translations by the author.

Parental Influences on Career Development Perceived by African American and Mexican American College Students

Teresa A. Fisher
Inna Padmawidjaja

This study examined parental factors that influence career development among African American and Mexican American college students. Analysis of student interviews revealed that parents are influential in the following career domains: encouragement, educational expectations, critical life events, vicarious learning, and work identity. Career development issues that counselors need to address are provided.

Parental influence on the career development of adolescents and young adults has been documented in the research literature. Recent studies have revealed numerous parental factors that have been instrumental in career development, such as concern and encouragement (Blustein, Walbridge, Friedlander, & Palladino, 1991; Fisher & Griggs, 1995; Kenny, 1990; Leung, Wright, & Foster, 1987), attitude and reinforcement patterns (Eisler & Iverson, 1986; Grotevant & Cooper, 1988; Hankin, 1986); expectations (Smith, 1981; Young, 1994); interest and aspiration (Astone & Mclanahan, 1991; Bitner, 1981; Crowder, 1992; Watson, 1986), and role modeling (Eisler & Iverson, 1986; Fisher & Griggs, 1995; Hackett, Esposito, & O'Halloran, 1989).

Although the majority of these studies were conduced with White, middle-class individuals, the results have often been used to make assumptions about the parental influence on the career development of racial and ethnic minorities in the United States. This has presented a possibly biased view of the particular parental components that may be crucial for ethnic minority youth.

The purpose of this study was to explore the parental influences that influence career development and choice among African American and Mexican American college stu-

Teresa A. Fisher is an assistant professor in the Division of Psychology in Education at Arizona State University, Tempe. Inna Padmawidjaja is a doctoral student at the Margaret Warner Graduate School of Education and Human Development, University of Rochester, New York. Correspondence regarding this article should be sent to Teresa A. Fisher, Arizona State University, Division of Psychology in Education, PO Box 870611, Tempe, AZ 85287-0611 (e-mail: T.A.Fisher@asu.edu).

dents. Little is known about minority students' perceptions of parental influence or the specific impact parents have on the career development of minority students. These are important career development factors that could prove valuable in the career preparation of the increasing numbers of ethnic minority group members in the United States.

The limited research in this area has shown that parental influence is important across ethnic groups (Hernandez, 1995; Lee, 1984; McNair & Brown, 1983), but specific types of parental factors may be more important for one cultural group than another (Kuvlesky, Wright, & Juarez, 1971; Lucas, 1997; Marjoribanks, 1991). For example, Lee's (1984) study with rural youth indicated that parent's expectations had a greater impact on the career choices of 10th-grade African American and Native American students than on the career choices of White students. Investigations on the impact of parental role models for rural youth revealed that this factor was the primary significant predictor for the career decision making of male and female African American adolescents, whereas White male students were influenced by other variables as well (McNair & Brown, 1983). A study (Clayton, Garcia, Underwood, McEndree, & Sheppard, 1993) examining family influences on career development for 8th graders, 12th graders, and community college students (*n* = 2,118) indicated that Mexican American students (66% of sample) rated parental influence on academic and career decisions higher than did other students. In addition, this study found that the Mexican American parents had higher educational aspirations for their children than they had for themselves.

Dillard and Campbell (1981) sampled 194 White, Latino, and African American students in grades 9 to 12 (32 Latinos, 57 White, and 105 African American). Their results showed that African American and Mexican American parents' career aspirations contributed significantly to their children's career development. White students seemed to be influenced more by nonparental factors (e.g., peers).

This article expands existing research by examining, retrospectively, African and Mexican American college students' perceptions of parental influences on their career development. These students were chosen because of their successful career paths (see Participants section). They had made detailed career decisions and were enrolled in a program focusing on their chosen profession. The authors

were aware that African Americans and Latinos have different sociodemographic characteristics and may not have the same pattern of parental influences. The emphasis was to identify major themes for future research, theory development, and counseling practice.

The design phase of this study was influenced by Krumboltz's (Mitchell & Krumboltz, 1996) social learning theory of career decision making. This theory, whose foundation stems from the work of Bandura (1986, 1997), considers learning experiences (e.g., instrumental, associative), genetic endowments (e.g., inherited characteristics that may affect academic and occupational goals), environmental conditions (e.g., family economic history), and task-approach skills (e.g., self-observations, problem orientation, and other learned cognitive and performance behaviors) to be important factors that contribute to one's career path. Combinations of these factors interact in different ways to produce a variety of choices and individual response patterns. The social learning theory was selected because of its comprehensive structure and the fact it provides a framework for assessing a wide range of personal, familial, cultural, and environmental factors that can account for one's career choice and development. A more detailed discussion of the social learning theory of career decision making can be found in Mitchell and Krumboltz (1996).

This descriptive study was guided by the following research questions: (a) What parental behaviors contribute to the career development of African and Mexican American students? (b) Are there culture-specific parent factors that influence the career development of African Americans and Latinos? An additional focus was to indicate what counselors and educators can do to help parents enhance the career development of African American and Mexican American students.

METHOD

Participants

Twenty African American and Mexican American students attending a large Midwestern university internship program were randomly selected for this study. The internship program was created to match college seniors with mentors who were active in the students' chosen profession. The following criteria were used to select students for the internship program: (a) interest in a specific graduate degree, (b) a B or better college grade point average, and (c) identification of and action toward their career goals. This particular internship program was chosen because it has a 100% success rate for past interns obtaining their specified career choice, thus providing a pool of students with excellent chances for their desired career attainment. Forty internship students (out of a total of 100) volunteered to participate in this study. After ethnic-gender categories were established among the 40 volunteers, 20 of them were randomly selected to be interviewed. The 20 participants ranged in age from 19 to 21 years and included 11 African Americans (9 young women and 2 young men) and 9 Latinos (3 young women and 6 young men). All participants were from the lower half of the middle-income range, as indicated by parents' income and educational background (Hauser & Featherman, 1977). Sixteen of the 20 participants indicated that the highest degree obtained by their custodial parent was a high school diploma.

Interview Protocol

Students' perceptions of career influences were obtained through semistructured interviews. This method of research gave the students an opportunity to describe in detail their subjective experiences with parents as well as with other career influences. The interview protocol is considered to be an excellent strategy for obtaining unique experiences from an untapped population (Spradley, 1979).

The authors used the four major social learning components to develop semistructured interview questions. The Appendix is a display of the key questions used to assess various domains of learning experiences (Questions 1, 2, 4, and 5), genetic endowment (Questions 3 and 7), task approach skills (Questions 6 and 7), and environmental conditions. This fourth component was incorporated into probes, as indicated by a P in the Appendix (due to space constraints, only some of the probe questions are listed).

As participants identified significant career influences, follow-up questions were asked to get detailed information regarding the specific nature of the influence. Other questions were included to give the students an opportunity to expand upon influences without responding to leading questions (Questions 8, 9, and

10). Several questions in the study stimulated responses regarding parental attitudinal and behavioral variables, including this: Who or what has had the most influence on your career plans? If students identified their parent(s), follow-up probes were used to enhance the comprehensiveness of the answers (e.g., What specific parental behaviors were helpful in your career decision? How was the experience helpful?). The probes were designed to obtain data about how parents' behavior influenced vocational choices as well as reinforced career explorations.

Procedure

Participants were told that the purpose of the interview was to discuss their perception of significant influences on their career choice and development. The interviews were conducted and tape-recorded by two doctoral students in education. They were well versed as to the nature of the study and the interview procedure. Each interviewer received extensive training on asking follow-up questions. The interviews took place in a university classroom and ranged from 1 to 2 hours in length.

Data Analysis

The 20 interviews were transcribed and coded by two graduate students in education. The investigators used pilot data to train coders to use thematic categories when analyzing interview transcripts. Ten students (seniors in college) who were not involved in the internship program participated in the pilot. The training of coders lasted 2 weeks, at which time a 95% coder reliability had been established.

The first part of the data analysis included examining patterns among the participant's responses (Fetterman, 1989) for the following probes: What specific parental behaviors were helpful in the participants' career planning, and in what way did they find the parental influences helpful? Each coder was required to individually identify major thematic categories among the responses. After the individual analysis of transcripts, the coders discussed their categories and potential themes that connect them.

Their identified categories were very similar; each coder used almost identical descriptions of parent roles (categories) that were viewed as influential for participants' career development. Consensus was used to identify

TABLE 1

Thematic Categories and Subcategories of Parental Influence

Thematic Category/ Subcategory	%	Selected Quotes
Encouragement		
Availability	65	"My parents were usually available to talk and listen to my plans."
Guidance and Advice	50	"I now realize that the advice and guidance my parents provided about life and goals actually paid off"
Acceptance	35	"They were always supportive of my career plans."
Autonomy	20	"I appreciate them for leaving my career choice up to me."
Educational Expectations	100	"My parents made school a top priority. They placed a huge emphasis on education because they wanted me to have achievements for myself and my race."
Critical Life Events	40	"When my dad was put on trial, I became very interested in a law career, to be helpful when others faced issues like this."
Vicarious Learning	60	"My parents had to drag themselves to work and constantly complained about their long hours and low pay. After watching them, I realized I wanted to work in a setting I felt good about."
Work Identity	25	"Ever since I can remember, I watched my Dad start his own businesses. He enjoyed being his own boss. I decided at an early age to follow his path and become an entrepreneur."

themes that would encompass these categories. To verify the meaning of each thematic category as well as its clarity, each coder was asked to write summary statements from the transcripts that reflected the meaning of the thematic category. This was done for each transcript. The similarity in meaning of summary statements among the coders suggested that the selected thematic categories were appropriate as well as exhaustive for all respondents (Miles & Huberman, 1984).

Table 1 includes the thematic categories, subcategories, and representative quotes that reflect parental behavior associated with a particular theme. Percentages under each theme reflect the frequency of endorsement by the 20 students.

The reliability check for the coding system used a random selection of coded transcripts. The average proportion of agreement using Cohen's (1960) kappa was .91 (Hollenbeck, 1978). The kappas ranged from .87 to 1.0 for the 8 thematic categories.

RESULTS

The results did not reveal any differences by ethnicity or gender. Table 1 describes thematic categories and subcategories of parental influ-

ence for each participant based on their responses to the research questions and probes. The largest reported category is encouragement, which comprises four subcategories: (a) availability, (b) guidance and advice, (c) acceptance, and (d) autonomy. The other four major categories identified were educational expectations, critical life events vicarious learning, and work identity. Following is a brief description of the themes. Quotes are included to reflect the specific nature of student perceptions.

In general, the thematic category of encouragement refers to the variety of parental support and reinforcement students perceived regarding their career planning and choice. Availability was the most frequently identified factor participants viewed as parental encouragement (65%). Students indicated that their parents were always accessible and ready to help. This was particularly evident when students discussed school-related topics. The following quote demonstrates this issue: "She would tell me things like 'if you need any help you know I'm always here.' She would keep saying that. She would ask me about school, and how was I doing. She took an active interest in what I was doing."

The parent role of providing guidance and advice was cited by 50% of the students as being an encouraging factor for their career development. Students particularly saw the beneficial aspects of having parents who were persistent about giving feedback on a variety of educational and career topics. The guiding role of parents was also perceived as being very constructive. As one student explained, "I had a lot of good experiences and I appreciate a lot of things that my parents have done. Even though at the time I didn't appreciate them . . . like them making us go to church every Sunday. There was no question whether you were going or not and if you were sick, you had to prove you were sick."

Of the participants, 35% believed that parental acceptance of their career choice was an influential component to career planning. This is reflected in the following student comment: "My parents were quite helpful, ever since high school. I was always asking, 'What do you think about this?' And they would provide feedback. For instance, I asked, 'What do you think if I go into education?' And they told me, 'Oh that's really great, why don't you try that if you really are interested, go right ahead.' So they are the ones who really motivated me."

Autonomy was a parental encouragement factor cited as contributing to student career development and choice by providing the freedom to choose a particular career. Twenty percent of the students in this study felt it was very beneficial that their parents did not force them to select specific career options. They found this lack of pressure a motivating force as they pursued their career path.

The thematic category of educational expectations reflected that all of the participants had parents who had high educational expectations and stressed the relationship between one's educational level and obtainable social and professional goals. Participants perceived that they were expected to be independent and to achieve a more successful and productive life than their parents were experiencing.

Students were aware that their parents faced several obstacles (e.g., racism, poverty) that prevented them from pursuing their desired level of education. Because their parents had few educational opportunities, they placed a high priority on the education of their children. Students reflected how their parents often indicated the individual benefits and racial-ethnic group advances that education can offer. Students were motivated to achieve as much education as possible. This sentiment is reflected in the following response: "I think my dad definitely wanted me to go to college. There wasn't a question in his mind since I was in kindergarten. Although my dad only went to the second or third grade and my mom up to the sixth, he always had an interest in school, but was not able to pursue it. He had a lot of influence on me, pushing me to go on and on a far as I can. Because of him, there was never a question in my mind about college."

Students described the theme of unexpected critical life events as directly influencing their parents and subsequently the students' career plans. Examples were serious parental illness or a social problem that dramatically changed the family's routine. Forty percent of the participants believed that parental critical events played a major role in their career development by providing insight for a particular career related to the event. Having parents who were in jail or who had high blood pressure motivated students to examine careers in law or medicine, respectively. These students derived constructive meaning from difficult life events, as the following two quotes illustrate: "When I was younger my father was put on trial for accepting bribes at the State Motor Vehicles Department. I found myself confused as well as outraged that my father was accused. Although he was acquitted, it affected me enough to seriously consider a law career." "My father has high blood pressure. I really wanted to find out how I could help people who had these problems. . . . I would say my family problems kind of heightened my interest in dietetics."

This vicarious learning theme reflects students learning indirectly from their parents the importance of seeking career opportunities that would make them comfortable psychologically and financially. Sixty percent of participants often observed their parents working any job just to make ends meet. They put in long hours at "dead-end" jobs for very little pay. The following quote demonstrates that students learned vicariously that it was important to pursue careers that would bring them some pleasure: "My dad worked long hours. . . . He didn't have a very exciting job— it was basically the same thing every day. I knew I didn't want that. I wanted to do something that I would be happy to go to work to in the morning and not be miserable."

Work identity involves the students' belief that their career direction was influenced by the type of career aspirations or occupation their parents had. Participants expressed the sentiment that pursuing an occupation similar to one's parents indicates that shared interests are developed as well as one's confidence—if my parents can do this, I can too. As one participant explained: "I am interested in becoming a lawyer, or something in the legal system. I got interested in law through my mother. She used to study law when she was living in Mexico, and it was something she really enjoyed and we used to talk about it often."

DISCUSSION

The results of this study give us insight into parental factors that contribute to the career development of an academically successful group of African and Mexican American undergraduates. The findings can help guide future research and serve as a resource for counselors working with this population. The participants' responses were supportive of existing research that has shown strong relationships between students' career autonomy and encouraged exploration of career interests (Lankford, 1995; Leung et al., 1987; Marjoribanks, 1991; Sankey & Young, 1996; Young & Friesen, 1992). Similar to other studies, high parent availability was a major factor in the development of positive parent-child relationships, which helped to maintain consistent communication about careers. In addition, the parental encouragement factors identified in this study helped the African American and Mexican American students effectively make decisions regarding their wide range of educational and career options.

Numerous studies have shown that being born to parents with limited education decreases one's expectations of attending college or obtaining a professional occupation (DeRidder, 1991; Mortimer, 1992; Office of Institutional Research, 1995). The current study did not support that finding. Instead, parents that were college educated as well as those who were not had high educational expectations for their children, and consequently were able to instill in them the desire to have experiences and accomplishments that would enable them to surpass their parents' educational and occupational level. These findings are consistent with results found among Latino college graduates (Clayton et al., 1993) as well as African Americans (Edwards & Polite, 1992; Ford, 1993; Hill, 1971; Hines & Boyd-Franklin, 1982).

This study suggests that the high parental educational expectations stemmed from a desire to protect offspring from hardships that the parents encountered, and to encourage them to take advantage of opportunities that would help them make a contribution to their ethnic group. Another explanation for these results could be the parents' desire to prepare their children for a world that does not expect them to succeed. Therefore the operating message may be, "I want you to show the world that your racial-ethnic group is as good as anyone else's." Students in this study internalized the parents' high expectations and used them as a motivation factor. This finding is noteworthy, especially because this theme was identified by all students, and the fact that such indications for racial-ethnic groups are often overshadowed by reports of low aspirations and high drop-out rates.

Critical life events has emerged as a key parental component in the career development of these participants. The students in this study wanted to avoid negative familial life events (e.g., being wrongfully accused of a crime) for themselves as well as others. They observed the hardships that accompanied these unanticipated situations and were able to use such events as a learning and motivational tool on the route to their career goals. These findings are supportive of existing research that has observed the impact of critical events on career decision making (Kenkel & Gage, 1982), career trajectories (Sweeting & West, 1994), and specific career choices (e.g., social workers, medical professionals; Rompf & Royse, 1994).

The influence of parental role models on the career development of adolescents and young adults has been well documented in the literature (Birk & Blimline, 1984; Eisler & Iverson, 1986; Grinstad & Way, 1993; Hackett et al., 1989). The general conclusion of these studies was that parents provided not only a source of identification for their offspring's career development, but also guided them to formulate feelings about occupations. Although research has shown strong relationships between parent and child occupational aspirations, (DeSantis & Youniss, 1991; Lankford, 1995; Smith, 1981), few have included minority students in these investigations. The results from this study suggest that African American and Latino students with college educated parents may also aspire to educational and occupational levels that are similar to their parents.

This exploratory study identified key parental factors that had an impact upon career development and choice for African American and Mexican American college students. Although this study did not introduce new categories of parental influences, it provides a glimpse of how one's culture can affect the nature and type of influence parents can have. For instance, when students from minority and dominant cultures attempt to meet the parental expectations placed on them, minority students may have the additional responsibility of obtaining a career status above their parents', to "move their race forward." Given the fact that existing studies show parents with low educational levels have difficulty motivating their children (DeRidder, 1991; Mortimer, 1992), future research is warranted to better assess how parents with a limited education are able to create a strong desire for education.

These findings also direct attention to the fact that certain family values have been overlooked by researchers who design value inventories for career development. Current value inventories do not capture the variables of moving the race forward or giving back one's racial-ethnic group (Betz & Fitzgerald, 1995). This study lends credence to the importance of creating value inventories that are more inclusive of family values embraced by ethnic minority populations.

Implications for Counseling

Although the results come from a limited sample of successful college students, they provide implications for theory development as well as the counseling profession. As mentioned, the research questions were partially guided by the social learning theory of career development (Mitchell & Krumboltz, 1996). The thematic categories identified in this study reflect three of the major social learning categories: genetic endowment, learning experiences, and environmental conditions. Genetic endowment incorporates one's ethnicity, gender, physical appearance, and other inherited characteristics as well as societal behavior directed toward these characteristics. The theme classified as educational expectations is associated with genetic endowment because of the emphasis parents place on advancing one's ethnic group through education. The students perceived that this belief was a direct reaction to negative societal treatment their parents received because of their ethnic group

membership. Learning experiences is represented by the critical life events and vicarious learning themes. Both of these are forms of associative learning, a major component of the social learning theory. The theme of work identity is associated with environmental conditions, which includes several social, cultural, and economic factors that are not directly controlled by individuals (e.g., financial resources). This theme was identified by students who perceived that they were affected by their parents' chosen or desired occupational choice. Choices were also influenced by the parent's social and economic resources. The relationship between the social learning components and identified themes indicate the feasibility of the theory for this population.

When using social learning theory as a career counseling tool for African American and Mexican American students, special consideration should be given to the interpretation of ethnic influences. Mitchell and Krumboltz (1996) incorporated this factor under their genetic endowment category, and it is viewed as a societal characteristic that could limit one's educational and occupational choices. In this study, ethnic influences were perceived as the prime motivation for high parental educational expectations. This was a self-imposed factor that parents used to push their children to achieve for themselves and to advance their racial-ethnic group. These two different dimensions of ethnic influences should be further researched to avoid conflicts in interpreting social learning theory for minority group members.

In the meantime, as career development models are being developed to become more inclusive of the unique aspects of different cultures, counselors need to be observant and sensitive to career decisions that have been influenced by one's ethnicity. For instance, counselors should assess whether or not minority students feel pressured to achieve because of their parent's desire for them to move their ethnic group "forward." This should be assessed in regard to the students' level of acculturation and ethnic identity (Hackett & Byars, 1996). Students who feel it is an honor to make contributions toward one's ethnic community need counselors to provide encouragement and resources that will help them realize their goals. Others, who feel this pressure is a burden, can benefit from a supportive and advocacy style of counseling (Osborne et al., 1998). This may involve counselors helping these students to acquire the necessary skills to identify the sources of support that are often found in the African American and Mexican American communities (Sue & Sue, 1990).

This research should help affirm counselors' commitment to involve parents in their children's career planning as early as possible. They need to help parents understand the important role they play in influencing their offspring's career development. Many parents are unaware of how to be encouraging or how to help their children learn about lifelong career development strategies. School counselors can be instrumental in this regard by getting parents to actively participate in the school's career education curriculum. Parents need to be familiar with the same career-planning activities that their children are exposed to, so they can be a supportive resource for career decision making (Fouad, 1995; Grinstad & Way, 1993; Hawks & Muha, 1991; McCracken & Fails, 1991; Middleton & Loughead, 1993).

Career workshops for parents could run simultaneously with those for students and focus on such issues as self-assessment, goal attainment, problem-solving skills, career resources, and the impact that one's gender and ethnicity can have on career expectations. Such active involvement by parents will enable them to become effective partners in their child's career and decision-making.

Limitations

The study discussed here has limitations because of its small volunteer sample and interview procedure. The authors worked diligently to train interviewers not to ask leading questions. Though the transcripts revealed that leading questions were avoided, it is difficult to determine the impact that nonverbal cues may have had. Furthermore, because of the variability in response time for participants, it is hard to train interviewers on the amount of time they should allot for responses. An impatient interviewer can limit the richness of the data.

This study should be replicated with a larger number of participants that are diverse regarding ethnic and gender categories, socioeconomic level, and geographic location. Such a population will provide an opportunity to observe parental influences on career development across income levels and between various subgroups of ethnic minorities. For instance, the Latinos in the current study only represented Mexican Americans. Research indicates that depending on the specific Latino subgroup, their level of acculturation, and ethnic identity, different career development factors can evolve (Arbona, 1995). This could also be the case for other ethnic subgroups.

A larger sample not constrained by volunteer status in a college internship program would also provide a better indication of parental influences on career development for ethnic-gender categories and non-college populations.

Given the important nature of this study for the career development of African-American and Latino students, the study should be expanded to provide a more detailed account of key parental factors that affect their behavior. Further research is warranted to identify the role parents may play in helping their children overcome familial critical events. This information could be invaluable as researchers acquire a better understanding of the resilient factors necessary for pursuing one's career goals in spite of adversity.

CONCLUSION

In this study, high parental expectations seemed to be motivated by one major factor, which was the desire to have their children surpass their own educational and occupational level, thus placing them in a position to make a contribution to their racial-ethnic group. This finding should receive further scrutiny in the context of Bandura's perceived collective efficacy, which is defined as "a group's shared belief in its conjoint capabilities to organize and execute the courses of action required to produce given levels of attainment" (Bandura, 1997, p. 478). Although these parents didn't work together intentionally, they all believed that their high educational expectations would result in the same common goal. Collective efficacy may be a viable concept to use in explaining this parental behavior. It would be extremely beneficial to obtain information from both students and parents regarding their perceptions of how parents affect their offspring's career planning, thus providing an opportunity to assess how well parents' intentions match the students' perceptions. Another important issue would be to determine if parental behaviors that influence career development are more beneficial at certain stages of a child's life.

Hopefully, this exploratory investigation has offered insight into the significant role parents play in the career development of African American and Mexican American students. Future research should continue to provide valuable information that will enhance the joint efforts of counselors and parents as they prepare our youth for their career goals.

REFERENCES

Arbona, C. (1995). Theory and research on racial and ethnic minorities: Hispanic Americans. In F. T. Leong (Ed.), *Career development and vocational behavior of racial and ethnic minorities* (pp. 37–66). Mahwah, NJ: Erlbaum.

Astone, N., & Mclanahan, S. (1991). Family structures, parental practices, and high school completion. *American Sociological Review, 56,* 309–320.

Bandura, A. (1986). *Social foundations of thought and action: A social cognitive theory.* Englewood Cliffs, NJ: Prentice-Hall.

Bandura, A. (1997). *Self-efficacy: The exercise of control.* New York: Freeman.

Betz, N. E., & Fitzgerald, L. F. (1995). Career assessment and intervention with racial and ethnic minorities. In F. T. Leong (Ed.), *Career development and vocational behavior of racial and ethnic minorities* (pp. 263–279). Mahwah, NJ: Erlbaum.

Birk, J. M., & Blimline, C. A. (1984). Parents as career development facilitators: An untapped resource for the counselor. *The School Counselor, 31,* 310–317.

Bitner, T. R. (1981). *The effect of parental influence on post secondary school career or education choices made by secondary school seniors.* Unpublished doctoral dissertation, Ball State University, Ohio.

Blustein, D. L., Walbridge, M. M., Friedlander, M. L., & Palladino, D. E. (1991). Contributions of psychological separation and parental attachment to the career development process. *Journal of Counseling Psychology, 38*(1), 39–50.

Clayton, K., Garcia, G., Underwood, R., McEndree, P., & Sheppard, R. (1993). *Family influences over the occupational and educational choices of Mexican American students.* Berkeley, CA: National Center for Research in Vocational Education.

Cohen, J. (1960). Weighted Kappa: Nominal scale agreement with provision for scaled disagreement or partial credit. *Psychological Bulletin, 70,* 213–220.

Crowder, V. G. (1992). *Women's participation in quantitative careers: An explanatory model.* Unpublished doctoral dissertation, University of Georgia, Athens.

DeRidder, L. (1991). *The impact of parents and parenting on career development.* (ERIC Document Reproduction Service No. ED 325 769)

DeSantis, J. P., & Youniss, J. (1991). Family contributions to adolescents' attitudes toward new technology. *Journal of Adolescent Research, 6*(4), 410–422.

Dillard, J. M., & Campbell, N. J. (1981). Influences of Puerto Rican, Black and Anglo parents' career behavior on their adolescent children's career development. *The Vocational Guidance Quarterly, 2,* 139–149.

Edwards, A., & Polite, C. K. (1992). *Children of the dream: The psychology of Black success.* New York: Doubleday.

Eisler, T. A., & Iverson, B. (1986, August). *Predicting career choice in college women: Empirical test of a theory based model.* Paper presented at the annual conference of the National Council of Family Relations, Dearborn, MI.

Fetterman, D. (1989). Ethnographic educational evaluation. In G. Spindler & L. Spindler (Eds.), *Interpretative ethnography of education.* Hillsdale, NJ: Erlbaum.

Fisher, T. A., & Griggs, M. B. (1995). Factors that influence the career development of African-American and Latino youth. *The Journal of Vocational Education Research, 20*(2), 57–74.

Ford, D. Y. (1993). Black students' achievement orientation as a function of perceived family achievement orientation and demographic variables. *Journal of Negro Education, 62*(1), 47–66.

Fouad, N. A. (1995). Career behavior of Hispanics: Assessment and career intervention. In F. T. Leong (Ed.), *Career development and vocational behavior of racial and ethnic minorities* (pp. 165–191). Mahwah, NJ: Erlbaum.

Grinstad, J. A., & Way, W. L. (1993). The role of family in the vocational development of family and consumer education teachers: Implications for vocational education. *Journal of Vocational Education Research, 18*(4), 43–80.

Grotevant, H. D., & Cooper, H. R. (1988). The role of family experience in career exploration: A lifespan perspective. In P. B. Baltes, D. L. Featherman, & R. M. Lerner (Eds.), *Lifespan development and behavior* (pp. 231–258). London: Erlbaum.

Hackett, G., & Byars, A. M. (1996). Social cognitive theory and the career development of African American Women. *Career Development Quarterly, 44,* 323–340.

Hackett, G., Esposito, D., & O'Halloran, S. (1989). The relationship of role model influences to the career salience and educational and career plans of college women. *Journal of Vocational Behavior, 35,* 164–180.

Hankin, E. K. (1986). *Women's mathematics oriented career choices in college.* Unpublished doctoral dissertation, Bryn Mawr College, Bryn Mawr, PA.

Hauser, R. M., & Featherman, D. L. (1977). *The process of stratification.* New York: Academic.

Hawks, B. K., & Muha, D. (1991). Facilitating the career development of minorities: Doing it differently this time. *Career Development Quarterly, 39,* 251–260.

Hernandez, T. J. (1995). The career trinity: Puerto Rican college students and their struggle for identity and power. *Journal of Multicultural Counseling and Development, 23,* 103–115.

Hill, R. (1971). *The strengths of Black families.* New York: Emerson Hall.

Hines, P. M., & Boyd-Franklin, N. (1982). Black families. In M. McGlodrick, J. K. Pearce, & J. Giordiano (Eds.), *Ethnicity and family therapy* (pp. 84–107). New York: Guilford.

Hollenbeck, A. R. (1978). Problems of reliability in observational research. In G. P. Sackett (Ed.), *Observing behavior: Vol. 2. Data Collection and analysis methods* (pp. 79–98). Baltimore: University Park.

Kenkel, W. F., & Gage, B. A. (1982). Life's predictable unpredictables and the career plans of youth. *Sociological Spectrum, 2,* 307–314.

Kenny, M. (1990). College seniors' perceptions of parental attachments: The value and stability of family ties. *Journal of College Student Development, 31,* 39–46.

Kuvlesky, W. P., Wright, D. E., & Juarez, R. Z. (1971). Status projections and ethnicity: A comparison of Mexican-American, Negro and Anglo youth. *Journal of Vocational Behavior, 1,* 137–151.

Lankford, B. (1995). *Family role in career development.* (ERIC Document Reproduction Service No. ED 389 878)

Lee, C. C. (1984). Predicting the career choice attitudes of rural black, White and Native American high school students. *Vocational Guidance Quarterly, 32*(3), 177–184.

Leung, J. J., Wright, B. W., & Foster, S. F. (1987, April–May). Perceived parental influence and adolescent post secondary plan. *The High School Journal,* 173–178.

Lucas, M. (1997). Identity development, career development, and psychological separation from parents: Similarities and differences between men and women. *Journal of Counseling Psychology, 44*(2), 123–132.

Marjoribanks, K. (1991). Family environment and cognitive correlates of young adults' social status attainment: Ethnic group differences. *Journal of Biosocial Science, 23*(4), 491–498.

McCracken, J., & Fails, E. (1991). *Comparison between the 1985 and the 1988 career plans of the same rural youth in Ohio.* (ERIC Document Reproduction Service No. 338 4530)

McNair, D., & Brown, D. (1983). Predicting the occupational aspirations, occupational expectations, and career maturity of Black and White male and female 10th graders. *Vocational Guidance Quarterly, 32*(1), 29–36.

Middleton, E. B., & Loughead, T. A. (1993). Parental influence on career development: An integrative framework for adolescent career counseling. *Journal of Career Development, 19*(3), 161–173.

Miles, M., & Huberman, A. (1984). *Qualitative data analysis.* Beverly Hills, CA: Sage.

Mitchell, L. K., & Krumboltz, J. D. (1996). Krumboltz's learning theory of career choice and counseling. In D. Brown & L. Brooks (Eds.), *Career choice and development* (3rd ed., pp. 233–280). San Francisco: Jossey-Bass.

Mortimer, J. (1992). *Influences on adolescents' vocational development.* Berkeley, CA: National Center for Research in Vocational Education.

Office of Institutional Research. (1995). *New Student Inventory Survey Results* (Research Monograph II). Tulsa, OK: Author.

Osborne, J. L., Collison, B. B., House, R. M., Gray, L. A., Firth, J., & Lou, M. (1998). Developing a social advocacy model for counselor education. *Counselor Education and Supervision, 37,* 190–202.

Rompf, E. L., & Royse, D. (1994). Choice of social work as a career: Possible influences. *Journal of Social Work Education 30,* (2), 163–171.

Sankey, A. M., & Young, R. A. (1996). Ego-identity status and narrative structure in retrospective accounts of parental career influence. *Journal of Adolescence, 19,* 141–153.

Smith, T. E. (1981). Adolescent agreement with perceived maternal and paternal educational goals. *Journal of Marriage and the Family, 43,* 85–93.

Spradley, J. P. (1979). *The ethnographic interview.* New York: Holt, Rinehart & Winston.

Sue, D. W., & Sue, D. (1990). *Counseling the culturally different* (2nd ed.). New York: Wiley.

Sweeting, H., & West, P. (1994). The patterning of life events in mid to late adolescence: Markers for the future. *Journal of Adolescence, 17*(3), 283–304.

Watson, D. S. (1986). *An analysis of selected factors influencing career choices of women in science.* Unpublished doctoral dissertation, University of Northern Colorado, Greeley.

Young, R. A. (1994). Helping adolescents with career development. *The Career Development Quarterly, 42,* 195–203.

Young, R. A., & Friesen, J. D. (1992). The intentions of parents in influencing the career development of their children. *The Career Development Quarterly, 40,* 198–207.

APPENDIX

Influences and Career Development: Student Interview

1. Now that you are on the career path of your chosen profession, can you reflect on how you became interested in this career? **(P)** Were there any specific events that stand out in your mind? When did you start thinking about this career?

2. Who or what has had the most influence on your career plans? **(P)** In what ways were they helpful?

3. Did you feel you had any options as to which career to explore? Explain.

4. Were there any specific programs in your community that helped you decide on a career? If so, please explain.

5. Were there any specific programs in your school that helped you decide on a career? If so, please explain. **(P)** Did you find high school subjects helpful for planning your career? What about college subjects? If yes, give some examples.

6. Did you perform as well as you expected to in school? **(P)** Explain. What would you do again? What would you do differently?

7. Do you feel confident about your success in your chosen profession? Explain.

8. What is the difference between you and someone with a similar background as yourself, but who does not have the same academic and career accomplishments? **(P)** What do you think would have made a difference in the lives of less successful youth?

9. What can be done to help others who have no clue about their future career direction?

10. What factors help youth make the transition from school to their chosen career?

Note. **(P)** = Probing question; asked on an as needed basis

From La Belle Sauvage[1] to the Noble Savage

The Deculturalization[2] of Indian[3] Mascots in American Culture

By Cornel D. Pewewardy

Introduction

Invented media images prevent millions of Americans from understanding the past and current authentic human experience of First Nations People. My opposition to the use of Indian mascots for sports teams has always been because these trappings and seasonal insults offend the intelligence of thousands of Indigenous Peoples in this country.

This article speaks to the American educator and discusses how, as educators, we are responsible for maintaining the ethics of teaching and for helping to eliminate racism in all aspects of school life. Therefore, the exploitation of Indian mascots becomes an issue of educational equity. What should educators know about the issues of American Indian mascots, logos, nicknames, and the tomahawk chop?

As someone who has spent his entire adult life teaching in and administrating elementary schools for Indigenous children, I see that the way Indian mascots are used today is about "dysconscious racism"

Cornel D. Pewewardy is an assistant professor in the Department of Teaching and Leadership, School of Education, University of Kansas, Lawrence.

> **... if you have seen the racial antics and negative behaviors portrayed by Indian mascots hundreds of times for most of your life, you may become absolutely numb to their presence. That's dysconscious racism.**

and a form of cultural violence, which operates primarily at the psychological level. According to Joyce King (1991) and Gloria Ladson-Billings (1990), dysconscious racism[4] is a form of racism that unconsciously accepts dominant white norms and privileges.

For example, if you have seen the racial antics and negative behaviors portrayed by Indian mascots hundreds of times for most of your life, you may become absolutely numb to their presence. That's dysconscious racism. The thousands of ways in which Indian mascots are used today in American sports culture is racist and should be eliminated, using education as the tool for liberation. However, I understand that many educators not familiar with equity issues are not equipped to teach such liberation.

The issues

Teachers should research the matter and discover that Indigenous Peoples would never have associated the sacred practices of becoming a warrior with the hoopla of a pep rally, half-time entertainment, or being a side-kick to cheerleaders. Even though it has become as American as apple pie and baseball, making fun of Indigenous Peoples at athletic events across the country is wrong!

From *Multicultural Education*, Spring 1999, pp. 6-11. © 1999 by Caddo Gap Press, Inc. Reprinted by permission of *Multicultural Education*, the magazine of the National Association for Multicultural Education.

Many schools around the country exhibit Indian mascots and logos, using nicknames and doing the tomahawk chop[5] in sports stadiums through inauthentic representations of Indigenous cultures. Many school officials state or say they are honoring Indigenous Peoples and insist their schools' sponsored activities aren't offensive, but rather a compliment. I would argue otherwise.

There's nothing in Indigenous cultures that I'm aware of that aspires to be a mascot, logo, or nickname for athletic teams. It would be the same as a crowd of fans using real saints as mascots or having fans dressed up as the Pope (Lady Pope's or Nuns) at a New Orleans Saints football game and doing the "crucifix chop" to the musical accompaniment of Gregorian chants while wearing colorful religious attire in the stands. What would be the reaction of Catholics around the country if that happened?

The behavior to which I object makes a mockery of Indigenous cultural identity and causes many young Indigenous people to feel shame about who they are as human beings, because racial stereotypes play an important role in shaping a young person's consciousness. Subjective feelings, such as inferiority, are an integral part of consciousness, and work together with the objective reality of poverty and deprivation to shape a young person's worldview.

Beginning with Wild West shows and continuing with contemporary movies, television, and literature, the image of Indigenous Peoples has radically shifted away from any reference to living people toward a field of urban fantasy in which wish fulfillment replaces reality (Deloria, 1980). Schools should be places where students come to *unlearn* the stereotypes that such mascots represent.

So why do some teachers allow their students to uncritically adopt a cartoon version of Indigenous cultures through the use of a mascot portrayed by sports teams? Dennis (1981) contends that people engage in racist behavior because they are reasonably sure that there is support for it within their society. Their cultural lens, for example, may be highly ethnocentric; yet no distortions are perceived in the field of vision.

To understand why this is racist, consider how euphemisms and code words for ethnic persons and groups are used: scalp, massacre, redskin, squaw, noble savage, papoose, Pocahontas, Cherokee princess. Bosmajian (1983) explains that while the state and church as institutions have defined the Indians into subjugation, there has been in operation the use of a suppressive language by society at large which has perpetuated the dehumanization of Indigenous Peoples. The English language includes various phrases and words which relegate the Indigenous Peoples to an inferior status: "The

only good Indian is a dead Indian"; "Indian Giver"; "drunken Indians," "dumb Indians," and "Redskins."[6] These words represent a new generation of ethnic slurs that are replacing the older, more blatant and abusive nicknames (Allen, 1990; Moore, 1976).

Children's self images are very impressionable, pliable, and susceptible to external forces, especially if they are steeped in violent and negative images (Fleming, 1996; Rouse & Hanson, 1991; Madsen & Robbins, 1981; Pushkin & Veness, 1973). They also respond accordingly to the respect they are shown with regard to their individuality, including their ethnicity and/or race (Paley, 1989). Unfortunately, for Indigenous Peoples, many false images of ethnicity still dominate the consciousness of the American psyche.

Howard (1983) asserts that in the American psyche, Indigenous People have fulfilled their historical mission. They existed to provide a human challenge to whites as they marched across the continent. Their resistance provided the stuff of myths of conquest and glory. Moreover, I have found that many ethnic images have been manufactured and created in the image of other racial groups. The manufactured "savage," "pagan," "retarded," "culturally deprived," non-European is the flipside of the European civilization myth. To affect ethnic images is to distort reality while creating a new and seductive reality of its own. Students in schools cannot be expected to understand the realities of modern American life and the prospect for future generations without understanding the popular images of the past and the present.

History of Manufactured Images

The challenge that we have today is to deconstruct a reality that has been manufactured by the American media and scholars. For many Americans there is something faintly anachronistic about contemporary Indigenous Peoples. Many people today look at Indigenous Peoples as figures out of the past, as relics of a more heroic age. Put somewhat differently, the modern presence of Indigenous Peoples has been hard to grasp for most Americans. It is only recently that Indigenous Peoples have begun to reclaim their own images and make their special presence known.

The portrayal of Indigenous Peoples in sports takes many forms. Some teams use generic Indigenous names, such as Indians, Braves, or Chiefs, while others adopt specific tribal names like Seminoles, Cherokees, or Apaches. Indian mascots exhibit either idealized or comical facial features and "native" dress ranging from body-length feathered (usually turkey)

head dresses to more subtle fake buckskin attire or skimpy loincloths. Some teams and supporters display counterfeit Indigenous paraphernalia, including tomahawks, feathers, face paints, symbolic drums and pipes. They will also use mock-Indigenous behaviors, such as the "tomahawk chop," dances, chants, drum beating, war-whooping, and symbolic scalping.

So-called Indian mascots reduce hundreds of Indigenous tribal members to generic cartoon characters. These "Wild West" figments of the white imagination distort both Indigenous and non-Indigenous children's attitudes toward an oppressed—and diverse—minority. The Indigenous portrait of the moment may be bellicose, ludicrous, or romantic, but almost never is the portrait we see of Indian mascots a real person (Stedman, 1982). Most children in America do not have the faintest idea that "Indigenous Peoples" are real human beings because of such portrayals.

The contradictory views of Indigenous Peoples, sometimes gentle and good and sometimes terrifying and evil, stem from Euro-America's ambivalence toward a race of people they attempted to destroy. For example, today, the perceptions and negative images of Indigenous Peoples by the American macroculture is a part of the history of the motion picture portrayals, which evolved from stereotypes created by the earliest settlers and chroniclers of this country. The treatment of Indigenous Peoples in the movies is the final expression of white America's attempt to cope with its uneasiness in the face of unconscious cultural guilt (Bataille & Silet, 1980).

Francis (1992) advocates that the *Indian* began as a white man's mistake, and became a white man's fantasy, because of white guilt, white fear, and white insecurity. Deloria (1994) asks the question "where did Westerners get their ideas of divine right to conquest, of manifest destiny, of themselves as the vanguard of true civilization, if not from Christianity?" Having tied itself to history and maintained that its god controlled that history, Christianity must accept the consequences of its past.

Social Construction of Reality

Furthermore, I contend that American racism as we inherit it today is the social construction of reality. Racism is the primary form of cultural domination in America over the past four hundred years. Prior to Columbus, what is known as the new world functioned for millennia without the race construct as we understand it today (Stiffarm & Lane, 1992; Mohawk, 1992). According to Banton (1998), the pre-Columbian European explorers in the Pacific had only fleeting contacts with the islanders, who often received them in friendship.

Their accounts were favorable. However, European writing inspired by these accounts went further and built the myth of the Noble Savage. This was of importance politically, for to believe that the savage is noble is to believe than man is naturally good. If evil does not have its origin in human nature, it must spring from the faulty organization of society.

In this context, Indigenous Peoples stood as the cipher for everything that was pristine and sublime. This fascination and its attendant desire for otherness was used by European intellectuals as an emblem that escaped the emotional and intellectual shackles of modernity. These notions of exotic innocence are no less stereotypical than the idea that Indigenous People are less civilized and more barbaric. Solomos and Back (1996) contend that this kind of identification is locked within the discourse of absolute difference which renders Indians exotic and reaffirms Indigenous Peoples as a "race apart." It was this danger which Frantz Fanon outlined when he argued that those Europeans who blindly adore the difference of the other are as racially afflicted as those who vilify it (Fanon, 1986).

According to Solomos and Back (1996), Darwinian arguments in favor of heredity and variation challenged the idea of the fixity of species, but by the late 19th and early 20th centuries themes derived from Darwin were used in debates about race in a variety of national contexts. This was evident, for example, in the popularity of Social Darwinism and of Eugenics during this period (Mosse, 1985; Dengler, 1991). We are well aware of the consequences of this theory upon our times. Genovese (1989) advocates that with the appearance of Darwinism, racism—or at least white racism—took a new course: "many white people were quite enthusiastic about Darwinism because, proclaiming the survival of the fittest, it confirmed their policy of expansion and aggression at the expense of the inferior peoples (p. 158)."

Gould (1996) contends that this construct came from Darwinian theory. Social scientists and other students of group life have furthered these ideas throughout the 20th century and much of their work has been used by the mass media. Together with schools, legal systems, and higher education institutions, these forces participate in a major way in legitimizing and reifying this invalid construct—the romanticized image of Indigenous Peoples. Consequently, race as a construct is now internalized by the world's masses. All these voices together have helped to perpetuate this ignorance and distortion.

The primary issue in American racism is hegemony.[7] I agree with Hilliard (1997) and Kane (1996) that racism is a mental illness. It is mental illness because it is a socially constructed system of beliefs created by advocates and inventors of hegemonic systems. It is a precursor to mental illness, among ethnic minorities, because it requires that the individual function with the academic falsification of their human record, distortion of cultural identity, and delusions of grandeur about white supremacy (Novick,1995).

Tinker (1993) asserts that even many Indigenous Peoples have internalized this illusion just as deeply as white Americans have, and as a result they discover from time to time just how fully Indigenous People participate today in their own oppression. At the ideological level, racism's link to mental illness requires continued systemic study and at the applied level, massive financial resources toward the deconstruction of the European colonial mindset need to be devoted to the structuring of domination. Conflicting ideological components, such as a defense of racial exploitation on one hand, or an assertion of racial equality on the other, must depend in part for their effectiveness upon a degree of correspondence with that ongoing construction (Saxton, 1990).

Racism is Detrimental to Children

Today, as a teacher educator, I show future teachers why Indian mascots are one cause for low self-esteem in Indigenous children. This is the point where this issue becomes *detrimental* to the academic achievement of students in school. To make my point clear, I point to the American Indian Mental Health Association of Minnesota's (1992) position statement supporting the total elimination of Indian mascots and logos from schools: "As a group of mental health providers, we are in agreement that using images of American Indians as mascots, symbols, caricatures, and namesakes for non-Indian sports teams, businesses, and other organizations is damaging to the self-identity, self-concept, and self-esteem of our people. We should like to join with others who are taking a strong stand against this practice."

Most of the resolutions to eliminate negative ethnic images came from grassroots people, mostly Indigenous parents. Resolutions to ban Indian mascots and logos from schools have also been drafted by American Indian organizations like the National Indian Education Association, Kansas Association for Native American Education, Wisconsin Indian Education Association, and Minnesota Indian Education Association. Other groups that have passed resolutions to ban Indian mascots and logos include the National Education Association, Governor's Interstate Indian Council,[8] United Indian Nations of Oklahoma, Great Lakes Inter-Tribal Council in Wisconsin, Oneida Tribe of Wisconsin, National Congress of American Indians, American Indian Movement, National Rainbow Coalition, NAACP, and the Center for the Study of Sports in Society.

More recently, the National Collegiate Athletic Association (NCAA) has issued a statement supporting the elimination of Indian names and mascots as symbols for their member institutions' sports teams (Charles Whitcomb, 1998). Yet these strong voices seemingly speak to deaf ears. As a result, the continued exoticization of people of color, particularly Indigenous Peoples, has been used to justify the control of entire communities (Kivel, 1996).

Power and Control

Because the powerful messages from state and national organizations have been ignored, the question must be asked: why do racial slurs in the form of Indian mascots and logos remain? I believe that the hidden agenda behind their use is about annihilation, both cultural and spiritual, and about intellectual exploitation. Therefore, the real issues are about power and control. These negative ethnic images are driven by those that want to define other ethnic groups and control their images in order to have people believe that their truth is the absolute truth.

Furthermore, it's the ability to define a reality and to get other people to affirm that reality as if it were their own. Remember that media commercials are carefully designed and expensively produced to stereotype groups and help us, as consumers, "realize" we are far less intelligent than we should be. This is an additive systemic approach to power and control.

Even new books about power and control such as Greene's (1998) The *48 Laws of Power,* this season's most talked-about all purpose personal-strategy guide and philosophical compendium, talk about economic indicators of success. Greene sets out to codify "the timeless essence of power, much as the great Florentine thinker Machiavelli did half a millennium ago in *The Prince.* Machiavelli never stooped to dispense mere get-rich-quick advice, and neither does Greene. Law 15 in Greene's The 48 Laws of Power reads:

> Crush your enemy totally. More is lost through stopping halfway than through total annihilation. Crush him, not only in body but in spirit.

Adler (1998) asserts that his rules are couched as grand abstractions about human nature "always say less than necessary," "assume formlessness," "pose as a friend, work as a spy." Adams (1995) contends that the easiest way to oppress the colonized is by keeping them weak, too weak to upset the system, but strong enough to fulfill their lowly role as menial workers to support the economy of corporate rulers.

Politics of Colonization

Through the politics of colonization, Indigenous Peoples were socialized into stereotypes of being seen as inferior, stupid, and lazy, thereby fulfilling the need to be everybody's mascot. This list of stereotypes of Indigenous Peoples are well known (i.e., University of Illinois' Chief Illinawic, Oklahoma's Eskimo Joes, Crazy Horse Malt Liquor, Land of Lakes Butter, Jeep Cherokee, Pocahontas, etc.).

While the Cleveland Indians, Atlanta Braves,Washington Redskins, Kansas City Chiefs, Florida State University Seminoles, Southeastern Oklahoma State University Savages, Wichita North High School Redskins, and many more academic institutions have resisted the pressure to change, scores of colleges, universities, and high school teams have adopted new names over the years. Stanford changed from Indians to the Cardinal. Dartmouth changed from Indians to The Big Green. Ohio's Miami University Redskins became the Red Hawks. If these colleges and universities can change, so can other educational institutions. In the Big Ten Conference, the University of Wisconsin and University of Minnesota athletic departments established policy that banned out-of-conference competition with universities that use Indian mascots names and logos, e.g., Marquette Warriors, who recently changed their name to Golden Eagles.

Several newspapers, including the *Minneapolis Star Tribune, Seattle Times, Portland Oregonian*, have instituted new policy on the use of racist overtones and words, such as "Redskin" in its reporting, particularly of sports events. Moreover, some radio announcers and stations will not use racially insulting words over the air.

Some large school districts across the nation (i.e., Dallas Public Schools, Los Angeles Public Schools) have eliminated Indian mascots from their school districts as the result of active advocacy parent and education groups working closely with school officials. Wisconsin and Minnesota have mandated that publicly funded schools not use mascots, names, or logos that have been deemed offensive to Indigenous Peoples.

While some colleges, universities, high schools, and middle schools have dropped their racially insulting Indian mascots and logos, no professional sports team has felt enough heat or, perhaps, has enough conscience or respect to take a similar step. However, the Washington Wizards succumbed to political pressure and changed their name from the Bullets to the Wizards, which suggests that changes are possible at this level. Change should be possible without the unsightful alumni and student backlashes that smear Indigenous complainants as activists or militants—even as politically correct minorities. This is apparently not consistent with the current fad of being "politically correct."

Negative imagery of Indigenous Peoples has been around for more than a century. However, the more serious controversy regarding it did not emerge until the past two decades. During this period, there has been a growing Indigenous consciousness and grass-roots transformation, while at the same time the general public and media have become more alert to the rapidly growing ethnic awareness and diversification of society. Consequently, racism in its overt and subtle forms has encountered greater resistance from the "politically correctness" movement of recent years.

Student's Right to an Equal Education

Most states make a commitment to provide the best public education for every student. The issue of equity is an important component of that commitment to educational excellence, ensuring access, treatment, opportunity, and outcomes for all students, based on objective assessment of each individual students' needs and abilities. Requirements and support for equity come from the state Legislature, the federal government, the private sector, community organizations, parents, school boards, and school district staff members.

Given this foundation, many of the issues pertaining to negative Indian mascots and logos displayed in programs and activities in schools comes under the category of "discrimination." The discrimination prohibition applies to: curricular programs, extracurricular activities, pupil services, recreational programs, and other (e.g., use of facilities, food service). While most states prohibit discrimination against students, many initial Indian mascots and logos complainants are dismissed as irrelevant by school officials, thereby one must follow a process of filing an official complaint as an "aggrieved person" (i.e., a student or parent of student who has been negatively affected) who is a resident of the school district.

Every pubic school district is required to have a complaint procedure adopted by the school board for residents to use. Some complainants of Indian mascots and logos have additionally filed complaints with the U.S. Department of Education's Office for Civil Rights, basing their discrimination on the student's sex, race, handicap, color, or national origin.

Conclusion

Understanding the contemporary images, perceptions, and myths of Indigenous Peoples is extremely important not only for Indigenous Peoples, but also for mainstream America. Most images of Indigenous Peoples have been burned into the global consciousness by fifty years of mass media. It was the Hollywood screen writers who helped to create the "frontier myth" image of Indigenous People today. It was, moreover, a revelation that had gone largely unrecorded by the national media and unnoticed by a public that still sees Indigenous Peoples mainly through deeply xenophobic eyes and the mythic veil of mingled racism and romance. Each new generation of popular culture has, therefore, reinvented their Indian mascot in the image of its own era.

Those of us that advocate for the elimination of mascots of Indigenous Peoples appreciate the courage, support, and sometimes the sacrifice, of all people who stand with us by speaking out and drafting resolutions against the continued use of Indian mascots in schools. When you advocate for the removal of these mascots and logos, you strengthen the spirit of tolerance and social justice in your community as well as model pluralism for all children. You provide a powerful teaching moment that can help to deconstruct the fabricated images and misconceptions of Indigenous Peoples that most school-age children have burned into their psyche by the American media.

If your team name were the Pittsburgh Negroes, Kansas City Jews, Redding Redskins, Houston Hispanics, Chicago Chicanos, Orlando Orientals, or Washington Whities, and someone from those communities found the invented name, stereotyped labels, and ethnic symbols associated with it offensive and asked that it be changed, would you not change the name? If not, why not? Let us further "honor" these groups with demeaning caricatures of a rabbi in a flowing robe, a Black Sambo image, a mascot who would run around in a Ku Klux Klan outfit. It's a mix of racism with sports enthusiasm under the guise of team spirit. Vickers (1998) asserts that Indigenous writers, artists, and activists on all fronts would be sure to condemn all the noxious stereotypes implied above.

I have made several points in this article and my previous messages to educators. Educators need to educate themselves about Indigenous Peoples and their communities. Doing so will help them see that as long as such negative mascots and logos remain within the arena of school activities, both Indigenous and non-Indigenous children are learning to tolerate racism in schools (Munson, personal communication, 1998). That's what children see at school and on television. As a result, schools only reinforce the images projected by popular culture (LaRocque, 1998). This is precisely what sports teams with mascots and logos of Indigenous Peoples teach children—that it is "acceptable" racism to demean a race or group of people through American sports culture.

Finally, I challenge educators to provide the intellectual leadership that will teach a critical perspective and illuminate the cultural violence associated with Indian mascots used in schools. Inaction in the face of racism is racism. As culturally responsive educators, we must understand that "enslaved minds cannot teach liberation."

Notes

1. Scores of early European writers—Peter Martyr, Montaigne, Rousseau, Chateaubriand—focused upon the innocent Indigenous Peoples as (1) naked, (2) childlike, (3) willing to share anything they possessed, (3) unaware of religion, and (5) unconcerned with laws or personal property. A sixth element, cannibalism, crept into some accounts—and into hundreds of illustrations—but since the practice did not fit a good-savage motif, it was smoothed over or simply disregarded by many theorists (Stedman, 1982). The character Poconhontas was created by these early European writers to elevate Indigenous women to a European monarchial mode like a royal princess. Through the nation's growing years Pocahontas the Nonpareil—intelligent, guileless, lovely, courageous—turned into Pocahontas the Imitated or La Belle Sauvage.

2. The first method of deculturalization segregation and isolation—was used with Indigenous Peoples. Indigenous Peoples sent to Indian Territory were isolated in the hope that missionary-educators would "civilize" them in one generation. Indigenous children sent to boarding schools were isolated from the cultural traditions of their tribe as they were "civilized." Forcing a dominated group to abandon its own language is an important part of deculturalization. Culture and values are embedded in language. Using a curriculum and textbooks that reflect the culture of the dominating group was another typical practice of state school systems and federal government programs. All these methods of deculturalization were accompanied by programs of Americanization (Spring, 1997).

3. Previous research focusing on aboriginal peoples in the United States have used American Indian, Indian, and Native American as the nomenclature for this population. This article subverts this tradition by instead using the terms "Indigenous Peoples" and "First Nations People." These terms are capitalized because they are proper nouns (particular persons) and not adjectives (words describing nouns). It is also capitalized to signify and recognize the cultural heterogeneity and political sovereignty of Indigenous Peoples in the western hemisphere (Yellow Bird, personal communication, 1997). In this respect, the con-

sciousness of the oppressor transforms Indigenous identity into a commodity of its domination and disposal (Freire, 1997). Ceasing to call Indigenous Peoples American Indians is more than an attempt at political correctness. It is an act of intellectual liberation and it is a correction to a distorting narrative of imperialist "discovery and progress" that has been maintained far too long by Europeans and Euro-Americans. Thus, American Indian and Indian are sometimes used interchangeably in the vernacular of this article only when trying to make a point in an attempt to liberate and combat linguistic hegemony, which is both a direct and indirect power block to the identity of Indigenous Peoples (Yellow Bird, personal communication, 1997).

4. Racism is defined as the unshared unilateral use of power that exploits, dominates, and tyrannizes people of color. The exploitation of cheap Black, Hispanic, or Chinese labor to maximize profits within a capitalist system is a classic example of racism as defined by this mode of thinking (Terry, 1996). Racism in America is rooted deeply in the very structure of society. It is not solely, or even mainly, a matter of personal attitudes and beliefs. Indeed, it can be argued that racist attitudes and beliefs are but accessory expressions of institutionalized patterns of white power and social control (Bower, Hunt & Pohl, 1981).

5. The "tomahawk chop" is a social phenomena that was created by those individuals who perceive the need for a supportive physical display of action (to cheer on one's favorite athletic team). It's the extension of a single arm out in front on an individual—swinging the hand and forearm in an up and down motion. The act of the tomahawk chop perpetuates an image of savagery and usually takes place in large crowds in sports stadiums accompanied by a so-called Indian war chant. The tomahawk chop is also a racist gesture because it perpetuates a stereotype that is not true for all Indigenous Peoples, and it certainly is not true in modern America. This invented act of cheerleading plays on the transformation of Indigenous spirituality, knowledge, objects, rituals into commodities, and commercial exploitation, as well as constitute a concrete manifestation of the more general, and chronic, marketing of Native America (Whitt, 1995).

6. "Redskins" is a word that should remind every American there was a time in United States history when America paid bounties for human beings. There was a going rate for the scalps or hides of Indigenous men, women, and children. These "redskin" trophies could be sold to most frontier trading posts. "Redskins" as used by the Washington National League football team, was a poor choice from the beginning. It was an unflattering name given to Indigenous Peoples by EuroAmericans. George Preston Marshall selected the name when he organized the Boston-based team in 1933. The fact that the name has become habitual or traditional for today's sports fans make it no more pleasant to Indigenous Peoples who hear it.

7. Hegemony, in this reading, becomes simply the establishment or preservation by a rul-

ing class of identification between class and group (Saxton, 1990).

8. The Governors' Interstate Indian Council (GIIC) began in 1947 when Minnesota Governor Luther Youngdahl expressed concern about federal government involvement in Indian affairs. As an alternative, he recommended that Native Americans in the states work together to address common concerns. For the past 45 years, the GIIC has worked on the state level to promote cooperation between states and their native people and to work toward solutions to their mutual problems. The Senate and House Committees on Indian Affairs rely on the GIIC input as do other Congressional committees and national associations. The Council consist of member states who send delegates to the annual meeting of the Council. GIIC regions represent the following: Northwest: WA, OR, ID, MT, WY, ND, SD, NE, AK; Southwest: CA, NV, UT, AZ, CO, NM, KS, OK, TX, HI; Northeast: MN, IA, WI, IL, MI, IN, OH, KY, NY, PA, NJ, DE, MD, WV, VA, VT, MA, CT, RI, NH, ME; Southwest: TN, MS, AL, NC, SC, GA, FL, AR, LA, MO.

References

Adams, H. (1995). *A Tortured People: The politics of colonization.* Penticton, British Columbia: Theytus Books Ltd.

Adler, J. (1998). The Prince Wants a Word With You. *Newsweek.* 73.

Allen, I.L. (1990). *Unkind Words: Ethnic labeling from Redskin to WASP.* New York: Bergin & Garvey.

American Indian Mental Health Association of Minnesota. (1992). *Position statement regarding the use of team mascot/namesakes that convey an image of the Native people of this land.* Minneapolis, MN: American Indian Mental Health Association.

Banton, M. (1998). *Racial Theories.* New York: Cambridge University Press.

Bataille, G.M., & Silet, C.L.P. (1980). *The Pretend Indians: Images of Native Americans in the movies.* Ames, IA: Iowa State University Press.

Bosmajian, H.A. (1983). Defining the American Indian: A case study in the language of suppression. In G. Goshghrian (Ed.). *Exploring Language.* Evanston, IL: Little, Brown, Inc.

Bowser, B.P., Hunt, R.G., & Pohl, D.C. (1981). Introduction. In B.P. Bowser & R.G. Hunt (Eds.)., *Impacts of Racism on White Americans.* Beverly Hills, CA: Sage Publications.

Deloria, V. (1994). *God Is Red: A Native View of Religion.* Golden, CO: Fulcrum Publishing.

Deloria, V. (1980). Preface. In G.M. Bataille & C.L.P. Silet (Eds.)., *The Pretend Indians: Images of Native Americans in the Movies.* Ames, IA: Iowa State University Press.

Dengler, C.N. (1991). In *Search of Human Nature: The Decline and Revival of Darwinism in American social thought.* New York: Oxford University Press.

Dennis, R.M. (1981). Socialization and Racism: The white experience. In B.P. Bowser & R.G. Hunt

(Eds.), *Impacts of Racism on White Americans.* Beverly Hills, CA: Sage Publications.

Fanon, F. (1986). *Black Skin, White Masks.* London, UK: Pluto Press.

Fleming, D. (1996). *Powerplay: Toys as popular culture.* New York: Manchester University Press.

Francis, D. (1992). *The Imagery Indian: The image of the Indian in Canadian culture.* Vancouver, British Columbia: Arsenal Pulp Press.

Freire, P. (1997). *Pedagogy of the Oppressed.* New Revised 20th-Anniversary Edition. New York: Continuum.

Genovese, S. (1989). The Myth of Racism. In J. Groebel & R.A. Hinde (Eds.), *Aggression and War: Their biological and social bases.* New York: Cambridge University Press.

Gould, S.J. (1996). *The Mismeasure of Man.* New York: W.W. Norton & Company.

Greene, R. (1998). *The 48 Laws of Power.* New York: Viking Press.

Hilliard, A.G. (1997). Psychology as Political Science and as a Double Edged Sword: Racism and counter racism in psychology. Speech given at the American Psychological Association Conference on Racism, Chicago, IL.

Howard, J.R. (1983). American Indians: Goodbye to Tonto. In J.R. Howard (Ed.), *Awakening Minorities: Continuity and change.* New Brunswick, NJ: Transaction Books.

Kane, E. (1996). *Seeing Racism as a Mental Health Issue.* Available: www.jsonline. com/ arch ive/ autoarc/ 970511seeingracismasmental.stm

King, J.E. (1991). Dysconscious Racism: Ideology, Identity, and Miseducation of Teachers. *Journal of Negro Education,* 60(2), 133–146.

King, J.E., & Ladson-Billings, G. (1990). Dysconscious Racism and Multicultural Illiteracy: The distorting of the American mind. Paper presented at the annual meeting of the American Educational Research Association, April 16–20, Boston, MA.

Kivel, P. (1996). *Uprooting Racism: How white people can work for racial justice.* Gabriola Island, British Columbia: New Society Publishers.

LaRocque, E. (1998). Transformation. In Joy Harjo & Gloria Bird (Eds.), *Reinventing the Enemy's Language: Contemporary Native Women's Writings of North America.* New York: W.W. Norton & Company.

Madsen, J.M., & Robbins, R. (1981). Native American Visual and Verbal Images in the Caldecott and Newbery Award Books. *Minority Voices.* 5(1/2), 17–39.

Mohawk, J. (1992). Looking for Columbus: Thoughts on the past, present and future of humanity. In M. Annette Jaimes (Ed.), *The State of Native America: Genocide, Colonization, and Resistance.* Boston, MA: South End Press.

Moore, R.B. (1976). *Racism in the English Language.* New York: Racism/Sexism Resource Center for Education.

Mosse, G. (1985). *Toward the Final Solution: A history of European Racism.* Madison, WI: University of Wisconsin Press.

Novick, M. (1995). *White Lies White Power: The fight against white supremacy and reactionary violence.* Monroe, MI: Common Courage Press.

Paley, V.G. (1989). *White Teacher.* Cambridge, MA: Harvard University Press.

Pushkin, I., & Veness, T. (1973). The Development of Racial Awareness and Prejudice in Children. (pp. 23–42). In P. Watson (Ed.), *Psychology and Race.* Chicago, IL: Aldine Publishing Company.

Rouse, L.P., & Hanson, J.R. (1991). American Indian Stereotyping, Resource Competition, and Status-based Prejudice. *American Indian Culture and Research Journal.* 15(3), 1–17.

Saxton, A. (1990). *The Rise and Fall of the White Republic: Class politics and mass culture in nineteenth-century America.* New York: Verso.

Spring, J. (1997). *Deculturalization and the Struggle for Equality: A brief history of the education of dominated cultures in the United States.* New York: McGrawHill.

Stedman, R.W. (1982). *Shadows of the Indian: Stereotypes in American culture.* Norman, OK: University of Oklahoma Press.

Stiffarm, L.A., & Lane, P. (1992). The Demography of Native North America: A question of American Indian survival. In M. Annette Jaimes (Ed.), *The State of Native America: Genocide, Colonization, and Resistance.* Boston, MA: South End Press.

Solomas, J., & Back, L, (1996). *Racism and Society.* New York: St. Martin's Press.

Terry, R.W. (1996). Curse or Blessing for the Elimination of White Racism? In B.P. Bowser & R.G. Hunt (Eds.), *Impacts of Racism on White Americans.* Thousand Oaks, CA: Sage Publications.

Tinker, G.E. (1993). *Missionary Conquest: The gospel and Native American cultural genocide.* Minneapolis, MN: Fortress Press.

Vickers, S.B. (1998). *From Stereotype to Archetype in Art and Literature.* Albuquerque, NM: University of New Mexico Press.

Whitcomb, C. (1998). Guest editorial—Use of Indian Mascots Shows Lack of Respect. *The NCAA News* (September 28, 1998), Available: www.geocities.com/~earnestman/ncaa_statement.htm

Whitt, L.A. (1995). Cultural Imperialism and the Marketing of Native America. *American Indian Culture and Research Journal.* 19(3), 1–31.

A Therapeutic Moment?
Identity, Self, and Culture
in the Anthropology of Education

Diane M. Hoffman
Curry School
University of Virginia

Identity is a key area for consideration in contemporary educational analysis and in the anthropology of education in particular. This article considers the need for critical inquiry into the notion of identity, suggesting that the field might reconsider the need and value of an approach that moves beyond identity toward consideration of cultural models of self and their implications. The discussion outlines three areas where self appears to be a useful construct (cultural therapy, multiculturalism, and transcultural comparisons of teaching and learning).

Problematizing Identity

To speak of education in the 1990s is inevitably to speak of identity. While the notion remains subject to varying interpretations linked to particular methodological and theoretical paradigms and to the wide variety of social, cultural, and political contexts in which it is analyzed, in many ways identity has become the bread and butter of our educational diet—an "everybody help yourself" construct, served up on nearly every scholarly table. In this article I suggest that a re-examination of our views of identity is in order, as a means to both more and better theory development as well as the promotion of more effective educational practices in situations of cultural and ethnic pluralism. While educational anthropologists have been at the forefront of efforts to promote cultural and ethnic identities as significant domains for consideration in education, noting the close link that exists between identity and school performances, at the same time the critiques of essentialized approaches to identity and culture that have emerged across disciplinary boundaries in recent years have yet to exert much influence on mainstream educational anthropology, where the dominant perspectives on identity stress understanding, respecting, and celebrating it, rather than holding it up for critical interrogation.

While we would not want to doubt the importance of valuing the diversity of cultural backgrounds students bring with them to school, at the same time we need to be more aware of how failure to interrogate discourses on identity can obscure long-standing educational problems, including those of minority achievement. Not only is the idea of identity potentially shaped by unexamined frames of reference grounded in universalizing assumptions about self and society that merit critical analysis, but, as McDermott (1987:364) reminds us, we constantly need to work "against" our culture in order to study it. This, I take it, includes constant questioning of the categories that we bring to our analyses. Without critical inquiry, our cultural categories then achieve the givenness that allows them to "acquire" their victims (McDermott 1993; McDermott and Varenne 1995).

To some extent, constructivist accounts of the fluid, situated, and negotiated character of real social lives in and out of schools have made a substantial contribution to the ways in which we conceptualize identity by questioning the fixedness of identity categories as well as their salience in social life (see Davidson 1996, 1997; Heath and McLaughlin 1993; Hemmings 1996; Phelan et al. 1993). Heath and McLaughlin point out that well-intentioned outsiders (teachers, social workers, administrators, anthropologists) often perceive "ethnic identity" or gender in ways that diverge from the perspectives of insiders—those who supposedly "have" the identities we are talking about. Heath and McLaughlin raise important issues concerning the salience of ethnic identity and gender in the lives of inner-city youth that respond to the presumptions of academics and others about the nature and importance of these concepts.

Critical ethnography has also made a contribution toward our understandings of identity in schooling, especially by situating identity within oppositional or contesting frames of power and social relations (see Levinson et al. 1996). By emphasizing the production of identities in education, we move away from the stasis implicit in social reproduction theories toward views that emphasize agency and individual "empowerment."[1]

Despite the contributions of these approaches (postmodernist, constructivist, critical ethnographic), what Hall (1995:2) critiques as the "irreducibility" of the construct of identity remains apparent. Identity is simply a given of one's existence—indeed,

the very thing that makes such existence in a social world possible. Rather, we require a base from which to question and critique this taken-for-grantedness of discourses about identity in schooling: the pervasive assumptions that we all know what identity is, that one identity is the same as (or as good as) another, that we all need well-defined and clear cultural, ethnic, or racial identities in order to be psychologically healthy, that the objective of culturally supportive educational process is to "protect" our identities. We need to begin by inquiring into what kind of selves undergird the construction of identities in social contexts, and how such selves may affect the kinds of identity issues that arise in educational contexts. In some sense it is ironic that where identity is indeed "on the borderlines" and in process, as it so often is in plural educational contexts, it is precisely there that so little of the effort toward its reconceptualization has occurred.

Identity and Self

A fundamental issue raised by anthropologists and anthropologically-minded psychologists many years ago concerned the enduring and pervasive importance of a psychocultural dimension to identity—in other words, a *self* (see DeVos 1978; Fogelson 1979; Hallowell 1955). While there is much debate as to the meaning of self and divergence in views of self depending on one's disciplinary frame, I understand self from a psychoanalytic perspective (following Goldberg 1979) as a culturally patterned way of relating to others; to the material, natural, and spiritual worlds; and to time and space, including notions of agency, mind, person, being, and spirit. Identities, on the other hand, reflect the self's situatedness in social roles—Whiting's notion of identity as "a person's perception of his or her place on the social structure" (1990:357). This perception is grounded in sociocultural categories such as race, ethnicity, class, and culture that allow the individual to position him- or herself relative to others within a particular social structure. While identity can often be a focus for reflection and awareness (for example, a woman may speak quite readily of her "identity as a mother/Latina/scholar"), the psychocultural dimensions of self are less frequently the object of conscious analysis or reflection, at least among certain individuals and cultural groups.[2]

There are, of course, dangers to describing self in this way—not the least of which is the potential for a kind of inner/outer matrix to organize our perceptions of self along culturally biased directions. As anthropological studies of self in a variety of cross-cultural contexts have shown (e.g., Geertz on self in Java, Bali, and Morocco [1983]), we cannot presume that there is an "inner self" separate from external roles or social iden-

tity. The point is that the relationship between self and identity needs to be explored, not assumed. As Blacking (1983) argues, it is impossible to even approach the understanding of identity in the absence of a coherent system of cultural ideas about the self and others: to understand the former, one must consider the latter—and, in particular, the ways in which Euro-American ethnopsychology has biased its understandings of identity through its presupposition of certain visions of autonomous and egoistic selfhood. Thus, it is crucial to consider just how self is related to identity, for it forms the base of assumptions about self-other relatedness upon which identities can be constructed.

It is currently fashionable, however, to dismiss self as a fiction of hegemonic discourses and structures, or to see it as constructed solely in terms of narrative(s) that presumably respond to the determining forces of culture and political systems. In part, the broad shift across the humanities and social sciences toward views of identity as constructed (and selves as shifting, groundless, artifactual/artificial) had led to a preoccupation with the politics of identity, the ways identities are "defined" from outside, manipulated, or otherwise situated in social structures. In the anthropology of education, this tendency is reflected in the ways in which we describe identity construction in schooling: construction occurs in response to social or academic pressures, systems, or structures; or to situated practices in classrooms, schools, or communities. It is rarely construction in response to cultural models of self—the discourses, norms, and values that continue to generate cultural patterning in the ways self develops in relation to others and otherness. The latter, while rightly questioned because of our fears of psychological determinism and "deficit" thinking, have been ignored in the grand quest to legitimate identity as a domain of inquiry and to acknowledge the place of power and politics in its development.

Instead, I argue, it is critical to resurrect a domain of inquiry in the anthropology of education that recognizes, in the words of the writer Gish Jen, that a person "is more than the sum of her social facts" (Jen 1997:19). What Jen insists on is that there can be a self that is *not* necessarily subsumed by public identities—a domain of what she calls the "inner person," and knowledge of that "inner person" must be taken to be as important as knowledge that can be publicly claimed and agreed upon.[3] I suggest that the anthropology of education might fruitfully redirect its attention to this domain of the "inner person" in its discussions of identity and schooling, and in particular, to do so by revisiting what has long been a central focus in the work of psychologically-oriented anthropologists in the field—the concept of self. While our concern for identities in recent years has led to a rich appreciation for the effects of cultural diversity in schooling, better understanding of the processes involved in identity construction in and through schools, and legitimate concern for the human experiences of suffering and inequity by those whose identities have not been respected, the question of self has been neglected (see Appel 1996 for a similar critique). In a sense, we have reduced our understanding of persons in the educational process to a singular concern for "defining 'truth' from the outside" and neglected the variety and complexity of cultural influences on the formation of self that, in fact, may "define 'truth' from the outside" and neglected the variety and complexity of cultural influences on the formation of self that, in fact, may "define 'truth' from the inside" (Jen 1997:19).

Background: Why Self?

The roots of contemporary concerns for the self in cultural context extend, of course, to earlier work in anthropology, with its long-standing concerns for understanding processes of enculturation and cultural transmission, notions that were more or less explicitly tied to specific cultural understandings of what it means to become a person in a particular cultural context. This focus eventually became one of the points of departure for the entire subfield of culture and personality in the 1940s and 1950s. Despite the emphasis on cultural contrasts, however, and the important work being done in the area of ethnopsychology, the whole notion of identity was not "up for grabs," as it were; one did, after all, become a Kwoma; one did finally assume the particular identity embedded in the practices and socialization techniques that one experienced. It is only in the more recent incarnations of the culture and personality theme—notably in cultural psychology—that identity has been reformulated and approached at a different level of analysis that attempts to account for both inter- and intrapsychic variability in the experience of self. While the shift in terminology from "identity" toward "self" in the 1980s may reflect a movement away from the discourses of the 1970s that were clouded with intergenerational conflicts and searches for "the real me," it also reflects a more subtle philosophical shift away from conceptualization of identity as group membership and boundary marker to identity as the confluence of social roles and social positioning that are more or less shifting and negotiable. Within this context, the self is experiencing a rebirth as both a focal point for cross-cultural comparison and an active, intentional agent in human life. It is not reducible to the roles it plays, the groups it "belongs" to, or to the identities it negotiates; it points, in sum, to something beyond identity.

Yet in current educational discourses, far too often self and identity are conflated, or a one-to-one correspondence between self and social role(s) is assumed that then becomes *faute de mieux*, one's "identity" (or "identities," in the case of the situated/multiple/shifting crowd). Given the slippery nature of both identity and self, it is quite understandable that for the purposes of most researchers, distinguishing between the two is not necessary. Yet from a theoretical perspective, we need to question the presumed isomorphism between self and identity so that we can address both sociostructural and psychodynamic dimensions, and so that we can see how cultural understandings of self interact with sociocultural contexts and structures to produce identities through such processes as schooling. Hence the need for an anthropology of education that teases out the possibilities—and problems—inherent in those points of non-correspondence between self and social behavior.

Specifically, greater attention to the self in anthropological studies of education may be useful for four reasons. First, if we take identities as socially constructed, we need to consider a range of influences on their construction, including those associated with indigenous cultural psychological models of the self. There is much anthropological evidence that there are indeed significant cross-cultural differences in the ways self is conceptualized and experienced (Ames et al. 1994; Geertz 1983; Marsella et al. 1985; Shweder 1990; Shweder and Bourne 1984). Cultures differ greatly in the manner in which they define the relationship between self and other, the degree to which they distinguish between "mind" and "body" (or have separate categories for each), and in the way in which they conceptualize agency and motivation as external or internally directed. One of the more persistent themes in this literature concerns the contrast between a self defined in terms of autonomy, individuation, and separateness and a self defined in terms of social embeddedness, where quite different qualities such as fluidity, social dependency, and diffuse boundaries are more characteristic (Geertz 1983; Markus and Kitayama 1991; Sampson 1988).[4] A number of researchers have noted that such differences in constructions of self may be linked to fundamental differences across cultural groups in other domains, including cognition, motivation, affect, and learning (see Greenfield 1994; Hoffman 1995; Markus and Kitayama 1991; Suarez-Orozco and Suarez-Orozco 1993; Tobin 1994). If so, we need to at least include consideration of cross-cultural differences in the self as a relevant area for inquiry in analysis of educational processes.

It is important to point out, however, that consideration of self is not totally unproblematic. In addition to the potential for implicit bias in understandings of self mentioned earlier, consideration of cultural differences may tread dangerously close to essentialism if it is supposed that there exist unchanging core "essences" of self that remain fixed across time and space. Rather, we need to be aware that cultural views of what constitutes self may exist on multiple levels with different significance, that these are always evolving in response to a variety of social forces and discourses, and that there may be great gaps between ideals reflected in discourse and the real "experiences" of self in everyday lives.

Moreover, indigenous psychologies of the self raise yet another difficult issue: just what qualifies as "indigenous," and how far does one have to go in specifying particular cultural perspectives? That is, need one insist on a separate psychology for every distinctive ethnic group, or even distinctive psychologies for subgroups within ethnic groups? In such cases one risks over-particularizing and setting up boundaries around ethnic cultures that may not reflect realities of mutual cultural interface. While indigenization is rightly perceived as an antidote to the overgeneralizing ethnocentrism of much of Western and particularly U.S. psychology, at the same time, in its more extreme forms it risks cultural reification and excessive particularism. The task would seem to be one of negotiating the delicate borderlands at the interface of cultures, where both difference and similarity coexist and where neither excessive generalization nor particularism accurately captures the nature of social life.

A second justification for a renewed attention to self and culture in considering identity stems from the perennial difficulty anthropologists and other social scientists have faced in adequately accounting for the problem of structure and agency. The need for an explanatory paradigm that can link the phenomenological richness of attention to individual and group patterns of behavior, value, and so forth with larger "macro"-level structural constraints and forces has been, arguably, one of the forces that has propelled anthropologists in the direction of critical studies. In this context, the cultural production and reproduction of identities has come to be considered a central issue in analyses of both formal and informal educational processes. As useful as this conceptualization of identity has been, attention to cultural scripts and understandings of self is important because one cannot presume that agency is understood in the same ways across all cultural contexts; indeed, cultures are quite variable in their formulations of the links between structure and agency. As Dissanayake (1996) observes in the case of Japan, the typical view of identities fashioned in the supposedly "group-oriented" culture of Japan is one that denies individual agency; yet as his analysis of Japanese films amply demonstrates, individual agency is, in fact, alive and well. Indeed, unless one moves beyond the views of identity in which group affiliation predominates, one cannot appreciate the ways self is, in fact, a locus for action, despite its apparent "invisibility" in normative discourses about group identification.[5]

Third, without consideration for cultural models of self, identity is frequently reduced to being either "pro" or "con" in relation to social structures: it is either seen as a product of dominant discourses and hegemonic practices; or, alternatively, a product of resistance to dominant perspectives and values. Identity is still a product—a casualty, if you will—of the battleground of cultural (re)production wherein competing visions of cultural capital, success, and "the educated person" (Levinson et al. 1996) are played out. Implicitly, identity becomes a political boundary marker, a distinguishing feature of group self-definition that fixes and encodes relations of dominance and subordination. While recognition of these themes is important, there is much more to the process. As Appel (1996) notes, lack of attention to the psychodynamics of socialization process—or, in other words, to the self in its psychosocial context—has led to one of the primary weaknesses in critical approaches to education: their inability to theorize identity formation in schooling. The critical tradition has largely ignored the warnings of DeVos (1992) and DeVos and Suarez-Orozco (1990), who remind us that the sociocultural context is intimately tied to the psychocultural; one cannot explain one without reference to the other.

A fourth justification for renewed attention to self is the emergence of a new field of inquiry called "cultural psychology" (Cole 1996; Shweder 1990) which attempts to take cultural activities or practices as key units of social analysis—transcending, it is hoped, the "artificial" dichotomization of context and subject, actor and object (Lave and Wenger 1991; Rogoff et al. 1995).[6] A key idea behind such approaches is the importance placed on identity formation through participation in activity: in Lave's words, "Learning . . . is a process of becoming a member of a sustained community of practice. Developing an identity as a member of a community and becoming knowledgeably skillful are part of the same process . . ." (Lave 1991: 65). While this approach highlights the importance of culture in the formation of identities in communities of practice, little explicit attention has been given to a prime arena for cultural/contextual difference: understandings of the self. Thus, we can ask, how and to what extent does the identity of a bricklayer in one culture differ from the identity of a bricklayer in another, for example? Or, how and to what extent does being a bricklayer in culture A share something with being a butcher in culture A? In other words, while we recognize that identities are "different" and "similar" in various ways across communities of practice, we have no systematic theoretical grounds to analyze and explore such differences/similarities. While rightly recognizing

the links between identity and learning, this approach still does not get at a more basic and interesting dimension of culture—its models for normative and experienced selves.

In this article I examine three fairly well-developed areas of anthropological inquiry in education that, as I see it, provide a particularly rich ground for exploration of identity and its relation to culture and self. These are cultural therapy, minority education and multiculturalism, and transcultural comparisons of teaching and learning. Each of these areas has generated substantial interest in the anthropology of education and each is in at least some ways deeply grounded in concerns about identity and its role in educational process. While the literature in each of these areas is extensive, rather than offer a comprehensive look at trends and themes, I focus selectively on studies that provide a window that has potential for opening up our discourses on self and culture in education.

Moving beyond Identity: Three Areas for Considering the Self

Cultural Therapy

In recent years, an explicit and welcome focus on the self in education has emerged under the rubric of "cultural therapy." As conceptualized by George and Louise Spindler (see Spindler and Spindler 1989, 1992, 1993, 1994), cultural therapy involves an exploration of the relationship between individual self and culture. In part, this is a most helpful approach, simply because it assumes that one *can* question that relationship, that cultural identity (for example) is *not* the finish line where all inquiry stops, as if people were locked into fixed patterns of feeling, thinking, and behaving determined by their identities, without the possibility of envisioning alternatives. As such, cultural therapy is an orientation toward examination of the implicit, tacit, unconscious, or unobserved aspects of culture as they function within the individual; by bringing these to consciousness, it can help to alleviate bias, distortion, and unproductive adaptations to cultural situations (such as schooling). It envisions a self in interaction with a culture (or cultures), instead of being subsumed by culture; it distinguishes between a "situated self" that responds to changing circumstances, an "enduring self" that reflects an individual's deeply held cultural values, ideals, and aspirations (Spindler and Spindler 1993).[7]

As a preliminary orientation, we can state that cultural therapy is a process of bringing one's own culture, in its manifold forms—assumptions, goals, values, beliefs, communicative modes— to a level of awareness that permits one to perceive it as a potential bias

in social interaction and in the acquisition or transmission of skills and knowledge—what we later refer to as "instrumental competencies." At the same time one's own culture, brought to this level of awareness, is perceived in relation to the other culture, so that potential conflicts, misunderstandings, and blind spots in the perception and interpretation of behavior may be anticipated. [1993:28]

By focusing attention on the self as a potential site of flexible adaptations to culture, rather than on a cultural identity that offers no points of discontinuity with culture, cultural therapy offers individuals a sense of options and choices in their cultural responses to situations and helps to move us beyond the determinism present in many writings on identity. According to the Spindlers, although cultural therapy is most useful for teachers, it can also be a form of "consciousness raising" for students that allows them to "clarify the steps necessary to obtain the instrumental competencies they need to gain access to opportunities in the school system (and hopefully the larger society)" (1993:29). Thus, for teachers and students, it is both a strategy of awareness and a strategy for empowerment, because it allows and encourages conscious choice and active response to situations that are potentially disempowering (such as schooling).

The notion has resonated among many contemporary anthropologists of education. Trueba (1993a, 1993b) has found in cultural therapy one possible solution to "healing" the difficulties that multiculturalism currently poses in the United States. The Spindlers' own edited collection of papers exploring the use of cultural therapy in real educational settings stands as a testimony to the potential power and use of the concept (see Spindler and Spindler 1994). To approach culture in an educational setting as amenable to therapeutic intervention—rather than simply as something to be understood or accounted for—represents a new development and raises valuable theoretical questions concerning the relationship between the individual self and culture. Just how "determined" are selves, in a cultural sense, and what might the link to identity be? Can we speak of behavioral and attitudinal change while retaining a clear sense of "identity," or does "identity" automatically change, too? How much do cultural models of the self influence persistence or change in subjective identities?

The notion of enduring and situated selves is quite helpful in approaching these questions, particularly since it locates therapeutic change in the situated self. An even more interesting set of theoretical questions arises when we consider this model in the light of indigenous cultural understandings of self. The latter encourage us to ask to what extent "enduring" and "situated" selves are culture-general or culture-specific,[8] and whether cultures distinguish equally between "types" of self based on situatedness or enduringness. In Japan, for example, the presence of a "layered" concept of self having inner, social interactional, and "boundless" dimensions (Lebra 1994) strongly mirrors the situated/enduring distinction; so does the traditional cultural model of self in Iran, with its clear distinction between the *zaher* (external or social self that is strongly "situated") and *batin*, the inner, "true" self that constitutes the core person and remains apart from the situated behaviors and expressions required by social interactions (Good and Good 1985). One wonders, however, whether this distinction would be equally useful in other cultural contexts (such as the Javanese or Balinese described earlier) where a sense of "inner self" is not as strongly marked (Geertz 1983). In sum, in positing a distinction between an enduring self and a situated self, cultural therapy points us toward consideration of the relevance of "self" in educational processes. It suggests that cultural differences in understandings of self are relevant in the analysis of individual and group responses to education and that adaptation needs to be seen in terms much more complex than identity shift, loss, affirmation, or conflict.

Multiculturalism, Identity, and Minority Educational Experience

The idea that we all need clearly defined identities to be psychologically healthy and successful in school is one that has been at the heart of educators' thinking for a long time (for example, Banks writes, "The individual who has a confused, nonreflective, or negative ethnic identification lacks one of the essential ingredients for a healthy and positive personal identity" [1988:43]). In contrast, as the Arabian poet Sami Ma'ari writes, "Identities are highly complex, tension filled, contradictory, and inconsistent entities. Only the one who claims to have a simple, definite, and clear-cut identity has an identity problem" (quoted in Gergen 1991).

This difference in how we look at identity is of particular import in the dialogue (or, perhaps, lack of it) between anthropologists of education and multicultural educators. While anthropologists have in recent years offered plentiful critiques of some of the more egregious misuses of culture in multiculturalism (see Gibson 1984; Hanna 1994; Perry 1992; Turner 19923; Ulichny 1996; Wax 1993), less has been said about the conceptualization and use of identity clarity/consistency (in an albeit well-intenioned effort to validate and "celebrate") remain unchallenged, except insofar as such identities as seen as "resisting" or, alternatively, "conforming" to schooling and other structures of power.[9]

Describing identity in terms of resistance/conformity, however, fails to capture

its complexity, and, in particular, the nuances of a psychological reality that many times allows (and perhaps even encourages) the coexistence of resistance and conformity at different levels and across different situations within the same person. This points us to a need for some consideration of dynamics of self. While the relationship between conformist/resistant identities and variable cultural understandings of self is not often elaborated, there is much suggestive work in this area. Ogbu's (1978, 1982, 1983, 1992) discussions of oppositional identity, often read as "culturalist" (Davidson 1996) or cultural/ecological, address indigenous cultural psychology in their appeals to "folk theories" of success and cultural background factors that lead to "inversion" or "adaptive" responses to schooling. While Ogbu can be accused of excessively categorical discussions of identity that fail to take account of the fact that among many minorities, an individual can experience both "opposition" and "conformity/adaptation" at the same time in responding to schooling (Davidson 1997; Hoffman 1988, 1989a), he also notes that even "oppositional" minorities can and should learn that adaptations to school need not require a "threat" to self (Ogbu 1992), thereby suggesting that there is a level of self that needs to be considered in analysis of the identities that emerge in schooling.

George and Louis Spindler, in the context of their studies on instrumental competencies in Germany (1987, 1989), have been concerned with the role of the self in mediating adaptations to change. Rather than simply speak of "change-resistant" or "change-oriented" identities, their attention to self allows a much more complete and complex view of how individuals respond to social change. Suarz-Orozco (1987) and Suarez-Orozco and Suarez-Orozco (1993) have also indicated that cultural understandings of self among Hispanics are an important consideration in understanding Hispanic responses to mainstream schooling and adaptation to life in the United States. Gibson's (1988) analysis of Punjabi adolescents' accommodations to mainstream schooling also represents an effort to come to terms with aspects of self in the cultural adaptation and learning process that goes beyond simplistic either-or discussions of identity that revolve around maintenance/loss or resistance/conformity.

Across all of these writings is the idea that in understanding cross-cultural experiences it is important to distinguish between socially situated and more or less "instrumental" (to use the Spindlers' term) behaviors, and a person's deeply held values, commitments, and ways of relating to others that may or may not be implicated or exemplified in social behavior. Moreover, cultural variations inhere in the extent to which there is an expected correspondence between these levels of social functioning. An important theme in some of these analyses is that there

are domains in which cultural behaviors commonly associated with particular identities are not necessarily fixed, leading—potentially—to situationally flexible adaptations of the self, rather than monolithic "conformist" or "resistant" identities. Education, in this view, shapes identity by shaping the patterns of self's relations to others, the expectations that exist for conformity between "situated" and "enduring" selves, and patterns of orientation to change. It is, at heart, a pedagogy of selfhood—a mirror for as well as a model of culturally envisioned self.

As might be expected, the ways self is mirrored in schooling becomes especially important in understanding minority educational experiences, especially since academic achievement and achievement "motivation"—another culturally loaded term—are highly dependent upon assumptions about the self and its relations to others, including autonomy and styles of social relatedness, the relation between performances and self, ideas about individual differences, and sources of self-esteem. As Suarez-Orozco and Suarez-Orozco (1993) point out, considering the case of Hispanic minorities in the United States, many mainstream assumptions about identity and its relationship to achievement are simply inaccurate. They write,

> The Hispanic case does not fit the majority (non-Hispanic) American paradigm for achievement motivation. The most motivated of these Hispanic immigrants are not individualists searching for self-advancement and independence. . . . In the case of Hispanic Americans, it has been argued, in a simplistic fashion, that a somehow asphyxiating cultural matrix orienting individuals heavily to the family is responsible for crippling achievement motivation. . . . [1993: 132–133]

Rather, the authors note, the strong wish to nurture parents and other family members, combined with a sense of responsibility and obligation to do so, is a more accurate explanation for the source of achievement motivation among Hispanics:

> Rather than encountering a pattern of rugged individualism and independence, we identified the emergence of a world-view that orients the self to others. . . . The assumptions that have guided pedagogical practice and curriculum strategies are based on an understanding of motivation relevant to largely white, middle-class students from the dominant culture. [1993: 133]

Similarly, for ethnic Koreans in the United States, a U.S. cultural psychology that stresses individualist and self-oriented motivation fails to explain the pervasiveness of the theme of self-sacrifice in discussions of education for Korean minority students, as well as the tight relationship held to exist between parental expectations and student achievement (see Kim 1993; Lee 1996; Sorensen 1994). Indeed, for Koreans in the United States, educational success is closely tied to notions of sacrifice—both on the part of parents for the children and children for parents (who are likely to place parental desires for success in education above their own personal interests [Kim 1993]). Rather than stress achievement for its own sake or for self-actualizing goals, the aim is to benefit the family, as a larger manifestation of self, according to the "cultural model of success" held by the Korean immigrant community. Academic achievement is therefore not just a "personal" affair but a communal one, tied closely to strong themes of collectivist identity and membership in an exclusive cultural community. Within this context, self-esteem is not so dependent on a sense of one's personal uniqueness, but upon a sense of connectedness or relatedness to others within the in-group and of fulfilling one's obligations to that group.

This may help to explain the apparent paradox of Korean ethnic cultural separatism alongside strong ideologies of participation/success in the U.S. mainstream. In fact, identity as a Korean in the United States is situated within a strong ideology of academic/career success in the U.S. mainstream. The two are not only not opposed, but functionally equivalent (see Kim 1993). Koreans in the United States thus do not seek "culturally congruent" experiences in schooling—that is, schooling that would reinforce their "Koreanness" or be based in the celebration of Korean heritage. Rather, they seek out an education that allows them to achieve success in the U.S. mainstream at the same time as the ethnic community promotes a rather exclusive cultural identification as Korean (see Lee 1994, 1996). In general terms, the idealized model of Korean ethnic identity is one in which pragmatic or instrumental adaptation occurs without occasioning undue conflict with "being Korean."[10]

As the Korean and Hispanic cases illustrate, it is important to consider cultural models of self in understanding academic performance; in neither case, however, do we see cultural models of self predetermining academic outcomes. It is especially important to note that while both cases illustrate socially situated and embedded ideals of self, the overall outcomes in terms of group levels of achievement are starkly different. There is thus nothing intrinsic about the relationship between cultural models of self and achievement per se. This points to the need to consider additional aspects of how self is negotiated in the context of different cultures, particularly in terms of how it incorporates or resists differences, and the extent to which changes in situational behaviors or adaptive strategies result in

threat or anxiety to a sense of cultural identity.[11] Some minorities may structure school experience in terms of its impacts on or relevance for cultural/self identity, with some groups experiencing a more tenuous and fragile sense of cultural self-survival (a "self" easily permeable to external influence, in DeVos's [1978] terms) and others viewing schooling as merely one instrumental means toward achieving occupational success, and therefore as not incompatible with the maintenance of distinct minority cultural values, and so on. In such cases, it is clearly not enough to simply look at identity from the outside and to assume that all identities are basically the same with similar outcomes in terms of academic performance (e.g., "resistant" identities correlate with low academic performance). Rather, we need to pay more attention to the variable ways in which indigenous cultures shape the self, and to the influences of such differences on the identities associated with educational performance.

Transcultural Comparisons of Teaching and Learning

Another potentially rich area for anthropological exploration in education concerns the comparative exploration of the relationship between educational values, beliefs, and practices and cultural views of self. If understandings of self differ across cultures (as many anthropologists and cultural psychologists argue), then we should be able to see these differences reflected in educational practices, and understand the latter better in the light of their relation to culturally normative views of self.

One case of interest concerns anthropological studies of Japanese education, where a rich discourse on self exists.[12] In Japan, it is almost impossible to speak of education without reference to an indigenous psychology of the self, where concepts of interpersonal dependency (amae), inner core self (hara), critical self-reflection (hansei), empathy (omoiyari), and persistence (gambaru) (among many others) reflect great concern for cultivating various qualities of the self, especially in its relations with others. Indeed, as has been well-documented in studies of Japanese early education, concern for the development of the whole child is prior to and viewed as foundational for later cognitive development and for the teaching of cognitive skills (see, for example, Lewis 1995; Peak 1991; Singleton 1989; Tobin et al. 1989; White 1987). Furthermore, Japanese cultural understandings of self are integrally related to teachers' conceptualizations of educational practice. Pedagogical approaches, views about learning, and patterns of authority and control in Japanese classrooms all reflect culturally normative views of self that differ, in many cases, from the assumptions that govern educational practices in the United States

(Hoffman 1995). Additionally, Azuma (1986) and Tobin (1994) clearly argue for more attention to self as a basis for understanding educational practices and later educational attainment among Japanese children.

In the United States, rich areas for the comparative exploration of self and its influences on education also exist, especially when we consider that education in a culturally plural context may involve competing or contrasting cultural understandings of self across mainstream and minority groups. Multicultural education as it is frequently conceptualized and practiced in the United States is one area where such implicit assumptions about self are strongly present, yet largely unrecognized (Hoffman 1996). For example, personal uniqueness, the desirability of aggressive self-affirmation, self-esteem boosting, and identification of self with abilities and performances all presuppose a certain model of self associated with the white U.S. middle class. Yet this view of self is certainly not shared by many other cultures, including many minority groups in the United States who are supposedly "supported" by multicultural education. Indeed, these assumptions may actively conflict with notions about self present in a different culture (where the understanding of self may emphasize commonalities across individuals rather than uniqueness, the cultivation of restraint in self-expression, and views of self-esteem that are not grounded in external attributes or performances).

In the contemporary United States, competing discourses of self also exist in many domains outside of formal schooling (with repercussions, inevitably, for schooling). Various media, community, and national discourses encode implicit values and visions concerning self. (For example, the pro-life/pro-choice debate can be read on one level as a debate about the separateness of selves and the role of choice in the maintenance of self. The treatment of the theme of "community" in educational reform agendas would be another interesting arena for consideration of implicit understandings of self.) Indeed, discourses about the self can be seen as overarching frames that shape practice and meaning in all areas of society—from the "We do it all for *You*" of the advertising world to the myth of "quality time" that justifies parental absence from children's lives. It behooves us all, especially anthropologists of education, to focus more of our attention on these hidden agendas for self-formation in social practices.

Conclusion—A Therapeutic Moment in the Field

The areas I have identified above as potent ones for moving beyond identity toward consideration of self in anthropological studies of education are not, by any means, the only ones; nor do they have walls around them. Cultural therapy, for example, if applied to students and seen in the context of a cultural ecological account of minority school failure such as that of Ogbu, provides an interesting way to temper what Ogbu sees as the "identity threat" that is implicated in the development of cultural inversion and "oppositional identities." That is to say, cultural therapy can suggest a more flexible model of self that distinguishes between situational responses and a more "enduring" inner core self, and move us beyond the stasis implied by the notion of "oppositional identity." Reconceptualizing identity and self in the context of minority education may highlight the importance of workable strategies to relate cultural self-identity to the demands of participation in the mainstream. Groups or individuals who systematically approach experiences of "otherness" (such as schooling) from a self-perspective that stresses the separability of situational behavior from enduring value orientations may be more flexible in their social adaptive behavior, without experiencing such behavioral adaptation as a "threat" to their identity. On the other hand, those individuals or groups who tend to stress consistency and identification between inner self and instrumental action without strategies to preserve a sense of cultural self-identity may be less predisposed toward such adaptive flexibility, since the inner self is perceived as far more permeable to the "threatening" influences of the outside. It is perhaps for this latter group that culturally responsive pedagogy may be most useful, for it may reduce the subjective sense of dissonance between self and the practices of mainstream schooling.[13]

Awareness of implicit models of self can also help us to examine assumptions regarding the nature of teacher-student relationships, good teaching practice, teacher authority, and classroom discipline. As Shimahara and Sakai (1995) illustrate in the case of Japanese and American teachers, differences in core cultural assumptions about children and relationships between children and teachers strongly influence how they go about teaching, even when their coursework and official teacher education preparation are strikingly similar. Other areas in which cultural understandings about self have significant influence concern the importance of critical versus noncritical (praise-oriented) views of self, conceptualizations of learning as basically an explicit or implicit process, and culturally-based oppositions between "rote learning" and "teaching students to think" (see Hoffman 1995). All of these educational practices are shaped by basic underlying and often tacit understandings of the nature of self and its relations to others, and they offer a rich area for anthropological comparison.

At the same time, we want to remain aware that ideas about the self do not exist in some cultural vacuum, divorced from larger societal and structural movements and forces. Their interconnectedness with such forces necessarily means that they become arenas for conflict and change. Indeed, attention to the tacit discourses of self present in educational change movements, for example, can deepen our appreciation for the political significance of situated identities and the ways they can be used to oppress (as well as liberate). If identity is seen in this way—as grounded in culturally normative, albeit changing, views of self that include a whole range of implicit values and understandings about what it means to be a person—it can remain a powerful idea, rich with hermeneutic significance and value. But if divorced from its bearings in self, it becomes a mere political sign whose only raison d'être is to erect boundaries and borders that pit "us" against "them." In such a world, neither communication nor exchange is possible, and identities become straitjackets that situate us within systems and groups from which there is no escape.

The danger lies in assuming that self is the new conceptual panacea. Like identity, in its reified, essentialized, and static manifestations—the kinds of meanings that unfortunately do plague contemporary educational discourses—self can ultimately be used in the service of the status quo, as yet another source for stereotyping and blanket generalizations about what "minority students need." The challenge for anthropologists of education, I maintain, is to keep that from happening, by constant questioning and self-criticism. For it is only by turning givens into questions that we can generate the momentum for change.

Diane M. Hoffman is an assistant professor of anthropology and comparative education at the Curry School, University of Virginia.

Notes

1. Yet given the new reductionism to power that we face in many areas of social analysis, we may question whether, in this politicizing move, we have truly moved toward genuinely transformative views of identity, or are merely playing the same melody in a different key. See Brown 1996 for critiques of power, dominance, and resistance as themes in contemporary social science, and LeCompte and deMarrais 1992 for an insightful critique of "empowerment" discourse.

2. There are certainly individual (and probably cultural) differences in the extent to which persons are conscious of the psychodynamic patterns of self; it would be misleading to say that self is always conscious. However, the existence of psychotherapy in a number of cultures around the world (both in its Western as well as in a variety of indigenous forms) points at least to the fact that people often do have aspects of "self" that are not immediately "conscious" or open to investi-

gation/reflection. I take this as some indication that there is some validity in speaking cross-culturally of a dimension of psychodynamic selfhood that is not completely equivalent to conscious social identifications.

3. Again, this does not mean that self is automatically "inner" and identity is automatically "outer." Rather, it means that the relationship between inner and outer (and, of course, whether or not there is a culturally conceptualized inner-outer in the first place) needs to be taken into account. Vygotskian perspectives on development that stress the social origins of self, as well as those of G. H. Mead and other social interactionists do speak clearly of inner-outer processes (e.g., "internalization"), which gives us something to think about in terms of what kinds of selves result from such processes, and whether cultural variations exist in this process of internalization that may produce cultural variations in self. Fundamental characteristics of how individuals relate to others—their degree of social embeddedness, for example—would seem to be an interesting area for analysis.

4. The broad theme of opposition in much of this literature between a self conceptualized as "individual" and one that is "socially embedded" is a topic of debate at present; see Battaglia 1995.

5. It should be noted that the idea of "self" in Japanese culture is a topic on which there is much disagreement, with some analysts stressing its constantly shifting, socially positioned characteristics (and denying any "essential" or "core" aspects) and others stressing the existence of a "modal" variety of self that can be called "Japanese." T. S. Lebra (1994), for example, characterizes the Japanese self as a layered self, where there exist clear levels that she calls "inner self," "social interactional self," and "boundless self." I believe it is important not to gloss over the existence of variable cultural "models" of self—one of which, in the Japanese case at least, encodes a comparatively high degree of socially flexible and shifting representation.

6. There are many other terms associated with this approach, such as "distributed cognition" and "situated social practice." While they do not all mean the same thing, they can be taken together as part of a new conceptual approach to learning and development that Cole (1996) calls "cultural psychology."

7. The Spindlers have also discussed a third type of self, the "endangered self" (1993:37). This self seems to emerge when there is some grave incompatibility between situated and enduring selves such that the enduring self is damaged by being violated too often and too strongly by the adaptive demands of the situated self.

8. George Spindler (personal communication, 1997) reminds us that the enduring/situated self is a non-culture-specific construct; if so, we need to consider possible variations in its form across cultural contexts.

9. There are, of course, some significant exceptions. Challenges to prevailing multiculturalist views of identity have come from Davidson 1996, 1997; Heath and McLaughlin 1993; Hoffman 1996; Kondo 1990; Segal and Handler 1995, among others. As noted earlier, work in the critical/postmodern vein has also

been strongly critical of assumptions about identity clarity, stasis, and so on.

10. While this may be the ideal, the reality is sometimes quite different. Experiences of "identity conflict" are not unknown among Koreans in the United States. On the contrary, especially among the second generation, parental expectations for retaining "Korean" identity, especially within the family, are intense, and often occasion conflict with "Americanized" social identities that are cultivated at school. This may in fact reflect the generational shift toward adoption of Americanized cultural understandings of self in which pragmatic/situational adaptations are less compatible with the maintenance of values and inner orientations that diverse from social behavior.

11. The case of Iranians in the United States provides another interesting illustration of the importance of situational modalities of self in the academic context (see Hoffman 1988, 1989a, 1989b, 1990).

12. The emphasis on self in the literature on education in Japan stands in stark contrast to the anthropological literature on education in the United States, where self is much less often a focus. In fact, the only area where a discourse on "self" is quite prevalent in U.S. education is educational psychology (and its popularized "self-help" variants), with its emphasis on "self-concept," "self-esteem," "self-fulfillment," "self-actualization," and so forth. Anthropological literature on education in the United States makes more frequent mention of "identity" than self. Furthermore, while the emphasis on self in the literature on Japanese education is remarkable, this does not mean that "identity" discourses are absent among Japanese. The latter is definitely not true, given the oft-noted and discussed phenomena of *nihonjinbunkaron* (theories of Japanese identity). Identity issues are becoming increasingly salient in the context of discussions in education about internationalization and international returnees. However, the emphasis on self remains, partially (as I see it) a result of the enduring influence of philosophies such as Confucianism and Buddhism on ideas of teaching and learning in Asian societies.

13. We should be well aware of the need to guard against the tendency for "deficit" interpretations to creep into any kind of comparative analysis, including the kind proposed here. One way to do this is to take to heart the idea that individuals, while "in" and "of" culture, are never isomorphic to culture. "Deficit" can thus never be attributed clearly to either "culture" or "individual."

References Cited

Ames, Roger, Wimal Dissanayake, and Thomas P. Kasulis, 1994, Self as Person in Asian Theory and Practice. Albany: State University of New York Press.

Appel, Stephen, 1996, Positioning Subjects: Psychoanalysis and Critical Educational Studies. Westport, CT: Bergin and Garvey.

Azuma, Hiroshi, 1986, Why Study Child Development in Japan? In Child Development and Education in Japan. Harold Stevenson, Hiroshi Azuma, and Kenji Hakuta, eds. Pp. 3–12. New York: W. H. Freeman and Company.

Banks, James A., 1988, Multiethnic Education: Theory and Practice. 2nd edition. Newton, MA: Allyn and Bacon.

Battaglia, Debbora, 1995, Rhetorics of Self-Making. Berkeley: University of California Press.

Blacking, John, 1983, The Concept of Identity and Folk Concepts of Self: A Venda Case Study. In Identity: Personal and Socio-Cultural. Anita Jacobson-Widding, ed. Pp. 47–65. Uppsala, Sweden: Almquist and Wiksell.

Brown, Michael F., 1996, On Resisting Resistance. American Anthropologist 98:729–749.

Cole, Michael, 1996, Cultural Psychology: A Once and Future Discipline. Cambridge, MA: Harvard University Press.

Davidson, Anne Locke, 1996, Making and Molding Identity in Schools: Student Narratives on Race, Gender, and Academic Engagement. Albany: State University of New York Press.

——1997, Marbella Sanchez: On Marginalization and Silencing. In Beyond Black and White: New Faces and Voices in U.S. Schools. Maxine Seller and Lois Weis, eds. Pp. 15–44. Albany: State University of New York Press.

DeVos, George A., 1978, Selective Permeability and Reference Group Sanctioning: Psychocultural Continuities in Role Degradation. In Major Social Issues—a Multidisciplinary View. Milton Yinger and Stephen Cohen, eds. Pp. 9–24. New York: Free Press.

——1992, Social Cohesion and Alienation: Minorities in the United States and Japan. Boulder, CO: Westview Press.

DeVos, George A., and Marcelo M. Suarez-Orozco, 1990, Status Inequality: The Self in Culture. Newbury Park, CA: Sage Publications.

Dissanayake, Wimal, 1996, Self, Agency, and Cultural Knowledge: Reflections on Three Japanese Films. In Narratives of Agency: Self-Making in China, India, and Japan. Wimal Dissanayake, ed. Pp. 178–201. Minneapolis: University of Minnesota Press.

Fogelson, Raymond D. 1979, Person, Self, and Identity: Some Anthropological Retrospects, Circumspects, and Prospects. In Psychosocial Theories of the Self. Benjamin Lee and Kathleen Smith, eds. Pp. 67–110. New York: Plenum Press.

Geertz, Clifford, 1983, From the Native's Point of View: On the Nature of Anthropological Understanding. In Local Knowledge: Further Essays in Interpretive Anthropology. Pp. 55–72. New York: Basic Books.

Gergen, Kenneth J., 1991, The Saturated Self: Dilemmas of Identity in Contemporary Life. New York: Basic Books.

Gibson, Margaret 1984, [1976] Approaches to Multicultural Education in the United States: Some Concepts and Assumptions. Anthropology and Education Quarterly 15:94–119.

——1988 Accommodation without Assimilation: Sikh Immigrants in an American High School. Ithaca, NY: Cornell University Press.

Goldberg, Arnold, 1979, The Self of Psychoanalysis. In Psychosocial Theories of the Self. Benjamin Lee and Kathleen Smith, eds. Pp. 3–22. New York: Plenum Press.

Good, Byron J., and Mary DelVecchio Good, 1985, The Interpretation of Iranian Depressive Illness and Dysphoric Affect. In Culture and Depression. Arthur Kleinman and Byron Good, eds. Pp. 369–428. Berkeley: University of California Press.

Greenfield, Patricia, 1994, Independence and Interdependence as Developmental Scripts: Implications for Theory, Research and Practice. In Cross-Cultural Roots of Minority Child Development. Patricia M. Greenfield and Rodney Cocking, eds. Pp. 1–40. Hillsdale, NJ: Lawrence Erlbaum Associates.

Hall, Stuart, 1995, Introduction: Who Needs Identity? In Questions of Cultural Identity. Stuart Hall and Paul duGay, eds. Pp. 1–17. London: Sage.

Hallowell, A. Irving, 1955, Culture and Experience. Philadelphia: University of Pennsylvania Press.

Hanna, Judith Lynn, 1994, Issues in Supporting School Diversity: Academics, Social Relations, and the Arts. Anthropology and Education Quarterly 25:66–85.

Heath, Shirley Brice, and Milbrey McLaughlin, 1993, Identity and Inner-City Youth: Beyond Ethnicity and Gender. New York: Teachers College Press.

Hemmings, Annette, 1996, Conflicting Images? Being Black and a Model High School Student. Anthropology and Education Quarterly 27:20–50.

Hoffman, Diane M., 1988, Cross-Cultural Adaptation and Learning: Iranians and Americans at School. In School and Society: Learning Content through Culture. Henry T. Trueba and Concha Delgado-Gaittan, eds. Pp. 163–180. New York: Praeger.

——1989a, Language and Culture Acquisition among Iranians in the United States. Anthropology and Education Quarterly 20:118–132.

——1989b, Self and Culture Revisited: Culture Acquisition among Iranians in the United States. Ethos 17:32–49.

——1990, Beyond Conflict: Culture, Self, and Intercultural Learning among Iranians in the U.S. International Journal of Intercultural Relations 14:275–299.

——1995, Models of Self and Culture in Teaching and Learning: An Anthropological Perspective on Japanese and American Education. Educational Foundations 9 (3):19–42.

——1996, Culture, Self, and Multicultural Education: Reflections on Discourse, Text, and Practice. American Educational Research Journal 33:545–569.

Jen, Gish, 1997, Who's to Judge? The New Republic, April 21:18– 19.

Kim, Eun Young, 1993, Career Choice among Second Generation Korean-Americans: Reflections of a Cultural Model of Success. Anthropology and Education Quarterly 24:224–248.

Kondo, Dorinne, 1990, Crafting Selves: Power, Gender, and Discourses on Identity in a Japanese Workplace. Chicago: University of Chicago Press.

Lave, Jean, 1991, Situating Learning in Communities of Practice. In Perspectives on Socially Shared Cognition. Lauren B. Resnick, John M. Levine, and Stephanie D. Teasley, eds. Pp. 63–84. Washington, DC: American Psychological Association.

Lave, Jean, and Etienne Wenger, 1991, Situated Learning: Legitimate Peripheral Participation. New York: Cambridge University Press.

Lebra, Takie S., 1994, Self in Japanese Culture. In Japanese Sense of Self. Nancy Rosenberger, ed. Pp. 105–120. Cambridge: Cambridge University Press.

LeCompte, Margaret D., and Kathleen Bennett de-Marrais, 1992, The Disempowering of Empowerment: Out of the Revolution and into the Classroom. Educational Foundations 6 (3):5–32.

Lee, Stacey 1994, Behind the Model Minority Stereotype: Voices of High and Low Achieving

Asian American Students. Anthropology and Education Quarterly 25:413–429.

——1996, Unraveling the "Model Minority Stereotype": Listening to Asian American Youth. New York: Teachers College Press.

Levinson, Bradley A., Douglas E. Foley, and Dorothy C. Holland, eds., 1996, The Cultural Production of the Educated Person: Critical Ethnographies of Schooling and Local Practice. Albany: State University of New York Press.

Lewis, Catherine, 1995, Educating Hearts and Minds: Reflections on Japanese Preschool and Elementary Education. Cambridge: Cambridge University Press.

Markus, Hazel R., and Shinobu Kitayama, 1991, Culture and the Self: Implications for Cognition, Emotion, and Motivation. Psychological Review 98 (2):224–253.

Marsella, Anthony J., George A. DeVos, and Francis L. K. Hsu, 1985, Culture and Self: Asian and Western Perspectives. New York: Tavistock.

McDermott, Ray, 1987, The Explanation of Minority School Failure, Again. Anthropology and Education Quarterly 18:361–364.

——1993, The Acquisition of a Child by a Learning Disability. In Understanding Practice: Perspectives on Activity and Context. Seth Chaiklin and Jean Lave, eds. Pp. 269–305. New York: Cambridge University Press.

McDermott, Ray, and Herve Varenne, 1995, Culture as Disability. Anthropology and Education Quarterly 26:324–348.

Ogbu, John, 1978, Minority Education and Caste: The American System in Cross-Cultural perspective. New York: Academic Press.

——1982, Cultural Discontinuities in Schooling. Anthropology and Education Quarterly 13: 290–307.

——1983, Minority Status and Schooling in Plural Societies. Comparative Education Review 27 (2):168–190.

——1992, Understanding Cultural Diversity and Learning. Educational Researcher 21 (8):5–14.

Peak, Lois, 1991, Learning to Go to School in Japan. Berkeley: University of California Press.

Perry, R. J., 1992, Why Do Multiculturalists Ignore Anthropologists? The Chronicle of Higher Education, March 4:52.

Phelan, Patricia, Anne Locke Davidson, and Hanh Cao Yu, 1993, Students' Multiple Worlds: Navigating the Borders of Family, Peer, and School Cultures. In Renegotiating Cultural Diversity in American Schools. Patricia Phelan and Anne Locke Davidson, eds. Pp. 52–88. New York: Teachers College Press.

Rogoff, Barbara, Jacqueline Baker-Sennett, Pilar Lacasa, and Denise Goldsmith, 1995, Development through Participation in Sociocultural Activity. In Cultural Practices as Contexts for Development. Jacqueline Goodnow, Peggy J. Miller, and Frank Kessel, eds. Pp. 45–66. San Francisco: Jossey-Bass.

Sampson, Edward, 1988, The Debate on Individualism: Indigenous Psychologies of the Individual and Their Role in Personal and Societal Functioning. American Psychologist 43(2): 15–22.

Segal, Daniel, and Richard Handler, 1995, U.S. Multiculturalism and the Concept of Culture. Identities: Global Studies in Culture and Power 1(4):391–407.

Shimahara, Nobuo K., and Akira Sakai, 1995, Learning to Teach in Two Cultures: Japan and the United States. New York: Garland Press.

Shweder, Richard, 1990, Cultural Psychology: What Is It? In Cultural Psychology: Essays on Comparative Human Development. James W. Stigler, Richard A. Shweder, and Gilbert Herdt, eds. Pp. 1–46. Cambridge: Cambridge University Press.

Shweder, Richard, and Edmund J. Bourne, 1984, Does the Concept of the Person Vary Cross-Culturally? In Culture Theory: Essays on Mind, Self, and Emotion. Richard A. Shweder and Robert A. Levine, eds. Pp. 158–199. Cambridge: Cambridge University Press.

Singleton, John, 1989, Gambaru: A Japanese Cultural Theory of Learning. In Japanese Schooling: Patterns of Socialization, Equality, and Political Control. James J. Shields, ed. Pp. 8–15. University Park: Pennsylvania State University Press.

Sorensen, Clark W., 1994, Success and Education in South Korea. Comparative Education Review 38(1):10–35.

Spindler, George, and Louise Spindler, 1987, Cultural Dialogue and Schooling in Schoenhausen and Roseville: A Comparative Analysis. Anthropology and Education Quarterly 18:3–16.

——1989, Instrumental Competence, Self-Efficacy, Linguistic Minorities, and Cultural Therapy: A Preliminary Attempt at Integration. Anthropology and Education Quarterly 10: 36–50.

——1992, The Enduring, Situated, and Endangered Self in Fieldwork: A Personal Account. In The Psychoanalytic Study of Society, vol. 17. Essays in Honor of George D. and Louise A. Spindler. L. Bryce Boyer and Ruth M. Boyer, eds. Pp. 23–28. Hillsdale, NJ: The Analytic Press.

——1993, The Processes of Culture and Person: Cultural Therapy and Culturally Diverse Schools. In Renegotiating Cultural Diversity in American Schools. Patricia Phelan and Ann L. Davidson, eds, Pp. 27–51. New York: Teachers College Press.

——1994, Pathways to Cultural Awareness: Cultural Therapy with Teachers and Students. Thousand Oaks, CA: Sage Publications.

Suarez-Orozco, Marcelo M., 1987, Towards a Psychosocial Understanding of Hispanic Adaptation to American Schooling. In Success or Failure: Learning and the Language Minority Student. Henry T. Trueba, ed. Pp. 156–168. Cambridge, MA: Newbury House.

Suarez-Orozco, Marcelo M., and Carola E. Suarez-Orozco, 1993, Hispanic Cultural Psychology: Implications for Education Theory and Research. In Renegotiating Cultural Diversity in American Schools. Patricia Phelan and Ann L. Davidson, eds. Pp. 108–138. New York: Teachers College Press.

Tobin, Joseph, 1994, Japanese Preschools and the Pedagogy of Selfhood. In Japanese Sense of Self. Nancy Rosenberger, ed. Pp. 21–39. Cambridge: Cambridge University Press.

Tobin, Joseph, David Wu, and Dana Davidson, 1989, Preschool in Three Cultures. New Haven, CT: Yale University Press.

Trueba, Henry T., 1993a, Cultural Therapy in Action. In Healing Multicultural America: Mexican Immigrants Rise to Power in Rural California. Henry T. Trueba, Cirenio Rodriquez, Yali Zou, and Jose Cintron, eds. Pp. 155–168. London: Falmer Press.

——1993b, Cultural Diversity and Conflict: The Role of Educational Anthropology in Healing Multicultural America. In Renegotiating Cultural Diversity in American Schools. Patricia Phelan and Ann L. Davidson, eds. Pp. 195–215. New York: Teachers College Press.

Turner, Terrance, 1993, Anthropology and Multiculturalism: What Is Anthropology that Multiculturalists Should Be Mindful of It? Cultural Anthropology 8:411–430.

Ulichny, Polly, 1996, Cultures in Conflict. Anthropology and Education Quarterly 27:331–364.

Wax, Murray, 1993, How Culture Misdirects Multiculturalism. Anthropology and Education Quarterly 24:99–115.

White, Merry, 1987, The Japanese Educational Challenge: A Commitment to Children. New York: Free Press.

Whiting, John W. M., 1990, Adolescent Rituals and Identity Conflicts. In Cultural Psychology: Essays on Comparative Human Development. James W. Stigler, Richard A. Shweder, and Gilbert Herdt, eds. Pp. 357–365. Cambridge: Cambridge University Press.

On the Teaching and Personal Construction of Educational Equity

By Patricia Terry Davidman and Leonard Davidman

Equity has been conceptualized, described, and defined in a variety of ways by various theorists, practitioners, and politicians. James Banks (1994, pp. 13–14) describes it as a basic element of pedagogy and major dimension of multicultural education (*equity pedagogy*). Christine Bennett (1995, pp. 16–17) links it strongly to academic performance in her discussion of *academic excellence and equity*, while we (Davidman & Davidman, 1997, pp. 13–14) present *educational equity* as one of seven fundamental goals of multicultural education.

And, Christine Whitman, the current Governor of New Jersey, and her staff, when they try to revise the costs of complying with their State Supreme Court's equity-related rulings, create their own "working" definition of equity (Karp, 1997). Yet, as different as some conceptions of equity are, we believe that most advocates of multicultural education would agree that educational equity is an essential feature of education that is or seeks to be multicultural.

However, while we can speak with confidence about the importance of educational equity within various models of multicultural education, we are less certain that advocates and professors of multicultural education would reach substantial agreement regarding the nature of educational equity, or the ways in which the concept should be taught in pre-service teacher education programs.

While we believe this possible variation in belief is worthy of study, we believe that an article about the nature of educational equity and the ways it should be presented to future and current educators is timely. In an earlier effort, we provided readers with an analysis of the different levels one could use to analyze and conceptualize

—Patricia Terry Davidman is an associate professor of education and Leondard Davidman is a professor of education, both with the University Center for Teacher Education at California Polytechnic State University, San Luis Obispo.

educational equity (Davidman & Davidman, 1997). In that work, (1) educational equity, the social construction of knowledge, and the empowerment of students, parents, and teachers were linked; and, (2) the strong support which *inequality* has enjoyed in our capitalistic democracy (to the detriment of educational equity) was examined.

In this essay, drawing on our previous work, we will: (1) introduce some general ideas about educational equity; (2) review the above-mentioned levels; and (3) show how the equity theorizing of Ken Sirotnick, Elliot Eisner, Bennett, and Patrice Leblanc Kohl and Elaine Witty can help educators gain additional insight into educational equity, and to a lesser degree the social and personal construction of knowledge. We will close with some speculative remarks about the relationship between educational equity and social justice.

General Ideas

Notions of educational equity and educational equality are quite complicated. Perhaps this is because at the core of each are meanings which are both similar and different. Why might this be the case? For one thing, in the educational literature some very different conceptions of educational equity have arisen out of the different ways different groups (i.e., ethnic minorities, women, English learners, disabled citizens) were intended to benefit from equity-oriented legislation and assistance programs. The perceived and real absence of a fair distribution of resources, rights, and opportunities in many states and school districts throughout the 20th century created the intellectual, legislative, judicial, and moral need to invent the idea of educational equity, as well as the policies, laws, and organizations that have contributed to its development.

Relatedly, this conceptual diversity illustrates how knowledge, in this case the concept of educational equity, is constructed by individuals and organizations who are influenced first by the core values and so-

cietal pressures of a culture in a given era, and secondly by their personal or collective interpretation of these factors. Thus, we are discussing here a very important and complicated idea, a concept whose meanings have been shaped by a diverse set of legislators, academicians, social activists, jurists, and educational leaders to name a few.

Finally, because of its importance to the mission of public education in a democracy, pre-service teacher candidates and graduate students in education should be encouraged to study the concept in a manner that allows them to come up with their own personal conception of, and rationale for, educational equity. Hopefully, the discussion below will facilitate this process.

Diverse Criteria and Levels for Educational Equity

When fleshing out the various meanings of educational equity, it is helpful to remember that it is an idea that can be discussed and defined in terms of various observable, measurable conditions, as well as conditions that are more difficult to measure. For example, if one accepts that equity is strongly related to fairness and that educational fairness is sometimes but not always synonymous with educational equality, an educator could analyze the degree of equity between two sixth grade classrooms in the same school district in terms of:

1. The allocation of financial, physical, and human resources in each classroom;
2. The amount of time per week each class has to learn specific topics like mathematics and art;
3. The content of the curricula addressed in each classroom;
4. The appropriateness of the pedagogy employed in each classroom;
5. The specific learning inputs and outcomes for both individuals and specific groups (girls, low-SES students,

African Americans, second language learners, students with IEPs); and

6. The morale of the learners in each class.

Of course, teachers need not look to another classroom to think about educational equity, and in most cases do not. Teachers can measure the relative allocation of resources and learning opportunities between individuals and groups in their own classrooms. In contrast, it may be necessary to carry out investigations regarding educational equity at the school district, county, state, and federal levels.

For example, it is quite possible that a concern for internal equity could produce a very fair allocation of resources and opportunity structure for learning in a rural, low S.E.S. school district. However, when compared with wealthier school districts in the same state, as occurred in Kentucky in 1989, a State Supreme Court could find that unequal funding or inequity was pervasive within the state, and on that basis rule that the *entire* statewide school system within the state was unconstitutional (Stephens, 1989).

In addition, at the federal level some investigations pertaining to educational equity have focused on whether or not a state or school district or university was providing, in the context of its educational programs and policies, equal protection of the laws. While it is not unconstitutional for one state to fund public education at a level dramatically below another state, it was and is unconstitutional for a single student or group of students within a state or several states to be denied equal protection of the laws as guaranteed by the Fourteenth Amendment to the U.S. Constitution.

Thus, in 1954 the U.S. Supreme Court, led by Chief Justice Earl Warren, struck down the legality of segregated schools, which had been established by the U.S. Supreme Court's 1896 decision in *Plessy v. Ferguson*. In *Brown v. Board of Education* Justice Warren wrote:

In these days, it is doubtful that any child may reasonably be expected to succeed in life if he is denied the opportunity for an education. Such an opportunity, where the state has undertaken to provide it, is a right which must be made available to all on equal terms. (Warren, 1954)

Here we see that a phrase pertaining to equality in the Fourteenth Amendment to the U.S. Constitution, coupled with (a) the high degree of inequality and oppression associated with legalized segregation, (b) the tenacity of NAACP lawyers led first by Charles Hamilton Houston and then Thurgood Marshall, and (c) the social pressures and opportunities of the post-World War II

era, led the Warren Supreme Court to construct a new interpretation of educational equality and, relatedly, new facts about the separate-but-equal logic and legality of *Plessy v. Ferguson*. Before *Brown v. Board of Education*, "separate but equal" was constitutional; after *Brown*, it was unconstitutional.

This example shows that the study of educational equity can lead to discussions regarding the genesis of pivotal U.S. Supreme Court civil rights decisions, and further that these discussions can be structured in a manner that reveals that knowledge is constantly being constructed, modified, and invented by individuals whose knowledge construction process is more or less influenced by the social, economic, and political events of a given era. Such discussions, while valuable in themselves, can also serve as stepping-stones to more explicit comparisons of competing conceptions of educational equity.

Competing Conceptions of Equity

In this section we will contrast the contributions of Sirotnick and Eisner, and then Bennett and Kohl and Witty, as we attempt to highlight the differences and similarities between selected conceptions of educational equity.

As we have noted elsewhere (1997, p. 78), "For Sirotnick, equity is concerned with the allocation of resources to groups, is assessed quantitatively, and is conceptually linked to the idea of excellence." Regarding the latter, Sirotnick has written that, "excellence is indicated by conditions, practices, and outcomes in schools that are associated with high levels of learning for most students in all valued goal areas of the common curriculum" (1990, p. 159). Utilizing this definition, Sirotnick states that

Equity is indicated when there are no systematic differences in the distributions of these conditions, practices, and outcomes based upon race, ethnicity, economic status, or any other irrelevant grouping characteristic. (1990, p. 159)

And, please note that when Sirotnick refers to race and ethnicity, etc., as an irrelevant grouping characteristic, he is not saying that these concepts are irrelevant in the real world of school districts and society; rather, he implies that these factors should be irrelevant in determining educational outcomes. It is noteworthy also that in Sirotnick's conception equity has a lot to do with similarity rather than difference of conditions.

In contrast to Sirotnick, "Eisner's equity theorizing focuses on the education that *individuals* receive, and his perception of what is fair and good in schooling dramatically differs from Sirotnick's conception" (1997, p. 79). For Eisner "equity is achieved in education not only by giving students an opportunity to come to school, it is also influenced by what they find when they arrive." He goes on to say that "school programs that create a very narrow eye of the needle through which all children must pass diminish educational equity" (Eisner, 1991, p. 17). Eisner concludes by noting that:

The genuinely good school does not diminish individual differences, it expands them. Virtue in the context of education is not achieved by bringing all children to the same destination; it is achieved by helping them learn how to become who they are. (1991, p. 17).

Regarding these seemingly antithetical conceptions we observed (1997) that when Eisner " . . . says that differences between individuals should be expanded, he does not mean that a genuinely good school should set out to increase the pre-schooling differences between various ethnic, racial, and socioeconomic groups." However, what his statement does make clear is that our perspective on what is real and important influences our interpretation of fairness and goodness. For example:

Sirotnick creates a conception aimed at reducing differences in test scores between *groups*, primarily because he believes these group differences are problematic and not inherently real or immutable. They are, to a great extent, created by societal conditions; and society, through its investment in schools, can significantly reduce these *group* differences. However, if Sirotnick had focused on what is good and fair for individuals, he might have written Eisner's essay. Schools, after all, are not formed to stamp out hubcaps. They are, we hope, involved in the design and implementation of curricula to develop creative individuals and thoughtful citizens who seek to improve their democratic legacy. (Davidman & Davidman, 1997, p. 79)

Suffice it to say here that Eisner's conception parallels the American core value of individualism. For Eisner, social groups may be interesting, but it is what happens to individuals that really matters. Sirotnick, with his group-oriented conception, more closely parallels the legislative and judicial interpretation of equity in the latter half of the 20th century. Equity-oriented programs reallocate resources and try to create equivalent conditions, outcomes, etc., for groups because individuals in specific groups have been and continue to be stigmatized and discriminated against because of their perceived group label(s).

We believe that both conceptions hold value for practitioners because, in fact, when most educators teach they respond directly to individuals and not social groups, and they should encourage these individuals to reach for their very own stars. But our work with individuals is informed by knowledge about social groups, and this is logical. For, as we have noted

... school practitioners ... do not only deal with real individuals. They also deal, directly and indirectly, with real social groups. These groups include students who are severely handicapped, or homeless, or Latino American, or African American, or female, or learning English as a second language, or some combination of these. Furthermore, with regard to these groups, classroom teachers and administrators have overlapping *and* different responsibilities vis-a-vis teaching, schoolwide evaluation, and policymaking. And, to fulfill these responsibilities professionally, they need more than an either-or conception of equity. They need a conception that helps them to work wisely and fairly with both individuals and groups, and a philosophy that enables them to do this without trampling on the constitutional rights of individuals or groups. (1997, pp. 79–80)

These educators need flexibility and balance, and they need teaching and administrative strategies which help them build classroom and schoolwide *unity* in settings where respect for individual and group diversity is manifest.

With this unity in mind, one of the positives in the work of Eisner and Sirotnick is their avoidance of creating an explicit us/them distinction about education equity. For Eisner equity is for all children, and for Sirotnick it could be; when and if we reach Sirotnick's ideal state of equity, a better society will be available to all.

But other knowledgeable multicultural education theorists construct a different and narrower response to the question: Whom is equity for? For instance, Bennett, in the opening pages of her text, *Comprehensive Multicultural Education: Theory and Practice,* writes that " ... the equity movement ... targets primarily ethnic minorities and the poor" (1995, p. 14), and adds that:

Although one's ethnic group is just one of a number of identity sources available, ethnicity is the heart of the

equity problem in this society. Therefore, discussions about achieving educational excellence require concern about those ethnic groups that have been consistently cut off from equal access to a good education. (1995, p. 17)

Bennett keeps her focus on ethnic groups, race, and culture because of her understandable concern that multicultural education can become overextended. "Multicultural education," she writes, "is the one area that focuses on diversity issues related to race and culture. If it becomes overextended, it is likely to lose its power in these areas" (1995, p. 16). Thus, we have a conception of equity where gender equity and equity for gay and lesbian students or religious minorities, while acknowledged as important, would take second place. And, we see how one's beliefs about the appropriate parameters for multicultural education can shape one's construction of a point of view about educational equity.

In contrast to a strong emphasis on ethnic groups, Kohn and Witty, in their informative and partial review of the equity literature, chose to focus on four equity areas: disabilities; ethnicity/race; socioeconomic status; and gender. They note that their selection of these groups " ... was not meant to slight any other equity groups; it was a decision based on the authors' areas of expertise and the reality of space constraints" (1996, p. 838).

For Kohl and Witty, "Equity addresses the primary goal of education in the United States—educating all children" (1996, p. 837). Working with this as a starting point, they were able to develop an expansive and, from our perspective, a more logical view regarding the question: Whom is educational equity for? In short, equity is to be created for various equity groups, and teachers and administrators in the settings in which they work should strive to create equity for all of the pertinent equity groups and individuals in their population of learners.

While they appear to diverge on which group or groups should be the focus of equity initiatives, Bennett and Kohl and Witty all make a clear distinction between equity and equality. Kohl and Witty state that, "Equity should not be confused with equality," and further that "equality calls for all children to be treated equally" (1996, p. 837). They clarify this assertion by observing that:

State equalization formulas for distribution of finances are an example; all children receive equal amounts of funding for schooling. However, equity focuses on the redistribution of funds to those who need it most. Here disadvantaged children receive more funding for education to de-

crease the gap between where they are and where average U.S. students are. (1996, p. 837)

In a similar vein, Bennett says that, "Equity in education means equal opportunities for all students to develop to their fullest potential," but also that "equity in education must not be confused with equality or sameness of result or even identical experiences" (1995, p. 16). Working the same theme, Carl Grant states that multicultural education is a philosophical concept and educational process that recognizes " ... that equality and equity are not the same thing: equal access does not necessarily guarantee fairness" (1994, p. 4).

In partial agreement but with some contrast, we believe that the concept of educational equity encompasses educational equality, and that educational equity will sometimes be achieved by creating educational equality. Thus, the two concepts will sometimes be the same thing—the condition of equality will be the condition of equity. For example, aiming for equity for exceptional learners, the poor, and second language learners will often lead to *different* teaching strategies, curricula, and financial costs. But in other important arenas such as gender equity, state funding of public schools, and graduation rates—the effort to create *equality* of condition and *equal* distribution of inputs and outputs is a significant part of the overall equity movement.

However, while some advocates strive to create quality of condition, others, quite appropriately, try to deliver *more* than equal funding to *overburdened* schools, schools that are typically low S.E.S. with high percentages of funds channeled into special education and security programs (Slavin, 1997). The argument here is that overburdened schools, in order to have equivalent amounts of money available for basic instruction in the "regular education" program for our most needy students, will need more money at the outset. But even here the argument for providing more than equal funding is intertwined with the idea of equality. If inequality of funding makes sense in this context, it is because it is aimed at a very difficult idea, namely equality of opportunity, or more realistically, leveling a playing field which will always be tilted toward inequality. In short, in different arenas creating equality, as well as inequality, of resources will contribute to educational equity.

The case of gender equity (for females) in sports activities at National Collegiate Athletic Association (NCAA) Division One campuses may illustrate the latter point. Presently, to determine if a university's athletic program is in compliance with the Title IX of the Education Amendments of 1972, the U.S. Department of Education's Office of Civil Rights utilizes three criteria

(Naughton, 1997). Naughton, in an article in the *Chronicle of Higher Education*, indicates, first, that the "substantial proportionality" test is one of three compliance criteria utilized by Office of Civil Rights staff, and, second, that:

> Although the phrase has never been legally defined, colleges at which the proportion of female athletes is no more than five percentage points less than the proportion of female undergraduates are generally considered to have met the test. (1997, p. A39)

In addition, Naughton reports that colleges that lack "substantial proportionality" can be found in compliance with Title IX if they are " . . . continually expanding athletic opportunities to the under-represented gender, or . . . meeting the athletic 'interests and abilities' of its student body." While much data in his article indicates that the 305 NCAA Division One sports programs reported on are far from achieving parity in male and female sports programs, for our purposes the key point is that the criterion for determining if sex discrimination is present in a university's athletic program *is not* equality of female athletic participation. In fact, in this instance, lack of sexual discrimination, or equity, is legally defined by a specific level of inequality, or of consistent actions which indicate a genuine desire to improve the situation. Thus, in the area of collegiate-level sports opportunities for women, at the present time it appears that unequal access does not necessarily indicate inequity.

It may be confusing to learn that the effort to fairly educate all of America's students produces initiatives which call for both equality and inequality of resources, but complex realities require complex ways of thinking. Furthermore, to set the stage for equity-oriented action at various levels of operation, change agents need an understanding of equity that is both clear and accurate. With clarity and accuracy in mind, we suggest that both equity-oriented educators and authors make several things clear—to themselves and others—when they attempt to create, advance, or report on equity-oriented initiatives.

First, which equity group or groups (African Americans, second language learners, women, the poor, etc.) are the focus of the initiative? Second, is the goal to equalize or unequally distribute resources across groups, or does the initiative encompass both? Third, which level or levels of operation (classroom, school, school district, etc.) is the initiative attempting to influence? Fourth, is the initiative attempting to modify inputs or outcomes, or both. And finally, with Eisner in mind, does the initiative focus on socially defined groups or individuals, or somehow both?

> *. . . if the terms that various advocates employ, such as educational equity, social justice, and critical pedagogy are not thoroughly analyzed, debated, and clarified . . . opponents might be better able to undermine the movement towards multicultural education.*

Final Thoughts

The terms which advocates of multicultural education create and use to explain and advance their multicultural agendas are obviously important. However, if the terms that various advocates employ, such as *educational equity, social justice,* and *critical pedagogy* are not thoroughly analyzed, debated, and clarified, advocates might lose sight of the diversity of opinion in their midst, and opponents might be better able to undermine the movement towards multicultural education.

We have endeavored here to bring more clarity to educational equity so that the words could more clearly inform and provoke action. However, in the 1990s, as we do this we see the goal of educational equity being overshadowed, and perhaps subsumed, by the goal of social justice. This might ultimately be constructive. But, theoretically and programmatically, what is social justice? How does it relate to educational equity? And, will social justice-oriented teaching incorporate, as Bob Peterson (1994) suggests: the teaching of activism for social justice; an emphasis on critiquing bias and attitudes; a questioning/problem-posing approach; dialogue; and a curriculum grounded in the lives of students?

Furthermore, in a society where inequality is deeply entrenched and widely supported, and where most efforts seem to contribute to the efficient management of inequality, what are some of the specific turning points and conditions which will let advocates know they have arrived at, or at least are heading towards the territory where social justice is to be found? We see now in the educational literature, in general, and the multicultural education literature specifically, a need for more clarity if this term is to serve as a meaningful goal for multicultural education.

For example, underlining the need for more clarity is the first paragraph in the definition of social justice provided in the *Dictionary of Multicultural Education* (1997):

> Social justice and social responsibility can be treated as synonymous concepts. These terms, to a great extent, concern institutionalized patterns of mutual action and interdependence that are necessary to bring about the realization of distributive justice. Citizens have a personal obligation mediated through political obligations, to help create a society in which the concerns for concrete needs of all persons and the creation of reciprocal interdependence are fundamental. (p. 247)

Although the definition becomes clearer in later paragraphs when the author alludes to the social justice work of César Chavez, Fannie Lou Hamer, John F. Kennedy, and Martin Luther King, Jr., we think that advocates for social justice-oriented teaching and social justice in society would better serve society if they would indicate the specific changes they would support to provide more social justice in schools and society.

For example, Woodrow Wilson, in his first inaugural address (March 14, 1913), indicated specific areas where legislation could create greater social justice. Wilson, hardly an advocate for racial justice as we know it, said:

> The firm basis of government is justice, not pity . . . there can be no equality of opportunity, the first essential of justice in a body politic, if men and women are not shielded in their lives, their very vitality, from the consequences of great industrial and social processes which they cannot alter, control, or singly cope with. Society must see to it that it does not itself crush or weaken or damage its constituent parts. The first duty of law is to keep sound the society it serves. Sanitary laws, pure food laws, and laws determining conditions of labor which individuals are powerless to determine for themselves are intimate parts of the very business of justice and legal efficiency.

We would like to know more specifically what educational strategies, community action, and social legislation a specific advocate of social justice would support. We see no reason to believe that all advocates of social justice will fall onto the same legislative page, and without specifics, we don't know what page advocates are on. Above all we need examples. In the abovementioned *Dictionary of Multicultural Education* definition, the author goes on to say:

> Social responsibility requires that human needs take priority over claims that derive from a system of role distribution in society. Justice demands equality and fairness in all private transactions, wages, and property ownership, as well as equal opportunity for all to participate in the public benefits generated by society, such as social security, health care, and education. (p. 247)

This is getting clearer. We are beginning to recognize a call for what we might call a socialistic-oriented democracy, but we're not sure. What does " . . . equality and fairness in all private transactions, wages, and property ownership" mean? Without specific examples of the type of changes or proposed legislation such equality and fairness would call for, one is left uncertain about the nature of social justice that is being advocated in a given era and society.

Finally, we note that by attending to the task of clarifying educational equity and social justice, we may, according to John Goodlad, be helping colleagues who work as teacher educators in departments, colleges, and schools of education. Goodlad and his colleagues, after an extensive study

of teacher education programs in the 1980s, concluded that the most critically important omission of these programs was " . . . a vision that encompasses a good and just society, the centrality of education to the renewal of that society, the role of schools [in] bringing this education equitably to all, and the kind of preparation teachers require for their stewardship of the nation's schools" (1994, p. 4). Producing such a vision with a group of colleagues is difficult but critically important work.

We suggest that the act of clarifying what social justice denotes will help to shape the vision of what it is that makes a society good and just. Furthermore, the development of this vision or visions should illuminate the relationship between educational equity and social justice as goals for multicultural education and may leave both K–12 teachers and professors of multicultural education in a better position to respond to questions about "the teaching of activism for social justice," why it is needed, and what it might look like in a second or 11th grade classroom. We shall return to such vision building in a future essay.

References

Banks, J. A. (1994). *Multiethnic Education: Theory and Practice*. (3rd ed.) Boston, MA: Allyn & Bacon.

Bennett, C. I. (1995). *Comprehensive Multicultural Education: Theory and Practice*. (3rd ed.) Boston, MA: Allyn & Bacon.

Davidman, L. & Davidman, P. T. (1997). *Teaching with a Multicultural Perspective: A Practical Guide*. (2nd ed.). White Plains, NY: Longman.

Eisner, E. W. (1991). "What really counts in schools," *Educational Leadership*, 48, 10–17.

Garcia, S. S. (1997). "Social Justice," in the *Dictionary of Multicultural Education*, editors: Carl A. Grant & Gloria Ladson-Billings. Phoenix, AZ: Oryx Press (pp. 247–248).

Goodlad, J. I. (1994). *Educational Renewal: Better Teachers, Better Schools*. San Francisco, CA: Jossey-Bass.

Grant, C. (1994, Winter). "Challenging the Myths about Multicultural Education," *Multicultural Education*, 2, pp. 4–9.

Karp, S. (1997). "Equity Suits Clog the Courts: Legal Battles for State Remedies Face Limitations," in *Funding for Justice: Money, Equity, and Public Education*, Milwaukee, WI.: Rethinking Schools.

Kohl, P. L. & Witty, E. P. (1996). "Equity challenges," Chapter 39 in the *Handbook of Research on Teacher Education* (2nd edition). Ed., J. Sikula, New York, NY: Simon & Schuster Macmillan (pp. 837–866).

Naughton, J. (1997). "Women in Division One Sports Programs: The Glass Is Half Empty and Half Full," *The Chronicle of Higher Education*, 43, no. 31, pp. A39–A40 (April 11, 1997).

Peterson, B. (1994). "Teaching for Social Justice: One Teacher's Journey," in *Funding for Justice: Money, Equity, and Public Education*, Milwaukee, WI.: Rethinking Schools.

Sirotnick, K. (1990). "Equal access to quality in public schooling: Issues in the assessment of equity and excellence." Chapter 9 in *Access to Knowledge: An Agenda for Our Nation's Schools*. Eds., J. I. Goodlad & P. Keating. New York, NY: The College Board.

Slavin, R. (1997). "Where Should the Money Go?" in *Funding for Justice: Money, Equity, and Public Education*, Milwaukee, WI: Rethinking Schools.

Stephens, R. (Chief Justice). (1989). *Rose v. Council for Better Education*, Opinion of the Court, 88–SC–804–TG.

Warren, E. (Chief Justice). (1954). *Brown v. Board of Education of Topeka*, 347 U.S. 483.

Wilson, W. (1973). "First Inaugural Address, in *Documents of American History* (Vol. II). Ed. H. S. Commager, New York, NY: Appleton Century Crofts. (Document #89, pp. 82–84).

Unit 5

Unit Selections

Key Points to Consider

❖ How can teachers best teach about human ethnicity and culture?

❖ How should teachers and students deal with xenophobic reactions when they occur?

❖ What are the similarities and distinctions between a "culture" and an "ethnic group"?

❖ Why is it more effective to integrate multicultural curriculum content into all aspects of a school curriculum?

❖ What are the varying ways in which multicultural education is defined? Which model of multicultural education do you prefer?

❖ What is the rationale for the existence of the multicultural educational effort in the elementary and secondary schools? Should all students be exposed to it?

❖ How can inservice teachers be better prepared to engage in multicultural instruction and learning experiences?

 **Links** **www.dushkin.com/online/**

These sites are annotated on pages 4 and 5.

Curriculum and instruction includes all concerns relative to subject matter to be taught and all pedagogical theory relating to methods of instruction. All pedagogical theory is based on some philosophical assumptions relating to what is worth knowing, and what actions are good. Every school curriculum is the product of specific choices among those available. Since classroom teachers are the "delivery systems" for a curriculum, along with whatever texts are used, teachers have the opportunity to interpret and add their own insights regarding the curricula they teach.

It is in the area of curriculum and instruction in the elementary and secondary schools, as well as in teacher education curricula, that a fundamental transformation must occur to sensitize all young people, including those living in isolated rural and small town communities, to the multicultural reality of our national civilization. There are several different approaches to multicultural educational programming in the schools. This area of study has developed steadily, in stages, since the events of the 1960s, 1970s, and 1980s forced a reassessment of our sense of social justice. There are programs in some school systems that merely include the study of the minority cultural groups living in their particular area, and this is often done through isolated, elective courses or units in required courses that students must take. This is not the approach to multicultural education that most current leaders in the field favor. Today, most experienced multicultural educators favor a more inclusive approach to the subject—the infusion of multicultural themes into the entire life of the school and all possible course content. Such an inclusive approach to multicultural education seeks to help students and teachers to develop a sense of social consciousness. This sense, coupled with a more global and integrated conception of our social reality, will empower them to make more critical assessments than have been made in the past about such distinctions as the disparity between public democratic rhetoric and the reality of some social groups, which still have not been accepted into society's mainstream.

An important focus of multicultural education is that a democratic nation has a moral responsibility to see that minority ethnic, cultural, or religious groups are not isolated or marginalized in the social life of the nation. The educational institutions of a nation tend to be the primary places where children and young adults learn about their national history, literature, and scientific achievement. Multicultural educational content is necessary in all American schools because students, even in the most culturally isolated rural and small town settings, do learn opinions and beliefs about ethnic, cultural, and religious groups other than their own. What students learn in the informal social relations of their home communities about other social groups is often factually misleading or incorrect. This is how our past heritage of racism and negative stereotypes of differing social groups evolved. There has been much progress in the area of civil rights in the past 40 years, but there has also been resurgent racism and intercultural misunderstanding. School is the one place children and adolescents go each day where it is possible for them to learn an objective view of the culturally pluralistic national heritage that is both their present and future social reality. All communities are linked in some way to the culturally pluralistic social reality of the nation. When students leave high school to go into military service, attend college, or attempt careers in other parts of the nation in the corporate sector, government, or the arts, they will encounter a multicultural world very different from their often isolated local community or cultural group.

Becoming a multicultural person is a process that any dedicated teacher should be willing to pursue. We need to help students of all cultural heritages to become effective citizens of our national communities. Xenophobia and cultural prejudice have no proper place in any truly democratic national community. The English language is not in trouble. We are in trouble only if we cannot live up to our self-proclaimed heritage as a "nation of immigrants." We must remember our national heritage. We must also remember that our forefathers acquired the lands of Native Americans, 34 percent of the territory of Mexico in 1848, and the island of Puerto Rico in 1898. With those acquisitions came responsibilities that we cannot avoid if we are a morally conscious people. All Americans deserve a fair representation of their respective cultural voices.

Teachers should help their students to recognize and respect ethnic and cultural diversity and to value the ways in which it enhances and enriches the quality of our civilization. Children and adolescents should also be made aware that each of them has the right to choose how fully to identify with his or her own ethnic or cultural group.

The essays in this unit reflect a wide variety of perspectives on how to broaden the multicultural effort in our schools. The authors seek to incorporate more intercultural and global content and experiences into the main body of curriculum and instruction. Educators will find that, taken together, these essays provide a very sound basis for understanding what multicultural curriculum and instruction should be about. They are relevant to coursework in curriculum and instruction, curriculum theory and construction, educational policy studies and leadership, history and philosophy of education, and cultural foundations of education.

Respect in the Classroom

Reflections of a Mexican-American Educator

To be effective, teachers must treat the culture, heritage, and language of all their students *con respeto.*

Eva Midobuche

To understand diversity and multicultural education, we must begin by respecting our students and their backgrounds. What makes me arrive at this conclusion? I am a career educator whose heritage is culturally and linguistically differ-

My Mexican-American culture was never included in books or on bulletin boards.

ent from mainstream U.S. culture. My experiences in classrooms at all levels force me to view multicultural education and issues of diversity with great sadness. Although my story is one of educational success, my school life was painful to the point that the scars have yet to completely heal. Why did my experiences differ so radically from those of other children? In our "land of equal opportunity," they shouldn't have. What was lacking in these experiences was respect.

Remembering

Growing up in the Southwest was itself not remarkable. However, growing up Mexican American made life a bit complicated. For example, I re-member asking my mother—in Spanish, of course—what the sign "No Dogs or Mexicans Allowed" meant at the country store near my hometown. Its meaning was inexplicable to a young child. Yet the sign was allowed to exist, beckoning our minds to it.

This blatant form of racism was there only if I looked for it. Too many times, however, racism found me instead.

During my early education, my Mexican-American culture was never described in books or illustrated on bulletin boards. Even the lunchroom was an uncomfortable place. I used to lie about what I had eaten for breakfast. I always said eggs, bacon, toast, milk, and orange juice, although I had really eaten something totally different but just as nutritious. Some of us Mexican-American students hid our lunches so that the other students would not make fun of us. What I wouldn't give today for a lunch of tortillas made by my mother's loving hands.

I don't think that my experiences as a culturally and linguistically diverse student were different from those of my Hispanic classmates. For instance, I remember when a rare snowfall excited a classroom full of elementary students. Our teacher became angry and called one of my friends to the front of the class. She commanded us to look at my friend's red canvas tennis shoes, which were wet from walking to school in the snow. The teacher made some terrible remarks about the kind of mother who would send her child to school in the snow with tennis shoes. Still standing in front of the class, my friend started to cry. Feeling her embarrassment and pain, I also began crying. The teacher told my friend to go home and change shoes. Through her tears, my friend said that she could not because those were her only shoes. The total disregard for a child's—and a family's—self-esteem (Benavides, 1992) now seems unforgivable. Didn't the teacher feel what my friend and the rest of the class were feeling? How could she not be aware?

I was told by adults and family around me that school taught us what we needed to know in life. As I sit and remember another teacher, I wonder what need she was addressing when she brought her granddaughter to our class one day. She asked her granddaughter, who was two grades behind our class and came from an English-speaking family of educators, to read from our textbook. The teacher's comment to her predominantly Mexican-American students who were struggling to learn English was, "See how much smarter she is than you. She can read at your grade level."

From *Educational Leadership,* April 1999, pp. 80-82. © 1999 by the Association for Supervision and Curriculum Development (ASCD). All rights reserved. Reprinted by permission.

I was often punished for speaking Spanish. I remember writing 25 lines of "I will not speak Spanish in

The teachers who had a positive impact on my life recognized and valued my culture and language.

school" for every word I spoke in my native tongue. I find it ironic that we now praise Vice President Al Gore and Texas Governor George Bush (Fineman, 1998) for their efforts in speaking Spanish to promote their politics with Hispanics. I was spanked for speaking the language they are now attempting to learn.

This lack of respect was rampant when I was in elementary school. It became so bad that I had nightmares, stomach cramps, and difficulty sleeping. My mother met with my teacher to explain what was happening. (My real problem was my fear of the teacher and of what she was doing to all of us.) Because my mother spoke no English, she had to find an interpreter. She explained to the teacher that I was having sleeping problems because I was not comfortable in school.

After my mother left, the teacher called me to the front of the classroom. She asked the class to point to me and call me "baby." She told the students that I was not mature enough to be in her class, that I was afraid of her, and that I was such a baby that my mother had to speak to her. I never again said anything to my mother. I even pretended to sleep through the night. I actually thanked God in my prayers when I got the chicken pox that year. Why not? It kept me out of school for two weeks. To this day, when I smell the perfume this teacher wore, my stomach gets butterflies.

Showing Respect

The teachers who were caring and respectful and who had a positive im-

pact on my life recognized and valued my culture and language. They taught me the skills (including English) to survive and to become a productive citizen. I remember my high school biology teacher, who always encouraged all of us. He repeatedly met with my parents, and though non-Hispanic, spoke in Spanish to answer their questions about whether to send me away to a four-year university. The respect that this man demonstrated through his use of my native language and his understanding of how difficult this decision was for Mexican parents was, in one word, inspiring.

Here was a human being who, although his culture was different from ours, well understood my parents and me. This teacher went out of his way to understand. The truly beautiful part of his understanding was that it didn't make us feel indebted to him. Somewhere he had learned that showing respect was part of being a good teacher. He even kept tabs on me as I progressed through undergraduate school, always counseling and inspiring me. This type of teacher, however, was rare in my experiences.

Colleges of education can nurture diversity by ensuring that they prepare their students in a multicultural environment.

The State of Multiculturalism Today

The teaching profession was changed since my time as a student. Multicultural education is part of state certification requirements and teaching programs. We know so much more about how children learn, feel, and behave—especially linguistically and culturally diverse children. Yet, we seem to have to push the profession very hard to put that knowledge to work.

As Nieto (1996, p. 354), points out, "When diversity is respected, it is used as the basis for much of the education offered."

I am appalled when I hear a university student who is preparing to become an English as a Second Language teacher adamantly state in social studies methods course that she will never teach about the historical contributions made by Mexicans, although the majority of her students will be of Mexican descent. She will, however, teach about the contributions made by Egyptians. I am disheartened when I hear a student who will be teaching culturally and linguistically diverse students say, "I'm nauseated by the amount of Spanish I hear." These prospective teachers have made public their true feelings. I sometimes feel that they are proud of these negative attitudes. They wear them as an emblem of their imagined superiority. These students can be challenged to think, read, discuss, and reflect. In the end, however, they often demonstrate a callous disregard for minority and majority students alike.

Colleges of education, as well as public schools, can nurture diversity by ensuring that they prepare their students and teachers in a multicultural environment. Universities must guarantee that their courses in multicultural education are rigorous and that they ask students with negative attitudes to consider additional preparation or an alternative to the teaching profession. School administrators must take a strong position in requiring that their teachers not only be knowledgeable about issues of diversity, but also actually incorporate these concepts into their teaching. How else will minority and majority children see their own self-worth and the relatedness of their lives?

The skills and concepts of multicultural education are needed by all teachers—not only those teaching in schools with a large minority population. Bilingual and English as a Second Language teachers should not be the only ones to shoulder the responsibility for creating an accepting society. The demographics of our national school enrollment reveal that almost every classroom will at some time have students from linguistically or culturally diverse backgrounds. Therefore, the knowledge and the skills for teaching in a diverse setting become essential.

Respect for All

Teachers who respect and appreciate the different cultures in the classroom accept, validate, and acknowledge the experiences, language, and traditions of linguistically or culturally diverse students. These students develop not only a sense of belonging but also a realistic and positive self-concept. They can then learn—and enjoy the experience.

Why should a teacher of culturally mainstream students incorporate multicultural concepts into the classroom? In the real world, all students will encounter people from diverse backgrounds. Learning about diversity helps students learn more about themselves as they examine the similarities and differences in other cultures and points of view. In turn, this exposure adds to the breadth of knowledge that a good teacher attempts to create. It also allows students to understand why people are different but still able to live in harmony.

In a word, multicultural education teaches respect. Respect leads to understanding. In turn, understanding leads to caring about our community and ourselves. Respecting children for who and what they are—especially the worth of their language and culture—will go far in helping children and their families develop the skills necessary to succeed.

Respecting the diversity of the classroom as it mirrors U.S. society shows us that multicultural education is necessary to our continuance. Perhaps no other country in the world contains so much ethnic, racial, cultural, and linguistic diversity. Increasingly, teachers will be required to show that they understand, accept, and respect this diversity. When a teacher commits to respect and does so with a complete passion for his or her students, only one result is possible: learning for all children.

I sometimes wonder how my life might be difficult if my teachers had respected me as a child. Possibly the distance between home and school would have been truly bridged *con respeto,* as pointed out by Valdés (1996). Perhaps my teachers might have understood me better and demonstrated genuine concern for my learning—making my pleas to God unnecessary.

References

Benavides, A. H. (1992). Whose culture? Teaching from a multicultural perspective in the bilingual/ESL classroom. *The Bilingual Review/La Revista Bilingüe, 17*(2), 184–186.

Fineman, H. (1998, July 13). Se habla español. *Newsweek,* 26–27.

Nieto, S. (1996). *Affirming diversity* (2nd ed.). White Plains, NY: Longman.

Valdés, G. (1996). *Con respeto: Bridging the distances between culturally diverse families and school.* New York: Teachers College Press.

Eva Midobuche is Assistant Professor at Arizona State University West, College of Education, 4701 W. Thunderbird Rd., P.O. Box 37100, Phoenix, AZ 85069–7100 (e-mail: Midobuch@asu.edu).

The Changing Face of Bilingual Education

As bilingual education shifts toward more instruction in English and less in native languages, we need to focus on what research tells us about effective practices.

Russell Gersten

The past year or so has brought a virtual avalanche of dramatic events in the field of bilingual education, portending a significant shift in how English language learners are taught in the United States.

In April 1998, Secretary of Education Richard Riley announced a major shift in policy, calling for a goal of English language proficiency in three

> **An unbiased review of research indicates that we do not have adequate information to determine the optimal time for a child to be taught academic content in English.**

years for virtually all English language learners. Riley asserted that "new immigrants have a passion to learn English, and they want the best for their children" (p. 2). A survey of 420 randomly selected members of the Association of Texas Educators (both inside and outside the field of bilingual education) found that the majority agreed with the secretary. They believed that children spend too much time in native language instruction (Tanamachi, 1998). Traub (1999) also argues that Latino students spend far too much time in native language instruction, concluding that, in its current form, "bilingual education seems

to be hurting" Latino students the most—"the one group it was initially designed to help" (p. 33).

This view stands in stark contrast to the position of several noted scholars in the field, who feel that English language learners should be taught all academic subjects in their native language for no fewer than five, and preferably seven, years (for example,

Cummins, 1994). These scholars believe that extensive academic instruction in the native language is necessary for students to benefit from mainstream classrooms.

Recent events indicate that some large school districts (for example, New York and Denver) and some states (for example, California) are seriously rethinking how they educate English language learners. Invariably, the initiatives call for students to enter English language academic instruction at a much earlier age, and they propose a significant reduction in academic instruction in native languages. An article in the *New York Times* re-

ports that "in response to years of criticism of the city's bilingual education programs... New York City plans to dramatically increase the amount of time devoted to English language development" (Archibold, 1998). The article concludes with a summary of major lawsuits. Lawsuits or threatened litigation in Sacramento, Denver, and Albuquerque convey the emotional tenor of the debate.

Increasingly, parents and teachers (most notably Jaime Escalante and Gloria Tuchman) have begun to question the small amount of time devoted to English language development in many bilingual education programs in the primary grades. Advocacy groups have consistently raised such issues as parental choice in the amount of English language instruction each child receives, how early a child is introduced to substantive English language instruction, and when a child should exit classrooms that use a great deal of native language instruction.

It seems reasonable to expect that after so much attention, controversy, and discussion, research would provide answers to questions such as these:

- At what age is it best to introduce academic instruction in English to young students?
- To what extent—if any—does native language instruction benefit

© Susie Fitzhugh

students' cognitive and academic growth?

• Which are the best instructional methods for developing English language proficiency?

Unfortunately, research findings have stubbornly failed to provide answers to the first two questions. Ironically, we have more research-based information on the third—and least emotional—of these guiding research questions.

Searching for Answers

An unbiased review of research addressing the first question indicates that we do not have adequate information to determine the optimal time for a child to be taught academic content in English.[1] This is not to say that researchers have not passionately de-

bated the issue or that they have not developed and disseminated a vast array of complex theories. This issue has been debated extensively and serves as the basis of some of the aforementioned lawsuits.

The cornerstone of most contemporary models of bilingual education is that content knowledge and skills learned in a student's primary language will transfer to English once the student has experienced between five and seven years of native language instruction. Yet absolutely no empirical research supports this proposition. Methodological problems so severe that the question cannot be adequately answered plague the research on the subject (August & Hakuta, 1997). These problems appear to be most severe in some of the larger studies intended to "answer" major policy questions.

The recent report released by the National Academy of Sciences, *Improving Schooling for Language Minority Children* (August & Hakuta, 1997), offers a laundry list of complaints concerning these studies:

> The major national-level program evaluations suffer from design limitations, lack of documentation of study objectives, poorly articulated goals, lack of fit between goals and research designs and excessive use of elaborate statistical designs to overcome shortcomings. (p. 138)

In addition, the report concludes that "it is difficult to synthesize the program evaluations of bilingual education because of the extreme politicization of the process" (p. 138). The report makes clear that the prevalence of writings by "advocates who are convinced of the absolute correctness of their positions" (p. 138) presents serious barriers to attempts to improve the quality of instruction for English language learners.

Trying to unravel the issues behind these conflicts and debates can be frustrating. Even the National Academy of Sciences report is of little immediate help. It is as filled with contradictions as most other writing in the field. For example, the authors savagely critique the research on effective schooling and classroom processes, yet report the findings from these seriously flawed studies as if they represented solid facts. Similarly, the authors indicate that there is no

Although Kirst was discussing California, similar problems have been noted in states such as Texas and Massachusetts. This concern with compliance as opposed to learning outcomes helps explain why the bilingual education knowledge base is so inadequate—which in turn contributes to many of the current problems in the field.

Increasingly, researchers argue that we need to focus on aspects of instruction that lead to improved learning outcomes as opposed to political labels that at best crudely describe complex instructional interventions. Several years ago, my colleagues and I received support from the U.S. De-

teachers use native language to help a child complete a task, to clarify a point, or to respond to a question.

Almost invariably, sheltered content instruction is coupled with instruction geared toward building the student's knowledge of the English language. In years past, this component has been referred to as ESL or ESOL. Increasingly, educators are using "English language development" (ELD). Historically, teachers focused on the formal structure of language (for example, grammar and mechanics). Critics routinely attacked this approach, however, because it failed to capitalize on the communication function of language, did not generate student interest, and resulted in very limited generalization.

The 1980s brought more "natural" conversational approaches to teaching English. These also attracted criticism, primarily because they did not necessarily help students learn the highly abstract, often decontextualized language of academic discourse. A movement began about 10 years ago to merge English language learning with content acquisition. The rationale is that students can learn English while learning academic content and that this type of learning will build academic language (Cummins, 1994)—that is, the abstract language of scientific, mathematical, or literary discourse. However, too often teachers merely "hope that language occurs [during lessons]. There is a risk during content instruction of neglecting language development" (Gersten & Baker, in press).

The erratic quality of ELD instruction is at the root of the growing dissatisfaction with current practice. Inadequate attention has been devoted to curriculum development, *pragmatic* teacher training and professional development, and applied research. In a recent professional work group that I conducted in California for the U.S. Department of Education (Gersten & Baker, in press), an educator from the district bilingual education office articulated the problem: "It's important for teachers to be clear about objectives and goals . . . yet an explicit

> We have made definite progress in understanding what instructional goals are feasible for English language learners and what specific classroom practices are likely to help meet these goals.

empirical support for the effectiveness of native language instruction in the early grades, yet still advocate its use. However, the report also demonstrates an awareness of the contradictory nature of the database by noting:

> It is clear that many children first learn to read in a second language without serious negative consequences. These include children who successfully go through early-immersion, two-way, and English as a second language (ESL)-based programs in North America. (p. 23)

Michael Kirst of Stanford University (Schnaiberg, 1998) recently provided some valuable insight into the problems within the bilingual education knowledge base. In discussing California, he noted:

> From its inception . . . in the 1970s, bilingual education has been oriented toward inputs, process and compliance. . . . The assumption was if you have this input, the outputs would take care of themselves. So . . . [we monitor] . . . whether you mounted the program, *and not its results.* (p. 16, emphasis added)

partment of Education to begin to articulate these components. Our charge was to synthesize the knowledge base on effective classroom practices that simultaneously promote English language development and academic learning. We intentionally eschewed the ongoing political debates. Our goal was to delineate specific techniques that teachers could use to simultaneously promote learning and English language development.

English Language Development

Although questions about optimal age remain unanswered, at some point all English language learners begin academic instruction in English. The initial transition is often called "content area ESOL," "structured immersion," or "sheltered content instruction." The common feature is teachers' use of English designed for students who are not proficient in the language. In sheltered instruction, teachers modulate their use of English so that it is comprehensible to the student and base their degree of support on their knowledge of that student. In some cases, statement of goals does not exist [in district or state curricular materials]."

I would argue, however, that we have made definite progress in understanding what instructional goals are feasible for this group of students and what *specific classroom practices are likely to help meet these goals.* In our two-year research synthesis project (Gersten & Baker, in press), we concluded that the beginning of an empirical knowledge base on effective instructional practices for English language learners exists. It is important to emphasize, however, that this knowledge base is emerging and should be the topic of controlled, high-quality classroom research.

Principles for Merging ELD with Content Area Learning

ELD programs must include the development of oral and written proficiency, the development of basic conversational English and academic language, and the systematic proactive teaching of conventions and grammar (Saunders, O'Brien, Lennon, & McLean, 1998; Fashola, Drum, Mayer, & Kang, 1996). As they undertake these tasks, teachers should keep in mind the following instructional principles derived from the limited research in this area.[2]

- Avoid oversimplifying with contrived, intellectually insulting material when teaching academic content in English. Subjects such as science and math can be excellent venues for merging English language development because all students are learning a new technical vocabulary and there is great potential to use concrete objects (Chamot, 1998).
- Use visuals to reinforce verbal content when teaching in English (Saunders et al, 1998; Reyes & Bos, 1998).
- Use both oral and written modalities frequently (Saunders et al., 1998).
- Employ strategic use of synonyms. Word choice and sentence structure need to be consistent

and concise during second language learning. Pay attention to use of metaphors and similes and other highly culture-specific phrases and expressions (Gersten & Jiménez, 1994).

- Focus on approximately five to eight core vocabulary words in each lesson. Some strategies include (1) carefully selecting words (evocative words that stimulate instruction, key words for understanding a story), (2) linking words or concepts to words known in the native language, (3) showing new words in print, and (4) using visuals (for example, concept maps) to depict concepts or word meanings (Saunders et al., 1998).
- Use native language during ELD strategically. At times, it might be helpful to use both native language and English during instruction; however, be aware of the risk of overreliance on simultaneous translations.
- During the early phases of language learning, modulate and be sensitive when providing feedback and correcting language usage; however, during later stages, identify errors and provide specific feedback to students (Reyes, 1992).

To date, much has evolved from grassroots experimentation and attempts by researchers to describe practices that appear to engage students and enhance their learning. Nonetheless, it is becoming increasingly clear that a set of practices exists that teachers can use to persistently, but sensitively, encourage students to learn content while expressing their ideas in a new language. This information may be particularly helpful as the shift toward greater emphasis on instruction in English takes effect.

[1]An unpublished meta-analysis by Jay Greene (1998) has been occasionally cited as support for native language instruction. However, when we examined his data, we found that his results show no benefits of native language instruction for Latino students in the elementary grades. We also noted numerous methodological problems in his meta-

analysis (Baker, Gersten, & Otterstedt, 1999). Thus we conclude that there is no empirical evidence of benefits to extensive native language instruction.

[2]For a more complete description see Gersten, Baker, and Marks (1998). The practices are embedded in programs such as Instructional Conversations (Echevarria & Graves, 1998), Bilingual CIRC (Calderon, Hertz-Lazarowitz, & Slavin, 1998), Cognitive Academic Language Learning Approach (Chamot, 1998), collaborative strategic reading (Klingner, Vaughn, & Schumm, 1998), Peer-Mediated Instruction (Arreaga-Mayer, 1998), and the Effective Strategies for Studying Literature model used successfully in Los Angeles schools by Saunders and colleagues (1998).

References

Archibold, R. C. (1998, June 21). Crew plans an overhaul of bilingual education. *New York Times*, p. 27.

Arreaga-Mayer, C. (1998). Language sensitive peer mediated instruction for culturally and linguistically diverse learners in the intermediate elementary grades. In R. Gersten & R. Jiménez (Eds.), *Promoting learning for culturally and linguistically diverse students: Classroom applications from contemporary research* (pp. 73–90). Belmont, CA: Wadsworth.

August, D., & Hakuta, K. (Eds.). (1997). *Improving schooling for language-minority children.* Washington, DC: National Academy Press.

Calderon, M., Hertz-Lazarowitz, R., & Slavin, R. (1998). Effects of bilingual cooperative integrated reading and composition on students making the transition from Spanish to English reading. *Elementary School Journal, 99*(2), 153–165.

Chamot, A. U. (1998). Effective instruction for high school English language learners. In R. Gersten & R. Jiménez (Eds.), *Promoting learning for culturally and linguistically diverse students: Classroom applications from contemporary research* (pp. 187–209). Belmont, CA: Wadsworth.

Cummins, J. (1994). Primary language instruction and the education of language minority students. In *Schools and language minority students: A theoretical framework* (2nd ed.). Los Angeles: California State University, National Evaluation, Dissemination and Assessment Center.

Echevarria, J., & Graves, A. (1998). *Sheltered content instruction: Teaching English-language learners with diverse abilities.* Des Moines, IA: Allyn & Bacon.

Fashola, O. S., Drum, P. A., Mayer, R. E., & Kang, S. (1996). A cognitive theory of orthographic transitions: Predictable errors in how Spanish-speaking children spell English words. *American Educational Research Journal, 33,* 825–844.

Gersten, R., & Baker, S. (in press). The professional knowledge base on instructional interventions that support cognitive growth for language minority students. In R. Gersten, E. Schiller, S. Vaughn, & J. Schumm (Eds.), *Research synthesis in special education.* Mahwah, NJ: Erlbaum.

Gersten, R., Baker, S., & Marks, S. U. (1998). *Productive instructional practices for English-language learners: Guiding principles and examples from research-based practice.* Reston, VA: Council for Exceptional Children.

Gersten, R., Baker, S., & Otterstedt, J. (1999). Further analysis of "A meta-analysis of the effectiveness of bilingual education," by J. P. Greene (1989). Technical Report No. 99-01. Eugene, OR: Eugene Research Institute.

Gersten, R., & Jiménez, R. (1994). A delicate balance: Enhancing literacy instruction for students of English as a second language. *The Reading Teacher, 47*(6), 438–449.

Greene, J. P. (1998). *A meta-analysis of the effectiveness of bilingual education.* Unpublished technical report. Austin, TX: University of Texas & the Thomas Rivera Policy Institute.

Klingner, J. K., Vaughn, S., & Schumm, J. S. (1998). Collaborative strategic reading during social studies in heterogeneous fourth-grade classrooms. *Elementary School Journal, 99*(1), 3–22.

Reyes, M. (1992). Challenging venerable assumptions: Literacy instruction for linguistically different student. *Harvard Educational Review, 62*(4), 427–446.

Reyes, E., & Bos, C. (1998). Interactive semantic mapping and charting: Enhancing content area learning for language minority students. In R. Gersten & R. Jiménez (Eds.), *Promoting learning for culturally and linguistically diverse students: Classroom applications from contemporary research* (pp. 133–152). Belmont, CA: Wadsworth.

Riley, R. W. (1998, April 27) *Helping all children learn English.* Washington, DC: U.S. Department of Education, Office of Public Affairs.

Saunders, W., O'Brien, G., Lennon, D., & McLean, J. (1998). Making the transition to English literacy successful: Effective strategies for studying literature with transition students. In R. Gersten & R. Jiménez (Eds.), *Effective strategies for teaching language minority students: Classroom applications from contemporary research* (pp. 99–132). Belmont, CA: Wadsworth.

Schnaiberg, L. (1998, April 29). What price English? *Education Week,* pp. 1, 16.

Tanamachi, C. (1998, July 18). Educators poll: Set bilingual time limit. *Austin American Statesman,* p. B1.

Traub, J. (1999, January 31). The bilingual barrier. *The New York Times Magazine,* pp. 32–35.

Author's note: This article was supported, in part, by the United States Department of Education, Office of Special Education Programs, grant number HO23E50013. Mark Harniss and Scott Baker contributed to the writing of this article.

Russell Gersten is Professor at the University of Oregon and Senior Researcher at the Eugene Research Institute, 132 East Broadway, Ste. 747, Eugene, OR 97401.

Research Alive

The Relationship between Culture and Cognitive Style: A Review of the Evidence and Some Reflections for the Classroom

Joan Thrower Timm
University of Wisconsin Oshkosh

Abstract

This column summarizes factors in cultural experience that affect approaches to learning and problem solving. It reviews the evidence over the past thirty years on cognitive style differences in culturally diverse groups in the United States including Asian, African, Latino, and Native Americans and reports recent research findings on the Hmong. Finally, it raises some issues to consider when working with students from different cultural backgrounds.

The possibility of a relationship between cultural experience and cognitive style has been supported, challenged, or rejected by anthropologists, psychologists, and educators. Indeed, the mere idea of such a relationship has been the subject of recent controversy and much debate. The controversy has arisen primarily out of a concern about biases in Western thought in reference to cultural differences. However timely, this concern has tended to be based on assumptions that confuse concepts of so-called "intelligence" with different approaches to learning which arise out of diverse socialization practices. As a result, even the mention of cultural cognitive style is sometimes interpreted as evidence of an arrogant and Eurocentric bias in regard to non-Western populations.

The debate has arisen out of a long series of studies in the fields of cultural anthropology, psychology, and education. These studies have focused on how thinking and learning occurs in various cultural contexts. While early studies were based on the cognitive developmental concepts of Piaget, others were derived from the pioneering work of Witkin and his associates (Witkin et al., 1973) and Berry (1976) on the relationship between culture and cognitive style. The long dialogue regarding the complexities and inter-relatedness of culture and cognitive processing is beyond the scope of this paper but has recently been addressed in a comprehensive review of cultural psychology by Michael Cole (1996).

Kraemer (1973) asserted that people sharing common primary experiences develop similar styles of cognitive processing including perceiving, conceiving, and judging. The concept of diverse cognitive styles arising out of different cultural experiences has been supported by Anderson (1988):

> Because the social, cultural, and environmental milieus of ethnic and racial groups differ, one should expect these differences to be reflected in their respective cultural/cognitive styles. Much of the literature in cross-cultural research supports this contention (p. 4).

More recently Shade (1997) has concurred with this view and has stated that:

> Culture, through the mediating process called cognitive style, determines the affective and cognitive behaviors which an individual selects to meet environmental demands. As environmental psychologists have been able to suggest, situations in which individuals find themselves tend to solicit the behavioral patterns necessary for survival within the confines of that situation. As such cognitive style has a significant impact upon an individual's competent performance in various behavioral settings (p. 10).

In addition, Shade (1997) maintains that culture influences not only cognitive processing but modes of communication and social interaction as well.

Basically, the literature on cultural considerations and cognitive style falls into three main categories: (a) an array of philosophical and historical essays about the relationship of culture and cognition; (b) a wide variety of research studies reporting differences in cognitive style and interactive modes among students from diverse groups both globally and in the United States; and (c) suggestions for taking cognitive style into account in teaching. The importance for teachers to know specific ways in which

From *Mid-Western Educational Researcher*, Spring 1999, pp. 36-44. Reprinted by permission of MWERA and the author.

cultural experience impacts cognitive style, however, generally has not been taken into account in discussions of implementing cognitive style in classroom settings. An example of this relationship between learning at home and learning at school is described later in this paper in regard to Hmong students in American schools.

Learning Style or Cognitive Style?

The term *cognitive style* needs to be differentiated from *learning style*. Because these terms have sometimes been used interchangeably, some confusion has arisen as to what degree they overlap or refer to similar or different issues.

Learning Style

The term *learning style* has been used to refer to different factors, some internal, some external, some cognitive, some emotional, some social, and some behavioral. Irvine and York (1995) consider learning styles to be "an umbrella term encompassing three distinct substyles: cognitive, affective, and physiological" (p. 484). Curry (1990) has pointed out this problem of ambiguity in regard to the term itself. Slavin (1997) refers to "Theories of Learning Styles" but switches to the term "cognitive style" without differentiating between them (p. 136).

Kagan (1964) distinguished between an impulsive and a reflective approach to learning. Entwistle (1981) later concurred about the importance of impulsivity or reflectivity in style. Fischer and Fischer (1979) referred to style as "a pervasive quality in the *behavior* (emphasis mine) of an individual" (p. 245). Shade (1989) distinguished between an analytic and a synergetic style.

Fischer and Fischer (1979) further identified and described ten different kinds of learners: the incremental learner, the intuitive learner, the sensory specialist, the sensory generalist, the emotionally involved, the emotionally neutral, the explicitly structured, the open-ended structure (d), the damaged (in self concept and social competence among other problems), and the eclectic learner.

Based on individual *preferences for different learning conditions,* Dunn and Dunn (1979) identified four parameters of learning style: environmental, emotional, sociological, and physical. These parameters, or "stimuli," were further broken down into eighteen "elements." Among these, the environmental elements were sound, light, temperature, and design (or physical arrangement of the room); the emotional elements were motivation, persistence, responsibility, and a need for structure; the sociological elements included a preference for working alone, with peers, with an adult, or a combination of these potential partners; and the physical elements referred to perceptual strengths (visual, auditory, tactile, kinesthetic), a need for "intake" (food, drink), time of day, and greater or lesser need for mobility.

Entwistle (1981) suggested that style refers to *information processing.* Similarly, Nieto described learning style as "the way in which individuals process and receive information" (1992, p. 111). The term *learning style* as used by Entwistle and Nieto in regard to information processing is synonymous with cognitive style. Gardner (1983) has suggested that culture, affect, and cognition interact and are conducive to multiple intelligences (logical-mathematical, spatial, musical, kinesthetic, and interpersonal), thus blurring the distinction between culture, style, and different *abilities.*

Perhaps the most comprehensive definition of learning style is that of the National Task Force on Learning Style and Brain Behavior (as cited in Keefe and Languis, 1983):

> Learning style is that consistent pattern of behavior and performance by which an individual approaches educational experiences. It is the composite of characteristic cognitive, affective, and physiological behaviors that serve as relatively stable indicators of how a learner perceives, interacts with, and responds to the learning environment. It is . . . molded by . . . the cultural experiences of home, school, and society (p. 1).

Another ambiguity in definitions of learning style is that the differences between style, strategy, and tactic have not always been clear. Entwistle (1988) suggested that strategy refers to *consistency in* (students') *approach* to different learning situations. Snowman (1989) suggested that tactic refers to the *observable activities or habitual responses* of students in learning situations. In view of these different interpretations of what learning style means, it is clear that different educators use the term "style" to refer to different processes and that in fact they are referring to behavior, preferences for different environments, strategies, or tactics.

In concordance with the concept of learning styles, a plethora of tests were created to measure "styles." Irvine and York (1995) report that more than thirty test instruments have been constructed. Some of these tests were designed for children, while others were created for adults and applied in both educational and business settings (Gregorc, 1982, for example). Research using these tests has been extensive. According to Irvine and York, several thousand studies were conducted between the mid 1980s and 1995. Curry (1990) has questioned both the validity and the reliability of many of these instruments. Timm (1996) has pointed out an additional problem in regard to learning style instruments. The forced choice format is based on an assumption that individuals have a fixed rather than an adaptive approach to learning situations and to problem solving. A final criticism of learning style instruments has been that they have low predictive value for achievement (Irvine and York, 1995). This, however, may be a spurious concern due to the fact that there is no reason to assume that one approach over another will necessarily result in success.

In spite of these problems in definition, test assumptions, and difficulties in utilizing test results in the classroom, the concept of learning styles does offer some important considerations about the relationship between cultural experience, individuality, and learning situations.

Cognitive Style

Correctly used, the term *cognitive style* derives from cognitive theory and refers to variations in information processing, perceiving, conceptualizing, analyzing, and problem solving procedures (Timm, 1996). Evidence suggests that cultures differ in respect to these processes. Ambiguities have occurred with the term cognitive style, however, similar to those associated with learning style. For example, Kuchinskas (1979) identified cognitive style "as the way an individual acts, reacts, and adapts to the environment" (p. 269).

In this review, the term *cognitive style* is used to refer to cognitive processes. Field independence or sensitivity, communication, and social interaction modalities are specified as such. Wherever the term *learning style* appears in this review, it is the term used by the author(s) under discussion.

Another interpretation of cognitive style (which also includes social and behavioral factors) is a concept known as *field independence/dependence,* first identified and described by Witkin and his associates (Witkin et al., 1971; Witkin et al., 1977; Witkin, 1979; Witkin and Goodenough, 1981) by means of the Embedded Figures Test (Witkin et al., 1973). The Children's Embedded Figures Test (Karp and Konstadt, 1971) was further developed from this test. These tests require the test taker to locate or identify basic geometric shapes embedded in surrounding complex patterns. Two important aspects of these tests have generally been overlooked in the literature. First, the shapes are basic configurations and, second, the tests are language free, thus eliminating the bias of linguistics, although directions for the test may be provided in different languages.

Because many studies have reported cultural differences in field independence/dependence, it is important to clarify these terms here. Chickering (1976) described field independence/dependence as differences in ability to distinguish figure from ground (or shape from pattern) and (by logical extension) a construct from its surrounding context. Field independent learners have been reported to be adept at identifying specific aspects of a situation and at separating concepts from context. Other characteristics include a preference to work independently, intrinsic motivation, and a desire for personal recognition. Heppner and Krauskopf (1987) further reported that field independent learners persevere longer and are more self-directive in their learning than field dependent learners. Field dependent learners tend to be situation specific in their orientation to learning, and tend not to separate concepts from context. Other characteristics include a preference to work with others, a need for extrinsic motivation, an orientation toward social cues, and a sensitivity to others. Heppner and Krauskopf (1987) have also reported that field de-

pendent learners adapt to new situations more easily than field independent learners. Recently the term *field sensitive* has been used rather than field dependent. It is important to note that field independence or dependence are *value free* designates and that they should not be confused with notions about intelligence, ability, or as predictors of academic performance. They are simply tendencies along a continuum by which individuals perceive, conceptualize, and problem solve in their approach to a learning situation.

Cultural Factors in Learning

In the definition of learning style by the National Task Force on Learning Style and Brain Behavior (cited above), reference is made to the relationship between style and cultural experiences. Guild (1994) has reported three different sources for research information about the relationship between culture and learning processes. These are: (a) observations and descriptions of learners from different cultural groups; (b) data based on test instruments administered to diverse student populations; and (c) direct discussion (including interviews). The major ways in which cultural experiences affect cognitive style have not always been made explicit in reports of students from diverse groups, however. These experiences include socialization or child rearing practices, cultural "tightness," ecological or environmental considerations, a written or oral/aural language tradition (Worthley, 1987; Bennett, 1990), and so-called "high" or "low" context cultures (Halverson, 1993).

Permissive socialization practices, which encourage individual experimentation or trying different ways of performing tasks, result in a wider flexibility of cognitive style. Strict socialization practices, with pressure to perform tasks according to traditional ways, result in less flexibility of style (Jahoda, 1980). Strict practices which focus on obedience also tend to result in an orientation to learning which is specific to the present situation (Nedd and Gruenfeld, 1976).

Cultural "tightness" refers to the degree of emphasis and value given to traditional routines. Cultural "looseness" refers to the degree of latitude given to variation in the performance of daily tasks or routines. Thus "tight" cultures tend to follow precisely various time-honored ways while "loose" cultures are less rigid and more flexible in regard to traditional procedures (Worthley, 1987).

Ecological adaptation refers to customs in relation to nature within any given culture (Berry, 1976). For example, some cultures rely on highly developed perceptual skills for survival. Cultures which depend primarily on agriculture and animal husbandry emphasize customary routines in order to survive. Child rearing practices focus on responsibility, conformity to customs, and the value of traditional ways. Cultures which depend primarily on hunting, gathering, and to some extent fishing for survival require more self-reliance and application of skills under varying circumstances. Child rearing practices, while teaching traditional methods, also tend to encourage more individual initiative.

Literate societies use written symbol systems for the transmission of knowledge. Learning is more abstract and decontextualized than in oral societies which follow a more active mode and use demonstration and role modeling in order to teach. Learning is through observation and is based on specific situations (Hvitfeldt, 1985).

In addition to the foregoing considerations, Halverson (1993) has described another factor—that of "high" and "low" context cultures. In high context cultures, learning is situationally based within a social context. Skills and procedures are demonstrated and learning depends to a large degree on observation. Learners also relate the learning process to their place in social groups and to their role in society. In low context cultures, learning is more detached from the immediate use of the information and procedures are described in verbal or written form. Learners are less oriented toward the applicability of the information being transmitted in terms of the immediate task or social situation than they are in high context cultures.

Cultural Diversity and Cognitive Styles

There is a steadily increasing body of evidence in support of the notion of different patterns in cognitive style including field independence/dependence among students from diverse cultural backgrounds. The following review focuses on diverse groups in the United States.

Asian Americans

Differences among Asian Americans have been reported in accordance with ethnic background.

The Hmong. As an example of the relationship between the cultural factors cited above and cognitive style, Timm and Chiang (1997) have described traditional Laotian Hmong culture and the cognitive style of Laotian Hmong students in the United States. In their former rural agricultural mountain communities in Laos, the Hmong approach to learning was situation specific. Strict socialization practices emphasized obedience and adherence to time honored procedures. The culture was "tight" with little latitude in routines. Ecologically, survival depended primarily on successful crops, although there was some hunting and fishing. As part of the socialization process, children participated in agricultural work as young as four years of age (Lee, 1986). Pressure for conformity was high in Hmong social organization, based on patrilineal clans with clear lines of male authority. Social roles were delineated along gender lines.

The culture was primarily oral and formal education was rare. Few villages had a school. Knowledge was handed down from generation to generation. It has been estimated that seventy percent of Hmong refugees were non-literate when they left Laos (Takaki, 1989). Thus, learning to use a written language was a profound problem which many faced in their relocation into literate societies such as the United States. The concept of writing was not unfamiliar to the Hmong, however. There have been "at least fourteen major attempts to develop writing systems for the Hmong language over the past one hundred years" (Smalley, 1990, p. 149) but Hmong students who did attend school were instructed in either Lao or French. The Hmong who cooperated with the United States during the Vietnam War gained some literacy in English (Duffy, 1997). The Romanized version of Hmong, developed in the early 1950s by two linguists (William Smalley and Linwood Barney) and a French priest (Yves Bertrais) and known as the Romanized Popular Alphabet (RPA), has become the most widely accepted and is the script used in the United States (J. Duffy, personal communication, January 12, 1998).

Finally, Hmong culture may be described as being high context. Learning was situationally based and children received their "education" at home and in the fields where they learned through observation. Procedures were demonstrated rather than discussed.

Hmong families in the United States continue to teach their children in the traditional way by using demonstration and relying on observational learning. At the same time, however, Hmong students are encountering curricular programs in American schools which transmit information in a decontextualized, written form and emphasize a more independent approach to learning. Using the Group Embedded Figures Test (available from Consulting Psychologists Press in Palo Alto) as the test instrument to determine field independent and field dependent cognitive styles, Timm and Chiang (1997) first reported a field dependent cognitive style consistent with Hmong situation specific learning experience. In a follow-up study, Timm, Chiang, and Finn (1998) found acculturating effects of length of residency in the United States and duration of time in American schools on Hmong students' cognitive style. Covariance statistical analyses yielded significant effects for both U.S. residency and years in American schools. In other words, evidence of Hmong cultural practices was found in the cognitive and social interaction styles of these students but shifts were also found from a situation specific or field dependent style to a more field independent style associated with the number of years the students had been living in the United States and attending American schools. Gender differences were also found in the shift in style with the boys moving into a field independent mode slightly ahead of the girls. This difference may be attributed to Hmong socialization practices in regard to gender roles (Timm et al, 1998).

Prior to the studies by Timm and Chiang (1997) and Timm et al. (1998), two earlier studies reported both cognitive and interaction styles consistent with Hmong cultural experiences. Hvitfeldt (1986) reported behaviors characteristic of a field dependent style in a literacy class for nonliterate and low literate Hmong adults, ranging from twenty to sixty-five years of age. These behaviors included consistent interpersonal interactions among the students, a reliance on contextual referents, and a personal relationship with the instructor. Using the Group Embedded Figures Test, Worthley (1987) reported a two-to-one ratio of field dependence over field independence among Hmong male high school and college students, ranging from seventeen to thirty-five years in age.

Other Asian students. Reid (1987) also found acculturating effects among other Asian students and reported that college ESL students who had been in the United States for more than three years were significantly more auditory in their learning style preference in comparison with students who had been in this country for shorter periods of time. Reid further reported visual learning style preferences among Korean, Chinese, and Arabic-American students in comparison with Japanese students.

In a study of learning style preferences among Chinese, Filipino, Korean, Vietnamese, and Anglo high school students, Park (1997) reported major preferences for an auditory style among Vietnamese and Chinese American students, and a minor preference among Korean, Filipino and Anglo students. Park also reported a minor visual learning style preference among the four Asian groups in contrast with Anglo students who showed a negative response to visual learning. There were also differences among the Asian groups, with the Chinese students being the most visual, followed by the Filipino and Korean, and the Vietnamese students being the least visual in their preference. Ewing and Yong (1993) also reported a visual preference among gifted American-born Chinese students.

Park (1997) further examined their students' preferences for group or individual approaches to learning. The Vietnamese students showed the highest preference for group learning, the Filipino students showed a minor preference for it, and the Chinese, Korean, and Anglo students did not prefer it. This is an important finding because cooperative learning approaches may work well with Vietnamese and Filipino students but not so well with Chinese, Korean, and Anglo students. Park reported that high achievers across all groups preferred an individual style and that low achievers preferred group learning.

Differences in socialization practices, social interaction styles, and educational values have been reported among other Asian American groups in reference to ethnicity and length of residency in the United States. Cabezas (1981) reported differences in socialization practices in the San Francisco area among Chinese and Filipino mothers born overseas in comparison with American born mothers. Rumbaut and Ima (1988) reported that Vietnamese, Chinese-Vietnamese, and Hmong parents in San Diego placed more emphasis on school achievement than Lao and Khmer (Cambodian) parents. These value differences may be attributed to their prior cultural experience. Lao refugees in the United States have tended to come from rural areas. The more educated and urban Lao refugees relocated in France following the takeover of Laos by communist forces after the Vietnam War. Likewise, many of the Khmer refugees who settled in the states were from rural areas of Cambodia and were less educated. The more educated Khmer were massacred during the Pol Pot regime. Consistent with Rumbaut and Ima, Timm (1994) reported that although Laotian Hmong families now living in the Midwest had come from rural areas where education was minimal, they have adopted a high value for education in regard to their children in the United States.

African Americans

Ogbu (1983) described an historical, caste-dominated society along racial lines in the United States by which exploitation has extended across economic, political and social experience. It is not surprising, therefore, that African American cultural patterns include values which emphasize group unity and mutual support (Staples, 1976). Jones (1979) added spirituality, spontaneity, and a preference for oral expression. Boykin (1986) suggested that African American culture contains nine themes: spirituality, harmony or interdependence with humans and nature, movement, "verve," affect, communalism or social connectedness, personal expression, oral tradition, and a focus on "social time." These aspects suggest that students may learn better through personal relationships with the teacher, cooperative learning modes, and oral strategies. In Shade's (1997) view, African American experience has led to "survivalisms" (p. 14) or an experiential wisdom among African Americans which is not shared by non-Blacks. According to Shade, the sources of African American culture include these survivalisms, European American mainstream society, and a culture of oppression which causes anxiety, over-identification with those in power, hostility, an ability to handle contradictions, and a preoccupation with issues of freedom and equality. Shade has suggested that "the kinship system (including protection and mutual support), world view, and social interactive behaviors have the greatest impact on learning style" (p. 15) and that African American culture and social stratification "serve as the transmitters of the cognitive and affective entry behaviors which come with the child to school" (p. 24).

Shade (1997) further reported an auditory processing mode, a precociousness sensori motor capability, a socially oriented (as opposed to an object centered) modality, and a preference for an interactive learning situation among Black children. She further suggested that perception (and therefore interpretation) of visual cues is affected by cultural experience. African Americans are more likely to be field dependent when tested on the Embedded Figures Test (Shade, 1986). This field sensitive finding is consistent with Gitter, Black, and Mostofsky (1972) who reported that African Americans are sensitive to social cues and adept at interpreting facial emotions. This social sensitivity impacts Blacks students' behaviors in the classroom (Shade). Ewing and Yong (1993) also found a preference for a visual learning mode among gifted African American students.

Mexican Americans

A sensitivity in the social interaction of Mexican Americans, together with an orientation to collective or collaborative efforts, reflects the traditional Mexican cultural values of close affiliation with family and community (Shade, 1997). Slonin (1991) suggested that Hispanic culture is based on cooperation, interpersonal relationships, a "relaxed" time perception, a preference for physical proximity, and traditional sex roles. Vasquez (1990) suggested that Hispanic American students' orientation of loyalty to family and groups may predispose them toward cooperative learning. Dunn and Dunn (1978) reported that Mexican American students were peer oriented and were more likely to perform well in cooperative group situations. In a large study of Mexican American immigrant and first generation elementary students and Anglo American elementary students (n=687), Dunn, Griggs, and Price (1993) found that the Mexican American students were more peer-oriented than were the Anglo students, with the Mexican American girls more peer oriented than the boys. They also found that the Mexican American boys had the strongest preferences for tactile learning and that the Mexican American girls in general showed less tactile learning preferences and a more varied approach to learning than the boys. Similarly, Ewing and Yong (1993) reported that gifted Mexican American students preferred a kinesthetic learning style over an auditory or visual one. Mori (1991) reported that Mexican students with higher English proficiency continued to show a stronger orientation for active learning in comparison with high English proficiency Japanese students who did not prefer this modality.

Saracho (1991) cautioned against making assumptions about cognitive style in Mexican American children, however. She asserted that, although a generally field dependent, prosocial orientation has been assumed in Mexican American children, field independence/dependence "is a relative rather than an absolute term (and that) extensive data must be collected and analyzed before accepting any generalizations" (p. 23). In a study of Mexican American kindergarten children from an agricultural community, Saracho found a range of field independence/dependence on The Children's Embedded Figures Test (CEFT). She also found significant differences in the children's play behavior and social competence. In other words, Saracho found both a diversity of cognitive styles and a range of social competency related to that stylistic diversity.

Saracho (1997) further suggested that both the amount of traditional procedures in child rearing and the degree of generational distance from migration to the United States both affect cognitive style. Several findings on differences in cognitive style among Mexican Americans in relation to Anglo contact support Saracho's view. Some of these findings are similar to the findings for Hmong students with regard to United States residency (Timm et al., 1998). For example, Buriel (1975) reported that first and second generation Mexican immigrants had cognitive

styles similar to traditional communities, but the third generation did not. Ramirez and Castaneda (1974) reported that Mexican American students were inclined toward a field sensitive learning style but that style varied in relation to assimilation, distance from Mexico, length of residence in the United States, impact of urbanization, and amount of prejudice encountered. Ramirez, Castaneda, and Herold (1974) studied three different types of communities: (a) Mexican American members with a primarily traditional Mexican culture; (b) dualistic with Mexican American cultures; and (c) Mexican American members with manifest values from Anglo-American culture. They reported that the students from the dualistic community were in between the more field dependent members of the traditional community and the less field dependent members of the Anglo-oriented community. Other studies have reported similar results from traditional and dualistic communities (Laosa and DeAvila, 1979).

This section has focused on Mexican American students but other students may experience shifts in their cognitive style in relation to type of community, demographic considerations, and length of residency in the United States. In light of Creason's report (1992) that 40% of Hispanic students drop out of school, there is clearly a need for more research in this area.

Native Americans

Smith and Shade (1997) cited some Native American cultural factors that are conducive to a field sensitive cognitive style and socially sensitive interactive style. Among these are a conviction of the inherent good of all people, a belief that all people are interconnected with each other and with nature, and a view that cooperation is important for solving problems. According to Pepper and Henry (1997), socialization among Native Americans tends to be permissive and children are encouraged to experiment and to explore. Discipline does not mean obedience, but development of self control whereby children come to regard non-interference as normal. "Respect for individual dignity and personal autonomy are valued and youngsters are taught not to interfere in the affairs of others" (p. 170). Socialization further emphasizes observational and contextually relevant learning. Thus a cognitive style emerges that includes a preference for visual processing, an informal and exploratory learning preference, and a sensitivity to social cues.

An association between culture, ecology, and cognitive style has been reported among Native Americans by Kleinfeld (1970). In a testing situation for visual memory which required the ability to recall complex visual patterns, rural Inuit native children of all ages outperformed urban White children. These results were attributed to the ecology of a sparse Arctic landscape and to socialization that included a hunting tradition, both of which require visual acuity and an ability to perceive slight variations in the environment. Berry (1971) also reported visual acuity among urban Inuit subjects, in spite of less hunting experience. This finding suggests that Inuit child rearing practices emphasize visual learning, imitation, and non-verbal instruction.

Phillips (1978) reported that Native American students show a preference for learning by observation before they attempt to perform a task themselves. According to More (1987), Native American students prefer a visual to verbal learning mode and use images to learn concepts. These characteristics suggest a field sensitive cognitive style. Caldwell (1989) and Kasten (1992) reported a preference for cooperation in learning situations among Native American students.

Gender and Social Class

Within diverse groups, cognitive style may be mediated by gender and socioeconomic status. In a large study (636 boys and 638 girls), Park (1997) reported gender differences in style preferences across auditory, visual, and tactile modes and a significant gender difference in kinesthetic preference, with the girls reporting a higher preference. Some findings of gender differences within groups are reported above for Hmong and Mexican American students. Social class differences are also sometimes overlooked in the reporting of cognitive styles. Blackwell (1975) reported that African Americans in the professional/middle class and skilled blue collar class are more oriented to achievement, social striving, and consumerism in comparison with the economically disadvantaged. In an early study of Chinese, Jewish, Black, and Puerto Rican children from middle class and low income homes, however, Stodolsky and Lesser (1967) reported different patterns in cognitive processes for each ethnic group regardless of social class. In other words, ethnicity appeared to influence cognitive style more than social class. Banks (1988) also reported similar findings of the effect of ethnicity over social class and further reported that ethnic differences remained even when social class had changed for the better. These findings suggest that the interrelationship between ethnicity, gender, and social class is a complicated one in which cognitive styles may not necessarily be assumed by one dimension alone.

Educational Implications

The research findings considered in this review raise some important issues for classroom application. First, not all students in any cultural group necessarily approach learning in the same way. As Irvine and York (1995) assert, stereotyping occurs when inaccurate or general characteristics of a group are ascribed to, or assumed, for individuals. Second, educators must remember that learning is a fluid process and that students' cognitive styles are not static but may change across time. Findings of acculturation effects among Mexican American, Hmong, and other Asian Americans suggest that individual differences

and acculturating experiences must be considered. Third, individuals may use different approaches to learning and problem solving, depending on the nature of the problem. Timm (1996) reported the following anecdote:

> . . . a teacher was required to take a widely marketed learning style test by her school administrator. During the test she considered how she approached the task of writing a report and answered the test items accordingly. Being suspicious of the test's validity, she asked to retake the test immediately. Because her hobby was sewing, this time she considered how she approached the task of creating a dress of her own design. The results of her two tests indicated two totally different learning styles (p. 190).

In other words, the creators of learning style tests have not generally taken into consideration the fact that people may use a variety of approaches that best suit the task at hand.

In spite of these caveats, the above review does reveal some general patterns for diverse groups. Shade (1997) suggested that cognitive processes are the result of socialization and cultural experiences and that the environment is interpreted through cultural filters and responded to accordingly. Thus, people who share common experiences develop similar processes of "conceiving, judging, and reasoning" (p. 134). Shade, Kelly, and Oberg (1997) offer a variety of teaching strategies for working in culturally responsive classrooms. As educators, we need to remember that our own interpretations, problem solving strategies, and communication styles are the result of our cultural experiences, but we sometimes forget our own ethnocentrism in these matters. And worse, we make judgments about the abilities of students that are filtered through our own cultural lenses.

I will close by sharing an incident, told to me by a Wisconsin teacher, that dramatically illustrates how a school task may be culturally biased and fail to take diverse cultural styles into account. Hmong students in a Wisconsin school were given a sorting test and asked to draw a circles around objects that did **not** belong. One test item included a picture of a hammer, a saw, a hatchet, and a fire. The "correct" answer was the fire because it was not a tool, but the Hmong students choose the hammer. Rather than assuming that the students were wrong, the teacher asked them why they had chosen the hammer. They told her that "you would use a saw or a hatchet to cut the wood for the fire but not the hammer." This context oriented and procedurally based answer is not surprising in Hmong culture. There is a lesson here for all of us.

References

Anderson, J. A. (1988). Cognitive styles and multicultural populations. *Teacher Education, 39*(1), 2–9.

Banks, J. A. (1988). Ethnicity, class, cognitive and motivational styles: Research and teaching implications. *Journal of Negro Education, 57*(4), 452–466.

Bennett, C. I. (1990). *Comprehensive multicultural education,* (2nd ed.). Boston: Allyn and Bacon.

Berry, J. (1971). Ecological and cultural factors in spatial perceptual development. *Canadian Journal of Behavioral Science, 3*(4), 324–336.

Berry, J. W. (1976). *Human ecology and cognitive style: Comparative studies in cultural and psychological adaptation.* New York: Wiley.

Blackwell, J. E. (1975). *The Black community: Diversity and unity.* New York: Dodd, Mead and Co.

Boykin, A. W. (1986). The triple quandary and the schooling of Afro-American children. In U. Neisser (Ed.), *The school achievement of minority children,* (pp. 57–92). Hillsdale, NJ: Lawrence Erlbaum Associates.

Buriel, R. (1975). Cognitive styles among three generations of Mexican-American children. *Journal of Class-Cultural Psychology, 6*(4), 417–429.

Cabezas, A. (1981). *Early childhood development in Asian and Pacific American families: Families in transition.* San Francisco: Asian, Inc.

Caldwell, A. J. (1989). *Cultural learning styles: American Indian students in the classroom.* Madison, WI: Wisconsin Department of Public Instruction.

Chickering, A. W. (1976). Commentary: The double bind of field dependence/independence in program alternatives for educational development. In S. Messick (Ed.), *Individuality in learning,* (pp. 79–89). San Francisco: Jossey-Bass.

Cole, M. (1996). *Cultural psychology: A once and future discipline.* Cambridge, MA: Harvard University Press.

Creason, P. (1992). Changing demographics and the importance of culture in student learning styles. (ERIC Document Reproduction Service No. Ed 361 270).

Curry, L. (1990). A critique of the research on learning styles. *Educational Leadership, 48*(2), 50–56.

Duffy, J. (1997, October). Ideologies of literacy: The historical development of reading and writing in Laos: 1921–1975. Paper presented at the meeting of The Mid-Western Educational Research Association, Chicago, IL.

Dunn, R. S. and Dunn, K. J. (1978). *Teaching students through their individual learning styles: A practical approach.* Reston, VA: Reston Publishing.

Dunn, R. S. and Dunn, K. J. (1979, January). Learning styles/teaching styles: Should they . . . can they . . . be matched? *Educational Leadership, 36*(4), 238–244.

Dunn, R., Griggs, S., and Price, G. E. (October, 1993). Learning styles of Mexican-American and Anglo-American elementary students. *Journal of Multicultural Counseling and Development, 21,* 237–247.

Entwistle, N. (1981). *Styles of learning and teaching.* Chichester: Wiley.

Entwistle, N. (1988). Motivational factors in students' approaches to learning. In R. Schmeck (Ed.), *Learning strategies and learning styles.* New York: Plenum.

Ewing, N. J. and Yong, F. L. (1993). Learning style preferences of gifted minority students. *Gifted Education International, 9*(1), 40–44.

Fischer, B. B. and Fischer, L. (1979). Styles in teaching and learning. *Educational Leadership, 36*(4), 245–254.

Gardner, H. (1983). *Frames of mind: The theory of multiple intelligences.* New York: Basic Books.

Gitter, A. G., Black, H., and Mostofsky, D. (1972). Race and sex in the perception of emotion. *Journal of Social Issues, 28*(4), 63–78.

Gregorc, A. F. (1982). *Transaction ability inventory.* Department of Secondary Education, University of Connecticut, Storrs.

Guild, P. (1994, May). The culture/learning style connection. *Educational Leadership, 51,* 16–21.

Halverson, C. B. (1993). Cultural context inventory: The effects of culture on behavior and work style. *The 1993 Annual: Developing Human Resources.* (131–139). San Diego, CA: Pfeiffer and Company.

Heppner, P. and Krauskopf, C. (1987). An information processing approach to personal problem solving. *Counseling Psychologist, 15*(3), 371–447.

Hvitfeldt, C. (1985). Picture perception and interpretation among preliterate adults. *Passage: A Journal of Refugee Education, 1*(1), 27–30.

Hvitfeldt, C. (1986). Traditional culture, perceptual style, and learning: The classroom behavior of Hmong adults. *Adult Education Quarterly, 36*(2), 65–77.

Irving, J. J. and York, D. E. (1995). Learning styles and culturally diverse students: A literature review. In J. A. Banks and C. A. M. Banks (Eds.), *Handbook of research on multicultural education,* (pp. 484–497). New York: Macmillan Publishing USA.

Johada, G. (1980). Theoretical and systematic approaches in cross-cultural psychology. In H. C. Triandis and W. W. Lambert (Eds.), *Handbook of cross-cultural psychology: Perspectives, Vol. 1,* (pp. 69–142). Boston: Allyn and Bacon.

Jones, J. M. (1979). Conceptual and strategic issues in relationship of Black psychology to American social science. In A. W. Boykin, A. J. Franklin, and J. F. Yates (Eds.), *Research directions of Black psychologists.* New York: Russell Sage Foundation.

Kagan, J. (1964). American longitudinal research on psychological development. *Child Development, 35*(1), 1–32.

Karp, S. A. and Konstadt, N. L. (1971). Children's embedded figures test. In H. A. Witkin, P. K. Oldman, E. Raskin, and S. A. Karp (Eds.), *A manual for the embedded figures tests,* (pp. 21–26). Palo Alto, CA: Consulting Psychologists.

Kasten, W. C. (1992). Bridging the horizon: American Indian beliefs and whole language learning. *Anthropology and Education Quarterly, 23*(2), 108–119.

Keefe, J. W. and Languis, M. (1983). Untitled article. *Learning Stages Network Newsletter, 4*(2), 1.

Kleinfeld, J. (1970). *Cognitive strength of Eskimos and implications for education.* University of Alaska. Institute of Social, Economic and Government Research.

Kraemer, A. J. (April, 1973). A cultural self-awareness approach to improving intercultural communication skills. (ERIC Document Reproduction Service NO. ED 079 213).

Kuchinskas, G. (1979). Whose cognitive style makes the difference? *Educational Leadership, 36*(4), 269–271.

Laosa, L. M. and DeAvila, E. A. (1979). Development of cognitive styles among Chicanos in traditional and dualistic communities. *International Journal of Psychology, 14*(2), 91–98.

Lee, G. Y. (1986). Culture and adaptation: Hmong refugees in Australia. In G. L. Hendricks, B. T. Downing, and A. S. Deinard (Eds.), *The Hmong in transition,* (pp. 55–72). Staten Island, NY: Center for Migration Studies.

More, A. J. (1987). Native-American learning styles: A review for researchers and teachers. *Journal of American Indian Education, 27*(1), 17–29.

Mori, S. (1991, Spring-Fall). ESL classroom personality. *Journal of Intensive English Studies (JIES), 5,* 37–54.

Nedd, A. N. and Gruenfeld, L. W. (1976). Field dependence-independence and social traditionalism: A comparison of ethnic subcultures of Trinidad. *International Journal of Psychology, 11*(1), 23–41.

Nieto, S. (1992). *Affirming diversity: The sociopolitical context of multicultural education.* New York: Longman.

Ogbu, J. U. (1983). Minority status and schooling in plural societies. *Comparative Education Review, 27,* 168–190.

Park, C. C. (1997). A comparative study of learning style preferences: Asian-American and Anglo students in secondary schools. Paper presented at the American Educational Research Association, Chicago, IL.

Pepper, F. C. and Henry, S. (1997). Social and cultural effects on Indian learning style: Classroom implications. In B. J. R. Shade (Ed.), *Culture, style, and the educative process,* (2nd ed.), (pp. 168–177). Springfield, IL: Charles C. Thomas.

Phillips, J. C. (January 16, 1978). College of, by, and for Navajo Indians. *Chronicle of Higher Education,* 10–12.

Ramirez, M. and Castaneda, A. (1974). *Cultural democracy, bicognitive development and education.* New York: Academic Press.

Ramirez, M., Castaneda, A., and Herold, P. L. (1974). The relationship of acculturation to cognitive style among Mexican Americans. *Journal of Cross Cultural Psychology, 5,* 424–433.

Reid, J. (1987). The learning style preferences of ESL students. *TESOL Quarterly, 21*(1), 87–111.

Rumbaut, R. and Ima, K. (1988). *The adaptation of Southeast Asian refugee youth: A comparative study.* Washington, DC: U.S. Department of Health and Human Services, Office of Refugee Resettlement.

Saracho, O. N. (1991). Cognitive style and social behavior in young Mexican American children. *International Journal of Early Childhood, 23*(2), 21–38.

Saracho, O. N. (1997). Cultural differences in the cognitive style of Mexican-American students. In B. J. R. Shade (Ed.), *Culture, style, and the educative process,* (2nd Ed.), (pp. 118–125). Springfield, IL: Charles C. Thomas.

Shade, B. J. R. (1986). Is there an Afro-American cognitive style? *Journal of Black Psychology, 13,* 13–16.

Shade, B. J. R. (1989). *Culture, style, and the educative process.* Springfield, IL: Charles C. Thomas.

Shade, B. J. R. (1997). *Culture, style, and the educative process,* (2nd Ed.). Springfield, IL: Charles C. Thomas.

Shade, B. J. R., Kelly, C., and Oberg, M. (1997). *Creating culturally responsive classrooms.* Washington, DC: American Psychological Association.

Slavin, R. E. (1997). *Educational psychology: Theory and practice,* (5th ed.). Boston, MA: Allyn and Bacon.

Slonin, M. B. (1991). *Children, culture, and ethnicity.* New York: Garland.

Smalley, W. A., Vang, C. K., and Yang, G. Y. (1990). *Mother of writing: The origin and development of a Hmong messianic scripts.* Chicago: The University of Chicago Press.

Smith, M. and Shade, B. J. R. (1997). Culturally responsive teaching strategies for American Indian students. In B. J. R. Shade (Ed.), *Culture, style, and the educative process,* (2nd Ed.), (pp. 178–186). Springfield, IL: Charles C. Thomas.

Snowman, J. (1989). Learning tactics and strategies. In G. D. Phy and T. Andre (Eds.), *Cognitive instructional psychology: Components of classroom teaching.* New York: Academic Press.

Staples, R. (1976). Black culture and personality. In R. Staples (Ed.), *Introduction to Black Sociology* (pp. 55–88). New York: McGraw-Hill.

Stodolsky, S. S. and Lesser, G. (1976). Learning patterns of the disadvantaged. *Harvard Educational Review, 37,* 546–553.

Takaki, R. (1989). *Strangers from a different shore.* Boston, MA: Little, Brown and Company.

Timm, J. T. (1994). Hmong values and American education. *Equity and Excellence in Education, 27*(2), 36–44.

Timm, J. T. (1996). *Four perspectives in multicultural education.* Belmont, CA: Wadsworth.

Timm, J. T. and Chiang, B. (1997). Hmong culture and cognitive style. In B. J. R. Shade (Ed.), *Culture, style, and the educative process,* (2nd Ed.), (pp. 105–117). Springfield, IL: Charles C. Thomas.

Timm, J. T., Chiang, B., and Finn, B. D. (1998). Acculturation in the cognitive style of Laotian Hmong students in the United States. *Equity and Excellence in Education, 31*(1), 29–35.

Vasquez, J. A. (March, 1990). Teaching to the distinctive traits of minority students. *The Clearing House, 63,* 229–304.

Witkin, H. A. (1979). Socialization, culture and ecology in the development of group and sex differences in cognitive style. *Human Development, 22*(5), 358–372.

Witkin, H. A. and Goodenough, D. R. (1981). *Cognitive styles: Essence and origins, field dependence and field independence.* New York: International Universities Press.

Witkin, H. A., Moore, C. A., Goodenough, D. R., and Cox, P. W. (Winter, 1977). Field dependent and field independent cognitive styles and their educational implications. *Review of Educational Research, 47*(1), 1–64.

Witkin, H. A., Oldman, P. K., Cox, P. W., Ehrlichman, E., Hamm, R. M., and Ringler, R. W. (1973). *Field-dependence-independence and psychological differentiation: A bibliography.* Princeton, NJ: Educational Testing Service.

Witkin, H. A., Oldman, P. K., Raskin, E., and Karp, S. A. (1971). *A manual for the embedded figures tests.* Palo Alto, CA: Consulting Psychologists Press.

Worthley, K. M. E. (1987). Learning style factor of field dependence/independence and problem solving strategies of Hmong refugee students. Unpublished master's thesis, University of Wisconsin Stout, Menomonie, WI.

Using Stories
TO INTRODUCE AND TEACH
Multicultural Literature

by Patricia Goldblatt

If stories can ease lost boys into adulthood and fledgling doctors into compassion, so it would seem that stories could also play a role in introducing migrants to a new and alien world, for stories are everywhere

In the story of *Peter Pan,* Pan takes the girl Wendy to Never-Never Land so that she can be a mother to the Lost Boys. The boys sit transfixed as Wendy spins her tales, enfolding and enchanting the lads. When the stories have facilitated the boys' development and growing up, Pan has no choice but to relinquish his troop. What powers of transformation do stories possess that cause these children to escape from the world of eternal childhood and adults to regain their innocent childhood perspective?

In *The Call of Stories: Teaching and the Moral Imagination* (1989), Robert Coles addresses the transformative nature of stories that allows children to enter and apprehend worlds beyond their own experience. Coles became aware of the power of stories when he met 15-year-old Phil. Phil had lost his father in World War II, his mother in a car accident, and the use of his limbs to polio, which had rendered him permanently paralyzed. Coles was surprised when Phil began to talk about *The Adventures of Huckleberry Finn.* Phil confided that this book has made him feel "different." He reflected,

> I forget about myself—no, I didn't actually. I joined up with Huck and Jim; we were a trio. They were really nice to me. I explored the Mississippi with them on the boats. I had good talks with them . . . they straightened me out. (Coles 1989, 35–36)

Phil went on to read *Catcher in the Rye,* explaining that the novel "got to me," lending purpose to one who was "flat out" (Coles 1989, 38). Phil came to believe that his own misfortune had caused him to see life sardonically: he was now able, like Holden, to spot the "phoniness," hypocrisy, and deceit of the world.

So impressed was Coles by Phil's forays and lessons learnt through short stories and novels that in 1974, Coles decided to integrate stories into a course at Harvard Medical School called "Literature and Medicine." Coles selected novels, short stories, and poetry written by and about physicians. By sampling from literature, young doctors vicariously comprehend, or are at least privy to, the human aspect of illness. More than statistics and body parts, stories written by or about doctors' decisions, personal conflicts, and confrontations impart knowledge that speaks to the medical students' hearts as well as to their heads.

If stories can ease lost boys into adulthood and fledgling doctors into compassion, so it would seem that stories could also play a role in introducing migrants to a new and alien world, for stories are everywhere, waiting to accost unsuspecting ears. Stories can present diverse aspects of our globe that are blatantly ignored, feared, deemed exotic, or merely taken for granted; these stories possess the power to inform our lives, opening our eyes to new perceptions and possibilities.

Visiting Ellis Island last summer, I was mesmerized by the stories of a park ranger who recreated the experiences of those hopeful travelers arriving at New York's infamous port. She described the six-second medical inspection that sealed the fate of many newcomers to the United States:

> If while ascending the stairs to the second level of the processing building at Ellis Island, a person—child or adult—cast their eyes upwards towards the ceiling, they were labelled as 'mentally defective,' and either returned to their country of origin, or confined in a mental hospital.

Why? The ranger explained the doctors' belief that every sane person knows above their heads is only ceiling and sky, and therefore there was no reason, indeed *only a lack of reason,* to cause a person to look upward while mounting the stairs.

Similarly, the musical *Ragtime,* an adaptation of the novel by E. L. Doctorow, depicts the story of immigrants' arrival and adjustment to a new world. Directors Terrence McNally and Garth Drabinsky have translated problems, worries, adjustments, and restrictions into the concrete impediments of gates, fences, locked doors, and surly, condescending officials. Visually and aurally, the play's symbolic representations convey to the viewer and listener the barriers encountered by those fleeing oppression in one country and the resultant frustration of discovering more limitations in the "new world." Instead of being relieved of fears and hostility, the play's travelers, on disembarking, feel depressed and lost. They are confused and perplexed, filled with regret and wonderment at what this land of "milk and honey" might offer their children. Both the stories of the Ellis Island ranger and the popular musical begin to address the painful transitions of the immigrant. Instead of ignoring the reality of those newcomers to America, authors and playwrights who write about these experiences impart validity to the newcomers' plight. Addressing the issues and hearing their voices cause us to empathize with their trials and tribulations: the stories make us aware that the issues are *real.*

To focus on these real problems, students from Somalia, Jamaica, and Sri Lanka at a high school in Toronto have created a drama program as a subsidiary of an already existing program called CultureLink. Improvising scenes, the students dramatize obstacles encountered by their peers: for example, obtaining directions on a bus when a bus driver cannot be bothered to understand a dialect or language foreign to him; or a guidance counselor's assessment that a newcomer will be incapable of tackling courses at university. One student reflected that these scenarios, although educating the audience about the trials faced by newcomers, also made her very aware that "these encounters based on skin color and accent left her feeling like an outsider in a country she was trying so hard to call home." Yet she emphasized that the audience viewing these skits shouldn't be scared and "if they see a newcomer struggling [in everyday life], they should help make newcomers feel welcome" *(The Toronto Star,* June 16, 1998).

Even now, many of the new arrivals' stories have not had a recognized place in the literary canon taught in the high schools of Canada and the United States. In *Culture and Imperialism,* Edward Said points out that novels focusing on colonization have always been written from the point of view of the colonizer. A popular choice in high school English courses, Joseph Conrad's *Heart of Darkness* does not even consider that the Africans of the Congo have a story to tell; they are only props, catalysts for the experiences and revelations of the British intruders, Kurtz and Marlowe. The reader experiences the tales and tribulations only from the point of view of the white man.

Mindful of this problem and of the needs of immigrants to Canada, in 1988 the Canadian Parliament passed the Canadian Multiculturalism Act, in which "the Constitution of Canada recognize[d] the importance of preserving and enhancing the multicultural heritage of Canadians . . . while working to achieve the equality of all Canadians in the economic, social, cultural and political life of Canada." In 1992, an amendment

to the Education Act required all boards of education to put in place anti-racist and ethnocultural equity policies. As a result of that policy, Mandarin Chinese, Hebrew, Sanskrit, and various other language and cultural programs are offered during and after school hours to students in Toronto public schools. In 1995, a policy document called The Common Curriculum stated that:

> the curriculum must reflect the diversity of Canadian society. Curriculum must present an accurate picture of the world in which students live and will work. Students' self-image and their attitudes to others are affected both by what is taught and how it is taught. Students are entitled to have their personal experiences and their racial and ethnocultural heritage valued, and to live in a society that upholds the rights of the individual. Students will also learn that their society is enriched and strengthened by its diversity. (19)

With the goals of multiculturalism in mind, educators were instructed to offer texts and curricula that extended greater connection to their students, course material in which all Canadians could recognize themselves, their families, and their former countries.

Even before these goals had been officially addressed, Linda Hutcheon and Marion Richmond selected stories by a variety of Canadians whose backgrounds were Polish, Tamil, Hungarian, Jewish, Indian, and Armenian, for an anthology titled *Other Solitudes.* The authors' diverse topics include suicide, spousal death, adjustment, language classes, letters home, longings, and forging new identities. "The multiracial and multiethnic nature of this country is made real . . . in the end [it] help[s us] understand that there are ways of seeing the world, and of writing in and about it, that may be different from our own—ways—whatever they might be—valuable because of that difference" (Hutcheon and Richmond 1990, 5).

In *Other Solitudes,* Himanji Bannerji describes the tensions faced by East Indian parents and children transplanted to a new environment. Bannerji's story, "The Other Family," portrays a little girl who is required to draw a picture of her family for an assignment in school. Excited and proud, the child shows her rendering to her mother, who becomes distraught and confronts her daughter:

> "Listen," said the mother, "this is not your family. I, you and your father are dark-skinned, dark-haired, I don't have a blond wig hidden in my closet, my eyes are black, not blue, and your father's beard is black, not red, and you do not have a white skin, a button nose with freckles, blue eyes and blond hair tied in a pony tail." *(Other Solitudes* 1990, 142–143)

The child and many of her immigrant classmates have produced similar images of their families, drawing on a schoolbook's images of what a family should look like. More importantly, they have had their efforts not only acknowledged but also applauded by their teacher. The mother in this story is frightened and yet terribly angered by the school as agent of socialization in her new country. She trembles to think about this process of assimilation and the insensitivity of the teacher, who will knowingly obliterate her daughter's past and with it, her child's identity. Although fiction, "The Other Family" addresses the problems of assimilation, acculturation, and adjustment made by immigrants from visible minorities. Bannerji bases his story on the experiences of real children.

The pain felt by Eva Hoffman in her revealing memoir, *Lost in Translation,* pinpoints the horror of having her Polish name changed because her schoolteacher in Vancouver is unable to pronounce it. In this way, Hoffman's identity is swept away. Her life's experiences, friendship, kinship, even the countryside of her 13 years lived in another land, another language are torn away in an instant. She writes:

> These new appellations, which we ourselves can't yet pronounce, are not us. They are identification tags, disembodied signs pointing to objects that happen to be my sister and myself. We walk to our seats, into a roomful of unknown faces, with names that make us strangers to ourselves. (Hoffman 1989, 105)

It is said that children are malleable, and whether by group pressure, a desire to fit in, or a real devotion to the new culture, perhaps they do inevitably adjust. However, the cost is high for Hoffman and her sister. I recently heard her speak in Toronto, pensively reading her words to an audience of rapt listeners. Years after her arrival to Canada, she was still repeating her story. Although an accomplished journalist, university professor, and author, Hoffman has recently decided to become a therapist. I could not help but wonder if those first traumatic experiences in Vancouver had rendered her vulnerable, severing her from the language in which her initial identity had been forged. Perhaps her desire now was to help others who had suffered as she had.

The plight of the elderly as well as the children newly arrived to this country is painful. Theirs is a story less told, but like Hoffman's, one redolent with loss. The title of Neil Bissoondath's short story "Security," published in *The Penguin Book of Caribbean Short Stories* (Markham 1996), is ironic because the experience of a man exiled from his former life is anything but secure. Bissoondath revisits the conflicts that exist both inside and outside a family that has departed its place of birth. Bissoondath's elderly protagonist, Alistair Ramgoolan, feels resentment and alienation in his strange new world; he longs for the friendship and traditions left home in India and Trinidad. Vijay, Alistair's successful businessman son, and Vijay's older brother, are too busy for the old man. Even Alistair's wife has deserted him for a job as a cook outside their apartment. Alistair moans that "everybody—even birds—needed a safe place to land . . . a point of reference from which they could assure themselves of their place in the world" (Markham 1996, 386).

In order to recreate his prior world, Alistair decides to celebrate *Divali,* the Indian festival of lights, in Canada. In addition to preparing traditional food and dressing in his *dhoti,* Alistair lights 20 sticks of incense and sets the room ablaze with two dozen candles, unfortunately triggering the fire alarm. Like a mischievous child, he is soundly scolded. Depressed, chastised, and embarrassed, Alistair retreats to the world of the television, where the excitement of *The Price Is Right* allows him finally

<hr/>

A Reading List of Multicultural Stories
(in order of presentation)

Coles, Robert. *The Call of Stories: Teaching and the Moral Imagination.* Boston: Houghton Mifflin, 1989.

Hutcheon, Linda and Richmond, Marion, eds. *Other Solitudes: Canadian Multicultural Fiction.* Toronto: Oxford University Press, 1990.

Hoffman, Eva. *Lost in Translation.* New York: Penguin, 1989.

Markham, E. A., ed. *The Penguin Book of Caribbean Short Stories.* London: Penguin, 1986.

Malouf, David. *Remembering Babylon.* New York: Vintage, 1993.

Mistry, Rohinton. *Such a Long Journey.* Toronto: McClelland and Stewart, 1991.

Andrews, W. L., ed. *African American Literature: Voices in a Tradition.* San Diego, Calif.: Harcourt, Brace, Jovanovich, 1992.

Yee, Paul. *Tales from Gold Mountain: Stories of the Chinese in the New World.* Toronto: Douglas & McIntyre, 1989.

Burgos-Debray, Elisabeth. *I, Rigoberta Menchú: An Indian Woman in Guatemala.* New York: Verso, 1984.

<hr/>

to obtain the dreams and longings unattainable in his present situation. Seeking a place of acknowledgement and understanding, a place free from conflicts or confrontations, people like Alistair Ramgoolan often purposefully distract themselves in order to dull the pain of separation from their previous life. Stories that examine the feelings of alienation cast light on and draw attention to the smiling individuals who pretend to cope, refusing to blame or even to acknowledge that their situations are desperate. Many sink wordlessly into depression in an attempt not to trouble the busy, seemingly well-adjusted, happy members of their family. Bissoondath's story focuses on the loneliness of the exiled.

From newly transplanted children and parents to those children born far from their parents' native land, people identified by racial characteristics often encounter thoughtless remarks and behavior that makes them feel they do not belong. A graduate student of Indian descent recently related his story: in spite of the fact that he had been born in Canada, he was constantly identified as a foreigner because of his Indian features. He lamented that his parents, at least, had the benefit of growing up in a country where they felt they belonged and were familiar with traditions, festivals, and celebrations that were part of their culture. In dark days in a new country, they could return in their minds to that place of acceptance and security. My student friend yearns for that lost country pictured so romantically in his parents' stories. He lives vicariously, as does Janet McIvor, a young schoolgirl in David Malouf's novel *Remembering Babylon.* Janet dreams of her mother's homeland of Scotland, wishing fervently to escape her life as a girl and an inhabitant of the dreary land of Australia. For her the stories in books are the passage out of her present situation:

> She pored over books, anything she could lay her hands on that offered some promise that the world was larger, more pas-

sionate, crueller—even that would be a comfort—than the one she was bound to. (Malouf 1993, 58)

For some young people, stories are a way of adopting another identity, of escaping who one is. In this sense, being presented with the reality of other cultures is at once an opportunity and a source of controversy. Kindler cites the example of Jan Kadar, a real little boy, five-and-a-half years old, of Polish descent. When his family moved form the United States to Vancouver, Canada, he became fascinated with the killer whales depicted on street banners. He met a sculptor of Haida totem poles and decided to integrate Haida imagery into his cultural heritage. When asked at school to introduce his class to artifacts of his personal heritage, he proffered drawings of totem poles, identifying himself with the Haida culture. His teacher berated him for not bringing perogies. His mother worried that multicultural studies might "brand children as mem-

> *We must suggest that our students reach out to past generations to reestablish valuable links and demand stories that reflect how people have successfully coped in their new lives in their new countries*

bers of distinct and closed societies" (Kindler 1994, 59). The questions are perplexing: to which culture do we belong, and must we be publicly identified and stereotyped by our natal origins, defining our separateness because of birth, race, or cultural traits? What role does school play in encouraging stereotypes that limit and restrict our sense of ourselves and our children?

Rather than encouraging students to renounce their links and feel shame or embarrassment at their unique traditions, their secret longings to be somewhere else—anywhere, but here—must be encouraged, fostered, and employed to promote dialogue. We must suggest that our students reach out to past generations to reestablish valuable links and demand stories that reflect how people have successfully coped in their new lives in their new countries. Stories that share traumas of anguish and separation proclaim that the newcomer is not alone in her resettlement.

Books that deal with universal issues of dating, parental conflict, and life choices allow new Canadians to comprehend that their needs, dreams, and aspirations—whether at home or in this new place—connect them with the inhabitants of all countries. In *Such a Long Journey,* by Rohinton Mistry, the family's problems are not cultural but a result of generational differences. In this story set in Bombay, a Parsi father and his bright son battle over the value of studying the arts versus studying technology, which will yield a brighter future of pos-

sibilities. One can parallel this novel's theme to a real-life situation in Montgomery, Alabama, where an African-American community chose a science magnet school over a performing arts one because the parents believed that science and technology would provide their children with socioeconomic mobility (Hanna 1994, 69–75). Gustad, the devoted but often domineering father in *Such a Long Journey,* shares these feelings. Besides the universal issue of future vocation, the novel is rich in ethnographic details, extending a world that is, for students, familiar yet different.

One of my students, an Indian girl named Jasmine, who had lived in Burma for several years, commented in an essay on the choice of using *Such a Long Journey* as required reading in class:

> *Such a Long Journey* allowed this reader to ask her parents and aunts about the culture and language of India, thus strengthening the relationships between younger and older generations.... Adding such books to the English curriculum helps minority students to relate their own background to school. It also helps other students learn about the variety of cultures that inhabit the schools.

For Jasmine, talking about her old world and having her peers' interest and respect focus on her as a special person reinforced her bonds with both worlds, old and new. At first a shy girl reticent to contribute her views in a class of mostly white upper-middle-class students, Jasmine's insider's information into Indian idiom and language facilitated her ease. The novel was successful on many levels: it spoke to universal problems between parents and children, it imparted information about Indian culture, and it encouraged students from cultures other than the dominant one to speak out and explain in a personal way different mores and traditions.

Carefully chosen books and textbooks can facilitate a student's improved understanding of herself and her classmates. *African American Literature* is a valuable anthology of poignant tales. It excerpts stories, poetry, and biographies that present the marginalized lives of more than 100 African Americans. In "Incidents in the Life of a Slave Girl," Harriet A. Jacobs recreates her place of hiding, the scurrying mice, the stifling space, the lack of air, and her desire to respond to the voices of her children on the other side of her closeted wall that acts as a prison but also a protective hiding space. She maintains, "I would have chosen this, rather than my lot as a slave, though white people considered it an easy one" (1992, 197). In her fiery proclamation at the Akron Conference in 1852 Sojourner Truth asserts her rights against the clergy who oppose women's rights and the white women who disdain her for her color and her position in society. She proclaims,

> Then that little man in black there, he says women can't have as much rights as men, 'cause Christ wasn't a woman! Where did your Christ come from? Where did your Christ come from? From God and a woman! Man had nothing to do with Him. (1992, 169)

These words spoken so long ago by an uneducated slave girl once named Isabella by her owners not only impart awareness of times past but also point out that there have always been individuals ready to confront and battle the injustices inflicted upon them. As role models, people from the past speak again, their voices remarkably echoing modern-day sentiments to reveal that there is an unbreakable chain among those who are oppressed. To people born in a particular country who might think these stories possess little interest or relevance to their lives, it must be underlined that freedoms, rights, and liberties are universal concerns for *all* peoples, and only aboriginal peoples are the indigenous ones. The issues of acceptance and love speak to the human condition, a condition we all must address.

In order to empathize with those pushed to the fringe of society, those misfits who whether by poverty, class, race, gender, or exceptionality have been alienated, stories provide insight into troubled lives. Stories have the power to inform us of another dimension of human experience. They facilitate our growth as people, as we read and vicariously experience the lives of those "others." Toni Morrison's excerpt from *The Bluest Eye* makes the reader privy to the feelings and madness of poor, sexually abused Pecola through the eyes of two sisters. The patent leather shoes, fluffy sweaters, and brightly colored knee socks worn by the rich set them apart from the narrators. The black girls know their place, or rather lack of it, and "step aside when [the white girls] want[ed] to use the sink in the girls' toilet" (1992, 69). Bemused, irritated, and fascinated, the narrators search for flaws in a world of privilege, desperately needing a way to secure their dignity. They discover that one of their oppressors, Maureen Peel (aptly nicknamed by them "Meringue Pie"), possesses a "dog tooth" and the scars of a sixth finger on each hand. Triumphantly, they rejoice at her imperfection. They realize that she, too, possesses secrets that set her apart. Bitterness and pain are offset by giggles and sharing with a sister, a loved one who knows the pain of not belonging. Yet for Pecola—lonely, sad Pecola—her only escape from life's affliction is a descent into soothing madness.

Not all story offerings in *African American Literature* are as contentious or as wrenching as Sojourner Truth's or Toni Morrison's. The excerpt from Maya Angelou's memoir *I Know Why the Caged Bird Sings* recreates that dreamy place of childhood, opening the doors to a magical place where life's sustaining visions are formed and kept safe as protections against the hostile universe of those who do not fit into society:

> The lamplight in the store gave a soft make-believe feeling to our world which made me want to whisper and walk about on tiptoe. The odors of onions and oranges and kerosene had been mixing all night and wouldn't be disturbed until the wooden slat was removed from the door and early morning air forced its way in with the bodies of people who had walked miles to reach the pickup place. (1992, 34)

The delicacy and fragility of this remembrance preserves that moment when a place or experience is crystallized and marks an epiphany, a magical point of beginning or ending in a life's journeys. Stored in the writer's mind, the smells and sounds of a special experience are kept safe, usable by the owner for inspiration or security, memories of a safe place, a home.

Stories that highlight the experiences of the outsider, the newcomer, extend links to readers and promote understanding between worlds. Rather than nostalgic views frozen in time, postcard images of happy "natives" marked by ethnic song and dance, "the meaning of being [the other] . . . beyond ethnicity and cultural talk" (Hutcheon and Richmond, 147) takes place in stories. Connecting a past life and a present reality entwines two relevant worlds. Like the AIDS Quilt that uses a traditional format to address contemporary issues, writings by immigrant and minority authors tell of a history too often ignored by today's young people.

Bridging times and worlds creates a hybrid culture. By conjoining worlds and by combining perhaps incongruent points of view and eras, something new and wonderful emerges. In his many stories of Chinese immigrants' adjustment to life on the prairie, Paul Yee combines past and present by blending his own Canadian experiences with those of his Chinese ancestors. He draws on a wealth of multicultural tales, personal experiences, and contacts with a variety of people. From Chinese folktales to *Red Riding Hood* and British Columbia's history of industrial capitalism, he interweaves past and present, near and far, here and there. Not stereotyping, ghettoizing, or promoting exotic and fossilizing ideas about cultures, he offers vibrant well-written stories to pierce the silence of the forgotten immigrant. The possibility of a "hybrid culture," one that accommodates, or at least suggests, a reconciliation of the world left behind and the one presently inhabited acknowledges the difficulties, but also the promise, of acceptance and belonging in a new world.

Then there are those stories that must be set down. More horrific than stories of adjustment or acculturation, stories of abuse and murder proclaim the reasons why people choose or were forced to emigrate. *I, Rigoberta Menchú* is that living testament to the trials and confrontations of the Guatemalan-born author's indigenous people. She speaks for them; Rigoberta is their voice. She tells the tale of the slaughter of her kinspeople. Exiled from her home, she is committed to raising awareness of the abuses in Guatemala. Spoken to the ethnologist Elisabeth Burgos-Debray, Rigoberta's tale documents the deaths of her mother, her father, her brothers and sisters, and her many friends; she relates a story of all her people:

> They tied him up, they tied his testicles . . . behind with string and forced him to run. And they left him in a well, I don't know what it's called, a hole with water and a bit of mud in it, they left him naked there all night. There were a lot of corpses in the hole with him and he couldn't stand the smell of all those corpses. My brother was tortured for more than sixteen days. They cut off his fingernails, they cut off his fingers, they cut off his skin, they burned parts of his skin. (Burgos-Debray 1984, 174)

These are experiences that we would prefer not to know, and yet hearing them, we have a duty to respond to Rigoberta's story. The words infiltrate our consciousness, making us aware of, and perhaps more willing not to judge but to view with compassion, those newcomers who have fled their homes and families.

Words. Stories. Glimpses. Ways to enter another's world and know it—maybe just a little. Karen Blixen, also known as the Danish writer Isak Dinesen, once said that she had been an armchair traveler, and for many that is the only way that they will ever visit, touch, or experience another life or world. The beauty of the story is that each single account reflects a human who perceives, sees, and explains her world in a personally unique fashion. Whether by testimony, descriptive imagery, reported, direct, rambling, broken speech and dialect, or a straightforward narrative, the story has the power to create the world of the writer, allowing it entrance into the world of the reader. Thus, it communicates and links two individuals who perhaps might never have met in actuality. Through marks on a page, universes are shared. For the newcomers to any country, knowing that stories can impart their experiences in another land and that they will be respected and acknowledged as persons with rights, traditions, and history aids in transitions that are most often painful. For those persons who have lived in one particular place, feeling ease and comfort in the conventions of their society, stories open doors of understanding. Stories are a gift: precious offerings from the world of one into the world of another. Lovingly wrapped in words and images, the real treasure of the story is what is revealed by the giver and understood by the recipient, that which opens the hearts of both.

WORKS CITED

Andrews, W. L., ed. *African American Literature: Voices in a Tradition.* 1992. San Diego, Calif.: Harcourt, Brace, Jovanovich.

Burgos-Debray, E. 1984. *I, Rigoberta Menchú: An Indian Woman in Guatemala.* New York: Verso.

Coles, R. 1989. *The Call of Stories: Teaching and the Moral Imagination.* Boston: Houghton Mifflin.

Conrad, Joseph. 1973. *Heart of Darkness.* New York: Penguin.

Hanna, J. 1994. "Issues in Supporting School Diversity: Academics, Social Relations and the Arts." *Anthropology and Education Quarterly* 25(1).

Hoffman, E. 1989. *Lost in Translation.* New York: Penguin.

Hutcheon, L. and Richmond, M., eds. (1990). *Other Solitudes: Canadian Multicultural Fiction.* Toronto: Oxford University Press.

Kindler, A. 1994. "Children and the Culture of a Multicultural Society." *Art Education* 47 (July).

Malouf, D. 1993. *Remembering Babylon.* New York: Vintage.

Markham, E. A., ed. 1996. *The Penguin Book of Caribbean Short Stories.* London: Penguin.

Ministry of Education, Ontario. 1987. *English Guidelines: Intermediate and Senior Divisions (Grade 7–12).* Toronto: The Queen's Printer.

___. 1995. *The Common Curriculum: Policies and Outcomes, Grade 1–9.* Toronto: The Queen's Printer.

Mistry, R. 1991. *Such a Long Journey.* Toronto: McClelland and Stewart.

Said, E. 1994. *Culture and Imperialism.* New York: Vintage.

Salinger, J. D. 1951. *Catcher in the Rye.* Boston: Little, Brown.

Twain, M. 1985. *The Adventures of Huckleberry Finn.* Berkeley: University of California Press.

Patricia Goldblatt is a teacher of English at Northern Secondary School in Toronto, Ontario and a regular contributor of articles and book reviews for *MultiCultural Review.*

Making the Most of the Classroom Mosaic:

A Constructivist Perspective

By Bruce Marlowe & Marilyn Page

Recently, we visited a student teacher in a small elementary school in the northwest corner of rural Vermont. Imagine our surprise to find a sign on the front door for parents written in Vietnamese! Schools are changing. And they are changing fast.

The arrival of new immigrant groups and the precipitous rise in poverty among children have both contributed to making our classrooms more diverse—and in more ways—than at any other time in our nation's history. In fact, children are the most diverse segment of American society.

Although student diversity makes teaching more challenging, this is only problematic if the focus is on how the teacher will deliver instruction rather than on how the students will learn. Classroom settings with students from different cultures, abilities, needs, and interests provide rich learning opportunities, in part, because they so clearly reflect one of the central tenets of constructivism: There is virtually an infinite variety of ways to know the world. The magnitude of student diversity underscores this point in ways impossible to ignore by even the most traditional of teachers.

How are Our Schools Changing?

Consider the following:

- Close to 60 percent of the nation's entire immigrant population entered the United States in the 1980s. A century ago, the nations that sent us the largest numbers of immigrants had a common

European culture (England, Ireland, Germany, Italy). The nations that send us the most immigrants now—and that are projected to do so through at least the year 2000—come from every corner of the globe. In rank order they are: Mexico, the Philippines, Korea, China, Taiwan, India, Cuba, the Dominican Republic, Jamaica, Canada, Vietnam, the United Kingdom, and Iran (Hodgkinson, 1995).

- As a group, children are America's poorest citizens. During the 1980s, the poverty rate for children reached an unprecedented 11 percent; by 1993, the level increased to 23 percent (or more than one in five school aged children) (Hodgkinson, 1993).

- The two largest minority groups are African-Americans (30 million) and Hispanic-Americans (20 million). Together they will comprise about one third of the total school enrollment by the year 2000; currently, non-European American students are the majority in the 25 largest school districts in the country (Hodgkinson, 1992).

- More than 15 percent of students in the schools of New York, Chicago, Los Angeles, Washington, D.C., and San Francisco are of limited English proficiency (Hodgkinson, 1992).

- The United States Bureau of the Census estimates that there are 329 languages other than English spoken in the United States (Sileo, Sileo, & Prater, 1996).

Do These Differences Affect Learning?

Simply put, "yes." There is overwhelming evidence that such factors as a student's

country of origin, cultural heritage, linguistic background, and religious beliefs, as well as the socioeconomic status of the student's parents, all, in their own way, influence learning.

Teachers who fail to recognize how the values of traditional schooling may clash with particular cultural values (Kugelmass, 1995) often face classrooms of disengaged, unmotivated, and/or disruptive learners who may find school irrelevant, or even hostile to their values.

The Problem

As suggested above, today's teachers are required to be sensitive to a wider range of multicultural differences than ever before. Most teachers in the United States are white. By century's end more than one third of the school-aged population will be nonwhite; "minority" students are already the majority culture in many large urban school districts.

Although eager to learn, teachers as a group believe they are unprepared to teach students from diverse cultures (Barry, 1995). Can teachers package content into a single format that all children can understand? Or should they continuously repackage the content for each of the cultural, religious, and ethnic groups represented in their classrooms?

Liberating Ourselves

Framing the issues in this way reveals just how potent teacher commitment is to thinking about teaching as information dispensing. As Barry (1995) reports, teachers are concerned primarily with how they will relate content in multiple ways to meet the

---

—*Bruce Marlowe and Marilyn Page are professors in the Education Department at Johnson State College, Johnson, Vermont.*

From *Multicultural Education*, Summer 1999, pp. 19-21. © 1999 by Caddo Gap Press, Inc. Reprinted by permission of *Multicultural Education*, the magazine of the National Association for Multicultural Education.

needs of a very diverse student body. It should come as no surprise that teachers feel that this is a daunting task for which they are ill prepared.

In fact, this is not a daunting task at all; it is an impossible one. Although some find this enormously distressing, we believe it is very liberating; as teachers, we cannot simultaneously be all things to all children. Nor can we present one approach based on a kind of average of student difference. Rather, we must reframe our questions about teaching and learning.

We must do so to allow for student exploration and inquiry in a way that allows them to connect content knowledge to what they already know. How is this possible for students with limited English proficiency? How can teachers meet the needs of Mexican-American children and children of Asian Pacific descent and African-American children, all of whom are in the same classroom?

Focusing on Students' Experiences

Ethnic differences are real, but continually seeking to alter our teaching style to conform to our beliefs about each student (based solely on his or her ethnic identity), perpetuates an overgeneralization about ethnic groups and puts the focus of the teaching/learning experience in the wrong place. Knowing that Asian children as a group are quieter and more submissive to authority will not enhance the learning of students of Asian descent if, as a teacher armed with this knowledge, you continue to focus on what you will do to cover the curriculum as opposed to focusing on the ways you can help your students connect content to the most important factors in student learning—the students' experiences and prior knowledge (Ausubel, 1968).

The value of constructivism is that it respects and allows each student to use his or her unique knowledge and experience in the learning process. This is so whether the student is from a 10,000 acre ranch in Billings, Montana, or a one-room flat in Springfield, Massachusetts.

Classroom Culture and Ethnic Culture: A Dynamic Relationship

Looking at Two Ethnic Groups: Vietnamese and Navajo

Many books that address the teaching of different ethnic groups describe Vietnamese (and in general Asian) children as being quiet, submissive, and reluctant to speak publicly, and Navajo children as being non-verbal, non-analytical, even disengaged. Review the table on the next page, but be advised: *The table is detrimental to the learning health of your students!*

In Traditional Classrooms

The traits described in the table appear primarily when the diverse classroom is one where the teacher dispenses knowledge. In these classrooms teachers of minority students spend more time talking to students than do teachers of white children; thus, minority children "spend considerably more time listening than being heard" (Moran, 1981, in McCarty et al, 1991, p. 54).

When communication is controlled by the teacher, when students are singled out to answer direct questions about subjects "for which they have little background knowledge" (Collier, 1972, p. 70), this very classroom culture reinforces submissiveness and makes certain minority groups appear, as groups, to be non-verbal, non-analytical, or disengaged.

In Constructivist Classrooms

The situation is different in constructivist classrooms. Where:

> . . . teachers and students share talk, where the expression of students' ideas is sought and clearly valued, where curricular content meaningfully incorporates the students' social environment, and where students use their cultural and linguistic resources to solve new problems, Native American students respond eagerly and quite verbally to questioning, even in their second language. (McCarty, et al, 1991, p. 53)

According to Steinberg (1996), Asian students outperform all other groups (including whites) on measures of school performance. They earn higher grades, do more homework, cut class less often, and report less mind-wandering. One of Steinberg's most striking findings, however, is that compared to all other ethnic groups, Asians frequently "turn to each other for academic assistance and consultation" (p. 47). They collaborate, they work in groups, they pose questions and work on them together. This is hardly what one would expect based on the table (see next page) which characterizes Asians as independent, passive, and reluctant to ask questions.

And in a study by McCarty et al (1991), the use of a pilot curriculum that emphasized open-ended questioning, collaborative group work, and student-directed learning (not exactly the approach suggested in the table) was shown to enhance student engagement, content mastery, and analytic reasoning in Navajo youth. As suggested in the table, this approach was widely considered to be antithetical to the Navajo "learning style." As Au pointed out (in McCarty, 1991) "Native American children may in no way be characterized as nonverbal. . . ." though " . . . there are settings in which they may appear so" (p. 53). Unfortunately, these settings are all too often our classrooms.

Two Approaches

Lets turn to a more practical example of these points. Think about the assumptions that inform and guide the different educational approaches presented below:

Approach 1: Monday–Thursday, a 10th grade biology teacher presents a 40-minute lecture each afternoon on the digestive system of sheep, their eating habits, and their grazing preferences. When a student asks a question about the content during the lectures, the teacher provides the answer.

> . . . as teachers, we cannot simultaneously be all things to all children. Nor can we present one approach based on a kind of average of student difference. Rather, we must reframe our questions about teaching and learning.

Ethnicity	Learning Style	Implications for Teaching
Asian	• quiet • submissive • obedient • prefer not to call attention to themselves • prefer to work independently • reluctant to engage in "free discussion" • prefer not to partake in brainstorming.	Didactic methods important, teachers should transmit information, strategies, exercises etc. through lecture. Teachers should understand if student does not ask questions, is reluctant to challenge assumptions/methods of teacher or otherwise appears unengaged.
Navajo	• non-analytical • nonverbal • visual learners • "doers" rather than "talkers" (McCarty, 1992) • may consider it rude to disagree in public • may not consider it worth the risk of hurting someone's feelings by stating an opinion in class.	Teacher should employ "right-hemisphere" approaches, emphasize dance, art, music. Often slow to respond verbally. Teachers should employ a lot of wait time after questions. Try to avoid asking direct questions which put students on the spot.

If the teacher poses a question to which a student responds incorrectly, the teacher provides the right answer, or turns to another student until she gets the correct response. She then moves on. On Friday, she gives a multiple choice test based on the information covered during the week. Her evaluation of a student's learning is based on the student's test score. Although she may never return to the subject of sheep for the remainder of the year, the teacher is confident that a high score indicates that a student has learned the material and that she has adequately "covered" the content.

Approach 2: Monday–Thursday, an elder Navajo sheep herder spends 40 minutes with tribal children each afternoon listening to their questions about sheep, their eating habits, and their grazing preferences. When a child asks a question, the elder replies, "What do you think?" and continues to encourage further observation, and inquiry (McCarty et al., 1991). On Friday, the elder asks the children to herd the sheep without him, to rely on one another, and to return prepared to demonstrate what they have learned. Gradually, children become responsible for the herding of sheep and their mastery of the content information is continuously tied to, and used as a foundation for, subsequent learning.

Though fictional and time-compressed, these scenarios encapsulate much of what we know about the importance of a constructivist perspective in diverse classroom settings: Children, regardless of their cultural heritage, are curious, active explorers and constructors of their worlds. Navajo children, however, may not appear so inclined. In Approach 1, in fact, they typically are characterized (as noted in the table above) as passive and disengaged. Yet, as McCarty and colleagues (1991) demonstrated, in educational settings that encourage children to tie new content to their own experience, that are conducive to give-and-take, and that facilitate exploration and experimentation, Navajo children, in fact, all children, are active learners who pose questions, make hypotheses, and draw conclusions based on their own analyses.

Traditional classroom settings may reinforce not only submissiveness in many cultures, but dependence as well. If you believe that children in Approach 2 know and will remember more about sheep than children in Approach 1, this suggests that a reasonable goal would be to set up your classroom in ways that encourage questioning, experimentation, and collaboration (with or without live sheep).

Where Do You Go From Here?

Reframing teaching in the ways we describe above is challenging and suggests several questions for teachers and other educational leaders. To help you on your journey towards making your diverse classrooms more student-centered, consider the following:

• Should students learn about cultural diversity even if they live in regions of the country that are fairly homogenous? If so, given the lack of diversity, what would be the context for learning?

• Should the make-up of your classroom, school, or district have some bearing on curriculum requirements?

• Given the projected increases in the number of Spanish-speaking students, should learning Spanish be required of all new teachers? Why? Why not?

References

Ausubel, D.P. (1968). *Educational psychology: A cognitive view.* New York: Holt, Rhinehart & Winston.

Barry, N.H. & Lechner, J.V. (1995). Preservice teachers' attitudes about and awareness of multicultural teaching and learning. *Teaching and Teacher* Education, 11(2), 149–161.

Collier, J.J., Laatsch, M., Ferrero, P. (1972). Film analysis of the Rough Rock Community school–phase one. (Manuscript on file at Rough Rock, Chinle, AZ)

Hodgkinson, H.L. (1992). *A demographic look at tomorrow.* Washington, DC: Institute for Educational Leadership Center for Demographic Policy.

Hodgkinson, H.L. (1993) American education: The good, the bad, and the task. *Phi Delta Kappan,* 84(8), 619–623.

Kugelmass, J.W. (1995). Educating children with learning disabilities in Foxfire classrooms. *Journal of Learning Disabilities,* 28(9), 545–553.

McCarty, T.L., Lynch, R.H., Wallace, S. & Benally, A. (1991) Classroom inquiry and Navajo learning styles: A call for reassessment. *Anthropology and Education Quarterly,* 22(1), 42–59.

Sileo, T.W., Sileo, S.P. & Prater, M.A. (1996, January). Parent and professional partnerships in special education: Multicultural considerations. *Intervention in School and Clinic,* 145–153.

Steinberg, L. (1996). *Beyond the classroom: Why school reform has failed and what parents need to do.* New York: Simon & Schuster.

Noteworthy Books

ABOUT LATINOS FOR
CHILDREN AND ADOLESCENTS

ISABEL SCHON

From the heartfelt bonds between a little Latina girl and her two grandmothers, to the poignant life of Latino youth in California's Central Valley, to a tender love story amid the sinking of the *U.S.S. Maine,* these recently published books provide engrossing insights into the dreams, trials, and aspirations of Latino people both in the United States and abroad.

Alvarez, Julia. *Something to Declare.* Chapel Hill, N.C.: Algonquin, 1998. 312 pp. ISBN 1–56512–193–7, $19.95. Gr. 9–adult.

With wit and her unmistakable candor, Alvarez relates in these 24 personal essays her childhood in her native Dominican Republic, where grandfather's blessings really made a difference, girls' only aspirations were to be good wives and mothers, and Dominicans learned the habits of repression, censorship, and terror under Trujillo's 31-year dictatorship. She also tells about her experiences with the English language as an adolescent in New York, and her adult life as a writer with an American husband in Vermont. Divided into two parts—"Customs" and "Declarations"—Alvarez's memoir will inspire and entertain adolescents as they appreciate her charisma and dedication to her art.

Chambers, Veronica. *Marisol and Magdalena: The Sound of Our Sisterhood.* New York: Hyperion, 1998. 191 pp. ISBN 0–7868–2385–2, $20.49. Gr. 6–9.

Maraisol lives in Brooklyn with her mother, who grew up in Panama, and can't imagine life without her best friend Magda. Despite both girls' problems with the Spanish language, they enjoy Panamanian food, dances, and other family traditions. Suddenly, Marisol finds out that she will be spending one year in Panama with Abuela, her grandmother, whom she has never met. In a lively first-person narrative, this novel recounts Marisol's experiences in her family's homeland as well as her search for her own father, a man who is vilified by both her mother and grandmother. This is indeed a joyous, if somewhat rose-colored, portrayal of a girl as she confronts the best of her black American and Panamanian cultural roots.

Ewing, Lynne. *Party Girl.* New York: Knopf, 1998. 110 pp. ISBN 0–679–89285–0, $16.00. Gr. 6–9.

Set in Los Angeles, where gang members fight over crumbling cement and potholed streets in a neighborhood divided by "hatred stronger than barbed-wire fences," this poignant view of gang life is an eloquent plea for a different lifestyle. As 15-year-old Kata mourns the death of her best friend, Ana, who had come from Mexico, she is engulfed by her own fears and determined to seek revenge. Amid pregnant teenagers, alcoholic mothers, and vicious boyfriends, this realistic novel will ring true to many adolescents in and out of gangs. The sprinkling of Spanish words and phrases adds a decidedly Latino ambience to this cautionary tale.

Jermyn, Leslie. *Peru.* Milwaukee, Wis.: Gareth Stevens, 1998. 32 pp. Series: Festivals of the World. ISBN 0–8368–2006–1, $18.60. Gr. 3–5.

The color, excitement, and traditions of festivals in Peru are described through a simple text and colorful photographs on every page. Like other titles in this series, this is not an in-depth discussion of "fiestas" in Peru; rather, it is a vivid introduction for the young to numerous celebrations in Peru such as *Inti Raymi* (the Inca festival of the sun), Corpus Christi, Puno Day, and others. The book includes a glossary and various craft activities, such as a sun god mask and *natilla* recipe.

King, Elizabeth. *Quinceañera: Celebrating Fifteen.* New York: Dutton, 1998. 40 pp. ISBN 0–525–45638–4, $15.99. Gr. 6–9.

The lovely Latino/Mexican rite of passage in which a *quinceañera,* a 15-year-old girl, is celebrated with a church ceremony and a big party is touchingly depicted through spectacular candid color photographs that show the elaborate preparations and wonderful *fiesta.* In an easy-flowing narrative with numerous Spanish words sprinkled throughout, the author provides a bit of the history and significance of the event and highlights the differences in celebrations in various Central American, Cuban, and Mexican families. The book is indeed a warm introduction to this joyous coming-of-age celebration with an unfortunate caveat that mars this otherwise wonderful scrapbook: The word *Quinceañera* is supposed to be used for the girl it honors, not for the celebration itself. Other Spanish-language linguistic aberrations will also irritate Spanish-speaking readers.

Leonard, Elmore. *Cuba Libre.* New York: Bantam, 1998. 343 pp. ISBN 0–385–32383–2, $23.95. Gr. 9–adult.

Set in Cuba during the period just before the Spanish-American War, when Cubans were struggling for independence, this easy-to-read, fastpaced novel intermingles adventure with a tender love story amid the sinking of the *U.S.S. Maine.* American interests in Cuba, the infamous prison in el Morro Castle, villainous General Weyler, and the contemptible Guardia Civil officers all appear in the novel. This is not a serious historical narrative but rather an action-packed love story with kind, courageous, and handsome protagonists who overcome nefarious characters in their search for each other. They also get to keep a bundle of the evil man's cash as the hero gets used to living in Cuba with his beloved Amelia, a New Orleans-born beauty. This is just right for reluctant readers of history—Cuban or otherwise.

Patent, Dorothy Hinshaw. *Quetzal: Sacred Bird of the Cloud Forest.* New York: Morrow, 1996. 40 pp. Illus. by Neil Waldman. ISBN 0–688–12662–6, $16.00. Gr. 5–8.

Patent combines the story of the beautiful quetzal, a unique bird with impressive tail feathers and brilliant iridescence, with the history of the Maya and other cultures of Mesoamerica. She explores ancient beliefs about the god Quetzalcoatl and the quetzal's life cycle, daily existence, and dangers for survival in a narrative brimming with natural and pre-Columbian history. The softly shaded colored-pencil drawings blend well with the tone and spirit of this tribute to the quetzal. It is unfortunate that a photograph of the beautiful quetzal is not included. Nonetheless, this appealing blend of nature, history, and lore will strike a chord with naturalists-to-be as well as historians-to-be.

Reinhard, Johan. *Discovering the Inca Ice Maiden: My Adventures on Ampato.* Washington, D.C.: National Georgraphic Society, 1998. 48 pp. ISBN 0–7922–7142–4, $17.95. Gr. 6–12.

In an engrossing first-person account, Reinhard, an anthropologist, narrates his 1995 discovery of the approximately 500-year-old Peruvian ice mummy on Mount Ampato and the subsequent retrieval and study of the girl who became known as the Inca "Ice Maiden." Stunning full-page color photographs of the Peruvian Andes and Inca archaeological sites add interest to this incredible discovery. A timeline, a glossary, and an index further complement this narrative, which provides interesting background information on the Inca empire as well as Inca customs and beliefs.

Soto, Gary. *Petty Crimes.* San Diego, Calif.: Harcourt Brace, 1998. 157 pp. ISBN 0–15–201658–9, $16.00. Gr. 5–7.

In a poignant manner, Soto describes the often-tragic lives of Latino youth as they engage in or are the victims of various petty crimes in California's Central Valley. Fourteen-year-old Priscilla takes what she wants whenever she wants it; 14-year-old Alma tries desperately to buy back her dead mother's clothes. While 13-year-old Mario is still an infant in the art of scramming, José, a born worker, finally comes to realize that there are many liars like his cousin Arnie. This collection of 10 stories will ring true to many adolescents. In his wonderful style, Soto condenses the pathos of life amid the trials of adolescence.

Tanka, Shelly. *Lost Temple of the Aztecs.* New York: Hyperion, 1998. 48 pp. Illus. by Greg Ruhl. Series: I Was There. ISBN 0–7868–0441–6, $16.95. Gr. 4–7.

The best parts of this book are the wonderful color photographs and numerous informative sidebars that describe the discovery of the Great Aztec Temple in Mexico City, the last few years of Moctezuma's empire, and the Spanish conquest, from 1519 to 1521. Unfortunately, the author's narrative sensationalizes the events and even Moctezuma's thoughts to such an extreme that the compelling story of the conquest of Mexico suffers by this unnecessary dramatization. Despite the regrettable narrative, the color photographs, illustrations, and appealing design make this an enticing introduction to the Aztecs and the Spanish conquest of Mexico.

Torres, Leyla. *Liliana's Grandmothers.* New York: Farrat, Straus & Giroux, 1998. 32 pp. Illus. By the author. ISBN 0–374–35105–8, $16.00. Ages 4–7.

In a sweet and simple tone, the reader is introduced to Liliana's grandmothers: Mima, who lives down the street in the United States, and Mama Gabina, who lives in South America and speaks only Spanish. Despite superficial differences between the two grandmothers, children will identify with the warm feelings elicited by both grandmothers as they do yoga exercises, feed the birds, eat a peanut butter and jelly sandwich, or prepare a big Latin American lunch. Torres's pastel double-page spreads affectionately convey the heartfelt bonds between Liliana and her two loving grandmothers, whether close or far away. This title is also available in Spanish.

Willard, Nancy. *The Tortilla Cat.* San Diego, Calif.: Harcourt Brace, 1998. 48 pp. Illus. by Jeanette Winter. ISBN 0–15–289587–6, $15.00. Gr. 3–5.

Doctor Romero, who can cure anything, loves his five children but refuses to consider any pets in the home except goldfish. When a bad fever kills his wife, he does his best to be both father and mother. As the children get sick with the deadly fever one by one, they are saved by a little gray cat carrying a tray with a single tortilla. Rational Doctor Romero refuses to believe in the magic cat until he too gets sick. Winter's framed acrylic illustrations perfectly complement the text's magical realism, in which members of this loving Latino family experience serious sickness and confront death. The ever-present afflictions and loss of a family member may bother some children (and their parents); others will enjoy the magical cat's tortillas that defeat even Papa's logic.

Isabel Schon is Director of the Center for the Study of Books in Spanish for Children and Adolescents at California State University, San Marcos.

Class Web Sites Can Offer Enhanced Access to

Information for Language Minority Parents and Students

By Joseph Slowinski

With the aid of information technology, classroom teachers can take steps to promote improved information access for minority language families. Several on-line resources can be added to a class Web site to enhance the language diversity offered.

In an effort to facilitate the development of multicultural class Web pages, I offer a few suggestions on how to add the power of a free on-line translator, links, and multilingual search engines to a teacher's classroom home page.

Alta Vista Babelfish
On-line Translation Tool

Alta Vista Babelfish, available at http://babelfish.altavista.com, is a free on-line translation service that provides translations of Web pages or inputted text. For educators with minority language students and parents, Babelfish can be utilized to locate Web pages on a variety of topics written in German, Spanish, Italian, French, or Portuguese.

To maximize the potential of Babelfish, educators can add a button that will send the URL to Babelfish directly when clicked. The page can then be translated. When using Alta Vista Babelfish on Web pages it is best to keep pages to maximum of four paragraphs of text. This will allow each page to be completely translated rather than partially.

To add Babelfish to a page, insert the following HTML code in the document:

```
<form action="http://babelfish.altavista.com/
    cgi-bin/translate?" method ="post">
<input type="hidden" name="doit"
    value="done">
<input type="hidden" name="urltext" value=
    "http://www.YOUR_PAGE_URL.html">
<input type="hidden" name="languagepair"
    value="en_fr">
<input type="Submit" value="What is typed
```

here will appear on button">
```
</form>
```

Remember to place the page's URL that you want to translate in the appropriate location in this code.

With translation capability on a teacher's Web site, all school and class information is offered to the language minority parents. This step will offer proof that an educator is interested in all children's academic success in the classroom and that s/he is interested in promoting communication with all parents. Consequently, this translation tool can be a catalyst for improved community relations.

One word of caution needs to be offered. Since Babelfish provides translation from a software package, the potential for some words to not translate properly is possible. Yet, this warning offers the classroom teacher or school principal the opportunity to go out into the language

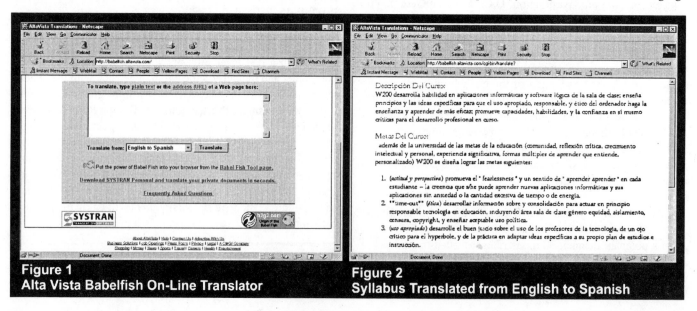

Figure 1
Alta Vista Babelfish On-Line Translator

Figure 2
Syllabus Translated from English to Spanish

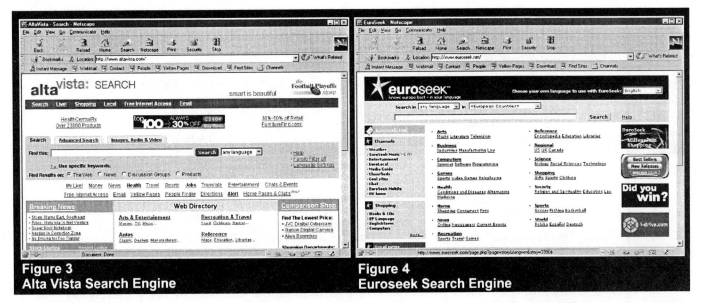

Figure 3
Alta Vista Search Engine

Figure 4
Euroseek Search Engine

minority community to ask for assistance in the translation project. This would only further develop rapport with the community. In addition, schools can provide print-outs of these on-line materials for those families that don't have access to the Internet at home.

Multilingual Search Engines

Some search engines offer the ability to search in more than twenty languages. For example, a classroom teacher can add a direct link from a Web site to these search engines in order to inform parents that these exist and can be used to access mother tongue documents. I suggest the use of two such search engines.

One example, Alta Vista Digital (http://www.altavista.com), can search for Websites in the following languages: Cesky, Chinese, Dansk, Deutsch, English, Eesti, Francais, Español, Greek, Hebrew, Islenska, Italiano, Japanese, Korean, Latviski, Lietuviskai, Magyar, Nederlands, Norsk, Português, Polski, Româna, Russkij, Svenska, and Suomi.

In addition to Alta Vista Digital, Euroseek (http://www.euroseek.net) can conduct searches in over 25 languages. Euroseek can search in the following languages: Brezhoneg, Balgarski, Català, Cesky, Cymraeg, Dansk, Deutsch, Eesti, Ellinika, English, Esperanto, Español, Euskara, Vlaams, Francais, Frysk, Galego, Gàidhlig, Hrvatski, Islenska, Ivrit, Italiano, Latviski, Lietuviskai, Magyar, Macedonski, Malti, Nederlands, Norsk, Português, Polski, Româna, Russkij, Slovencina, Slovenscina, Shqip, Srpski, Svenska, Suomi, and Türkçe.

With access from a class or school Web site to these search engines, the world of information is available to minority language families. In addition, teachers can find Web sites published in the mother tongue that could aid the child with assistance on homework and other projects. These pages can become links from the class page in order to provide additional academic support for all children in the classroom.

Conclusion

Classroom teachers and schools have an obligation to provide access to classroom and school information for minority languages students. Information technology can offer enhanced access to this information through a creative teacher, on-line free translation services, as well as links to resources in the mother tongue. Access to the Internet remains an issue for American families. Yet, teachers can provide printed copies of Web pages and resources for those families without Internet access. As we approach the new millennium, educators can better serve the needs of limited English families through the adoption of multilingual resources and the broadening of class Web pages.

—Joseph Slowinski is an associate instructor in the School of Education at Indiana University, Bloomington.

How To Locate Multilingual Web Resources

How to Find Educational Web Sites Published in a Variety of Languages

1. Visit the Babelfish Web page and type the English word or phrase in the Babelfish window.

2. Choose translate from English to one of five languages. Click the translate button.

3. When the term or phrase is returned highlight and copy. Go to Alta Vista (http://www.altavista.com) or Euroseek (http://www.euroseek.net), paste the term in the search window and choose search in the appropriate.

4. If using Alta Vista search, all links are translatable by simply clicking translate.

5. If using Euroseek, you should first open up a new browser window as to work with two Web sites simultaneously. After the search returns links, you must copy the search URL and paste this into Babelfish. Choose translate from English to language of choice. Once search is translated all links will automatically load into Babelfish for translation.

Unit 6

Key Points to Consider

❖ How can educators develop a better sense of cross-cultural conflicts and values?

❖ What can be learned about teacher education from children's educational experience in other countries?

❖ What are some effective ways to overcome the obstacles in a parent-teacher relationship?

❖ What are some of the dynamics of the language revitalization programs currently taking place in various parts of the country?

❖ How can educators better meet the needs of multiracial and multiethnic children?

 **Links**   **www.dushkin.com/online/**

These sites are annotated on pages 4 and 5.

Each year we try to focus in this section of this volume on selected special topics that have been of particular interest to those who live or work in multicultural settings. Topics are also chosen if they have a direct bearing on issues of equality of educational opportunity.

There is change in the journal literature as well as some thematic continuity from year to year. The articles in this unit this year reflect a broad variety of topics that we believe readers will find informative and interesting. The first article reflects on and describes the career of a heroic child therapist during the Holocaust, Friedl Dicker-Brandeis, who was a prisoner at the Terezin concentration camp during the Holocaust. The article also notes the work of other scholars who have researched the lives of victimized children during the Holocaust.

It is important and a poignant concern to witness how parents and others attempt to help children cope with adversity. There is great relevance in this for the field of multicultural education in American and other nations. The role of teachers and therapists in helping parents and other significant others in the lives of children challenged by adverse circumstances should always be a concern of all educators.

Other themes that run through this unit this year deal with the roles of parents and teachers as they attempt to understand each other's concerns and perceptions of what is happening in the education of students. Cultural bridges can be crossed successfully by positive parent-teacher conferences. Overcoming the obstacles to constructive parent-teacher relations is a very important concern for all educators. Examples of the need to understand the values of students' cultures are explored in the articles in this unit—a theme that runs in many ways and many directions through the essays. Examples of collaborative efforts of parents and teachers working together in the best interests of the children are to be found in the articles in this unit this year.

Perspectives on the expanding roles of teachers to enhance students' racial and ethnic identities are of great relevance to all educators, but especially to teachers of children from cultures other than their own. Native American, Hispanic, and African American perceptions of what the roles of teachers should be are explored here. International perspectives on how teachers can assist their students in expanded ways are explored also. A case study is included on how teachers attempt to assist the lives of students beyond simply classroom instruction in Baroda, India. Other articles in this unit touch on this theme.

A concern for how cultural groups give testimony and voice to their visions of the world is also reflected in these essays. The theme of how people use language to express their cultural heritage also runs through these essays. The relationships and differences between cultural groups is expressed. How to help people whose linguistic voices have been ignored in schools is a very serious concern to multicultural educators. The importance of the role of language in the shaping of personal identity as well as in learning one's culture is of great concern to those who feel that their voices and values have been denied or ignored in mainstream schools. Sociological, anthropological, and psychological research on how alienated cultures might restore cultural groups' respective knowledge of their heritage is an important contribution to the field of multicultural education as well as to efforts to raise levels of cultural understanding and acceptance in society as a whole.

How cultural groups show resistance to efforts to deny their voices as well as their cultural heritages will always be a concern of multicultural educators. There are several important issues raised in this context, one of which is how we stereotype or deny the existence of the great many varieties of groups within particular cultures. Of particular relevance to this is how we fail to meet the needs of multiracial and multiethnic children and adolescents in the schools. We cannot simply stereotype with one identity the children in schools into African American, Hispanic, Asian, Native America, "white," or "other."

We must recognize that cultures come together, they meet and merge, and out of these cultural unions come multiracial and multiethnic populations who do not fit neatly into one of the above categories. The numbers of interracial and interethnic marriages are on the increase, and a trend toward this has been developing for several decades. This is not a new development, but it is one the federal government has not yet adequately addressed, nor have most school systems. The unique needs of multiracial and multiethnic students must be addressed more effectively in teacher education as well as at all levels of schooling. We are becoming more and more a multiracial and multiethnic society.

So, as the reader may discern, a broad spectrum of issues is addressed in the essays in this unit. We hope that they will be perceived as useful in strengthening our understanding of multicultural education.

The essays in this unit are relevant to courses in educational policy studies, multicultural education, and cultural foundations of education.

Special Topics in Multicultural Education

PRACTICAL PROFESSIONAL PRACTICE

Children and Play in the Holocaust: Friedl Dicker-Brandeis— Heroic Child Therapist

Hilda R. Glazer

Although Terezin was the model concentration camp of the Germans, the environment was extremely repressive; the world of children deported there was shattered. Fifteen thousand children passed through the gates; 100 survived. Despite the conditions, play and art were still part of the lives of children at Terezin. This article explores play and art and Friedl Dicker-Brandeis's vital role in these activities in the camp.

Even during World War II in the repressive environment of the Terezin concentration camp, children were encouraged to process their experiences through play and art. Much of the evidence that supports this thesis has been recorded by those who existed in Terezin (*Theresienstadt* in German). In particular, evidence exists that Friedl Dicker-Brandeis, recognizing the therapeutic value of play, worked to provide opportunities for art and organized play for children at Terezin. The world of the children deported to Terezin was shattered and lacked balance and stability; at Terezin, time and space were distorted and fear was an ever present emotion (Makarova, 1990). The world of the children of Terezin was changed. In this environment, interaction with adults in play and art became a significant feature. This article reviews research on play during the Holocaust and interprets the value of play activities to the survival of the person and the humanness of the individual.

Ghetto Theresienstadt was established in November 1941 by the first head of Reich Security, Reinhold Heydrich (Troller, 1991). This camp was unique in that the Germans insisted that it was really a country club, an old folk's home, and a vacation spot for favored Jews (Green, 1969). According to the United States Holocaust Memorial Museum (1995), of the more than 15,000 children interned at Terezin, only 100 survived the Nazi regime.

Hilda R. Glazer is the acting chair of the Division of Psychology at Walden University in Minneapolis, Minnesota. Correspondence regarding this article should be sent to Hilda R. Glazer, Walden University, 155 Fifth Avenue South, Minneapolis, MN 55401 (e-mail: hglazer@waldenu.edu).

PLAY IN THE LIVES OF THE CHILDREN OF THE HOLOCAUST

To examine the world of the child during the Holocaust from a perspective of trauma provides a framework for this discussion. *The Diagnostic and Statistical Manual of Mental Disorders*, fourth edition (*DSM-IV*; American Psychiatric Association, 1994) characterized post-traumatic stress disorder as a reaction to experiencing, witnessing, or confronting events that involve actual or threatened death, serious injury, or threat to the physical integrity of self or others. Play therapy has been shown to provide the traumatized child with the opportunity to restructure traumatic events to provide them with meaning, to gain control over such events, and to gain a sense of control or psychological safety (Frick-Helms, 1997).

Play represents children's attempts to organize their experiences and their world (Landreth, 1991). Children are much more likely to be comfortable using toys and play, as opposed to language, to express themselves and to show how they feel about people and events (Kottman, 1995). According to Landreth, the process of play can provide the opportunity for the child to experience control even though the reality of his or her circumstances may dictate otherwise. Play involves the child's physical, emotional, and mental self in creative expression (Landreth). Children use metaphorical devices to separate play from reality until the reality is bearable (Frick-Helms, 1997). Moustakas (1959) noted that in the case of the disturbed child, it is his or her way of reacting to the situation and to the therapist that enables him or her to work through attitudes and to reorganize them. The result is that through play children gain a better understanding of himself or herself as a person and a better understanding of the reality of the world. The Holocaust and internment in camps obviously had an impact on children's emotional and relational connection to their parents because children want and need a haven of safety and love provided by their parents. The value of play to the children of the Holocaust is seen in the descriptions of play and the uses of play by children during this time. The understanding of the therapeutic value of play can be seen in the actions of adults to provide children with the opportunity for play and for expression through art and toys.

CHILDREN'S PLAY IN THE HOLOCAUST

The lives of the children were harsh; as noted, of the 15,000 who passed through Terezin only 100 survived. The United States Holocaust Memorial Museum Calendar (1995) stated: "But before they died, they lived as children do: simply, fully and even at times, joyfully. In the harsh conditions of Theresienstadt, the children played" (p. 2). According to Green (1969), "In their hopeful minds they saw butterflies, and flowers, and the joyful life they had left behind; and they painted these and wrote about them" (p. 138). Eisen (1988) noted that, knowing that exercise and play were important during normal times, the prisoner-administrators and prisoner-educators in the ghettoes and the camps quickly began to use play as a re-creative and therapeutic intervention technique during times of exceptional mental and physical duress:

> Children's play constituted a part of this quest for survival. Civic leaders as well as educators hoped that play would surround the children with a protective cloak—a spiritual shelter from which the wounds of the ghetto would not seem as horrifying. (p. 42)

The Jewish prisoners responsible for the care of the children knew the value of play. There seemed to be value in children's play not only for the child but also for the adult who watched the children at play. Adults saw that children's play had the power not only to ease but to promote mental adaptation of the adult population to the novel demands of the ghetto existence. Providing opportunities for play was part of a conscious escape mechanism through which the adult population of the camps attempted to transcend in spirit both the physical walls and the walls of terror (Eisen, 1988).

In Terezin, the adults organized play and games, and the children recognized and appreciated these efforts (Eisen, 1988). At the same time, there were efforts by children themselves to create a "play world"; after the war, there was evidence of this in every hide-out, ghetto, and camp. This play world was fostered also, to a large measure, by the absence of parents who would have provided children with a stable environment under normal conditions. Eisen cited an example of this creativity in the description of a young girl who, hiding in Italy, created a fantastic play world with the help of scissors and a cardboard box.

Surviving camp children later noted that during the period when their caretakers were disappearing from their lives, their own psychic lives turned more inward or toward their favorite toys (Eisen, 1988). The toys of children took on special significance. Green (1969) described a psychological transference process that took place in which the children perceived that they were receiving love from an inanimate object instead of a loved one. Eisen felt that they were sharing their emotions with the worn-out dolls and that the broken toys were good listeners. This was, perhaps, the attempt of the children to use their play to move them beyond the walls of Terezin or to recreate in their play the unconditional love of those no longer in their lives.

The play of children in the camps were described by Eisen (1988) as reflecting the children's unique cognitive development levels and the confined context in which they were reached. Hungry, battered, and terrorized, the children retained their humanness and their respect for life; their actions reaffirmed the primacy of existence by attempting to find equilibrium in an irrational world. Eisen further suggested that the children may have also used play as a form of protest or deliberate opposition, which may have meant that the children achieved a heroism that transcended the ordinary definition and understanding of the term for their actions signified the ultimate spiritual resistance.

Describing the play of children in the camps, Eisen (1988) stated that the powers of adaptation and survival were closely connected with the children's ability to enact atrocities and thus facilitate a process of accommodation to the almost unbearable reality. It seemed evident that children's behavior in play articulated skills necessary for survival. For example, girls in the Lodz ghetto enacted the hardships of their mothers as they tried to secure food.

Eisen (1988) hypothesized that the functional significance of fantasy play was not that it offered an opportunity to avoid coping with reality but that it assisted in "reality assimilation"—information processing. Eisen stated that a survivor of Terezin rationalized, in retrospect, that playing was more than passing time; it helped her and many other children in the camp to clarify, rationalize, and accommodate reality; "it interchanged fantasy and

reality so that we could at least try to survive" (p. 115).

CHILDREN'S ART IN THE HOLOCAUST

Children's art in the camps was done in secret and then hidden; it has become part of the "clandestine art" of the Holocaust (Costanza, 1982). Costanza noted that there was something bizarre in many of the art works of such children such as the presence of discomforting elements; unnatural and oversized forms replaced the child, who is usually the largest shape in children's drawings; death images appeared in many of the works; and, in one case, an entire page was smudged by a sooty gray. In these drawings, faces rarely smile, and oversized tears flow from little eyes to make an inadvertent pattern over the entire page. Black strokes from odd-sized chimneys dissect these blue and green childscapes.

After the way, two suitcases filled with paintings, poems, and drawings were found at Terezin and at other camps; these artifacts are now housed in several Holocaust museums and have been copied and printed in various publications. Many of these surviving pictures from Terezin are scenes of frolic in playgrounds despite the fact that no real playgrounds existed in the camp. To engage in the kind of play shown in the drawings, the children's imaginations had to transcend the barbed wire fences. These pictures are arresting in the wish they express to carry the unfortunate children back to a happier time and place. Eisen (1988) held that it was as if the children could not reflect on the immediate present but only a fantasy world where anything could happen.

FRIEDL DICKER-BRANDEIS: CHILD THERAPIST IN TEREZIN

It is difficult to identify many of the individuals who worked with children in the ghettoes and the camps. Of those who are known to have worked with children in art and play, the activities and efforts of Friedl Dicker-Brandeis (also known as Friedl Brandeis) stand out. She was an artist, an intellectual, and a political activist before the war. When the pattern of Nazi anti-Semitism began to emerge, Dicker-Brandeis obtained a visa to Palestine, but did not use it. Reasons for this can only be hypothesized; she may not have wanted to leave loved ones behind or she may have believed that her decision would not end in death. In December 1942, she and her husband were rounded up and sent by transport to Terezin, where she remained for 2 years before being transferred to Auschwitz, her final destination (Hurwitz, 1991).

Dicker-Brandeis saw the principal aim of teaching to be the liberation of concealed sources of children's creativity, the development of their fantasies and imaginations, and the possibility of authentic self-expression as well as enhancement of independent judgment and observation, which, in their sum, contribute to the consolidation of self-confidence and independence. She believed that children should be given an opportunity for self-expression in their play and in their art. Makarova (1990) viewed her as an art therapist who used art to confront the disorders in children's psyches and developed art therapy protocols for her children. She believed that for children under the age of 10, drawing and painting are the primary expressions of self-determination (Brandeis, n.d.). Her awareness of the developmental needs of children influenced the techniques that she used as did her realization that one cannot dictate the ideas of the child (Brandeis). Makarova stated that Dicker-Brandeis believed her goal to be the restoration of the shaken consciousness of the children of Terezin. Dicker-Brandeis was also aware of the therapeutic use of children's creative expression for psychic relaxation and objectification of conflicting experience, notions, and psychic states, and, therefore, analyzed the children's drawings and evaluated the children from this viewpoint. Her premise was that art should open children up or preserve their self-determination as a source of energy, and stimulate their fantasies and enforce their judgment and observation. Dicker-Brandeis believed that the child should freely express what he or she wants to say about himself or herself and that it is through free expression and spontaneous play that an art therapist can obtain invaluable insight into the child's experience.

Dicker-Brandeis believed that the internal and external events of a child's life are a source of imagery; she identified the child's stage of development and encouraged group activities because of their positive socializing effect on children and their continuing development. She believed in the ability of children to find their own way and to discover ways

to express those impulses that reflect their uniqueness as individuals (Hurwitz, 1991). To help children to do this, she used a variety of play and art therapy techniques. For example, using storytelling, Dicker-Brandeis asked children to select an object from the story that had been mentioned twice and to draw it (Makarova, 1990). Another technique was to provide children with a list of objects that they were to use in their drawings to compose a story. These techniques build on the child's natural inclination to communicate through story and metaphor (Muro & Kottman, 1995). Additionally, Kottman (1995) noted that the child's metaphor can be used to gain insight into and to process thoughts, feelings, and attitudes.

Spontaneous drawing lessons were an important vehicle for Dicker-Brandeis. Makarova (1990) reported that spontaneous drawing helped Dicker-Brandeis enter the child's inner world and to perceive the emotions and motivation of the child. An example of disclosure through spontaneous drawings was seen in the case of a 9-year-old girl who was able to express her feelings about the involuntary sex she had seen (Makarova, 1990). This use of art technique parallels the use of art techniques in Adlerian play therapy to help the child gain insight into her or his lifestyle (Kottman, 1995). Dicker-Brandeis also used mutual projects in her work with the children at Terezin such as making dolls and using them as puppets in a play. Another technique was that of collective creative work, in which groups of children produced a work or completed a task; Makarova believed that the objective was a lesson in exactness and tolerance.

Some of the basic principles of the therapeutic relationship were seen in the approach of Dicker-Brandeis to her work with children. The critical importance of the establishment of a trusting relationship was noted by Makarova (1990) as one of the important elements of Dicker-Brandeis's work. Her compassion and tender attitude, and the love that the children had for her are also considered important therapeutic factors in her work.

CONCLUSION

The value of play and art in the lives of children, particularly in a world of fear and death, is validated by the experience of the children of Terezin. The value of the relationship, as exemplified by Friedl Dicker-Brandeis, is also validated. It is the relationship that is the critical element of play, survival, and healing. It was said of Dicker-Brandeis that her work in the camp was the culmination of her lifelong endeavor in that it was there that she helped hundreds of children to find genuine human wealth in the inhuman condition of their existence in a concentration camp (The State Jewish Museum in Prague, 1988).

REFERENCES

American Psychiatric Association. (1994). *Desk reference to the diagnostic criteria from DSM-IV.* Washington, DC: Author

Brandeis, F. (n.d.). *Kinderzeichenen.* Jerusalem, Israel: The Central Archives for the Disaster and the Heroism, Yad-Washem.

Costanza, M. S. (1982). *The living witness: Art in the concentration camps and ghettos.* New York: The Free Press.

Eisen, G. (1988). *Children and play in the holocaust: Games among the shadows.* Amherst, MA: The University of Massachusetts Press.

Frick-Helms, S. (1997). "Boys cry better than girls": Play therapy behaviors of children residing in a shelter for battered women. *International Journal of Play Therapy, 6,* 73–91.

Green, G. (1969). *The artists of Terezin.* New York: Hawthorn Books.

Hurwitz, A. (1991). Friedl Dicker-Brandeis: The art educator as hero. In Massachusetts College of Art (Ed.), *Seeing through "paradise": Artists and the Terezin concentration camp* (pp. 71–81). Boston: Massachusetts College of Art.

Kottman, T. (1995). *Partners in play: An Adlerian approach to play therapy.* Alexandria, VA: American Counseling Association.

Landreth, G. L. (1991). *Play therapy: The art of the relationship.* Muncie, IN: Accelerated Development Press.

Makarova, E. (1990). *From Bauhaus to Terezin: Friedl Dicker-Brandeis and her pupils.* Jerusalem, Israel: Holocaust Martyrs' and Heroes' Remembrance Authority, The Art Museum.

Moustakas, C. E. (1959). *Psychotherapy with children: The living relationship.* Greeley, CO: Carron.

Muro, J. J., & Kottman, T. (1995). *Guidance and counseling in the elementary and middle schools: A practical approach.* Madison, WI: WCB, Brown, and Benchmark.

The State Jewish Museum in Prague (1988). *Friedl Dicker Brandeis: 1898–1944 exhibition to commemorate the 90th anniversary of her birthday.* Prague: Author.

Troller, N. (1991). *Theresienstadt: Hitler's gift to the Jews.* Chapel Hill, NC: University of North Carolina Press.

United States Holocaust Memorial Museum (1995). *1996 Calendar.* Washington, DC: Author.

Bridging Cultures with a Parent-Teacher Conference

When teachers acknowledge and adapt to different cultural values, they can work collaboratively to strengthen the learning environment of the whole community.

Blanca Quiroz, Patricia M. Greenfield, and Marie Altchech

A Latina immigrant mother remembers a parent-teacher conference with her daughter's 1st grade teacher:

> I couldn't understand what the teacher was trying to communicate when she commented on my daughter's performance. I particularly recall two confusing comments that this teacher made: "Your daughter is very sociable" and "Your daughter is outstanding in. . . ." My tendency as a Mexican mother was to feel very happy she was sociable; after all, that was what I was fostering. However, I did not know what to do about her being "outstanding"; I had tried to show my daughter not to "show off," but it seemed that it was not working.

Parent-teacher conferences are a prime situation for cross-cultural miscommunication.

Parent-teacher conferences are a prime occasion for cross-cultural communication. The issue of being "outstanding" is fraught with cross-cultural misunderstanding between teachers and Latino immigrant parents. The opening vignette illustrates two cultural models at play (Raeff, Greenfield, & Quiroz, in press).

Cross-Cultural Conflicts About Values

The teacher expressed an individualistic perspective: She assumed that the primary goal of development is to become an outstandingly competent individual. The mother interpreted "outstanding" as "standing out," something to be avoided in her culture. She was expressing an important element of the collectivistic model, which exphasizes fitting into and being a contributing member of a group.

Each cultural model consists of a set of assumptions that the group takes for granted and therefore does not recognize as cultural in origin. Each model also defines a set of criteria for evaluating child development and for guiding socialization; these models sometimes conflict when Latino immigrants enroll their children in public schools in the United States. For example, *educación*, the Spanish cognate for *education*, primarily refers to instruction in correct social demeanor, in contrast, the English equivalent, *education*, refers primarily to academic instruction (Reese, Balzano, Gallimore, & Goldenberg, 1995).

Culture lies in values and practices, not in ethnic labels.

This conflict does not occur with every Latino parent. It is as presumptuous to assume that all Latinos hold the same developmental and socialization goals as it is to assume that everyone should hold the developmental goals of mainstream U.S. education. Latinos are very diverse, differing in social class and education before immigration, rural or urban origin, country of origin, acculturation, and race. Therefore, teachers need to *explore* cultural values systems, not *assume* them. Nonetheless, the sociohistorical, socioeconomic, and sociocultural conditions experienced by large numbers of recent immigrants from Mexico and Central America provide a basis for a common pattern of adaptation and collectivistic cultural values (for example, Raeff, Greenfield, & Quiroz, in press; Valdés, 1996.)

From *Educational Leadership,* April 1999, pp. 68-70. © 1999 by the Association for Supervision and Curriculum Development (ASCD). All rights reserved. Reprinted by permission.

Likewise, teachers' behavior is not specific to a particular ethnic group. Latino teachers, like others, undergo an individualizing process that is part of higher education and teacher training (Delgado-Gaitan, 1994; Greenfield, Raeff, & Quiroz, 1996; Raeff, Greenfield, & Quiroz, in press; Rothstein-Fisch, Trumbull, Quiroz, & Greenfield, 1997). Culture lies in values and practices, not in ethnic labels.

Latino immigrant families are very interested in their children's education (Delgado-Gaitan, 1994; Goldenberg & Gallimore, 1995). However, parents from Mexico and El Salvador who ar-

dividualistic groups has been heightened.... Now not only do I realize that there are differences, but also I greatly appreciate the concept that a bridge must be constructed so that I do not value one over the other.

However, this leads to a conflict. What should be the ultimate goal of a teacher? Should it be to facilitate the academic success of my students? Or should it be to facilitate the collectivistic mode valued by the Hispanic families I work with? Maybe it could be a combination of both goals.

I feel that the parent conference situation is not easily resolved. First, I have a time constraint of 15 minutes in a room where other fami-

tural value in which children respect and look up to their parents as authority figures.

A culturally compatible format. The next year, the teacher developed a successful social format for the parent-teacher conference. In a later Bridging Cultures workshop, she described her approach:

> In the prescribed practice of parent conferencing, teachers allot 10 to 15 minutes for each parent. They use this time to review a child's academic progress, report card, social skills, and state test scores. Most of the time, other parents are waiting, or several parents arrive at the same time. In many circumstances, the appointment time is not when the parents show up. Teachers repeat generic information at each conference. This type of conferencing tends to be threatening for most parents.
>
> To incorporate the concept of collectivism, I redesigned my parent conferencing into group conferences. For families who couldn't attend, I arranged a separate time. I divided my children by ability levels and language into our English-speaking group and two Spanish-speaking groups. My paraprofessional translated for the Spanish language groups. I prepared the children for their part in the conferencing by role playing the student and parent parts during the previous week.
>
> Most of the parents arrived on time and sat with me in a circle. The children presented their parents, mostly mothers, with a folder that contained test scores, their report card, a parents' tips list, and a hard-to-understand booklet for interpreting test scores. I explained the percentiles and stanines of the Stanford 9 or Aprenda and how the parents could use the results to know which academic areas are strong and which need improvement. I explained the report card format and the meaning of the marks and discussed my expectations for the next quarter. I also discussed what I could do to help students progress academically as well as how the parents could help at home.
>
> A comfortable and warm feeling came across during the conferencing. Many parents had questions that benefited the others. The children, once the group session was over, excitedly escorted their parents and siblings to their desks to share

> **In the interdependent perspective of Latino immigrant parents, education is a tool not for developing the individual potential of each child, but for enabling each child to help the family as a whole.**

rive with little education do not necessarily realize that they and their children will be asked to give up collectivistic values in pursuit of educational achievement. In the interdependent perspective of Latino immigrant parents, education is a tool not for developing the individual potential of each child, but for enabling each child to help the family as a whole.

The Bridging Cultures Project: A Teacher Responds

Bridging Cultures (Greenfield, Raeff, & Quiroz, 1998) is an ongoing cross-cultural professional development effort that allows a group of California teachers and researchers to collaboratively apply research on cross-cultural value conflict in schools to the education of children from Latino immigrant families (Rothstein-Fisch, 1997; Trumbull et al., 1997). During a Bridging Cultures workshop, one teacher-participant responded to our analysis of her conferences with Latino immigrant parents:

> My awareness of the cultural differences between collectivistic and in-

lies are waiting.... Second, I *am* responsible for the academic-social progress of each child. I show parents how well their children are doing or where improvement is necessary. My conflict arises with understanding what kind of success this child should be striving for. If it's academic, it may conflict with the family's definition of success as a supportive member of [the] family. But parents explain to me that they immigrated here "to better their lives," so perhaps academic achievement is in alignment with this goal.

The Child-Led Versus the Group Conference

During the Bridging Cultures workshops, teachers proposed alternative practices for conducting parent-teacher conferences, and experimentation ensued.

A culturally incompatible format. The teacher previously quoted experimented with the child-led conference. Despite its current popularity, this format turns out to be incompatible with Latino culture: By putting the child in the leadership role, the child-led conference violates the collectivistic cul-

and discuss their portfolios. Thy took their parents on a tour of the room to show their displayed work.

The group conferencing was relaxing for the parents. It was a less threatening environment than the individual conferencing style; parents supplied support and were company for one another. This format provided a group voice from the parents rather than an individual voice. After one hour, parents could sign up for a private conference or ask a few questions privately.

My new format was successful. I saw all 28 parents in three days. The conference design impressed my principal, who asked me to lead a staff development program on the subject. I see this conferencing format as an evolving process.

Achieving Harmony

The Latino parents interpreted the teacher's ability to coordinate the group conference as a display of the social skills appropriate to her position as the leader of her classroom domain. From the parents' perspective, the teacher demonstrated that she could integrate a group of individuals into a harmonious multiparty interaction with explicit and common goals. At the same time, she let children play the role of active participants, a role valued by the school. Latino parents often value harmonious group interaction more highly than one-on-one interaction. In contrast, the individualistic worldview places high value on individual attention and privacy and sees one-on-one interaction as the ideal for social interaction; the social format of the standard parent-teacher conference reflects this value.

Initially, this teacher focused on the pragmatic difficulties of integrating different values into a parent-teacher conference, achieving the accomplishments she expected, and interpreting the parents' goals. Through the Bridging Cultures workshop process and through her own experimentation, she realized that she did not need to convert to someone else's cultural orientation to understand and accommodate that person's needs and perspectives. Goals that initially seemed incompatible became mutually

reinforcing in her new group-conferencing format. She gave the parents of each group of similarly achieving students an overview of academic progression on the group level, without singling out individuals. She used a family process—parent-child communication—to present parents with their children's individual work. And she provided an opportunity for parent-teacher consultation on individual problems.

Most important, however, was the teacher's realization that including families' cultural perspective on social interaction could benefit students as well as herself. This process is not easy. To accept that one's own perceptions are not the only ones or even the better ones requires humility. These qualities can be threatening to people raised in a culture that places high priority on building and protecting self-esteem.

One important outcome of the Bridging Cultures process was the participants' realization that, as educators, they function under the implicit assumptions of their own cultural framework. This step is necessary to build respect for differences and a sincere acknowledgment that diversity has value.

References

Delgado-Gaitan, C. (1994). Socializing young children in Mexican-American families: An intergenerational perspective. In P. M. Greenfield & R. R. Cocking (Eds.), *Cross-cultural roots of minority child development* (pp. 55–86). Hillsdale, NJ: Erlbaum.

Goldenberg, C., & Gallimore, R. (1995). Immigrant Latino parents' values and beliefs about their children's education: Continuities and discontinuities. In P. Pintrich & M. Maehr (Eds.), *Advances in achievement motivation* (Vol. 9, pp. 183–228). Greenwich, CT: JAI Press.

Greenfield, P. M., Raeff, C., & Quiroz, B. (1996). Cultural values in learning and education. In B. Williams (Ed.), *Closing the achievement gap: A vision for changing beliefs and practices* (pp. 37–55). Alexandria, VA: ASCD.

Greenfield, P. M., Raeff, C., & Quiroz, B. (1998). Cross-cultural conflict in the social construction of the child. *Aztlán, 23,* 115–125.

Raeff, C., Greenfield, P. M., & Quiroz, B. (in press). Conceptualizing interpersonal relationships in the cultural contexts of individualism and collectivism. In S. Harkness, C.

Raeff, & C. M. Super (Eds.), *The social construction of the child: The nature of variability: New directions in child development.* San Francisco: Jossey-Bass.

Reese, L., Balzano, S., Gallimore, R., & Goldenberg, C. (1995). The concept of *Educación:* Latino family values and American schooling. *International Journal of Educational Research, 23,* 57–81.

Rothstein-Fisch, C. (1997). *Bridging cultures in the classroom: A module for pre-service teachers.* San Francisco: WestEd.

Rothstein-Fisch, C., Trumbull, E., Quiroz, B., & Greenfield, P. (1997, June). *Bridging cultures in the classroom.* Poster session presented at the Jean Piaget Society for the Study of Knowledge and Development, Santa Monica, CA.

Trumbull, E., Greenfield, P., Rothstein-Fisch, C., Quiroz, B., Altchech, M., Daley, C., Eyler, K., Hernandez, E., Mercado, G., Pérez, A. I., & Saitzyk, P. (1997). *Bridging cultures between home and school: A guide.* San Francisco: WestEd.

Valdés, G. (1996). *Con respeto: Bridging the distances between culturally diverse families and schools.* New York: Teachers College Press.

Author's note: The Bridging Cultures project is sponsored by WestEd, the federally funded education research and development laboratory for the Western U.S. region. The teachers are from the Los Angeles Unified School District, the Ocean View School District in Oxnard, and the Los Nietos School District in Whittier. The researchers are from UCLA, WestEd, and California State University, Northridge.

Blanca Quiroz is a doctoral student at Harvard University in the Graduate School of Education, Cambridge, Massachusetts. **Patricia M. Greenfield** (e-mail: greenfield@psych.ucla.edu) is Professor of Psychology at UCLA, Los Angeles, CA 90095. **Marie Altchech** is a teacher at Stoner Avenue School in the Los Angeles Unified School District.

Editor's note: A longer version of this article appeared in *Connections,* a newsletter of the Urban Education Studies Center, University of California, Los Angeles, at Corrine A. Seeds University Elementary School.

Expanding Roles of Teachers for the 21st Century

An Indian Context

American educators, in their attempts to clarify
their expanding roles, need to examine further
the kaleidoscope of teachers' roles in
other societies and other settings.

Navaz Peshotan Bhavnagri and Thrity G. Vaswani

Navaz Peshotan Bhavnagri is Associate Professor, Early Childhood Education, Wayne State University, Detroit, Michigan. Thrity G. Vaswani is Reader (i.e., Associate Professor), Faculty of Social Work, Maharaja Sayajirao University, Baroda, India.

Many teacher educators, school administrators, education reformers, teachers, social policy pundits, and politicians in the United States are reflecting on the question, "How should we best prepare our teachers for the 21st century?" They further ponder, "How can we learn from other countries and then adapt what we learn to our conditions?" U.S. educators already have learned and applied much from other countries' practices, such as Italy's Reggio Emilia early childhood programs (Edwards, Gandini, & Forman, 1998; Hendrick, 1997). As American educators attempt to clarify their expanding roles, they need to examine further the kaleidoscope of teachers' roles in other societies and other settings. This article examines the rationale for expanding teachers' roles, using preschool education in the slums[1] of Baroda, India, as an

Note: The authors wish to thank Girdhar Vaswani, Executive Director of Baroda Citizens Council, for giving us permission to interview the organization's personnel and use their library, and for making the necessary support services available.

From *Childhood Education,* Annual Theme 1999, pp. 297-303. Reprinted by permission of the authors and the Association for Childhood Education International. © 1999 by the Association.

illustrative study, and its implications for teacher preparation in the 21st century United States.

RATIONALE FOR EXAMINING TEACHERS' EXPANDING ROLES

There are five justifications for examining teachers' expanding roles. First, although the social conditions that have paved the way for teachers assuming ever-larger roles have existed for several decades, more recent legislation has precipitated this change. The Personal Responsibility and Work Opportunity Act of 1996 "ended welfare as we know it," according to President Clinton. Therefore, while the responsibility for administering child welfare programs is now delegated to the individual states, the states will receive 20 percent less federal support to execute these programs (Sherman & Viggiani, 1996). Some child advocates fear a resulting dramatic reduction of services to poor children and families (Children's Defense Fund, 1997). In addition, other pending bills (both at the federal and state levels) on health care, Medicaid, and foster care also may reduce services to poor families. Teachers, as caring individuals, will be picking up the slack of providing these social services; increasingly, they will have to act as child advocates and dependable resource persons for their needy pupils. States also may reduce their education budgets, to compensate for the larger amount spent on social services. Consequently, fewer teachers and other personnel may be hired, and those currently teaching may be compelled to perform even more roles that extend beyond teaching.

Second, the current philosophy in early and elementary childhood education is to educate the "whole child" and promote "total development" (e.g., Barbour & Seefeldt, 1993; Bredekemp & Copple, 1997; Hart, Burts, & Charlesworth, 1997; Hendrick, 1996, 1998). To promote physical and motor development, teachers need to have an indepth knowledge of developmental milestones, first aid and basic health education, immunizations, and prevention of childhood diseases (i.e., teachers need to expand their role to include that of a pediatrics nurse). To promote social and emotional development, teachers also need to have a sound knowledge of social and personality development; how peers, media, and community affect the child; and guidance and counseling (i.e., the role of a counselor).

Third, national standards for early childhood and elementary education emphasize that working with parents and the community is an integral component of teacher preparation (Association for Childhood Education International, 1997a, 1997b; National Association for the Education of Young Children, 1996). Thus, these standards explicitly acknowledge that teachers have to take on the roles of community worker, counselor, resource person, liaison, and advocate.

Fourth, Bronfenbrenner (1979) contends that our knowledge of human development is limited to the child's microsystems (i.e., the immediate environment in which the child is present). Relatively little is known regarding the child's mesosystem (i.e., the links between any two of the child's microsystems), exosystems (i.e., the setting in which the child is absent but that still influences his development), and macrosystems (i.e., societal, cultural, ideological, and philosophical values and belief systems that influence his development). Educators need to exert a positive influence not just on the microsystem (e.g., school or home), but also on all of the child's other systems. For example, the teacher has to be an effective communicator, parent educator and supporter, and thereby strengthen the child's home-school relations—the child's mesosystems. The teacher also has to be a community worker to strengthen the child's micro- and exosystems, and to work as a child's advocate to strengthen the child's macrosystem.

Fifth, teachers are the only other adults besides parents who daily spend significant amounts of time with children. Teachers not only have a high frequency of interactions, they also have opportunities to develop emotionally close, influential, and committed relationships with their pupils (Hyson, 1994). Teachers and other adults can positively inspire children by their own examples, and they can inculcate many virtues in them. Mahatma Gandhi, when asked about which "works" influenced his life, replied that while he had little recollection of books he had read or the "lessons" he had learned in school, he did feel that the vital teaching force throughout his life was the individuals who inspired him by the examples of their own lives, and that these people were always standing beside him (Bainbridge, 1996). Thus, teachers wield enormous influence as they take on the roles of friend, mentor, confidant, counselor, spiritual guide, and social activist.

In the slums of one Indian city, 17 preschool teachers carry out all these roles. (It is beyond the scope of this article to discuss the status of early childhood education in all of India. For such details see: Bhavnagri, 1995; Department of Education, 1986; Joshi, Mohite, & Verma, 1991; National Institute of Public Cooperation and Child Development, 1984; Verma, 1979; Verma & Mohite, 1991.)

PRESCHOOL EDUCATION IN THE SLUMS OF BARODA

Baroda, the 21st-largest city in India, with a population of 1.5 million, is about 130 kilometers (nearly 80 miles) northwest of Mumbai (previously named Bombay). Because of the city's strategic location, it was transformed into a major industrial center during the 1960s. Industrialization brought an influx of migrants and a subsequent growth of slums. In 1966, a voluntary, nonpolitical, nonprofit, secular, development organization called Baroda Citizens Council (B.C.C.) was established, with initial support from a Quaker group called American Friends Service Committee. The goal of B.C.C. is to involve the urban poor community in solving their problems by developing local leadership, competence, and faith in themselves, and by making effective use of available resources (Baroda Citizens Council, 1996).

About 15 years ago, B.C.C. opened up balwadis in the slums. ("Bal" means child and "wadi" means a garden—thus, a "garden for children." The balwadis serve 2- to 6-year-olds, while kindergartens in the U.S. typically serve 5-year-olds.) In 1985, the program gained momentum. Today, B.C.C. sponsors 17 balwadis serving 39 percent of the 3- to 6-year-olds in Baroda's slums. Another 35 percent of urban 3- to 6-year-old slum children attend balwadis funded by Integrated Child Development Scheme (ICDS). ICDS is the Indian government's largest developmental project, and is the world's largest early childhood government-sponsored program for the poor. (See Bhavnagri, 1995, and National Institute of Public Cooperation & Child Development, 1992, regarding ICDS and its resemblance to Head Start.) Despite ICDS's wide reach, it is still unable to help all slum preschoolers. Therefore, B.C.C. offered

its preschool programs in Baroda's slums. Unfortunately, about one fourth of the slum children do not receive benefits from any program (Baroda Citizens Council, 1996).

The authors used multiple methodologies and sources to ensure the credibility of their findings about the preschools run by B.C.C. and the teachers' roles. First, three focus groups were conducted in the Gujarati language, since all teachers were proficient in it. Besides taking detailed notes, the authors audiotaped these sessions to capture the teachers' voices. The authors also interviewed the Executive Director of the B.C.C. Next, the authors visited the preschools and the community services in the slums, followed by visits to the parents' homes. They also attended weekly planning meetings. Finally, they examined the children's cumulative records and the agency's other publications.

Both authors offered expertise in child development, early childhood education and social work, gained from Indian institutions of higher education. They also had university and preschool teaching experiences in India. The first author also brought an outsider's perspective, based on her graduate studies at an American university and her years of university teaching experience in the United States.

EXPANSIVE ROLES OF TEACHERS IN INDIAN SLUMS

Education of the Child

Description of the Urban Slum Child. About 85 percent of preschool slum children in Baroda suffer from varying degrees of protein and calorie deficiency; iron deficiency anemia; Vitamin A deficiency, which causes dryness of the eyes and, in extreme cases, blindness; and iodine deficiency, which adversely affects physical and mental development (Foneska & Malhotra, 1994). Some of the children were low-birthweight babies, because their mothers suffered from nutritional anemia.

A lack of 100 percent safe drinking water, poor physical conditions of the home, and the general conditions of the slums further contribute to poor health. Fonseka and Malhotra (1994) report that the rural children who migrate to urban slums have worse health than their rural counterparts, even though they generally eat better food and more regularly. Thus, the unhealthy slum environment may affect their well-being. Fonseka and Malhotra also report that even though more slum children are enrolled in school, the non-enrollment rate in slums is nine times greater, and the

photos courtesy of authors

Children working collaboratively in a small group, building a tower with alphabet blocks.

dropout rate 20 percent greater, than in non-slum schools.

The preschoolers whom we observed all were clean, with well-groomed hair, despite the limited availability of water for bathing. Their clothes were handwashed, but not ironed. As many of these children have continuously runny noses, due to poor health, some of them had a cotton handkerchief safety-pinned to their clothing.

Role of a Child Educator. First, the preschool teachers develop a curriculum. Since commercial materials are limited in quantity and variety, the teachers make materials such as indigenous dolls, paper-rolled beads, woven baskets, board games, and matchbox alphabets. They receive training in constructing such materials from a university extension program. They take children on outings to provide experiential learning. For example, the children from all B.C.C. preschools meet in public gardens to celebrate their annual children's festival with games, a magic show, a puppet show, gifts, and a picnic. The teachers educate the children about healthful foods by cooking, and talking about, nutritious snacks. They also conduct thematic units on food.

Role of a Child Advocate. The preschool teachers identify, assess, and advocate for those children with special needs who have not received proper medical attention. The city's complex and bureaucratic government health system is very confusing and intimidating to parents, who often are illiterate, and thus, feel powerless. Therefore, the B.C.C. teachers go with these children and their families to government hospitals for physiotherapy, occupational therapy, x-ray appointments, appointments with orthopedic doctors, and even surgery. The B.C.C. teachers have special badges that allow them direct access to medical services, facilitating their roles as liaisons for slum dwellers. In addition, through years of experience, they have accumulated a deep understanding of how the hospitals work. The B.C.C. teachers are able to expedite medical services by reading signs and filling out forms for illiterate parents, explaining technical jargon used by medical personnel, and clearly articulating patients' concerns. They also assist families in applying for bus and rail concession passes for the handicapped, and by visiting the appropriate offices to process the applications.

These teachers believe they should be advocates because, as one teacher said, "It is our responsibility to be vigilant and take notice of the needs of the community. We need to note which family has had a birth of a handicapped child and which child in the community has now come of age, such that it is safe and appropriate to operate. We then have to follow through on these cases."

They are also advocates for street children who do not attend school. In 1998, 110 street children were reached through B.C.C.'s seven non-formal education classes. ("Non-formal education" refers to schooling provided by agencies other than private and public schools.) These children were admitted up to 15 years of age because of their difficult circumstances. The B.C.C. teachers reported that they must regularly remind the street children to continue attending non-formal classes. As many street children do not have birth certificates, a necessity for school admission, the B.C.C. teachers have to provide documentation that these children have received non-formal education. Such documentation substitutes for birth certificates and allows the children to enroll in regular schools.

Education of the Families

Description of the Family. B.C.C. offers expansive services (e.g., programs on health and economic development, and programs targeting women, handicapped children, street children, and preschoolers) to almost 13,500 families. Seven hundred and thirty-five of these families receive preschool education through the B.C.C. balwadis. Eighty-two percent are Hindu families, 17 percent are Muslim families, and one percent are Christians or from other religious faiths. The average size is 4.87 children per family. These families are predominantly nuclear (82 percent). Only a few families (18 percent) have other relatives residing with them. Both parents work in these families. India is similar to other developing countries in that older siblings are the caregivers for younger children when adults work outside the home (Bhavnagri, 1994; Whiting & Edwards, 1988). More recently, however, slum parents are sending their children to school in greater num-

One of the slums where B.C.C. teachers work.

bers. As a result, the older siblings are not available to babysit. Therefore, preschools such as those run by B.C.C. are needed.

Eighty percent of the men and 60 percent of the women in these families are literate (i.e., they have primary education and above). Women's literacy is critical because it is positively related to their children's education, language and cognitive development, and health and nutrition (Levine, 1987; UNICEF, 1992). These families earn on average Rs. 260 per month (i.e., approximately 6 dollars, when the rate of exchange is Rs. 44 = 1 dollar). Western research indicates that economic hardships (McLoyd, 1990) and the day-to-day "hassles" of parenting (Crinic & Greenberg, 1990) are major stressors for poor families, contributing to children's social incompetence (McLoyd, 1990).

Role of a Family Life Educator. B.C.C. teachers perform home visits for several reasons. They want to know, for example, why a child has not been attending the preschool lately. If the child is absent because of health reasons, as is often the case, then the B.C.C. teachers ask the parents to bring their child to the clinic. The teachers also need to remind parents to pay their fees. They may also persuade mothers to limit the size of their families. With one exception, all of the teachers interviewed reported that they prefer to discuss issues with the mothers during home visits. The teacher who preferred to speak with the fathers explained, "Far too often women say, 'I will have to check with my husband and get back with you.' I therefore prefer to go on a home visit when the head of the household is at home. I tell the fathers, 'If you save 50 paisa, which is only half a rupee a day, then you can save 15 rupees a month! That is plenty towards your child's fee. If you smoked a little less each day, then the savings on the bidis [i.e., Indian cigarettes] is the extra money you saved.' "

During their parent conferences, the teachers educate the families regarding the importance of cleanliness. They remarked to us, "We often have to remind parents to send their child to school clean. Clothes should be clean. Give him a handkerchief and pin it to his shirt for wiping his runny nose." They also emphasize literacy, recommending that the parents provide writing materials at home.

They have group meetings at which mothers, grandmothers, or older sisters attend. Fathers usually cannot attend because the meetings are held in the afternoon. Some teachers with whom we spoke believed that many fathers are unlikely to attend the evening meetings either, because, as

one said, "Once they come home they are with the bottle and [they] drink through the evening."

Education of the Community

Description of the Slum Community. The slum population in Indian cities has grown two to three times faster than the rate for the overall urban population. Baroda is in Gujarat State, which is the second most urbanized state in the nation. Approximately one quarter of the urban population in Gujarat State lives in slums (Government of Gujarat, 1994). In 1998, Baroda had 360 slum pockets (G. Vaswani, personal communication, August 15, 1997).

These neighborhoods are not lawless or depraved. They are made up of rural, migrant families that are struggling to make a living. They work in the informal unorganized sector, and they contribute to the city's economy. Some community members have visibly improved their lot after working in the city. They were able to purchase radios, televisions, bicycles, motorbikes, refrigerators, gas operated cooking stoves, fans, and western style furniture. Then, there are less fortunate people who are merely trying to eke out a living. They use firewood or kerosene stoves, eat and sleep on the floor, have no electricity or furniture, and possess only the most necessary clothing and cooking utensils.

The slum environment is not generally hygienic. While it does receive municipal public services, these services may not be evenly distributed across the entire slum. Although most city slums have potable water, paved streets, drainage, electricity, street cleaning, and garbage collection, all of these services and infrastructure need improvement. Research indicates that the ecology of neighborhoods greatly affects the quality of children's lives (e.g., Berg & Medrich, 1980; Brooks-Gunn, Duncan, & Aber, 1997; Garbarino, Dubrow, Kostelny, & Pardo, 1992; Skogan, 1990).

Thanks to B.C.C.'s continuous efforts to promote self-reliance among slum dwellers, the slums where B.C.C. operates have more amenities (e.g., drinking water, bathrooms, toilets, drainage, electricity) than other slums. Moreover, 72 percent of the slum dwellers where B.C.C. operates are owners of their shelters. B.C.C. works in 33 out of the 360 identified slum pockets, and it has preschools in 17 out of these 33 slums.

Role of an Environment Educator. The teachers organize community meetings on sanitation projects that influence the health of the children they serve. They invite a B.C.C. expert to speak about how to acquire low-cost toilets, soak pits for kitchens, UNICEF-designed water pumps, and community drainage systems. Teachers make follow-up visits to motivate the community to sustain these projects. During focus groups, the teachers reported, "We live in the neighborhoods where we work. So we end up visiting various community members daily, [one person] or another. We end up visiting their homes sometimes twice in a day, on our way to and from our [own] homes and as we run family errands in our neighborhood. We encourage them to construct inexpensive latrines in their homes. We always talk about cleanliness, reinforcing in them [the need] to keep the environment clean, so [that] we don't have problems in the community. We say, 'Eradicate filthiness.'"

In the past, the teachers from the U.S. also lived and worked in the same community, and so they too were intimately involved in their community's welfare and viewed community education as their responsibility (e.g., Wiggin, 1923). Such involvement is much less common today.

Role of an Economic Adviser. The B.C.C. teachers encourage many slum families to save. They say, "If you save, we then give you loans for latrines, health needs, and hospital costs." They further monitor these families, making sure they make monthly deposits to the B.C.C. credit and savings association. The teachers often end up visiting the families twice a day to ensure that regular deposits are made. Friends or relatives of these families cannot provide financial assistance, nor do the families have any collateral to offer a bank. In the past, they used to take loans from money lenders, who charged an interest rate four times higher than the B.C.C.'s.

B.C.C. serves 13,000 slum households and 60 percent of households (about 8,000) are enrolled in the savings plan. Sixty percent of savings plan members are women. It has been frequently observed that women in emerging nations spend their savings on children's needs (e.g., school fees, uniforms, and books), while men spend their savings on personal luxury items (e.g., transistor radios, clothing for themselves, and eating out). The B.C.C. teachers encourage women to save and thereby help ensure the education of the children they serve.

Role of a Health Educator. These teachers also educate the community to immunize all children under 5 against tuberculosis, polio, tetanus, diphtheria, and measles. Teachers even give booster shots and oral vaccines. One hundred percent of the children in the B.C.C. preschools are immunized, compared to a range of 89 percent to 96 percent of the children in the rest of the community. This remarkably high level of immunization

is evidence of the teachers' effectiveness as health educators.

These teachers assist doctors at the B.C.C. clinic on alternate Saturdays, helping to distribute calcium, iron, and multivitamins; draw blood from patients and make laboratory slides, to check for malaria and anemia; register mothers at the postnatal clinic; and check that mothers and their newborns keep their postnatal check-ups. The infant mortality rate in Baroda is 61 per 1,000 live births, but in the Baroda slums, it is 100 per 1,000 live births. In the slums where these teachers provide health education, the rate has dropped to 85 per thousand (Baroda Citizens Council, 1996).

One of the teachers' comments serves as a good summary: "All these roles are interrelated. We start a discussion [with a community member] on one topic and we find ourselves talking about our other roles. We then end up taking on all other roles together."

TEACHER PREPARATION FOR THE 21ST CENTURY

The lesson we can extrapolate from these Indian teachers is how to collaborate effectively with other professionals (e.g., health, public transportation, public school, and social service professionals). Corrigan (1996) states that, "Tomorrow's school teachers . . . and other educators need to learn how to collaborate with partners in other human service professions such as health care, social work, and criminal justice, who serve the same clients" (p. 143). The following reasons necessitate interprofessional collaboration in the United States.

First of all, children under 6 are the poorest Americans. The poverty rate in this group has been rising since the 1970s; it remains high today (National Commission on Children, 1990). Children in this group are at a great risk of impaired health, school dropout, school failure, and delinquency (National Center for Children in Poverty, 1990). Thus, they are vulnerable, like the Indian slum children, and they need support services from multiple agencies. Therefore, teachers need to form partnerships with other professionals to promote the total well-being of these children, and to increase the likelihood of their academic and developmental success.

Second, rapid immigration, industrialization, and urbanization in the United States during 1890–1917 led to terrible living conditions and poor health of immigrant children. At that time, teachers were able to assume an expanded role of assisting other welfare services (Levine & Levine, 1992), as do the B.C.C. teachers of today. Immigrant and poor minority children are once again on the increase in U.S. schools (U.S. Bureau of the Census, 1997); therefore, teachers will have to work again with multiple agencies to ensure their success.

Third, incentives already exist for forming such partnerships. In order to enforce public laws 94–142 and 94–457, which are aimed at optimizing the education and development of children with special needs, teachers are expected to work collaboratively with other professionals. Fourth, "Goals 2000" challenges schools to form partnerships with parents and the community, state and federal agencies, national and nonprofit organizations, and corporations to ensure that all children are equally served.

To sum up, teachers alone cannot meet all of children's needs, but when they team up with other professionals they can certainly make a difference. However, if the teachers of tomorrow are not trained in coordinating their efforts with other professionals on interdisciplinary teams, then their effectiveness will be limited. They will not be able to receive support from these professionals, nor will they be able to offer support to other professionals. They will continue to feel stressed, overworked, and overwhelmed. Some may even feel resentful, exploited, and burnt out, and may finally leave the profession. Therefore, teacher education must prepare teachers to work with other professionals and across agencies in family-centered, community-based, and full-service schools (e.g., Corrigan & Udas, 1996; Dryfoos, 1994; Lawson, 1994; Office of Educational Research & Improvement, 1995).

On a final note, although teacher preparation for interprofessional collaboration of novice teachers is absolutely critical, it is only the first step. Novice teachers, when they enter the world of work, need additional support and mentoring from their administrators and colleagues, so they can take on this challenge of performing multiple roles and successfully collaborating with other professionals. Administrators' and colleagues' scaffolding and collaboration can empower and mobilize these new teachers to work closely with other professionals in the welfare, legal, medical, business, religious, and political systems. For it is really true, "It *does* take a village to raise a child."

1. The word "slum" is typically used in India. It is a commonly accepted term used by the Indian government, American philanthropic organizations, and other international donor agencies that work in poor and congested urban neighborhoods in India.

References

Association for Childhood Education International. (1997a). Preparation of early childhood teachers. *Childhood Education, 73,* 164–165.

Association for Childhood Education International. (1997b). Preparation of elementary teachers. *Childhood Education, 73,* 166–167.

Bainbridge, R. (1996). The teacher as evolutionary energy. In N. C. Dowsett, S. R. Jayaswal, M. S. Srinivasan, & Vijay. (Eds.), *The true teacher* (pp. 30–41). Pondicherry, India: Sri Aurbindo Institute of Research in Social Sciences.

Barbour, N., & Seefeldt, C. (1993). *Developmental continuity across preschool and primary grades: Implications for teachers.* Olney, MD: Association for Childhood Education International.

Baroda Citizens Council. (1996). *Annual report 1995–96.* Baroda, India: Author.

Berg, M., & Medrich, E. A. (1980). Children in four neighborhoods: The physical environment and its effects on play and play patterns. *Environment & Behavior, 12,* 320–348.

Bhavnagri, N. P. (1994). Child development and household behaviors. In R. Bourah, K. Cloud, S. Seshadri, T. S. Saraswathi, J. Peterson, & A. Verma (Eds.), *Capturing complexity: An interdisciplinary look at women, households, and development* (pp. 210–227). New Delhi: Sage Publications.

Bhavnagri, N. P. (1995). An interview with Professor Amita Verma: A leader in early childhood education in India. *Childhood Education, 71,* 156–160.

Bredekemp, S., & Copple, C. (Eds.). (1997). *Developmentally appropriate practices in early childhood programs.* Washington, DC: National Association for the Education of Young Children.

Bronfenbrenner, U. (1997). *The ecology of human development.* Cambridge, MA: Harvard University Press.

Brooks-Gunn, J., Duncan, G., & Aber, J. L. (Eds.). (in press). *Neighbourhood poverty: Context and consequences for children.* New York: Russell Sage.

Children's Defense Fund. (1997). *The state of America's children: Leave no child behind.* Washington, DC: Author.

Corrigan, D. (1996). Teacher education and interprofessional collaboration: Creation of family-centered community-based integrated service systems. In L. Kaplan & R. A. Edelfelt (Eds.), *Teachers for the new millennium: Aligning teacher development, national goals, and high standards for all students* (pp. 142–171). Thousand Oaks, CA: Corwin.

Corrigan, D., & Udas, K. (1996). Creating collaborative, child and family centered education, health and human services systems. In J. Sikula (Ed.), *Handbook of research on teacher education* (pp. 893–921). New York: Macmillan.

Crinic, K. A., & Greenberg, M. T. (1990). Minor parenting stresses with young children. *Child Development, 61,* 1628–1637.

Department of Education, Ministry of Human Resource Development, Government of India. (1986). *National policy on education: Programme of action.* New Delhi, India: Author.

Dryfoos, J. G. (1994). *Full service schools: A revolution in health and social services for children, youth, and families.* San Francisco: Jossey-Bass.

Edwards, C., Gandini, L., & Forman, G. (Eds.). (1998). *The hundred languages of children: The Reggio Emilia approach—advanced reflections.* Norwood, NJ: Ablex.

Fonseka, L., & Malhotra, D. D. (1994). India: Urban poverty, children and participation. In C. S. Blanc (Ed.), *Urban children in distress: Global predicaments and innovative strategies* (pp. 161–215). Florence, Italy: UNICEF; Langhorne, PA: Gordon and Breach.

Garbarino, J., Dubrow, N., Kostelny, K., & Pardo, C. (1992). *Children in danger: Coping with the consequences of community violence.* San Francisco: Jossey-Bass.

Government of Gujarat. (1994). *State programs of action for the child in Gujarat.* Gandhinagar, India: Author.

Hart, C. H., Burts, D. C., & Charlesworth, R. (Eds.). (1997). *Integrated curriculum and developmentally appropriate practice.* Albany, NY: State University of New York.

Hendrick, J. (1996). *The whole child: Developmental education for the early years.* Englewood Cliffs, NJ: Prentice Hall.

Henrick, J. (Ed.). (1997). *First step toward teaching the Reggio way.* Upper Saddle River, NJ: Merrill.

Hendrick, J. (1998). *Total learning: Developmental curriculum for the young child.* Upper Saddle River, NJ: Merrill.

Hyson, M. C. (1994). *The emotional development of young children: Building an emotion-centered curriculum.* New York: Teachers College Press.

Joshi, A., Mohite, P., & Verma, A. (1991). Early childhood education in India: The research scene. *Perspectives in Education, 1*(1), 3–13.

Lawson, H. (1994). Towards healthy learners, schools, and communities. *Journal of Teacher Education, 45,* 62–70.

Levine, A., & Levine, M. (1992). *Helping children: A social history.* New York: Oxford University.

Levine, R. (1987). Women's schooling, patterns of fertility, and child survival. *Educational Researcher, 16,* 21–27.

McLoyd, V. C. (1990). The impact of economic hardship on black families and children: Psychological distress, parenting, and socioemotional development. *Child Development, 61,* 311–346.

National Association for the Education of Young Children. (1996). *Guidelines for preparation of early childhood education.* Washington, DC: Author.

National Center for Children in Poverty. (1990). *Five million children: A statistical profile of our poorest young citizens: Summary report.* New York: Author.

National Commission on Children. (1990). *Just the facts: A summary of information on America's children and their families.* Washington, DC: Author.

National Institute of Public Cooperation and Child Development. (1984). *Perspective plan in child development 1980–2000.* New Delhi, India: Author.

National Institute of Public Cooperation and Child Development. (1992). *National evaluation of integrated child development services.* New Delhi, India: Author.

Office of Educational Research & Improvement. (1995). *School-linked comprehensive services for children and families: What we know and need to know.* Washington, DC: Author.

Sherman, L. V., & Viggiani, P. (1996). The impact of federal policy changes on children: Research needs for the future. *Social Work, 41,* 594–600.

Skogan, W. (1990). *Disorder and decline: Crime and the spiral decay in American neighborhoods.* Berkeley, CA: University of California.

UNICEF. (1992). *Strategies to promote girls' education: Policies and programmes that work.* New York: Author.

U.S. Bureau of the Census. (1997). *Statistical abstract of the United States, 1997.* Washington, DC: Author.

Verma, A. (1979). Child development and child welfare: Research and policy. *Indian Journal of Social Work, XLVII*(1), 25–30.

Verma, A., & Mohite, P. (1991). Research in early childhood education: A trend report. In M. B. Bush (Ed.), *Fourth survey of research in education: 1983–1988* (Vol 2). New Delhi, India: National Council of Educational Research and Training.

Whiting, B. B., & Edwards, C. P. (1988). *Children of different worlds: The formation of social behaviour.* Cambridge, MA: Harvard University.

Wiggin, K. D. (1923). *My garden of memory: An autobiography.* Boston, Houghton Mifflin.

APPENDIX: FOCUS GROUP GUIDE

Introduction

All of you know us both. I worked with you four years ago, when I visited you from the United States. At that time, I conducted inservice workshops for all of you. I then played the role of a teacher. Today, I am going to play the role of a learner. All of you are going to educate me about your work in the preschools run by B.C.C. Although your preschools are in different slums of Baroda, all of you have the same roles and responsibilities, because you work under the auspices of the same organization. We have divided you into small groups, to facilitate the discussion and to provide amble time and opportunity for you to express your viewpoints. So feel free to exchange your views with each other.

You also know Thrity. She teaches Family and Child Welfare in the School of Social Work. She teachers her students about how to improve the conditions of poor urban children and families who live in slum areas. Therefore, she, too, is here to learn from your experiences.

We have divided our roles. I will be the facilitator of our discussions by raising questions on various issues related to your work. Thrity will be the recorder and will take notes. Additionally, she may facilitate me if I need any special help in my communications. She is very familiar with your local expressions and technical jargon. We will also tape the discussions to provide us with details and with an exact recording of what you said. Does anyone have any objections to our audio-taping? (No one expressed any objections.) So, now let us begin. Let us go around and start introducing ourselves. Tell us where you work, the years of experience you have and any other information about you that you think is pertinent. (The introductions were done next.)

Questions and Comments

1. Let us start with you all describing your work. Why don't you tell us about a typical day in your balwadi? What is your daily time table?
2. What goals or purpose do you have?
3. When you teach, how do you go about planning your lessons? What is your method?
4. It is our understanding that you not only work directly with the children, but also reach out to their parents. Can you share that with us?
5. Do you limit yourself to the parents of the children who attend your preschool, or do you also work with members of the community who are not parents of these children? Tell us any work you do with other community members.
6. Discuss some of the opportunities you have had to learn and grow on the job. Share with us information regarding any inservice training that you have received.
7. Do you think you are making any difference through your work? What are your satisfactions and dissatisfactions on your job?

Conclusion

We really enjoyed this discussion. You gave us so many detailed descriptions with specific examples, and so we learned a lot. I am so glad I got an opportunity to reacquaint myself with you. It was nice seeing you all again. You gave so much of your time and we really appreciated that.

Thank you very much.

How to Overcome Obstacles to Parent-Teacher Partnerships

ALTHIER LAZAR and FRANCES SLOSTAD

Parent-teacher partnerships bring a community of adults together to work toward a common goal—helping students succeed. When these partnerships are based on genuine respect and mutual sharing of ideas, a web of support is created to provide students the best opportunity to thrive in school (Henderson 1988: Chavkin and Williams 1988: Epstein and Dauber 1991). Teachers are more likely to forge partnerships with parents if they see families as important resources of support and when they welcome and involve caregivers as equal partners (Shick 1997; Hoover-Dempsey and Sandler 1997). Yet, teachers' perceptions of parents and parent involvement, shaped by culture, history, and schooling practices, can inhibit these home-school linkages. By describing the educational climate that influences teacher-parent partnerships, we wish to help teachers critically examine their ways of perceiving parents and parent involvement so they can navigate past conditions that have limited these collaborations. We see teachers and administrators as the principal reformers in making parent-teacher partnerships possible.

Evidence Supporting Parent-Teacher Collaboration

Research clearly indicates that student achievement is maximized through parent involvement. Henderson (1988) reviewed forty-nine studies of parent involvement programs and reported numerous benefits, including "higher grades and test scores, long-term academic achievement, positive attitudes and behavior, more successful programs, and more effective schools" (60). Chavkin and Williams (1988) extended this description of the Henderson study to include "an increase in student attendance, a reduction in dropouts, an improvement of student motivation and

Althier Lazar is an assistant professor of education, and Frances Slostad is an assistant professor of education and coordinator of the Graduate program in Elementary Education, both at West Chester University, West Chester, Pennsylvania.

self-esteem and more parent and community support for schools" (87).

Children's academic success depends on the degree to which teachers understand and accept the divergent cultures of the communities they serve (Delpit 1995; Chisholm 1994; Ladson-Billings 1994; Heath 1983). The number of school-aged minority children is expected to increase by more than 30 percent by the year 2000 (Chisholm 1994). Several studies have found that collaboration with the caregivers from nonmainstream cultures helps teachers gain the cultural competence they need to enhance student motivation and achievement (Ladson-Billings 1995; Delpit 1995; Shockley 1994; Cairney and Munsie 1995). Delpit, for instance, urges Anglo teachers to invite parents and community spokespeople to come to school to share stories of home and community life so the teachers will be better prepared to teach "other people's children."

So important are parents in the fabric of educational support that both state and federal agencies are now calling for greater collaboration between parents and teachers. The Goals 2000: Educate America Act specifically states, "Every school will promote partnerships that will increase parental involvement and participation in promoting the social, emotional, and academic growth of children" (U.S. Department of Education 1994). In addition. teacher accreditation agencies now require teachers to meet these federal standards. The NCATE standards state that "beginning teachers must be able to collaborate with parents and agencies in the larger community for supporting student learning and well being" (Morris et al. 1995). Although these findings clearly indicate a growing movement toward parent-teacher collaboration, real application is complicated by a range of factors.

Obstacles to Parent-Teacher Collaboration

Socio-Historical Factors

Can you remember back to your first day of school? Even though your parents were primarily responsible for your early language and learning experiences, your caregiver ceased to be your primary teacher once you entered first grade, and the distinction between parenting and teaching increased as you grew older. By the time you entered high school, your parents and teachers assumed very different roles in your life. Their relative statuses also differed. Hierarchical relationships, with teachers often dominating over parents, have been so much a part of our culture they are almost never questioned (Burke 1985).

Maybe you hear teachers complain about how parents do not help their children with homework. You might also hear parents accuse teachers of being too lazy, expecting too much, or being too lenient. According to Mary Henry (1996), parents and teachers today engage in frequent "we-they" battles: "Educators argue that there has been a decline in parenting in today's society and parents blame schools for increasingly neglecting their primary purpose—to teach" (45-46).

Adversarial relationships between teachers and parents are rooted in the earliest days of our schooling culture. Since America's colonial period, educators have blamed parents for their seeming inability to support children's intellectual, social, and moral development. For example, laws passed in Puritan America suggest that the establishment did not fully trust parents to educate their own children (Tyack 1967). If parents neglected their duties to raise moral and literate children, the state could take these "delinquent" youngsters away from their parents. In the common schools of the early 1800s, teachers warned immigrant children not to emulate the language and customs of their parents, a practice that divided home and school. "When children entered the doors of the public school, they passed into a world unfamiliar to their elders, one that seemed to teach them to scorn inherited traditions" (230). During the industrial revolution, schooling practices stressed uniformity and discipline partly because of what educators considered to be a "lack of 'family-nurture' and the weakening moral influence of both the nuclear and extended family" (317).

One hundred years later, we continue to blame parents, especially those from low-income and minority backgrounds, for the academic failures of children. How often do you hear teachers complain, "Kids are failing in school because *those* parents never read to them!" Underlying such comments is the assumption that poor and minority parents do not care about supporting their children's academic progress. Many teachers tend to believe that parents in those communities neither value education highly nor provide their children with the intellectual and motivational prerequisites for learning in school (Ascher 1988). This assumption is narrow and largely inaccurate. Parents, by and large, care very much about the educational needs of their children. Then why do these negative perceptions of parents and parent involvement persist? One reason is that that our schools of education have not adequately educated teachers to understand parents and to network with them. Another reason is that district policies and traditions of schooling limit teachers' access to parents.

The Failure of Teacher Education

Teachers' fears and apprehensions about parent involvement stem from a fundamental flaw in teacher education. Teachers have not been provided with adequate educational support to invite and maintain partnerships with parents. A review of the teacher education literature reveals that very little attention is given to preparing teachers to work with parents and other adults (Foster and Loven 1992; Midkiff and Lawler-Prince 1992). Fero and Bush (1994) concluded that "perhaps there is no other factor for which most new teachers are less prepared" (8), and furthermore, Swap (1993) reports, "Teachers, parents, and administrators have generally received limited information about how to work together effectively. Information about creating effective parent involvement programs is rarely incorporated in pre-service preparation programs" (26). More recently, Epstein (1995) noted that "most educators enter schools without an understanding of family background, concepts of caring, or the framework of partnerships . . . most teachers and administrators are not prepared to understand, design, implement, and evaluate practices of partnerships with the families of their students" (21).

Given the lack of attention to this area in both undergraduate and graduate education, teachers cannot help but feel uneasy about parents and unprepared to invite parent collaboration. Teacher educators must consider revamping the curriculum to include parental involvement projects as part of field experiences. For those already teaching, professional development is urgently needed.

School Culture Systems That Divide Home and School

Even when teachers work to develop insight into the way parents approach involvement, however, school systems generally do not reward teachers for those efforts and, in fact, have traditionally distanced parents and teachers (Burke 1985; Henry 1996). When was the last time your school district administrator encouraged you and members of your faculty to take a university course on parent involvement? Can you even imagine a system that awards you incentive pay for your exemplary work with parents? In the current educational climate, these ideas seem absurd.

The organizational nature of schools and the levels of support from school districts to reward teachers' efforts in home-school networking are often restrictive. Some teachers believe they do not have the authority to work with parents collaboratively unless given permission to do so by the central office and school board. In addition, some school districts perpetuate the divide between home and school by excluding parents from most forms of education decision making (Henry 1996). The parent-teacher conference, for example, dictated by schools and held on school turf, is especially intimidating for low-income or minority parents. Parents have little say in arranging for alternative ways of communicating with teachers. Furthermore, parents are rarely asked to participate in decisions about curriculum and instruction, evaluation, or hiring, school-controlled decisions that are generally based on the needs of the greater, majority culture (Henry 1996).

Issues for Teachers of Older Children

The belief that parent involvement is an "elementary school thing" is pervasive in our schooling culture. Unlike elementary teachers, many secondary teachers do not view parent involvement and parent-teacher communication as critical to students' academic success (Broderick and Mastrilli 1997). Teachers often interpret students' increasing need for autonomy as a sign that students do not need or desire parent-teacher collaboration as a form of

Teachers who regularly partner with parents believe these partnerships actually reduce the stress of teaching.

support (Eccles and Harold 1993). However, teens are better served when parents and teachers work together to support them—without compromising students' need for autonomy (Dauber and Epstein 1993).

The size and bureaucratic nature of schooling at the secondary level also limit teachers' access to students and, consequently, their parents. For example, many middle school and high school teachers teach twenty-five to thirty different students each class period, so they could conceivably teach over one hundred different students per day. These teachers are less likely to see the feasibility of getting to know their students and their students' parents than are elementary school teachers who serve only one class of students for the entire day. Also, the complexity of the secondary-level curriculum, the fragmented day, and the added extracurricular choices make it difficult to connect with students and their families.

A decline in parent involvement is also influenced by the high level of academic work required at the secondary level and by parents' uncertainties about their ability to help their children academically (Chavkin and Williams 1993; Dauber and Epstein 1993; Scott-Jones 1987). Actually, adolescents are particularly vulnerable to stresses associated with middle and high school and are in most need of support from both parents and teachers at that time (Hoover-Dempsey and Sandler 1997).

Research finds that parents are a valuable resource to aid teachers in determining effective interventions for teens who may need help to achieve (Jackson and Cooper 1992). Dauber and Epstein (1993) report that parents of middle school students who were doing better academi-

cally indicated more school-related contact with teachers than parents of children who were doing less well.

The Need for Systemic Change

Overcoming Assumptions about Parents

So far, we have examined some of the factors that limit parent-teacher partnerships. We believe teachers can overcome obstacles by understanding parents and the possibilities of parent involvement and by agitating for systemic change in the ways that schools involve parents. First, knowing about the perceptions and motivations of parents helps teachers recognize that the assumption of parental lack of interest is misplaced. For example, parents in low-income communities vary considerably in their beliefs about supporting their children's education. Some low-income parents do not see their role as including active school involvement and believe schooling is best left up to teachers (Lareau 1989), while others take a far more active role in the schooling process (Clark 1993; Segal 1985). Moreover, the ways parents view their roles is shaped by the circumstances and norms of particular cultures. Most African Americans, for example, tend to view education as the way to a better life and thus value academic achievement (Ritter, Mont-Reynaud, and Dornbusch 1993).

As we discussed earlier, parents' beliefs about their own effectiveness as teachers or tutors (their "sense of efficacy") is also a factor that shapes parent involvement, and this is especially true for parents of older children. Parents with a low sense of efficacy tend to avoid helping their children because they do not want to face their own inadequacies, or they assume that their involvement will not produce positive results (Bandura 1989). Efficacy is lowest for those who do not graduate from high school; differences between high school and college graduates were not found to be significant (Bandura 1989).

Teachers who understand the significance of role and efficacy in parent involvement are in a better position to invite parents to support their children's education (Hoover-Dempsey and Sandler 1997). Many parents feel they should or can support their children's development, but they simply do not know how to do so (Tharp and Gallimore 1988). Parents who fall into this category are teachers' most valuable, if untapped, resource.

Overcoming Assumptions about Parent Involvement

Our work with teacher interns and cooperating teachers suggests that parent outreach is often taken as a well-intentioned yet unreasonable extra chore. You might feel this way if you were a teacher who had to write daily lessons for several classes of students, assess the varied abilities of students, attend committee meetings, and chair student organizations. When and how are you supposed to partner with parents?

We find that teachers who regularly partner with parents believe these partnerships actually reduce the general level of stress associated with teaching. Teachers who send out brief, weekly newsletters to parents describing classroom and homework activities or grading procedures keep all parents and students "on the same page," averting confusion and cutting down the time spent explaining and defending practices and policies. Inviting parents to provide input on their child's performance through phone calls, written comments, or during conferences actually helps teachers to solve classroom conflicts and to examine teaching practices that best meet the needs of their students. Teachers who invite parent commentary are more likely to understand the social-situational context that shapes a student's performance in school (Lazar and Weisberg 1996).

Even if inviting parent input makes good practical sense, you might think that doing so will take away from your authority as a teacher. What if parents criticize your instructional methods, curriculum decisions, or classroom management techniques? You have worked hard to serve children through your pedagogical knowledge and mastering of your content area. You believe you should be in charge of your own classroom. Inviting parent involvement, however, does not mean that parents will walk all over you or take charge of your classroom. We find that teachers do not lose professional status and authority by inviting parent input; in fact, they gain it by relating well to parents, trusting parents, and using information from parents about their children. Of course, the possibility does exist that parents will in fact criticize your teaching decisions. We find, though, that most parents who take time to volunteer in the classroom are genuinely interested in helping the teacher and the students.

Some teachers fear they might not be able to handle conflicts with parents. For instance, you might not know how to interact with a parent who is angry or overbearing. You might think that avoiding contact altogether reduces the chance of having a confrontation with a parent. Actually, just the opposite is true. Avoiding parent contact increases the likelihood that miscommunication and conflict will occur. Think how confused parents would be if they did not have any sense of what was happening in a classroom where their child was failing, or how resentful they might be if the teacher never solicited their opinions or never listened to their views.

Conclusion

In the current education climate, many parents and teachers find themselves in separate worlds, often with parents maintaining a distinct "outsider" status. Given the factors that constrain parent-teacher collaboration, it can seem that forging relationships with parents is too difficult to do. Yet teachers cannot fully achieve their teaching goals without such help.

We believe that you can work toward changing those practices and policies that seem to limit parent-teacher collaboration. The first step is to inquire about the ways in which your school and district invite parent involvement. Are your attempts to attract parental support consistent with those of the larger school and district? What changes are needed to attract parent involvement on a school and district level? Are the practices and policies of schools systematically designed to keep caregivers at a distance? How can you lobby for professional development funding to improve your school district's parent involvement program?

You may not be able to solicit the support of all parents. But, until you actually communicate with parents, find out more about parents' views toward school involvement, and investigate how the school and the larger district can support your efforts to partner with parents, the possibilities for collaborating with parents will be limited. If you welcome parents as potential partners, and if parents assume a significant role in working with you, your students will have the best shot at succeeding in school.

REFERENCES

Ascher, C. 1988. Improving the school-home connection for poor and minority urban students. *Urban Review* 20:109–23.

Bandura, A. 1989. Regulation of cognitive processes through perceived self-efficacy. *Developmental Psychology* 25:729–35.

Broderick, P.C., and T. Mastrilli. 1997. Attitudes concerning parent involvement: Parent and teacher perspectives. *Pennsylvania Educational Leadership* 16:30–36.

Burke, C. 1985. Parenting, teaching, and learning as a collaborative venture. *Language Arts* 62:836–43.

Cairney, T. H., and L. Munsie. 1995. Parent participation in literacy learning. *Reading Teacher,* 48:392–403.

Chavkin, N. F., and D. L. Williams, Jr. 1988. Critical issues in teacher training for parent involvement. *Educational Horizons* 66:87–89.

——. 1993. Minority parents and the elementary school: Attitudes and practices. In *Families and schools in a pluralistic society,* edited by N. F. Chavkin, 73–84. Albany: State University of New York Press.

Chisholm, I. M, 1994. Preparing teachers for multicultural classrooms. *Journal of educational issues of language minority students* 14:43–67.

Clark, R. M. 1993. Homework-focused parenting practices that positively affect student achievement. In *Families and schools in a pluralistic society,* edited by N. E Chavkin, 85–106. Albany: State University of New York.

Dauber, S. L., and J. L. Epstein. 1993. Parents' attitudes and practices of involvement in inner-city elementary and middle schools. *In Families and schools in a pluralistic society.* edited by N. F. Chavkin, 53–71. Albany: State University of New York Press.

Delpit, L. 1995. *Other people's children.* New York: New Press.

Eccles, J. S., and R, D. Harold. 1993. Parent-school involvement during the early adolescent years. *Teachers College Record* 94:586–87.

——. 1994. Family involvement in children's and adolescents' schooling. Paper presented at the Family-School Links Conference, Pennsylvania State University.

Epstein J. L. 1995. School/families/community partnerships: Caring for children we share. *Phi Delta Kappan* 76:101–702.

——. 1997. *School, family, and community partnerships.* Newbury Park, Calif.: Sage.

Epstein, J. L., and S. L. Dauber. 1991. School programs and teacher practices of parent involvement in inner-city elementary and middle schools. *Elementary School Journal* 91:291–305.

Fero, F., and B. Bush. 1994. Beginning teacher perceptions of parent's role in an educational setting. Paper presented at the Annual Meeting of the Association of Teacher Educators.

Foster, J. E., and R. G. Loven. 1992. The need and directions for parent involvement in the 90's: Undergraduate perspectives and expectations. *Action in Teacher Education* 14:13–18.

Heath, S. B. 1983. *Ways with words: Language, life, and work in communities and classrooms.* New York: Cambridge University Press.

Henderson, A. 1988. Good news: An ecologically balanced approach to academic improvement. *Educational Horizons* 66:60–62.

Henderson, V. L., and C. S. Dweck. 1990. Motivation and achievement. In *At the threshold: The developing adolescent,* edited by S.S. Feldman and G. R. Elliott, 308–29. Cambridge, Mass.: Harvard University Press.

Henry, M. 1996. *Parent-school collaboration: Feminist organizational structures and school leadership.* Albany, N.Y.: State University of New York Press.

Hoover-Dempsey, K. V., and H. M. Sandler. 1997. Why do parents become involved in their children's education? *Review of Educational Research* 67 (1): 3–42.

Jackson, B., and B. Cooper. 1992. Involving parents in improving urban schools. *NASSP Bulletin* 76 (543): 30–38.

Jones, L. T., and J. Blendinger. 1994. New Beginnings: Preparing future teachers to work with diverse families. *Action in Teacher Education* 16:79–88.

Ladson-Billings, G. 1994. *The dreamkeepers: Successful teachers of African American children.* San Francisco: Jossey-Bass.

Lareau, A. 1989. *Home advantage: Social class and parental intervention in elementary education.* New York: Falmer Press.

Lazar. A., and R. Weisberg. 1996. Inviting parents' perspectives: Building home-school partnerships to support children who struggle with literacy. *Reading Teacher* 50:2–10.

Midkiff, R. B., and D. Lawler-Prince. 1992. Preparing tomorrow's teachers: Meeting the challenge of diverse family structures. *Action in Teacher Education* 14:1–5.

Morris, V., S., Taylor, J. Knight, and R. Wasson. 1995. Preparing preservice teachers to take leadership roles in parent involvement programs in schools. Paper presented at the 1995 annual meeting of the Association of Teacher Educators, Detroit, Michigan.

Ritter, P. L., R. Mont-Reynaud, and S. M. Dornbusch. 1993. Minority parents and their youth: Concern, encouragement, and support for school achievement. In *Families and schools in a pluralistic society,* edited by N. F. Chavkin, 107–20. Albany: State University of New York.

Scott-Jones, D. 1987. Black families and literacy. In *Advances in reading/language research: A research annual. Literacy through family, community, and school interaction,* edited by S. B. Silvern, 173–200. Greenwich, Conn.: JAI Press.

Segal, M. 1985. A study of maternal beliefs and values within the context of an intervention program. In *Parental belief systems: The psychological consequences for children,* edited by I. E. Sigel, 271–86. Hillsdale, N.J.: Erlbaum.

Shick, K. 1997. Involving families in the professional preparation of educators. *Clearing House* 70:265–268.

Shockley, B. 1994. Extending the literate community: Home-to-school and school-to-home. *Reading Teacher* 47:500–502.

Swap, S. 1993. *Developing home-school partnerships from concepts to practice.* New York: Teachers College Press.

Tharp, R. G., and R. Gallimore. 1988. *Rousing minds to life: Teaching, learning, and schooling in social context.* New York: Cambridge University Press.

Tyack, D. B. 1967. *Turning Points in American Educational History.* New York: John Wiley and Sons.

U. S. Department of Education, 1994. *Strong families, strong schools: Building community partnerships for learning.* Washington, D.C.: U.S. Department of Education.

Sizing it Right:

Class-Size Reduction and Student Achievement

by Nancy L. Waymack and Darrel W. Drury

As districts and states struggle to identify the most appropriate strategies for raising student achievement, class-size reduction (CSR) has emerged as an increasingly popular alternative. President Clinton has made CSR a major part of his education plan, proposing to spend more than $12 billion in the next seven years to help districts reduce class size.[1] In addition, several states have begun launching CSR programs of their own. Most of these initiatives have been embraced enthusiastically by the voting public, teachers, and parents alike, but despite the groundswell of support, questions remain concerning the details of such proposals. This Policy Research Brief draws heavily upon the latest round of research examining this important issue, much of it just recently published.[2] Collectively, these studies corroborate the success of CSR and offer insights into its underlying causal mechanisms, but point to the need for more focused, flexible approaches.

Evidence from the STAR Experiment

The strongest evidence for CSR to date is an experiment commissioned in the late 1980s by the Tennessee legislature, known as the Student-Teacher Achievement Ratio (STAR) study. In the STAR experiment, students and teachers in 79 Tennessee schools were randomly assigned to three types of classes:

1. small classes with 13–17 students;
2. regular classes with 22–25 students; or
3. regular classes with a full-time teacher's aide. The study continued for four years—kindergarten through third grade—and achievement data on both criterion- and norm-referenced tests were collected each year. Researchers reported significant test-score gains for students enrolled in smaller classes, across *all subject areas* and for *each year* of the experiment, but found no effect associated with the addition of a teacher's aide. The observed gains were most pronounced for minority and underprivileged students.[3]

A recent reanalysis of the STAR data, applying a more sophisticated statistical approach that addresses several design problems in the original study, supports these basic conclusions. However, the reanalysis also suggests that the main benefit of CSR manifests itself by the end of the first year of a child's exposure to small classes. Researchers have interpreted this as evidence that there is a one-time school socialization effect due to small classes that raises the level of a student's achievement in the first year, followed by smaller positive effects in subsequent years.[4]

> **R**esearchers reported significant test-score gains for students enrolled in the smaller classes, across all subject areas and for each year of the experiment...

Although the marginal impact of CSR on achievement seems to decline after a child's first year of exposure to small classes, recent studies demonstrate that the cumulative benefits of small classes are persistent. For example, the latest round of STAR research—which follows subjects through secondary school—has found that students originally assigned to small K–3 classes are more likely to have college aspirations, as evidenced by their higher rate of participation in college entrance examinations. Consistent with previous STAR findings, this difference is most pronounced for minority students and for those eligible for free or reduced-price lunch.[5] These latest analyses also suggest that, compared with their peers assigned to regular-size classes, students exposed to small K–3 classes complete more advanced coursework in secondary school, have lower dropout rates, are more likely to graduate on schedule, and are more likely to graduate in the top tenth of their classes.[6]

Additional Class-Size Research

Other recent studies lend further support to the STAR findings. Examining fourth- and eighth-graders' performance on the National Assessment of Educational Progress (NAEP), one investigation concludes that students in small classes—defined as fewer than 20 students—perform better than those assigned to regular-size classes, even after controlling for other factors that might influence test scores. According to the study, students assigned to smaller classes can expect to progress at a faster rate than those assigned to larger classes—33 percent and 12.5 percent faster for fourth- and eighth graders, respectively. Even more striking, fourth-graders assigned to smaller classes in inner-city schools can expect to progress 75 percent faster than their peers in larger classes.[7]

New findings from Wisconsin's Student Achievement Guarantee in Education (SAGE) program also attest to the effectiveness of class-size reduction. The SAGE program—which targets schools with 50 percent or more of their students in poverty—limits class sizes to 15 for grades K–3. A recently published study evaluates data from two years of the program's four-year phased implementation. (The program began in 1996 with kindergarten and has expanded each year to include additional grades.) According to the study, first-grade students in SAGE classrooms significantly outperformed their counterparts in other classrooms. While the advantage associated with smaller classes did not grow in second grade, neither did it decrease. Equally important, because the effect was strongest for African Americans, the black-white achievement gap narrowed in SAGE classrooms, while it widened in those classrooms unaffected by the program.[8]

Explaining the Effect

With mounting evidence of the effectiveness of smaller classes, researchers have begun to turn their attention to the underlying mechanisms that might account for the relationship between class size and academic gains. Analyses of the behavioral benefits associated with the STAR experiment revealed that students in small classes displayed more initiative, greater effort toward their schoolwork, and less disruptive and inattentive behavior in class, even *after* they had returned to normal-size classes in the fourth grade.[9]

Similarly, in the SAGE study, questionnaire and interview data have been analyzed to reveal any changes in teacher and student behavior occurring in response to class-size reduction. SAGE teachers report spending

Students in small classes displayed more initiative, greater effort toward their schoolwork, and less disruptive and inattentive behavior in class, even after they had returned to normal-size classes in the fourth grade.

more time on individualized instruction, doing more hands-on activities, and including more discussion in their teaching than they had previously. In interviews, teachers say that, as a result of smaller classes, they are able to gain a more intimate understanding of their students' personalities and better gauge their progress on specific tasks. They also report that they spend less time on discipline and that their students display more on-task, attentive, and involved behavior. Yet, while smaller classes seem to promote a more intimate learning environment and increase students' focus on learning, there is little evidence that teachers significantly alter their pedagogical approach.[10]

Research looking further into the behavioral effects of class-size reduction is limited, and most recent studies examine secondary, rather than elementary schools, where CSR policies traditionally have been targeted. Nonetheless, this research is useful in shedding light on how teachers and students change their behavior in smaller classes. A recently published account of the effects of class size on the teaching methods of high-school math teachers finds that those in smaller classes shift a modest amount of time from administrative and disciplinary duties to more individualized instruction and review.[11] Another high-school study suggests that class size may be more influential in determining the use of time among math teachers than among science teachers, that the impact of class size is less pronounced in classes with more than 20 students, and that the effects of CSR are stronger when coupled with more planning time for teachers.[12]

The Cost of Class-Size Reduction

Despite growing evidence of the advantages associated with class-size reduction, some question its cost-effectiveness.[13] To be sure, reducing class size on a large scale will require significant up-front expenditures. The costs fall into three major categories: (1) salaries for additional teachers; (2) the cost of building new or expanding existing facilities; and (3) operational costs, including the cost of classroom equipment and support staff. But if smaller classes result in less student retention, fewer children with special education needs, or early detection of learning disabilities, these costs may be offset by reductions in future expenditures. Unfortunately, such benefits are difficult to measure and lag far behind the initial investment.

The cost of hiring additional teachers is one of the most expensive elements of most class-size reduction proposals. In most districts, teachers' salaries vary with their qualifications and experience. If substantial numbers of teachers who have left the profession return to meet the new demand, the cost will be greater than if all new hires are recent graduates. But, even if the majority of teachers hired are newly certified, they will require additional professional development—adding to their initial cost—and as this cohort becomes more experienced, their salaries will increase, ensuring that the cost of CSR will grow with time.[14]

Each additional teacher will, of course, require a classroom in which to teach as well as the basic tools of the profession. Combined, the facilities and operational costs created under CSR have the potential of taxing the resources of even the most advantaged districts. Alternative scheduling systems—such as year-round schooling or block scheduling—may, however, lessen the blow somewhat.[15]

The details associated with different class-size reduction initiatives significantly alter the resources needed to achieve full implementation. A key factor influencing the cost of any such proposal is its starting point. For example, reducing first-grade class sizes to 18 would require substantially less funding in a state with a present limit of 20 students per class than in a state with a current limit of 24. The timing of CSR initiatives can have a large impact on costs as well. If the movement to reduce class size comes at a time when enrollment is down, the costs will obviously be lower than during a period of booming enrollment.[16]

The flexibility available in a policy also has a significant impact on its cost. Policies that mandate specific numeric caps for each grade level will significantly increase costs, as compared with policies that allow for averages across grade levels, schools, and districts. For example, a state that mandates an average maximum class size of 18 in grades K–3 will pay less for its CSR program than one that imposes an equivalent cap on each grade level individually. More rigid CSR policies also make the staffing needs of schools and districts more sensitive to fluctuations in enrollment.[17]

Finally, the cost of class-size reduction is highly dependent upon the population targeted. Most proposals under consideration by state legislatures across the country target specific populations, namely elementary-school children in grades K–3. Focusing CSR policies on inner-city or minority children—those for whom smaller classes seem to bring the most benefit—would significantly reduce the cost of such programs.

In combination, these factors can produce substantial variation in the costs associated with class-size reduction programs. One report estimates that a national proposal to reduce class size to 18 in first through third grades over the next decade could cost more than $6 billion per year. Adding flexibility to the proposal could reduce the cost to around $5 billion per year. Implementing the proposal on a targeted basis—i.e., only in schools in which over 50 percent of students are eligible for free or reduced-price lunch—would reduce the cost even further.[18]

It is important to realize that class-size reduction is just one of several approaches to increasing student achievement, not an end in itself. In allocating scarce resources, policymakers should always compare the costs and benefits of alternative reform strategies, and CSR is no exception. Yet, based on the evidence presented here, flexible, targeted, class-size reduction programs are likely to fare well in such comparisons. By targeting children in the early grades who are most likely to benefit from smaller classes—i.e., those enrolled in heavily minority or inner-city schools—states and districts can effectively boost academic performance and reduce the gap between advantaged and disadvantaged students.

About the Authors

Nancy L. Waymack, a former research analyst at NSBA, currently serves as budget analyst for the District of Columbia Public Schools. Darrel W. Drury is director of policy research at NSBA.

Endnotes

[1]Class-size reduction (1999). *http://www.ed.gov/offices/OESE/Class Size/.*

[2]Much of the research presented in this Policy Research Brief is based on articles published in the Summer 1999 issue of *Education Evaluation and Policy Analysis.*

[3]Finn, J. D., & Achilles, C. M. (1999). Tennessee's class-size study: Findings, implications, misconceptions. *Educational Evaluation and Policy Analysis. 21*(2).

[4]Kruger, A. B. (1998). Experimental estimates of education production function. Working paper #379. Cambridge, MA: National Bureau of Economic Research.

[5]Kruger, A. B., & Whitmore, D. M. (1999, April). The effect of attending a small class in the early grades on college attendance plans. Executive summary presented at STAR press conference, Washington, DC.

[6]Pate-Bain, H., Fulton, B. D., & Boyd-Zaharias, J. (1999, April). Effects of class-size reduction in the early grades (K–3) on high school performance: Preliminary results from project STAR. Tennessee's longitudinal class-size study. Summary presented at STAR press conference. Washington, DC.

[7]Wenglinsky, H. (1997). *When money matters: How educational expenditures improve student performance and how they don't.* Policy Information Perspective. Princeton, NJ: Policy Information Center, Educational Testing Service.

[8]Molnar, A., Smith, P., Zahorik, J., Palmer, A., Halbach, A., & Ehrle, K. (1999). Evaluating the SAGE program: A pilot program in targeted pupil-teacher reduction in Wisconsin. *Educational Evaluation and Policy Analysis, 21*(2).

[9]Finn & Achilles (1999).

[10]Molnar et al. (1999).

[11]Betts, J. R., & Shkolnik, J. L. (1999). The behavioral effects of variations in class size: The case of math teachers. *Educational Evaluation and Policy Analysis, 21*(2).

[12]Rice, J. K. (1999). The impact of class size on instructional strategies and the use of time in high-school mathematics and science courses. *Educational Evaluation and Policy Analysis, 21*(2).

[13]Hanushek, E. (1999). Some findings from an independent investigation of the Tennessee STAR experiment and from other investigations of class-size effects. *Educational Evaluation and Policy Analysis, 21*(2).

[14]Brewer, D. J., Krop, C., Gill, B. P., & Reichardt, R. (1999). Estimating the cost of national class-size reductions under different policy alternatives. *Educational Evaluation and Policy Analysis, 21*(2).

[15]McRobbie, J., Finn, J. D., & Harman, P. (1998, August). Class-size reduction: Lessons learned from experience. Policy Brief #23. WestEd. *http://www.wested.org/policy/ pubs/ full_text/pb_ft_csr23.htm.*

[16]Brewer et al. (1999).

[17]Brewer et al. (1999).

[18]Brewer et al. (1999).

TESTIMONIES
of Latin American Women
An Annotated Bibliography

by Marjorie Agosín

The works listed and annotated below explore the experiences of Latin American women active in the struggle for social justice in the late twentieth century. Most of the works are by Latin American women; several others are biographies or oral histories of women activists in Latin America or else critical studies of the testimonial genre.

Though autobiographical works constitute perhaps the most visible representation of testimonial literature, one may find testimonial works of fiction, poetry, drama, collective biography, and oral history. What all these works have in common is the act of bearing witness, of connecting the writer's personal struggles to the broader struggle for social justice in Latin America. These works detail lives of desperate poverty and the dreams of poor people for a better life for themselves and their community. The writers (and speakers, in the case of the biographies and oral histories) also describe their quest for economic, social, and political justice in the face of military repression, with its ever-present consequences of torture, disappearance, and death. Finally, these women talk of their struggles as a challenge to a traditional patriarchal culture.

Barrios de Chungara, Domitila and Viezzer, Moemar. *Let Me Speak! Testimony of Domitila, a Woman of the Bolivian Mines.* New York: Monthly Review Press, 1979.

One of the earliest testimonial works by a woman in Latin America in the twentieth century, this autobiography documents and bears witness to the life of Barrios, an organizer on behalf of the wives of the miners as well as the miners themselves. Her account of her struggle to improve conditions in the mines is an essential read in order to understand the grassroots activism of the poor, mostly indigenous, Bolivian peasants and laborers and the issues of gender, ethnicity, and class that influenced their struggle.

Fisher, Jo. *Mothers of the Disappeared.* Boston: South End Press, 1989.

This groundbreaking book is one of the earliest studies of the Mothers of the Disappeared in Argentina. Fisher has worked very closely with the Mothers, and it is clear that her knowledge is both theoretical and practical. The book represents oral testimonies by the Mothers as well as important observations about women's resistance movements in Latin America; Fisher places the Mothers' struggle within the context of Latin American popular struggles for human rights.

Gugelberg, George and Kearns, Michael. "Voices for the Voiceless: Testimonial Literature of Latin America." *Latin American Perspectives* 18:3 (Summer 1991): 3–14.

This issue of *Latin American Perspectives* presents essential articles that explore the theoretical aspects of the testimonial genre. Written mostly by academics, the articles are an important source of reference for further study.

Hooks, Margaret. *Guatemalan Women Speak.* Washington, D.C.: Epica, 1993.

This collection of testimonials includes the voices of Guatemalan women and their struggles. Hooks's work serves as an excellent companion to Jo Fisher's study of women activists in Argentina.

Jara, René and Vidal, Hernan. *Testimonio y literatura.* Monographic series of the Society for the Study of Contemporary Hispanic and Lusophone Revolutionary Literatures, No. 5.

From *MultiCultural Review*, March 1999, pp. 41-43. © 1999 by Greenwood Publishing Group, Inc., Westport, CT. Reproduced with permission.

Minneapolis, Minn.: Institute for the Study of Ideology and Literatures, 1982.

This is one of the first academic publications in the United States to explore the nature of testimonial writings, the theoretical issues surrounding first-person witnesses, and issues concerning those who serve as scribes to these witnesses. Several prominent academics in the field have contributed articles to this monograph, which is available only in Spanish.

Jesus, Carolina María de. *Child of the Dark: The Diary of Carolina María de Jesus.* New York: Mentor Books, 1962.

This is an important and powerful autobiography of Carolina María de Jesus's life in the *favela* (slum) of Sao Paulo. The testimony is written in the form of a diary, and the reader can engage with the struggles as well as the hopes of this woman living in absolute poverty. Yet her will to write and to create amidst a cruel existence reminds us of the tenacity of the human spirit.

Küppers, Gaby, ed. *Compañeras: Voices from the Latin American Women's Movement.* London: Latin American Bureau, 1994.

This is a valuable oral history collection that highlights the voices of women activists from diverse parts of Latin America and brings to light the different discussions involved in understanding the role of feminism in the region. There are important articles discussing the connection between women's rights and human rights as well as articles dealing with the political imagination of Latin American women.

Levine, Robert M. and Sebe, José Carlos, et al. *The Life and Death of Carolina María de Jesus.* Albuquerque: University of New Mexico Press, 1995.

This is an intriguing and thought-provoking biography that explores the beginnings of de Jesus's life as an activist and writer, her impact on the Brazilian media, and her eventual return to a life of destitution after a brief moment of success (a period she chronicles in her own testimonial *I'm Going to Have a Little House: The Second Diary of Carolina María de Jesus*). Levine and Sebe offer a poignant and provocative study that comments on the nature of race, class, and gender within Brazilian society.

Marin, Lynda. "Speaking Out Together: Testimonials of Latin American Women." *Latin American Perspectives* 18:3 (Summer 1991): 51–68.

This article explores the unique contributions of Latin American women past and present.

Mellibovsky, Matilde. *Circle of Love Over Death: Testimonies of the Mothers of the Plaza de Mayo.* Willimantic, Conn.: Curbstone Press, 1997.

Undoubtedly one of the most lyrical and powerful testimonials written about the Mothers of the Plaza de Mayo, Mellibovsky's work is from the point of view of the Mothers themselves. The author is one of the founding members of the movement, and she successfully combines the private and the

political in this memoir. The book contains vivid and haunting descriptions of the personal lives the women lead and the nature of their political participation.

Menchú, Rigoberta. *I, Rigoberta Menchú: An Indian Woman in Guatemala.* New York: Routledge, 1985.

In one of the classic works of Latin American testimonial literature, Menchú describes her coming of age amid the Guatemalan military's repression of her Quiché people. She details the murder of her father, mother, and brother for their pro-labor activities and her own political and personal struggles. She discusses how she had to learn Spanish, the oppressor's language and an alien language to her people, in order to raise global awareness of the plight of indigenous people in Guatemala.

Meyer, Doris. *Life on the Lines.* Berkeley: University of California Press, 1994.

Meyer offers an essential oral history anthology that presents the testimonies of Latin American writers, many of them women, their literary vocation, and the way they integrate literature and culture.

Partnoy, Alicia. *Tales of Disappearance and Survival in Argentina.* New Brunswick, N.J.: Rutgers University Press, 1986.

This is an important collection of fictionalized vignettes based on Partnoy's true experiences as a disappeared, and then "appeared," person in an Argentine concentration camp. The stories are powerful and vivid and give the reader a clear understanding of life in prison, human solidarity, and hope.

Patai, Daphne. *Brazilian Women Speak: Contemporary Life Stories.* New Brunswick, N.J.: Rutgers University Press, 1988.

Patai provides a very eclectic collection of women's oral histories from several sectors of Brazilian society. The oral histories are candid and fascinating to read. Patai also documents the ways in which these interviews were conducted and offers insights into the nature of testimonial works.

Poniatowska, Elena. *Massacre in Mexico.* Columbia: University of Missouri Press, 1991.

Poniatowska's oral history of the Mexican army's massacre of peaceful student demonstrators in 1968 is a classic of the genre. She chronicles this tragedy through interviews with student leaders, family members of victims, and witnesses to the shooting. Poniatowska is the author of several other important testimonial works, including *Until We Meet Again* (Pantheon, 1987), a novel based on the testimony of a woman from Mexico City's slums who endures both grinding poverty and domestic violence. After her abusive husband's death she comes to challenge the roles assigned to her because of her gender and social class.

Randall, Margaret. *Sandino's Daughters: Testimonies of Nicaraguan Women in Struggle.* London: Zed Press, 1982.

Randall provides one of the most important documents of Nicaraguan women who participated in the struggle against the Somoza dictatorship. She captures the voice of the women and engages the reader in their personal and political struggles.

Sepúlveda, Emma. *Testimonio y literatura.* Santiago, Chile: Editorial Ergo Sum, 1997.

This collection of essays published in Spanish explores the nature of testimonial literature in Latin America and analyzes recent works in the genre, with emphasis on works written by women.

Sklodowska, Elzsieta. *Testimonio hispanoamericano: Historia, teoría poética.* New York: Peter Lang, 1992.

Sklodowska offers a key study, published in Spanish, of the testimonial as a genre and its relevance to Latin American literature in general.

Stephens, Lynn. *Women and Social Movements in Latin America.* Austin: University of Texas Press, 1998.

This is an original comparative study that addresses crucial theoretical as well as practical issues about the nature of political activism, grassroots struggles, and collective identity.

Stephens describes the ways in which women have organized for human rights in the Americas, using stories of the women themselves.

Tierney, Leigh Nancy. *Robbed of Humanity: Lives of Guatemalan Street Children.* Philadelphia, Pa.: Pangaea, 1997.

This is one of the first books to document the lives of Guatemala's many street children. The book's originality lies in its ability to let the children speak for themselves. Tierney records the lives of the children through their own voices, in the form of poetry.

Wright, Ann. *Rigoberta Menchú: An Indian Woman in Guatemala.* London: Verso, 1984.

Along with Menchú's own autobiography, this is perhaps the best known book taught in North American colleges and universities that narrates the life of this Nobel Prize-winning organizer and activist. Wright narrates Menchú's life history from her birth to her becoming an activist. The biography is poignant and well written as it describes Menchú's struggle for justice for her family and her people.

The Issue of "Authenticity" in California Language Restoration

LEANNE HINTON
JOCELYN AHLERS
University of California at Berkeley

Two language revitalization programs in California are described here with a focus on how new words can be developed in a way authentic to a given language which reflects traditional values and thoughts. The importance of combining classroom approaches with community-based programs is also discussed.

In linguistic anthropology, the relationship between language on the one hand and cultural values and practices on the other is a central issue. This relationship is a major concern for communities attempting language restoration. Indigenous peoples the world over are involved in a growing effort to revitalize their languages. The reasons for this are multifaceted; but certainly the related notions of group identity and culture are among the most important. As put by Herriman and Burnaby, "Language, as much as anything, can capture the essence of group membership. If belonging to a group means sharing its culture, then language is a primary means by which the culture is articulated.... Language is therefore the principal medium for expressing civility, communality and shared values" (1996:10).

For many indigenous people, then, one important reason for linguistic revitalization is to get back to old values and customs. Yet we cannot say that the relationship between language and culture is deterministic or automatic. Language (like culture) is changeable, and if it is not abandoned in favor of

another language, it may still change to express new culture and new values. In the changed world in which native language activists find themselves, one can barely find anything to speak about that does not touch on modern culture. As Welsh speaker and teacher Gerald Morgan says,

> Technological change is wreaking havoc with minority languages as they get swamped with loan words and calques. Welsh slate quarrying, and coal mining, and traditional agriculture had huge vocabularies, most of which are in desuetude. Traditional diet is replaced by burgers and pasta! [And] there is great ignorance of the names of birds and wildflowers. [Personal communication, February 4, 1997]

Can use of the heritage language succeed in reflecting the traditional worldview in any way, or does it become a hollow shell, inside of which can be found nothing but the dominant culture?

When considering "authenticity," it is possible to focus either on linguistic form, such as pronunciation or grammar, or on the expression of traditional

values. We will demonstrate how language restoration activists in California have found ways to express traditional values and worldview even while allowing massive change of linguistic form and vocabulary.

Language Revitalization in the Classroom

For some endangered languages for which the educational system was once a tool of language destruction, it has now become a tool for language revitalization. Where one generation was punished for speaking the language in the schoolroom, another generation is given lessons in how to speak, read, and write the same language or even given all instruction in the language. In such places as New Zealand and Hawai'i, the same schools that assisted in the demise of a language have now created a new generation of young speakers.

Despite the wonderful successes in such places, the classroom alone is insufficient for the goals of language revitalization and can in fact be detrimental in certain ways. For one thing, the school system, regardless of what language is used, is still charged with teaching the subjects demanded by the dominant culture and educating children to become productive members of that culture. Furthermore, there is a culture of the classroom itself that differs fundamentally from any indigenous community's traditional culture of learning (Kramsch 1993). Communities with school-based language revitalization programs are aware of these problems and make strong efforts to ensure that traditional culture and values are given a place in the school, but the fact remains that the other culture and the other values are strongly present.

And along with this, the language itself, of necessity, changes drastically. Changes in the sound system, intonation, and grammatical structure occur as a result of mass bilingualism and language interference. The functional requirements on school language lead to new discourse genres (such as oral reports on books or particular scholastic topics), conversational styles (such as strict turn taking where, even with a large class of students, conversation is always directed at the teacher and a student who wants a turn must raise her or his hand and wait to be called on), and literary forms (such as written reports, short stories, or arithmetic problems). And there are massive changes in vocabulary to accommodate the need to discuss the subjects taught in school—science, math, and government, to name a few. A vast new vocabulary must be developed to accommodate standard educational topics. The new vocabulary can be so overwhelming that native-speaking elders may have difficulty understanding the speech of children in classroom immersion programs. As one Maori educator said, the elders complain, "Sure, we have a new generation of speakers—but all they talk about is English concepts!"...

Another consideration is what the functions of a language are. A language in full use has genres, conventions, styles, and registers for many different contexts—some for school, some for informal peer interaction, and others for family interaction, traditional storytelling, oratory, or commercial transactions. A language that is kept alive only in the schools is both stylistically and conceptually restricted.

Language revitalization in the schools is, all in all, a very limited sort of revitalization. As Fishman says, in

a discussion of revernacularization (the reestablishment of a language as the medium of informal daily communication in the home),

> Schools are normally programmed and not inter-generational, and mother-tongues are inter-generational and not programmed. You see, they have almost completely opposite constellations of forces.... We can organize for languages of school; we can organize for languages of church; we can organize for languages of government.... Yet none of the foregoing result in informal, inter-generational mother-tongue transmission. All those thousands of years that Hebrew was transmitted through formal institutions did not help it to become a mother-tongue.... Vernacularization is the opposite of institutionalization. [1996: 192–193; see also Fishman 1991 for further arguments on the claim that a successful revitalization program must go beyond school-based settings]

For many reasons, including the considerations above, combining classroom programs with broader-based community language revitalization programs is ideal. In community-based language learning, it is easier to incorporate traditional activities and traditional values (and traditional language!) into the learning situation. Although the development of new vocabulary and other sorts of changes are inevitable in these situations too, it is nevertheless easier for individuals to adhere to the traditions they value, being free from the institutional demands that are present in the school. Learning can take place in traditional locations, doing traditional activities. Furthermore, the community-based language programs can develop principles for vocabulary modernization based on traditional values. These principles can in turn have applicability in the classroom as well.

The California Situation

California has more indigenous languages than almost any other part of the world; some fifty different languages still have speakers (Hinton 1994). But there are at least thirty and maybe more that have no speakers left; and every one of the approximately fifty languages still spoken is in what Michael Krauss labels a "moribund" state (1992). No language endemic to California is being learned at home by children; most are spoken only by elders.

But as in much of the rest of the indigenous world, the peoples of California are aware of the problem and are working on it. For most of the endangered languages, and even for a large number of the languages with no speakers, there are tribal members who have taken it on themselves to learn the language and to develop teaching programs for their communities. Through written, audio, and video documentation, language curriculum development, after-school programs, family classes, language camps, and mentored learning, California Indians are fighting to keep their languages alive.

While immersion schools are a goal of a number of California tribes, they have not yet become a reality. The languages have too few speakers, the communities are too dispersed (often being landless), and the support systems in universities that are present in places like Hawai'i, New Zealand, Ireland, and Wales (where people can major in the language, and curriculum for schools can be developed) are missing in California because of its very linguistic diversity. Funding is a more difficult problem as well: whereas Hawai'i and New Zealand are willing to muster financial resources for their one indigenous tongues, how can fifty or more different languages representing very small constituencies ever hope to all have the clout to receive adequate funding?

But through the community programs, the number of professional-age speakers is increasing to the point where there is hope for immersion school development within the next few years. In the meantime, these community language programs have a number of advantages, especially their ability to tie the language to traditional activities and values.

We will discuss two intertribally based language revitalization programs here: the Master-Apprentice Language-Learning Program, founded by the Native California Network (NCN) and now administered by a committee of native Californians called the Advocates for Indigenous California Language Restoration (AICLS), and the California Native Language Restoration Workshop, a program developed at the University of California at Berkeley in summer 1996 for native Californians whose languages have no speakers. Hinton worked with NCN to develop both of these programs. Ahlers has assisted in training sessions for the master-apprentice program and in the summer workshop.

The Master-Apprentice Language-Learning Program

The master-apprentice program is a program of mentored learning for adults. Teams consisting of an older native speaker and a younger tribe member spend up to twenty hours per week together, living their daily lives together while speaking only their heritage language. The goal is proficiency for the younger adult, who was accepted into the program because of a demonstrated commitment to language teaching as well as learning. Training workshops for the master-apprentice program not only teach immersion techniques to the teams but also stress methods of expanding the learning situation within the community. The teaching and learning methodology is designed to be an orally based, informal approach that can be learned readily by people with no formal language-teaching background. The teams are taught how to utilize gesture, action, and context to meet their communication needs without resorting to English; the speakers are taught the fundamental importance of repetition; and the learners are taught how to elicit language from the speakers. The teams are shown how language can be transmitted through participation in daily activities, such as cooking and eating, washing clothes, or going on a drive, and traditional activities such as the gathering of wild plants, basketry, and ceremonials. Over the past four years, this program has trained close to fifty teams for over twenty different languages. The degree of learning varies from team to team, depending on personal traits (such as talent for language learning and degree of personal commitment to it) and circumstances (such as how close the team members live to each other and how many other time commitments they have). But it can be said with some satisfaction that a number of new learners are now quite fluent in the language of heritage. (A full explanation of the program can be found in Hinton 1997.)

The California Native Language Restoration Workshop

The "Breath of Life, Silent No More" California Native Language Restoration Workshop has been held annually since June 1996, each year introducing 20 California Indians representing 16 different languages to linguistic materials held in the Berkeley archives and teaching them linguistic fundamentals to help them learn how to find, pro-

nounce, and utilize useful words and phrases as the first step in language restoration. Here the techniques are of necessity completely different from those in the master-apprentice program, for there are no native speakers of the languages being studied. The program is oriented toward the use of archival written materials but focuses on teaching the participants how to pronounce the language material out loud and how to extract phrases that can be useful in daily conversation.

Anyone learning a language with no speakers and no pedagogical materials, and beginning the process of re-introducing that language to the community, must of course continue to speak English for most communication needs. However, useful phrases can be inserted into the stream of conversation as they are learned. The participants in the workshop learn greetings, and simple utterances like "yes" and "no," or command forms. When such materials can be found, they learn prayers, short stories, or songs. (A full description of this program can be found in Hinton 1996.)

Most of the participants in both the California programs dream of a day when their language, like Hebrew, or the promise of Hawaiian, Irish, and Maori, can be brought into use again as the mother tongue of their communities. However, the fulfillment of this dream, if it ever comes, is generations away. In the meantime, the languages will survive as second languages.

Language Change in the Revitalization Process

It is obvious that when the new generation of speakers begins their learning as adults, in a situation in which input is usually insufficient for complete learning, there will be important changes in the language. Like all language learners, the second-language learners of native California simplify their languages in various ways. Although continued learning will bring expanded mastery of many complexities of the languages, realistically we have to expect that many of the specialized constructions will be lost in transmission. Interference from English, their dominant language, also influences the adult learners' speech.

In a foreign language learning situation, a learner may always display errors and interference patterns and may never gain full command of the language. However, in foreign language learning, the language learner's mistakes will never have an impact on the

language as a whole because of the existence of native speakers elsewhere. In the situation of language revitalization in small speech communities, the new learners will one day be the sole bearers of the language, and therefore all of the patterns of simplification, interference, and incomplete learning that remain extant in the learners' speech will be a permanent part of that language.

Not all of the changes that occur in the restoration process involve simplification and interference. Some are consciously engineered changes involving lexical development. In any language being brought into modern usage, there have to be lexical changes so that speakers can discuss the full range of topics in their present-day world. Besides the loss of old vocabulary for customs and objects no longer in use, there has to be development of new vocabulary for the new situations of daily life that a living language must express. Although the need for new vocabulary is not as extreme as in the schools, it is nevertheless a common daily experience for the teams to try to express something for which a word does not already exist in the language. Here we can see one of the differences between the master-apprentice program of California and the statewide classroom-based approach in Hawai'i and New Zealand. In the California situation, words are being created one by one, through informal agreement between the master and apprentice. These usages can spread slowly through the community, but there is no authoritative body needed to regulate the process. This is a major difference from the classroom approach in the larger school systems of Hawai'i and New Zealand, where the creation of new vocabulary must be regulated in order to maintain homogeneity of the curricula across schools.

Attitudes toward Language Change

Just about all younger speakers of Native American languages everywhere have been criticized by elders for mistakes. There is a certain stage in language shift when this phenomenon actually hastens language decline, when young semispeakers decide not to speak the language any more because of the pain of criticism. While the elderly native speakers of California languages still show vestiges of this critical attitude, which itself comes from the pain of hearing their language misspoken, the state is in fact emerging out of this period. Most elders have not heard anyone speak their language for many years now and find themselves overjoyed to hear even a few words from the younger members of their communities. The master-apprentice program stresses patience and supportive, noncritical methods of correction of learners, and the elders have easily taken on these methods.

Many language learners in California are extremely willing to use the language as much as possible, even when it means imperfect usage. Karuk apprentice Terry Supahan puts it this way: "I am interested in communication, not preservation." He means that he wants to use his language and hear it used by others, even if it is mispronounced and grammatically impoverished. One of the participants in the first language restoration workshop, Cody Pata (Nomlaki), went so far as to compose a speech in what he called "Pidgin Nomlaki," inserting the Nomlaki vocabulary he had learned into an English grammatical frame, including the use of English suffixes on Nomlaki roots. (Pata had lived in Hawai'i for a number of years and had become quite proficient in both Hawaiian and Hawaiian Creole English, locally called Pidgin. The latter was his inspiration for Pidgin Nomlaki.) Pata's speech provides an example of the ways in which the definition of "authenticity" is less rigid in the minds of language activists in cases in which the language being revitalized is so close to death. In such an instance, the focus of speakers is on using the language whenever and however possible rather than on the correctness of the usage.

Traditional Values and Worldview as Linguistic Authenticity

Despite this extreme (perhaps, to some, even shocking) willingness on the part of California Indian second-language learners to sacrifice authenticity of linguistic form, there are certain ways in which they have a conservative attitude. Most learners emphasize that the main motivation for language learning, for them, is the retention or regaining of traditional values and worldview (although most language learners do not fully understand, any better than the rest of us, where in language those values are located.)

Because of this attitude, it behooves those of us who consult with minority groups on language learning methods

to think deeply about how learners can incorporate worldview and value systems into the learning process. The obvious and much used way to do this is to combine language learning with cultural experience. This is certainly being done by most of the language learners we know. They combine language learning with traditional ceremonials, song, prayer, basketry, food gathering, and many other traditional practices. The vocabulary and discourse practices that go along with these activities are areas in which tradition is embedded in language.

Of course, culture itself is no more static than language, and present cultural practices have changed greatly from what they once were. Culture is also more than an enumerated set of ceremonials and practices; it is also daily life. Separating out those aspects of daily life that are "native" from those aspects of daily life that are practiced by the same people but are not "native" is perhaps an impossible task. But while schools often try to separate the native from the nonnative practices, with much input from education professionals who may not themselves be native to the community, the California programs leave such judgments up to the participants themselves. So too must the values themselves be found (consciously or unconsciously) by the participants, not the program designers.

Going back to the issue of modernization, another way in which learners demand authenticity is in the manner of the development of new vocabulary. New vocabulary comes to a language either through borrowing or through processes of word formation. Every language has ways to form new words, through such familiar processes as compounding and descriptive-phrase formation. Authenticity can be maintained in vocabulary development through the analysis and teaching of traditional processes of word formation.

Metaphor and Metonymy

As pointed out by Mojave apprentice Parris Butler, not just any compound or phrase will do for new vocabulary. Some new item, such as a computer, might be seen in a different light by a traditional elder than it would by some young apprentice thoroughly steeped in Western culture. It is how the elder might see new items that learners would like to incorporate into new vocabulary. Within each language, the creation of new words must take into account two processes—formal and cognitive. By formal, we mean the process by which parts

of words are put together to form whole words. By cognitive, we mean the thought processes behind the naming of an item. So by following the example of established processes of word formation, both formal and cognitive, it is possible to maintain traditional worldviews in the creation of new words. Speakers of Hupa, an Athapaskan language spoken in northern California, have done this, as we will show.

Hupa provides a good example of the use of these kinds of processes for several reasons. Like most Athapaskan languages, it has, throughout its history and for a variety of social reasons, developed a great number of new words. This means that there is a large amount of data to be studied in analyzing the processes by which new words were traditionally created. Hupa is also (again, like most Athapaskan languages) very resistant to borrowings, which means that speakers have looked to other ways of creating new words in modern language use.

In studying older words to discover the kinds of processes used in their creation, we have found several cognitive strategies. The most frequent of these is metonymy, whereby a salient feature is used to stand for the entire object. This process is also used in English, in sentences such as "The White House issued a statement today," in which the White House is used as a salient symbol of the presidency to stand for the president. Hupa tends to use a particular type of metonymy that Ahlers has named "associated action frame (AAF) metonymy" (1996). Using this type of metonymy, Hupa speakers associated an object with an action that was typically performed with that object. This allowed them to name the object with the word for the action. This fits in well with the formal process used to create words in Hupa, which is typically to use a third-person present verb form. So by focusing on a salient action, the verb form can be used to name the associated noun. The following are some examples of this:[1]

dahch'iwile:l	"arrows" (literally "he holds them up")
k'iwinya'n	"acorn" (lit. "what someone eats")
t'anq'-ts'isday	"acorn camp" (lit. "in the fall—she stays there")
xatL'e'-na:mat'	"bat" (lit."at night—it flaps around")

In each case, an action that is performed with the object, or that the object prototypically performs (as with the bat), is used to name that object.

Hupa speakers continue to use this process in the creation of words for modern items. They follow not only the conventional formal structure (third-person singular verb forms) but the cognitive structure (AAF metonymy) as well:

'miq'it-k'iwiLiw	"butter" (lit. "on top—it is smeared")
mitah-'a:iL'e:n	"baking powder" (lit. "amongst it—someone scatters it")
miL xosah' no:l na: ng'	"candy" (lit. "with mouth it makes it taste good")
me' si-liq'	"pie" (lit. "into it is flopped")

In these cases, new vocabulary items have been created using standard cognitive processes. This can be taken one step further in cases when not only is a typical cognitive process used to name something but traditional items are invoked in the name. For example, new foods can be named in comparison to a traditional food:

ne:de'tl-nehwa:n	"beans" (lit. "like pine nuts")
k'iqade'-nehwa:n	"carrot" (lit. "a willow root it resembles")

One of the master-apprentice teams evoked this principle in a word they developed themselves for "spaghetti": te' qi.wil q'ots' qi-ye: jo:-ne: wha:n, literally "in the water it is dunked, looks like eel strings." The traditional food, eel tendons, looks like spaghetti when fried. Similarly, traditional games can be evoked to name new games. The word for playing cards is yiman'dil-mikine, literally "white people—their sticks," using the traditional stick game to name the new item.

The metaphor system of a language can also be studied, both to gain a greater understanding of traditional worldview and to find ways of expressing new ideas. By metaphor, we mean a cognitive process whereby one (typically abstract) domain is understood in terms of another (typically concrete) domain (Lakoff 1987, 1993; Lakoff and Johnson 1980). This process is common to all languages and reflects a general human cognitive trait. For example, Hupa uses the

metaphor "life is a journey," which can be found in many languages, including English. In this metaphor, life (the abstract domain) is conceptualized as a journey across a landscape. On this landscape, objects are understood to be events in a person's life. However, the actual expression of the metaphor is different in Hupa than in English. In the case of Hupa, life is a journey that is made on foot. Therefore, Hupa has expressions such as minejit na'asiya, meaning "middle aged, middle of his life," literally "center his walking." This metaphor is related to the metaphor "marriage is a journey," which created the following: nayaseL, meaning "[they are] walking together" or "they're married" (lit. "the middle of his trip"). This metaphor could therefore be exploited in the creation of words for "divorce," for example. In general, novel extensions of metaphors such as the above could be used to express new ideas.

Lessons for the Classroom

Compared to school immersion programs, with their immediate and constant need for new vocabulary to translate, for example, math curriculum or biology textbooks in a timely manner, the demand for new words in language learning situations outside the classroom is relatively gentle. But the very way in which vocabulary development is approached in these situations can provide lessons for the educational system as well. It is possible to reconcile the desire to create new vocabulary and to modernize a language with the desire to retain the expression of traditional worldviews. Through careful study of the metonymic and metaphorical systems of a language, language activists can gain an understanding of the ways in which new words can be created that invoke the traditions of language speakers. In using accepted formal structures and conventional cognitive processes, and in referring to traditional objects and actions, it is possible to modernize a language while still retaining that which makes the language an expression of the culture that uses it.

In sum, although the school is a very effective institution for teaching a language when it has ceased to be the mother tongue of a community, it nevertheless has limitations by its very nature as an institution. As Fishman (1996) points out, the school alone can never achieve the regaining of

mother tongue status for a language. Nor can the school teach all the topics, styles, and registers that socially complete language makes use of. A community that is really serious about language revitalization must not leave the battle to the schools but must develop programs for the home and community. This article has been about programs stationed entirely in the community, which so far have only an indirect and tenuous relationship to schools. The ideal, and the aim of the California programs, is a multifaceted effort involving schools as well as other community venues.

Even if the school is an inherently limited institution with built-in structures that restrict its capacity for full language revitalization, the community programs themselves can provide some inspiration for classroom goals and methods. The statement above about vocabulary development is one case in point. But beyond that, school personnel must (and often do) think about the values that a community wants to transmit to its children and at the same time must realize that these values may not be fully understood by school staff or even be fully articulable by community members. Values are transmitted through the actions of social living. School itself, taking up so much of a child's day, removes the child from the family and community aspects of education that transmit those values. The better school programs invite community members into the classroom to teach aspects of traditional culture, but these guests are as restricted by the school environment as the students and teachers are. Very little of the traditional culture and value system can be taught in the school away from the environment where traditional activities normally take place. For example, a student may be taught to make a basket in the schoolroom and how to utter the vocabulary associated with basket making but may not learn when, where, and how to gather the materials, how to respect and pray over the plants that give the materials, and how to care for and harvest the plants so that they will give new shoots next year. An apprentice learning basketry as part of the master-apprentice program can learn all these things, for the student's learning does not take place in a classroom but, rather, takes place wherever the student and teacher go, whatever they do.

All this suggests that an important goal for the school committed to teaching values along with language is to get children out of the classroom and into the community as part of their schooling, so they have the opportunity to converse with native speakers about the things native speakers usually talk about and to do what they do, rather than the things schools talk about and do.

Leanne Hinton is a professor of linguistics at the University of California at Berkeley. **Jocelyn Ahlers** is a doctoral candidate in linguistics at the University of California at Berkeley.

Notes

1. The Hupa examples are written in the official Hupa writing system. A full explanation of the writing system can be found in Golla 1996.

References Cited

Ahlers, Jocelyn, 1996, Metonymy and the Creation of New Words in Hupa. *In* The Proceedings of the 1996 Meeting of the Berkeley Linguistics Society, vol. XXII.

Fishman, Joshua, 1991, Reversing Language Shift: Theoretical and Empirical Foundations of Assistance to Threatened Languages. Clevedon, UK: Multilingual Matters.

——1996, Maintaining Languages: What Works? What Doesn't? *In* Stabilizing Indigenous Languages. Gina Cantoni, ed. Pp. 186–198. Flagstaff: Northern Arizona University Press.

Golla, Victor, 1996, Hupa Language Dictionary. 2nd edition. Hoopa, CA: Hoopa Valley Tribal Council.

Herriman, Michael, and Barbara Burnaby, eds. 1996, Language Policies in English-Dominant Countries. Philadelphia: Multilingual Matters, Ltd.

Hinton, Leanne, 1994, Flutes of Fire: Essays on California Indian Languages. Berkeley, CA: Heyday Books.

——1996, "Breath of Life—Silent No More": The Native California Language Restoration Workshop. News from Native California 10(1): 13–16.

——1997, Survival of Endangered Languages: The California Master-Apprentice Program. International Journal of the Sociology of Language 123: 177–191.

Kramsch, Claire, 1993, Context and Culture in Language Teaching. Oxford: Oxford University Press.

Krauss, Michael, 1992, The World's Languages in Crisis. Language 68(1): 4–10.

Lakoff, George, 1987, Women, Fire, and Dangerous Things. Chicago: University of Chicago Press.

——1993, The Contemporary Theory of Metaphor. *In* Metaphor and Thought, 2nd edition. Andrew Ortony, ed. Pp. 202–251. Cambridge: Cambridge University Press.

Lakoff, George, and Mark Johnson 1980, Metaphors We Live By. Chicago: University of Chicago Press.

Dissin' "the Standard": Ebonics as Guerrilla Warfare at Capital High

SIGNITHIA FORDHAM

University of Maryland, Baltimore County

This article analyzes the discourse styles, including the linguistic practices, of a group of African American high school students and offers a twofold conclusion: (1) Ebonics or Black English is the norm against which all other speech practices are evaluated by the students at the research site and (2) "the standard"—that is, the standard English dialect—is constructed as a vernacular. As a vernacular, this discourse is not privileged; indeed, it is "dissed" (disrespected) and is only "leased" by the students on a daily basis from nine to three. This linguistic practice is centrally implicated in the postulated guerrilla warfare at the school. With data from a predominantly African American high school in Washington, D.C., the effects of this practice on African American academic achievement are documented. Several policy implications are also noted.

Black people [talk to] each other, like, as if they were enemies. And you know, you can be good friends [with another Black person], but you [talk to] them like an enemy. Well, another person [a non-Black person] would consider it as treating them as an enemy, but we call it friendship. Like we tease each other, and hit on each other, and talk about each other all the time—that's considered friendship. And that's what [the dominant society] call[s] abnormal. But that's the way most Black people I know who are friends *are*. They say, if you can talk about their mother and get away with it, you *must* be their friend. . . .

Norris, February 18, 1983[1]

They do it in the classrooms, they do it in the hallways, they do it when talking to teachers, they even do it in English classes. What they do every day at Capital High is use Ebonics. Ebonics, also known as Black English, Black Dialect, and African American Vernacular English (AAVE), "is Euro-American speech with an Afro-American meaning, nuance, tone, and gesture [reflecting] the conditions of [Black] servitude, oppression and life in America" (Smitherman 1977:2, see also Lippi-Green 1997). Further, according to Smitherman, it is spoken by "80 percent of American Blacks, at least some of the time" (1977:2). For example, Korey insisted, "I don't do no book reports" (Fordham 1996:300). However, limiting one's analysis or interpretation for the above statement to a comparison of how it parallels or deviates from the usage approved in the standard dialect captures only a small portion of what is central to the analysis offered here. Moreover, because Ebonics, like all natural speech varieties, is systematic and rule governed (Dillard 1972; Linguistic Society of America 1997; Smitherman 1969; Wolfram 1969), understanding the rules is critical but insufficient.

Not all Capital students communicate in Ebonics. A few of Capital's students use the standard dialect most of the time. However, they are the exceptions rather than the rule. Most students at the school resist the requirement that they learn to speak and communicate in "the standard" English dialect, especially in the school context. Their resistance to this state-approved curriculum requirement is their way of "dissin'" or disrespecting this dialect.[2] Thus, dissin' the standard is at the core of the guerrilla warfare at the school and is fundamentally revealed in both the students' refusal to discontinue their use of Ebonics as the language of communication while at or in school and their wholesale avoidance of the standard dialect in most other contexts.

My analysis of how students managed and maintained these competing discourses had its genesis in a conversation with Rita, one of the high-achieving females in my research group, when I asked her to talk about her recent Pre-Scholastic Achievement Test (PSAT) scores (she received the highest verbal score in the school—96 percent—and she scored at the 75th percentile on the math component). I vividly recall the jolt I experienced when she used the Ebonics speech variety to tell me about her performance on the exam. Her use of Ebonics was unexpected, pronounced, and severely exaggerated, compelling me—her listener—to revisit the dialect usage recorded in poems written by such authors as Paul Lawrence Dunbar and Langston Hughes and the narratives of enslaved people as represented in John Blassingame's 1979 *The Slave Community*.

Rita's response had an enormous impact on my perceptions of contemporary African

American students' academic performance and how their discourse style (not just their linguistic practices) is a marker of a Black identity. Rita had never used the linguistic component (see below) of the Ebonics register in our previous verbal exchanges. Indeed, she, more than most of the other students, often talked disparagingly about how her peers frequently equated high academic performance with "acting White" (Fordham 1996; Fordham and Ogbu 1986). The linguistic component of varied Black discourse styles is not often used in direct conversations with school officials who are identified as professionals—especially if the adults are not well known. I met these criteria. Hence, I was astounded and, frankly, flabbergasted when she used the Ebonics register to talk with me—an official adult stranger—in this manner.[3]

Time away from the research site has helped me to understand this violation and to offer an empirically grounded explanation. Initially, I did not (could not) believe Rita's response was engendered by a fear of the loss of her Black identity. Nevertheless, the persistence of the practice was compelling: from that day on, every time I mentioned her PSAT scores, grade point average, and so on, she responded by reverting to the exaggerated dialect practices noted above. Rita did not limit this response pattern to me. I watched her respond to Ms. Yanmon, her counselor, and other adults in a similar way when they mentioned her PSAT performance or any of the other markets of her academic distinction. Rita's discourse "parody" was instructive in that it compelled me to a greater understanding of how Ebonics is the anchor in the maintenance of guerrilla warfare at Capital High.

Rita's response pattern was atypical. Most students at Capital used the standard dialect in the presence of school officials who were categorized as strangers, and they continuously lapsed into the Black discourse style in other contexts. For example, Ms. Apropos, an English teacher and one of the school's strongest proponents of the consistent use of the standard dialect, was constantly thwarted by her students' apparent failure to either learn or practice the rules of the standard. This was the dominant response even immediately following her carefully choreographed lessons discussing specific grammatical rules and principles. Capital students' general refusal to demonstrate mastery of the recently studied principles produced much angst and teacher frustration. Indeed, Ms. Apropos was in a constant emotional struggle with her students, uncertain about the value and impact of her standard dialect lessons. While her students were carefully taught and were able to demonstrate on exams and other measures their mastery of the rules, they chose to appear not to know them in their conversations with each other.

Moreover, because the annually required course in English was the most visible target of the guerrilla warfare at the school—in part because it is the only course required of every student, every year, in the District of Columbia Public School System—Holt's 1972 notion of *inversion* in Black American discourse practices is applicable here: "Words and phrases were given reverse meanings and functions changed.... The purpose of the game was *to appear to but not to*" (1972:154, emphasis added).[4] While most Capital students also sought to avoid other components of the curriculum—including social studies and the mathematics curricula beyond the introductory level (trigonometry, calculus, unified math, etc.)—it was the obligatory English curriculum that was particularly bothersome, not because of a perceived difficulty beyond that of other subjects but because of the minefield of conflicts it engendered among the students at the school.[5]

As the above examples suggest, this inquiry deviates from traditional linguistic analyses (see, for example, Baratz and Baratz 1970; Dillard 1972; Labov 1972; Rickford 1992; Stewart 1970) in that not only is it much broader in scope, but it is also not limited to the actual act of speaking. Therefore, it is less preoccupied with the way Black speakers conjugate the verb "to be," whether they say "dis" for "this," "dat" for "that," or "ax" for "ask." Following Gee's notion of discourses, this analysis includes the students' "ways of behaving, interacting, valuing, thinking, believing, speaking, and often reading and writing" (1990:xix). Not surprisingly, then, in this conceptualization, the reader is compelled not only to consider Korey's words—"I don't do no book reports"—for example, but, in addition, to include these other issues in the analysis of what he is conveying through the use of language.

This analysis proceeds as follows: I begin by outlining a conceptual frame for how Capital students' commitment to a Black identity is centrally embedded in their linguistic repertoire, compelling them to "diss" "the standard" dialect by only leasing rather than internalizing it from nine to three. Following the work of theorists who are beginning to reframe the discourse practices of African Americans as weapons in the war of the weak (see Scott 1985) rather than deficiencies (Delpit 1988, 1995; Dyson 1995; Foster 1989, 1990; Gates 1994; Gee 1990, 1992; Holt 1972; Scott 1985), I assert that, at Capital High, students wrestle with two strains of an embodied discourse style: Ebonics as "rhetorical resistance" (Dyson 1995) in the latent, yet ongoing, subversive war of Black identity maintenance. Following that, I present several case studies of Capital students' discourse practices in order to empirically document how both the high- and the underachieving students' use of the standard as a leased or rented discourse is variously manifested at Capital High. The conclusion offers several policy implications.

The Conceptual Frame: Dissin' the Standard

Language is a, or perhaps *the*, basic medium of group identity, welding disparate individuals into a closely knit, bonded social group (Holt 1972). When members of a recognized group opt to use language in ways not sanctioned by the group, they impel themselves into direct confrontation with the group's norms and mores.

Language is central to the maintenance of group identity within African American communities. Ebonics and the language practices of the students at Capital High are the most visible evidence of the hypothesized guerrilla warfare. It is against this background that I propose *leasing the standard* as a metaphor for the linguistic practices of Capital High students (and many other members of the African American community) because it reflects both their reluctance to be "mastered by . . . the . . . definitions of caste built into the [White] semantic/social system" (Holt 1972:154) and the strategies they use to appropriate the discourse that marks one as using the standard dialect. In addition, this proposed leasing metaphor enables me to use Gee's 1990 notion of discourses in documenting why and how Ebonics has become the standard in many predominantly Black schools while the traditional "standard" (English) is reinvented as a *vernacular* in these same contexts.

As I use it here, "the standard" (English dialect) means *more* than a structured language, *more* than its phonology, syntax, and lexicon. Here the standard includes, but is also broader than, Gee's notion of discourses as well as Hymes's notion of "speech community" (1971), Gumperz and Cook-Gumperz's "mismatch hypothesis" (1994), and Ogbu's "oppositional or ambivalent language frames" (1996). In this expanded sense, "the standard" incorporates both attitudes and styles of speaking as well as behavior. Of specific interest here are issues involving values of hostility and opposition to Ebonics or AAVE and other nonverbal features of the Black discourse repertoire, including rejection of the kinetic element in Black idiom (Kochman 1972:160, 1981). Thus it comes as no surprise that the standard, understood in this broad sense, might be resisted by African Americans because its definitions of caste, which stigmatize Black speech, extend easily to other practices associated with Black people.

Capital students' commitment to a Black identity compels them to diss the standard because it is viewed as an inappropriate speech form. Indeed, dissin' the standard is so pervasive among African Americans that

one is compelled to rethink and even invert what linguists and other researchers have generally accepted as nonfalsifiable: the language practices of Black people as a vernacular. The irony is that as a speech act practiced among the students at Capital High, what linguists have generally labeled "standard English" (see Dillard 1972; Labov 1972; Lippi-Green 1997; Smitherman 1973, 1977; Stewart 1970) is used and understood to be a vernacular, that is, a socially stigmatized dialect. For example, Capital students' discourse practices embody and reflect the practices identified in the above vignette, that is, friends stalk each other linguistically and behaviorally (e.g., "play the dozens" [Foster 1974]), and, if this practice is not perceived to be a sign of friendship, it is, at the very least, constructed as a benign social act *within most African American communities*. Nevertheless, this Black discourse style violates the polite linguistic (as well as broader discourse) practices (e.g., "May it please the court" and "Johnny, don't you think you should be doing your homework?") that are sanctioned and celebrated in both the system of public schooling and the larger U.S. community.

The point I want to emphasize here is not the structure in AAVE, that is, not whether the subjects and verbs agree or disagree (although in the standard English variety, that, too, is also very much a marker of a native speaker), but the way in which the speakers' discourse styles convey meaning and both conceal and make manifest a perception of power. Among most dominant group members, for instance, Black discourse practices mark the speaker as lacking civility, cultural graces, or good taste. Because this kind of language usage is deemed inappropriate, Black people's continuous use of such linguistic markers promotes academic and social failure.

Following Foucault (1977) and Fiske (1993:74), I argue that what is seen as normal is a product of power. The discourse of power—the standard dialect—is more than verbalized speech patterns. It constitutes, in addition, a contested site for self-definition, resistance, and accommodation. As popularly constructed in the United States, "standard English" suggests the phonology, syntax, and lexicon of modern American English.[6] Represented as an innocuous but important dialect, it is simply the standard (Lippi-Green 1997): no more, no less.

Antipathy to Ebonics or Black discourse traditions is, at least in part, a reaction to its deviation from "the standard." As Ebonics is not limited to the formal school curriculum at Capital High, this enmity is visible in other institutionalized school practices, coming from school officials which constantly admonish students to temper their voices, to speak in modulated tones, to act like ladies and gentlemen, and generally to appropriate not only standard English grammar but the

entire power discourse identified with school and classroom teachers—regardless of race or ethnicity—and by extension the dominant White community. But most Capital students reject the "dressage" valued by this "imagined community" (Anderson 1991)—that is, values of grace and dignity, implying silence and passivity (in linguistic as in other behavior).[7] Those students who embrace the linguistic dressage sanctioned at the school enhance their achievement potential; on the other hand, if they do not reject it, they are accused by their peers of "acting White." The vast majority of the student population values the form of interaction and the kind of talking that emphasize visibility, possession of voice, and a semantic code outside the mainstream culture (see Smitherman 1977). Black students at Capital High do use standard English—some more than others—but to most of them it is a socially stigmatized dialect (just as in the wider society AAVE is a socially stigmatized dialect).

I postulate that most Black students at Capital High lease standard English, return it, and lease it again during the next class session. They do not seek to own it, to internalize it. By using the standard only episodically between nine and three, the students display their awareness that it is deemed crucial to academic success. Further, by leasing rather than taking ownership of this school-approved discourse style, they also demonstrate their commitment to Ebonics and the prominent discourse practices in the African American community. This identified language resistance suggests that Black students do not want to own something they collectively identify as having been a historical instrument of Black enslavement, oppression, and dehumanization.[8] By engaging in this form of resistance, I argue, these students also reveal the tenacity with which they cling to a Black identity, its imagined cultural traditions and practices. For some students, leasing the standard is a successful, albeit contested, terrain, evoking undesired tensions and contradictions. More critically, this practice also enables them to retain effective ownership of a (less powerful) Black discourse even while temporarily and episodically embracing the "imagined" nation-states' approved discourse practices (see Anderson 1991:5). Black people who choose discourses that mimic those of Whites while in predominantly Black contexts may well be marginalized as power seekers and, furthermore, as people who might use power just as the larger society has historically done, to exploit and dehumanize other African Americans.

Discourse Styles: Inversion and Rhetorical Resistance

Leasing the discourse of power at schools is not a simple, dichotomous, full-scale switching between one dialect (Ebonics) and another (standard English), for standard English and Ebonics are distinguished not only by relatively minor grammatical differences but also by a much more overarching rhetorical and stylistic divergence. Capital students who seek to pursue academic excellence struggle to maintain a delicate balance between the discourse traditions promulgated by the school and those of their sociocultural situation, past and present. To explicate this point, I explore here certain discourse practices associated with African-descended American citizens, arguing that such practices embody reluctance to become, symbolically, the Other.[9]

In a seminal analysis, Holt (1972:154) brilliantly asserts that once Black Americans were freed from official enslavement, language became the major vehicle for perpetuating the legitimation of the subsequent stages of oppression (see also Lorde 1990). Language thus replaced slavery as the social mechanism that would ensure the continued exploitation of Black people. Those who were either unwilling or unable to accept and embrace the discourse practices of the power brokers in the larger society were tracked for failure, academic and otherwise. The existence of Black American—specific discourse practices adumbrates a contested social context, riddled with conflict, uncertainty, and an ongoing guerrilla-like struggle. Inherent in the idea of leasing rather than taking ownership of a language is a flotilla of contradictory expectations and possible outcomes.

"Appearing to but not to be" standard English speakers is one way African American adolescents can negotiate contradictory values centering around academic success and failure. This contradiction is inherent in "appearing to but not to" in order to maintain a Black identity. It is also one way to avoid becoming mired in the tangled vines of the larger society's oppressive social structure. Thus, for Black adolescents at Capital High, leasing rather than internalizing the discourse of power enables them to minimize the dissonance endemic to group subordination.

Lorde (1990:287) acknowledges that "appearing to but not to be" standard English speakers is important because the master's unique language code will never dismantle his or her power. The dominant discourse is thus ineffective in fighting oppressive social conditions, she argues, because language propels us to comprehend the world through a specific culture and its texts (see also Gates 1994).

Scott (1985, 1990) offers an even broader perspective for the linguistic warfare at Capital High.[10] Insisting that in modern state systems, subordinated populations engage in revolutionary practices through the use of what he labels "weapons of the weak," Scott compels us to confront power struggles and complex rivalries within state systems through language and other discourse prac-

tices. His analysis is particularly compelling in the case of African Americans because Black people's physical survival was and is contingent on minimizing their exposure to the unadulterated terror and physical violence of the dominant state system (see hooks 1992). In contexts controlled by the norms and standards of (an) Other, African-descended Americans learned that masking linguistic meaning was (and still is) a central weapon (Holt 1972) in their struggle to transform their living conditions. Hence, speaking a standard version of English compels Black adolescents to forsake the power embodied in the "duality, connotations, and denotations that developed within black [English] usage" (Holt 1972:154). Gilmore (1985), for example, describes how a teacher in an urban elementary school sought to "whiten" the writing and speech vocabulary of the students in her Academic Plus class. Gilmore (1985:125) laments this teacher's decision to presume ignorance on the part of the students and, in response to this perception, delete the richness of their linguistic constructions and by extension aspects of the students' Black selves. Similarly, Smitherman (1977:218) notes how classroom teachers' disdain for Black students' linguistic practices silences and kills their academic effort.

Hegemonic Discourse Practices: Speaking "the Standard" as Acting White

Most of the students at Capital High define "acting White" as when Black people "try to behave in a way that is more acceptable to White people."[11] In a preliminary analysis of the responses of fewer than 100 survey respondents to the issue of what it means to "act White," 79.2 percent of the ninth graders identified speaking the standard English dialect as an "acting White" behavior,[12] over 72 percent of the 11th grade high achievers defined speaking the standard English dialect in a similar manner. While these data compel us to focus our lens on the verbal practices or behaviors of Black Americans, the analysis offered here suggests that if Black Americans try "to behave in a way that is more acceptable to White people" as opposed to ways that closely approximate their perception of how Black Americans ought to behave is only a smidgen of what it means to act White. This is an inevitable outcome primarily because the core of U.S. life is institutionalized on the norms of the White rather than the Black community.

Acting White, then, is a metaphor for power relationships that addresses the historical exclusion of Black Americans from the core of U.S. life through the institutionalization of what the larger society unabashedly terms "all-American" norms. It is a notion that evokes the rampant, though per-

haps unconscious, oppression to which Black Americans have been subjected. The danger in acting White is captured in Gramsci's (1971) notion of hegemony, that is, the tendency of diverse members of a presumably bounded state system to unwittingly uphold the existing system of power relations through the everyday practices sanctioned by those who have been or are currently in power. At issue here is how African Americans and other people of color are symbolically propelled to dissolve or reconstruct their identities in order to be seen as powerful people.

For most Black American adolescents, acting White is quintessential evidence of symbolically becoming a dominant Other: a powerful rather than an oppressed person. Acting White is resisted at Capital because it suggests identity deflection or impersonation—the act of representing an Other in the presence of other Black people (see Fordham 1993, 1996).

The central issue is one of appropriateness. There are times when acting White is absolutely indicated and sanctioned by all segments of both the Capital High community and the Black American community at large. For example, in responding to a classroom teacher, one is applauded and even respected for being able to display facility in the discourses of the academy, when one chooses to. What many Capital community residents find problematic, however, is the uncritical, self-conscious adoption of the discourse of power rather than Ebonics when interacting with (or when inappropriate in the presence of) other Black people. A practicing professional (lawyer, teacher, doctor, government bureaucrat, etc.) is expected to lease the appropriate discourse practices of the powerful in institutional contexts. Indeed, among such members of the Black community, being unable to use appropriately the discourse practices of the larger society marginalizes the speaker in both cultural contexts. On the other hand, to use these same practices when interacting with other African Americans outside these institutional settings marks one as acting White.

Capital High students have a long and varied list of ways by which it is possible to act White, including playing golf, going to the country club, going to a museum, hiking, dancing to the lyrics rather than the music of a song, and speaking standard English (in inappropriate contexts). Acting White extends also to the pursuit of academic excellence. At Capital, many students are enormously conflicted by the assumption that to get good grades is to act White. On the one hand, acting White may be perceived as unavoidable in order to achieve success as defined by the larger society, both in school and, later, in the adult work force (see Scheurich 1993). Embracing the cultural principles promulgated by the larger society (including its definitions of success) constitutes uncritical acceptance of the dominant U.S. aesthetic and moral system, which unwittingly reproduces the conditions that are inevitably oppressive of the Black self (Scheurich 1993). Many Black American adolescents find this possibility particularly abhorrent. They refuse to comport themselves as commodities to be traded in pursuit of success when that pursuit also involves a flight from the Black self.

Refusing the Standard: Avoidance as Successful Failure

As I have noted elsewhere (Fordham 1996:39–40), while resistance is the common weapon the high- and underachieving students use in constructing a Black (school) identity, the specific ways they resist do not converge and are noteworthy. Among the high achievers, for example, resistance is manifested as conformity to school rules and practices in order both to achieve academic success and to negate state-supported claims of Black intellectual inferiority (see Jencks 1972; Jensen 1969, 1973; Herrnstein and Murray 1994; Shockley 1970). The students involved in school desegregation (e.g., the nine students at Central High School in Little Rock, Arkansas [see Beals 1994]; see also, for example Fulwood 1996; Hunter-Gault 1992), for example, were explicitly expected to conform to the then-extant school norms and practices of the larger society, not only for themselves but as representatives for the entire Black community. This was not a new expectation. Moreover, because members of the African American community have been indelibly marked by their ancestors' enslavement, the descendants of those Americans have incorporated into their cultural practices an organizational structure that celebrates group rather than individual achievement, honoring what I have labeled elsewhere the "fictive kinship system" (Fordham 1988, 1996).

In striking contrast, my Capital High study indicates that the underachieving students resist the larger society's claims of Black intellectual deficits through avoidance. Avoidance includes lack of attendance, tardiness, refusing to study or participate in class, disobeying clearly established rules of conduct and behavior (i.e., collaborating with peers rather than working alone), and so on. Black students use avoidance as the primary weapon in their attempts to maintain a perception of what it means to possess Black intellectual integrity in a setting controlled by the norms and values of a dominating Other (Fordham 1996). Given their widespread utilization of resistance by avoidance, in assigning failure to these students one must also consider the default bottom. The following examples are illustrative of this claim.

Like every other high school student in the D.C. Public School System, Korey had to take a course from the English curriculum annually.[13] Because English is one of the required courses that most of the students at the school would avoid were it possible to do so, the strategies they adopt to help them survive what they cannot avoid are extremely illuminating. As avoidance is not possible, many of the underachieving students did the next best thing: they bypassed essential components of the English curriculum. For Korey, that component was the book report.

The year I began this study, Korey was enrolled in eleventh grade English.[14] His decision to avoid the required book report was significant because the book report was the most critically important component of his English class, far more important than the mechanical requirements (e.g., defining vocabulary words, completing other lower-level assignments, including answering the questions at the end of the chapters, participating in classroom discussions, etc.) which he readily completed. This act alone made him extremely vulnerable to failure.

Korey's assertion—"I don't do no book reports"—is a typical example of the way most of the underachieving students practiced guerrilla warfare at the school. In refusing to complete the book report for his English class, he saw himself as resisting what was likely to transform his identity. Korey's primary school response was to avoid any aspect of the curriculum that might tamper with his perception of who he was as a Black person. There were some requirements in his English class that he refused to do, regardless of the academic price he might pay. At the same time he prided himself on being a well-behaved student, admitting that if he were not, his English teacher, Ms. Blumberg, probably would have given him an F the previous semester, rather than the D she gave him, when he opted not to submit a book report. When I probed further, trying to get at the real issues influencing his decision to avoid that component of his English class, I got the following response: "'Cause I didn't do no book report. ... I do my work. I just don't do no book report" (interview, June 15, 1983).

Sadly, the underachievers' refusal to lease the discourse practices that they view as foreign and hostile to their own identity is influential in marking them for academic and social failure. For example, Dawn—another underachieving student in the research sample—did not fit the normative female pattern, either physically or socially: she was not only very tall—six feet two inches—but something other than thin. She was also an athlete. Her intention was to go to college, where she planned to major in broadcast journalism. This, she acknowledged, entails learning and practicing as much standard English as possible. However, like most of the other underachieving students in my sample, she devoted very little of her time to homework and studying and even less time to her obligatory English classes. In fact, she acknowledged that she spent only about one hour and 15 minutes completing all assigned homework (in seven classes) on a nightly basis:

> **Signithia Fordham:** About how long does it take you to do your homework?
> **Dawn:** About an hour and 15 minutes.
> SF: Do you usually have homework in each class?
> D: Not usually, but most of the time I'll just sit down and just look over something. ... I'll look over mostly the classes that I like. [Laughter.] But when it's time for me to have a test or something like that, then I know I have to sit down and read over it.
> SF: What classes do you like"
> D: None of them! [Laughter.] [Interview, March 22, 1983]

Like Dawn—and many of the other students—Karl devoted as little time as possible to mastering or internalizing the standardized school discourses. When asked why he was failing many of the required courses, he noted that he did not

> study for Math, I know Math—I got homework to do, I do that. Science—do Science homework. Study in Science, go over my notes and stuff. And the [assigned] chapter—read the chapter. English—sometimes I study for the spelling [tests], sometimes I don't. Today I got caught cheating [on the English quiz], right?—cheating on the test? And the teacher said she was going to fail me for the year—just because she caught me cheating, right?—she caught me cheating twice. ... 'Cause I didn't study for the test. [And] she caught me. It wasn't no big thing—hey! you get caught cheating. It ain't nothing but a F—[a] zero. [Interview, March 15, 1983]

Hence, the academic failure of most Capital students is embedded in their resistance by avoidance to the state-sanctioned school discourse practices. By refusing—at a bare minimum—to lease these discourse practices, they are failing academically, albeit essentially by default.

Leasing a Dialect: Containing Standard English

As the above cases indicate, school presents students with contradictions that they cannot escape. School success demands that they adopt the very discourse practices they perceive as ineffectual and pallid (Scheurich 1993). In their passage from prepubescence and puberty into adult status, though, most students realize the political reality in which they participate. Adopting the behavioral trappings of the academy is acting White, and Black people who act White may be thought to be seeking (perhaps inadvertently) to delegitimize, evade, or repress the knowledge attendant to an African American cultural system. Caught between the imperatives of colliding cultural systems, some students refuse to display a critical symbol of the pursuit of power in the school context—using the standard English dialect—with implications in marginal to low academic performance.

Many at Capital High attempt to lessen the conflict these colliding systems evoke by seeking only to lease standard English from nine to three while retaining ownership of the discourse practices generally used in the Black American community. They do not do so easily, but those who manage it participate in a type of inversion that resonates with the discourse practices of ancestors who had various ways of "seeming to but not to." It is both a resistance that preserves the essential Black self and a means of social mobility. Here I present two typical approaches to not only the language usage practices of the high-achieving students at the school but, in addition, the broader Black discourse practices and the contradictions imposed on the Capital students.

Maggie, a high achiever, was well aware of the dialect contrasts present in her speech community. In discussing her mother's speech practices, Maggie suggested a rejection of bidialectalism, a refusal to be seen as both Us and Them—concurrently—primarily because, as she saw it, such passing behaviors are disingenuous at best. She asserted that her mother sounded White when she was talking on the phone or in contexts outside their home:

> She just talks like that on the telephone, I'll put it like that. When she talks, she puts on airs, you know, sounds White, so you can't tell whether she's White or Black. But when she's around the house, she talks, you know, regular; but when she's out around other people, anywhere out besides the house, she talks in a proper manner.... When my mother [speaks in the standard English dialect] it appears that she's trying to be someone she's not. [Interview, February 25, 1983]

Maggie experienced her mother's speech practices as fraudulent—"She's trying to be someone she's not"—and saw that as deceptive: "You can't tell whether she's White or Black." Rather than viewing her mother's

linguistic practices as evidence of appropriate code switching within a multidialect society, she saw them as acting White and therefore inappropriate.

In contradistinction, Maggie declared that she rarely participated in such linguistic fraud. Indeed, she insisted, "I talk the same way all the time [in all contexts]" (interview, February 25, 1983). More important, she categorized her constant linguistic behavior as a more appropriate, more correct—or more standard—way to structure a Black identity. To a large extent, Maggie's characterization of her linguistic practices is correct. In some instances, however, she was forced to lease the school-sanctioned standard English dialect in interactions with teachers and other school officials, and she could be heard switching just as her mother did.

Norris, a brilliant student, had learned to camouflage his academic achievement by leasing standard English from nine to three so that his peers did not feel threatened by him. He used "Black Street Speech" (Baugh 1983) as a standard and standard English as a vernacular dialect. Consequently, neither his cohorts who were underachieving nor those who were performing as well as he obstructed his academic efforts. He was therefore able to pursue his goals virtually unmolested by his peers.

At Berkeley Elementary, which was, in Norris's terms, filled with "hoodlums, thugs, and the dregs of society," he had been academically ahead of most of the students in his class and in the school. At the same time, however, realizing that he had to live with those students, he planned a course of action that would minimize any obstacles to his academic future. Norris deliberately chose for friends individuals whose resistance to dominant discourse practices was greater than his. Those peers, he reasoned, would act as camouflage in exchange for his help on homework assignments and tests. He was not picky about who they were. He simply wanted them to keep the other kids from beating him up or verbally harassing him so that he would be free to pursue his dream of academic excellence:

> I didn't want to, you know, be with anybody that was like me [academically], 'cause I didn't want to get beat up. The school I went to, Berkeley, was really rough, see? It was really rough. So I had to hang with people that were tough, you know? Lived in the projects and everything, and known tough and everything. So I used to hang with them. If anybody ever came in my face and wanted to pick on me, they'd always be there to help me. So I always made sure I had at least two or three bullies to be my friends. Even though if it does mean I have to give up answers in class.... I was willing to give up a little to get

a lot. So I did that for elementary school. [Interview, January 11, 1983]

Norris's alliance with the "bullies and hoodlums" in elementary school was a successful strategy. His close association with peers whose behavior clearly indicated they were not committed to the school-sanctioned discourse empowered him by removing any question about his loyalty to Blackness and Black Americans.

In junior high school he chose to embellish this strategy. In addition to making alliances with bullies, he adopted a clown or comedic persona (one component of which was the use of Black Street Speech [Baugh 1983]) that suggested that he was not very skilled academically. Wearing this mask (appearing to but not to) protected him from the scorn of those who discounted school-sanctioned skills. The merging of these strategies remained a part of his school persona:

> I had to act crazy then . . . you know, nutty, kind of loony. They say, "He's crazy." Not a *class* clown to get on the teachers' nerves, I never did that to the . . . around *them*. I'd be crazy. But as soon as I hit the classroom door, it was serious business. . . . Only the people who knew me knew my crazy side; when they found out I was smart, they wouldn't believe it. And the people that knew that I was smart, they wouldn't believe it if they were told that I was crazy. So I went through [school] like that. I'm still like that *now*, though. [Interview, January 11, 1983]

In acting a role, Norris became a discourse chameleon, merging with the surrounding context. Among friends, he behaved as if he were crazy; among classmates who were not close friends but were seeking the same academic goals as he, he conveyed an image of a standard English speaker and an academic competitor. He moved from one discourse to another in order to alternately mask and display his academic abilities. He realized that he had to fake it in order to make it (Granfield 1991), and, as noted in this article's opening vignette, Norris understood and appreciated the nuanced stylistic differences in the discourse practices of Black Americans and those of the dominant population.

At 17, Norris made a profound observation about contrasting cultural norms, an observation that, unfortunately, his teachers and other school officials were not as adept at discerning, if their practices were a true reflection of their understanding. These nuanced meanings and subtle discourse practices were either ignored or not understood. If his understanding was widely recognized by teachers and school officials, it could allow them to be much more successful at helping the students they know and desire to see achieve academically.

Like most other students at the school, both Norris and Maggie spoke standard English, at least intermittently between nine and three. Both recognized the discontinuity between the two discourses. Maggie strongly criticized her mother's shifting speech practices and declared that she, unlike her mother, was a greater warrior in the linguistic guerrilla war because she talked the same way all the time. Norris fully acknowledged his efforts to lease the standard discourse for school purposes. This is extremely telling. Unlike that of many of his peers, Norris's future was fairly well charted. He was performing well in school, and he realized that he had to continue to do so in order to go to college, especially because his mother was not financially able to send him to school. While Maggie and Norris differed in their perceptions, they shared the common element of leasing the standard discourse style—Norris more willingly than Maggie, which may account for his greater academic success—using it almost exclusively for instrumental purposes.

While Korey's, Dawn's, and Karl's strategies present a striking contrast that reflects how most of the underachieving students achieve successful academic failure through avoidance, Maggie's and Norris's strategies for leasing standard English minimize the appearance of social distance between them and other academic strivers and also demonstrate their continuous allegiance to the Capital community in spite of their school success. Their use of Black Street Speech (Baugh 1983) as a standard discourse allowed them to avoid the predictable cacophony—or worse, silence—that accrues to Black adolescents who opt to use the standard English vernacular in inappropriate contexts. As noted above, resistance—as conformity—is the academically successful students' weapon of choice in their efforts to maintain a Black identity and in fighting the ongoing linguistic war.

Conclusion

Among the students at Capital High, the standard version of English is inverted, reinvented as a vernacular that they lease on a daily basis in order to achieve specific academic goals. Use of this vernacularized dialect is one of the primary reasons a Black American can be accused of acting White. Because acting White is stigmatized and unavoidable, students who desire to achieve academic success must find ways to cope with the knowledge that to survive economically they must master the discourse style that guarantees their continued subjugation while at the same time confronting the fact that for any social group seeking to be free

of human degradation, liberation begins with language (Holt 1972:156).

Indeed, the argument made here is that Ebonics, or the language practices of the students at the school, is the most visible evidence of this on-going guerrilla warfare. This analysis also suggests that in concurrently leasing the discourse that represents power—the standard dialect—while seeking to maintain ownership of what is generally referred to as Ebonics, Capital High students demonstrate (perhaps unconsciously) an understanding that this is not a pristine, dichotomous, full-scale switching between one dialect and another. This is critically important because standard English and Ebonics differ not only in relatively minor grammatical ways but in much more overarching rhetorical and stylistic terms.

The fact that African American adolescents are engaged in an ongoing war through language does not mean that they are conscious of it—or, if they are aware of it, that they feel free to discuss it publicly. On the contrary, at Capital High, the students' language use fit Scott's (1985) description of a "weapon of the weak." Their resistance to adopting the standard version of English as their standard was not generally constructed as such by either school officials—most of whom, ironically, were Black—or the larger Black and White populations in Washington. Neither of these populations appeared to see African American adolescents' use of the Black discourse style as a deliberate, self-conscious linguistic practice. Rather, the students' failure to embrace the standard English discourse was generally understood as group incompetence, an inability to perform a culturally sanctioned task (Inkeles 1968; Ogbu 1981): to speak the standardized English dialect. This perception, as Lee (1994) asserts, persists despite the fact that it is well documented that the Black discourse style increases rather than diminishes the longer Black students are in school. Paradoxically, African American adults—parents, teachers, and other school officials—usually unwittingly contribute to the continuation of this below-the-surface warfare. These adults seek to teach their children to make the power discourse their standard. Generally, their children reject these efforts. A more viable approach, however, might be to recognize and actively promote a strategy that some students have already adopted: to embrace standard English as a lingua franca for instrumental purposes. This limited utilitarian use has an undesired side effect: validation of its vernacular status.

What can we do to end the larger guerrilla warfare encoded in these discourse practices? How might we alter social policies and practices in such a way that African American adolescents' daily stigmatization of the standardized version of English is discontinued? What can we do to maximize African American adolescents' academic effort,

thereby diminishing academic failure? Obviously, I do not have complete answers. Nevertheless, it does seem to me that we must first understand the *meaning* of the linguistic practices of African American adolescents. I have offered a first step here. While understanding this meaning does not necessarily imply acceptance, it does suggest, at the very least, a questioning of the conventional explanation: linguistic deficiencies vis-à-vis Black American speakers. What I have suggested here is that conventional explanations miss the mark. They miss the mark, I argue, because they minimize the functioning of Black Americans' discourse practices as instruments of rhetorical resistance that nurtures the liberation of a people and reinforces their Black identity. Given the centrality of Black resistance in the situation presented here, successful policy makers will discontinue the extant ineffective practice of disregarding cultural and identity issues.

Hence, repairing or altering Black students' penchant for Ebonics is, as I have argued here, largely counterproductive. This just does not work, period. Indeed, instead of trying to repair the linguistic practices of Black American adolescents, successful policy makers will redirect their energies toward minimizing the linguistic warfare inherent in the ongoing convention of marginalizing and stigmatizing the Black self, thereby compelling it to unwittingly engage in the dissin' of its own funeral.

Signithia Fordham is an associate professor of anthropology in the Department of Education at the University of Maryland, Baltimore County.

Notes

Acknowledgments. The research on which this analysis is based was initially funded by grants from the National Institute of Education (NIE-G-82-0037), the Spencer Foundation, a dissertation fellowship from the American University in Washington, D.C., a Spencer Postdoctoral Fellowship, and a National Science Foundation Minority Research Grant (MRI). I am grateful for this financial assistance. I wish to thank the faculty, staff, and students at Capital High (who can not be individually identified because of my contract with the District of Columbia Public School System), their parents, and all other adults in the Capital community for allowing me to represent their lives. In addition, I wish to thank Professors Iris Carter Ford, Renee Larrier, and William Leap for helpful comments and suggestions on successive drafts on this article. I am especially grateful to Linda Chalfant, Maria Phillips, and Professors Carolyn Adger and Linda Hoyle for editorial assistance. I am solely responsible for the ideas and claims made in this final version. Some portions of this analysis appear in Fordham 1988.

All proper nouns designating either people or places connected to the research site are pseudonyms. I capitalize *Black* and *White,* contrary to *Anthropology & Education Quarterly* style.

1. Norris was one of the 12 high-achieving students (there were also 21 under-achieving students) who served as key informants for the multiyear research study on which this analysis is based. (For a more detailed discussion of the research design and techniques, see Fordham 1996).

2. *Dissin'* is a shortened version of the word *disrespecting.* Its use among African-descended Americans is intended to convey great angst regarding one's personal sense of violation. Thus, as I use it here, *dissin'* deviates from the common media practice of confining its usage to a description of how it leads to physical violence. As I use it here, *dissin'* suggests a perception of psychic and physical violence to the Black self, with a greater emphasis on the psychic terror African Americans have historically endured (see hooks 1992: 165–178).

3. I do not mean to suggest that Black speakers—male and female—do not make grammatical errors when talking with adults. They do. Rather, what is being emphasized here is the degree to which Rita went to demonstrate this connection.

4. Holt discusses inversion at more length as follows.

Words and phrases were given reverse meanings and functions changed. Whites, denied access to the semantic extensions of duality, connotations, and denotations that developed within black usage, could only interpret the same material according to its original singular meaning. White interpretation of the communication event was quite different from that made by the other person in the interaction, enabling blacks to deceive and manipulate Whites without penalty. This form of linguistic warfare protected the subordinated, permitted the masking and disguising of true feelings, allowed the subtle assertion of self, and promoted group solidarity. The purpose of the game was to appear to but not to. [1972:154]

5. Someone is sure to suggest that this practice is not unique to the students at Capital High, which is probably true. Given the unique history of any social group, including Americans of African ancestry, the way in which intergroup members respond to the same phenomena have different meanings and implications (see Castile and Kushner 1981; Spicer 1980). Therefore, while the avoidance behaviors described here may exist in other school contexts, among other stu-

dents, it is unlikely to have exactly the same meaning to the two student groups.

6. In addition to the usual dictionary definitions, Lippi-Green offers the following responses to her requests for definitions of "the standard" (English):

Standard English is . . .

having your nouns and verbs agree. . . .

the English legitimatized by wide usage and certified by expert consensus, as in a dictionary usage panel. . . .

what I learned in school, in Mrs. McDuffey's class, in Virginia, in the mid-seventies. It really bothers me when I read and hear other people who obviously skipped her class. . . .

the proper language my mother stressed from the time I was old enough to talk. [1977:55]

7. I am indebted to Paglia (1994) for the concept of dressage. She attributes it to Jacqueline Bouvier Kennedy Onassis: "the closest thing to royalty that America has never seen" (1994:12). Paglia asserts that dressage is a "form of radical minimalism, of hierarchial stillness and repose, so entrenched, so well synchronized in the personhood of the aristocratic horseperson that the rider's signals to the horse are completely invisible" (1994:12). Her analysis is analogous to Tracy's (1991) argument regarding how to measure success and power among academic women: silence and invisibility.

8. Elsewhere (Fordham 1996:39–40) I have offered a detailed analysis of how African American students at Capital High exhibited resistance: through conformity to and avoidance of school rules.

9. I am indebted to Professor Michael Dyson (1995) for the idea of discourse styles as inversion and rhetorical resistance.

10. While some linguists question the applicability of Scott's (1985, 1990) analyses to speech and perhaps even language and power (see, for example, Gal 1995), I argue that they are appropriate here because speech and language are only a small portion of what Gee (1990) describes as discourses and the discourse of power.

11. Student Research Questionnaire, Black Student School Success Research Project, page 27. During the second year of the multiyear study at the school, I developed and administered an in situ research questionnaire to more than 600 students, representing a cross section of ninth through 12th graders. This definition was one of seven options offered to question number 122 of a 201-item, three-part research instrument. This response pattern represents a preliminary analysis of a randomly chosen sample.

12. At the time of the study reported here, all persons admitted as ninth graders at the school were officially designated "high achieving."

13. While many of my examples are from the English curriculum, I want to stress that there is nothing unique or extremely difficult about the English classes at the school. The English curriculum stands out because it is the only component of the curriculum that has an annual requirement for every student, regardless of which academic track he or she takes.

14. All students in the ethnographic component of the Capital High study were 11th graders.

References

Anderson, Benedict, 1991, Imagined Communities: Reflections on the Origins and Spread of Nationalism. Revised edition. London: Verso.

Baratz, Stephen S., and Joan C. Baratz, 1970, Early Childhood Intervention: The Social Science Base of Institutional Racism. Harvard Educational Review 1: 29–50.

Baugh, John, 1983, Black Street Speech: Its History, Structure, and Survival. Austin: University of Texas Press.

Beals, Melba Pattillo, 1994, Warriors Don't Cry: A Searing Memoir of the Battle to Integrate Little Rock's Central High School. New York: Pocket Books.

Blassingame, John W., 1979, The Slave Community: Plantation Life in the Antebellum South. 2nd edition. New York: Oxford University Press.

Castile, George P., and Gilbert Kushner, 1981, Issues in the Analysis of Enduring Cultural Systems. In Persistent Peoples: Cultural Enclaves in Perspective. George P. Castile and Gilbert Kushner, eds. Pp. xv–xxii. Tucson: University of Arizona Press.

Delpit, Lisa, 1988, The Silenced Dialogue: Power and Pedagogy in Educating Other People's Children. Harvard Educational Review 54: 280–298.

———, 1995, Other People's Children: Cultural Conflict in the Classroom. New York: The New Press.

Dillard, John L., 1972, Black English. New York: Random House.

Dyson, Michael Eric, 1995, Making Malcolm: The Myth and Meaning of Malcolm X. New York: Oxford University Press.

Fiske, John, 1993, Power Plays; Power Works. London: Verso.

Fordham, Signithia, 1988, Racelessness as a Factor in Black Students' School Success: Pragmatic Strategy or Pyrrhic Victory? Harvard Educational Review 58(1): 54–84.

———, 1993, "Those Loud Black Girls": (Black) Women, Silence, and Gender "Passing" in the Academy. Anthropology and Education Quarterly 24: 3–32.

———, 1996, Blacked Out: Dilemmas of Race, Identity and Success at Capital High. Chicago: University of Chicago Press.

———, 1998 Speaking Standard English from Nine to Three: Language as Guerrilla Warfare at Capital High. In Kid's Talk: Strategic Language Use in Later Childhood. Susan M. Hoyle and Carolyn Temple Adger, eds. Pp. 205–216. New York: Oxford University Press.

Fordham, Signithia, and John U. Ogbu, 1986, Black Students' School Success: Coping with the "Burden of 'Acting White.'" The Urban Review 18(1): 176–206.

Foster, Herbert, 1974, Ribbin', Jivin', and Playin' the Dozens: The Unrecognized Dilemma of Inner-City Schools. Cambridge, MA: Ballinger.

Foster, Michèle, 1989, "It's Cookin' Now": A Performance Analysis of the Speech Events of a Black Teacher in an Urban Community College. Language in Society 18: 1–29.

____, 1990, The Politics of Race: Through the Eyes of African American Teachers. Journal of Education 172: 123–141.

Foucault, Michel, 1977, Language, Counter-Memory, Practice: Selected Essays and Interviews. Donald F. Bouchard, ed. and trans. Ithaca, NY: Cornell University Press.

Fulwood, Sam III, 1996, Waking from the Dream: My Life in the Black Middle Class. New York: Anchor Books.

Gal, Susan, 1995, Language and the Arts of Resistance. Cultural Anthropology 10(3): 407–424.

Gates, Henry Louis, Jr., 1994, Colored People: A Memoir. New York: Alfred A. Knopf.

Gee, James P., 1990, Social Linguistics and Literacies: Ideology in Discourses. London: Falmer Press.

____, 1992, The Social Mind: Language, Ideology and Social Practice. New York: Bergin and Garvey.

Gilmore, Perry, 1985, "Gimme Room": School Resistance, Attitude, and Access to Literacy. Journal of Education 167: 111–128.

Gramsci, Antonio, 1971, Selections from the Prison Notebooks of Antonio Gramsci. London: Lawrence and Wishart.

Granfield, Robert, 1991, Making It by Faking It: Working-Class Students in an Elite Academic Environment. Journal of Contemporary Ethnography 20: 331–351.

Gumperz, John, and Jennie Cook-Gumperz, 1994, Language in Education: Changing Views of Anthropological Perspectives. In International Encyclopedia of Education, vol. 6. Toren Husen and T. Neville Postlethwaite, eds. Pp. 3235–3238. London: Pergamon Press.

Herrnstein, Richard J., and Charles Murray, 1994, The Bell Curve: Intelligence and Class Structure in American Life. New York: The Free Press.

Holt, Grace Sims, 1972, "Inversion" in Black Communication. In Rappin' and Stylin' Out: Communication in Urban Black America.

Thomas Kochman, ed. Pp. 152–159. Urbana: University of Illinois Press.

hooks, bell, 1992, Black Looks: Race and Representation. Boston: South End Press.

Hunter-Gault, Charlayne, 1992, In My Place. New York: Vintage Books.

Hymes, Dell, 1971, On Linguistic Theory, Communicative Competence, and the Education of Disadvantaged Children. In Anthropological Perspectives on Education. Murray L. Wax, Stanley Diamond, and Fred. O. Gearing, eds. Pp. 51–66. New York: Basic Books.

Inkeles, Alex, 1968, Social Structure and the Socialization of Competence. Harvard Educational Review, Reprint Series, 1: 50–68.

Jencks, Christopher, 1972, Inequality: A Reassessment of the Effects of Family and Schooling in America. New York: Basic Books.

Jensen, Arthur R., 1969, How Much Can We Boost IQ and Scholastic Achievement? Harvard Educational Review, Reprint Series, 2: 1–123.

____, 1973, Educability and Group Difference. London: Methuen.,

Kochman, Thomas, 1972, The Kinetic Element in Black Idiom. In Rappin' and Stylin' Out: Communication in Urban Black America. Thomas Kochman, ed. Pp. 160–169. Urbana: University of Illinois Press.

____, 1981, Black and White Styles in Conflict. Chicago: University of Chicago Press.

Labov, William, 1972, Language in the Inner City: Studies on the Black English Vernacular. Philadelphia: University of Pennsylvania Press.

Lee, Felicia R., 1994, Lingering conflict in the Schools: Black Dialect vs. Standard Speech—Grappling with Ways to Teach Young Speakers of Black Dialect. The New York Times, January 5: A1, D22.

Linguistic Society of America, 1997, LSA Resolution on the Oakland "Ebonics" Issue. Annual Meeting of the American Association for Applied Linguistics, Chicago, January.

Lippi-Green, Rosina, 1997, English with an Accent: Language, Ideology, and Discrimination in the United States. New York: Routledge.

Lorde, Audrey, 1990, Age, Race, Class, and Sex: Women Redefining Difference. In Out There: Marginalization and Contemporary Cultures. Russell Ferguson, Martha Gever, Trinh T. Minh-ha, and Cornel West, eds. Pp. 281–288. Cambridge, MA: MIT Press.

Ogbu, John, 1981, On Origins of Human Competence: A Cultural Ecological Perspective. Child Development 52: 413–429.

____, 1996, Speech Community, Language Identity and Language Boundaries. Prepared for "Language and Environment: The Impact of Cultural, Social and Political Factors on Promoting Second Language Learning in Immigrant Housing Areas," Botkyrka, Stockholm, Sweden, June 17–19.

Paglia, Camille, 1994, Jackie's Ride. New Republic 210(24): 12–13.

Rickford, John R., 1992, Grammatical Variation and Divergence in Vernacular Black English. In Internal and External Factors in Syntactic Change. Marinel Gerritsen and Dieter Stein, eds. Pp. 175–200. Berlin: Mouton de Gruyter.

Scheurich, James Joseph, 1993, Toward a White Discourse on White Racism. Educational Researcher 22(8): 5–10.

Scott, James C., 1985, Weapons of the Weak: Everyday Forms of Peasant Resistance. New Haven, CT: Yale University Press.

____, 1990, Domination and the Arts of Resistance: Hidden Transcripts. New Haven, CT: Yale University Press.

Shockley, William, 1970, A "Try Simplest Cases" Approach to the Heredity-Poverty-Crime Problem. In Psychological Factors in Poverty. Vernon L. Allen, ed. Pp. 141–146. Chicago: Markham.

Smitherman, Geneva, 1969, A Comparison of the Oral and Written Styles of a Group of Inner-City Black Students. Ph.D. dissertation, Department of Linguistics, University of Michigan.

____, 1973, White English in Blackface, or, Who Do I Be? The Black Scholar, May–June: 32–39.

____, 1977, Talkin' and Testifyin'. Boston: Houghton Mifflin Co.

Spicer, Edward H., 1980, The Yaqui: A Cultural History. Tucson: University of Arizona Press.

Stewart, William A., 1970, Toward a History of Negro Dialect. In Language and Poverty: Perspectives on a Theme. Frederick Williams, ed. Pp. 351–379. Chicago: Markham.

Tracy, Laura, 1991, The Secret between Us: Competition among Women. Boston: Little, Brown and Co.

Wolfram, Walter, 1969, A Sociological Description of Detroit Negro Speech. Washington, DC: Center for Applied Linguistics.

Meeting the Needs of Multiracial and Multiethnic Children in Early Childhood Settings

Francis Wardle[1,2]

Early childhood programs have been in the forefront of implementing a multiracial curriculum. Early childhood educators need to extend these approaches to support and embrace multiracial and multiethnic children. These are children whose biological parents crossed traditional U.S. Census categories to have children. To meet the unique needs of these children and their families, early childhood educators need to engage in staff training, provide classroom materials, work closely with parents, and challenge the single race approach to multicultural education.

KEY WORDS: diversity; multicultural; multiracial; multiethnic; interracial; U.S. Census and OMB categories; single race.

INTRODUCTION

Early childhood and school programs continue to make strides in meeting the needs of an ever more diverse population. Multicultural, anti-bias programs, responding to welfare reform, providing for the needs of homeless children, and full inclusion of children with physical, mental, and learning disabilities, are all examples of this commitment to diversity. Now programs are also beginning to meet the needs of a previously ignored group of students: multiethnic and multiracial children (Morrison & Rogers, 1996).

According to Root (1996), the number of multiracial babies is increasing faster than the number of single race babies. There have been over 100,000 biracial (Black/White) babies born every year since 1989, and a total of 1 million first generation biracial babies have been born since then (Root, 1996). This increase in births is also true among non-Black/White biracial and biethnic babies, such as White/Hispanic, Hispanic/Asian, and White/Native American. This article will address the needs of young children whose biological parents come from two or more traditional racial/ethnic groups (Cruz-Janzen, 1997). The terms multiracial and multiethnic will be used as the best current descriptors of these children; interracial and interethnic will be used for their families.

WHO SHOULD MULTICULTURAL EDUCATION INCLUDE?

One reason multicultural education has been slow to respond to the needs of this population is because, historically, multiracial children in this country have been viewed as having the same identity as minority children (Cruz-Janzen, 1997; Daniel, 1992; Wardle, 1991). The "one drop rule" has declared anyone with any Black heritage as Black (Daniel, 1992). Similar rules of hypodescent (the notion

[1]Adjunct Faculty, University of Phoenix (Colorado).
[2]Correspondence should be directed to Francis Wardle, 2300 S. Krameria Street, Denver, Colorado 80222.

From *Early Childhood Education Journal*, Vol. 26, No. 1, 1998, pp. 7-11. © 1998 by Kluwer Academic/Plenum Publishers. Reprinted by permission.

of defining identity based on any amount of non-White heritage) necessitates other mixed race children belong to the racial or ethnic group of their parent of color (Cruz-Janzen, 1997). Native American identity is tied to tribal membership, which differs from tribe to tribe. Many argue this historical process of classifying children of multiracial and multiethnic heritage has worked well and does not need to be changed (Banks & Banks, 1993).

The U.S. Census Bureau's categories, and the categories mandated by the OMB (Office of Management and Budget) for use by all Federal programs, are based on the belief that all U.S. citizens fall into one of the existing racial or ethnic categories. Thus, the U.S. population is broken into five exclusive categories: African American, Native American, Hispanic, Asian American (or Pacific Islander), and White. Consequently, our multicultural programs—training, college classes, curriculum materials, and activities—were developed to support individual knowledge, belonging, and pride in one of these groups (Banks & Banks, 1993).

It is well documented that racial and ethnic identity, and developing concepts about racial and ethnic diversity, are developmental tasks that begin in early childhood (Phinney, 1991; Poston, 1990). Theorists and researchers have also established that a central part of a child's sense of positive self-esteem is based on the child's racial/ethnic identity; and, finally, that a child with a high self-esteem does better in school (Matiella, 1991; Ogbu, 1987; Phinney, 1991).

Multicultural books, college diversity classes, training and conference sessions rarely address the needs of multiracial and multiethnic children, because most educators still adhere to the notion these children belong to the racial and ethnic group of their parent of color. Some scholars involved in studying racial diversity do not believe these children constitute a separate cultural group (Bullivant, 1993; Thorton, 1992). Thus, it is only natural that most teachers of young children automatically follow this thinking (Cruz-Janzen, 1997; Daniel, 1996; Morrison & Rodgers, 1996).

However, many psychologists believe multiracial and multiethnic children have a more difficult time determining racial identity in this society than children of single race heritage (Bowles, 1993; Gibbs, 1989; McRoy & Freeman, 1983). Because this society places such an emphasis on racial and ethnic identity

and affiliation, children of mixed parentage often feel disloyal and confused; they have a sense of not knowing where they belong. There is also a growing movement of multiracial individuals and interracial parents who are challenging the "one drop rule," insisting on an identity that embraces every part of a person's ethnic, racial, and national background (Benjamin-Wardle, 1991; Cruz-Janzen, 1997; Daniel, 1992; Brown & Douglass, 1996; Root, 1996).

Limited research is beginning to show that multiracial and multiethnic children not only have identity needs that are different from single race children, but they are also suffering in our early childhood and school programs because these unique needs are not being met (Bowles, 1993; Bradell, 1987; Cruz-Janzen, 1997; Poston, 1990; Wardle, 1992). More and more experts, along with many parents, believe that children who identify with both parents' heritages and cultures from an early age will have fewer identity problems later on (Baptiste, 1985; Benjamin-Wardle, 1994; Bowles, 1993; Funderburg, 1994; Morrison & Rodgers, 1996). They suggest children who accept and embrace their total ethnic, racial, and cultural heritage will not succumb to the tug of racial loyalties and group affiliations.

Educators need to find ways to respond to this new-found need for empowerment of multiracial children and interracial parents. Teachers, caregivers, and administrators must support multiracial and multiethnic children's total identity and heritage. This is particularly challenging because of the history of multiracial people in this country, the confining nature of the U.S. Census and OMB categories, and the dearth of advice, books, and curriculum materials (Cruz-Janzen, 1997; Wardle, 1996).

STAFF TRAINING

Early childhood and school programs wishing to address this issue need to provide training for staff. Because programs that include this population challenge much of our history and the way we have viewed race and ethnicity within our multicultural curricula, the training needs to be thorough and include specific topics (Wardle, 1996):

- Staff attitudes toward interracial and interethnic marriage, and multiracial and multiethnic identity;

- The concept of race and ethnicity in this country and the world;
- Ideas/techniques on how to support the healthy development of multiracial and multiethnic children;
- Techniques for working with interracial and interethnic parents;
- The history of multiracial and multiethnic people in this country, including historical heroes;
- The relationship between minority issues and multiracial and multiethnic programs—commonalities and differences:
- Curriculum ideas, activities, and resources.

The training should be provided by someone knowledgeable and sensitive to the topic. This might be a person who provides multicultural education for a program, or someone who teaches at the local college level. It can also be accomplished by attending a session at an early childhood conference. Finally, there may be someone on your staff (probably a multiracial person, or member of an interracial family) who would enjoy making this his or her special area of expertise.

Trainers will have to access current resources: books (Root, 1992, 1996; Spickard, 1989), articles, Internet sites, and interracial support groups. (Internet sites include, http://csbc.cncfamily.com—Center for the Study of Biracial Children; http://www.webcom.com/-intvoice/editor,html—Interracial Voice newsletter; http://www.geocities.com/CapitolHill/Lobby5006/—links to a variety of multiracial websites.) Trainers should also attend as many training and conference sessions as possible.

CURRICULUM

Like traditional multicultural curriculum, multiracial and multiethnic content must be integrated within the overall classroom curriculum. This avoids the tourist approach to diversity. Content should include (Morrison & Rogers, 1996; Wardle, 1993, 1996):

- Interracial families—two-parent, foster, adoptive, and blended;
- Racial/ethnic identity development and self-esteem;
- Teaching about culture, race, and diversity;
- Mixing of traditions, nationalities, language, and religions;

- Multiracial and multiethnic heroes;
- Interracial/multiracial books;
- Other classroom materials;
- Responding to bias and harassment;
- Federal and school forms;
- Field trips and classroom visitors.

IMAGES OF INTERRACIAL AND INTERETHNIC FAMILIES

Multiracial and multiethnic children believe they are invisible (Cruz-Janzen, 1997). One reason for this is because they don't see themselves in books, posters, articles, newsletters, communication boards, people sets, magazines, TV, videos, advertising materials, games, and home-school connections (newsletters, calendars, program descriptions, and other communications). They need to see images of themselves and their families, because they are invisible in the rest of society.

Teachers and caregivers must look for new books that include these families. Because of the dearth of materials, programs will need to make many products that show multiracial children and their families: school-home communication pieces, pictures for the wall, calendars, artwork, books, doll sets, puzzles, and family journals (individual books created by students about all aspects of their family heritage. These books should include drawings, paintings, dictated accounts, artifacts from home, newspaper clippings of family members, etc.). Interracial and interethnic families are also sources for resource ideas. Programs need to pressure educational companies—especially those that claim to provide multicultural materials—to provide classroom materials for these children.

SINGLE RACE ACTIVITIES AND CELEBRATIONS

Many early childhood programs and schools celebrate holidays that highlight a single culture: St. Patrick's Day; Cinco de Mayo; Black History Month; Chinese New Year; Jewish holidays; Kwanzaa; various Native American ceremonial days, etc. These activities can be difficult for multiracial and multiethnic children, unless they are conducted in a truly inclusive manner. They should be celebrated in such a way that every child feels included, and can benefit from the activity (Davidman, 1995). For example, a harvest festival that includes a Pueblo Corn Dance, European harvest songs, a display of products grown by the school and home, and other celebrations giving thanks for the fruits of the land, could be presented. A multiracial or multiethnic child should never be placed in a position to deny part of his/her background. Cultural celebrations should be a time when the multiracial and multiethnic child can support the part of his heritage being celebrated (Wardle, 1996). A child of Hispanic-English heritage can identify with the struggle of his Hispanic relatives during the September 16 celebrations. On November 5, she can celebrate Guy Fawkes Day, to enjoy her English heritage.

RESPONDING TO BIAS

Multiracial and multiethnic children receive a variety of harassment, from benign questions that want to know, "well, what are you, anyway?" to more direct insults regarding their mixed heritage. Teachers need to quickly and sensitively respond to these incidences, while providing accurate information to other children about race, biology, and genetics. For example, teaching about how animals and people reflect the physical features of both parents (height, skin color, features, etc.).

One of the strengths of having multiracial and multiethnic children in a program is to expose all children to the richness of diversity, and to challenge the concept of single categories and groupings. For example, there are families that include relatives from two or more countries; families where several different languages are spoken; people who have identities in more than one religion, and many people with dual citizenship. Multiracial and multiethnic children should not continually have to justify who they are; and they should not be required to select a single racial or ethnic label or group because others are more comfortable with this approach. Educators must help our children appreciate the diversity and complexity of all people.

FEDERAL AND SCHOOL FORMS

One of the most difficult realities for interracial parents is the realization there is no government category for their children (Graham, 1996). Head Start, child care, and school application forms are often the first place these parents directly face the realization their children are invisible (Cruz-Janzen, 1997); in late elementary school, many multiethnic and multiracial children are faced with this reality as they complete forms independently (Benjamin-Wardle, 1994). These forms pose a dilemma for almost all early childhood and school programs (any that receive Federal funds).

It is most important for educators to understand and be sensitive to the concerns of interracial parents. Some parents believe these forms are an official denial of their child's full heritage by their school and country (Graham, 1996). Other interracial parents view racial labels as a funding game, and will pick and choose the race of their child, depending on the quota needed by the program they wish their child to enter.

Program personnel can do two things when addressing this issue: talk with their funding representative to determine how accurate a count is needed (programs vary in their requirements, from accurate data to general estimates) and talk with individual parents. Based on these two discussions, educators can then try to reach an approach satisfactory to all involved. However, this might not be possible. While there currently is no multiracial category, the U.S. Census has recently decided to allow people to check as many racial categories as they choose. It is not clear whether this change will be reflected on school forms.

CURRICULUM MATERIALS AND ACTIVITIES

One of the best ways for children to develop healthy ethnic and racial identities is through lots of opportunities to explore their unique physical features (Derman-Sparks, 1989). This is achieved through projects that use mirrors and different colored paints (including accurate flesh colored paints); dramatic play materials of all kinds, including combs, barrettes and ribbons for hair, a variety of dolls, superheroes and miniature people; and a collection of books, magazines, photographs, and curriculum materials. Activities that involve mixing paints, light, fabrics, crayons, felt pens, and plastics will help biracial children understand the natural and normal concept of mixing colors. Other activities include mural painting and collages, collecting family stories and histories, and creating books and journals (Morrison & Rogers, 1996).

Field trips and classroom visits can also greatly enhance this multicultural curriculum. Interracial and interethnic parents should be asked to provide suggestions. Classes can visit local museums, bookstores, community stores, festivals, and different areas of the city. Classroom storytellers, Black cowboys, people from different parts of the world, and neighborhood leaders should present information about each part of the child's heritage. Educators then need to help multiracial and multiethnic children integrate this diverse information into their own unique backgrounds, heritage, and identities.

CONCLUSIONS

School and early childhood professionals continue to meet the needs of an ever more diverse population. Multiracial and multiethnic children are part of this population, and have unique needs that early childhood educators are just now beginning to address. Serving the needs of these children and their families is a particular challenge because of the history of multiracial people in this country, the lack of information, the dearth of staff training resources and curriculum, and the scarcity of classroom resources. But, to fulfill our commitment to diversity and to empowerment of all children and families we serve, schools and early childhood programs need to take the lead in supporting the healthy identity development of this ever increasing population.

REFERENCES

Banks, J. A., & Banks, C. A. M. (Eds.) (1993). *Multicultural education: Issues and perspectives.* Boston, MA: Allyn and Bacon.

Baptiste, P. (1985). The contemporary interracial child. *Communique,* April, 1–7.

Benjamin-Wardle, M. S. (1991). 14 year old speaks out, proving that teens have concerns, too. *New People, 1*(6), 6.

Benjamin-Wardle, M. S. (1994). Ethnic clubs exclude others. *New People, 4*(2), 6.

Bowles, D. D. (1993). Biracial identity: Children born to African American and White couples. *Clinical Social Work Journal, 21*(4), 417–428.

Brandell, J. R. (1988). Treatment of the biracial child: Theoretical and clinical issues. *Journal of Multicultural Counseling and Development, 16,* 176–187.

Brown, N. G., & Douglass, R. E. (1996). Making the invisible visible: The growth of community network organizations. In M. P. P. Root (Ed.), *The multiracial experience* (pp. 323–340). Newbury Park, CA: Sage.

Bullivant, B. M. (1993). Culture: Its nature and meaning for educators. In J. A. Banks & C. A. M. Banks (Eds.), *Multicultural education: Issues and perspectives* (pp. 29–47). Boston, MA: Allyn and Bacon.

Cruz-Janzen, M. (1997). *Curriculum and the Ethnic and Racial Self Concept of Biethnic and Biracial Persons.* Unpublished doctoral dissertation, University of Denver, Denver, CO.

Daniel, G. R. (1992). Passers and pluralists: Subverting the racial divide. In M. P. P. Root (Ed.), *Racially mixed people in America* (pp. 91–108). Newbury Park, CA: Sage.

Davidman, L. (1995). Multicultural education: A movement in the search of meaning and positive connections. *Multicultural Education,* Spring, 8–12.

Derman-Sparks, L. (1989). *Anti-bias curriculum.* Washington, D.C.: NAEYC.

Funderburg, L. (1994). *Black, white, other: Biracial Americans talk about race and identity.* New York: Morrow.

Gibbs, J. T. (1989). Biracial adolescents. In J. T. Gibbs, L. N. Hung, & Associates (Eds.), *Children of color: Psychological intervention and minority youth* (pp. 322–359). San Francisco: Jossey-Bass.

Graham, S. R. (1996). The real world. In M. P. P. Root (Ed.), *The multiracial experience* (pp. 37–48). Newbury Park, CA: Sage.

Matiella, C. A. (1991). *Positively different: Creating a bias-free environment for children.* Santa Cruz, CA: ETA Associates.

McRoy, R., & Freeman, E. (1986). Racial identity issues among mixed race children. *Social Work in Education, 8,* 164–174.

Morrison, J. W., & Rodgers, L. S. (1996). Being responsive to the needs of children from dual heritage backgrounds. *Young Children, 52*(1), 29–33.

Neugebauer, B. (Ed.) (1992). *Alike and different.* Washington, D.C.: NAEYC.

Ogbu, J. U. (1987). Variability in minority school performance: A problem in search of explanation. *Anthropology and Education Quarterly 18,* 312–334.

Phinney, J. S. (1991). Ethnic identity and self-esteem: A review and investigation. *Hispanic Journal of Behavioral Science, 13*(2), 193–208.

Poston, W. S. C. (1990). The biracial identity model: A needed addition. *Journal of Counseling and Development, 69,* 152–155.

Root, M. P. P. (Ed.). (1996). *The multiracial experience.* Newbury Park, CA: Sage.

Spickard, P. R. (1989). *Mixed blood.* Madison: University of Wisconsin Press.

Thorton, M. C. (1992). Is multiracial status unique? The personal and social experience. In M. P. P. Root (Ed.), *Racially mixed people in America* (pp. 321–326). Newbury Park, CA: Sage.

Wardle, F. (1987). Are you sensitive to interracial children's special needs? *Young Children, 43*(2), 53–59.

Wardle, F. (1991). Interracial children and their families: How social workers should respond. *Social Work in Education, 13*(4), 209–279.

Wardle, F. (1992). *Biracial identity: An ecological and developmental model.* Denver, CO: Center for the Study of Biracial Children.

Wardle, F. (1993). Interracial families and biracial children. *Child Care Information Exchange, 90,* 45–48.

Wardle, F. (1996). Multicultural education. In M. P. P. Root (Ed.), *The multiracial experience* (pp. 380–384). Newbury Park, CA: Sage.

LOOKING AT THE SCHOOLS

Public Agenda Asks African-American and White Parents About Their Aspirations and Their Fears

BY STEVE FARKAS AND JEAN JOHNSON

Editor's Note: Does a chasm separate African-American and white parents when they talk about what they want from the public schools? That's not the finding of the latest Public Agenda report, entitled Time To Move On. *The report, on which the following article is based, reveals some divisions, but it also finds that African-American and white parents are in solid agreement on what constitutes a good K-12 education and on the steps schools must take to provide it.*

MOST AMERICANS seem to believe in the concept of equal education for every child, regardless of race or ethnicity. Surveys tell us that only a handful question the goals of the civil rights movement, and only fringe elements say they would like to return to the days of segregated schools and separate lunch counters. Most Americans also say they believe that the dream envisioned by the Rev. Martin Luther King, Jr. has yet to be fully achieved.

When we move from the theoretical to the practical, however, the apparent consensus dissolves. Policies designed to promote integration and improve public education for minority youngsters often breed bitter controversy. As a nation, we seem to agree on what should be, but not on how we can get there. Indeed, some observers believe that the nation is now in "pause" mode when it comes to issues of school integration and equal educational opportunity.

Steve Farkas and Jean Johnson are senior vice presidents of Public Agenda, a nonpartisan organization that conducts in-depth research on how the public views critical policy issues. Portions of First Things First, *an earlier report on public education, appeared in the Winter 1994–95 issue of* American Educator.

Against this backdrop, Public Agenda and the Public Education Network (PEN) joined together to take a fresh look at how parents—black and white—see this often vexing complex of issues. The result, *Time To Move On: African-American and White Parents Set an Agenda for Public Schools,* expresses the aspirations and concerns of African-American and white parents, who want to secure a good education for their children in today's schools. It reports the results of in-depth telephone surveys of eight hundred African-American and eight hundred white parents, as well as findings from focus groups and individual interviews with parents and public education professionals.

Why didn't we also include Hispanic and Asian parents in this study? Partly because of limited funding and the high cost of research comparing the views of multiple subgroups of the general population. But this limitation also reflects Public Agenda's decision that if the study is to be helpful, it must focus sharply on very specific questions about race.

What follows is a summary of the key findings from *Time To Move On.*

The order in which we present these findings is perhaps unusual: The perspective of African-American parents comes first, followed by that of white parents, and we conclude with areas of common ground. But we hope this order will allow readers to absorb each group's thinking in context.

As researchers, we attempted to capture the views we heard as accurately and honestly as possible. We hope that in so doing, we can launch a renewed discussion of these difficult issues—one less encumbered by the weight of miscues and faulty assumptions. In the coming months, we will use this research as the context for community discussions on these issues to be sponsored by PEN and its network of Local Education Funds.

Finding One
The Message from Black Parents:
Academics First and Foremost

For African-Americans parents, the most important goal for public schools—the prize they seek with single-minded resolve—is academic achievement for their children. These parents believe in integration and want to pursue it, but their overriding concern is getting a solid education for their kids. Many spoke about jarring experiences with racism over the years, but despite these experiences, their focus is resolutely on the here and now. They want to move beyond the past and prepare their children for the future.

■ By an 8-to-1 margin, African-American parents say raising academic standards and achievement in the nation's schools is a higher priority than achieving more diversity and integration.

■ In their own children's schools, by an overwhelming 82 percent to 8 percent, black parents want the schools to make raising academic standards and achievement the foremost priority.

■ While 41 percent of black parents agree that kids get a better education in a racially integrated school, 51 percent say school integration makes little difference, and 5 percent say it makes for a worse education.

■ Sixty-three percent of African-American parents say the statement, "Too much is made of the differences between blacks and whites and not enough of what they have in common" comes *very* close to how they feel.

■ Only 41 percent of black and 34 percent of white parents say it is *excellent* or *good* to take black kids out of failing schools and send them to schools that are successful but mostly white.

Finding Two
The Current Political Agenda:
Time-Honored or Timeworn?

African-American parents are firmly committed to promoting diversity in the schools, but they express serious doubts about some of the most frequently debated policies. As they see it, approaches such as affirmative action in school hiring are double-edged swords: They accomplish some goals, but they can have negative consequences and can distract schools from their main task. In fact, black parents are decisive in opting for quality, regardless of race, in hiring teachers and school superintendents. Given the heated controversies surrounding standardized tests, one might also expect black parents to distrust them. However, most accept standardized tests as valid measures of student achievement, and most say that community discussions about education might be improved by less emphasis on race.

■ Ninety-seven percent of black and white parents agree that "our country is very diverse, and kids need

---

African-American parents' laser-like focus on academic achievement reflects a deep anxiety about how their children fare in the nation's schools.

---

to learn to get along with people from different cultures and ethnic backgrounds."

■ Seventy-five percent of African-American parents and 59 percent of white parents believe it is absolutely essential for schools to teach about the contributions blacks and other minorities have made to American history.

■ Three-quarters of African-American (73 percent) and white (77 percent) parents say, "Too often, the schools work so hard to achieve integration that they end up neglecting their most important goal—teaching kids."

■ Three-quarters of African-American parents say race should not be a factor when choosing a teacher or superintendent for a predominantly black school district.

■ But sixty-eight percent of black parents express concern that because of cultural differences, white teachers are not likely to understand how to deal with African-American students. Nearly seven in ten also think teachers and principals have lower expectations for black students due to racial stereotypes.

■ Forty-four percent of African-American parents say standardized tests measure "real differences in educational achievement," while another 18 percent say whites tend to do better because black students have low expectations of themselves. Only 28 percent think "the tests are culturally biased against black students." Nearly eight in ten black parents want differences in black and white achievement test scores publicized, since this may help to set reforms in motion to solve the problem.

■ Seven in 10 black parents say good discussions about schools "should be about what's good for students—there's no need to bring up race."

Finding Three
Black Student Achievement:
An Educational Crisis

African-American parents' laser-like focus on academic achievement reflects a deep anxiety about how their children fare in the nation's schools. They believe that far too many black children are not learning enough, and far too many of the schools they attend are unacceptably deficient. As one parent put it: "It's not just psychological, it's a fact. The mostly white schools have more resources, strong parents, computers. They're able to put money into those schools, and parent interest is there. They can't hire just any teacher." African-American parents believe that the problem of inadequate schools for their children is at a crisis point. White parents also believe African-American youngsters attend poorer schools and are less likely to do well academically. They see the problem as limited to poor, urban areas, however, and they do not call the situation a *crisis*.

■ The majority of black (56 percent) and white (54 percent) parents think *less than* half of black students are in good schools with good teachers. By contrast, 74 percent of black and 63 percent of white parents say *more than* half of white students are in good schools with good teachers. While only one in five says most white students are doing poorly in school, almost half say most blacks are doing poorly.

■ Six in ten African-American parents do not think underachievement among black students is confined to inner cities, whereas 56 percent of white parents do. Half of black parents say the problem affects students regardless of family income, but 64 percent of white parents believe it is mainly focused on low-income families.

■ More than half of African-American parents say the failure of black students to do well in schools is "a crisis and must be addressed quickly," but just over three in ten white parents say the same, although many say it's a serious problem. Few African-American and white parents say, "The problem is exaggerated."

■ Sixty percent of black parents would switch their kids to a private school if they could afford to do so.

Finding Four
White Parents: Will My Children Have to Pay the Price?

The views of white parents on race and the public schools are complex and often ambivalent. They want African-American children to receive a good education that will allow them to succeed, and they firmly believe that good schools are something any child deserves. They take pride in refusing to judge people on the color of their skin and in being more tolerant than earlier generations of white Americans. But they also have anxieties: They describe a struggle to find good schools, and they are nervous about any changes that they believe could endanger their quality. Many white parents fear that an influx of African-American students into a school would bring social and academic problems. Most say it is not the students' race but the socioeconomic status of their families that concerns them. They are deeply uncomfortable about admitting what troubles them, how-

ever, because they fear if they voice their concerns they will be labeled racists.

■ Sixty-one percent of white parents say, "One of the main reasons I live in this neighborhood is the quality of its schools," and slightly more than eight in ten agree that "since parents often pick a neighborhood for its schools, it's wrong to force them to send their kids elsewhere to achieve racial integration."

■ Sixty-one percent of white parents say if a large number of black students started attending a mostly white public school there might be discipline and safety problems, lower reading levels, or more social problems. But 71 percent say a school can prevent problems. Fifty-two percent say a private school would do a better job of maintaining discipline and order in a similar situation.

■ Eighty-two percent of white parents say they don't care about the race of the children in their schools so long as they come from good, hard-working families.

■ Nearly nine in ten black and white parents (86 percent) say, "It is society's responsibility to make sure black students have teachers and schools that are just as good as those of white students."

■ Seven in ten white parents and eight in ten black parents feel failing inner-city schools can overcome their problems with better resources, programs, and teachers.

■ Nearly three-quarters of African-American and white parents say, "It is hard for whites to talk honestly about problems in the African-American community because they are afraid someone will accuse them of being racist."

Finding Five
Integration: It's All in the Details

Both black and white parents say integration is valuable, but on closer examination, white—and to some extent, black—fears emerge. Both groups believe integrated schools improve race relations and enhance their children's ability to thrive in a diverse world. But they are also wary of associated costs: that schools will be distracted from academics; that bitter disputes will emerge; that their own children will end up paying the price. Whites are fearful that integration will bring troubled children into local schools; blacks fear their children will be thrown into hostile and contentious school environments. Most parents want integration to occur naturally and are optimistic that things can improve. Ironically, relatively few have direct experience with efforts to achieve school integration.

■ Nearly eight in ten African-American parents and close to seven in ten white parents say it is important that their own children's schools be racially integrated.

■ About six in ten black and white parents favor achieving integration through magnet schools, and 69 percent of black and 60 percent of white parents favor "redrawing district lines to combine mostly black and mostly white districts into one district."

■ Most black (73 percent) and white (65 percent) parents say black kids are usually the ones to bear the burden of integration.

■ Sixty-nine percent of African-American parents and 62 percent of white parents say, "Efforts to integrate often backfire because white people end up leaving the schools or the communities that try to integrate."

■ Sixty-nine percent of black and 81 percent of white parents say, "Given time, neighborhoods and schools will become more integrated on their own—you really can't force them."

■ About seven in ten African-American (66 percent) and white (74 percent) parents consider themselves better than their parents at dealing with people of different races. And about half of parents in both groups think their kids do a better job than they do.

Finding Six
Of Like Minds: African-American and White Parents Set an Agenda for Public Schools

Despite many differences in their experiences and concerns, white and African-American parents have strikingly similar visions of what it takes to educate kids: involved parents, top-notch staff, and schools that guarantee the basics, high academic expectations, standards, safety, and order. White and black parents also share considerable common ground over how to help black children and failing schools improve.

■ Black and white parents come within five percentage points of each other on nine of twelve questions dealing with the absolutely essential characteristics of good schools, such as teaching good work habits, teaching standard English, and guaranteeing safety and order.

■ About nine in ten African-American (88 percent) and white (92 percent) parents say, "Kids learn best when their families stress the importance of education; respect for the value of school begins at home."

■ Sixty-three percent of black and 76 percent of white parents think a student from a supportive family who attends a poor school is more likely to succeed than a student from a troubled family who goes to a poor school.

■ Eighty-three percent of black and 67 percent of white parents say they need to keep a close eye on teachers and schools to make sure their kids are treated well.

■ African-American parents are more likely than white parents to think it's absolutely essential for schools to expect all kids to go on to college (51 percent to 31 percent).

■ Fifty-five percent of black and 52 percent of white parents say it is the responsibility of the family, not the school or society, to address the problem when black students underachieve.

When asked about ways to fix failing schools and help African-American students who are doing poorly in school, there is a great degree of consensus among African-American and white parents. Solutions—such as expanding preschool programs to help prepare low-income black children for school, requiring parents of failing students to attend programs to teach them how to help their children learn, and having tough repercussions for students in possession of drugs or weapons or who are persistent troublemakers—receive high levels of support from both groups of parents. Solutions that would give families financial aid so they could move their children from failing public schools to private schools and charter schools attract somewhat less support.

Final Thoughts

Quotes, soundbites, and news headlines related to race and education debates can lead those following the issue to sense a great divide between the hopes of African-American and white parents for our nation's schools. While *Time To Move On* outlines some important areas of differences, it also identifies the many areas in which black and white parents are in close agreement. Their agendas are clear: African-American and white parents want safe and orderly schools to provide a solid background in the basics, have higher academic standards overall, and strong teaching staffs; and they want parents to get involved.

Copies of the study, which was carried out with funding from the W.K. Kellogg, Charles Stewart Mott, Rockefeller, and Surdna Foundations, are available from Public Agenda for $12.50 (including shipping and handling). Complete questionnaire results may also be obtained from Public Agenda for $42.50. For questions, contact Public Agenda (212/686-6610 or www.publicagenda.org).

Unit Selections

Key Points to Consider

❖ Describe the corporate interests in the future of schooling in America as identified by Irving Buchen in "Business Sees Profits in Education: Challenging Public Schools" and discuss the already-developing trends mentioned in this article.

❖ What would be possible if schools permitted teachers more autonomy in how they assess their students?

❖ What can teachers do to help students develop a sense of social consciousness and social responsibility?

❖ How can teachers help students to develop their talents and to develop a vision of hope for themselves? How can teachers help students to develop a sense of public service?

❖ What are the most important challenges confronting multicultural educators as we enter the new century?

 **Links** **www.dushkin.com/online/**

These sites are annotated on pages 4 and 5.

We are situated as people in the context of a social matrix of many dimensions, including social class, gender identity, culture, race, age, ideological position, life experiences, and beliefs. We have a special obligation to encourage our students to create the best visions for their lives that they can imagine and to help them lift up their voices and their spirits in the pursuit of their dreams. We must do this for all students, not just the marginalized. No child or teenager should have to feel unwanted or hopeless. As matters of social conscience and moral principle, we must recognize and affirm our duty as teachers to make the best effort possible to teach our students well.

We look forward to a future of multicultural education with a degree of optimism, although aware that there are serious challenges before us. The winds of xeneophobia are blowing across the land again; concern regarding immigration is at a fairly high level. Yet this concern was present in all earlier decades in American history when rates of immigration were running at as high levels as they are now. We all agree that there is much work to be done to accomplish the goals of multicultural education. There is, however, great hope that these goals will be achieved as our population moves steadily toward becoming ever more unique as a multicultural civilization. We are going to become less and less like western Europe and more and more a very unique national wonder such as the world has not seen before. The next 30 to 40 years will bring that vision into reality.

We need a vision for the future of our schools that includes a belief in the worth and dignity of all people. We need to clarify our vision in such a way that it has a holistic character, which takes into account the ever more culturally pluralistic social reality that we are becoming. As part of this effort we need to consider the French revolutionary concept of fraternity. Fraternity and its female counterpart, sorority, refer to brotherhood and sisterhood. We need a new birth of fraternity and sorority in our national life that will enable us to truly care about what happens to one another. We need very much to communicate that sense of caring to the young people who attend our schools, for they truly are our social future. The teaching profession needs a good dose of fraternity and sorority as well. Teachers need to work together in solving problems and supporting their respective professional efforts on behalf of students.

The future of teaching and learning from a multicultural perspective should include more emphasis on cooperative learning strategies that encourage students to develop a sense of community and fraternity that will transcend competition with one another and create a sense of trust and caring among them. We need to stop making students compete with one another and encourage them to work together. We need to learn to team together and teach together more than we have in the past, and we need to have the professional autonomy (independence of professional judgment) to be able to do so at our own discretion and not because someone told us to.

There needs to be more democratization of the day-to-day governance structures of schools so that competent teachers can enjoy the same levels of personal, professional autonomy that their colleagues in teacher education enjoy. A multicultural vision of the future of education will embrace the concept that the strengths and talents of all students need optimum development. The problems and weaknesses of all students need resolution and assistance. We need to see young people as a treasured human resource whose needs for safety, health, and cognitive and affective development are to be met by our best efforts as educators. A multicultural vision of our educational future will include an acceptance by educators of an expanded conception of their responsibility to their students to include a commitment to each student's best possible development as a person; we will see our clients whole. We will be concerned about more than their intellectual development, although this is our primary role; we will also see schooling as having a therapeutic mission. Diverse cultural backgrounds and learning styles will be accepted and nurtured as brothers and sisters in a shared national community of educational interests.

The future will also see less dependence on standardized, system-wide, behavioral objectives and more emphasis on permitting teachers at the local school level to develop models for assessing whether or not their students are achieving their educational goals. There will be more informal teacher-customized approaches to evaluation of student learning and less reliance on rigid, statewide, standardized learning objectives. Individual school faculties will be permitted to modify their schools' learning objectives for their students, and students will receive more individualized assessment and feedback on their progress in school.

Finally, a multicultural vision of the future of education will include a strong commitment to develop a powerful, critical sense of social consciousness and social responsibility between teachers and students. Students will be encouraged and assisted to define and to reconstruct their personal worlds so that they are empowered to see the world as it is, and to make it better if they can. Educational settings of society are important terrain in the struggle to reconstruct public life along more egalitarian social policy lines. A multicultural vision of our educational future will encourage teachers to adopt a pedagogy of liberation that champions the development of critical social awareness among students and which empowers them to evaluate critically all that they may experience. Education will have a liberating intent; the goal will not be just to teach children to reason critically, but to reason critically in the light of a clear vision of social justice worthy of all of their rights as citizens. The struggle to see a multicultural vision for our schools adopted by the teaching profession has always been closely aligned with the broader struggle for civil liberties and human dignity.

For Vision and Voice: A Call to Conscience

By Irving H. Buchen

Business Sees Profits in Education: Challenging Public Schools

Private enterprise is competing for America's $600 billion education market. In the future, a child's favorite teacher may be "MaMaMedia."

Education in the United States is undergoing a rapid and dramatic series of changes caused by private enterprise moving into the field.

Education attracts the private sector for three reasons. First, it can be financially rewarding: Education is estimated to be a $600 billion market, more than the budget for the Department of Defense. The biggest single market is kindergarten through twelfth grade (K-12), valued at $310 billion in 1998. Additionally, lifelong learning and training programs for businesses and organizations are growing areas.

Second, education has received such bad press that confidence in the established system is low, in spite of all the internal efforts at reform. In response to public education's many failures, home schoolers and charter schools have increased, and both are customers for educational products and services. Home-schooling parents regularly attend regional con-

ferences at which exhibitors offer their products and services.

Third, education is there for the taking: The general attitude is that professional, public educators have had sufficient time to turn the system around. They have no one but themselves to blame for corrective intervention from the private sector, even if that intervention is financially motivated, and especially since these actions promise to achieve results.

Almost all of the new educational products and services now being marketed bear the stamp of technology. Such technology replaces teachers altogether or reduces their number, thus solving several critical weaknesses in traditional education. For instance, replacing teachers reduces the high cost of an excessively labor-intensive instructional process while still serving the same number of students. Then, too, it eliminates tenure, which unfortunately locks in instructors who do not have the

training or knowledge to keep up with changing fields and new approaches. Finally, technology, like the best of teachers, is infinitely patient and reassuring. It accommodates the speed of each student and his or her level of learning. It never wearies.

Below is a description of the many different companies competing for the educational market, grouped by the main technology they use. Because the situation is in flux, not all the major players may appear here. The aim is not to produce a definitive picture but rather to demonstrate the extent to which education is changing.

Satellite Links

Channel One, viewed by over 8 million students, provides a 12- to 15-minute newscast and review of current events adjusted for different age groups. This service, free for

Originally published in May 1999 issue of *The Futurist*, pp. 38-44. Published with permission of the World Future Society, 7910 Woodmont Ave., Bethesda, MD 20814 .wfs.org

> Replacing teachers reduces the high cost of a labor-intensive process while serving the same number of students.

schools, is sponsored by advertisers. Feedback from students as to what designer labels they prefer and what advertising they enjoy seeing on TV is then sold as marketing data.

The **Educational Management Group** provides virtual voyages for over 4,000 classrooms. For $30,000, the company equips classrooms with a live satellite link and interactive speaker phones so that students can ask questions directly to a traveling series of TV crews visiting sites all over the world. Visits include archaeological sites, underwater explorations, scientific labs, and artists' studios.

Software

Lucas Learning was launched in the fall of 1998. The company uses the Star Wars format to teach 10- to 14-year-olds basic scientific principles. For example, their first software product is *Star Wars Droid Works*. Set on the floor of a robot factory, it takes students through all the principles and applications of energy, light, magnetism, engineering, and motion necessary to design and build robots.

The Learning Company and Broderbund: The result of a recent merger between Broderbund Software (which produces *Carmen San Diego* and *Myst*) and the Learning Company (which produced *MayaQuest*), this new company has almost doubled its registered users to about 20 million. Some of the most popular software programs are *ClickArt*, *Family Tree Maker*, *The Print Shop*, *Games Strategies*, *Red Orb Kids*, and

Mudball Wall (which builds the logic skills of eight- to 12-year-olds).

The Computer Curriculum Corporation is the largest K-12 software provider. CCC's 50 different programs are both student- and teacher-friendly. The company provides programs that monitor the needs and progress of individual students as well as an entire class, enabling teachers to diagnose student deficiencies and give weekly progress reports. One of the newest teacher aids is a program that helps to manage and coordinate school lesson plans.

MindQ Publishing has been extremely successful in the adult computer development market. Currently used by over 200 companies such as IBM, Sun, and Microsoft, MindQ trains employees in Java programming skills with its software *Java Academy*. MindQ provides CD-ROM for individual instruction at home, or it can design an entire computer

curriculum tailored to the needs of a specific company.

The Internet

Most of the companies offering educational products and services on the Internet are targeting businesses for employee and management training. **Cyber School** claims to have 30,000 student employees involved in computer training, live chat sessions, diagnostics, and personal tutoring by e-mail. **Pensare** uses a game format to simulate actual corporate situations for its 16,000 management trainee users. **The Executive Committee (TEC) Worldwide** is dedicated to making it less lonely at the top: Its 5,000 CEO members can contact nearly 350 peer advisory groups in order to share problems, exchange ideas, or swap war stories. **Productivity Point**

©PHOTODISC, INC.

International trains about 1 million employees at some 150 training centers around the United States, but its training is also available through distance education.

For kids, there's **MaMaMedia**, an Internet educational company that claims to have 90,000 registered users under age 12. Created by MIT graduates, MaMaMedia seeks parental, rather than teacher, endorsement of its content and linkages. The company's learning themes emphasize the "three X's": exploration, expression, and exchange. This company offers a program to link pen pals; teaches *Java Studio* skills such as drawing, painting, and photography; and provides Web pages where teen-agers can chat about their learning and living.

For adults, there's the soon-to-be-launched **Knowledge University**, which plans to offer post-secondary education and training to corporations and individuals. This new venture is owned by mega-supplier Knowledge Universe, to be described in greater detail later.

As for other universities in the United States, 65% were offering on-line courses in 1998, up from 25% in 1995, according to the Gartner Group, an information

THE LEARNING COMPANY

Math games: New software from The Learning Company allows six- to nine-year-olds to practice counting money and making change while rescuing Sam the Lion from a tricky pirate trap.

THE LEARNING COMPANY

The computer as teacher: Educational entrepreneurs offer learning software like *Schoolhouse Rock* (right). First and second graders learn reading, math, science, and more with games that take them through real life situations, like grocery shopping.

Young learner shows off phonics toy: The LeapFrog company goes after its share of the $1 billion educational toy market with products that teach reading, spelling, the alphabet, and more.

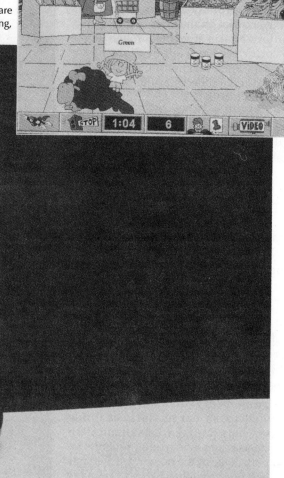

LEAPFROG, INC

technology consulting firm in Stamford, Connecticut. The group projects that figure will rise to 80% by 2001.

Tutoring

Score! is owned by the test prep company Kaplan Educational Centers. It offers personal coaching to some 20,000 students. The system is based on a sports model, which emphasizes study teams; teachers function as cheerleaders. Real life and electronic mentors offer one-on-one academic and career counseling. The company's database contains up-to-date information on future careers. Los Angeles just selected Score! to provide tutoring at 25 public schools.

Sylvan Learning Systems recently partnered with MCI to create over 100 pilot centers where students can receive highly sophisticated technology training after school. Over 40 such centers, dubbed the Caliber Learning Network, have served over 30,000 students. Sylvan will soon aggressively market its services; it will especially try to attract home schoolers during their off hours.

Computerized Testing

Computerized testing methods that can provide instruction or suggestions based on an individual's test results are further diminishing the role of the teacher. **Micro-Cat,** originally developed for the U.S. Marine Corps, evaluates reading, grammar, and math skills. **HyDrive,** designed by the Educational Testing Service (ETS) and the U.S. Air Force, tests both knowledge and problem-solving ability; it also gives corrective feedback. **Compass** recommends study plans based on a student's test results; it was created by textbook publisher Addison Wesley. Finally, **E-Rater** automatically scores essays for syntax, vocabulary, and organization. It is still being developed by ETS: The goal is for 85% agreement between E-Rater and human evaluations.

Books, Toys, and Television

Although less reliant on cutting-edge technology, the following companies, products, and services are also entering the education market:

The British publishing giant **Pearson** owns Penguin Books and the *Fi-*

> *Blues Clues'* 5 million weekly viewers outperform nonviewers on standardized tests.

nancial Times. Through a series of acquisitions, mergers, and alliances, it also owns or manages the education divisions of Simon & Schuster, Addison Wesley, Prentice Hall, and others. It is the biggest educational publisher in the world. Using its financial base, Pearson has developed a series of software programs on investment banking and financial risk management. It also offers training software for subjects from typing to linguistics.

Zany Brainy is an educational, upscale toy store with franchises all over the United States. Zany Brainy has designed special educational programs for parents and kids, usually using or demonstrating their teaching toys. The stores are equipped with computers where kids can access *e-line,* the company's monthly newsletter for kids. Another toy company, **LeapFrog,** teaches reading, spelling, and the alphabet with hand-held toys that combine touch, sight, and sound. based on a phonics system developed by Stanford professor Robert Calfee, LeapFrog toys are marketed directly to schools and through toy stores.

The *Blue's Clues* series, from cable TV company Nickelodeon, has over 5 million weekly viewers, which is higher ratings than *Barney* or *Sesame Street.* This show's viewers outperform nonviewers on standardized tests. On *Blue's Clues,* viewers join the host in solving a problem by searching for clues—indicated by pawprints of the cartoon puppy "Blue"—and putting the clues together.

Children's Discovery Centers of America claim some 20,000 students who learn language skills, logical thinking, and cooperative play. The Centers seek to address the "whole child." One of their techniques is to give each child plenty of physical space and permission to move around, which they believe liberates a child's thinking.

Administrative Approaches

Entrepreneurs, teachers, and parents are seeking to improve education through administrative, organizational, and methodological changes in addition to technological improvements. The following is a summary of these efforts.

The Edison Project

This method is probably the most controversial and invasive: Public

The Education Market

Type of Product/Approach	Estimated Market Share (in millions)
Tutoring	$37,500
Books	5,600
Toys	1,000
Administration	1,000
Software	683
Satellite Links	151
Internet	64

Sources: Simba Information, Inc., P.O. Box 7430, Wilton, Connecticut 06897. Telephone 1-203-834-0033.
Smith Barney Inc., 388 Greenwich Street, New York, New York 10013. Telephone 1-212-816-6999.

schools are actually taken over and run by the Edison Project at a profit. Chris Whittle, president of the Edison Project, was also the creator of Channel One. The Edison Project features courses such as "Technology as a Second Language"; requires more hours of school attendance, including summers; and regularly assesses both teacher and student performance. Edison now manages an estimated 48 schools and projected a profit of $125 million for 1998.

Charter Schools

Usually much smaller than the comparable elementary, middle, or high school from which they draw students, these alternative schools are "chartered" by boards of education to operate. The charter authorizes the school to operate and to receive public funds. There were 800 charter schools in the United States in 1998. Normally a group of parents is heavily involved. When a student transfers to a charter school, the district loses funding because the educational allotment for that student is given to the charter school.

It is too soon to gauge the effectiveness of charter schools, but proponents believe that the special attention and smaller size will automatically make a difference. Most states limit the number of charter schools, but a recent breakthrough in California may spread to other states: A coalition of parents and business executives, led by John Doerr, the Kleiner Perkins venture capitalist, succeeded in removing California's charter school cap. Doerr's major corporate partner in this venture was Tech-Net, a Silicon Valley political activist group.

Online Courses Generate Red Ink

Universities may be rushing to offer online education, but they aren't making any money at it, according to the director of New York University's online programs.

Calling the lack of profit a "dirty little secret," Gerald A. Heegar, dean of Continuing and Professional Studies at NYU, told *The New York Times* that online higher education doesn't yet have a business model that works. But universities are spending $50,000 or more to create and support each Internet class because they believe online education will be profitable in the future, and they want to stake out their share now.

Related to the issue of profit is the question of who should own online courses—the university or the faculty. Advocates for faculty note that, once a professor creates an online course, he or she becomes dispensable: The course can be used again and again, and another instructor can be assigned to answer questions and grade papers. NYU holds ownership rights to its online courses, but Penn State is splitting revenue with the faculty members who develop the courses.

Source: "More Colleges Plunge Into Uncharted Waters of On-Line Courses" by Karen W. Arenson. *The New York Times* (November 2, 1998).

Home Schooling

Although the estimated number of home-schooled students is about 1 million, many believe the actual number is higher. Part of the difficulty in estimating is that home schooling is growing. Originally impelled by parents whose religious views led them to object to the way certain subjects were taught, home schooling has caught on with parents who are concerned about their children's safety and quality of learning. Many home schoolers are located in areas with no viable private or parochial school alternatives.

Home-schooling parents have transformed the movement by affiliating with each other and aggressively petitioning local schools to provide them with access to laboratories, gymnasiums, art studios, theaters, and libraries. The net result is that home schooling is not as isolated as it was initially. Above all, technology has been the supreme equalizer by providing home schoolers with educational products that often surpass those available in regular schools. Finally, the homeschool calendar is flexible and can include family vacations as school and study time. Home schooling is at least as successful as regular schooling, and

Student Preference Should Dictate Technology

Some educators believe that distance education, such as courses offered on video or the Internet, is inferior to traditional education, but that isn't true, according to Thomas L. Russell of North Carolina State University, author of *No Significant Difference Phenomenon*. Russell's comparative studies show that when technology is used to teach it neither improves nor hinders the learning.

Some students prefer to learn via one technology rather than another, and it isn't always the newest technology that works best, Russell told a recent workshop of the Distance Education & Training Council.

The council concludes that, "until any of the old and new technologies can prove their superiority through comparative research, it is best to look at other factors—student preferences, access, cost—as the principal criteria. The ideal distance educational world would then offer each course through a variety of equally effective modalities."

Source: Distance Education & Training Council, 1601 18th Street, N.W., Washington, D.C. 20009. Telephone 1-202-234-5100; Web site http://www. detc.org.

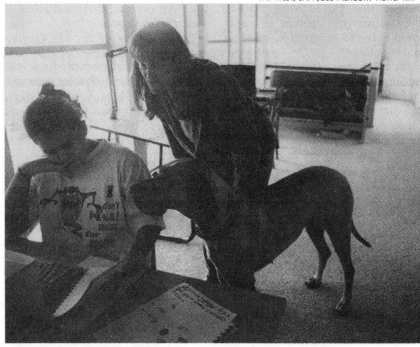

PAT WEST, *SAN JOSE MERCURY NEWS/* KRT

Schooling at home: Bobbi Sitkin helps her daughter, Mollie, age 11, with her homework at their home in Linden, California. The Sitkin family teaches their children at home, but once a month they travel to The Charter Learning Center in San Carlos, California, a public school that uses nontraditional teaching methods.

often superior, as measured by standardized tests.

Knowledge Universe

With revenues of over $1 billion, Knowledge Universe is the most extensive educational competitor and supplier—a mega-brand. The brainchild of Larry Ellison, billionaire CEO of Oracle, and Michael Milken of junk-bond fame, the company aims to provide a lifetime of educational products and services.

Knowledge Universe already owns in whole or in part five of the companies discussed above: Children's Discovery Centers of America, MindQ's *Java Academy*, Knowledge University, TEC Worldwide, and LeapFrog. These companies are estimated to be worth $4 billion-$6 billion. Knowledge Universe has also identified 31 additional industry

segments for acquisition. One such candidate is Nobel Education Dynamics, which operates 100 preschools and over 30 private schools; Nobel will take over its first charter school in 1999.

The Future of Education

Clearly, the three R's will be supplemented by the three T's: Technology, Teaming, and Transference. The Edison Project is correct: Technology is a new language and deserving of its own curriculum. Pensare and Score! rightly emphasize cooperative and collaborative learning—the educational version of corporate problem-solving teams. This approach to learning also builds community and social skills. New approaches and concepts such as linkages, bridging concepts, and systemic wholes not only improve the learning process, they allow the student to apply knowledge to unanticipated areas and situations.

All indications are that public education will lose control of the field. Private competition, home schooling, and charter schools are draining off students, often good ones. Charter schools take away per capita dollars as well. Software programs are threatening to replace teachers. Testing will become a province of automated technology, often in partnership with textbook publishers and software developers. Finally, the lure of so much money

LUKE FRAZZA/AFP

Charter schools gain support: U.S. President Bill Clinton with parent Sue Bragato at the San Carlos Charter School in San Carlos, California. Activists in California recently removed the state's charter school limit.

will attract even more venture capitalists, who will aggressively carve up the future education market.

But perhaps the biggest surprise may be the decision by a number of educators—especially those who have long been advocates for school reform—to give up tenure, join the entrepreneurial movement, start their own charter schools, seek employment with Edison or KU, or create their own educational companies. Two examples:

The recent book *Extra Life: Coming of Age in Cyberspace* by David S. Bennahum tells the story of one of the author's former teachers. Edward Moran left Horace Mann High School after 23 years to teach adults through the Global Knowledge Network, which provides continuing education to corporate employees.

Moran will never go back to public education.

Former teacher Robert Helmick created Real Education, which provides over 50 universities with online courses. Real Education employs 135 people and hires more each month, many former teachers. Helmick estimates that it takes a university 100 to 600 hours to put a course online. He can do it in 40 hours at a cost of about $3,000 per course. His courses are multimedia, interactive, and designed to run on even slow, inexpensive computers. This specialized niche filled by Real Education is part of the larger transformation taking place.

Of course, others will resist. Arthur Steinert, analyst for Edu Ventures, says, "Despite all the money spent on technology, there are still many technophobes and Luddites among the ranks of teachers." But there will be a comprehensive sorting out. Diehards will hang on if they can until retirement. Others will leave, like Edward Moran. Many who might have entered public education will turn instead to this new emerging educational market, in which the lines between public and private will be less clear.

About the Author
Irving H. Buchen is professor of management and communications at Walden University and a senior associate at COMWELL, a human resource consulting group. His address is 8650 Kilkenny Court, Ft. Myers, Florida 33912. E-mail ibuchen@msn.com.

An Outsider's View Inside

21st Century Directions for Multicultural Education

Offering Transnational, Transcultural
Visions of a Shared Heritage
and a Common Future

By David B. Willis

Introduction:

Audiences, Participants, Publics

Gaijin. Outside Person. Outrider. Living in a society where one is perpetually Other, where severe challenges to personal, cultural, and gender identity are forever being sharply played out, a society deeply xenophobic, yet crying out for cultural translators to help their "internationalization" (kokusaika), throws issues of multicultural education from the American context, from the context of my home (or at least one of them), into sharp, provocative contrast. My own perspectives have been drawn from a deep, intimate, and ultimately humbling experience of this culture, Japan, and likewise with India, the two com-

---

David B. Willis is a professor of Cultural Studies at Soai University, Osaka, Japan.

plex cultural settings where I have spent most of the 22 years of my professional life as an expatriate, an alien, an outcaste, a marginal person, an alien, Other.

The work of James A. Banks and his colleagues in multicultural education deeply attracted me in the late 1980s as having signal relevance to issues of human community on a global scale. The terrifying dramas of the 20th Century, of nationalism and genocide, of racism, imperialism, of human and ecological destruction played out on a massive scale leave us witness to two possible directions for humanity, one of cynical and weary despair, and the other, the only one that is really viable, of hope.

Looking from the outside (ten years teaching social studies in international schools in Japan and India, 12 years as an educational anthropologist/comparative educator teaching cultural studies at a Buddhist women's university in South Osaka), I could see

sparks of this hope in the discourses and practices of multicultural education. Now the field is coming of age. In this essay I will address linkages from the outside-inside, across borders, across times, across spaces, across places.

Transformative Discourse:

Answering the Critics of
Multicultural Education

How do the recent new directions of multicultural educators address criticisms that have been made of multicultural education? What areas need further scholarly development, focus, and attention? What directions are Banks and his collaborators taking us as we enter this new century and new millennium?

Christine Sleeter (1995) has identified important critiques of multicultural education from both the right and the left in an elegant model of scholarship that should be reviewed carefully by all of us. How has recent research answered some of these critiques? First, the eloquent presentation of the scholarly origins of multicultural education provided by Banks (1996), Banks and Banks (1995), and others should dispel criticism of any "suspicious extremist origins." Second, the emphasis on joining many communities around the issues, as exemplified by recent authors and their subjects, should quiet (if not silence) critics who say that multicultural education has a potential for divisiveness.

As many of the essays in Banks' recent book (1996) highlight, group values focused on sharing, generosity, and community are challenging the real source of divisiveness, the traditional Western emphasis on the individual, what Native Americans see as "chaotic and extreme individualism." Third, the intellectual rigor of multicultural education has clearly been demonstrated (though, of course, we need more). Fourth, the persistent and pernicious link between underachievement and genetics/lack of effort, used as an argument against any kind of affirmative action (an important part of multicultural education) no longer requires the dignity of a response. As Martin Carnoy (1994), Alejandro Portes and Ruben G. Rumbaut (1990), and recent statistics have borne out, when there is relative equality of opportunity there is hard work and achievement.

Critics of the left have more compelling arguments which must eventually be addressed. The major difference with multicultural educators is strategy. If we are to reach the vast middle of people whose sympathies could be with us, but whose information is stilted and limited by a conservatively manipulated media, we must choose the timing, context, and content of our messages carefully. And we must make strenuous efforts to get our messages out to the mainstream media, as documented by Carlos Cortes (1995) in his examination of the knowledge construction process as it appears in the mass media and by Carl Grant, who addresses myths about multicultural education which must be deconstructed (1994).

The severe problems of textbook depictions and the need for their active deconstruction/reconstruction have been eloquently stated by James Loewen in *Lies My Teacher Told Me, Everything Your American History Textbook Got Wrong* (1995). Now is the time to actively participate as multicultural educators in the re-construction of these messages (hooks, 1994). There is a great need to focus our activities on the mainstream intellectual mass media, which has such a great impact on the attitude formations of the masses and on key policy-makers. Our task in general is thus what Lila Abu-Lughod (1991) has called "a shift in gaze to include phenomena of connection."

Future Needs of the Metadiscipline:

Psychology and Multicultural Education; Diversity, Identities, and the Individual

Mestizaje es grandeza.
(Mixture is greatness).

One of the key issues which needs to be addressed in multicultural education is identity, its creation, its substances, and its transformations, usually thought to be the province of psychology.[1] Multicultural education has shown us a variety of strategies, both for relating to outsiders (who are increasingly on the inside) and for re-constituting one's own identity (which is seen to be more and more on the outside, on display to curious Others). Boundaries, cultural and national, are easily re-drawn and even more easily crossed, letting us know in subtle (and some not-so-subtle) ways about the new postmodern era we have entered. We have begun a time where "Borderlands" are less and less on the margin and more and more at the heart of contemporary discourse.

One of the most powerful discourses concerning boundaries that has appeared at the end of the 20th Century is that of mixed-race individuals. Their conversations deserve special attention from multicultural educators. The stunning perspectives presented by these powerful voices illuminate new paths in the practice of freedom (Williams, 1996; Zack, 1993; Root, 1992; Spickard, 1989; Rosenblatt et al., 1995; Scales-Trent, 1995; Funderburg, 1994; Obama, 1995).

Cosmopolitans, those people who are mixed-bloods and/or of mixed cultures and who have relationships with a plurality of cultures, the more the better, also deserve our attention. These people see diversity as meaning the coexistence of cultures, often within the multiplicity of their own identity. Their orientation is transnational or transcultural, the difference being a matter of degree of commitment. Transculturalism, to use the Swedish scholar Ulf Hannerz's phrase (1990, p. 239), is "first of all an orientation, a willingness to engage with the Other. It is an intellectual and aesthetic stance of openness toward divergent cultural experiences, a search for contrasts rather than uniformity."

As a new diaspora, transnationals/transculturals act as agents who "continuously inject new meaning-streams" into the discourses of contemporary societies (Appadurai, 1990, p. 11). The first transnational experience is that of being made the Other. "Nobody is born as the Other. People are made into the Other" (Essed, 1996). Transnationals and transculturals also bring a central force to the modern world: deterritorialization. Their experiences and views can perhaps teach us about the conditions of growing social disjunctures. They may show us how the globalization of culture is not the same as its homogenization.

Locals may carry a (nationalistic) air of provincialism in today's world. For cosmopolitans, on the other hand, orientation and competence are key skills. Cosmopolitans are especially adept at "managing meaning." This competence is both generalized and specialized: "There is the aspect of a state of readiness, a personal ability to make one's way into other cultures, through listening, looking, intuiting and reflecting. And there is cultural competence in the stricter sense of the term, a built-up skill in maneuvering more or less expertly with a particular system of meanings and meaningful forms" (Hannerz, 1990, p. 239).

These people demonstrate an expansion of the concepts of identity and loyalty that are critical if we wish to see the transition to a humane world system (Castenell & Pinar, 1993). For them national identity is less important than what can be called a transnational or transcultural identity: they are more than simply in the world—they are with the world. And as Robert Hughes has put it (1993), "The future . . . will lie with people who can think and act with informed grace across ethnic, cultural, linguistic lines. . . . In the world that is coming, if you can't navigate difference, you've had it." Multiple identity patterns are thus very important (Essed, 1996), beginning with a planetary identity and including national, class, ethnic, religious, local, and family identities. Each should be vivid and intense.

> It is, after all, on the subject of boundary construction where multiculturalism has had its severest critics. But most of those critics have misunderstood what a border means.... Borders are not where something stops. Borders are where something begins.

Society and Multicultural Education:

Creoles, Diasporas, Mixing

Missing from the discourse of multicultural educators are the authentic voices of Creole communities, contemporary diaspora, and international/transnational contexts. This is the intersection of multicultural education and society, connections, crossroads. And these communities and individuals tell us much about these crossroads.

Cherry McGee Banks and others have discussed borders and border crossings (Banks, 1996), but we need more exploration of identity in the context of society and connections. It is, after all, on the subject of boundary construction where multiculturalism has had its severest critics. But most of those critics have misunderstood what a border means and what those activities (including those called Afrocentric and similar, related terms) are all about. Borders are not where something stops. Borders are where something begins.

There is a great need, too, to connect with powerful scholarship of today in the active Borderlands. Examples include Gloria Anzaldua (1987), Oscar J. Martinez (1994), L. A. Urrea (1993), T. Todorov (1982, 1993), Arjun Appadurai (1990, 1991), Etienne Balibar and Immanuel Wallerstein (1993), and especially Benedict Anderson (1994). The transformation of the idea of the margins of societies is now becoming apparent. Marginality is now seen as conveying power and originality, as helping societies to move for-

ward. The margins are now becoming the center.

The borders of multicultural education must themselves be expanded. I must admit to having had some initial discomfort with the word "national" in NAME when I first joined. It just seemed too parochial and narrow, but if we take "national" to mean "nations" in the sense of the American Indian interpretation, then I can be comfortable with the term, a read which takes us beyond political borders, boundaries which are in any event so very porous these days.

We can no longer see diverse cultural flows simply as bilateral exchanges or bilateral antagonisms. Cartesian dualism, binary logic, either/or, fails us when trying to understand culture and contemporary social dynamics. Terms such as homogeneity/ heterogeneity, group/individual, unity/diversity do little to inform us about complex cultural processes. Ultimately they position any discussion of societies in a subject/object context that elevates the subject in his/her position of observation at the expense of the "voice" of the object.

Instead, we can conceptualize global culture not in terms of homogenizing processes, but "more in terms of the diversity, variety, and richness of popular and local discourses, codes and practices which resist and play-back systemicity and order" (Featherstone, 1990, p. 2). We should see particularities and differences as **both** parts of humanity, of a generative frame of unity where diversity can take place.

In border regions, when one side is dominant there are strong demands for acculturation and assimilation, but when the two sides are more closely together in power, even relatively equal, the main form of intercultural relations is transculturation. This is the practice of freedom.

What we are witnessing is a kind of "global compression" which has resulted in the present high degree and persistence of global complexity and increased cultural conflicts. Globalization also entails—at the local and international levels—(1) reduced cultural homogeneity, (2) increased cultural disorder, and (3) the formation of true transnational cultures (sometimes called "third" culture). As cultures which were formerly isolated pockets of relative homogeneity are linked, increasingly diverse portraits of the Other are created as well as reactions that reinforce one's own special identity (Featherstone, 1990, p. 6).

A theme which emerges from this discussion is that freeing students and

teachers from their cultural and ethnic boundaries, enabling them to cross cultural borders, is an important goal of education. One of the most powerful lessons we can teach to students is that they are boundary-makers, that they are in control of the act of creation of how they see the world. And as the Reverend Jesse Jackson so often notes, these creators, like James and Cherry Banks, help us "Keep hope alive."

Politics and Multicultural Education:

Activists and Praxis

We are really just at the beginning, a provocative and well-articulated beginning to be sure, but we need to bring other great American heroes like Frederick Douglass, John Brown, the radical Helen Keller (the Helen Keller whom we never hear about) and many others into the limelight, those heroes and heroines who have had an active influence on policymaking and who have been too invisible too long. And not only Americans. Martin Luther King, for example, learned from Mahatama Gandhi, who in turn learned from Tolstoy, Jesus, and Buddha. We need to broaden our horizons.

Another area in great need of investigative scholarship and documentation is the work "behind-the-scenes," the political maneuvering and changes, for example, in state certification requirements, teacher education programs, and other areas where requirements concerning Multicultural Education and Multiethnic Understanding have been instituted. This is the front-line work of multicultural educators and those programs which are particularly outstanding. Exemplars, such as California's Curriculum Guidelines and teacher certification requirements as well as the work of colleges of education (the Universities of Washington and Wisconsin come to mind) deserve recognition in the form of scholarly research. How have multicultural educators been able to effect transformations that have led us away from institutionalized racism and towards reconciliation and understanding? Of course the work of key leaders must be recognized, but so too should the work of the troops.[2]

World cultures are now linked globally and technologically. Politically, we are also linked in terms of class divisions and inequality created and maintained by social and political institutions. These should be the new objects of our inquiry. The 20th century was an era of nationalism and horrifying abuses (as well, of course, of various positive contributions to our well-being when compared to previous centuries). The 21st century has already shown itself to us, above all, as an era of haves and have-nots. As educators we need to enter, provoke, and transform those spaces of haves where certain wedge issues can move us to the realization of the values of tactical humanism. We need to speak directly to social and political institutions and to exactly how they should be reformed. As the Dutch Surinamese scholar Philomena Essed has said (1996), we must make implicit boundaries explicit.

As multicultural educators we have a particular duty to seek those spaces where "educating the democratic mind" (Parker, 1996) of both adults and students can have a deep impact. To do this it is important to create bonds on the basis of common racial and cultural experiences. These transnational/transcultural experiences indicate strategies of political cooperation, what Philomena Essed (1996) has termed "making room for the power that emerges from sharing cultures and experiences and for the power that emerges from drawing from one's own specific cultural or personal characteristics within such cooperation." We are, ultimately, concerned with the ethical framework of a common humanity (Soedjatmoko, 1994).

Economics and Multicultural Education

Economics and multicultural education is another area in need of attention. The relationships of class, income, and ethnicity need to be studied by multicultural economics educators. Carnoy's work is a good example (1994). Like it or not, this is the world we live in, a world with high emphasis on market forces, a single world time, and accelerating competition. There is a need, on the one hand, to show that multicultural education is cost effective. Carnoy's work, again, as well as the raft of statistics released in early 1997 showing great gains by at least some sections of non-White communities (and Portes and Rumbaut's work on immigrants, 1990) are very likely related to strategies found in multicultural education such as empowerment and transformative knowledge. On the

other hand, deep structural economic inequalities which have arisen from institutional racism need to examined by scholars of multicultural education.

We need to study the power of the consumer in the marketplace of ideas. The neoliberal stress on consumer power means fewer taxes and fewer government programs, which means that old ways of reaching larger audiences are questionable. Yet there are also opportunities here for multicultural educators. We are not going to change this system of economic inequality, but we can utilize some of the methods and approaches of capitalism to reach those larger audiences. Our era is, after all, supposed to be democratic capitalism.

The growing concentration of wealth, information, and power in the hands of a small elite is a global multicultural issue in which racism and class go hand-in-hand. The "savage inequalities" which Jonathan Kozol (1991) has so eloquently spoken about are global in the scale of their oppressions. And they are increasing. As Sleeter (1995) has said, "the work to come is political in addition to being pedagogical." Our goals are no longer "national" goals, nor are they "international" goals. They are human goals.

Technology and Multicultural Education

The 21st Century is already upon us, an era of greater and greater communication linkages. There is a need for exploration, utilization, and documentation of the impacts of technology, particularly of the World Wide Web, on our lives and work as multicultural educators. Recently I activated seven well-known Internet search engines, looking for information on multicultural education. The results indicate both paucity today and potentially tomorrow in terms of reaching vast audiences. Access as an issue is exploding, with the expectation that the current number of users of the Web (57 million) will reach well over 700 million people by the year 2000. While still only a fraction of human beings on the planet, these 700 million "haves" need to be reached by us. Access to multicultural ideas and ideals is a key issue if transformations leading to a just world are to take place. Multicultural technologists are sorely needed to help us transform the field of multicultural education in ways that can best utilize these new potentials.

Multicultural Education and Context:

The World, Borders, and Future Directions

Living in the Borderlands (is) . . . a numinous experience. It is always a path/state to something else.
—Gloria Anzaldua

Now is the time to expand our vision beyond the United States, to other countries, beyond the national message for our national American society. This expansion should be not only to world contexts but to multiple ethnoscapes, the Tamil anthropologist Arjun Appadurai's term for our world today. These ethnoscapes are profoundly interactive. The transnational communities in our midst who are forever mobile and moving are especially rich ethnoscapes for a living, dynamic multiculturals.

The struggles of multicultural education, human rights education, and peace education in Africa, China, India, Southeast Asia, Australia and Oceania, Latin America, Russia, North America, and Europe now need to be linked. Promising beginnings have been made by James Lynch et al. (1992), Lynch (1989), Banks and Lynch (1986), and the section on International Perspectives on Multicultural Education found in the *Handbook of Research on Multicultural Education* (1995), as well as the work of Daniela Gioseffi (1993) and Rushworth M. Kidder (1994).

Looking at our planet from the outside during the early space voyages told us more about ourselves than all the previous explorations, that we are all in this together. It is now time for the human sciences to catch up with this startling vision of unity, if not coherence.

Anzaldua (1987) has given us eye-opening insights into the many Borderlands we encounter: physical, psychological, sexual, spiritual.[3] As Ulf Hannerz has said (1990, p. 237), the world culture today "is marked by an organization of diversity rather than by a replication of uniformity . . . the world has become one network of social relationships, and between its different regions there is a flow of meanings as well as of people and goods."

The world historian William McNeill's discussion of polyethnicity as the norm rather than the exception in human history (1986) is an important touchstone here, too. This polyethnicity infuses those it comes in contact with a peculiar sort of "cultural capital" (Bourdieu & Passeron, 1977; Apple, 1981). Language is the primary vehicle of this "cultural capital," creating a polyphony of authentic voices, many of whom *do* understand each other. In our world today multilingual speakers far outnumber monolinguals, despite impressions to the contrary. This is a central point of multiculturalism: "Ethnic identity is twin skin to linguistic identity" (Anzaldua, 1987, p. 59).

Cultural Capital

It should be noted that this metaphor of "cultural capital" describes an individual's relative success in the educational system. The cultural capital that members of Creole and diasporic communities, people we can also call transnationals and transculturals, accumulate is a phenomenal collection of cross-cultural skills, languages, and symbols. These symbols can be associated with ideology, ethnic and group membership, and social status.

The real significance of the growth of transnational cultures lies in the mediating possibilities they offer. They are bridgeheads for entry into other territorial cultures. Another way of looking at transnationals is to see them as "decontextualized cultural capital" (Hannerz, 1990, p. 246). Angela Davis, exemplifying the spirit of resistance of such individuals, has described herself as being given enough "rope" attached to the "anchors" locating her in her primary communities to enable her "to move into other communities" (cited in Hollinger, 1995).

Taking this larger perspective enables us to see the workings of a multicultural society like the United States in a new light. We might even venture that these transnational cultures are central catalysts for social change in national cultures. It is Creoles, members of diaspora, and mixed peoples, more often than not, who hold up the social mirror for the rest of us, giving us a vision of ourselves and our culture, a vision sometimes fraught with a sense of peril and crisis—and of the rich possibilities derived from multiple experiences.

Where is culture located, we must ask? The location of culture today is not in some pure core inherited from the past but at the edges of contact. Pure culture, as we have seen in Serbian Bosnia, Rwanda, and a host of other examples, only means death and destruction, an ethnic cleansing of the richly fertile complexities of the borderlands. Today the core itself is rapidly being defined by the margins. The margins are becoming the center. We are entering a polycentric age, for individual identities, for group identities, for national identities, and for planetary identities (Buell, 1994).

There are vast implications for multicultural education here, an education which will eventually become the core of all learned curricula. What globalization is doing is increasingly apparent: strengthening the forces of localization. Cultural identities may look like they are threatened from above, but their roots are actually being reinvigorated from below, from the transactional power of communities and crossroads.

Understanding the Nature of Culture

Hannerz (1990, p. 239) has noted that cultures are not the hard-edged, easily-separated pieces of a mosaic but phenomena that tend to overlap and mingle. The boundaries we draw around them are frequently arbitrary. Robert Hughes (1995) has given us an insightful commentary on this mingling in the American context. Moreover, the impact of social history and cultural geography on multicultural education needs to be looked at more deeply in terms of the whole society in any given context, and not just individual group studies.

Culture is not a box. It is a fluid concept, an everchanging phenomenon, a live part of us. And one of the most important parts of culture, an area where we can find common ground is values. We need to have concerns with shared moral values. Concerns with multiple identities. Hybrid identities. The very concepts of culture are in a profound process of redefinition, as the cultural critic Homi Bhabba has put it (1997) and as Andrew Wright (1994) has so thoughtfully articulated for America's particular political and social landscapes.

Even the continued use of ethnic categories becomes problematic for a number of reasons, not the least of which being that Creole, "Halfie," or Double communities are growing explosively. The focus on "culture" now needs to shift to multiple cultures, to processes such as class analysis and inequality.

We now need to begin looking at cultures in terms of processes, especially at those crossroads, at those transnational, transcultural flows where we come into contact with each other. To continue to look at cultures as separate tribes is the equivalent of what has been criticized as "Orientalism." Where we are meeting and interacting is where we are articulating what the common culture is. An important need for multicultural educators is to identify this common multi-culture and present a clear theory of a multicultural society.

Sitting Down at the Table Together:

Themes, Choices, Values

Linking past, present, and future, James A. Banks' vision of the current status and future prospects of multicultural education is especially important for all of us. Characterized by a powerful commitment, unflagging energy, and great passion, Banks is like those earlier "giants on whose shoulders we stand." A giant in our midst, Banks is leading us towards new understandings of how we can support the struggles for empowerment, knowledge transformation, liberation, and human freedom.

Clues as to where he is taking us are evident in his emphasis on leadership through values, those core instrumental beliefs which drive our behavior as human beings. Actively encouraging, empowering, and transforming classroom teaching in the communities in which we live through values derived from the transformative knowledge of marginalized academic communities is a key goal. As Banks says, transformative knowledge makes explicit its value premises and its connection to action to improve society.

One of the most important values that Banks has brought to his work is an emphasis on cooperation and reconciliation, on working together, on sharing, as the roots of human relations. This is a radical paradigm shift in the approach to race relations, which since the days of Robert E. Park has seen conflict as the basic defining imperative of human relations. Park and others saw the formation of ethnic communities in America as defined by the Social Darwinist cycle of competition, conflict, accommodation, and assimilation. By and large this is the view still held by most Americans, a view that is essentially dysfunctional for the long-term interests of the society.

This is not to say that conflict will not happen, but that the direction, shaping, and expressing of values, which will clash with other value systems, should be towards functional conflict that has as its philosophical touchstone reasoned, explicit, and conscious shared values of equality and equity.

In linking communities and knowledge construction, community participation and involvement are essential components. How teachers and students mediate school knowledge to their communities are signal qualities of the transformative educational experience. Community support for transformation is evidenced by the African-American community's financial support for Carter G. Woodson's organization and activities and the participation and involvement of the Springfield Plan begun in 1939. Joining one another and not fighting each other was important then and now.

Respect, dignity, and humility have been missing for much of U.S. history. James Banks tries to bring these values to the fore in the ways in which we structure our educational system and, ultimately, our human relations. There is a need for respect in American society (and in other world societies). Banks gives us mentors and models whom we can respect and emulate. Banks is himself, of course, a great mentor, as shown by his support for his graduate students. The high standards of scholarship to which he holds these authors is indeed exacting and impressive.[4]

We should be rightly suspicious of traditional commentaries from humanism, the model of the universal human looking all too white and all too American (sometimes European). But something close to these values, what Abu-Lughod (1991) calls "tactical humanism," is the best hope we have. Tactical humanism must recognize carefully what we are studying, how we write, and for whom we write. It is the florescence of the new theoretical orientation of "practice" or "action" or "praxis" (Ortner, 1994; Bourdieu, 1977). James A. Banks and other "giants" of multicultural education are leading us in this 21st century direction.

Notes

1. Early work can be found in Jean Phinney and Mary Jane Rotheram (1987).
2. Catherine Cornbleth and Dexter Waugh (1995) provide an excellent introduction to this arena concerned with Multicultural Education and policymaking.
3. Two outstanding new journals appeared in the 1990s which take Borderland themes as their core: *Diaspora* and *Public Culture*.
4. There are few scholars who would so clearly state that a major goal of their research project is the mentoring of graduate students, that "The work of graduate students is an integral part of the project." Nurturing of one's students in this way is truly the mark of a great teacher.

References

Abu-Lughod, Lila. (1991). Writing against culture. In Fox, Richard G., Ed. *Recapturing Anthropology: Working in the Present*. Santa Fe, NM: School of American Research.

Anderson, Benedict. (1994). *Imagined Communities: Reflections on the Origin and Spread of Nationalism*. London, United Kingdom: Verso.

Anzaldua, Gloria. (1987). *Borderlands: The New Mestiza = La Frontera*. San Francisco, CA: Aunt Lute Books.

Apple, Michael W. (Ed.). (1981). *Cultural and Economic Reproduction in Education: Essays on Class, Ideology and the State*. London, United Kingdom: Routledge & Kegan Paul.

Appadurai, Arjun. (1990). Disjuncture and difference in the global cultural economy, *Public Culture*, Vol. 2, No. 2, Spring, pp. 1–24.

Appadurai, Arjun. (1991). Global ethnoscapes: Notes and queries for a transnational anthropology. In Fox, Richard G., Ed. *Recapturing Anthropology: Working in the Present*. Santa Fe, NM: School of American Research.

Balibar, Etienne & Wallerstein, Immanuel. (1993). *Race, Nation, Class: Ambiguous Identities*. London, United Kingdom: Verso.

Banks, James A. (1995), Multicultural education and curriculum transformation, *Journal of Negro Education*, Vol. 64, No. 4, pp. 390–400.

Banks, James A. (1993). Multicultural education as an academic discipline, *Multicultural Education*, Winter 1993, pp. 8–11, 39.

Banks, James A. & Banks, Cherry A. McGee, Eds., (1995). *Handbook of Research in Multicultural Education*. New York: Macmillan.

Banks, James A. & Lynch, James, Eds. (1986). *Multicultural Education in Western Societies*. London, United Kingdom: Holt.

Bhabha, Homi. (1997). Life at the Border: Hybrid Identities of the Present. *New Perspectives Quarterly*, Vol 14, Number 1.

Bourdieu, Pierre. (1977). *Outline of a Theory of Practice*. R. Nice, trans. Cambridge, United Kingdom: Cambridge University Press.

Bourdieu, Pierre & Passeron, Jean-Claude. (1977). *Reproduction in Education, Society and Culture*. Richard Nice, trans. London, United Kingdom: Sage.

Buell, Frederick. (1994). *National Culture and the New Global System*. Baltimore, MD: The Johns Hopkins University Press.

Carnoy, Martin. (1994). *Faded Dreams: The Politics and Economics of Race in America*. New York: Cambridge University Press.

Castenell, Louis A. & Pinar, William F. (1993). *Understanding Curriculum as Racial Text-Representations of Identity and Differences in Education*. Albany, NY: State University of New York Press.

Cornbleth, Catherine & Waugh, Dexter. (1995). *The Great Speckled Bird: Multicultural Politics and Education Policymaking*. New York: St. Martin's Press.

Cortes, Carlos. (1995) Knowledge Construction and Popular Culture: The Media as Multicultural Educator. In James A. Banks and Cherry A. McGee Banks, Eds., (1995) *Handbook of Research in Multicultural Education*. New York: Macmillan.

Dirks, Nicholas B., Eley, Geoff, & Ortner, Sherry B., Eds. (1994). *Culture/Power/History: A Reader in Contemporary Social Theory*. Princeton, NJ: Princeton University Press.

Essed, Philomena. (1996). *Diversity: Gender, Color, & Culture*. Trans. by R. Gircour. Amherst, MA: University of Massachusetts Press.

Featherstone, Mike. (1990). Global culture: an introduction. In Featherstone, Mike, ed., *Global Culture—Nationalism, Globalization and Modernity*. London, United Kingdom: Sage.

Fitzgerald, Thomas K. *Metaphors of Identity: A Culture-Communication Dialogue*. Albany, NY: State University of New York Press.

Fox, Richard G., Ed. (1991). *Recapturing Anthropology: Working in the Present*. Santa Fe, NM: School of American Research.

Funderburg, Lise. (1994). *Black, White, Other: Biracial Americans Talk About Race and Identity*. New York: William Morrow.

Gates, Henry Louis, Jr., and West, Cornel. (1996). *The Future of the Race*. New York: Alfred A. Knopf.

Gioseffi, Daniela, Ed. (1993). *On Prejudice: A Global Perspective*. New York: Anchor Books.

Goldberg, David Theo, Ed. (1994). *Multiculturalism: A Critical Reader*. London, United Kingdom: Blackwell.

Grant, Carl. (1994). Challenging the myths about multicultural education, *Multicultural Education*, Winter 1994, pp. 4–9.

Hannerz, Ulf. (1990). Cosmopolitans and locals in world culture. In Featherstone, Mike, ed., *Global Culture—Nationalism, Globalization and Modernity*. London, United Kingdom: Sage.

Herrnstein, R. J., and Murray, C. (1994). *The Bell Curve: Intelligence and Class Structure in America*. New York: The Free Press.

Hollinger, David A. (1995). *Postethnic America: Beyond Multiculturalism*. New York: Basic Books.

hooks, bell. (1994). *Teaching to Transgress: Education as the Practice of Freedom*. New York: Routledge.

Hughes, Robert. (1993). *Culture of Complaint: The Fraying of America*. New York: Warner Books.

Kidder, Rushworth M. (1994). *Shared Values for a Troubled World: Conversations with Men and Women of Conscience*. San Francisco, CA: Jossey-Bass.

Kozol, Jonathan. (1991). *Savage Inequalities*. New York: Crown.

Lemert, Charles, Ed. (1993). *Social Theory: The Multicultural & Classic Readings*. Boulder, CO: Westview Press.

Lind, Michael. (1995). *The Next American Nation: The New Nationalism and the Fourth American Revolution*. New York: The Free Press.

Loewen, James W. (1995). *Lies My Teacher Told Me: Everything Your American History Textbook Got Wrong*. New York: Touchstone.

Lynch, James. (1989). *Multicultural Education in a Global Society*. London, United Kingdom: Falmer.

Lynch, James, Modgil, Celia, & Modgil, Sohan, Eds. (1992). *Cultural Diversity and the Schools Series*, Volumes 1–4. Bristol, PA: Falmer Press.

Martinez, Oscar J. (1994). *Border People: Life and Society in the U.S.-Mexico Borderlands*. Tucson, AZ: University of Arizona Press.

McCarthy, Cameron and Crichlow, Warren, Eds. (1993).*Race, Identity, and Representation in Education.* New York: Routledge.

McNeill, W. H. (1986). *Polyethnicity and National Unity in World History.* Toronto, Ontario, Canada: University of Toronto Press.

Obama, Barack. (1995). *Dreams from My Father: A Story of Race and Inheritance.* New York: Times Books.

Ortner, Sherry B. (1994). Theory in anthropology since the sixties. In Dirks, Nicholas B., Eley, Geoff, & Ortner, Sherry B., Eds. (1994). *Culture/Power/History: A Reader in Contemporary Social Theory.* Princeton, NJ: Princeton University Press.

Parker, Walter C., Ed. (1996). *Educating the Democratic Mind.* Albany, NY: State University of New York Press.

Phinney, Jean, & Rotheram, Mary Jane, Eds. (1987). *Children's Ethnic Socialization: Pluralism and Development.* Newbury Park, CA: Sage.

Portes, Alejandro, & Rumbaut, Ruben G. (1990). *Immigrant America: A Portrait.* Berkeley, CA: University of California Press.

Root, Maria P. P., Ed. (1992). *Racially Mixed People in America.* Newbury Park, CA: Sage.

Rosenblatt, Paul C., Karis, Terri A., & Powell, Richard D. (1995). *Multiracial Couples: Black and White Voices.* Thousand Oaks, CA: Sage.

Ruiz, Vicki L. & DuBois, Ellen Carol. (1994). *Unequal Sisters: A Multicultural Reader in U.S. Women's History.* New York: Routledge.

Scales-Trent, Judy. (1995). *Notes of a White Black Woman: Race, Color, Community.* University Park, PA: The Pennsylvania State University Press.

Sleeter, Christine (1995) An Analysis of the Critiques of Multicultural Education. In James A. Banks and Cherry A. McGee Banks, Eds., (1995) *Handbook of Research in Multicultural Education.* New York: Macmillan.

Sleeter, Christine E. and Grant, Carl A. (1987). An analysis of Multicultural Education in the United States. *Harvard Educational Review,* 7, 421–444.

Sleeter, Christine E. & McLaren, Peter L, Eds. (1995). *Multicultural Education, Critical Pedagogy, and the Politics of Difference.* Albany, NY: State University of New York Press.

Smith, Anthony D. (1990). Towards a global culture? In Featherstone, Mike, ed. *Global Culture—Nationalism, Globalization and Modernity.* London, United Kingdom: Sage.

Soedjatmoko. (1994). *Transforming Humanity: The Visionary Writings of Soedjatmoko.* West Hartford, CT: Kumarian Press.

Spickard, Paul R. (1989). *Mixed Blood: Intermarriage and Ethnic Identity in Twentieth Century America.* Madison, WI: University of Wisconsin Press.

Takaki, Ronald. (1994). *From Different Shores: Perspectives on Race and Ethnicity in America.* New York: Oxford University Press.

Taylor, Charles, & Guttman, Amy. (1994). *Multiculturalism: Examining the Politics of Recognition.* Princeton, NJ: Princeton University Press.

Todorov, T. (1982). *The Conquest of America: The Question of the Other.* Trans by R. Howard. New York: HarperCollins.

Todorov, T. (1993). *On Human Diversity: Nationalism, Racism, and Exoticism in French Thought.* Cambridge, MA: Harvard University Press.

Urrea, L. A. (1993). *Across the Wire: Life and Hard Times on the Mexican Border.* New York: Anchor World Views Press.

Williams, Gregory Howard. (1995). *Life on the Color Line.* New York: Penguin.

Wright, Lawrence. (1994). Annals of politics: One drop of blood, *The New Yorker,* July 25, pp. 46–55.

Zack, Naomi. (1993). *Race and Mixed Race.* Philadelphia, PA: Temple University Press.

Photo by Laura McLaren

Peter McLaren

A Call for Multicultural Revolution

Peter McLaren is one of the most influential representatives of critical pedagogy, both nationally and internationally. A major exponent of the work of the late Paulo Freire, McLaren is considered one the nation's leading critical educational theorists. His work covers a wide range of topics, from film criticism, to hip-hop, to the pedagogy of Che Guevara. His writings have been translated into eleven languages. McLaren is a professor at the Graduate School of Education and Information Studies at the University of California, Los Angeles. Following is an interview with McClaren and five reviews of McLaren's book, *Revolutionary Multiculturalism: Pedagogies of Dissent for the New Millennium* (Boulder, CO: Westview Press, 1997) by faculty who focus on the use of that book with education students. This collection was assembled for *Multicultural Education* by Gustavo E. Fischman, who conducted the interview with McLaren and invited and edited the five reviews.

CHALLENGES & HOPES

MULTICULTURALISM AS REVOLUTIONARY PRAXIS

Gustavo E. Fischman Interviews Peter McLaren

Gustavo E. Fischman: It is difficult to put a label on your work because you have written in so many different fields, ethnography, literacy, critical pedagogy, educational policy, curriculum, and sociology, but it appears to me that multiculturalism is a topic that crosses almost all your books and articles despite the disciplinary approach that happens to frame your project at any particular time?

As of Fall 1999, Gustavo E. Fischman is an assistant professor in Curriculum and Instruction at the College of Education, Arizona State University, Tempe.

Peter McLaren: That is true.

Gustavo: Among your many works, I recall four books that have multiculturalism in their title: *Multicultural Education and Critical Pedagogy* (edited with Christine Sleeter), *Critical Multiculturalism* (edited with Barry Kanpol), *Multiculturalismo Critico*, that you did for Cortez Publishers and the Paulo Freire Institute in São Paulo, Brasil (and which I understand has a wide readership in Brasil), and your most recent book, *Revolutionary Multiculturalism*. There are also other books and several articles of yours that are very prominent in the field of multicultural education: *Life in Schools: Critical Pedagogy and Predatory*

Culture, and Between Borders (edited with Henry Giroux).

Peter: Yes, all my books deal to a greater or lesser extent with issues of race, class, gender, sexuality, the state, and power and capitalist exploitation. My readers know this and I have been fortunate to be able to publish so much since coming to the United States from Canada in 1985.

Gustavo: Multicultural education is a vast, complex, and not homogeneous pedagogical movement. Where do you locate your works within the field?

Peter: I have learned a lot from Jim Cummings, Enrique Trueba, James Banks, Gloria Ladson-Billings, Sonny San Juan,

Emily Hicks, Carl Grant, Sonia Nieto, Rudolfo Chávez Chávez, Herman Garcia, Rudy Torres, David Theo Goldberg, Warren Crinchlow, Cornel West, bell hooks, Cameron McCarthy, Christine Sleeter, Antonia Darder, Joyce King, Donaldo Macedo, Joe Kincheloe, Henry Giroux, and a host of other scholars and activists. They are superb and committed scholars. What makes my work a bit different is that it is underwritten by a serious critique of global capitalism and works out of a Marxist problematic.

Some people have accused me of stressing class issues to the exclusion of race, ethnicity, and gender, for instance, because I am a working class white guy from *el Norte del Norte* (Canada), but quite honestly I do believe that capitalist exploitation is the motor of the kind of systematic, institutionalized racism that has been so perniciously present in Western industrialized and post-industrialized nations. With all of our talk about racist formations, racialized discourses, binary thinking, Eurocentric tropes and conceits, and floating signifiers (which is fine, as far as sophisticated scholarly exegesis goes) we have forgotten—all too perilously—that racism and sexism are predicated upon the economic exploitation of the many by the few.

The academy is a vicious and hypocritical place that breeds neoliberals masquerading as leftist multiculturalists and opportunists trying to pass themselves as selfless "solidarists" in the struggle for justice. People working across differences and building alliances are exceptions. Antonia Darder—who has initiated the call for the creation of the California Consortium for Critical Pedagogy—is one of those rare and exceptional scholars.

Gustavo: As a multiculturalist, how do you come to terms with your own whiteness?

Peter: My whiteness (and my maleness) is something I cannot escape no matter how hard I try. Early economic hardship cannot eradicate my whiteness because as Mike Dyson notes, there is always a "negative culpability" on the part of whites, in the form of pleasure that some poor whites derive from not being black. Poor whites (whites in general) still occupy a privileged space on the comparative racial taxonomy. In pursuing these questions, in living my own life as a traitor to whiteness, I cannot become lazy by failing to interrogate the epistemological, political, and ethical assumptions of my own practice. If all whites are racists at some level, then we must struggle to become anti-racist racists. We must always rethink our positionalities, platforms, and affiliations, without defaulting the main game, which is to resist and transform the market system based on the maximization of corporate profits. After all, it was this system that enslaved millions of

Africans in the United States and still disproportionately exploits people of color worldwide.

Of course it is not capitalism alone that achieved this. Exploitation is also made possible by systems of classification that grew out of religion, social and natural sciences frameworks that justified slavery, and other forms of oppression on the basis of the supposedly sacred and/or scientific inferiority of certain groups of people. While battling the leviathan of United States transnational capitalism and its neocolonial clientele, and the alienation and exploitation that marks so many cultural practices of this society, the struggle ahead must include inventing life forms for ourselves where racism, sexism and homophobia have no place, where joy and love can flourish, and where we can live unfettered by the determinism of capitalist progress. This is no simple romantic anti-capitalism I am endorsing, but a challenge grounded in the tough task of historical materialist analysis and the imperative of class struggle.

Gustavo: What you just said reminds me of that in a recent issue of *Educational Theory*, you were criticized for using a language that includes a clear call for the educational left to rethink class struggle in light of global capitalism. The language seems quite close to traditional Marxists positions and a clear dismissal of identity politics.

Peter: I am not an old-style manifesto Marxist, as some of my critics in the *Educational Theory* issue that you mentioned have suggested, nor am I a postmodernist as other people seem to think (possibly because an article I wrote in 1986 was the first to deal with postmodernism in a U.S. educational journal—so I have been told). I do learn a lot from my critics, but in this case they appeared insistent on reading much into my text that was not there. A deeper and more nuanced reading of my essay would—I hope—reveal the following. I am not against identity politics. After all, as Robin Kelley has so lucidly pointed out, identity politics has always been central to working class movements. It has greatly enriched our conception of class. We

should not forget that African-American social movements have been in solidarity with workers, black male abolitionists supported women suffrage, black radicals a century ago lent a helping hand to Irish

> **My whiteness** (and my maleness) is something I cannot escape no matter how hard I try. . . . [I come to terms with my whiteness] in living my own life as a traitor to whiteness, I cannot become lazy. . . . If all whites are racists at some level, then we must struggle to become **anti-racist racists.**

self-determination and worked against the Chinese Exclusionary Act. Kelley also notes that in those alliances, gender and class can be conceived as "affiliations" that build unity by supporting other peoples' struggles.

My point was that some versions of postmodernist and poststructuralist theorizing tend to ignore the perils of global capitalism and the misery it is creating for so many people throughout the world. My argument is that we need to re-set our sights on anti-capitalist struggle before the noose around our neck is drawn too tightly. I invited readers to see how global capitalism colonizes, commodifies, and fetishizes across race, class, gender lines. Even though I explicitly stated that class should not be privileged over race, gender, or sexuality—and that the important issue is to understand how capitalism has reterritorialized race, class, and gender formations—some critics saw my latest works as a call for returning to the old days of Bowles and Gintis, or they claimed, rather ludicrously, that I blamed postmodern theory for the current success of global capitalism! Frankly, I still think we can learn much from the early work of Bowles and Gintis.

I think that, in general, there are postmodernist educators who will raise an objection to the "subjunctive mode" of my address—the "we should" do this or do that. They are, understandably, concerned that efforts at revolutionary praxis may contain hidden oppressions, or that the cure I propose is perhaps worse than the disease. But all that they offer in the place of revolutionary praxis is assuming an "ironic mode of address" or recognizing the indeterminacy of agency, or the multiple locations of subjectivity, and so on.

Well, I would rather build momentum against global exploitation on the basis of provisional directive than on the basis of linguistic indeterminacy, or the announcement of the impossibility of critical pedagogy to contribute to the struggle against exploitation and the process of liberation. I am not saying that the left is not immune to tragic mistakes, but I prefer a platform to an anti-platform if you are going to attempt an internationalist movement against the powerful global machinery of capital.

Gustavo: Let me clarify a point here. Are you stipulating a view of liberation that is limited to the Marxist or to a superconscious revolutionary agent?

Peter: I think these criticisms are important. But to elaborate my answer to your question, let me say that I believe that the very conceptions available to thought—especially in our educational institutions—are insufficient to teach what it means to live a revolutionary life. One has, in a word, to live it. And to this cause, critical pedagogy attempts to bring the self up against the limits of reason. Let me say that I certainly recognize that freedom is not altogether "free." All concepts of freedom—whether constructed by myself, or others (Marxists, feminists, environmentalists, and many other committed intellectuals and social movements)—are constrained by the knotted pathways of the psyche, where the machineries of desire (whether they are structured like a language or not I will leave to the Lacanians to answer) wrestle with socially imposed standards and established criteria.

Critical pedagogy and revolutionary multiculturalism recognize the violence that shadows the modern subject and it does not try to create a calculable, uniform or transparent subject of revolutionary idealism, purged of its inner contradictions. I do not wish to insulate the subject from the process of its own self and social formation, its genealogy of interiorization. After all, revolutionary multiculturalists need to reflect upon the patriarchal, teleological, and Eurocentric assumptions that shape our standards of freedom. But we should not eliminate the injunction to self-discipline. Resistance at some level needs to be disciplined if it is to have a global sweep. It should be open-ended, too—in other words, it should be combinative. But above all it should be committed and determined, and not susceptible to giving in to nominal concessions from the capitalist class.

Gustavo: Peter, you make a distinction between ludic and resistance postmodernists, correct? Not all postmodernist theorizing is capital friendly.

Peter: Correct. The work of Teresa Ebert has been very helpful in this regard. The distinctions have to do with whether postmodern discourses sufficiently challenge

Revolutionary Multiculturalism: Pedagogies of Dissent for the New Millennium by Peter McLaren (Boulder, CO: Westview Press, 1997.) Five reviews of this book appear on the pages following this interview.

the ruling frameworks of patriarchal capitalism that deploy sexual or racial difference to justify the unequal distribution of wealth and power. Ludic postmodernism basically examines semiosis in a context that does not seriously consider capitalist social relations of production. Resistance postmodernism is more likely to locate racism and patriarchy beyond the rhetoricization and troping of capitalism and within class, gender, and ethnic divisions of property and struggle over profit and surplus labor. Ludic postmodernism, on the other hand, takes the existing capitalist order to extremes—as if greed and consumerism would somehow secure its transcendence. We need to ask ourselves how we can sustain unalienated production and reproduction.

We cannot—we must not—think that equality can occur in our schools or society in general without at once and the same time demanding and participating in political and economic revolution. No sphere of domination must remain unassailed by the project of liberation. We need to remain steadfast, we cannot embark in a flight from being, that is, a flight towards the world of commodities that can only objectify being. We need to remember that we

do not own ourselves, we don't belong only to ourselves. We belong to being. Because we belong to being, we need not covet the fruits of capital, for they are also the fruits of exploitation. Exploitation violates being. To find our multicultural soul is always an exercise of praxis, not ownership. It is an act conjugated with love in the interests of social justice. I am not trying to be metaphysical here since I connect objectified being with labor, with the laboring and toiling body, with the alienated worker, with the commodification of labor, with the exploited and the oppressed.

Gustavo: I think that you agree with the idea that critical pedagogy is not a transparent practice or a set of clear-cut guidelines that we can find in a manual. The paradox, however, seems to be that every programmatic attempt to do critical pedagogy must necessarily begin with a position, an action, a positivity, a project, and that inescapably contains some form of exclusion. How, then, can critical pedagogy sustain itself without contradicting its very premises?

Peter: Critical educators must always ask themselves—without flinching—tough questions: What is the hidden history of otherness contained within our narratives of liberation? Whom do they exclude, marginalize, repress? How can we regather what has been lost and fill the empty space of despair with revolutionary hope? Hope stipulates an Other who stands before us. Where, after all, can we search for a praxis of transformation that emerges from the plasma of revolutionary love, if not in the space of dialogue, the space of the Other. The many truths that emerge from the history of struggle spoken to us by Che Guevara, Leon Trotsky, Rosa Luxemburg, Emma Goldman, Malcolm X, Paulo Freire, and others—those truths, however partial, are still valid. The challenge before us, *compañero,* is to create new spaces in which to realize them. This invariably involves class struggle on a global basis.

I have often asked myself, Gustavo, is liberation the aggregate of infusible yearnings? Yearnings too manifold and incommensurable to bring to the table of freedom? Is liberation from domination an impossibility? Is there some psychological armor that, under capitalism, insulates us from the Other? I believe in the end that there are many different ways for us to become subjects and to resist becoming objects. One of the key challenges ahead must center around indigenous struggles for liberation, and critical pedagogy has much to learn from these movements, such as the Zapatistas in Chiapas. *Hasta la victoria siempre campañero.*

Revolutionary Multiculturalism

A Multivocal Review [With E-mails from a Class on Multiculturalism]

By Karen Anijar

The many situations that Dr. McLaren has faced should be in a made-for-TV movie. —student narrative

Electronic Chimeras

A student wrote me an e-mail last year: "You can call Peter McLaren, the author of *Revolutionary Multiculturalism,* a lot of things, but one thing you cannot call him is boring." McLaren is one of education's most inventive, and original thinkers, who consistently theorizes and agonizes around complex themes with sophistication, style, wit, and intelligence. And *Revolutionary Multiculturalism* is McLaren's most ambitious, most personal project thus far. This work in all of its power and originality (replete with moments of incredible brilliance and moments of incredible indulgent excess) is especially significant at this particular historical juncture.

Within the context of a public political pedagogy my critique of *Revolutionary Multiculturalism* isn't as consequential as what the book represents to and for students of education who ultimately are (in the best of all possible worlds) the cultural and intellectual workers who negotiate the difficult terrain of the public schools.

California Dreaming . . . Wake Me Up When the Nightmare Is Over

The students whose words comprise the body of this review live and work in Southern California. Los(t) Angeles or Los (en) Angeles, (as McLaren is), is in the best of times a Balkanized metropolitan mosaic, on a Hegelian freeway of despair. A mosaic (like a mirror which can only reflect) and Los Angeles are static metaphors. You can not transform a mosaic, or a mirror, although mirrors and Los Angeles can sustain illusions with equal elan. The mirror, like a mosaic, can be shattered into thousands of pieces. Some of those broken fragments have jagged edges. Edges that are sharp and painful.

"I am a fourth-generation Californian, and very proud of it," declares Nancy. "I have seen what has happened to California not only in Education but economically

Karen Anijar is an assistant professor in the College of Education at Arizona State University, Tempe.

and many other ways. My deep opinion is that outsiders have been the primary cause of the down slide. The very large numbers of illegal immigrants [sic], people from other states here for a free hand out, and people that want to make a name for themselves to be known as a defender of the poor and helpless but that have no ability or foresight to think ahead before they make their decisions."

McLaren's passionate plea in *Revolutionary Multiculturalism* "emanates, is framed, and is situated," Lori insightfully writes, "in time and place and is informed by a deep rich sense of social commitment and justice." "For me, someone who always wanted to be a teacher," Donna decides "I take what McLaren says with the utmost seriousness." She continued, "I have to reconsider, and reflect, and think about who I am and what I am doing. I think of the damage that has been done, and have to ask am I responsible? McLaren might want to take out his guero eyes, but I can not rip out my heart, which pounds in anger, I will not turn a blind eye."

John was moved, "When McLaren reminded me that 'one percent of the population' is 'controlling the lives of the rest by exploiting their labor and by colonizing their capacity to resist—to dream or to think otherwise,' (McLaren, 1997:23), I became angry. VERY ANGRY! We need to 'wage nothing less than war,' [and] my weapon will be the schools."

Clarion Calls

"I will be reading it again and again. I want to put Peter McLaren's ideas into ACTION! What *Revolutionary Multiculturalism* has done for me, is to help me see my role as a teacher in a deeper and more profound way. I could go on for several more pages about specific ideas in this book that 'fired me up.' Noam Chomsky's ideas, 'dismantling Whiteness'(McLaren, 1997:279), bringing back the art programs to our schools, and, especially, the 'democratic-socialist feminist political imaginary,' (McLaren, 1997:279), among many others, but I don't wish to type ALL NIGHT! Because I intend to start to wake up in the morning go into my classroom and begin to really do the most important labor of all . . ." (Sam)

In *Revolutionary Multiculturalism* McLaren sounds a clarion call for critical pedagogues

to reexamine their Marxist roots. McLaren does not nostalgically (nostalgia is a conservative impulse) seek a return to the days when a class analysis was privileged above and beyond any other exigencies. However, he does ask us to negotiate the territories and the intersections between class race, gender, and ethnicity as they interanimate in continual process. Process is the operative word. "At times," writes Marisol, "(R)eading McLaren makes me feel as if time had been rolled back and I was attending a political meeting at the University of Mexico, and then I was taken aback by the thought that not too many things have changed in these 20 odd years. Racism and discrimination exists perhaps with even greater force than before . . . his book above all else put me back in touch with the Marx I thought I knew and had lost touch with. I feel moved and inspired seeing that some people still care enough to fight against the social forces that refuse to change."

Duke Nuke-Em's and Pat My Bucanan

"Tell me do you and your little Marxist friends get together and disparage Jefferson and Lincoln? I bet the only president people of your ilk admire is Slick Willy. I can not believe I spent my hard earned dollars on this book. And I am very angry that I have to take this class to listen to this Marxist rhetoric. . . . Some cultures are superior to others . . . that is the way it has always been . . . think back to Western Civilization. . . . oops I bet people like McLaren and you never took Western Civilization" (Katie).

The disingenuous duplicitous mean-spirited form of neo-fascism that exists, persists, and subsists in a post 187-209-Unz initiative universe, is often obscured under a cloud (a very polluted one indeed), a peace-corps of neo-benevolence, a celebration of *vive la diferance* (as long as you do my windows and don't make too much trouble). The reactions to the book, triggered reaction (literally) with several students, whose politics emerged in their responses. I remember as a child we used to tease other kids: "Guess what, your epidermis is showing." McLaren's book triggers the same sort of impulse: "Guess what, your ideology is showing."

Believe It or Not

Nat "came away from the book with" the question McLaren kept returning to ask: "Can we use new ways of organizing subjectivity to create a self-reflexive social agent capable of dismantling capitalist exploitation and domination?" (1997:95). I hope so. I need to believe that we can. I know we can. Because as Susan emphasizes, "We have an ethical responsibility to transform the world. It is through that responsibility that we begin to recognize root causes and begin to repair the damage done, doing justice and paying our debt to the young people of the world" (1997: 30).

A THEORETICAL ROLLER COASTER

A REVIEW OF REVOLUTIONARY MULTICULTURALISM

By Marta P. Baltodano

As a graduate student and later as a teacher educator, I have followed the academic and theoretical developments of Peter McLaren. I have to admit though, that I approached his writings with more suspicion than admiration. My initial reaction was an automatic rejection of his theories based on his personal location as a white male academician who came from a world (the very *Norte*), where the notion of blatant repression and violent political movements in third world countries— particularly Latin America—is deeply romanticized. It was hard for me to understand how the critical pedagogy advocated by McLaren could have any legitimacy within my own experience as a third world feminist, child of the Nicaraguan revolution, and witness of horrendous human rights abuses.

However, through the process of engaging in McLaren's "texts" and getting to know him personally, I have come to admire his contradictions. I came to appreciate his leading contributions to the field of critical pedagogy, his admission of his privileged perspective on critical educational theory, and particularly, his refusal to remain stagnated in the different boxes and categories where people have attempted to locate him. His willingness to integrate every critique of his work in this process of personal renovation is admirable.

I have seen McLaren constantly re-examining his understandings in terms of identity construction, critiques of feminism, racialized scholarship, Latino and Rap culture, and more recently global capitalism.

The readers of *Revolutionary Multiculturalism* are invited to take on a theoretical roller coaster. In it, we may experience and sense the perils, ups and downs of McLaren's voyage as an ethnographer, dense theorist, essentialist, Marxist, race *traitor,* postmodernist, poststructuralist, post-colonialist and radical academician.

McLaren's description of post-Fordist practices, "fast capitalism," and the reconceptualization of the notion of difference in the context of the hegemonic politics of consumption, are key themes throughout the book. But there is more. This book is also an experiment, a test to the fluidity and coherence of McLaren's theories in different cultural sites in an attempt to move away from the generalized paralysis that has afflicted his colleagues in the educational Left.

In light of this attempt, we can read McLaren's appealing arguments about: The role of North American intellectuals; the role of critical ethnographers; the integration of Baudrillard in his post-Fordist analysis (with Zeus Leonardo); his rethinking of the politics of race; his examination of Rap and Latino culture; and the gradual resurrection and integration of Marxism into critical pedagogy as a way of resisting the essentialist forces that have pervaded critical educational theory.

As one of the founding fathers of the critical pedagogy movement, McLaren's recent reconceptualization and infusion of political economy in his pedagogical analysis are among the strongest challenges to the ineffectiveness of most of today's critical educational theory and its discourse on diversity. *Revolutionary Multiculturalism* brings together the different stages of McLaren's theoretical and philosophical self, before moving on to a different ideological terrain and taking a "critical" distance from his predecessors and colleagues. And this is good news, because this distance could provide the much-needed perspective that may help in transforming this book, from one more display of rhetorical skills into a key element in turning the educational Left towards a different direction.

Marta P. Baltodano is a post-doctoral fellow in the Teacher Education Department at Claremont Graduate University, Claremont, California.

DISSENT, IDENTITY, & CRITICAL PEDAGOGY

A REVIEW OF REVOLUTIONARY MULTICULTURALISM & CRITICAL PEDAGOGY AND PREDATORY CULTURE

By Lourdes Diaz Soto

Lourdes Diaz Soto is a professor in the College of Education at The Pennsylvania State University, University Park

Among Peter McLaren's greatest gifts as a scholar is his ability to speak in the voice of the marginalized, disenfranchised, Latina, immigrant, bilingual, and bicultural. As a Latina, and a marginalized, bilingual scholar, I often find that McLaren's work continues to impact not only my work and my life but that of my students' and readers who can identify with the silenced and the marginalized.

In *Revolutionary Multiculturalism*, McLaren includes the plight of los olvidados ("the forgotten ones") and relays how he tries to hide his despair and his rage toward the system from his students. The marginalized ones and los olvidados can also empathize with the weight of a "heavy soul" who has toiled in the fields of social and educational activism. It may be that one of the reasons he is able to speak with the voice of the "other" can be attributed to his own description: "I have remained outside the mainstream, in the margins, in the folds of legitimacy or even credibility by normative standards. I think radical intellectuals work better in the borderlands, between worlds" (p. 226).

McLaren envisions "spaces of hope" but he is also able to uncover how "the kindling of fascism lies in the furnace of U.S. democracy, waiting for a spark to ignite a firestorm of state repression" (p. 6). In the chapter entitled, "Unthinking Whiteness, Rethinking Democracy" for example, the historical context and alliances with white supremacy by our nation are examined in light of gabachismo ("whiteness") and engabachamiento ("marginalized groups forced to act white") and viewed as an integral part of racist oppressive elements. McLaren quotes the words of John Silber, Pat Buchanan, Abraham Lincoln, Thomas Jefferson, Benjamin Franklin, Ward Connely, David Duke, Woodrow Wilson, Warren G. Harding (who was inducted into the Klu Klux Klan in a ceremony at the White House), and Pat Robertson, who all help create the myth of the superiority of white people. McLaren adds:

> The task ahead for those of us who wish to reclaim the dignity offered by true justice is to revivify democratic citizenship in a era of diminishing returns. It is to create critical citizens who are no longer content in occupying furtive spaces of private affirmation but who possess the will and the knowledge to turn these spaces into public spheres through the creation of new social movements and anticapitalist struggle. (p. 7)

The discussion about issues of identity constitute some of the more interesting and important contributions of this work. Not only does McLaren note how white youth searching for identity are able to "find meaning" only as it relates to their ability to hate nonwhites but he also debunks the notion that identities can be "fluidly recomposed, rearranged, and reinvented." McLaren notes:

> We are not autonomous citizens who can fashionably choose whatever ethnic combinations we desire in order to reassemble our identity. Al-

though the borders of ethnicity overlap and shade into one another, it is dishonest to assert that pluralized, hybridized identities are options available to citizens in the same way. (p. 7)

For the "other," for the Latina, for los olvidados, for women of color, for black males, for non-voting children, for the poor, and for many of us it appears not only dangerous but perhaps even unethical to continue to promote the notion of a "fluid identity" in postmodern discourse. For the privileged, the idea of a move toward a pluralistic reinvented identity may appear logical but for the "other" who has lived the daily reality of a social context embedded in racist, sexist, and socioeconomic differences it is an impossibility.

Two recent examples that help make McLaren's point about identity come to mind. At the university where I teach, a male former colleague relayed how he carefully socialized his children to become an integral part of the "American dream." His goal was to ensure that his Asian children walked, talked, and spoke like the mainstream privileged white society. He was careful to maintain an English-only speaking home environment; he sent his children to distant, elite, expensive private schools; and went to great lengths in socializing his children in ways that would diminish any spark of cultural and linguistic memory. Imagine this father's ultimate shock when he was confronted by his adult children and they relayed their painful experiences to him. These adult children understand that their Asian ancestry signifies that they will never be accepted by the privileged ones. These adult children are continually searching for their Asian identities and are thirsty for knowledge about their grandparents' language and culture. I saw my colleague cry when he retold this story at a committee meeting where we had struggled with issues of language and culture. He had in the past made sarcastic remarks when discussions centered on issues of home language and home culture, but not on that day.

One of my doctoral students also told us a story about identity that remains a revelation about children's early identity acquisition. My student is a visiting scholar from Myanmar who developed a warm friendship with a local family of Japanese origin. He relayed how the young girls in this family are making plans to have surgical eye operations so that their eyes will look more like the rounded mainstream eyes of Caucasian communities. Other doctoral students in the course confirmed how this surgical eye operation is in vogue for young Asian females. It is shocking to think that young women are willing to undergo painful operations in order to alter

their appearance while hoping to enter the mythical American dream of the mainstream privileged world. It saddens my heart and my spirit when I think about how young children are affected by the prevalent white supremacist element in America. Often times the examples are not as obvious since children are carefully, slowly socialized by multiple experiences and environments including schools, communities, and the media.

McLaren calls for a move "beyond the politics of diversity and inclusion" with additional emphasis "on the social and political construction of white supremacy and the dispensation of white hegemony" (p.8). It may be that this is our greatest challenge as educators and cultural workers as we chart our paths toward pedagogy of the oppressed and pedagogy of the oppressor. Our nation continues to be led by increasingly militant conservative and mean-spirited agents who silence the voices and lives of so many in order to maintain privileged positions by disregarding the terrifying implications and daily human realities that surround ethnic exclusion. Who are these conservative, right wing Republicans who seem compelled to add to the military budget yet are unable and unwilling to meet the needs of children and mothers? Who are these conservative, right wing Republicans who feel compelled to focus on William Jefferson Clinton's sexual escapades as opposed to the work of the people and for the people? Who are these conservative right wing Republicans who cannot envision free health care, quality child care, free higher education, and a decent living wage for families?

A recent visit to the U.S. Holocaust Memorial Museum in Washington, D.C. reminded my daughter and I of how Nazi Germany evolved in a systematic, deliberate manner and how the common German citizens participated in the persecution that led to the annihilation of six million Jews and millions of others including Gypsies, the handicapped, Poles, homosexuals, Jehovah's Witnesses, Soviet prisoners of war, Communists, and political dissidents. *Revolutionary Multiculturalism's* "truth-telling" continues to uncover the insidious nature of our present postmodern condition. What is most alarming about the Holocaust and current events is the deafening silence of so many for so long. McLaren notes:

> If we do nothing to contest the Republican initiative that will place children of those on social assistance in orphanages, how will we be able to resist when the initiative calls for forced sterilization? Or internment camps for illegal Latino/as? We need to remember that few spoke out when Jewish students were forced

out of German universities or when Jewish faculty were expelled. (p. 46)

Lest our readers think these ideas are far fetched, I invite them to watch the film *La Operacion* as it documents how one third of the women in Puerto Rico have been sterilized as a part of a 1937 policy based on the principles of eugenics. According to the Agency for International Development, the practice of sterilization was implemented as a means of preventing a revolution that would impede industrial and capitalist interests. Included in the project was research by the Family Planning Association which tested the first oral contraceptives at 20 times the current dosages on Puerto Rican women living in housing projects. The 550 percent profits reaped by industrial corporations have been earned on the backs of Puerto Rican women who were "encouraged" to attend sterilization clinics in the factories and who were visited in their homes by sterilization advocates. The women themselves were not fully informed nor did they understand what was taking place as a part of the government sanctioned programs.

English-only advocates have also been unmasked by their own memos (Crawford, 1992) when they too called for the forcible sterilization of Latinas. We are living under increasingly fascist elements and yet so few are willing to dissent and challenge the interests of the privileged ones, such as the conservative, right wing Republicans clutching tightly the reigns of power with the menacing whip of the oppressor.

McLaren calls on Freirian-based educators in higher education to raise more questions relating to race and gender so that these areas will serve as the central focus for "social transformation." Questions that he raises in this regard include: How have pedagogical practices been colonized by racialized discourses? How have racial and dominant discourses been reproduced by white supremacist discursive regimes? How are racist discourses reproduced in schools? How do forms of rationality work within the discourse of colonialism?

The issue for us as educators is that schooling continues to reproduce a stratified, differential caste-like system based upon socioeconomic standing, race, and gender. While some of us dissent and take up these questions in higher education, others continue to hide their heads in the sand and ultimately sleep with the fascist element. How many existing higher education programs are for privileged students only? McLaren envisions educators as active agents of social change but observes that

. . . emancipatory praxis has been largely orphaned in our institutions

of education as educators are either unable or refuse to name the political location of their own pedagogical praxis. (p.52)

As my non-critical colleagues continue to insist on the need for more "objectified knowledge," more "balanced perspectives," I continue to feel the burning pain of a racist historical legacy. For colleagues in the field of education who maintain that it is important to maintain a "neutral" stance, I can only say that neutrality is what condones the silencing and the radical right wing elements. As I have reported elsewhere (Soto, 1997), the "neutral" proponents were actually instrumental in helping to dismantle a school program that was benefiting 1200 second-language learners. Teachers in this school district report that these very same children today are being expelled or placed in special education classes disproportionately even as I write this piece. It is clear that the words of Pastor Martin Niemoller continue to hold true today:

First they came for the socialists, and I did not speak out because I was not a socialist. Then they came for the trade unionists, and I did not speak out because I was not a trade unionist. They came for the Jews, and I did not speak out because I was not a Jew. Then they came for me, and there was no one left to speak for me.

McLaren, while advocating for the development of the ethical self, defines *revolutionary multiculturalism* not merely as reforming capitalist democracy but of *transforming* capitalist democracy as a part of a project that is socialist-feminist and challenges historically fossilized racist, sexist, and anti-poor practices, and the process of "othering." He envisions the need to reinvent the deep structures of the political, the economic, the cultural, and ultimately the powerful elements that continue to oppress *los olvidados,* the marginalized, the bilingual, and women of color.

I think the reader will also appreciate the chapter "Ethnographer as Postmodern *Flâneur.*" In this piece, McLaren interrogates the discourses that locate him as "gringocentric" and informed by "gueroconsciousness" while sharing his daily readings of the world as he travels from West Hollywood, East Los Angeles, a former Gestapo headquarters in East Berlin, Paris, Mexico, Nebraska, Brazil, Argentina, and Japan. He adds, "We begin speaking for ourselves only when we step outside of ourselves-only by becoming other. It is in recognizing ourselves in the suffering of others that we become ourselves" (p. 112).

In *Critical Pedagogy and Predatory Culture,* the reader is taken on a journey of

readings with Peter McLaren, Paulo Freire, Henry Giroux, and Kris Gutierrez. In this volume radical pedagogy, critical multiculturalism, and postcolonial pedagogy are presented within a backdrop that unmasks existing postmodern "predatory culture." "Predatory culture" is "a field of invisibility—of stalkers and victims—precisely because it is so obvious. Its obviousness immunizes its victims against a full disclosure of its menacing capabilities" (p. 2). McLaren details "frozen memories detached from the historical context" (p. 13), and how schools in the predatory culture "keep youth stupid." McLaren talks about what he feels is the real danger facing education within predatory culture as

. . . not simply the refusal of the general public to recognize its embeddedness in relations of power and privilege at the level of everyday life, but rather that the public prefers to act as if there exist few-or no-such political linkages. The danger is not an apathetic nation, nor a cynical one, but rather the ability of the public sphere to exist relatively uncontested. (p. 13)

The vision of hope and possibility within this book lies in its call for a liberation lived within solidarity where victims can overcome their oppression and where schooling is immersed in an emancipatory praxis where "the individual and personal is always situated in relation to the collective and communal" (p. 23).

My graduate students and I embarked on a journey during the fall semester of 1998 to critically reflect and deconstruct the "word and the world." Our goal as cultural workers has been to forge a collaborative utopian vision as we explore our own identities, locations, notions of dissent, and the risk-taking that is an integral part of our work. How much are we willing to sacrifice on our journey as educators, multiculturalists, bicultural pedagogues, women of color, Puerto Rican males, mothers, men of color, Puerto Rican women, white women, lesbians, Central Americans, Koreans, Taiwanese speakers, single parents, poor whites, African American females, fathers, Mandarin speakers? Does our risk-taking include personal sacrifice and possibly even death?

We stand in places of safety and privilege because of those who came before us and those who are with us today carrying the weight of racism, sexism, and marginalization. How can we forge the "ethical self" and implement our dreamspaces of equity and justice while still surviving the oppressors bitter whip? For my students and for me the issue becomes how to implement action/praxis within the very colonized hostile environments we find ourselves in, not only in institutions of higher learning, but in our postmodern communities, and in our children's/students' schools.

—I would like to thank the students in my graduate seminar entitled "The politics of bilingual education" during the Fall of 1998 for their illuminating critical dialogues that continue to serve as spaces of hope within an increasingly mean-spirited national context.

References

Crawford, J. (1992). *Hold your tongue.* New York: AddisonWesley.

McLaren, P. (1997). *Revolutionary multiculturalism.* Boulder, CO: Westview Press.

McLaren, P. (1995,1997). *Critical pedagogy and predatory culture.* New York: Routledge.

Soto, L.D. (1997). *Language, culture, and power. Bilingual families and the struggle for quality education.* Allbany, NY: State University of New York Press.

Revolutionarily Speaking:

A Multiculturalism for Social Justice

By Marc Pruyn

I'm a white man who teaches social studies. Actually, more accurately put, I'm a pan-ethnic critical pedagogue who teaches social studies informed by radical multiculturalism and critical pedagogy. But, looking like a white guy, I'm usually treated like one. This gets me in the door with my twenty-something teacher education students. But soon, after healthy doses of Peter McLaren, Enid Lee, Louise Derman-Sparks, James Loewen, bell hooks and Howard Zinn, the tide turns—at least among a quite vocal numeric minority of both the white and Chicana/o students we serve at my institution.

I have been accused of "hating whites" and being a race traitor. Students have tearfully implored me not to have race as one of the foci in my course, announcing that, "But, Dr. Pruyn, I never owned slaves!"—as if racism were something relegated to our distant past. This past semester, a student actually rose and unabashedly asked the doctoral student teaching one of my sections, "What does race have to do with social studies?" Indeed, it is exactly for these reasons and examples that we need the "revolutionary multiculturalism" called for by Peter McLaren.

Revolutionary Multiculturalism continues the reflection initiated in McLaren's *Critical Pedagogy and Predatory Culture,* and it is a clarion call to engage in a struggle for social justice grounded in a criticalist neo-Marxist philosophical and political approach. In this way McLaren understands and seeks to counteract the homogenizing and *seemingly* omnipotent forces of postmodern predatory capital and its headlong plunge into the ultra-commodification and super-exploitation of the racialized, classed, gendered and homopho-

basized lives it has created for us during its bloody tenure.

McLaren argues that multiculturalism as it is largely practiced in current contexts needs to move beyond its calls for "diversity" and "inclusion" within the curriculum and in society. We need to move beyond the assimilationist position of asking to be invited into the master's house (or canon). If multiculturalism is to be successful, it needs to challenge the "white, Anglo, heterosexual male of bourgeois privilege" (p. 214) that is at the center of this society's socially constructed and stylized portrayal of "whiteness," Americana and white supremacy.

McLaren's point—drawing on Gramsci's notion of hegemony—is that "white is right" in our society. And that is what we as multicultural educators must confront on a daily basis. White (and male and straight and wealthy and fluent English-speaking) is normal. All else, in our late capitalist and whitened society is wrong, different and abnormal. What did the MSNBC headline read after Tara Lipinski unexpectedly beat U.S. Olympic teammate Michelle Kwan at the last Winter Games? "American Beats Kwan!" White is right. All else is "Other" odd, different, exotic, un-American.

As McLaren notes, "whiteness has located itself in those discourses of the public and the popular in such a way (whiteness is everywhere and nowhere) that our definition of the normal and the commonsensical has been colonized" (p. 46). "Whiteness" needs to be unseated from its transparent yet exalted seat of dominance and the socially constructed notion of race itself needs to be critically examined.

The Clash had it right, nearly twenty years ago, when they sang about those

"Washington bullets again" and implored us not to forget. And is all well? Is it okay to forget? (Or to *never learn,* as in the case of our students?) McLaren says, "No!" *La lucha continua.* There is still struggle. Maybe now more than ever. As the bombs continue to fall on people of color simply because they live under a U.S.-created "despot"; as young men continue to be tortured and left for dead in the middle of the night for being gay; and as young women continue to be forced to work long hours at sub-minimum wages and in slave-like working conditions in L.A. sweatshops and the *Maquiladoras* of Ciudad Juárez; the struggle does continue.

McLaren, in citing the *abuelito* of critical pedagogy, Paulo Freire, notes that, "revolutions do not occur just because we create them in our own minds" (139). Indeed they don't. McLaren, in this work, forwards concrete pedagogical and political suggestions toward revolutionizing multiculturalism. *Revolutionary Multiculturalism provides* us (and our students) with many of the theoretical and pedagogical tools necessary for understanding how exploitations surrounding race, class, gender and sexual orientation relate to both predatory capitalism and postmodernism. Through this approach, and with an unflinching and unapologetic opposition to white supremacy and global capitalism, McLaren helps us to strengthen and expand the struggle for social, multicultural and economic justice that our current times demand.

—Marc Pruyn is a member of the faculty at New Mexico State University, Las Cruces.

DICTIONARIES AND CRITICAL LENSES:

STUDENTS READING REVOLUTIONARY MULTICULTURALISM

By Troy Richardson

The class began in the usual way with several informal conversations circulating about the final assignment, the unseasonably warm weather, and some comments on the weeks spent reading Peter McLaren's *Revolutionary Multiculturalism*. Students were primarily relating to each other, and indirectly to me, the length of time they had spent reading the assigned chapters 1, 6 and 8. As they conversed I noticed they were not framing the chapters as "inaccessible," rather the majority of these students were commenting that the chapters were "packed" with issues they as educators needed to consider and their desire to "get it all" had lead them to invest more time with the text.

While several students did comment they had dictionaries close at hand as they read, overall their remarks ran counter to the critique of many teacher educators who suggest that McLaren's writings are remote and isolated from those whom he wishes to assist. On the contrary, the majority of students, who also happened to be educators with much teaching experience, suggested the issues which arose in our formal discussions of *Revolutionary Multiculturalism* were "necessary considerations."

My reflections of that class discussion offer insights not only on the student receptions of this book, but also on the importance of locating some of the themes outlined in *Revolutionary Multiculturalism* within the context of a semester-long study of identity, language, culture, economics, class interests, etc.

From chapter 1, "Writing From the Margins: Geographies of Identity, Pedagogy and Power," co-authored with Henry Giroux, my students found the succinct outline of McLaren and Giroux's interpretation of critical pedagogy especially helpful in understanding the dimensions of multiculturalism not only as a personal journey, but as a daily endeavor we must commit ourselves to and nurture in our students.

In our discussions of Chapter 6, "Global Politics and Local Antagonisms: Research and Practice as Dissent and Possibility," co-authored with Kris Gutierrez, students focused on the analysis of consumer identities. We reflected on how these various forms of the media intersect, inform and otherwise dictate to our students their value relative to their personal appearance. I related to my students some of the comments of Santee poet and activist John Trudell (*Stickman*. New York: INANOUT Press, 1994) who suggests that advertisements and the entire advertising industry are a constant attack against self worth. Trudell comments that we are constantly told that we will be better, people will like us more if we consume this or that product. Like McLaren and Gutierrez, Trudell links this attack on self worth to those he describes as the "industrial ruling class" or who McLaren and Gutierrez identify as "extraterritorial economic elites," (McLaren, pg. 195, 1997).

While appreciating the insights offered here, my students and I recognized the powerful agency with which our students do act and participate in the "global amusement culture" (McLaren, pg. 198) we both willingly and unwillingly engage. This participation, of course, operates in various ways, including forms of resistance, but it has come about in part due to technological advances of the late twentieth century. The ability of students to access information at a speed which has never before been available, and to make their own judgements about that information, has radically transformed the nature of intercultural communication and contributed to a social reconstruction my students and I suggest we are only beginning to understand.

While we noted some of the problems with the global amusement culture, including the fetishization of technology and the ability/desire to remain to some extent anonymous in such experiences, we cannot deny the impact of this medium in re-configuring the ways in which children and young adults participate in and change the local and global political, economic and socio-scapes they inhabit. We discussed, for example, the power and will of young people participating in an M.I.T initiative which has worked to place computer and Internet capabilities in the hands of young adults across class, gender, national, and ethnic boundaries. This effort has allowed students to participate in positive social change by organizing youth labor organizations, redistributing food, and other material goods as well as raising awareness about social, political and economic issues which are affecting them and their communities everyday.

We also discussed the work of one elementary class in Colorado which has raised money to purchase freedom for peoples enslaved in contemporary Africa and other parts of the world. What started with a class project hoping to free one or two individuals has lead to the emancipation of over 1,000 enslaved persons. In the end it may have been that my students and I needed to regain a sense of something positive occurring within and through our work as educators. There is more happening in our classrooms than just brainwashing. Through a discussion of these teacher and student actions, we became inspired by the ways in which educators can initiate the praxiological and dialogical pedagogy McLaren and Gutierrez call for.

Finally, my students and I turned to chapter 8, "Unthinking Whiteness, Rethinking Democracy: Critical Citizenship in Gringolandia." Here our conversations almost exclusively centered on McLaren's notions of whiteness. Using the framework of social constructionism (Berger, P.L. & T. Luckman. *The Social Construction of Everyday Life: A Treatise on the Sociology of Knowledge*. Garden City, NY: Doubleday 1966; Gergen, K.J. "The Social Constructionist Movement in Modern Psychology" *American Psychologist* 49:266-275, 1985), my students and I examined specific forms of knowledge, language, and culture which have been normalized and thus appear natural to us and our students. As our discussion progressed, my students reflected on their own socialization process, commenting on the ways in which whiteness operates in their own lives. Indeed, they struggled with themselves and each other about taking the difficult stand against whiteness.

McLaren's writings provided my students a provocative entry to begin their journey. We especially found it helpful to focus our attention on actualizing the comments of Lopez, whom McLaren quotes on page 272, by taking his three steps of disassembling whiteness in our everyday lives which might serve as a model for our students.

As I collected my things at the end of the discussion, I was both surprised and excited to find my students as engrossed as I had hoped they would be in their engagement of *Revolutionary Multiculturalism*. I had honestly been quite anxious to begin a conversation of this text, due to my feeling that the success of the course somehow hinged on the reception of *Revolutionary Multiculturalism*. That is to say, had my readings and class discussions provided enough theoretical, cultural and philosophical context for my students so that McLaren's work would be met with an eager intrigue—and yet would they also read him with a critical lens so as to avoid becoming McLarenite ideologues? From all indications we together seemed to find this balance.

Troy Richardson is a member of the faculty at the College of Education at the University of Utah, Salt Lake City.

Who Shall Have the Moral Courage to Heal Racism in America?

By G. Pritchy Smith

The arc of a moral universe is long, but it bends toward justice.
—Martin Luther King, Jr.

I want to thank the National Association for Multicultural Education (NAME) Planning Committee of the 1997 Annual Conference for this opportunity to share some of my thinking about education in the United States and its role in creating a more fair, just, democratic, and antiracist society. Before I begin, let me say that I consider this opportunity to speak at the NAME conference one of the highest honors that I will ever receive in my career as an educator. I have titled this address "Who Shall Have the Moral Courage to Heal Racism In America?"

Some of you in the audience, at this very moment, may be asking yourselves, "Why in the world is this white boy with the ponytail standing before the microphone? What in the world does **he** know about racism?" Before I have finished today, I hope I have convinced most of you that "the problem of racism" in the United

G. Pritchy Smith is professor of curriculum and instruction in the College of Education and Human Services at the University of North Florida, Jacksonville, Florida.

This article is the transcript of his keynote address at the 7th Annual NAME Conference in Albuquerque, New Mexico, on October 31, 1997. At the end of Smith's address, a deeply moved audience spontaneously burst into a standing ovation. The tone of his message is personal and conversational. It speaks to the heart. With the exception of some minor editorial changes, his address is printed as closely as possible as originally spoken.

States is the responsibility of us all, **most especially** the responsibility of those of us who are white, and **absolutely** the responsibility of every one of this nation's educators.

The truth is that only a fool would voluntarily choose to speak on the topic of racism at a national conference. After all, racism is a difficult topic to talk about. However, I chose to speak on racism for that very reason and others—because it is **so difficult to talk about** and because the conversation about racism **must be** a part of the broader discipline of multicultural education. I am also speaking on the topic of racism because of something Rose Duhon-Sells, the Mother of NAME, said to me over 20 years ago.

In order to understand the story behind why I am standing before the microphone today, you have to know the bigger story of my relationship to Rose Duhon-Sells. Rose and I became friends about 20 years ago when she heard me deliver an address in Memphis. You see, for many years now, Rose has seen me as "that white boy who is good to call on when you need someone to tell white folks what to do so they'll do right for a change."

Rose's perception may be true, but I can tell you that I am not before this microphone today **just** "to tell us white folks what we ought to do." I am here today to talk to **all** of us. When I say I am here today to speak to **all** of us, I mean every person in this room who has ever felt marginalized, every person who has ever felt locked out, every person who has ever felt like other people considered them "different," "low-down," or "no-good," simply because somebody else did not like "who we were" or "what we believed."

When I say **all** of us, I also mean those of us who have often felt confused regarding how to do the right thing about racism. But when I say I am before this microphone today to talk to all of us, I mean, most of all—**those of us who teach**. No matter how different we may be from each other, we are here as well-intentioned people who have dedicated our careers to teaching others.

I am going to talk about racism but not about racism alone. Indeed, it is true that racism cuts deeply into the fabric of this society, but it is the bigger beast of bigotry that wields the sword that continues to prune back this nation—that prevents this nation from flowering into the full democracy it could become. In my mind, bigotry is bigotry—whether it is based on race, ethnicity, or culture, or whether it is based on income level, gender, sexual orientation, or any other characteristic that marks one as "different."

Those of you in the audience who have heard me speak before know that I always do two things. The first is that I always tell a story, no matter who the audience is, for I believe it is in the voices of ordinary people that we find the great lessons of life played out. The second thing I do is tell the audience exactly what I am going to talk about. So, after I have told a story I am going to ask you to think along with me on **two** subtopics: (1) How racism and its peculiar characteristics play themselves out in the American education system from public schools through institutions of higher education; and (2) What teachers must do—what public and private education's responsibilities are—to recreate America as an antiracist, more fair, just, and democratic society.

T.J. and the Education of a White Boy

I am not an authority on racism, but I have been affected by it all my life from childhood to the present and I have thought about **racism and education** since I was an undergraduate student at the University of Texas in 1959. The story I have selected to provide as a context for the "meat" of my address is a personal story. My personal experience, after all, if not the best, is the only lens I have for examining racism. When I first wrote this story a few years ago, I titled it "T.J., A Great Teacher: The Education of a White Boy." It is the story of an experience I had at the University of Texas in the summer of 1959, an experience that would change profoundly for the rest of my life the way I would look at the world around me.

I was enrolled that summer in a Foundations of Education course. In that class was Thomas Jefferson Johnson, who preferred to be called "T.J." for short. For the most part, schools were segregated in Texas. In fact, in all my 15 years of schooling I had prior to that class, T.J. was my first African-American classmate. In the beginning, perhaps T.J. was only a curiosity to me, but something told me that I wanted to know this young man better. One day when I was on the way to class, T.J. called out to me from where he was sitting under one of those grand spreading oak trees on the University of Texas campus. "Hey, Smith, you want a cup of coffee?" The idea sounded good to me. After all, I was growing up, I was 20 years old, and I was away at college, drinking coffee now like a regular grown-up man, something college students did in those days whether they really liked coffee or not.

T.J. pulled from his briefcase a thermos and poured me a cup of coffee. We began to have coffee together under that oak tree almost like a ritual, sometimes before and sometimes after class. At these meetings where we would drink coffee and talk, I learned that T.J. was a French teacher in a segregated black high school in Abilene, Texas. He was at the University of Texas to complete a degree and get a teaching certificate. I began comparing myself to T.J. I was chagrined that his vocabulary of English words far exceeded mine and that his pronunciation in French seemed flawless to me, a white boy, who even though I had had fourteen credit hours of college level French, still pronounced such phrases as "MUR-SEA BOW-COOO, MAY-MWA-SELLE" with those long flat, dipthonged Texas vowel sounds. I could see that T.J. seemed more sophisticated and more intelligent than me. Sometimes T.J. talked about becoming "a great teacher" as if teaching were a special calling. I had never before heard anyone talk about teaching as T.J. did. And he also said things that frightened me sometimes. He used phrases I had never heard before like "the movement" and "freedom for the People."

You see, in order to understand the importance of my encounter with T.J., you have to remember what it was like in 1959. Neither T.J. nor I were really supposed to be at the University of Texas—T.J. because he was Black and I because I was what some of the White fraternity boys called "white-trash." After all, I was not the son of a banker, a doctor, a lawyer, or some well-to-do business man. I was straight off the farm. I was so politically naive that it had not even occurred to me that the reason T.J. and I were drinking coffee from a thermos bottle was that there were no integrated cafes or lunch-counters where the two of us could sit down together in the Austin, Texas, of 1959.

One Friday night about mid-way through the semester, I was strolling by myself down Gaudalupe Street, known as "the drag" to college students in those days. As I passed the Longhorn Theatre, a movie house, I noticed a strange phenomenon. The line of people in front of the Longhorn Theatre stretched the entire length of the block, and I noticed the line was really a double line of partners, one black and one white. Then I heard someone call out, "Pritchy, over here, over here!" I looked around to see T.J. standing in this unusual line of people. I walked over and he asked, "Why don't you join us, Pritchy?" I asked in return, "What in the world are you doin'?" He retorted, "We're trying to integrate the theatre, fool. This is how it works. You see, we stand in line in tandem, a black and white, and tie up the line so that people who really want to see the movie give up and go on home instead of standing in line all night to get their tickets. When we get to the ticket window, my white partner here asks if he and I can buy a ticket. Of course, the ticket seller always says no and we go back to the end of the line and start over. It's a kind of boycott. The theatre owner is either going to have to integrate the theatre or go broke."

T.J. asked again, "Pritchy, why don't you join us?" I faltered as I tried to speak. I stammered "I, uh, uh, I don't know. I don't think so. I . . . uh." After all, at twenty-years old I had never in my life taken a public action against anything. I had never even stood up for myself when I had been done a wrong, much less ever stand **up** or **against** authority that had done someone else a wrong. I remember clearly in less than a second the expression on T.J.'s face changed. His smiling face became stoic and hard. His eyes transformed suddenly from the happy twinkle I had known to a piercing, cold, steely stare. With eyes of ice he looked straight into my eyes and said "Pritchy, if you are not in this line, you are in the wrong line."

Then he looked away from me. I felt my scalp tighten. I felt chills run up my spine. I began to back away, almost stumbling from the impact of his words on me as I continued walking down the street. As I walked, his words kept ringing in my ears. I kept hearing over and over in my head "Pritchy, if you are not in this line, you are in the wrong line." I thought about those words all weekend, again and again. I tried to understand what was happening inside me. I had no prior social context within which to place this experience. You have to remember that this was prior to Dr. Martin Luther King, Jr. and Montgomery and Selma.

T.J.'s words worried me all weekend. On Monday, I started to class early. I had to see T.J. I went to the oak tree, but T.J. was not there. I went to class. T.J. was not in class. The next class day, T.J. was neither at the oak tree nor in class. A week passed. No T.J. Then the following week, T.J. was seated in the classroom. Acting like nothing had happened the week before, I said "Hi, T.J. Let's have coffee after class." T.J. did not look at me. He didn't speak. He looked past me with the same icy eyes I had seen on that Friday night in front of the theatre. After class, without a word he walked past me and out the door. T.J. had cut me out of his world.

Another week passed. Finally, when I could stand the inner turmoil no longer, I joined the boycott, an experience that was to affect me forever. Some bad things happened before the protest ended. For example, one night policemen leaped from trucks, swinging their nightsticks. I had never seen policemen swing nightsticks as they plunged into a panicked crowd, hitting men and women in their stomachs and heads. I was terrified by the shrieks and cries from the panicked crowd of protesters and even more terrified by the blood that was being splattered on me as the police hit people, coming closer and closer to me where I was pinned by the crowd against the building. I could see that these uniformed men were not just trying to breakup a protest. They wanted to kill us. I was lucky that night. I survived without injury, but it was that night that I realized, for the first time, that police in those days were there to preserve a racist social order, not to protect protesters who were exercising their Constitutional right to assemble peacefully.

Not all of the time T.J. and I spent together was as frightful or even serious, for that matter. Although we worked hard that summer mimeographing and passing out flyers and always making certain we took our turn at the boycott down at the Longhorn Theatre, we had some fun too. Some Saturday nights we would go to Floyd's Blue Note Club on the Hill, one of the black sections of Austin, located near Hustin-Tillotson College, Austin's only historically black college. If we were lucky, we might catch someone famous like Jimmy Reed wailing his own kind of blues, live, at Floyd's. After Floyd's closed about 2:00 a.m., we would cap off the night at Earl's Chicken Shack, an after-hours club where two hungry under-aged young men could eat and get one last drink of whiskey before the sun came up.

On other occasions, T.J. would be in one of his mischievous moods. During these times, he would pull some prank on me, stamp both feet like he was going to laugh himself to death, and then say, "Smith, you are one dumb white boy." I did not mind though. Somehow it did not seem like an insult.

At the end of that hot summer, in August, T.J. and I parted ways. T.J. had to return to Abilene to start a new school year, even though, as T.J. said, "Most of the kids at the Negro School will be picking cotton until the end of September." We met one last time under the oak tree. The Longhorn Theatre was still segregated. We felt surrounded by the kind of sadness a person experiences when he tries as hard as he can but does not win, the sadness of an unachieved triumph. It was the feeling Langston Hughes must have been trying to capture when he wrote about "a dream deferred." As hard as we had tried, we felt like we had failed. We did not know at that moment that it would be nearly another year before the owner of the Longhorn Theatre would stand before the crowd of protestors to announce that henceforth the doors of the theatre would be open to all. It would be a great moment of triumph with the crowd cheering and tossing their caps and signs into the air—a moment of joy that T.J. would not be there to experience.

We had met at the oak tree to have one last cup of coffee and say goodbye, but we did not know how. When it became time for T.J. to leave, there was an awkward uneasy moment, as if both of us were groping for some words that would sound right—like so often happens when men "just don't know how to act." Then T.J. broke the silence and said, "Smith, you're O.K. for a white boy. You're gonna be alright."

I stood there a good long while watching T.J. grow smaller as he walked down the street toward the bus station. I remember feeling like something in the world had changed that summer—like I was not ever going to be the same again, like maybe I knew for the first time that people have a choice. They can stand in the wrong line. Or they can stand in the right line.

On that last day I would see T.J., there was no way we could have known that T.J., just five years later, would be killed in the Vietnam war. It was just a few years ago, in fact, that I found myself standing before the Vietnam Memorial in Washington D.C.,

weeping almost uncontrollably as I touched my fingers to the letters of his name carved in the stone. The only words I could whisper aloud were "T.J., you did become a great teacher."

I learned many things from T.J. and our experience with the boycott, far too many things, in fact, than I can tell about in the limited time I have for delivering this address. However, the most important thing I learned was about myself. I found out that it would take far more than just learning to like the taste of coffee to become a man. I learned that "I could not stand up as a man until I stood up, first, for someone else," that " I would not become a man until I stood against injustice." It was this single lesson that would enable me later on in life to understand the full meaning of Martin Niemuller's famous words when I would read them for the first time. I am referring to Niemuller's passage about his inaction in Nazi Germany when he said:

First they came for the Jews and I did not speak out because I was not a Jew. Then they came for the communists and I did not speak out because I was not a communist. Then they came for the trade unionists and I did not speak out because I was not a trade unionist. Then they came for me, and there was nobody left to speak out for me.

The experience taught me also to question this society. It enabled me to begin to understand what James Baldwin (1963) was saying in his famous 1963 speech, "A Talk to Teachers," when he said:

Now if I were a teacher . . . dealing with Negro children . . . I would try to teach them . . . that those streets, those houses, those dangers, those agonies by which they are surrounded are criminal. . . . I would teach (the Negro child) that he doesn't have to be bound by the expediencies of any given (government) administration, any given policy, any given time—that he has the right and the necessity to examine everything. (p. 60)

The experience helped me understand what Lerone Bennett, the African-American historian, meant when he wrote that "an

educator in a system of oppression is either a revolutionary or an oppressor" (as cited in Hale, 1978, p. 7). It was my experience at the University of Texas that enabled me not to respond to James Baldwin and Lerone Bennett by calling them "radical" or "militant," as did so many of my peers, but to respond, instead, by beginning to question the injustices in this society.

Ultimately, my experience with T.J. along with other experiences would lead to my belief that education must be multicultural and social reconstructionist. So, therein lies the thesis of my address—in the story I have just told lies the genesis of my thinking about what the responsibilities are of public and private education, K–higher education, to heal the racism that makes a mockery of this democratic society. Many times since I first met T.J., over 37 years ago, I have asked myself why I learned more lessons about racism outside the classroom than in the classroom at the University of Texas. I have asked myself, "Why has racism been a taboo topic in a teacher's education?" I have asked, "Why has the study of racism and antiracism not been a part of the civic education of young people in our schools?" Today, there seems to be a considerable amount of disagreement in our profession as to what a teacher should know and believe about racism.

So, let me turn from the story of T.J. to the substance of my address, which is an attempt to answer the question, "Who shall have the moral courage to heal racism in America?"

Who Shall Have the Moral Courage to Heal the Racism and Bigotry in America?

Before we can begin to answer the question—Who shall have the moral courage to heal the racism and bigotry in America?—we must examine the nature of racism, not only with regard to how racism has played itself out in the history of the United States, but also some of the *peculiar* characteristics of racism.

The first peculiar characteristic of racism is its historical tenacity. Racism is a very old problem. It has been with us in the Americas since the first Europeans set foot here. Despite the presence of some European Americans who always fought against racism, it has found expression in the official U.S. government policy of genocide in the treatment of First Americans,

. . .in the story I have just told lies the genesis of my thinking about . . . the responsibilities . . . of . . . education . . . , to heal the racism that makes a mockery of this democratic society.

the enslavement of people of African descent, the Chinese Exclusion Act, the internment of Japanese Americans and the seizure of their property during World War II, and the almost continuous resistance to civil rights for people of color in the United States.

Although it is an old problem that has been ignored, particularly in our history books, it has not gone away. James W. Loewen's (1995) study of the twelve most frequently used high school American history books found that only one linked the causes of slavery to white racism. I suspect that, when W.E.B. Du Bois (1968) said 100 years ago that "the problem of the 20th century is the problem of the color line" (p. 221), he had no idea that the "color line" would also be the great problem of the 21st century. Racism seems not to be the type of problem that goes away if we ignore it.

In addition to being a very "old problem," a second peculiar characteristic of racism is that it is a problem that so many people deny even exists, no matter how much experiential or empirical evidence proves its existence. On the one hand, people like Morris Dees (1996) of the Southern Poverty Law Center and news reporters remind us almost daily that racism and bigotry run rampant in our American society. Consider these recent events in our public schools:

◆ In suburban Greenwich, Connecticut, five white high school students encode the words "kill all niggers" into the school's yearbook captions.

◆ Some students at Manhattan's Norman Thomas High School send a Jewish teacher a note that includes a swastika and the words "kill all the Jews."

◆ The principal of Randolph County High School, in Alabama, in 1994 threatens to cancel a high school prom because interracial couples might attend and refers to a mixed race student as a "mistake" her white and black parents should not have made.

◆ In Lake County, Florida, the school board, controlled by Christian Fundamentalists, votes that teachers **must** teach that "America is a superior culture."

Consider, also, that hate crimes and harassment based on race have steadily been reported since the mid-1980s with increasing, not diminishing, frequency on university and college campuses, some of which are considered the most prestigious of our Big Ten and Ivy League institutions (Lennon, 1988).

Consider this list of events in our larger society:

◆ The FBI reported over "7,000 victims of hate crimes in 1994 alone." (Dees, 1996, p. 4).

◆ Studies continue to show that prestigious banks and loan institutions continue to disapprove mortgage loan applications on the basis of race.

◆ Television sting operations continue to expose employment agencies, realtors, and property and rental companies that discriminate on the basis of race.

◆ In February, 1996 a white law enforcement officer in the State of Maryland refuses to give mouth-to-mouth resuscitation to an African American woman and she dies.

◆ No sooner than the horrifying images of the Rodney King beating begin to fade, we see on our televisions uniformed men beating our Latino brothers and sisters along a California freeway. Then, this year in 1997, police officers in Brooklyn's 70th precinct station house allegedly sodomize with a toilet plunger Abner Louima, a Haitian immigrant.

◆ National leaders show no shame in showing their bigotry in public. As Dees (1996) notes, "Republican Senator Alphonse D'Amato mocks 'little Judge Ito' " (p. 4); Republican "House majority whip Dick Armey refers to his Congressional colleague Barney Frank as 'Barney Fag' "; and "Republican Presidential contender Bob Dornan calls some of his political adversaries 'lesbian spear chuckers' " (p. 4).

◆ GOP Presidential Primary candidate Pat Buchanan says in a 1996 campaign speech, "Women are simply not endowed by nature with the same measures of single-minded ambition and the will to succeed in the fierce competitive world of Western capitalism."

With this kind of misguided moral leadership among political leaders, who shall have the moral courage to heal racism in America?

On the other hand, despite the evidence to the contrary, a majority of white Americans deny the existence of racism and bigotry and deny the resulting effect of discrimination. For example, the National Conference (1994) found in its survey on intergroup relations, titled *Taking America's Pulse,* that a majority of white Americans believe the citizens of color in the United States simply are not discriminated against. The same poll, however, found that African Americans, Latino Americans, and Asian Americans believed just the opposite—that bigotry and discrimination continue to be the reality.

In addition to being a very old problem, and a problem that people deny exists, a third **peculiar** characteristic or racism is that it is a problem that no one seems to own. Although the same National Conference poll found that prejudice against other racial groups exists in all ethnic and racial groups, most of the research tells us that it is only a minority of Americans who will

admit to being prejudiced. White Americans are less likely than persons of color to own up to and admit their prejudices. For example, another poll found that only 21 percent of white Americans would go on record as considering themselves biased against people of other races but that twice as many African Americans (41 percent) would claim their prejudices (Edwards, 1995).

Well, there you have it—the enigma and irrationality of racism. In short, what I have just said is that racism is **a very old, non-existing problem that no one owns**. So, who shall have the moral courage to heal this "old, non-existing problem that no one owns"? If the answer to this question is educators, let us examine the students in teacher education programs for a moment.

Teacher Education Students

By now those of us at this conference who are teacher educators can almost quote from memory Nancy Zimpher's (1989) well-known and often referenced profile of the "typical preservice teacher." That is, the typical preservice teacher is a monolingual white female from a low-middle or middle-class suburban or rural home who wants to teach children who are just like herself. Other demographic profiles tell us that 90 percent of our preservice teachers are white and less than 10 percent are students of color (AACTE, 1987). Research tells us that many of our preservice teachers simply do not have the prerequisite attitudes or life-styles patterns regarding diversity that would enable them to teach children who are different from themselves (Ahlquist, 1991; Beyer, 1991; Ladson-Billings, 1991).

In fact, most preservice teachers say they don't want to teach minority children, **except as a last resort** (Contreras, 1988). In truth, most of our students were socialized by their families to live monoracial and monocultural lifestyles as the preferred norm. Some of other studies tell us that a majority of our preservice teachers believe that the home background of minority public school students is so bad that it just can't be overcome by education. Personally, I am far less worried about the home backgrounds of minority students in schools than I am about the "backgrounds" of cultural and racial illiteracy of our teacher education students. Finally, another body of research literature tells us that the attitudes and lifestyle patterns of preservice teachers are extremely resistant to change (Grant & Secada, 1990).

Some of us are shocked—astounded sometimes—by the depth of bigotry among so many of our preservice teachers presently in training. My own assessment of today's preservice teachers in undergraduate training is that among them is the largest, most outspoken group of racists I have en-

It is important for our students to see us having interracial friendships . . . [and] . . . most importantly, . . . to see us not merely as nonracists . . . but . . . antiracists. . . .

countered since the beginning of my teaching career at the university level in 1967, almost 30 years ago. Not all of our students are racists, of course, but too many are. From my own university classroom experiences, my estimate is that about one-third of our teacher education students are **hard-core intractable racists.** Another third of them I would classify as **moderate racists,** young people who are relatively unaware of their racism, who, in fact, are blind to their own racism, and have not even given much thought to their racial attitudes. Another 20 percent I would classify as **non-racists,** young people whom we might describe "as good kids who want to do the right thing" but are rather passive and quiet about their thoughts on race. Another 10 to 12 percent, perhaps three or four out of every class of 30, arrive in my classes as **antiracists,** young people who have the prerequisite belief system to become social reconstructionists—young people who want to reconstruct a fairer, more just, antiracist democracy. This profile of the preservice teacher begs us to ask the question: "Who shall have the moral courage to heal racism in America?"

Ourselves, Educators

Let us turn from our students for a moment and look at ourselves—the public and private school teachers and the college professors. If we are honest with ourselves, we are very much like the preservice teachers. Ninety-five percent of professors of education are white European Americans; and as Haberman (1992) has noted, less than five percent of us have taught in an "urban" school and only 10 percent of the universities where we work are located in the great urban centers of racial and cultural diversity. With respect to other college professors and K–12 teachers, most of us are monolingual and live monocultural lifestyles. Our closest friends are likely to be of the same race. We are likely to attend same-race churches, live in same-race neighborhoods, and, particularly if we are white, send our children to predominately white, middle-class suburban schools with limited racial integration. Yet, like the teacher education students and other college students, some of us depart from this profile norm.

Who, then, shall have the moral courage to heal racism in America? If the answer to this question is "those of us who teach," what, then, must we do?

What Must Educators Do?

Many of us assembled here at this conference agonize over this "race thing." Those of us who teach teachers in the universities agonize over the moral dilemma we face each year when we graduate teachers whose racism and other forms of bigotry is so strong and deep that they cannot help but do damage to the children they will teach.

What must universities and teacher educators do to prepare antiracist teachers for diverse classrooms? I can tell you it will take far more than just "culturally diverse field experiences" prescribed by the standards of the National Council for Accreditation of Teacher Education. First, we must take ownership of this problem, this disease we call racism and its related viruses that constitute the many mutations of bigotry, and we must set goals and missions for our teacher education programs that clearly state our moral intent that we are not willing to accept the minimum standard of teachers who are just tolerant and without bias, but that we intend to graduate teachers who are antiracists, who are social activists against bigotry—teachers who will create a new world order where racism and bigotry are unacceptable. My point here is that our mission statements should express the moral imperative that we are not preparing teachers to teach in the world as it is but we are preparing teachers to change that world.

The second thing we must do is infuse what I call "the knowledge bases for diversity" into the center and forefront of the teacher education and liberal arts and humanities curriculum. Limitations on my time today do not enable me to describe all 13 of these knowledge bases in detail. Let me simply refer you to the description of these knowledge bases in the forthcoming book sponsored by the American Association of Colleges of Teacher Education.[1] I must, however, take enough time to describe two of these 13 knowledge bases.

The first knowledge base I speak of is the one I have called in my writings "Knowledge Base 8: The Foundations of Racism." No teacher should graduate from a teacher preparation program without having thoroughly studied **the foundations of racism.** In this knowledge base:

(a) Preservice teachers must study the true history of prejudice, discrimination, and racism in the United States;

(b) They must study the theory and research on how racism is integrated into one's identity and personality structure;

(c) They must study the effects of racism on members of the dominant white culture and on members of minority cultures;

(d) They must study the theory and research on "changing bigoted attitudes"; and

(e) They must examine a variety of antibias and antiracist curricula that have been developed for use in the K–12 school curriculum.

In addition to the knowledge base on racism and other forms of bigotry, we must infuse into our teacher education programs the knowledge base on the **educational policies and practices that are harmful to minority and low-income students**—what I have called "Knowledge Base 9" in my scholarship. This knowledge base enables preservice teachers to understand institutionalized racism and other forms of institutionalized bigotry in the educational system.

In this knowledge base preservice teachers must study the research on the harmful and inequitable effects of using standardized tests to allocate educational opportunity, tests that favor the white middle class students and disproportionately disfavor minorities and low-income students. They must study the use of ability grouping and curriculum tracking to segregate students by race under the same school roof. They must study the negative effects of racially segregated schools. They must study the use of inequitable funding formulas that cheat minority and low-income students out of equal opportunities for high quality education and the use of school choice, privatization, and vouchers to create even greater inequities and racial segregation in the educational system.

In short, this knowledge base exposes attempts of those who have power and privilege to create a meritocractic rather than a democratic educational system. As we teacher educators and other college professors present these two knowledge bases, we must own up to our own absence of courage to root out the racism and bigotry institutionalized in our own admission and certification policies that use standardized instruments that have no predictive validity but have, as my own research has found, eliminated over 100,000 minority candidates from the teaching profession.[2]

If educators do not do these things, then who will have the moral courage to heal racism in this society?

Finally, let me turn to what educators must do at a personal level—as individuals. Over the long term, what we teach may not be nearly as powerful as what we model.

It is likely that long after our students have forgotten the specific facts, the formal theories, and skills, what they will remember most of all is how we teachers lived our personal lives. So it is important that we model a multicultural and multiracial lifestyle. It is important for our students to see us having interracial friendships. It is important for our students to see that not only do we believe that a racially integrated education is superior to a segregated education but that we actually send our children to integrated schools. And, most important of all, our students must see us not merely as nonracists, but they must see that we are antiracists, actively engaged in our communities fighting racism and other forms of bigotry. In the final analysis, we must look into ourselves—as Ghandi put it, "We must be the change we wish to see in the world."

A Final Word

We multicultural educators have a vision of what America can become. We believe that education can be a powerful force to make this a more democratic society. That vision is in danger today. I do not have to tell the committed in this audience that these are turbulent political times and, as Carl Grant (1992) has said, "We are in a war for the minds of our children." Neither do I have to tell you that new, foul breezes are once again flapping the banner of racism over this nation. I do not have to tell you that the banner of racism is flying proudly over the right wing halls of the Republican-controlled Congress in Washington at this very moment. I do not have to tell those of you who know your history that much of the "Contract with America," the assault on affirmative action, and such initiatives as California's Proposition 209 are nothing more than a thinly disguised package of Jim Crow laws just like those passed by Congress and state legislatures to reserve Reconstruction after the Civil War. You know that. I know that. America stands at a crossroads today. We shall either become a great multicultural society—the first truly multicultural and multiracial democracy on the planet—or we shall revert to our most sinister persona that describes the worst part of our historical past, a compassionless society in which only the elite have power and privilege and in which we judge people not by the content of their character but by their race, their culture, their gender, their exceptionality, or their sexual orientation. We can be a better nation than that.

It will not be easy to do what we must do. But if we change the knowledge bases that teachers study and if we, ourselves, model an antiracist lifestyle, we will give the next generations of teachers and students the moral courage they need to do likewise. No one has described what we must do any better than Robert F. Kennedy (1966) when he said:

> Each time a person stands for an ideal, or acts to improve the lot of others, or strikes out against injustice, he or she sends forth a tiny ripple of hope. And crossing each other from a million different centers of energy and daring, those ripples build a current that can sweep down the mightiest walls of oppression and resistance.
>
> Few are willing to embrace the disapproval of their fellows, the censure of their colleagues, the wrath of their society. Moral courage is a rarer commodity than bravery in battle or great intelligence. Yet is it the one essential vital quality for those who seek to change a world that yields most painfully to change.

So, who shall have the moral courage to heal racism in America? The answer is "us"—we multicultural educators, we social reconstructionists. It is the only answer we can afford to give. It is from us that the next generation of teachers and their students must learn the simple lesson that T.J., "that great teacher," taught so well—"If you are not in this line, you are in the wrong line."

Notes

1. The knowledge bases for diversity referenced in the text of this address may be found in *Knowledge Bases for Diversity in Teacher Education*, a manuscript presently targeted to be published as a book by the American Association for Colleges of Teacher Education (AACTE) in 1998.
2. More information regarding research on the use of admission tests and certification tests to eliminate minority teachers can be found in the following citation: Smith, G. P. (1988, Spring) Tomorrow's white teachers: A response to the Holmes Group. *Journal of Negro Education*, 58 (2), 178–194.

References

Ahlquist, R. (1991). Position and imposition: Power in a multicultural foundations class. *Journal of Negro Education*, 60 (2), 158–169.

American Association of Colleges for Teacher Education (1987). *Teaching teachers: Facts and figures*. Washington, DC: American Association of Colleges for Teacher Education.

Baldwin, J. (1963, December 21). A talk to teachers. *Saturday Review*, pp. 42–44, 60.

Beyer, L. E., (1991). Teacher education, reflective inquiry, and moral action. In B. R. Tabachnick & K. M. Zeichner (Eds.), *Inquiry-oriented practice in teacher education* (pp. 113–129). New York: Falmer Press.

Contreras, A. (1980). Multicultural attitudes and knowledge of education students at a midwestern university. In C.A. Heig (Ed.), *Multicultural education: Knowledge and Perceptions* (pp. 63–78). Bloomington, IN: Indiana University, Center for Urban and Multicultural Education.

Dees, M. (1968, spring). Break the chain. *Teaching Tolerance*, 5 (1), p. 4.

Du Bois, W. E. B. (1968) *The souls of Black folks*. In *Three Negro classics* (p. 221). New York: Avon (Original work published 1905).

Edwards, A. (1995, November 10). Race in America. *Family Circle*, pp. 83–84, 86–87.

Grant, C. (1992). *Unpublished speech*. ATE Summer Workshop, University of Wisconsin, Parkside.

Grant, C. A., & Secada, W. G. (1990). Preparing teachers for cultural diversity. In W. R. Houston, M. Haberman, & J. Sikula (Eds.), *Handbook of research on teacher education* (pp. 403–422). New York: Macmillan.

Haberman, M. (1992). Unpublished speech. ATE Summer Workshop, University of Wisconsin, Parkside.

Hale, J. (1978). Cultural influences on learning styles of Afro-American children. In L. Morris (Ed.), *Extracting learning styles from social/cultural diversity* (pp. 7–27). Norman, OK: Southwest Teacher Corps Network (Grant No. G007–700–119, Teacher Corps, U.S. Office of Education, Department of Health, Education, and Welfare).

Kennedy, R. F. (1966, June 6). *Day of Affirmation address*. South Africa: University of Capetown.

Ladson-Billings, G. (1991). When difference means disaster: Reflections on a teacher education strategy for countering resistance to diversity. Paper presented at the annual meeting of the American Educational Research Association, Chicago, IL.

Lennon, T. (Producer), (1988). *Racism 101* [video recording]. (Available from PBS Video, Alexandria, VA).

Loewen, J. W. (1995) *Lies my teacher told me: Everything your American history textbook got wrong*. New York: New Press. The National Conference (1994). *Taking America's pulse: A summary report of The National Conference survey on intergroup relations*. New York: The National Conference.

Zimpher, N. (1989). The RATE Project: A profile of teacher education students. *Journal of Teacher Education*, 40 (6), 27–30.

AE Article Review Form

We encourage you to photocopy and use this page as a tool to assess how the articles in **Annual Editions** expand on the information in your textbook. By reflecting on the articles you will gain enhanced text information. You can also access this useful form on a product's book support Web site at **http://www.dushkin.com/ online/.**

NAME: DATE:

_____

TITLE AND NUMBER OF ARTICLE:

_____

BRIEFLY STATE THE MAIN IDEA OF THIS ARTICLE:

_____

LIST THREE IMPORTANT FACTS THAT THE AUTHOR USES TO SUPPORT THE MAIN IDEA:

_____

WHAT INFORMATION OR IDEAS DISCUSSED IN THIS ARTICLE ARE ALSO DISCUSSED IN YOUR TEXTBOOK OR OTHER READINGS THAT YOU HAVE DONE? LIST THE TEXTBOOK CHAPTERS AND PAGE NUMBERS:

_____

LIST ANY EXAMPLES OF BIAS OR FAULTY REASONING THAT YOU FOUND IN THE ARTICLE:

_____

LIST ANY NEW TERMS/CONCEPTS THAT WERE DISCUSSED IN THE ARTICLE, AND WRITE A SHORT DEFINITION:

ANNUAL EDITIONS revisions depend on two major opinion sources: one is our Advisory Board, listed in the front of this volume, which works with us in scanning the thousands of articles published in the public press each year; the other is you—the person actually using the book. Please help us and the users of the next edition by completing the prepaid article rating form on this page and returning it to us. Thank you for your help!

ANNUAL EDITIONS: Multicultural Education 00/01

Here is an opportunity for you to have direct input into the next revision of this volume. We would like you to rate each of the 40 articles listed below, using the following scale:

1. Excellent: should definitely be retained
2. Above average: should probably be retained
3. Below average: should probably be deleted
4. Poor: should definitely be deleted

Your ratings will play a vital part in the next revision. So please mail this prepaid form to us just as soon as you complete it. Thanks for your help!

RATING

ARTICLE

1. Americanization and the Schools
2. "Celebrating Diversity vs. Preparing for the Mainstream"? Should We Consider Another Choice?
3. Celebrating Diversity vs. Preparing for the Mainstream: A Pseudo-Controversy?
4. The Violence That Creates School Dropouts
5. Paying Attention to Our Children: Educational Dilemmas for Americans
6. Prospective Teachers' Attitudes toward Urban Schools: Can They Be Changed?
7. Predictors of Success in Urban Teaching: Analyzing Two Paradoxical Cases
8. Service Learning Helps Future Teachers Strengthen Caring Perspectives
9. Why Aren't Teachers Using Effective Multicultural Education Practices?
10. A Different Mirror: A Conversation with Ronald Takaki
11. The Idolatry of Multicultural Education: A Prophetic Pragmatic Alternative?
12. Why Standardized Tests Threaten Multiculturalism
13. Failing to Marvel: The Nuances, Complexities, and Challenges of Multicultural Education
14. Reducing the Effects of Racism in Schools
15. Culturally Authentic Bias
16. Parental Influences on Career Development Perceived by African American and Mexican American College Students
17. From La Belle Sauvage to the Noble Savage: The Deculturalization of Indian Mascots in American Culture
18. A Therapeutic Moment? Identity, Self, and Culture in the Anthropology of Education
19. On the Teaching and Personal Construction of Educational Equity
20. Respect in the Classroom: Reflections of a Mexican-American Educator
21. The Changing Face of Bilingual Education

RATING

ARTICLE

22. The Relationship between Culture and Cognitive Style: A Review of the Evidence and Some Reflections for the Classroom
23. Using Stories to Introduce and Teach Multicultural Literature
24. Making the Most of the Classroom Mosaic: A Constructivist Perspective
25. Noteworthy Books about Latinos for Children and Adolescents
26. Class Web Sites Can Offer Enhanced Access to Information for Language Minority Parents and Students
27. Children and Play in the Holocaust: Friedl Dicker-Brandeis—Heroic Child Therapist
28. Bridging Cultures with a Parent-Teacher Conference
29. Expanding Roles of Teachers for the 21st Century: An Indian Context
30. How to Overcome Obstacles to Parent-Teacher Partnerships
31. Sizing It Right: Class-Size Reduction and Student Achievement
32. Testimonies of Latin American Women: An Annotated Bibliography
33. The Issue of "Authenticity" in California Language Restoration
34. Dissin' "the Standard": Ebonics As Guerrilla Warfare at Capital High
35. Meeting the Needs of Multiracial and Multiethnic Children in Early Childhood Settings
36. Looking at the Schools
37. Business Sees Profits in Education: Challenging Public Schools
38. An Outsider's View Inside: 21st Century Directions for Multicultural Education
39. A Call for a Multicultural Revolution
40. Who Shall Have the Moral Courage to Heal Racism in America?

(Continued on next page)

We Want Your Advice

BUSINESS REPLY MAIL
FIRST-CLASS MAIL PERMIT NO. 84 GUILFORD CT

POSTAGE WILL BE PAID BY ADDRESSEE

Dushkin/McGraw-Hill
Sluice Dock
Guilford, CT 06437-9989

ABOUT YOU

Name   Date

Are you a teacher? ☐   A student? ☐
Your school's name

Department

Address   City   State   Zip

School telephone #

YOUR COMMENTS ARE IMPORTANT TO US !

Please fill in the following information:
For which course did you use this book?

Did you use a text with this *ANNUAL EDITION*? ☐ yes ☐ no
What was the title of the text?

What are your general reactions to the *Annual Editions* concept?

Have you read any particular articles recently that you think should be included in the next edition?

Are there any articles you feel should be replaced in the next edition? Why?

Are there any World Wide Web sites you feel should be included in the next edition? Please annotate.

May we contact you for editorial input? ☐ yes ☐ no
May we quote your comments? ☐ yes ☐ no